THE SOCIALIST FEMINIST PROJECT

A CONTEMPORARY READER
IN THEORY AND POLITICS

EDITED BY NANCY HOLMSTROM

To all the women and men engaged in socialist feminist struggles,
by that name or another

Library of Congress Cataloging-in-Publication Data available from the publisher

ISBN 1–58367–068–8 (paper)
ISBN 1–58367–069–6 (cloth)

Monthly Review Press
122 West 27th Street
New York, NY 10001

Designed and typeset by Illuminati, Grosmont
Manufactured in Canada

10   9   8   7   6   5   4   3   2   1

CONTENTS

PART III

WAGE LABOR AND STRUGGLES

INTRODUCTION

NANCY HOLMSTROM

Some would say socialist feminism is an artifact of the 1970s. It flowered with the women's liberation movement, as a theoretical response to what many in the movement saw as the inadequacies of Marxism, liberalism, and radical feminism, but since then it has been defunct, both theoretically and politically. I think this view is mistaken and the volume will show why.

Socialist feminism should be seen as an ongoing project. It is alive and well today and it existed before the women's liberation movement as well—though, both now and then, not necessarily in that name. It has sometimes been called Marxism, sometimes socialist feminism, sometimes womanism, sometimes materialist feminism, or feminist materialism, and sometimes is implicit in work that bears no theoretical labels. Though the term "socialist-feminist" can be used more narrowly, as I will explain, I am going to characterize as a socialist feminist anyone trying to understand women's subordination in a coherent and systematic way that integrates class and sex, as well as other aspects of identity such as race/ethnicity or sexual orientation, with the aim of using this analysis to help liberate women. As Barbara Ehrenreich said in 1975 the term socialist feminism "is much too short for what is, after all, really socialist, internationalist, antiracist, antiheterosexist feminism." The major purpose of this book is to show the strengths and resources—both theoretical and political—of this ongoing socialist-feminist project.

Today the project is more pressing than ever. "[T]he need of a constantly expanding market for its products chases the bourgeoisie over the whole surface of the globe.... transforming the world in its own image," was the *Communist Manifesto*'s prescient description of what is now referred to as "globalization." "The Battle of Seattle" against the World Trade Organization (WTO), and the demonstrations that have followed in Davos, Quebec City, Genoa and wherever world economic leaders meet, express peoples' growing awareness of and protest against capitalism as a global force beyond democratic control. The brutal economic realities of globalization impact everyone across the globe—but women are affected disproportionately. Displaced by rapid economic changes, women bear a greater burden of labor throughout the world as social services are cut, whether in response to structural adjustment plans in the Third World or to so-called welfare reform in the United States. Women have been forced to migrate, are subject to trafficking, and are the proletarians of the newly industrializing countries. On top of all this they continue to be subject to sexual violence and in much of the world are not allowed to control their own processes of repro-duction. How should we understand these phenomena and, more importantly, how do we go about changing them? Feminist theory that is lost in theoretical abstractions or that depreciates economic realities will be useless for this pur-pose. Feminism that speaks of women's oppression and its injustice but fails to address capitalism will be of little help in ending women's oppression. Marxism's analysis of history, of capitalism, and of social change is certainly relevant to understanding these economic changes, but if its categories of analysis are under-stood in a gender- or race-neutral way it will be unable to do justice to them. Socialist feminism is the approach with the greatest capacity to illuminate the exploitation and oppression of most of the women of the world.

The broad characterization of socialist feminism I am using allows for a range of views regarding the relationship among the many facets of our iden-tities. Some of us would make class fundamental from an explanatory point of view, while others would refuse to give a general primacy to any one factor over others. Despite these differences in our perspectives, in the broad sense of "socialist feminism" that I am using here all socialist-feminists see class as central to women's lives, yet at the same time none would reduce sex or race oppression to economic exploitation. And all of us see these aspects of our lives as inseparably and systematically related; in other words, class is always gendered and raced. One purpose of this volume is to promote conversation, dialogue, and debate among these different perspectives, but it is important to see that the conversation takes place within a common project that underlies the differ-ences. The project has a long history.

What we now call feminism came to public attention in the eighteenth century, most notably in Mary Wollstonecraft's *A Vindication of the Rights of Woman* (1792), where she argued for equal opportunity for women based on a rational capacity common to both sexes, expressing "the wild wish to see the sex distinction confounded in society." Her feminist aspirations came together with socialistic aims in the thinking of a number of utopian socialists, whose visions of socialism included not only sexual equality in the family and society at large, but the end of the sexual division of labor—Wollstonecraft's "wild wish," which is radical even today. Karl Marx and Friedrich Engels shared these aspirations, and deep-ened the critique of naturalistic justifications of all social hierarchies. But Marx and Engels were impatient with blueprints for a good society and focused instead on developing a theory of history, society, and social change which would be the basis for the realization of these ideals. It is worth pausing briefly to consider what Marx and Engels said, since Marxism has had a great influence on feminism, whether it has been appropriated, rejected, or transformed.

To summarize many volumes in a paragraph: according to Marxism's historical materialist approach, history is a succession of modes of production, like feudalism and capitalism, each constituted by distinctive relations between the direct producers and the owners of the means of production who live off the labor of the producers. History, says the opening lines of the *Communist Manifesto*, is "the history of class struggles ... freeman and slave ... lord and serf ...," in a word, oppressor and oppressed." But, although oppression and exploitation are common to all class societies, the relations between oppressor and oppressed have varied; in other words, exactly how each ruling class manages to live off the labor of the producers differs from one mode of production to another and each must be understood in its own terms.

> The specific economic form in which unpaid surplus labor is pumped out of the direct producers determines the relations of rulers and ruled.... It is always the direct relationship of the owners of the conditions of production to the direct producers ... which reveals the innermost secret, the hidden basis of the entire social structure, and with it ... the corresponding specific form of the state.[1]

Not only the state, but the family, art, philosophy, and religion—even human nature—all take different forms in different modes of production. Marx goes on to say that what is basically the same economic basis can show "infinite variations and gradations in appearance," depending on specific historical conditions, which have to be studied in detail. In other words, within capitalism different forms of government and art and family are possible because capitalism is not the only influence. Nevertheless, the relations of production have an explanatory primacy within Marxist theory because they constitute the framework within which other influences occur. And this is because the relations of production provide the "laws of motion" distinctive to each given mode of production. Thus capitalism, the mode of production most studied by Marx, is understood to be a unique historical form aimed at the maximization of profit in a competitive market system. This forces capitalists to strive continually to develop the productivity of labor and technology; for, according to Marx's theory, profit has its origin in wage labor. Though, unlike in slavery or serfdom, labor is legally free in capitalism, workers in capitalism are also free of any means of subsistence of their own; this forces them to work for capitalists and produce the profit that drives the system. Given these essential characteristics of all capitalist societies, while different and changing forms of government are possible, the constraints of capitalism rule out possibilities such as a true monarchy or a workers' government. Just what forms of family are possible within capitalism has been a matter of some debate.

Given the concepts' centrality in their theory, Marx and Engels focused on the oppression and exploitation inherent in the relationship between wage laborers and capitalists. They paid less attention to other forms of labor—for example, the labor of peasants or of women in the family—and to other kinds of oppression simply because they were not as central to their project of understanding capitalism and overturning it. Marx and Engels believed that if they could understand how capitalism worked and help make workers conscious of their oppression they could contribute to workers' self-emancipation. They believed that the *self*-emancipation of the working class—men and women, of all nations, races, and creeds—would be the basis for the end of all other forms of oppression. With the establishment of the first real democracy, the rule of the immense majority—that is, socialism—class oppression and antagonism would be replaced by "an association, in which the free development of each is the condition for the free development of all." As to how such a society would be organized, they pointed to the Paris Commune of 1870 as "what a workers' government would look like," but otherwise said very little.

Tragically, the first successful socialist revolution took place in Russia—a country that lacked the large working class and the material development that Marx saw as necessary for socialism—and no successful revolutions followed in Western Europe where these necessary conditions did exist. In the early years of the revolution when Alexandra Kollontai was in the government and women were organized independently within the Communist Party, remarkable gains were made for women, from the end of legal restrictions on sexual behavior, including homosexuality and abortion, to preventing women's jobs being given to returning soldiers (they were allocated on the basis of need rather than sex), to the provision of communal restaurants, laundries, and childcare. However, most of these gains were eliminated later on and women were certainly not emancipated in the Soviet Union. But this does not show, as many commentators would have it, that "socialism failed women." Men were not liberated either. This was far from the socialism-from-below that the classical Marxists had envisioned. Whatever the inadequacies of Marxist theories on what they called "the woman question," there was no opportunity to correct them, for, as Marx had predicted in *The German Ideology*, without the necessary conditions for socialism "all the old crap"—exploitation and oppression—would return. And indeed it did, in the form of Stalin's dictatorship, which expropriated the name of Marxism, established a mode of production Marx had never foreseen, and destroyed the vision of socialism for millions of people.

In the mid-1970s many women within the women's liberation movement found themselves dissatisfied with the prevailing analyses of women's oppression. Liberalism was not radical enough, and radical feminism ignored economic realities. But Marxism was tainted, as Adrienne Rich describes, "by the fear that class would erase gender once again, when gender was just beginning to be understood as a political category."[2] Seeking to combine the best of Marxism and radical feminism, these women developed a theory they called socialist feminism. When socialist feminism is intended in this way—as differentiated from Marxism—"Marxist feminism" is then understood as a perspective which gives primacy to class oppression as opposed to other forms of oppression, or, going further, that reduces sex oppression to class oppression. (Radical feminism asserts the reverse relationship.) While the terms "Marxist feminism" and "socialist feminism" can be used in these narrower senses, the distinctions are to some extent verbal. As Rosemarie Tong concedes in *Feminist Thought: A More Comprehensive Introduction*,[3] not everyone will agree with her classification of feminists into "Marxist" or "socialist." For Tong, "[a]lthough it is possible to distinguish between Marxist and socialist-feminist thought, it is quite difficult to do so." While there are theoretical differences among socialists and feminists on various issues, which in some contexts are important, *the terms* "Marxist" or "socialist" or "materialist" do not necessarily denote different perspectives. In *Feminist Politics and Human Nature*[4] Alison Jaggar suggests that socialist feminism may be a more consistent Marxism. Which term a feminist chooses to describe herself reflects her particular understanding of Marxism and her theoretical and political milieu, and perhaps her personal experience, as much as it does the substance of her position. For example, Margaret Benston's classic 1969 article "The Political Economy of Women's Liberation"[5] is described as a Marxist feminist analysis of household labor because she used Marxist categories and clearly saw herself as writing within a Marxist theoretical framework. In fact, Benston modified Marxist categories in ways that other feminists would say showed that Marxism was inadequate and needed a distinctive socialist-feminist theory.[6] Her article stimulated quite a debate regarding how to understand household labor within Marxist/socialist-feminist terms—the so-called domestic labor debate.

In the 1990s the term "materialist feminism" gained currency, coined by feminists who wanted to give some grounding in social realities to postmodernist theory. However, materialist feminism is "a rather problematic and elusive concept," in Martha Gimenez's apt characterization, in that sometimes it is used more or less as a synonym for "Marxist" or "socialist-feminist" combined with discourse analysis (as in the work of Rosemary Hennessy), while it is also used by cultural feminists who want nothing to do with Marxism.[7] Yet another term that does not necessarily signal a distinct theoretical perspective regarding the relationship among class, sex, and race is "womanist," a term preferred by some women of color who feel that "feminist" is too one-dimensional and who want to indicate solidarity with men of color as well as with women. Similarly, those who call themselves "multicultural" or "global" feminists would be socialist feminists in my broad sense. Feminists use a particular term to situate themselves within particular debates.

It is "socialist feminism" in the narrower sense that has declined. Developed by feminists who accepted Marxism's critique of capitalism but rejected the view that women's oppression was reducible to class oppression—which is how they understood the Marxist analysis—they argued that women's position in today's society was a function of both the economic system (capitalism) and the sex–gender system, which they called patriarchy. Some socialist feminists preferred to speak of one system they called capitalist patriarchy. But whether they preferred one system or two, the key claim was that the mode of production had no greater primacy than sex–gender relations in explaining women's subordination. Many saw the Marxist emphasis on wage labor rather than on all kinds of labor, especially mothering, and on the relations of production rather than on the relations they called "the relations of reproduction" (sexuality and parenting), as sexist. Convinced that "the personal is political" they wanted to give theoretical and political attention to issues of sex, sexuality, and relations in the family, which some utopian socialists had addressed but which most Marxists ignored.

This distinctively anti-Marxist version of socialist feminism declined, I believe, for both internal and external reasons. Socialist feminists of the 1970s had criticized liberal and Marxist writers for using categories that were "genderblind": "the individual" in liberalism, "the working class" in Marxism. Such categories ignore sex differences among individuals and workers, feminists argued, and hence neither liberalism nor Marxism could explain women's oppression. But women of color could and did make the same criticism of feminism, including socialist feminism, for using race-blind categories: "working class women," or simply "women." To accommodate race oppression (and heterosexism and other forms of oppression), there seemed to be two choices. If we need to posit "a system of social relations" to explain sexism, as they argued, then to explain racism (and other forms of oppression) we would have to posit systems beyond capitalism and patriarchy. This option raised a number of questions, including: What exactly constitutes a "system"? How many is enough? How are they related? How does the resulting perspective differ from simple pluralism? The other option was to go back to a theory like Marxism which aims to be all-inclusive. Since socialist feminists had distinguished themselves from Marxists because they were unclear how to integrate different forms of oppression without reducing one to the other, this did not seem an attractive option, but neither did the multiplication of systems. Hence there was and remains a lack of clarity, and disagreement as to exactly how different forms of oppression are related. Most of the writers included in this volume simply show their interconnectedness without addressing directly and theoretically the question of precisely how they are related and whether one has explanatory primacy.

Socialist feminism as a theoretical position distinct from Marxism also declined for external reasons, both intellectual and political. On the intellectual front, it would be difficult to overemphasize the influence postmodernism has had in the academic world. Starting from valid critiques of many theories' overgeneralizations and neglect of historical and political context, postmodernists ended up arguing from very anti-theoretical positions. Their emphasis on the local and particular, their attack on what they call "totalizing narratives" and on the very notion of truth and causality, were deeply discouraging to feminists trying to develop a coherent and systematic theory of women's oppression. The insight associated with postmodernism (though actually it was not new), that social and political power influence science, led many to scepticism. Also, despite the inconsistency, it led many to claim that everything is socially constructed, thereby eliminating the distinction between sex and gender that had been so central to feminist critiques of gender relations. But if the body disappears in significations, what is the basis for arguing for reproductive rights? Given that some of postmodernism builds on insights associated with feminism and presents itself as radical, its effect was disorienting to say the least.

Turning to political causes, the decline of women's liberation and other social movements had a profound impact. The explosion of writing by feminists of all persuasions (indeed the creation of these "persuasions") was a product of the women's movement of the 1960s and 1970s. Consider the fact that a number of very influential articles of this period began as position statements for activist groups (the Redstockings' Manifesto, the Combahee River Collective's State-ment) or as collective papers (Heidi Hartmann's and Gayle Rubin's—two of the most influential of this period). New movements stimulated new theorizing; for example, the gay and lesbian movements gave rise to the academic field Queer Studies. With the move of many activists into social policy and service work for women, into academia, and into families and middle age, this essential active stimulation was lost. It is not coincidental that the hottest feminist theorizing of the last decade was of a highly academic sort—postmodernism—while the domi-nant politics have been the most local and particularistic form of identity poli-tics. Moreover, of course, we have to appreciate the context in which all this has taken place: namely, the general rightward political drift throughout the world during the 1980s and much of the 1990s.

My own opinion is that critiques of Marxism as sexist for focusing on relations of production and for ignoring labor in the family are misguided, given the primary aim of Marxist theory, as explained above. It was not sexism that led Marx to say that in capitalism women's household labor was unproductive, for he said the same thing about a carpenter working for the government. Although both are obviously productive in a general sense, Marx was seeking to under-stand what is productive from the point of view of capitalism—that only labor produces surplus value. Moreover, to understand how various aspects of society, including different forms of oppression, interrelate—and, more important, how to change them—we need a theory that addresses these questions. That is precisely what historical materialism aims to do both in its sociological aspect and in its account of historical change. Hence it remains vitally important. Though any theory developed over a century ago needs some revision, in my opinion Marxism's basic theory does not need significant revision in order to take better account of women's oppression. However, I do believe that the theory needs to be supplemented. Feminists are justified in wanting a social theory that gives a fuller picture of production and reproduction than Marx's political economic theory does, that extends questions of democracy not only to the economy but to personal relations. They are also justified in wanting to pay attention to the emotional dimensions of our lives, both to understand how oppression manifests itself in the most intimate aspects of our lives and also, most importantly, to give a more complete vision of human emancipation. The potential is there in Marxism. Marx's subtle understanding of how economic relations penetrate into our very being make him "a great geographer of the human condition," in Adrienne Rich's characterization. But these insights were underdeveloped. Furthermore, Marx's and Engels's commitment to a genuinely democratic socialism led them to ignore questions of what socialism would look like, saying they did not want to "write recipe books for the cooks of the future." But what economic democracy would look like is an extraordinarily complicated question and explorations would have been helpful. Moreover, this omission made it easier to equate socialism with what existed in the Soviet bloc or in the social welfarist capitalism of Western Europe. Today we need these prefigurative visions of socialism more than ever and feminists have much to contribute to them.

Socialist feminist theorizing (in the broad sense) is flourishing, particularly in empirical work by historians and other social scientists, a sample of which is included in this volume. This work has been influential, showing that feminist theory is still a collective enterprise, as its practitioners always stress. What is now called "intersectionality"—that is, the recognition that a woman's position is always a function of her class, ethnicity, and so on, as well as her sex—is paid at least lip service by most feminists. Often, however, this recognition is expressed simply as a list of "isms," of which "classism" is given least attention or else is conflated with racism so that white is invariably coupled with middle class, and black with poor. It is only in the work that I am calling socialist feminist in the broad sense that these aspects are integrated coherently and systematically. A socialist-feminist perspective also informs what activism there is, including, most significantly, labor activism. While this is probably due more to the fact that the workforce of the United States is increasingly female and minority than to the influence of socialist-feminist theory, nevertheless it is significant. Even NOW (the National Organization of Women) is considerably more class and race conscious than it was in its early days when it focused on the ERA (Equal Rights Amendment) and the legalization of abortion while virtually ignoring the Hyde Amendment which denied the use of Medicaid funds for abortion.

I believe the time is right for a positive reappraisal of the socialist-feminist perspective. The brutal economic realities of globalization make it impossible to ignore class, and feminists are now asking on a global level the kinds of big questions they asked on a societal level in the 1970s. A number of developments in the United States are also significant in this regard. Most important is the fact that the increasingly female and minority composition of the workforce makes it more apparent that sharp splits between class oppression and sex or race oppression, or between workplace and community issues, are untenable practically and theoretically. The commitment of the new leadership of the AFL–CIO to organizing has raised peoples' interest and their hopes. Students across the country have become active around the issue of sweatshops and have linked up with labor groups around the world. A conference was held at Harvard a few years back on Students and Labor. This was followed by a long and successful Campaign for a Living Wage, at Harvard, in the spring of 2001. Two conferences on Academics and Labor have taken place. The academic focus on cultural issues to the exclusion of politics is beginning to seem one-sided, even self-indulgent, to more and more people. I believe the grip of postmodernism and identity politics is loosening as attacks have increased from all quarters. Even within identity politics there is some indirect attention to class, as for example in "white trash" literature. However, we must not leave these criticisms to the right (and to those on the left such as Todd Gitlin). It is essential to retain the insights of the 1960s. Socialist theory and practice that failed to give serious attention to issues of gender, race/ethnicity, and sexuality would have little credibility today. And so, in addition to criticism, it is important to offer positive examples of analyses that integrate class with those other aspects of identity. This volume does this. It is also important to pursue theoretical discussion within the broad socialist-feminist perspective regarding the relationship between class and other aspects of identity and the meaning of "material" and "economic." The recent internal critiques of postmodernism by feminists who have tried to take it in a more realist and materialist direction have broadened this discussion. With economic questions once again central to many feminists' agendas, and with the apparent decline of postmodernism, this is an opportune time to reconsider how Marxism can help us comprehend the global reality of women's oppression and how Marxism itself needs to be revised or supplemented.

FOREMOTHERS/FATHERS

In order to demonstrate my thesis that socialist feminism is an ongoing project with a history, this volume includes, in the opening section, some excerpts from socialist-feminist writings from the nineteenth and early twentieth centuries. Since the best-known socialist-feminist writings are from the second wave of the 1960s and 1970s, readers may be surprised not to see them included. Had space permitted, I would have included a selection. They are, however, readily available elsewhere. Since the primary purpose of this volume is to show the ongoing strength and resources of the socialist-feminist perspective, the overwhelming majority of the articles included are of quite recent origin. Although I have tried to include as many topics and voices as possible, my own point of view inevitably guided the selection; I am keenly aware of how much I had to leave out. But that just confirms my point about how much good socialist-feminist work is going on today!

SEX, SEXUALITY, AND REPRODUCTION

It seemed appropriate to begin the book with a section on this topic, since one of the most striking innovations of second-wave feminism was its attention to such issues previously ignored by almost all political thinkers. The insight that "the personal is political" means that even the most personal, intimate, and seemingly individual areas of our lives reflect the inequalities of power in society at large. As Dorothy Allison shows us vividly and poignantly, from the inside, class shapes our identities and gets into our most intimate relationships. Micaela di Leonardo and Roger Lancaster explore the history and political economy of debates on sexuality and society, issues they insist are crucial for left scholarship and practice. Emily Martin shows how scientific views on the impact of menstruation on women's capacity to work have a political-economic basis, including the diagnosis of PMS (premenstrual syndrome) as a medical problem. Rosalind Petchesky argues that despite the growing international commitment to reproductive rights as a human right, they cannot be achieved unless they are understood to be indivisibly connected to economic justice. Finally Rosemary Hennessey argues that historical materialism is a more adequate basis for understanding sexual identity than cultural materialism.

FAMILY: LOVE, LABOR, AND POWER

The family is another topic ignored by most political thinkers that has been a central focus of feminist writing. But what is the family? It is not a biological unit but an enormously varied and evolving site of love, labor, and power as well as reproduction. Judith Stacey focuses on the "varied and evolving" part of this description for the United States, and Temma Kaplan explains how and why fatherless families are becoming the norm in global capitalism. Ann Ferguson's concept of "sex-affective production" illuminates the labor involved in all families, while Purvi Shah and Cherríe Moraga address the power inequalities within families and the way race/ethnicity intersects with gender, a point Janice Haaken extends to differing understandings of family violence and strategies for dealing with it. In contrast to universalistic conceptions of patriarchy, Deniz Kandiyoti shows how women struggle to achieve the best situation for themselves within the constraints of different kinds of systems of male domination. Stephanie Coontz critiques the limitations of Marx and Engels's analysis of the family but credits them with insights about the family as a site of cooperation, conflict, and contradiction, which are developed by later thinkers including our authors.

WAGE LABOR AND STRUGGLES

The notion that "women's work" is in and around the home is belied by the fact that most women do paid work as well as unpaid; indeed women are the bulk of the workforce in the newly industrializing countries. But gendered and racialized ideologies, along with economic constraints, conspire to make certain paid work "women's work"—or particular kinds of women's work—and to render women's economic contributions insignificant or even invisible. As Evelyn Nakano Glenn showed for African-American women in her classic article "From

Servitude to Service Work,"[8] Chandra Talpade Mohanty shows for Third World women workers in the new global division of labor, and suggests possibilities for transnational solidarity. Leslie Salzinger and Elizabeth Oglesby provide additional illustrations from Latin America of how the production of goods and profit is simultaneously the production of gendered people. Nancy MacLean recounts the struggles of trade-union women in the United States for equality, showing the centrality of that history to feminism. Jo Bindman and Kamala Kempadoo discuss sex work and its many variations, from slavery to temporary part-time work, and the growing movement of sex workers around the world.

ECONOMICS, SOCIAL WELFARE, AND PUBLIC POLICY

Why are women sometimes loyal to oppressive systems? How have women fared in revolutions? Are women best served by gender-neutral laws and policies? Maxine Molyneux's influential discussion of different kinds of "interests" helps us to address these questions. Mimi Abramovitz shows how disastrous recent changes in welfare laws have been for women and how they are fighting back, while Angela Davis draws connections between private violence and the increasing public imprisonment of women, showing the racialized nature of both, and suggests that alliances should be forged between the anti-violence, women's prison, and human rights movements. On a positive note, Chris Tilly and Randy Albelda offer a strategy and agenda to achieve economic equality for women.

POLITICS AND SOCIAL CHANGE

What kinds of political strategies, movements, and changes are most and least promising in the struggle for social justice for women? Sheila Rowbotham takes us back to the heady days of the women's liberation movement in Britain when radical women first organized around their own interests as women. Since women are never only women but also a particular class, race/ethnicity and sexuality, a crucial political question for women is how movements organized around these different facets of our identities intersect. Leith Mullings and Elizabeth Martínez show the limitations for women of nationalist movements, while Ellen Meiksins Wood discusses the relationship between capitalism and different emancipatory projects, arguing that class is the only system of domination that is constitutive of capitalism. Along the same lines, Johanna Brenner argues that the women's movement and the civil rights movement made similar gains but have reached similar impasses, which can only be overcome by a broad anti-capitalist movement, the elements of which have begun to form. Cynthia Enloe shows how many women's lives are dominated by the military in manifold interconnected but often invisible ways, and Mary Hawkesworth shows that, contrary to democratization theory, the end of communism has not meant an improvement in political and economic conditions for most women, but in fact a worsening.

NATURE, SOCIETY, AND KNOWLEDGE

Having begun with the most personal topics, we conclude with the most abstract and universal topics to which a socialist-feminist approach also provides unique insights. Nancy Hartsock reformulates her influential idea of a feminist standpoint, adapted from Marx, the promise of which can be seen in Patricia Hill Collins's work on black feminist epistemologies[9] and other works on situated knowledge. The age-old question of whether women (and therefore men) have distinct natures can be fruitfully addressed, I contend, using Marx's approach to human nature. The politics of nature are addressed by ecofeminist Val Plumwood, who offers a theoretical approach unifying opposition to the domination of people and of nature, while Meera Nanda explores the dangers for women of some postcolonial ecofeminist thinking regarding rationality, culture, and development. Finally, Julie Sze shows the contribution that Asian-American feminists can offer to the struggle for environmental justice.

All in all our articles make clear that socialist feminism is alive and well and has tremendous potential to theorize and to build an alternative to the brutal system of global capitalism that threatens to destroy the very planet on which we live.

NOTES

1. *Capital*, vol. 3 (New York: International Publishers, 1967), 791.
2. Adrienne Rich, "Credo of a Passionate Skeptic," *Monthly Review* 53, no. 2 (June 2001), 25–31.
3. *Feminist Thought: A More Comprehensive Introduction*, 2d ed. (Boulder, CO: Westview Press, 1998).
4. Alison Jaggar, *Feminist Politics and Human Nature* (Totowa, NJ: Rowman & Allanheld, 1983).
5. Margaret Benston, "The Political Economy of Women's Liberation," *Monthly Review* 21 (September 1969).
6. See Nancy Holmstrom, "'Women's Work,' the Family and Capitalism," *Science and Society* 45, no. 2 (Summer 1981).
7. Martha Gimenez, "Marxist Feminism/Materialist Feminism," www.matfem, 1998.
8. Evelyn Nakano Glenn, "From Servitude to Service Work: Historical Continuities in the Racial Division of Reproductive Labor," *Signs: Journal of Women in Culture and Society* 18, no. 1 (1992), 1–43.
9. Patricia Hill Collins, *Black Feminist Thought*, 2d ed. (New York: Routledge, 2000).

FOREMOTHERS/FATHERS

Utopian socialists, followers of Robert Owen[1]

You look forward, as I do, to a state of society very different from that which now exists, in which the effort of all is to outwit, supplant and snatch from each other; where interest is systematically opposed to duty; where the so-called system of morals is little more than a mass of hypocrisy preached by knaves but unpractised by them, to keep their slaves, male as well as female, in blind uninquiring obedience; and where the whole motley fabric is kept together by fear and blood. You look forward to a better state of society, where the principle of benevolence shall supersede that of fear; where restless and anxious individual competition shall give place to mutual co-operation and joint possession; where individuals, in large numbers male and female, forming voluntary associations, shall become a mutual guarantee to each other for the supply of all useful wants ... where perfect freedom of opinion and perfect equality will reign amongst the co-operators; and where the children of all will be equally educated and provided for by the whole ... This scheme of social arrangements is the only one which will completely and for ever ensure the perfect equality and entire reciprocity of happiness between women and men.

William Thompson to Anna Wheeler, 1825

The uniform injustice ... practised by man towards woman in the family confounds all notions of right and wrong... Every family is a centre of absolute despotism, where of course intelligence and persuasion are quite superfluous to him who has only to command to be obeyed: from these centres, in the midst of which all mankind are now trained, spreads the contagion of selfishness and the love of domination through all human transactions ... This great obstacle must be removed before any real advance can be made to human happiness: not even Co-operation, without it, would produce happiness or virtue.

William Thompson, 1826

Be it known to the world that a female union is begun in Derby, and that the tyrants have taken flight at it, and have brought forth a document for the females to sign or *leave their employment*, not only to those who are employed in the factory, but to *the servants in their own houses also.* Here is a specimen of knavish tyranny; but, be it known that we have refused to comply with their request ... In consequence of this, there is a great number more added to the turnout ... Sisters! awake, arise ... from lodges in very town and hamlet. Mothers of families, and maidens, come forward and join in this our glorious cause, and we will defy the power of our adversaries; and let the first lispings of your innocent offsprings be *union! union!*

Anonymous letter to *The Pioneer*, February 22, 1834

A woman's wage is not reckoned at an average more than two-thirds of a male ... and we believe in reality it seldom amounts to more than a third (and wives have no wages at all). Yet, is not the produce of female labour as useful? ... The industrious female is well entitled to the same amount of remuneration as the industrious male.

Frances Morrison, 1834

It is time the working females of England began to demand their long-suppressed rights. In manufacturing towns, look at the value that is set on woman's labour, whether it be skilful, whether it be laborious, so that woman can do it [*sic*]. The contemptible expression is, it is made by woman and therefore cheap? Why, I ask, should woman's labour be thus undervalued? Why should the time and the ingenuity of the sex ... be monopolized by cruel and greedy oppressors, being in the likeness of men, and calling themselves masters? Sisters, let us submit to it no longer ... unite and assert your just rights!

Frances Morrison, 1834

... running the labor of the women against the men ... has been successfully done in the cotton manufacture, and the consequence is that there is now very little employment in it which will pay a man living wages. One of our earliest endeavours must be to root out this abominable practice of degrading the labor of females in order to destroy the value of the males' ... What is the antidote? Why merely for you to acknowledge the natural equality of women; include them in your schemes of improvement and raise them as high in the scale of sense and independence as yourselves.

John Doherty, 1834

The means for effecting the ecclesiastical emancipation of woman appear to us to consist in the formation of a "woman's society" in every city, town and village possible. In this society women might converse, discuss, and speak upon their rights, their wrongs, and their destiny; they might consult upon their own welfare and that of the great human family, and thus prepare each other for the mission of the apostile in society at large.

Catherine Barmby, 1841

... gentleness and force ... we wish to behold united in every human individual, without relation to sex. In fine, to be a true communist, or Socialist, the man must possess the woman-power as well as the man-power, and the woman must possess the man-power as well as the woman-power. Both must be equilibrated beings.

Goodwyn Barmby, 1840s

Flora Tristan, French utopian socialist

A universal union of working men and women ... is to be a bridge erected between a dying civilization and the harmonious social order foreseen by superior minds... I demand rights for women because I am convinced that *all the ills of the world come from this forgetfulness and scorn that until now have been inflicted on the natural and imprescriptible rights of the female.* I demand rights for women because that is the *only way that their education will be attended to* and because on the education of women depends that of men in general, and *particularly of the men of the people...*

Workers, under present conditions, you know what happens in your households. You, the man, *the master having rights* over your wife, do you live with her contentedly? Speak: are you happy?

No, no. It is easy to see that in spite of your rights, you are neither *contented* nor *happy.*

Between master and slave, there can only be fatigue from the weight of the chain that binds one to the other. Where the absence of liberty makes itself felt, happiness cannot exist. [...]

"RÉSUMÉ OF THE IDEAS CONTAINED IN THIS BOOK" whose purpose is to:

1. CONSTITUTE THE WORKING CLASS by means of a compact, solid, and indissoluble UNION.
2. Arrange for the representation of the working class before the nation by a defender chosen by the WORKERS' UNION and salaried by it, in order to establish firmly the fact that this class has its need to exist, and to secure acceptance of this fact by the other classes.
3. Secure recognition of the *legitimacy of arms as a form of property.* (In France twenty-five million proletarians have no property except *their arms.*)
4. Secure recognition of the legitimacy of the *right to work* for *all men* and *all women.*
5. Secure recognition of the legitimacy of the right to moral, intellectual, and professional education for *all men* and *all women.*
6. Explore the possibility of *organizing work* under the present social conditions.
7. Construct in each department PALACES OF THE WORKERS' UNION, where children of the working class will be instructed, intellectually and profession-ally, and where working men and women who have been injured at their jobs, and those who are infirm or aged, will be cared for.
8. Recognize the urgent need to provide *women of the people* with a moral, intel-lectual, and professional education, so that they may become moralizing agents of the *men of the people.*
9. Recognize, *in principle, the legal equality* of men and women as being the only means of constituting the UNITY OF HUMANITY.

Flora Tristan, *The Workers' Union,* 2d ed., 1844

[I]t is absolutely essential that the people depend on themselves alone; if they entrust their interests to the bourgeoisie they will lose out once again.

Flora Tristan, *Le Tour de France*, 1843

Charles Fourier, French utopian socialist

In every society, the degree of female emancipation (freedom) is the natural measure of emancipation in general. This applies perfectly to society today. The contemporary mass struggle for the political equality of women is only one expression and one part of the general liberation struggle of the proletariat, and therein lies its strength and its future. General, equal and direct suffrage for women will—thanks to the female proletariat—immeasurably advance and sharpen the class struggle. That is why bourgeois society detests and fears women's suffrage, and that is why we want to win it and will win it. And through the struggle for women's suffrage we will hasten the hour when the society of today will be smashed to bits under the hammer blows of the revolutionary proletariat.

Charles Fourier, *Théorie des Quatre Mouvements, Œuvres Complètes*, Paris, 1841–45

Sisters of America! your socialist sisters of France are united with you in the vindication of the right of women to civil and political equality. We have, moreover, the profound conviction that only by the power of association based on solidarity—by the union of the working classes of both sexes to organize labour—can be acquired, completely and pacifically, the civil and political equality of women, and the social right of all.

Letter of Pauline Roland and Jeanne Deroin, French utopian socialists, to the American women's convention, 1851

Marx and Engels

The direct, natural, and necessary relation of person to person is the *relation of man to woman*. In this *natural* relationship of the sexes man's relation to nature is immediately his relation to man, just as his relation to man is immediately his relation to nature—his own *natural* function. In this relationship, therefore, is *sensuously manifested*, reduced to an observable *fact*, the extent to which the human essence has become nature to man, or to which nature has to him become the human essence of man. From this relationship one can therefore judge man's whole level of development. It follows from the character of this relationship how much *man* as a *species being*, as *man*, has come to be himself and to comprehend himself; the relation of man to woman is *the most natural* relation of human being to human being. It therefore reveals the extent to which man's *natural* behaviour has become *human*, or the extent to which the *human* essence in him has become a *natural* essence—the extent to which his *human nature* has come to be *nature to him*. In this relationship is revealed, too, the extent to which man's *need* has become a *human* need; the extent to which, therefore, the *other* person as a person has become for him a need—the extent to which he in his individual existence is at the same time a social being.

Karl Marx, *Economic and Philosophical Manuscripts*, 1844

Abolition of the family! Even the most radical flare up at this infamous proposal of the Communists.

On what foundation is the present family, the bourgeois family, based? On capital, on private gain. In its completely developed form this family exists only among the bourgeoisie. But this state of things finds its complement in the practical absence of the family among the proletarians, and in public prostitution.

The bourgeois family will vanish as a matter of course when its complement vanishes, and both will vanish with the vanishing of capital.

Do you charge us with wanting to stop the exploitation of children by their parents? To this crime we plead guilty.

But, you will say, we destroy the most hallowed of relations, when we replace home education by social.

And your education! Is not that also social, and determined by the social conditions under which you educate, by the intervention, direct or indirect, of society, by means of schools, &c.? The Communists have not invented the intervention of society into education; they do but seek to alter the character of that intervention, and to rescue education from the influence of the ruling class.

The bourgeois clap-trap about the family and education, about the hallowed co-relation of parent and child, becomes all the more disgusting, the more, by the action of Modern Industry, all family ties among the proletarians are torn asunder, and their children transformed into simple articles of commerce and instruments of labour.

But you Communists would introduce community of women, screams the whole bourgeoisie in chorus.

The bourgeois sees in his wife a mere instrument of production. He hears that the instruments of production are to be exploited in common, and, naturally, can come to no other conclusion than that the lot of being common to all will likewise fall to the women.

He has not even a suspicion that the real point aimed at is to do away with the status of women as mere instruments of production.

For the rest, nothing is more ridiculous than the virtuous indignation of our bourgeois at the community of women which, they pretend, is to be openly and officially established by the Communists. The Communists have no need to introduce community of women; it has existed almost from time immemorial.

Our bourgeois, not content with having the wives and daughters of their proletarians at their disposal, not to speak of common prostitutes, take the greatest pleasure in seducing each other's wives.

Bourgeois marriage is in reality a system of wives in common and thus, at the most, what the Communists might possibly be reproached with, is that they desire to introduce, in substitution for a hypocritically concealed, an openly legalized community of women. For the rest, it is self-evident that the abolition of the present system of production must bring with it the abolition of the community of women springing from the system, *i.e.*, of prostitution both public and private.

Karl Marx and Frederick Engels, *The Manifesto of the Communist Party*, 1848

ᛁebel, leading German socialist

endeavor to found a society in which all the means of production are the of the community, a society which recognizes the full equality of all *without distinction of sex.*

> August Bebel, *Woman in the Past, Present and Future*, 1885

Independently of the question whether a woman is oppressed as a proletarian, in this world of private property she is viewed almost exclusively in terms of her gender. Any number of restrictions and obstacles unknown to man exist for her and restrict her in every situation. Much of what is permitted to a man is forbidden for a woman. An entire slew of social rights and freedoms which everyone enjoys are considered errors or crimes when done by a woman. A woman suffers as a social being and because of her gender, and it is difficult to decide in which of these roles she suffers the most.

> August Bebel, *Women and Socialism*, 1891

The favorite objection raised against them is that they are not fit for such pursuits, not being intended therefor by Nature. The question of engaging in the higher professional occupations concerns at present only a small number of women in modern society; it is, however, important in point of principle. The large majority of men believe in all seriousness that, mentally as well, woman must ever remain subordinate to them, and hence, has no right to equality. They are, accordingly, the most determined opponents of woman's aspirations.

> August Bebel, *Women and Socialism*, 1891

The tyranny of men over women is similar to the tyranny of the bourgeoisie over the proletariat; in many ways the former is even worse. The proletarian man sells his labor-time to his employer for a limited amount of time only, and if the situation does not please him, he can in most cases seek another, better employer. A wife, however, is tied to her husband forever and lives every hour and everyday in strife with him; she must wear her chains until the day she dies. The proletarian man is much more independent vis-à-vis other men. He can more easily demand respect and justice through coalitions with his colleagues. The situation is completely different for women. She must put up with all sorts of injustices, and the legal system protects her much less completely than it protects the proletarian man and in any case only in the most difficult of situations. When things progress this far, a separation is necessary, but it is a separation which leaves the women in misery and isolation, while the man is in the pleasant situation of taking another wife.

> August Bebel, "Über die gegenwärtige und künftige Stellung der Frau," 1878

Working-class women have more in common with bourgeois women or aristocratic women than do working-class men with men of other social classes.

> August Bebel, "Über die gegenwärtige und künftige Stellung der Frau," 1878

Frederick Engels

According to the materialistic conception, the determining factor in history is, in the last resort, the production and reproduction of immediate life. But this itself is of a twofold character. On the one hand, the production of the means of subsistence, of food, clothing and shelter and the tools requisite therefore; on the other, the production of human beings themselves, the propagation of the species. The social institutions under which men of a definite historical epoch and of a definite country live are conditioned by both kinds of production: by the stage of development of labour, on the one hand, and of the family on the other.

Frederick Engels, *The Origin of the Family, Private Property and the State*, 1884,
Preface to the first edition

That woman was the slave of man at the commencement of society is one of the most absurd notions that have come down to us from the period of Enlightenment of the eighteenth century. [...]

The overthrow of mother right was the *world-historic defeat of the female sex*. The man seized the reins in the house also, the woman was degraded, enthralled, the slave of the man's lust, a mere instrument for breeding children. This lowered position of women, especially manifest among the Greeks of the Heroic and still more of the Classical Age, has become gradually embellished and dissembled and, in part, clothed in a milder form, but by no means abolished.

The first effect of the sole rule of the men that was now established is shown in the intermediate form of the family which now emerges, the patriarchal family. [...]

This was the origin of monogamy, as far as we can trace it among the most civilized and highly-developed people of antiquity. It was not in any way the fruit of individual sex love, with which it had absolutely nothing in common, for the marriages remained marriages of convenience, as before. It was the first form of family based not on natural but on economic conditions, namely, on the victory of private property over original, naturally developed, common ownership. The rule of the man in the family, the procreation of children who could only be his, destined to be the heirs of his wealth—these alone were frankly avowed by the Greeks as the exclusive aims of monogamy. [...]

The first class antagonism which appears in history coincides with the development of the antagonism between man and woman in monogamian marriage, and the first class oppression with that of the female sex by the male. Monogamy was a great historical advance, but at the same time it inaugurated, along with slavery and private wealth, that epoch, lasting until today, in which every advance is likewise a relative regression, in which the well-being and development of the one group are attained by the misery and repression of the other. It is the cellular form of civilized society, in which we can already study the nature of the antagonisms and contradictions which develop fully in the latter. [...]

We are now approaching a social revolution in which the hitherto existing economic foundations of monogamy will disappear just as certainly as will those of its supplement—prostitution. ... Since monogamy arose from economic causes, will it disappear when these causes disappear?

One might not unjustly answer: far from disappearing, it will only begin to be completely realized. For with the conversion of the means of production into social property, wage labour, the proletariat, also disappears, and therewith, also, the necessity for a certain—statistically calculable—number of women to surrender themselves for money. Prostitution disappears; monogamy, instead of declining, finally becomes a reality—for the men as well. [...]

What will most definitely disappear from monogamy, however, is all the characteristics stamped on it in consequence of its having arisen out of property relationships. These are, first, the dominance of the man, and secondly, the indissolubility of marriage. [...]

Thus, what we can conjecture at present about the regulation of sex relationships after the impending effacement of capitalist production is, in the main, of a negative character, limited mostly to what will vanish. But what will be added? That will be settled after a new generation has grown up: a generation of men who never in all their lives have had occasion to purchase a woman's surrender either with money or with any other means of social power, and of women who have never been obliged to surrender to any man out of any consideration other than that of real love, or to refrain from giving themselves to their beloved for fear of the economic consequences. Once such people appear, they will not care a rap about what we today think they should do. They will establish their own practice and their own public opinion, conformable therewith, on the practice of each individual—and that's the end of it.

Frederick Engels, The Origin of the Family, Private Property and the State, 1884

Rosa Luxemburg, leader of the German socialist movement[2]

The women of the possessing classes will always be rabid supporters of the exploitation and oppression of workingpeople, from which they receive at second hand the wherewithal for their socially useless existence. ... The women of the proletariat, on the contrary, are independent economically; they are engaged in productive work for society just as the men are. Not in the sense that they help the men by their housework. ... This work is not productive within the meaning of the present economic system of capitalism, even though it entails an immense expenditure of energy and self-sacrifice in a thousand little tasks. This is only the private concern of the proletarians, their blessing and felicity, and precisely for this reason nothing but empty air as far as modern society is concerned. Only that work is productive which produces surplus value and yields capitalists profit—as long as the rule of capital and the wage system still exists. From this standpoint the dancer in a café, who makes a profit for her employer with her legs, is a productive workingwoman, while all the toil of the woman and mothers of the proletariat within the four walls of the home is considered unproductive work. This sounds crude and crazy but it is an accurate expression of the crudeness and craziness of today's capitalist economic order; and to understand this crude reality clearly and sharply is the first necessity for the proletarian woman.

For it is precisely from this standpoint that the workingwomen's claim to political equality is now firmly anchored to a solid economic base. Millions of proletarian women today produce capitalist profit just like men—in factories, workshops, agriculture, homework industries, offices and stores. They are productive, therefore, in the strictest economic sense of society today. [...]

After all this, the political disenfranchisement of proletarian women is all the baser an injustice because it has already become partly false. [...]

When wide circles of society are seized by a sense of injustice—says Friedrich Engels, the cofounder of scientific socialism—it is always a sure sign that far-reaching shifts have taken place in the economic basis of society, and that the existing order of things has already come into contradiction with the ongoing process of development. The present powerful movement of millions of proletarian women who feel their political disenfranchisement to be a crying injustice is just such an unmistakable sign that the social foundations of the existing state are already rotten and that its days are numbered.

Rosa Luxemburg, "Women's Suffrage and Class Struggle," 1912

Clara Zetkin, leading German socialist and leader of international working women's movement

There is a women's question for the women of the proletariat, of the middle bourgeoisie, of the intelligentsia, and of the Upper Ten Thousand; it takes various forms depending on the class situation of these strata.

What form is taken by the women's question among the women of the Upper Ten Thousand? A woman of this social stratum, by virtue of her possession of property, can freely develop her individuality; she can live in accordance with her inclinations. As a wife, however, she is still always dependent on the man. [...]

When the women of these circles entertain a desire to give their lives serious content, they must first raise the demand for free and independent control over their property. This demand therefore is in the centre of the demands raised by the women's movement of the Upper Ten Thousand. These women fight for the achievement of this demand against the men of their own class—exactly the same demand that the bourgeoisie fought for against all privileged classes: a struggle for the elimination of all social distinctions based on the possession of wealth. [...]

And how does the women's question manifest itself in the ranks of the small and middle bourgeoisie, and in the bourgeois intelligentsia? ... In these circles the woman does not enjoy equality with the man as owner of private property, as obtains in the higher circles. Nor does she enjoy equality as a workingwoman, as obtains in proletarian circles. The women of these circles must, rather, first fight for their economic equality with the men, and they can do this only through two demands; through the demand for equality in occupational education and through the demand for sex equality in carrying on an occupation. Economically speaking, this means nothing else than the realization of free trade and free competition between men and women. The realization of this demand awakens a conflict of interest between the women and the men of the middle class and the intelligentsia. [...]

We would do the bourgeois women's movement an injustice if we ascribed it only to purely economic motives. No, it also has a very much deeper intellectual and moral side. The bourgeois woman not only demands to earn her own bread, but she also wants to live a full life intellectually and develop her own individuality. It is precisely in these strata that we meet those tragic and psychologically interesting "Neva" figures, where the wife is tired of living like a doll in a doll house, where she wants to take part in the broader development of modern culture; and on both the economic and intellectual–moral sides the strivings of the bourgeois women's-righters are entirely justified.

For the proletarian woman, it is capital's need for exploitation, its unceasing search for the cheapest labour power, that has created the women's question... This is also how the woman of the proletariat is drawn into the machinery of contemporary economic life, this is how she is driven into the workshop and to the machine. She entered economic life in order to give the husband some help in earning a living—and the capitalist mode of production transforms her into an undercutting competitor; she wanted to secure a better life for her family—and in consequence brought greater misery to the proletarian family. [...]

The woman of the proletariat has achieved her economic independence, but neither as a person nor as a woman or wife does she have the possibility of living a full life as an individual. For her work as wife and mother she gets only the crumbs that are dropped from the table by capitalist production.

Consequently, the liberation struggle of the proletarian woman cannot be—as it is for the bourgeois woman—a struggle against the men of her own class. She does not need to struggle, as against the men of her own class, to tear down the barriers erected to limit her free competition. Capital's need for exploitation and the development of the modern mode of production have wholly relieved her of this struggle. On the contrary; it is a question of erecting new barriers against the exploitation of the proletarian woman; it is a question of restoring and ensuring her rights as wife and mother. The end-goal of her struggle is not free competition with men but bringing about the political rule of the proletariat. Hand in hand with the men of her own class, the proletarian woman fights against capitalist society. To be sure, she also concurs with the demands of the bourgeois women's movement. But she regards the realization of these demands only as a means to an end, so that she can get into the battle along with the workingmen and equally armed.

Clara Zetkin, "Proletarian Women and Socialist Revolution," 1896

Eleanor Marx, English socialist

[...] in Lancashire and Yorkshire, where the women almost without exception belong to unions, pay regular dues and of course also draw benefits from them, they have absolutely no part in the leadership of these organizations, no voice in the administration of their own funds, and up to now have never become delegates to their own union's congress. Representation and administration lie wholly in the hands of men workers.

The main reason for this apparent indifference and apathy on the part of the women can easily be discerned; it is common to a large part of all women's organizations and we cannot ignore it here. The reason is that even today women still have two duties to fulfil: in the factory they are *proletarians* and earn a daily wage on which they and their children live in large part; but they are also *household slaves*, unpaid servants of their husbands, fathers and brothers. Even before going to the factory early in the morning, women have already done so much that if the men had to do it they would consider it a right good piece of work. Noon hour, which promises the men some rest at least, means no rest for the women. And finally evening, which the poor devil of a man claims for himself, must also be used for work by the even poorer devil of a woman. The housework must be done; the children must be taken care of; clothes must be washed and mended. In short, if men in an English factory town work ten hours, women have to work at least sixteen. How then can they show an active interest in anything else? It is a physical impossibility. And yet it is in these factory towns that on the whole women have it best. They make "good" wages, the men cannot get along without their work, and therefore they are relatively independent. It is only when we come to the towns or districts where woman labour means nothing but sweating work, where a great deal of *home work* is the rule, that we find the worst conditions and the greatest need for organization.

In recent years, much work has been done on this problem, but I am duty-bound to say that the results bear no relation to the efforts made. However, the relatively small results, it seems to me, are not always due to the miserable conditions under which most of the female workers live. I think, rather, an important part of the reason is the way most of the women's unions have been established and led. We find that most of them are led by people from the middle class, women as well as men. No doubt these people mean well up to a certain point, but they cannot understand and do not want to understand what the movement is about. They see the misery about them, they feel uneasy, and they would like to "ameliorate" the conditions of the unfortunate workers. But they do not belong to us.

Eleanor Marx, "On the Workingwomen's Movement in England," 1892

[...] there is no more a "natural calling" of woman than there is a "natural" law of capitalistic production, or a "natural" limit to the amount of the labourer's product that goes to him for means of subsistence. That in the first case, woman's "calling" is supposed to be only the tending of children, the maintenance of household conditions, and a general obedience to her lord; that, in the second, the production of surplus value is a necessary preliminary to the production of capital; that, in the third, the amount the labourer receives for his means of subsistence is so much as will keep him only just above starvation point: these are not natural laws in the same sense as are the laws of motion. They are only certain temporary conventions of society, like the convention that French is the language of diplomacy. [...]

Both the oppressed classes, women and the immediate producers, must understand that their emancipation will come from themselves.

Eleanor Marx and Edward Aveling, *The Woman Question*, 1887

Edward Carpenter, English socialist and freethinker

[...] is it possible for Woman ever to be worthy of her name, unless she is free?

To-day, or up to to-day, just as the wage-worker has had no means of livelihood except by the sale of his bodily labor, so woman has had no means of livelihood except by the surrender of her bodily sex. She could dispose of it to one man for life, and have in return the respect of society and the caged existence of the lady or the drudge, or she could sell it night by night and be a "free woman," scorned of the world and portioned to die in the gutter. In either case (if she really thinks about the matter at all) she must lose her self-respect. What a choice, what a frightful choice!—and this has been the fate of Woman for how long? [...]

Here there is no solution except the freedom of woman—which means of course also the freedom of the masses of the people, men and women, and the ceasing altogether of economic slavery. There is no solution which will not include the redemption of the terms "free woman" and "free love" to their true and rightful significance. Let every woman whose heart bleeds for the sufferings of her sex, hasten to declare herself and to constitute herself, as far as she possibly can, a free woman. Let her accept the term with all the odium that belongs to it; let her insist on her right to speak, dress, think, act and above all to use her sex, as she deems best; let her face the scorn and the ridicule; let her "lose her own life" if she likes; assured that only so can come deliverance, and that only when the free woman is honored will the prostitute cease to exist. And let every man who really would respect his counterpart, entreat her also to act so; let him never by word or deed tempt her to grant as a bargain what can only be precious as a gift; let him see her with pleasure stand a little aloof; let him help her to gain her feet; so at last, by what slight sacrifices on his part such a course may involve, will it dawn upon him that he has gained a real companion and helpmate on life's journey. [...]

The nearer Society comes to its freedom and majority the more lovingly will it embrace this great soul within it, and recognizing in all the customs of the past the partial efforts of that soul to its own fulfillment will refuse to deny them, but rather seek, by acceptance and reunion, to transform and illumine them all. ... If society should at any future time recognize—as we think likely it will do—the variety of needs of the human heart and of human beings, it will not therefore confuse them, but will see that these different needs indicate different functions, all of which may have their place and purpose. If it has the good sense to tolerate a Nature-festival now and then, and a certain amount of animalism let loose, it will not be so foolish as to be unable to distinguish this from the deep delight and happiness of a permanent spiritual mating; or if it recognizes in some case, a woman's temporary alliance with a man for the sake of obtaining a much-needed child, it will not therefore be so silly as to mark her down for life as a common harlot. It will allow in fact that there are different forms and functions of the love-sentiment, and while really believing that a life-long comradeship (possibly with little of the sexual in it) is the most satisfying form, will see that a cast-iron Marriage-custom which, as to-day, expects two people either to live eternally in the same house and sit on opposite sides of the same table, or else to be strangers to each other—and which only recognizes two sorts of intimacy, orthodox and criminal, wedded and adulterous— is itself the source of perpetual confusion and misapprehension.

No doubt the Freedom of Society in this sense, and the possibility of a human life which shall be the fluid and ever-responsive embodiment of true Love in all its variety of manifestation, goes with the Freedom of Society in the economic sense. When mankind has solved the industrial problem so far that the products of our huge mechanical forces have become a common heritage, and no man or woman is the property-slave of another, then some of the causes which compel prostitution, property-marriage, and other perversions of affection, will have disappeared; and in such economically free society human unions may at last take place according to their own inner and true laws. [...]

Perhaps it will only be for a society more fully grown than ours to understand the wealth and variety of affectional possibilities which it has within itself, and the full enchantment of the many relations in which the romance of love by a tender discrimination and aesthetic continence is preserved for years and decades of years in, as it were, a state of evergrowing perfection.

Edward Carpenter, Love's Coming-of-Age, 1911

Emma Goldman, Russian/American anarchist leader

I did not believe that a Cause which stood for a beautiful ideal, for anarchism, for release and freedom from conventions and prejudice, should demand the denial of life and joy. I insisted that our Cause could not expect me to behave as a nun and that the movement should not be turned into a cloister. If it meant that, I did not want it. "I want freedom, the right to self-expression, everybody's right to radiant, beautiful things."

Emma Goldman, Living My Life, 1931

Woman's development, her freedom, her independence, must come from and through herself. First, by asserting herself as a personality, and not as a sex commodity. Second, by refusing the right to anyone over her body; by refusing to bear children, unless she wants them; by refusing to be a servant to God, the State, society, the husband, the family, etc., by making her life simpler, but deeper and richer. That is, by trying to learn the meaning and substance of life in all its complexities, by freeing herself from the fear of public opinion and public condemnation. Only that, and not the ballot will set the woman free, will make her a force hitherto unknown in the world, a force for real love, for peace, for harmony; a force of divine fire, of life-giving; a creator of free men and women.

Emma Goldman, "Woman's Suffrage," 1914

What is really the cause of the trade in women? Not merely white women, but yellow and black women as well. Exploitation, of course; the merciless Moloch of capitalism that fattens on underpaid labor, thus driving thousands of women and girls into prostitution.

Nowhere is woman treated according to the merit of her work, but rather as a sex. It is therefore almost inevitable that she should pay for her right to exist, to keep a position in whatever line, with sex favors. Thus, it is merely a question of degree whether she sells herself to one man, in or out of marriage, or to many men.

[...] It would be one-sided and extremely superficial to maintain that the economic factor is the only cause of prostitution. There are others no less important and vital. That, too, our reformers know ... I refer to the sex question, the very mention of which causes most people moral spasms.

It is a conceded fact that woman is being reared as a sex commodity, and yet she is kept in absolute ignorance of the meaning and importance of sex. Everything dealing with that subject is suppressed, and persons who attempt to bring light into this terrible darkness are persecuted and thrown into prison. Yet it ... is due to this ignorance that the entire life and nature of the girl is thwarted and crippled. We have long ago taken it as a self-evident fact that the boy may follow the call of the wild; that is to say, that the boy may, as soon as his sex nature asserts itself, satisfy that nature; but our moralists are scandalized at the very thought that the nature of a girl should assert itself. To the moralist, prostitution does not consist so much in the fact that the woman sells her body, but rather that she sells it out of wedlock.

... This double standard of morality has played no little part in the creation and perpetuation of prostitution. It involves the keeping of the young in absolute ignorance on sex matters, which alleged "innocence," together with an overwrought and stifled sex nature, helps to bring about a state of affairs that our Puritans are so anxious to avoid or prevent.

Not that the gratification of sex must needs lead to prostitution; it is the cruel, heartless, criminal persecution of those who dare divert from the beaten track, which is responsible for it.

Emma Goldman, "The Traffic in Women," 1910

Marriage is primarily an economic arrangement, an insurance pact. It differs from the ordinary life insurance agreement only in that it is more binding, more exacting. Its returns are insignificantly small compared with the investments. In taking out an insurance policy one pays for it in dollars and cents, always at liberty to discontinue payments. If, however, woman's premium is a husband, she pays for it with her name, her privacy, her self-respect, her very life, "until death doth part." Moreover, the marriage insurance condemns her to life-long dependency, to parasitism, to complete uselessness, individual as well as social. [...]

Love, the strongest and deepest element in all life, the harbinger of hope, of joy, of ecstasy; love, the defier of all laws, of all conventions; love, the freest, the most powerful moulder of human destiny; how can such an all-compelling force be synonymous with the poor little State and Church-begotten weed, marriage? [...]

Some day, some day men and women will rise, they will reach the mountain peak, they will meet big and strong and free, ready to receive, to partake, and to bask in the golden rays of love. What fancy, what imagination, what poetic genius can foresee even approximately the potentialities of such a force in the life of men and women. If the world is ever to give birth to true companionship and oneness, not marriage, but love will be the parent.

Emma Goldman, "Marriage and Love," 1916

Alexandra Kollontai, leading Russian Bolshevik

Among the many problems that demand the consideration and attention of contemporary mankind, sexual problems are undoubtedly some of the most crucial. ... One of the tasks that confront the working class in its attack on the "beleaguered fortress of the future" is undoubtedly the task of establishing more healthy and more joyful relationships between the sexes.

What are the roots of this unforgivable indifference to one of the essential tasks of the working class? How can we explain to ourselves the hypocritical way in which "sexual problems" are relegated to the realm of "private matters" that are not worth the effort and the attention of the collective? Why has the fact been ignored that throughout history one of the constant features of social struggle has been the attempt to change relationships between the sexes, and the type of moral codes that determine these relationships; and that the way personal relationships are organized in a certain social group has had a vital influence on the outcome of the struggle between hostile social classes?

The tragedy of our society is not just that the usual forms of behaviour and the principles regulating his behaviour are breaking down, but that a spontaneous wave of new attempts at living is developing from within the social fabric, giving man hopes and ideals that cannot yet be realized. We are people living in the world of property relationships, a world of sharp class contradictions and of an individualistic morality. We still live and think under the heavy hand of an unavoidable loneliness of spirit. ... Because of their loneliness men are apt to cling in a predatory and unhealthy way to illusions about finding a "soul mate" from among the members of the opposite sex. [...]

The "crude individualism" that adorns our era is perhaps nowhere as blatant as in the organization of sexual relationships. A person wants to escape from his loneliness and naïvely imagines that being "in love" gives him the right to the soul of the other person. [...]

The claims we make on our "contracted partner" are absolute and undivided. We are unable to follow the simplest rule of love—that another person should be treated with great consideration. New concepts of the relationships between the sexes are already being outlined. They will teach us to achieve relationships based on the unfamiliar ideas of complete freedom, equality and genuine friendship. [...]

The "sexual crisis" is made worse by the two characteristics of the psychology of modern man:

1. The idea of "possessing" the married partner.
2. The belief that the two sexes are unequal, that they are of unequal worth in every way, in every sphere, including the sexual sphere. [...]

The sexual crisis cannot be solved unless there is a radical reform of the human psyche, and unless man's potential for loving is increased. And a basic transformation of the socioeconomic relationships along communist lines is essential if the psyche is to be re-formed. This is an "old truth" but there is no other way out.

Alexandra Kollontai, "Sexual Relations and the Class Struggle," 1911

Sylvia Pankhurst, English socialist and feminist

I regarded the rousing of the East End as of utmost importance... My aim was not merely to make some members and establish some branches but the larger task of bringing the district as a whole into a mass movement from which only a minority could stand aside... The creation of a women's movement in that abyss of poverty would be a call and a rallying cry to the rise of similar movements in all parts of the country... I was anxious too to fortify the position of the working women when the vote should actually be given; the existence of a strong self-reliant movement amongst the working women would be the greatest aid in safeguarding their rights in the day of settlement. Moreover, I was looking to the future; I wanted to rouse these women of the submerged tenth to be fighters on their own account, despising platitudes and catch cries, revolting against the hideous conditions about them and demanding for themselves and their families a full share of the benefits of civilization and progress.

Sylvia Pankhurst, *The Suffragette Movement*, 1931

***

One must write not only for oneself. But for others. For those far-away, unknown women who will live then. Let them see that we were not heroines or heroes at all. But we believed passionately in our goals and we pursued them. We were sometimes strong and sometimes we were very weak.

Alexandra Kollontai[3]

NOTES

1. These excerpts are from Barbara Taylor, *Eve and the New Jerusalem: Socialism and Feminism in the Nineteenth Century* (New York: Pantheon, 1983).
2. The following are all taken from Hal Draper and Anne G. Lipow, "Marxist Women versus Bourgeois Feminism," in *Socialist Register 1976* (London: Merlin, 1976).
3. Quoted in Barbara Evans Clements, *Bolshevik Feminist: The Life of Alexandra Kollontai* (Bloomington: Indiana University Press, 1979).

PART I

SEX, SEXUALITY, AND
REPRODUCTION

A QUESTION OF CLASS

DOROTHY ALLISON

The first time I heard "They're different than us, don't value human life the way we do" I was in high school in Central Florida. The man speaking was an army recruiter talking to a bunch of boys, telling them what the army was really like, what they could expect overseas. A cold angry feeling swept over me. I had heard the word *they* pronounced in that same callous tone before. *They*, those people over there, those people who are not us, they die so easily, kill each other so casually. They are different. We, I thought. *Me.*

When I was six or eight back in Greenville, South Carolina, I had heard that same matter-of-fact tone of dismissal applied to me. "Don't you play with her. I don't want you talking to them." I and my family, we had always been *they*. Who am I? I wondered, listening to that recruiter. Who are my people? We die so easily, disappear so completely—we/they, the poor and the queer. I pressed my bony white trash fists to my stubborn lesbian mouth. The rage was a good feeling, stronger and purer than the shame that followed it, the fear and the sudden urge to run and hide, to deny, to pretend I did not know who I was and what the world would do to me.

My people were not remarkable. We were ordinary, but even so we were mythical. We were the *they* everyone talks about—the ungrateful poor. I grew up trying to run away from the fate that destroyed so many of the people I loved, and, having learned the habit of hiding, I found I had also learned to hide from myself. I did not know who I was, only that I did not want to be *they*, the ones who are destroyed or dismissed to make the "real" people, the important people, feel safer. By the time I understood that I was queer, that habit of hiding was deeply set in me, so deeply that it was not a choice but an instinct. Hide, hide to survive, I thought, knowing that if I told the truth about my life, my family, my sexual desire, my history, I would move over into that unknown territory, the land of they, would never have the chance to name my own life, to understand it or claim it.

Why are you so afraid? my lovers and friends have asked me the many times I have suddenly seemed a stranger, someone who would not speak to them, would not do the things they believed I should do, simple things like applying for a job, or a grant, or some award they were sure I could acquire easily. Entitlement, I have told them, is a matter of feeling like we rather than they. You think you have a right to things, a place in the world, and it is so intrinsically a part of you that you cannot imagine people like me, people who seem to live in your world, who don't have it. I have explained what I know over and over, in every way I can, but I have never been able to make clear the degree of my fear, the extent to which I feel myself denied: not only that I am queer in a world that hates queers, but that I was born poor into a world that despises the poor. The need to make my world believable to people who have never experienced it is part of why I write fiction. I know that some things must be felt to be understood, that despair, for example, can never be adequately analyzed; it must be lived. But if I can write a story that so draws the reader in that she imagines herself like my characters, feels their sense of fear and uncertainty, their hopes and terrors, then I have come closer to knowing myself as real, as important as the very people I have always watched with awe.

I have known I was a lesbian since I was a teenager, and I have spent a good twenty years making peace with the effects of incest and physical abuse. But what may be the central fact of my life is that I was born in 1949 in Greenville, South Carolina, the bastard daughter of a white woman from a desperately poor family, a girl who had left the seventh grade the year before, worked as a waitress, and was just a month past fifteen when she had me. That fact, the inescapable impact of being born in a condition of poverty that this society finds shameful, contemptible, and somehow deserved, has had dominion over me to such an extent that I have spent my life trying to overcome or deny it. I have learned with great difficulty that the vast majority of people believe that poverty is a voluntary condition.

I have loved my family so stubbornly that every impulse to hold them in contempt has sparked in me a countersurge of pride—complicated and undercut by an urge to fit us into the acceptable myths and theories of both mainstream society and a lesbian-feminist reinterpretation. The choice becomes Steven Spielberg movies or Erskine Caldwell novels, the one valorizing and the other caricaturing, or the patriarchy as villain, trivializing the choices the men and women of my family have made. I have had to fight broad generalizations from every theoretical viewpoint.

Traditional feminist theory has had a limited understanding of class differences and of how sexuality and self are shaped by both desire and denial. The ideology implies that we are all sisters who should only turn our anger and suspicion on the world outside the lesbian community. It is easy to say that the patriarchy did it, that poverty and social contempt are products of the world of the fathers, and often I felt a need to collapse my sexual history into what I was willing to share of my class background, to pretend that my life both as a lesbian and as a working-class escapee was constructed by the patriarchy. Or, conversely, to ignore how much my life was shaped by growing up poor and talk only about what incest did to my identity as a woman and as a lesbian. The difficulty is that I can't ascribe everything that has been problematic about my life simply and easily to the patriarchy, or to incest, or even to the invisible and much denied class structure of our society.

In my lesbian-feminist collective we had long conversations about the mind/body split, the way we compartmentalize our lives to survive. For years I thought the concept referred to the way I had separated my activist life from the passionate secret life in which I acted on my sexual desires. I was convinced that the fracture was fairly simple, that it would be healed when there was time and clarity to do so—at about the same point when I might begin to understand sex. I never imagined that it was not a split but a splintering, and I passed whole portions of my life—days, months, years—in pure directed progress, getting up every morning and setting to work, working so hard and so continually that I avoided examining in any way what I knew about my life. Busywork became a trance state. I ignored who I really was and how I became that person, continued in that daily progress, became an automaton who was what she did.

I tried to become one with the lesbian-feminist community so as to feel real and valuable. I did not know that I was hiding, blending in for safety just as I had done in high school, in college. I did not recognize the impulse to forget. I believed that all those things I did not talk about, or even let myself think too much about, were not important, that none of them defined me. I had constructed a life, an identity in which I took pride, an alternative lesbian family in which I felt safe, and I did not realize that the fundamental me had almost disappeared.

It is surprising how easy it was to live that life. Everyone and everything cooperated with the process. Everything in our culture—books, television, movies, school, fashion—is presented as if it is being seen by one pair of eyes, shaped by one set of hands, heard by one pair of ears. Even if you know you are not part of that imaginary creature—if you like country music not symphonies, read books cynically, listen to the news unbelievingly, are lesbian not heterosexual, and surround yourself with your own small deviant community—you are still shaped by that hegemony, or your resistance to it. The only way I found to resist that homogenized view of the world was to make myself part of something larger than myself. As a feminist and a radical lesbian organizer, and later as a sex radical (which eventually became the term, along with "pro-sex feminist," for those who were not anti-pornography but anti-censorship, those of us arguing for sexual diversity), the need to belong, to feel safe, was just as important for me as for any heterosexual, nonpolitical citizen, and sometimes even more important because the rest of my life was so embattled.

The first time I read the Jewish lesbian Irena Klepfisz's poems,[1] I experienced a frisson of recognition. It was not that my people had been "burned off the map" or murdered as hers had. No, we had been encouraged to destroy ourselves, made invisible because we did not fit the myths of the noble poor generated by the middle class. Even now, past forty and stubbornly proud of my family, I feel the draw of that mythology, that romanticized, edited version of the poor. I find myself looking back and wondering what was real, what was true. Within my family, so much was lied about, joked about, denied, or told with deliberate indirection, an undercurrent of humiliation or a brief pursed grimace that belied everything that had been said. What was real? The poverty depicted in books and movies was romantic, a backdrop for the story of how it was escaped.

The poverty portrayed by left-wing intellectuals was just as romantic, a platform for assailing the upper and middle classes, and from their perspective the working-class hero was invariably male, righteously indignant, and inhumanly noble. The reality of self-hatred and violence was either absent or caricatured. The poverty I knew was dreary, deadening, shameful, the women powerful in ways not generally seen as heroic by the world outside the family.

My family's lives were not on television, not in books, not even comic books. There was a myth of the poor in this country, but it did not include us, no matter how hard I tried to squeeze us in. There was an idea of the good poor— hard-working, ragged but clean, and intrinsically honorable. I understood that we were the bad poor: men who drank and couldn't keep a job; women, invariably pregnant before marriage, who quickly became worn, fat, and old from working too many hours and bearing too many children; and children with runny noses, watery eyes, and the wrong attitudes. My cousins quit school, stole cars, used drugs, and took dead-end jobs pumping gas or waiting tables. We were not noble, not grateful, not even hopeful. We knew ourselves despised. My family was ashamed of being poor, of feeling hopeless. What was there to work for, to save money for, to fight for or struggle against? We had generations before us to teach us that nothing ever changed, and that those who did try to escape failed.

My mama had eleven brothers and sisters, of whom I can name only six. No one is left alive to tell me the names of the others. It was my grandmother who told me about my real daddy, a shiftless pretty man who was supposed to have married, had six children, and sold cut-rate life insurance to poor black people. My mama married when I was a year old, but her husband died just after my little sister was born a year later.

When I was five, Mama married the man she was to live with until she died. Within the first year of their marriage Mama miscarried, and while we waited out in the hospital parking lot my stepfather molested me for the first time, something he continued to do until I was past thirteen. When I was eight or so, Mama took us away to a motel after my stepfather beat me so badly it caused a family scandal, but we returned after two weeks. Mama told me that she really had no choice: she could not support us alone. When I was eleven I told one of my cousins that my stepfather was molesting me. Mama packed up my sisters and me and took us away for a few days, but again my stepfather swore he would stop, and again we went back after a few weeks. I stopped talking for a while, and I have only vague memories of the next two years.

My stepfather worked as a route salesman, my mama as a waitress, laundry worker, cook, or fruit packer. I could never understand, since they both worked so hard and such long hours, how we never had enough money, but it was also true of my mama's brothers and sisters who worked hard in the mills or the furnace industry. In fact, my parents did better than anyone else in the family. But eventually my stepfather was fired and we hit bottom—nightmarish months of marshals at the door, repossessed furniture, and rubber checks. My parents worked out a scheme so that it appeared my stepfather had abandoned us, but instead he went down to Florida, got a new job, and rented us a house. He returned with a U-Haul trailer in the dead of night, packed us up, and moved us south.

The night we left South Carolina for Florida, my mama leaned over the back seat of her old Pontiac and promised us girls, "It'll be better there." I don't know if we believed her, but I remember crossing Georgia in the early morning, watching the red clay hills and swaying grey blankets of moss recede through the back window. I kept looking at the trailer behind us, ridiculously small to contain everything we owned. Mama had packed nothing that wasn't fully paid off, which meant she had only two things of worth: her washing and sewing machines, both of them tied securely to the trailer walls. Throughout the trip I fantasized an accident that would burst that trailer, scattering old clothes and cracked dishes on the tarmac.

I was only thirteen. I wanted us to start over completely, to begin again as new people with nothing of the past left over. I wanted to run away from who we had been seen to be, who we had been. That desire is one I have seen in other members of my family. It is the first thing I think of when trouble comes— the geographic solution. Change your name, leave town, disappear, make yourself over. What hides behind that impulse is the conviction that the life you have lived, the person you are, is valueless, better off abandoned, that running away is easier than trying to change things, that change itself is not possible. Sometimes I think it is this conviction—more seductive than alcohol or violence, more subtle than sexual hatred or gender injustice—that has dominated my life and made real change so painful and difficult.

Moving to Central Florida did not fix our lives. It did not stop my stepfather's violence, heal my shame, or make my mother happy. Once there, our lives became controlled by my mother's illness and medical bills. She had a hysterectomy when I was about eight and endured a series of hospitalizations for ulcers and a chronic back problem. Through most of my adolescence she superstitiously refused to allow anyone to mention the word *cancer*. When she was not sick, Mama and my stepfather went on working, struggling to pay off what seemed an insurmountable load of debts.

By the time I was fourteen, my sisters and I had found ways to discourage most of our stepfather's sexual advances. We were not close, but we united against him. Our efforts were helped along when he was referred to a psychotherapist after he lost his temper at work, and was prescribed drugs that made him sullen but less violent. We were growing up quickly, my sisters moving toward dropping out of school while I got good grades and took every scholarship exam I could find. I was the first person in my family to graduate from high school, and the fact that I went on to college was nothing short of astonishing.

We all imagine our lives are normal, and I did not know my life was not everyone's. It was in Central Florida that I began to realize just how different we were. The people we met there had not been shaped by the rigid class structure that dominated the South Carolina Piedmont. The first time I looked around my junior high classroom and realized I did not know who those people were—not only as individuals but as categories, who their people were and how they saw themselves—I also realized that they did not know me. In Greenville, everyone knew my family, knew we were trash, and that meant we were supposed to be poor, supposed to have grim low-paid jobs, have babies in our teens, and never finish school. But Central Florida in the 1960s was full of runaways and immigrants, and our mostly white working-class suburban school sorted us out not by income and family background but by intelligence and aptitude tests. Suddenly I was boosted into the college-bound track, and while there was plenty of contempt for my inept social skills, pitiful wardrobe, and slow drawling accent, there was also something I had never experienced before: a protective anonymity, and a kind of grudging respect and curiosity about who I might become. Because they did not see poverty and hopelessness as a foregone conclusion for my life, I could begin to imagine other futures for myself.

In that new country, we were unknown. The myth of the poor settled over us and glamorized us. I saw it in the eyes of my teachers, the Lion's Club representative who paid for my new glasses, and the lady from the Junior League who told me about the scholarship I had won. Better, far better, to be one of the mythical poor than to be part of the *they* I had known before. I also experienced a new level of fear, a fear of losing what had never before been imaginable. Don't let me lose this chance, I prayed, and lived in terror that I might suddenly be seen again as what I knew myself to be.

As an adolescent I thought that my family's escape from South Carolina played like a bad movie. We fled the way runaway serfs might have done, with the sheriff who would have arrested my stepfather the imagined border guard. I am certain that if we had remained in South Carolina, I would have been trapped by my family's heritage of poverty, jail, and illegitimate children—that even being smart, stubborn, and a lesbian would have made no difference.

My grandmother died when I was twenty, and after Mama went home for the funeral I had a series of dreams in which we still lived up in Greenville, just down the road from where Granny died. In the dreams I had two children and only one eye, lived in a trailer, and worked at the textile mill. Most of my time was taken up with deciding when I would finally kill my children and myself. The dreams were so vivid, I became convinced they were about the life I was meant to have had, and I began to work even harder to put as much distance as I could between my family and me. I copied the dress, mannerisms, attitudes, and ambitions of the girls I met in college, changing or hiding my own tastes, interests, and desires. I kept my lesbianism a secret, forming a relationship with an effeminate male friend that served to shelter and disguise us both. I explained to friends that I went home so rarely because my stepfather and I fought too much for me to be comfortable in his house. But that was only part of the reason I avoided home, the easiest reason. The truth was that I feared the person I might become in my mama's house, the woman of my dreams— hateful, violent, and hopeless.

It is hard to explain how deliberately and thoroughly I ran away from my own life. I did not forget where I came from, but I gritted my teeth and hid it. When I could not get enough scholarship money to pay for graduate school, I spent a year of rage working as a salad girl, substitute teacher, and maid. I finally managed to find a job by agreeing to take any city assignment where the Social Security Administration needed a clerk. Once I had a job and my own place far away from anyone in my family, I became sexually and politically active, joining the Women's Center support staff and falling in love with a series of middle-class women who thought my accent and stories thoroughly charming. The stories I told about my family, about South Carolina, about being poor itself, were all lies, carefully edited to seem droll or funny. I knew damn well that no one would want to hear the truth about poverty, the hopelessness and fear, the feeling that nothing I did would ever make any difference and the raging resentment that burned beneath my jokes. Even when my lovers and I formed an alternative lesbian family, sharing what we could of our resources, I kept the truth about my background and who I knew myself to be a carefully obscured mystery. I worked as hard as I could to make myself a new person, an emotionally healthy radical lesbian activist, and I believed completely that by remaking myself I was helping to remake the world. For a decade, I did not go home for more than a few days at a time.

When in the 1980s I ran into the concept of feminist sexuality, I genuinely did not know what it meant. Though I was, and am, a feminist, and committed to claiming the right to act on my sexual desires without tailoring my lust to a sex-fearing society, demands that I explain or justify my sexual fantasies have left me at a loss. How does anyone explain sexual need?

The Sex Wars are over, I've been told, and it always makes me want to ask who won. But my sense of humor may be a little obscure to women who have never felt threatened by the way most lesbians use and mean the words *pervert* and *queer*. I use the word "queer" to mean more than lesbian. Since I first used it in 1980 I have always meant it to imply that I am not only a lesbian but a transgressive lesbian—femme, masochistic, as sexually aggressive as the women I seek out, and as pornographic in my imagination and sexual activities as the heterosexual hegemony has ever believed.

My aunt Dot used to joke, "There are two or three things I know for sure, but never the same things and I'm never as sure as I'd like." What I know for sure is that class, gender, sexual preference, and prejudice—racial, ethnic, and religious—form an intricate lattice that restricts and shapes our lives, and that resistance to hatred is not a simple act. Claiming your identity in the cauldron of hatred and resistance to hatred is infinitely complicated and, worse, almost unexplainable.

I know that I have been hated as a lesbian both by "society" and by the intimate world of my extended family, but I have also been hated or held in contempt (which is in some ways more debilitating and slippery than hatred) by lesbians for behavior and sexual practices shaped in large part by class. My sexual identity is intimately constructed by my class and regional background, and much of the hatred directed at my sexual preferences is class hatred—however much people, feminists in particular, like to pretend this is not a factor. The kind of woman I am attracted to is invariably the kind of woman who embarrasses respectably middle-class, politically aware lesbian feminists. My sexual ideal is butch, exhibitionistic, physically aggressive, smarter than she wants you to know, and proud of being called a pervert. Most often she is working class, with an aura of danger and an ironic sense of humor. There is a lot of contemporary lip service paid to sexual tolerance, but the fact that my sexuality is constructed within, and by, a butch/femme and leather fetishism is widely viewed with distaste or outright hatred.

For most of my life I have been presumed to be misguided, damaged by incest and childhood physical abuse, or deliberately indulging in hateful and retrograde sexual practices out of a selfish concentration on my own sexual satisfaction. I have been expected to abandon my desires, to become the normalized woman who flirts with fetishization, who plays with gender roles and treats the historical categories of deviant desire with humor or gentle contempt but never takes any of it so seriously as to claim a sexual identity based on these categories. It was hard enough for me to shake off demands when they were made by straight society. It was appalling when I found the same demands made by other lesbians.

One of the strengths I derive from my class background is that I am accustomed to contempt. I know that I have no chance of becoming what my detractors expect of me, and I believe that even the attempt to please them will only further engage their contempt, and my own self-contempt as well. Nonetheless, the relationship between the life I have lived and the way that life is seen by strangers has constantly invited a kind of self-mythologizing fantasy. It has always been tempting for me to play off of the stereotypes and

misconceptions of mainstream culture, rather than describe a difficult and sometimes painful reality.

I am trying to understand how we internalize the myths of our society even as
we resist them. I have felt a powerful temptation to write about my family as
a kind of morality tale, with us as the heroes and middle and upper classes as
the villains. It would be within the romantic myth, for example, to pretend that
we were the kind of noble Southern whites portrayed in the movies, mill workers for generations until driven out by alcoholism and a family propensity for
rebellion and union talk. But that would be a lie. The truth is that no one in my
family ever joined a union.

Taken to its limits, the myth of the poor would make my family over into
union organizers or people broken by the failure of the unions. As far as my
family was concerned union organizers, like preachers, were of a different class,
suspect and hated however much they might be admired for what they were
supposed to be trying to achieve. Nominally Southern Baptist, no one in my
family actually paid much attention to preachers, and only little children went to
Sunday school. Serious belief in anything—any political ideology, any religious
system, or any theory of life's meaning and purpose—was seen as unrealistic. It
was an attitude that bothered me a lot when I started reading the socially
conscious novels I found in the paperback racks when I was eleven or so. I
particularly loved Sinclair Lewis's novels and wanted to imagine my own family
as part of the working man's struggle.

"We were not joiners," my aunt Dot told me with a grin when I asked her
about the union. My cousin Butch laughed at that, told me the union charged
dues, and said, "Hell, we can't even be persuaded to toss money in the collection plate. Ain't gonna give it to no union man." It shamed me that the only
thing my family wholeheartedly believed in was luck and the waywardness of
fate. They held the dogged conviction that the admirable and wise thing to do
was keep a sense of humor, never whine or cue, and trust that luck might
someday turn as good as it had been bad—and with just as much reason.
Becoming a political activist with an almost religious fervor was the thing I did
that most outraged my family and the Southern working-class community they
were part of.

Similarly, it was not my sexuality, my lesbianism, that my family saw as most
rebellious; for most of my life, no one but my mama took my sexual preference
very seriously. It was the way I thought about work, ambition, and self-respect.
They were waitresses, laundry workers, counter girls. I was the one who went
to work as a maid, something I never told any of them. They would have been
angry if they had known. Work was just work for them, necessary. You did what
you had to do to survive. They did not so much believe in taking pride in doing
your job as in stubbornly enduring hard work and hard times. At the same time,
they held that there were some forms of work, including maid's work, that were
only for black people, not white, and while I did not share that belief, I knew

how intrinsic it was to the way my family saw the world. Sometimes I felt as if I straddled cultures and belonged on neither side. I would grind my teeth at what I knew was my family's unquestioning racism while continuing to respect their pragmatic endurance. But more and more as I grew older, what I felt was a deep estrangement from their view of the world, and gradually a sense of shame that would have been completely incomprehensible to them.

"Long as there's lunch counters, you can always find work," I was told by my mother and my aunts. Then they'd add, "I can get me a little extra with a smile." It was obvious there was supposed to be nothing shameful about it, that needy smile across a lunch counter, that rueful grin when you didn't have rent, or the half-provocative, half-pleading way my mama could cajole the man at the store to give her a little credit. But I hated it, hated the need for it and the shame that would follow every time I did it myself. It was begging, as far as I was concerned, a quasi-prostitution that I despised even while I continued to rely on it. After all, I needed the money.

"Just use that smile," my girl cousins used to joke, and I hated what I knew they meant. After college, when I began to support myself and study feminist theory, I became more contemptuous rather than more understanding of the women in my family. I told myself that prostitution is a skilled profession and my cousins were never more than amateurs. There was a certain truth in this, though like all cruel judgments rendered from the outside, it ignored the conditions that made it true. The women in my family, my mother included, had sugar daddies, not johns, men who slipped them money because they needed it so badly. From their point of view they were nice to those men because the men were nice to them, and it was never so direct or crass an arrangement that they would set a price on their favors. Nor would they have described what they did as prostitution. Nothing made them angrier than the suggestion that the men who helped them out did it just for their favors. They worked for a living, they swore, but this was different.

I always wondered if my mother hated her sugar daddy, or if not him then her need for what he offered her, but it did not seem to me in memory that she had. He was an old man, half-crippled, hesitant and needy, and he treated my mama with enormous consideration and, yes, respect. The relationship between them was painful, and since she and my stepfather could not earn enough to support the family, Mama could not refuse her sugar daddy's money. At the same time the man made no assumptions about that money buying anything Mama was not already offering. The truth was, I think, that she genuinely liked him, and only partly because he treated her so well.

Even now, I am not sure whether there was a sexual exchange between them. Mama was a pretty woman, and she was kind to him, a kindness he obviously did not get from anyone else in his life. Moreover, he took extreme care not to cause her any problems with my stepfather. As a teenager, with a teenager's contempt for moral failings and sexual complexity of any kind, I had been convinced that Mama's relationship with that old man was contemptible. Also,

I knew that I would never do such a thing. But the first time a lover of mine gave me money and I took it, everything in my head shifted. The amount was not much to her, but it was a lot to me and I needed it. While I could not refuse it, I hated myself for taking it and I hated her for giving it. Worse, she had much less grace about my need than my mama's sugar daddy had displayed toward her. All that bitter contempt I felt for my needy cousins and aunts raged through me and burned out the love. I ended the relationship quickly, unable to forgive myself for selling what I believed should only be offered freely—not sex but love itself.

When the women in my family talked about how hard they worked, the men would spit to the side and shake their heads. Men took real jobs—harsh, dangerous, physically daunting work. They went to jail, not just the cold-eyed, careless boys who scared me with their brutal hands, but their gentler, softer brothers. It was another family thing, what people expected of my mama's people, mine. "His daddy's that one was sent off to jail in Georgia, and his uncle's another. Like as not, he's just the same," you'd hear people say of boys so young they still had their milk teeth. We were always driving down to the county farm to see somebody, some uncle, cousin, or nameless male relation. Shaven-headed, sullen, and stunned, they wept on Mama's shoulder or begged my aunts to help. "I didn't do nothing, Mama," they'd say, and it might have been true, but if even we didn't believe them, who would? No one told the truth, not even about how their lives were destroyed.

One of my favorite cousins went to jail when I was eight years old, for breaking into pay phones with another boy. The other boy was returned to the custody of his parents. My cousin was sent to the boys' facility at the county farm. After three months, my mama took us down there to visit, carrying a big basket of fried chicken, cold cornbread, and potato salad. Along with a hundred others we sat out on the lawn with my cousin and watched him eat like he hadn't had a full meal in the whole three months. I stared at his near-bald head and his ears marked with fine blue scars from the carelessly handled razor. People were laughing, music was playing, and a tall, lazy, uniformed man walked past us chewing on toothpicks and watching us all closely. My cousin kept his head down, his face hard with hatred, only looking back at the guard when he turned away.

"Sons-a-bitches," he whispered, and my mama shushed him. We all sat still when the guard turned back to us. There was a long moment of quiet, and then that man let his face relax into a big wide grin. "Uh-huh," he said. That was all he said. Then he turned and walked away. None of us spoke. None of us ate. He went back inside soon after, and we left. When we got back to the car, my mama sat there for a while crying quietly. The next week my cousin was reported for fighting and had his stay extended by six months.

My cousin was fifteen. He never went back to school, and after jail he couldn't join the army. When he finally did come home we never talked, never had to. I knew without asking that the guard had had his little revenge, knew too that my cousin would break into another phone booth as soon as he could, but do it sober and not get caught. I knew without asking the source of his rage, the way he felt about clean, well-dressed, contemptuous people who looked at him like his life wasn't as important as a dog's. I knew because I felt it too. That guard had looked at me and Mama with the same expression he used on my cousin. We were trash. We were the ones they built the county farm to house and break. The boy who was sent home was the son of a deacon in the church, the man who managed the hardware store.

As much as I hated that man, and his boy, there was a way in which I also hated my cousin. He should have known better, I told myself, should have known the risk he ran. He should have been more careful. As I grew older and started living on my own, it was a litany I used against myself even more angrily than I used it against my cousin. I knew who I was, knew that the most important thing I had to do was protect myself and hide my despised identity, blend into the myth of both the good poor and the reasonable lesbian. When I became a feminist activist, that litany went on reverberating in my head, but by then it had become a groundnote, something so deep and omnipresent I no longer heard it, even when everything I did was set to its cadence.

By 1975 I was earning a meager living as a photographer's assistant in Tallahassee, Florida. But the real work of my life was my lesbian-feminist activism, the work I did with the local women's center and the committee to found a women's studies program at Florida State University. Part of my role, as I saw it, was to be a kind of evangelical lesbian feminist, and to help develop a political analysis of this woman-hating society. I did not talk about class, except to give lip service to how we all needed to think about it, the same way I thought we all needed to think about racism. I was a determined person, living in a lesbian collective— all of us young and white and serious—studying each new book that purported to address feminist issues, driven by what I saw as a need to revolutionize the world.

Years later it's difficult to convey just how reasonable my life seemed to me at that time. I was not flippant, not consciously condescending, not casual about how tough a struggle remaking social relations would be, but, like so many women of my generation, I believed absolutely that I could make a difference with my life, and I was willing to give my life for the chance to make that difference. I expected hard times, long slow periods of self-sacrifice and grinding work, expected to be hated and attacked in public, to have to set aside personal desire, lovers, and family in order to be part of something greater and more important than my individual concerns. At the same time, I was working ferociously to take my desires, my sexuality, my needs as a woman and a lesbian more seriously. I believed I was making the personal political revolution with my life every moment, whether I was scrubbing the floor of the childcare center, setting up a new budget for the women's lecture series at the university, editing the local feminist magazine, or starting a women's bookstore. That I was constantly exhausted and had no health insurance, did hours of dreary unpaid work and still sneaked out of the collective to date butch women my housemates thought retrograde and sexist, never interfered with my sense of total commitment to the feminist revolution. I was not living in a closet: I had compartmentalized my own mind to such an extent that I never questioned why I did what I did. And I never admitted what lay behind all my feminist convictions—a class-constructed distrust of change, a secret fear that someday I would be found out for who I really was, found out and thrown out. If I had not been raised to give my life away, would I have made such an effective, self-sacrificing revolutionary?

The narrowly focused concentration of a revolutionary shifted only when I began to write again. The idea of writing stories seemed frivolous when there was so much work to be done, but everything changed when I found myself confronting emotions and ideas that could not be explained away or postponed until after the revolution. The way it happened was simple and unexpected. One week I was asked to speak to two completely different groups: an Episcopalian Sunday school class and a juvenile detention center. The Episcopalians were all white, well-dressed, highly articulate, nominally polite, and obsessed with getting me to tell them (without their having to ask directly) just what it was that two women did together in bed. The delinquents were all women, 80 percent black and Hispanic, wearing green uniform dresses or blue jeans and workshirts, profane, rude, fearless, witty, and just as determined to get me to talk about what it was that two women did together in bed.

I tried to have fun with the Episcopalians, teasing them about their fears and insecurities, and being as bluntly honest as I could about my sexual practices. The Sunday school teacher, a man who had assured me of his liberal inclinations, kept blushing and stammering as the questions about my growing up and coming out became more detailed. I stepped out into the sunshine when the meeting was over, angry at the contemptuous attitude implied by all their questioning, and, though I did not know why, so deeply depressed I couldn't even cry.

The delinquents were another story. Shameless, they had me blushing within the first few minutes, yelling out questions that were part curiosity and partly a way of boasting about what they already knew: "You butch or femme?" "You ever fuck boys?" "You ever want to?" "You want to have children?" "What's your girlfriend like?" I finally broke up when one very tall, confident girl leaned way over and called out, "Hey, girlfriend! I'm getting out of here next weekend. What you doing that night?" I laughed so hard I almost choked. I laughed until we were all howling and giggling together. Even getting frisked as I left didn't ruin my mood. I was still grinning when I climbed into the waterbed with my lover that night, grinning right up to the moment when she wrapped her arms around me and I burst into tears.

That night I understood, suddenly, everything that had happened to my cousins and me, understood it from a wholly new and agonizing perspective, one that made clear how brutal I had been to both my family and myself. I grasped all over again how we had been robbed and dismissed, and why I had worked so hard not to think about it. I had learned as a child that what could not be changed had to go unspoken and, worse, that those who cannot change their own lives have every reason to be ashamed of that fact and to hide it. I had accepted that shame and believed in it, but why? What had I or my cousins done to deserve the contempt directed at us? Why had I always believed us contemptible by nature? I wanted to talk to someone about all the things I was thinking that night, but I could not. Among the women I knew there was no one who would have understood what I was thinking, no other working-class woman in the women's collective where I was living. I began to suspect that we shared no common language to speak those bitter truths.

In the days that followed I found myself remembering that afternoon long ago at the county farm, that feeling of being the animal in the zoo, the thing looked at and laughed at and used by the real people who watched us. For all his liberal convictions, that Sunday school teacher had looked at me with the eyes of my cousin's long-ago guard. I felt thrown back into my childhood, into all the fears I had tried to escape. Once again I felt myself at the mercy of the important people who knew how to dress and talk, and would always be given the benefit of the doubt, while my family and I would not.

I experienced an outrage so old I could not have traced all the ways it shaped my life. I realized again that some are given no quarter, no chance, that all their courage, humor, and love for each other is just a joke to the ones who make the rules, and I hated the rule-makers. Finally, I recognized that part of my grief came from the fact that I no longer knew who I was or where I belonged. I had run away from my family, refused to go home to visit, and tried in every way to make myself a new person. How could I be working class with a college degree? As a lesbian activist? I thought about the guards at the detention center. They had not stared at me with the same picture-window emptiness they turned on the girls who came to hear me, girls who were closer to the life I had been meant to live than I could bear to examine. The contempt in their eyes was contempt for me as a lesbian, different and the same, but still contempt.

While I raged, my girlfriend held me and comforted me and tried to get me to explain what was hurting me so bad, but I could not. She had told me so often about her awkward relationship with her own family, the father who ran his own business and still sent her checks every other month. She knew almost nothing about my family, only the jokes and careful stories I had given her. I felt so alone and at risk lying in her arms that I could not have explained anything at all. I thought about those girls in the detention center and the stories they told in brutal shorthand about their sisters, brothers, cousins, and lovers. I thought about their one-note references to those they had lost, never mention-ing the loss of their own hopes, their own futures, the bent and painful shape of their lives when they would finally get free. Cried-out and dry-eyed, I lay watching my sleeping girlfriend and thinking about what I had not been able to say to her. After a few hours I got up and made some notes for a poem I wanted to write, a bare, painful litany of loss shaped as a conversation between two women, one who cannot understand the other, and one who cannot tell all she knows.

It took me a long time to take that poem from a raw lyric of outrage and grief to a piece of fiction that explained to me something I had never let myself see up close before—the whole process of running away, of closing up inside yourself, of hiding. It has taken me most of my life to understand that, to see how and why those of us who are born poor and different are so driven to give ourselves away or lose ourselves, but most of all simply to disappear as the people we really are. By the time that poem became the story "River of Names"[2] I had made the decision to reverse that process: to claim my family, my true history, and to tell the truth not only about who I was but about the temptation to lie.

By the time I had taught myself the basics of storytelling on the page, I knew there was only one story that would haunt me until I understood how to tell it—the complicated, painful story of how my mama had, and had not, saved me as a girl. Writing *Bastard Out of Carolina*[3] became, ultimately, the way to claim my family's pride and tragedy, and the embattled sexuality I had fashioned on a base of violence and abuse.

The compartmentalized life I had created burst open in the late 1970s after I began to write what I really thought about my family. I lost patience with my fear of what the women I worked with, mostly lesbians, thought of who I slept with and what we did together When schisms developed within my community; when I was no longer able to hide within the regular dyke network; when I could not continue to justify my life by constant political activism or distract myself by sleeping around; when my sexual promiscuity, butch/femme orientation, and exploration of sadomasochistic sex became part of what was driving me out of my community of choice—I went home again. I went home to my mother and my sisters, to visit, talk, argue, and begin to understand.

Once home I saw that as far as my family was concerned, lesbians were lesbians whether they wore suitcoats or leather jackets. Moreover, in all that time when I had not made peace with myself, my family had managed to make a kind of peace with me. My girlfriends were treated like slightly odd versions of my sisters' husbands, while I was simply the daughter who had always been difficult but was still a part of their lives. The result was that I started trying to confront what had made me unable really to talk to my sisters for so many years. I discovered that they no longer knew who I was either, and it took time and lots of listening to each other to rediscover my sense of family, and my love for them.

It is only as the child of my class and my unique family background that I have been able to put together what is for me a meaningful politics to regain a sense of why I believe in activism, why self-revelation is so important for lesbians. There is no all-purpose feminist analysis that explains the complicated ways our sexuality and core identity are shaped, the way we see ourselves as parts of both our birth families and the extended family of friends and lovers we invariably create within the lesbian community. For me, the bottom line has simply become the need to resist that omnipresent fear, that urge to hide and disappear, to disguise my life, my desires, and the truth about how little any of us understand—even as we try to make the world a more just and human place. Most of all, I have tried to understand the politics of *they*, why human beings fear and stigmatize the different while secretly dreading that they might be one of the different themselves. Class, race, sexuality, gender—and all the other terms with which we categorize and dismiss each other—need to be excavated from the inside.

The horror of class stratification, racism, and prejudice is that some people begin to believe that the security of their families and communities depends on the oppression of others, that for some to have good lives there must be others whose lives are truncated and brutal. It is a belief that dominates this culture. It is what makes the poor whites of the South so determinedly racist and the middle class so contemptuous of the poor. It is a myth that allows some to imagine that they build their lives on the ruin of others, a secret core of shame for the middle class, a goad and a spur to the marginal working class, and cause enough for the homeless and poor to feel no constraints on hatred or violence. The power of the myth is made even more apparent when we examine how, within the lesbian and feminist communities where we have addressed considerable attention to the politics of marginalization, there is still so much exclusion and fear, so many of us who do not feel safe.

I grew up poor, hated, the victim of physical, emotional, and sexual violence, and I know that suffering does not ennoble. It destroys. To resist destruction, self-hatred, or lifelong hopelessness, we have to throw off the conditioning of being despised, the fear of becoming the *they* talked about so dismissively, to refuse lying myths and easy moralities, to see ourselves as human, flawed, and extraordinary. All of us—extraordinary.

NOTES

1. *A Few Words in the Mother Tongue: Poems, Selected and New* (Portland, OR: Eighth Mountain Press, 1990).
2. Dorothy Allison, *Trash* (Ithaca, NY: Firebrand Books, 1988).
3. Dorothy Allison, *Bastard Out of Carolina* (New York: Dutton, 1992).

GENDER, SEXUALITY, POLITICAL ECONOMY

MICAELA DI LEONARDO
AND ROGER LANCASTER

The threads of gender and sexuality run through all contemporary political debates, whether national or international. In the U.S. in particular, living as we do in the midst of a dominant identity politics that stresses immutable gender, sexual preference, and race/ethnic/national identities while eliding class, it is difficult to maintain a long historical vision of the shifting intersections of sex and politics. Many observers have held the identity-based "new social movements" responsible for the decline of organized left politics. This perspective, coupled with media commodifications and other misappropriations of our common history, has made it difficult to see both how integral clear understanding of gender and sexuality are to socialist thought and action, and how contentious feminist and gay scholarship and politics have been and are. (The importance and contentiousness of race analyses are far more recognized.) In what follows, we contextualize changing scholarly understandings of—and divisions over—gender and sexuality since the 1960s within the particularly American political-economic shifts that made those changes possible. We focus here primarily on the rise of the second wave of feminism and of gay liberation. In other, longer work, we include as well the central role of anticolonial and race liberation movements in reshaping our visions of sex.

THE SECOND WAVE

The renaissance of feminist thought and activism, now more than a quarter-century in the making, was spurred by a concatenation of historical political-economic shifts. In the U.S., postwar economic expansion led to greatly increased demands for labor, and thus to women's rising labor force participation rate. The very possibility of supporting themselves without reliance on father or husband allowed many women to challenge male societal dominance, while the low pay, low status, and minimal prospects for advancement that characterized most "women's jobs" in that era stimulated feminist reaction. At the same time, the ongoing war in Vietnam gave rise to a nationwide protest movement, a movement deeply affected by and working in concert with civil rights/black power. The demographic bulge of a 1960s college-age cohort laid a further material basis for youth-based rebellion. Feminists drew both personnel and practices from these other contemporary movements, and the relatively youthful profile of feminist activists enhanced their emphasis on issues of sexuality, body, and reproduction.

Early second-wave theorists and activists, following Simone de Beauvoir's postwar "made, not born" promulgation, coined the sex/gender distinction that has since become widespread. Assigning to "sex" the biological realities of differing male/female physiologies, and to "gender," a term theretofore largely used in formal grammar, the layering of enculturated notions of proper sex roles, feminists were thus able to query arguments for the "natural" status of female subjection to male control, confinement in the home, responsibility for housework and childcare, sexual passivity, and automatic heterosexuality.

"The personal is political" is of second-wave coinage, but its very specific meaning has become attenuated and vitiated in recent years. The nineteenth- and early-twentieth-century woman movement—as it was then labeled—largely had not challenged prevalent household divisions of labor and dominant notions of aggressive, sexual males and passive, maternal, nonsexual females, and the scholarly establishment that asserted and rationalized such practices and ideologies. They reserved their fight for the scaling of public sphere walls—for the vote, for entrance into higher education and the professions, for a voice in the reform of government. Second-wave feminists expanded the definition of the political to "sexual politics": to include the struggle on the domestic front for women's control over their own reproduction, for parity in household labor, for equal involvement of male and female parents in childcare, and for admission of women's equal sexual needs and rights. In this vein, they illuminated the entirely social—and male-dominant—ideologies of women's sexual passivity, of "female frigidity," "female neurosis," a variety of mother-blaming psychological constructs, and notions of universally "correct" feminine body types, bodily self-presentation, and body grooming and adornment. They challenged the male bias of the "sexual revolution" of the 1960s; rediscovered Kinsey's work on female sexuality; unearthed early-twentieth-century feminist work on female sexual response; and engaged in their own survey research on female and male sexuality and sexual relationships. Also, activists revealed the serious consequences of male bias in medical practice and campaigned for reforms, including more and better research on breast cancer, contraceptive methods, the physiology of menopause, and the elimination of unnecessary hysterectomies, Cesarean sections, and radical mastectomies.

The dominant analytic mode of this period, however, both as subject and as rhetoric, was the focus on women's labor. Feminists stripped away the veils of "feminine role" from women's underemunerated and undervalued work, whether unpaid in households or in the paid labor force, whether in Great Neck, Gujarat, Guam, or Soviet Georgia. They expanded the notion of labor, following Marx and Engels, to include the work of reproducing human beings, encompassing both their gestation and their nurturance to adulthood. The labor emphasis allowed feminists to envision women's lives outside the "affective role" assigned to them by Parsonian sociology. (This model defined men's roles as "instrumental," reproducing the dichotomous immanent/transcendent model de Beauvoir had analyzed and protested.) In the process of analyzing women's work activities across time and around the world, feminists newly saw households as sites of labor and consumption practices inflected unequally through gender; perceived the model of sexual services exchanged for financial support implicit in "traditional" heterosexual marriage; and investigated pornography, prostitution, sex tourism, and other forms of sex work as large-scale industries in which women, some younger men, and children provided the exploited labor for high-profiting male (and a very few female) entrepreneurs.

As productive (to pun) as the "laborizing" of feminist theory was in this period, it revealed inherent limits, and these limits showed themselves very clearly in considerations of sexuality and reproduction. The work analogy, derived from orthodox or vulgar Marxism, was fundamentally reductionist—it reduced all practice, agency, or activity down to "work," narrowly conceived; it defined sexuality and reproduction narrowly as "really" and "only" about economic exchange and exploitation. Just as more ordinarily envisioned labor—in a factory or an office—can reflect at the same time exploitation, cooperation, and fundamental human satisfaction wrested from constraining circumstances, so can, and often are, women's and men's sexual, household and reproductive experiences. The practices of consciousness-raising groups, powerfully liberating as they were, enhanced the implicit and sometimes explicit model that women's sometimes positive evaluations of men and their "traditional" roles invariably revealed a simple "false consciousness." Thus Shulamith Firestone's aphorism, "Love is the victim's response to the rapist."

The labor mode proved a theoretical weakness in another, more indirect and non-Marxist thread of analysis. A cluster of feminist theorists focused on the notion that because of their reproductive bodies, women necessarily universally care for children and are excluded from the public sphere, leading their lower status lives in the domestic domain. Sherry Ortner elaborated on this frame from a Lévi-Straussian structuralist perspective, and alleged that women universally are associated with nature (through childbirth and cooking), men with culture (through the public sphere and politics); and thus, as humans universally identify their project as the transcendence of nature through culture, women are associated with primitiveness, non-humanness, and therefore have lower status than men. Nancy Chodorow's feminist Freudian analysis complemented Ortner's. Chodorow alleged that, psychoanalytically speaking, women's universal sole childminder role causes children to devalue women; in order to alter the human psyche and thus women's status, men must engage in childcare. Michelle Rosaldo's feminist Weberian frame contended in the same vein that, universally, the less rigid the division between public and domestic spheres and the greater women's presence in public, the higher women's status would be.

All of these schemata were based on the notion of a transhistorical and cross-cultural unchanging "women's work" of childbirth, childcare, cooking, and housework, work done in a more or less separate women's domestic sphere. But, in fact, the very notion of "woman's sphere" is itself a Western historical construct, an artifact that became hegemonic in the Victorian era. Moreover, women by no means perform the same labors across time and space; even the work of caring for children is not solely women's, and involves very different activities in differing times and places. "Public" and "domestic" are not in any way universal human social divisions. Finally, as Carol MacCormack and Marilyn Strathern's edited 1980 volume *Nature, Culture, Gender* lays out in painstaking detail, human constructions of nature, culture, and gender not only do not universally identify women with nature, men with culture—many cultures simply do not construe the universe through a "nature/culture" dichotomy at all. "Nature" itself, as we understand it in the contemporary West, is a product of the anticlerical and antimonarchy struggles of the Enlightenment, a category of challenge that also encompassed struggles over the social meanings of gender difference. Thus not only is the "labor" frame incomplete and reductionist as the sole basis for feminist analyses of gender, sexuality, and the body; universalizing schemata partially based on the notion of "women's bodies in labor" are empirically flawed. Certainly, women's public political participation and male involvement in the care of children cannot be bad things in any society. But the Western feminist *idée fixe* of the trapped housewife/mother as universal Woman served ill as a basis for understanding the lives of most of the world's women, present and past.

While feminist social scientists were working their ways out of early universalizing schemata, historians, ironically, were vigorously moving forward through the incorporation of anthropological or ethnographic understandings of the contingency and specificity of social forms, E. P. Thompson's pioneering early-1960s *The Making of the English Working Class* laid the basis for the growth of cultural history, or the serious consideration of changing *mentalités* and cultural productions as inherently part of larger economic and political history. This frame allowed the blossoming of histories of gender and sexuality. Work in feminism was stimulated particularly by Carroll Smith-Rosenberg's essay "The Female World of Love and Ritual," published in the premier issue of *Signs* in 1975. Smith-Rosenberg, in reviewing an archive of nineteenth-century letters among middle-class and better-off white American female friends and kinswomen, asserted both a nineteenth-century separate women's sphere and evidence of passionately romantic attachments between women, attachments lasting entire lifetimes and unaffected by heterosexual marriage. Historians' deep immersion in "anthropologizing" the past, in the notion that "the past is another country," allowed the writing of the histories of varieties of gender and sexual arrangements in Western and other histories. It allowed, in particular, the critical explication of changing hegemonic constructions of gendered bodies with the rise of Western science. Anthropologists, building on theoretical frames from symbolic/interpretive anthropology and a variety of Marxist traditions, began, especially with the rise of gay studies, to provide detailed ethnographies and analyses of Western and non-Western gender–sexual–body constructions.

THE PROBLEMATICS OF CULTURAL FEMINISM

Smith-Rosenberg's landmark essay, however, not only heralded a new scholarly sensitivity to widespread homosocial attachments but also indexed the devolution of American radical feminism into contemporary cultural feminism, a shift that both was influenced by and paralleled the rightward tilt of American and Western politics generally, since the mid-1970s. Alice Echols, in her documentary history *Daring To Be Bad* has described this historical shift from "a political movement dedicated to eliminating the sex–class system" to "a countercultural movement aimed at reversing the cultural valuation of the male and devaluation of the female." "Valuing women," certainly a component of any feminist program, was transformed in the changing political climate into a celebration of characteristics assumed to be inherent to women's universal nature—nurturance, altruism, cooperativeness, pacifism, and benevolent or absent sexuality. This insistent portraiture coincided with the related gendered portrait of all men as inherently competitive, violent, and oppressive to women, and thus with a shift away from consideration of variations across time and space in women's and men's status and lives—away from analysis of the roles of varying, historically contingent institutions and politics in determining relative power and the characteristics of human gender relations.

Feminist political activism in this era, particularly in its anti-militarist and environmental wings, increasingly operated with this Manichean symbolism (e.g. "Take the toys away from the boys," "Love your mother"). And much feminist scholarship reflected and further spurred this shift. Psychologist Carol Gillian, in her bestselling *In a Different Voice*, asserted that women "not only define themselves in a context of human relationships but also judge themselves in terms of their ability to care." This feminist essentialist stance neatly recuperates the Victorian vision of woman as the "angel on the hearth," the morally superior domestic being whose influence cleanses the father/husband/son returning from the vicious, competitive marketplace. And this vision parallels the Victorian construct in its presumption either of women's inherent passionlessness or of sexual needs that (unlike men's) somehow never involve harm or inconvenience to others. Certainly, in some historical moments, in some places, women have appeared thus to themselves and others; but in many others they have not. Theft, the use of one's sexuality for material gain or to damage others, the abandonment of children, torture, murder, sexual abuse—all of these activities have been engaged in by at least some women in most past and present societies, and these actions are not necessarily explained away by prevalent male domination. Also, the "nurturant" and "unselfish" activities of caring for home and children often involve a great deal of self-seeking. Children, after all, until very recently in the industrialized West, labored for their parents and as adults owed them—often especially their mothers—loyalty, labor, and cash.

Cultural feminism thus denies the sameness pole of the enduring sameness/ difference antinomy in the history of Western feminism, and fuses the construction of women's difference to a morality play in which women act only as heroines and victims. It fails to challenge the gender-functionalist leitmotif in Western political thought; it fits uncommonly well, in fact, with contemporary antifeminist politics, which valorizes women in their "traditional" role. We shall see, as well, that in asserting a universalist category "woman," cultural feminism simultaneously invites disproof on the grounds of women's diversity, and shapes that disproof to the problematic structures of contemporary identity politics. Most important for our project here, however, is the role of cultural feminism in the "feminist sex wars" of the 1980s.

As we have seen, both asserting women's right to sexual pleasure and protesting the prevalence of sexual violence against women were high on the agenda of the early feminist second wave. Between 1970 and 1975, for example, bestselling American books included Kate Millett's *Sexual Politics* (1970), which detailed contemporary male writers' misogynist, often sexually violent, portraiture; Shulamith Firestone's apocalyptic *The Dialectic of Sex* (1970), which excoriated the myth of romantic love and suggested a science-fiction future of test tube pregnancies; Germaine Greer's *The Female Eunuch* (1970), a gorgeous romp through literary history in the service of upholding a vision of women's randy capacity for pleasure and damning male sexual misogyny; Erica Jong's picaresque, wildly successful, and rather badly written roman-à-clef, *Fear of Flying* (1973), which contributed the phrase "zipless fuck" to American culture; and, finally, Susan Brownmiller's Second Sex-like passionate summary tome on rape, *Against Our Will* (1975). Activists demanded sexual freedom, lesbian rights, reproductive control, abortion on demand and freedom from sexual fear. They (we) inaugurated Take Back the Night Marches, campaigned against violent pornographic representations of women in mass media, founded and worked in rape crisis centers and battered women's shelters, lobbied for legislative changes, discussed female sexual desires (including desires for other women), and challenged men—individually and collectively—to reform their sexual behavior. By the waning of the decade, though, with the rigidification of cultural feminism, the sexual-freedom/freedom-from-sexual-fear unity of second-wave feminism began to unravel.

At one end of the new divide, writers like Susan Brownmiller, Catherine MacKinnon, and Andrea Dworkin focused overwhelmingly on violence against women, and in particular on pornography as the key or only feminist issue. MacKinnon, a legal scholar, and other anti-pornography feminists cooperated with the Christian right in efforts to write and/or influence legislation to outlaw print and video sexual representations in the U.S. and Canada. These feminists, in their obsessions with pornography and red-light districts, have tended ironically to neglect the issues of real-world rape, battery, and sexual abuse, and the concerns of women and men who serve and advocate for victims of these crimes. Nevertheless, their hyperbolic pronouncements have gained them access to mass media, where they often represent "the feminist perspective." Catherine MacKinnon in particular has come to stand for the feminist perspective on sexuality in the contemporary U.S.—in fact, she lays claim to it in *Feminism Unmodified*, in which she states, "In my view—you will notice that I equate 'in my view' with 'feminism'." Let us, then—with the aid of Mariana Valverde's 1989 analysis in *Feminist Studies*—consider MacKinnon's view of human sexuality.

MacKinnon envisions sexuality alone as the fulcrum of women's oppression, and unequal sexual experience as a transhistorical and cross-cultural constant: "I would argue that sexuality is the set of practices that inscribes gender as unequal in social life." She declares roundly that "what defines woman as such is what turns men on," thus denying, as Valverde notes, "the social and economic roots of women's oppression"—not to mention erasing all female sexual agency from human history. Inevitably, this essentialist, anti-historical stance leads to a denial as well of any variation in sexual experience across history and by race, class, or nationality—and, indeed, to a denial of the equal (or even any) importance of those categories to an analysis of the human condition. In an essay that addresses her critics, MacKinnon evades charges of ignoring class and race, but holds the historians' objection up to ridicule, and ignores, for example, the complicated new scholarship on the political uses of pornography in modernizing Europe:

> For such suggestions, feminists have been called antihistorical. Oh, dear. We have disrespected the profundity and fascination of all the different ways in which men fuck us in order to emphasize that however they do it, they do it. And they do it to us. If that hasn't changed all that much, enough to fit their definition of what a history has to look like, I submit to you that that is not our fault.

Unlike many other cultural feminists, who focus on women's heroic resistance, MacKinnon's theoretical frame disallows it, thus denying women, Valverde points out, "any position, however precarious, from which to reclaim or invent nonpatriarchal sexual desires." MacKinnon includes lesbianism in her broadbrush indictment of heterosexual sex, as "so long as gender is a system of power, and it is women who have less power, like any other benefit of abstract equality, it can merely extend this choice to women who can get the power to enforce it." Valverde concludes that

> [t]he eventual result is a construction of sexuality as uniformly oppressive, a picture of relentless male violence drawn with the twin brushes of feminist functionalism (all

phenomena are explained as serving a purpose for patriarchy in general) and philosophical pessimism. Resistance, subversion, and pleasure are written out of the account.

While the anti-pornography group has been relatively uninterested in women's lives as mothers, a great deal of cultural feminist energy in both popular culture and scholarship has gone into the fetishization of motherhood. The presumptions that the acts of giving birth and rearing children are always experienced identically, that males never care for children, and that continuous, attentive altruistic "maternal thinking," as philosopher Sara Ruddick has labeled it, best describes female consciousness across space and time have been widespread in Western popular culture since the Victorian era. Cultural feminists simply tapped into this broad ideological "Madonna and Child" vein, attempting to "spin" it toward a greater valorization of women's lives. Perhaps the best critique of this sentimentalizing and ethnocentric perspective is political essayist Katha Pollitt's essay "Marooned on Gilligan's Island," which takes on Sara Ruddick, Carol Gilligan, and linguist (*You Just Don't Understand*) Deborah Tannen:

> But the biggest problem with all these accounts of gender is that they credit the differences they find to universal features of male and female development rather than to the economic and social positions men and women hold, or to the actual power differences between individual men and women.

Pollitt points out that the cultural feminist *Weltanschauung* misdescribes the realities of motherhood even in the contemporary U.S.:

> Ruddick claims to be describing what mothers do, but all too often she is really prescribing what she thinks they ought to do ... But mothers feature prominently in local struggles against busing, mergers of rich and poor schools and the opening in their neighborhoods of group homes for foster children, boarder babies and the retarded.... The true reasons may be property values and racism, but what these mothers often say is that they are simply protecting their kids.

Cultural feminist pieties give us no tools to comprehend the actions and understandings of mothers living in extreme poverty; nor do they help us engage with the gendered realities of reproduction, global demographic trends, and neo-Malthusian population theories. Cultural feminism capitulates to bad, misogynist science in its insistence on women's utterly different nature. It cannot comprehend the necessity of a carefully historical, sociology-of-knowledge approach to gender and science. Nor can it at all comprehend the varying realities of sexual violence against women—and men—around the globe today. It gives us no purchase whatsoever on the varying and changing ways in which race is inscribed in gendered sexuality. Finally, it is well to remember that many women of all races and nationalities, gay and straight, do pursue and find sexual pleasure. As Cindy Lauper reminded us, girls just wanna have fun.

At the other end of the growing ideological abyss—although far less often represented in popular culture—are most feminist and gay scholars of sexuality and reproduction, as well as free-speech advocates. The two American "feminist sex bibles" of the 1980s—the anthologies *Powers of Desire* and *Pleasure and Danger* (1983, 1984)—brought together many of these researchers across many disciplines. While individuals may have disagreed on a number of issues, they came together in the common projects of open investigation of female sexual desires; in recognition of the ubiquitous (but not necessarily identical or universal) constraints on women; in a commitment to detailed historical and cross-cultural research on the varieties of female and male sexual lives; and, finally, in open acknowledgement that gender is by no means the only meaningful human division to be considered in sexual theory and research—the analytic categories of class, caste, race/ethnicity, sexual orientation, age, reproductive status, religion, and nationality may be as necessary as gender to the understanding of sexuality in particular places and times. In line with the growing divide among feminists, neither volume dealt at length with issues of violence against women—except as they intersect with American race stratification. Nevertheless, unlike the cultural feminists and MacKinnon, these scholars, who sometimes took on the label "pro-sex feminists," recognized and deplored the newly dominant notion that feminists must choose to identify sex only with pleasure or with terror. "We oscillate between two perspectives," warned the *Powers of Desire* editors, "on the one hand, a self-righteous feminine censoriousness; on the other, a somewhat cavalier libertinism, which deals but minimally with vulnerability." *Pleasure and Danger* editor Carole Vance underlined the realities of extraordinary variation in women's—even in any one woman's—sexual experience:

> For some, the dangers of sexuality—violence, brutality, and coercion, in the form of rape, forcible incest, and exploitation, as well as everyday cruelty and humiliation—make the pleasures pale by comparison. For others, the positive possibilities of sexuality—explorations of the body, curiosity, intimacy, sensuality, adventure, excitement, human connection, basking in the infantile and non-rational—are not only worthwhile but provide sustaining energy. Nor are these positions fixed, since a woman might choose one perspective or the other at different points in her life in response to external and internal events.

Finally, the commitment to history not only kept these scholars more intellectually honest than the cultural feminists; it revealed to them the embeddedness of Western sexual ideologies in the stream of time, and thus the value of considering ourselves in the context of a century of Western feminist history. Ellen Carol Du Bois and Linda Gordon's insightful 1984 essay "Seeking Ecstasy on the Battlefield" laid out the extraordinary parallels between the late-nineteenth-century social purity movement, which focused on prostitution and fostered the notion of women's innate passionlessness, and contemporary cultural feminism, which focuses on pornography and is silent on the issue of female sexual pleasure:

> [S]ocial purity politics, although an understandable reaction to women's nineteenth-century experience, was a limited and limiting vision for women ... Today, there seems

to be a revival of social purity politics within feminism ... a feminist attack on pornography and sexual "perversion" in our time, which fails to distinguish its politics from a conservative and antifeminist version of social purity, the Moral Majority and "family protection movement." The increasing tendency to focus almost exclusively on sex as the primary arena of women's exploitation, and to attribute women's sexual victimization to some violent essence labeled "male sexuality" is even more conservative today because our situation as women has changed so radically.

Many other scholars have investigated the connections among American and European women's sexual radicalism or resistance, class divisions, political organization, and evolving sexual moralities over the past two centuries; and yet others have begun to investigate the interpenetrating realms of sexuality and politics in the states we used to label the Third World. Alice Echols's summary commentary on the feminist political present draws from this historical depth:

> The cultural feminists ... appeal to women's sense of sexual vulnerability and the resilience of gender stereotypes in their struggle to organize all women into a grand and virtuous sisterhood to combat male lasciviousness ... [T]he antipornography crusade functions as the feminist equivalent of the anti-abortion movement—reinforcing and validating women's traditional sexual conservatism and manipulating women's sense of themselves as culture's victims and its moral guardians.

The issue of lesbianism, as well, has been central to the "feminist sex wars," but in order to understand its ramifications we must first engage with the rise of gay rights and gay studies.

GAY REVOLUTION AND THE QUEERING OF THEORY

> As human beings we are unique among animals in having a largely unspecified potential. Besides the basic biological needs for food, water and rest, we have needs which are specifically human and subject to conscious development: the need for relationship, the need to create and build. We are all erotic beings. We experience our lives as a striving for satisfaction. We experience our lives sexually, as enlivened by beauty and feeling. At base we have a need for active involvement and creation, the need to give form and meaning to our environment and ourselves.
>
> Red Butterfly, *Gay Liberation*

Like feminism, the modern movement for gay/lesbian emancipation draws on a long, rich history. It comes after centuries of dissident sexual subcultures and cunning resistance to various gender hegemonies. It absorbs lessons from a counter-canon of "underground" or "coded" literary, artistic, and social expression—a presence which occasionally has broken into the open as a love which dared speak its name. And it builds on many-stranded traditions of sexological, liberal, left, and social-democratic campaigns for homosexual rights and social tolerance, beginning most visibly with such early figures as Magnus Hirschfeld, Havelock Ellis, Edward Carpenter, Edward Westermark, and Karl Ulrichs.

Gay history, however, is hardly continuous. Certainly, the mid-twentieth century represents an abrupt pause in the visibility of this political tradition. Stalinism in the USSR and Eastern Europe, Nazism in Germany and Central Europe, and McCarthyism in the U.S. all vigorously repressed homosexual speech, politics, representation—and activity. Each drew on pseudo-scientific theories to prove that homosexuality was a grave moral, medical, or psychological threat to national stability and social well-being. Each dispatched state powers to the ends of homosexual detection, persecution, imprisonment, brainwashing, physical maiming—and, in some cases, execution. During that long interregnum that commenced before World War II and began to dissipate in the late 1960s, queer bodies, bent desires, were very much the objects of legal regulation, social supervision, political surveillance, scientific curiosity, and "medical" or psychiatric invasion. In the U.S., as late as the 1960s, lesbians and gay men were subjected to hormonal "therapies," electroshock treatment, and even frontal lobotomies.

Even at its most tolerant, the (Cold) War Family of the 1950s scarcely provided a fertile ground for openly homosexual politics. Although small clusters of brave and dedicated people like the Mattachine Society endured state surveillance and political repression, the open expression of gay/lesbian politics on a substantial scale awaited the opportunity of a political opening. But whatever else gay history shows, it is that things are not always what they seem. Although the period from 1945 to 1969 was one of unprecedented, national-level persecutions, it was also preceded by the large-scale mobilizations of the Federal Works Projects—and, of course, by the military draft of the Second World War. As Allan Bérubé has shown, these mobilizations drew young adults out of small-town isolation and provincialism, giving many their first taste of relative freedom. The expansive same-sex environments thus created afforded many the opportunity for sexual experimentation—and for new modes of self-fashioning.

The collective experience of the Second World War had many unanticipated effects. War production by "Rosie-the-Riveters" is now widely understood as an early (though halted) stimulus to feminist thinking. Black Americans, mobilized in the fight against fascism, returned home to face Jim Crow segregation—a collective experience of disjuncture which strengthened pre-existing demands for civil rights. And in bringing together lesbians and gay men of all classes and regions, these vast military mobilizations also presaged and encouraged the first wave of gay migration to environments of greater personal freedom and individual autonomy—the big cities—a trend that ran directly counter to the pervasive suburbanization of the American landscape in the postwar years. It was this pattern of urban concentration which eventually made possible the organization of gays and lesbians as a coherent political bloc. In unprecedented numbers, gays and lesbians settled in liberal, tolerant, and "Bohemian" neighborhoods, and their concentration in cities like San Francisco and New York allowed the accumulation of a new scale of community resources: in informal networks, in gay neighborhoods, and in social institutions like gay bars and meeting places.

The newly emergent gay liberation movement drew on a subculture which had been expanding, in spite of social censure and police harassment, since the end of the Second World War. (Not by accident, the routine police harassment of patrons at a gay bar—the Stonewall Inn—provided the push that set the movement in motion.) And it capitalized on the life cycle of that demographic bulge, the Baby Boom, whose masses simultaneously began entering young adulthood and seeking exit from the enclosures of sexual and political McCarthyism. Taking cues from the civil rights movement, from feminism, and from the militant antiwar movement, the Gay Liberation Front creatively confronted a repressive psychoanalytic establishment, attacked sodomy laws (with limited although by no means complete success), challenged the most visible forms of discrimination, forged tentative alliances with other political movements, and urged gay men and lesbians to collective self-disclosure—in the process, converting a covert practice into the basis for a radical politics, and capturing the imagination of millions with slogans like "Out of the closets and into the streets."

In those heady days, the Gay Liberation Front and other groups made no apologies about the scope of gay revolution. One slogan urged: "Two, four, six, eight; Smash the family, church, and state." Since the gay movement is so often invoked as the example par excellence of a "new social movement"—a genre of mobilization tied to fragmentary identities and supposedly seeking small-scale, personalistic, everyday changes as opposed to totalizing, systemic, macropolitical transformations—it is good to remember that gay liberation in fact expressed a totalizing, global perspective, and that it analytically linked oppression in the sphere of sexuality with oppression in other arenas, most notably gender, but also race and class. The perspective of gay liberation was anything but "narrow"—its vision was, in the words of one activist, a revolution more total than feminism and more terrifying than death itself. Echoing Marx and Engels's vision of a stateless, classless society, some militants and theorists envisioned a long-term revolution that would change personal life and social institutions so thoroughly that even the very categories of struggle and mobilization, "heterosexual" and "homosexual," would come to an end. The subsequent turn to a gradualist, rights-oriented approach, the quasi-ethnic focus on identity and the florescence of a gay consumer sub-economy, even the more recent celebrations of resistant marginality over politicized identity, can each be viewed in various ways, depending on one's perspective: as political retreats in the face of a less-than-revolutionary situation; as necessary developments in a process of maturation; as cooptations by a repressively tolerant consumer society; or as extremes in a necessary and dialectical tacking back and forth between utopian dreams and pragmatic advances. Whatever the case, the gay movement was launched and nurtured by anything but a "micropolitical" vision.

As was the case with feminism, political practice implied a social theory. And like second-wave feminism, the early models of gay/lesbian studies represented a turning of the tables on conventional theory. If various disciplines had obsessed for decades over the "causes" of and "cures" for homosexuality, new and empowering scholarship inquired instead into the causes and structures of homosexual oppression, and explored scenarios for gay liberation. If previous theory had always assumed not just a heterosexual perspective but a hetero-normalizing perspective, then just seeing matters from a gay or lesbian point of view constituted a radical break with previous hegemonizing models. In thus exposing the coercive dynamics of heterosexual normativity—in institutions such as the family, religion, psychology, and medicine—gay/lesbian studies opened new possibilities for the critical study not simply of gay and lesbian sexualities but also of sexualities in general.

Like early second-wave feminism, early versions of gay theory tended toward expansive universalism and open generalization. It was assumed that homosexuality, like womanhood, was a readily demarcated and already-known thing—an identity subject to historical and cultural variations, surely, but singular, unequivocal, and stable at the core. In some of these models, a homosexual or lesbian identity is seen, explicitly or implicitly, as "essential" or "given"—that is, as a tendency either universally given in all people, or present among a minority in all societies. In other paradigms, heterosexism serves as a universal framework of culture: a system of oppression intricately articulated with other systems of power, and as enduring as its nearest relative, sexism. Gayle Rubin's 1975 essay "The Traffic in Women," for example, a tour de force of Marxism, structuralism, and Freudo-Lacanian theory, draws on analogies with political economy to hypothesize a universal "sex–gender system." Rubin associates the universal presence of gender asymmetry with a system of compulsory heterosexuality. The one implies and mandates the other: the taboo on same-sex behavior both bars women from phallic power and mandates heterosexual alliance—the traffic in women. At the same time, the system of gender inequality requires an enforced and coercive production of dichotomous gender differences—an equilibrium that can only be enforced by a strict taboo on homologous couplings. Although overstated in their universalist scope, such arguments were mainstays of lesbian feminism, and signaled early on the possibilities of collaboration between feminism and gay/lesbian studies.

In the 1970s and 1980s, an expanding literature treated the forms and functions of homosexual stigma—in history, in society. Clearly, the denigration of homosexuality regulates and reinforces gender norms—just as gender norms regulate and reinforce homosexual stigma. But, although a taboo on homosexual activity is old, nothing seems implicit, necessary, or universal about it. As Weeks, Goodich, Boswell, Greenberg, and others have shown, homosexual oppression has a history. It comes into existence under certain circumstances; its force waxes and wanes over long periods of time; its definitions and configurations shift; it is both produced within and productive of certain kinds of struggles and projects. It is uniquely tied to the history of the West as "the West"—indeed, to its very designation apart from "the rest"—and, once established, provides a resource perpetually available to the authoritarian projects of institutions.

In Europe, the persecution of sodomy intensified during the twelfth and thirteenth centuries: first among the clergy themselves, and then on a larger social scale, as the church extended its influence over the laity. The ensuing anti-sodomy campaigns of church and secular authorities have been analyzed in various regards. Most obviously, they participated in the increasing regulation of sexual activity and family life. But these campaigns, which shaped important elements of Western culture, were also dynamically connected with broad political and economic developments. Portrayals of sexually dissolute lives were commonly invoked in political discourse; such representations mobilized popular resentments against the privileged aristocracy to the advantage of the rising burghers. Harnessed to class conflict, hostility to sodomy thus played a role in the decline of feudalism and in the rise of the bourgeois class.

The menace of sodomy was also a leitmotif of Christian campaigns against both Islam and heresy. European languages still carry traces of this history. Thus the term "bugger" was derived from "Bulgar" (Bulgarian) as an index of heresy, an implication of Islam, and an uneasy marking of the frontier of the Christian West. Similarly, for a long time the ambiguous term "sodomy" was synonymous with religious heresy (the Other within) and evocative of paganism or Islam (the alien without). The absolute and unconditional prohibition of homosexual acts—and the perceived encirclement of Europe by sodomitical cultures—was both unique to the West, and defined a distinctive and self-conscious masculinity of imperialism. In short, the taboo on homosexual intercourse played a variegated role in the rise of capitalism, in the self-definition of the West, in the cultivation of religious and political intolerance, in the emergence of the modern nation-state, in the discourses and the forms of colonialism, and in authoritarianism of all kinds.

Parallel to a stream of feminist writing, one tendency of the gay studies literature is recuperative, even celebratory. An enduring task of gay history and ethnography is to discover hidden lives and to reclaim forgotten voices. The practices of "reclamation" and "uncloseting," however, raise questions when they are applied to histories very remote or to cultures very different from the contemporary Western setting that gave rise to this imperative.

In the footsteps of anthropologist Ruth Benedict, a certain style of study looks for homosexuals and lesbians in other cultures and historical periods. These studies usually take one of two narrative forms. In one variant, gays and lesbians live happily because their society is more tolerant and enlightened than our own—and thus provides a model to be emulated. Alternatively, other gays and lesbians in other cultures persevere in the face of social intolerance and circumstantial adversity—and thus are *themselves* good role models. Obviously, in either case, the cultural self is being written into history or ethnography. The writer, the readers, project themselves into other cultures and periods, exploring the possibilities of another life there—a leap of identification.

Such leaps are perhaps necessary, but they are not quite adequate conditions for serious study. Historical studies of oppression and empirical studies of sexuality soon encountered an enormous range of historical difference and cross-cultural diversity. For if the homosexual taboo is not universally or invariably present, then what of the identity it both prohibits and necessarily implies? And even where taboos are present, if they are cast in terms different from modern Western homophobia, then is the object of profanation necessarily the same as our own? Such questions of designation posed serious problems—and generated exciting innovations—in a field which had once assumed that "a rose is a rose is a rose," and that homosexuality could be understood as an undifferentiated, uniform, and universal tendency.

What to make, for instance, of the premodern Sodomite, whose labeling bears some affinity to that of the modern homosexual, but whose identity scarcely revolves around the same sun of sexual object choice? Although both Sodomite and homosexual are clearly stigmatized on the basis of some sexual activity, the former is a "sinner" (as all men are sinners!), whereas the latter is medically and psychologically defined as either "degenerate" or "different." (It is not even clear that Sodomites were consistently labeled in terms of same-sex intercourse, and much of the confusion over the definition of "sodomy," even in legal circles today, participates in this ambiguity.) And what to make of man–boy love in classical antiquity? Clearly, Greek pederasty involved two males. But whereas Greeks approved, even endorsed, sexual relations between adult men and rank inferiors—women, slaves, adolescent boys—sexual intimacy between two adult free men (the very definition of male homosexuality today) was considered repugnant. How to understand the various practices reported in parts of Melanesia? There, semen is understood as a substance that is acquired, not produced; thus, older, affinal youths or young men inseminate younger boys in order to "grow" them into men. In these societies, semen is properly, necessarily, transacted between males. What would be improper there would be the flow of semen in the wrong generational direction. And what to make of the Native North American berdache and similar trans-gendered statuses? Whitehead has argued that although berdaches were once glossed as Native American homosexuals, their status is better understood as an intermediary gender (which sometimes implies bi- or homosexual patterns) than as a "homosexual niche."

As the gay studies literature developed and expanded, its object of inquiry tended either to slip away or to transmute into hitherto unimagined identities and unposed questions. By the 1980s, then, it had become increasingly apparent that it made little sense to speak of homosexuality—and heterosexuality—as "universal" forms with minor, superficial variations. What sophisticated scholarship discovered was not cultural and historical variations on a theme but, rather, deep thematic variation. In that sense, the "end of the homosexual" (and of the correlative heterosexual, too) thus came about in theory before it came about in practice.

At the same time, a parallel approach to identity emerged in the field of gender. Citing Simone de Beauvoir and renouncing all the romantic and essentialist themes that had accrued as "cultural feminism," Monique Wittig's manifesto of lesbian materialist feminism threw down the gauntlet: "One is not born a woman"—and one should not aspire to be one, either. Soon, authors began putting not just "Woman" but also "women" and even "sex" in quotation marks to signify the arbitrariness of their invention as cultural categories. In an inter-disciplinary crucible of politics and scholarship, and in a shared space between feminist theory and gay/lesbian studies, a new approach emerged. The more social specificities and cultural differences come to the fore of investigation, the more problematic become such already-given and already-understood rubrics such as "men," "women," "gay," "straight." The "Cyborg" literature—which exploits the myth of a being who blurs the distinctions between humans, ani-mals, and machines (see especially Donna Haraway)—and the recent wave of Queer Theory, which likewise throws all boundaries into question, both gather in and extend these tropes of feminist and gay/lesbian scholarship, further problematizing the notion of stable core identities, and urging caution toward categorical traps.

The debates over "lesbian sexuality" in the 1980s bore on these new insights. A group of lesbian scholars and activists, with Gayle Rubin in a leadership role, argued strongly against the then-dominant vision of women's/lesbians' sexual feelings and actions as profoundly different from (gay or straight) men's: as innately cooperative, benevolent—"vanilla" in their parlance. These theorists objected to the counterempirical claim that some women did not also have violent, overwhelming sexual feelings and desires to engage in extreme behavior, including (mutually agreed-upon) lesbian sadomasochism. These claims whipped (as it were) the antipornography feminists into a frenzy, culminating in their disruption of the 1982 Barnard College Scholar and the Feminist Conference because of the published views of some of the participants. Once again, the Moral Mother's dead hand weighed like a nightmare upon the living, demand-ing, in the name of feminism, that women repress sexual feelings; even, in the name of a putative core female identity, that women repress their own discus-sions of variations in female sexuality.

We have focused here on the development of essentializing identity-politics strands in feminist and gay theory and practice, the tendencies most dominant and harmful in the contemporary public political realm. Since the 1980s, how-ever, the academic world has been overwhelmed by poststructuralist/postmodern interpretations. The domain of gender/sexuality in particular has been swamped by work extending the denial of stable core sexual identities to the denial of any identities at all, and of the reality of the material world to boot. Within this frame, the intelligent insight that gender and sexuality are socially constructed tips over into a rudderless idealism that denies our human embodiment in ongoing political economy. While MacKinnon's gender-Manicheanism, for example, may have easy access to the *New York Times* and certain precincts of law, inside the ivy walls purely discursive analyses of gender and sexuality rule the academic roost for all the world as if discourse were not embodied in, produced by, and affecting the lives of real, material human animals. Historian Lisa Duggan has gently guyed this state of affairs in her *Social Text* essay "Queering the State," which hilariously imagines various postmodern academic stars attempting to communicate to the public on *Oprah*.

In between the ahistorical and ethnocentric essentialisms of identity politics and the necessary-but-insufficient idealist work of the "turn to language" lie evolving left scholarship and politics on sexuality—the tradition we have traced in these pages. Historical political-economic work and associated activism may not at the moment be winning the megaphone war in either forum of the public sphere. But the gender/sexuality domain they illuminate is for that reason no less crucial to a larger political vision. We on the left should not leave home— or go home—without it.

PREMENSTRUAL SYNDROME, WORK DISCIPLINE, AND ANGER

EMILY MARTIN

There are so many roots to the tree of anger that sometimes the branches shatter before they bear.

Audre Lorde, "Who Said It Was Simple," in *Chosen Poems Old and New*, 1982

There is an enormous outpouring of interest—the publishing of magazine and newspaper articles, popular books and pamphlets, the opening of clinics, the marketing of remedies—devoted to premenstrual syndrome.

The dominant model for premenstrual syndrome (PMS) is the physiological/ medical model. In this model, PMS manifests itself as a variety of physical, emotional, and behavioral "symptoms" which women "suffer." The physical cause comes from "a malfunction in the production of hormones during the menstrual cycle, in particular the female hormone, progesterone. This upsets the normal working of the menstrual cycle and produces the unpleasant symptoms of PMT" (premenstrual tension, another term for PMS).[1] Astonishingly, we are told that "more than three quarters of all women suffer from symptoms of PMT." In other words, a clear majority of all women are afflicted with a physically abnormal hormonal cycle.

It seems probable that this view of PMS has led to an improvement from the common dismissals "it's all in your mind," "grin and bear it," or "pull yourself together." Yet, entailed also in this view of PMS are a series of assumptions about the nature of time and of society and about the necessary roles of women and men.

Let us begin by returning to the nineteenth century, when menstruation began to be regarded as a pathological process. Because of ideas prevailing among doctors that a woman's reproductive organs held complete sway over her between puberty and menopause, women were warned not to divert needed energy away from the uterus and ovaries. This view of women's limited energies ran very quickly up against one of the realities of nineteenth-century America: many young girls and women worked exceedingly long and arduous hours in factories, shops, and other people's homes. The "cult of invalidism" with its months and even years of inactivity and bed rest, which was urged on upper-class women, was manifestly not possible for the poor. This contradiction was resolved in numerous ways. For example, according to Edward Clarke's influential *Sex in Education* (1873), female operatives suffer less than schoolgirls because they "work their brain less."

If men like Clarke were trying to argue that women (except working-class women) should stay home because of their bodily functions, feminists were trying to show how women could function in the world outside the home in spite of their bodily functions; indeed, it is conceivable that the opinions of Clarke and others were in the first place a response to the threat posed by the first wave of feminism.

The relationship between menstruation and women's capacity to work was a central issue in the nineteenth century. When the focus shifted from menstruation itself to include the few days before menstruation, whether women could work outside the home was still a key issue. It is generally acknowledged that the first person to name and describe the symptoms of premenstrual syndrome was Robert T. Frank in 1931.[2] Two aspects of Frank's discussion of what he called "premenstrual tension" deserve careful attention. The first is that he carried forward the idea, which flourished in the nineteenth century, that women were swayed by the tides of their ovaries.

Frank reserved X-ray treatment for the most severe cases, but it was not long before the perceived influence of female hormones on a woman was extended to include her emotional states all month long. It was not until the 1970s that some researchers began to insist that women's moods had important social, cultural, and symbolic components and that even though *correlation* between biochemical substances and emotional changes can be observed, "the direction of causality is still unclear. Indeed, there is abundant evidence to suggest that biochemical changes occur in *response* to socially mediated emotional changes."[3]

The second aspect of Frank's study that deserves attention is his immediate interest in the effect of premenstrual tension on a woman's ability to work.[4] It seems exceedingly significant that Frank was writing immediately after the Depression, at a time when the gains women had made in the paid labor market because of the First World War were slipping away. Pressure was placed on women from many sides to give up waged work and allow men to take the jobs.[5]

Can it be accidental that many other studies were published during the interwar years that showed the debilitating effects of menstruation on women?[6] Given this pattern of research finding women debilitated by menstruation when they pose an obstacle to full employment for men, it is hardly surprising that after the start of the Second World War a rash of studies found that menstruation was not a liability after all.[7]

After the Second World War, just as after the First, women were displaced from many of the paid jobs they had taken on.[8] The pattern seems almost too obvious to have been overlooked so long, but as we know there was a spate of menstrual research after the Second World War that found, just as after the

First, that women were indeed disabled by their hormones. Research done by Katherina Dalton in the 1940s was published in the *British Medical Journal* in 1953,[9] marking the beginning of her push to promote information about the seriousness of premenstrual syndrome.

Although Dalton's research fitted in nicely with the postwar edging of women out of the paid workforce, it was not until the mid- to late 1970s that the most dramatic explosion of interest in PMS took place. This time there were no returning veterans to demand jobs for which women were suddenly "unqualified"; instead, women had made greater incursions into the paid workforce for the first time without the aid of a major war. Laws has suggested that the recent burgeoning of emphasis on PMS is a "response to the second wave of feminism." This is a plausible suggestion.[10]

Turning to the premenstrual symptoms women themselves report, what views of the world of work are represented in their words? An overriding theme in the changes women articulate is a loss of ability to carry on activities involving mental or physical discipline. It is understandable that in a society where most people work at jobs that require and reward discipline of mind and body, loss of discipline would be perceived negatively. Marx showed long ago that in a system in which an owner's profit is based on how much value can be squeezed out of laborers' work, the amount of time laborers would have to work and what they did (down to the precise movements of their hands and bodies) would be controlled by factory owners. Indeed, historically, when legislation forced a shortening of the working day, owners found it necessary to intensify labor during the hours remaining.

Braverman and others have shown how scientific management, introduced in the late nineteenth century, has contributed to the deskilling and degradation of work: creative, innovative, planning aspects of the work process are separated from routine manual tasks, which are then extremely subject to finely tuned managerial control.[11] We are perhaps accustomed to the notion that assembly-line factory work entails a bending of workers' bodies in time and space according to the demands of "productivity" and "efficiency," but we are less accustomed to realize that deskilling, leading to monotony, routine, and repetition, has increasingly affected not just clerical occupations and the enormous service industry[12] but the professions as well.

With respect to work, then, the vast majority of the population and all but a very few women are subjected to physical and mental discipline, one manifestation of what Foucault calls a "micro-physics of power," "small acts of cunning" in the total enterprise of producing "docile bodies."[13] What many women seem to report is that they are, during premenstrual days, less willing or able to tolerate such discipline. An obvious next question is whether the incidence of PMS is higher among women subjected to greater work discipline.[14] One would also like to know whether there is any correlation between the experience of PMS symptoms (as well as the reporting of them) and factors such as class and race. Unfortunately, PMS literature all but ignores these kinds of question.

Perhaps part of the reason a more sophisticated sociological analysis has not been done is that those who comment on and minister to these women do not see that women's mental and physical state gives them trouble only because of the way work is organized in our industrialized society. Women are perceived as malfunctioning and their hormones out of balance rather than the organization of society and work perceived as in need of a transformation to demand less constant discipline and productivity.

Many PMS symptoms seem to focus on intolerance for the kind of work discipline required by late industrial societies. But what about women who find that they become clumsy? Surely this experience would be a liability in any kind of social setting. Perhaps so, and yet it is interesting that most complaints about clumsiness seem to focus on the difficulty in carrying out the mundane tasks of keeping house: "I must break a glass every month. But that's when I know I'm entering my premenstrual phase."[15] Is there something about housework that makes it problematic if one's usual capacity for discipline relaxes?

Perhaps the need for discipline in housework comes from a combination of the desire for efficiency and a sense of its endlessness, a sense described by Simone de Beauvoir as "like the torture of Sisyphus ... with its endless repetition: the clean becomes soiled, the soiled is made clean, over and over, day after day. The housewife wears herself out marking time: she makes nothing, simply perpetuates the present."[16] Not only sociological studies[17] but also novels by women attest to this aspect of housework:

> First thing in the morning you started with the diapers. After you changed them, if enough had collected in the pail, you washed them. If they had ammonia which was causing diaper rash, you boiled them in a large kettle on top of the stove for half an hour. While the diapers were boiling, you fed the children, if you could stand preparing food on the same stove with urine-soaked diapers. After breakfast, you took the children for a walk along deserted streets, noting flowers, ladybugs, jet trails. Sometimes a motorcycle would go by, scaring the shit out of the children. Sometimes a dog followed you. After the walk, you went back to the house. There were many choices before nap time: making grocery lists; doing the wash; making the beds; crawling around on the floor with the children; weeding the garden; scraping last night's dinner off the pots and pans with steel wool; refinishing furniture; vacuuming; sewing buttons on; letting down hems; mending tears; hemming curtains. During naps, assuming you could get the children to sleep simultaneously (which was an art in itself), you could flip through *Family Circle* to find out what creative decorating you could do in the home, or what new meals you could spring on your husband.[18]

Here is Katharina Dalton's example of how a premenstrual woman reacts to this routine:

> Then quite suddenly you feel as if you can't cope anymore—everything seems too much trouble, the endless household chores, the everlasting planning of meals. For no apparent reason you rebel: "Why should I do every thing?" you ask yourself defiantly. "I didn't have to do this before I was married. Why should I do it now?"[19]

A woman who drops things, cuts or burns herself or the food in this kind of environment has to adjust to an altogether different level of demand on her time and energy than, say, Beng women in the Ivory Coast. There, albeit menstrually instead of premenstrually, women specifically must not enter the forest and do the usual work of their days—farming, chopping wood, and carrying water. Instead, keeping to the village, they are free to indulge in things they usually have no time for, such as cooking a special dish made of palm nuts. This dish, highly prized for its taste, takes hours of slow tending and cooking and is normally eaten only by menstruating women and their close friends and kinswomen.[20] Whatever the differing demands on Beng as opposed to Western women, Beng social convention requires a cyclic change in women's usual activities. Perhaps Beng women have fewer burned fingers.

For the most part, women quoted in the popular health literature do not treat the cyclic change they experience as legitimate enough to alter the structure of work time. However, several of the women I interviewed did have this thought. One woman got right to the heart of the matter with simplicity:

> Some women have cramps so severe that their whole attitude changes; maybe they need time to themselves and maybe if people would understand that they need time off, not the whole time, maybe a couple of days. When I first come on I sleep in bed a lot. I don't feel like doing anything. Maybe if people could understand more. Women's bodies change. (Linda Matthews)

Given that periodic changes in activity in accord with the menstrual cycle are not built into the structure of work in our society, what does happen to women's work during their periods? Much recent research has attempted to discover whether women's actual performance declines premenstrually. The overwhelming impression one gets from reading the popular literature on the subject is that performance in almost every respect does decline. Yet other accounts make powerful criticisms of the research on which these conclusions are based: they lack adequate controls, fail to report negative findings, and fail to report overall levels of women's performance in comparison to men's.[21] Still other studies find either increased performance or no difference in performance at all.[22]

Some women we interviewed expressed unforgettably the double message that women workers receive about PMS:

> I grew up thinking you shouldn't draw attention to your period; it makes you seem less capable than a man. I always tried to be kind of a martyr, and then all of a sudden recently I started hearing all this scientific information that shows that women really do have a cycle that affects their mood, and they really do get into bad moods when they have their periods. I don't know whether all of a sudden it gives legitimacy to start complaining that it's okay. (Shelly Levinson)

I think the way out of this bind is to focus on the women's experiential statements—that they function differently during certain days, in ways that make it harder for them to tolerate the discipline required by work in our society. We could then perhaps hear these statements not as warnings of the flaws inside women that need to be fixed but as insights into flaws in society that need to be addressed. This consideration gives rise to the question of whether the decreases reported by women in their ability to concentrate or discipline their attention are accompanied by gains in complementary areas. Does loss of ability to concentrate mean a greater ability to free-associate? Is loss of muscle control a gain in ability to relax? Does decreased efficiency mean increased attention to a smaller number of tasks?

Here and there in the literature on PMS one can find hints of such increased abilities. One woman reports: "no real distress except melancholy, which I actually enjoy. It's a quiet reflective time for me." Others find they "dream more than usual, and may feel sexier than at other times of the cycle."[23] A sculptor described her special abilities when she is premenstrual. "There is a quality to my work and to my visions which just isn't there the rest of the month. I look forward to being premenstrual for its effect on my creativity."[24] Another woman said:

> Sometimes I'll cry at the drop of a hat, but it's a good crying. I'll be watching something tender on TV or my children will do something dear, and my eyes fill up. My heart is flooded with feelings of love for them or for my husband, for the world, for humanity, all the joy and all the suffering. Sometimes I could just cry and cry. But it strengthens me. It makes me feel a part of the earth, of the life-giving force.[25]

We can gain some insight into how women's premenstrual and menstrual capacities can be seen as powers, not liabilities, by looking at the ethnographic case of the Yurok.[26] Thomas Buckley has shown how the Yurok view of menstruation (lost in ethnographic accounts, until his writing) held that

> a menstruating woman should isolate herself because this is the time when she is at the height of her powers. Thus, the time should not be wasted in mundane tasks and social distractions, nor should one's concentration be broken by concerns with the opposite sex. Rather, all of one's energies should be applied in concentrated meditation on the nature of one's life, "to find out the purpose of your life," and toward the "accumulation" of spiritual energy.[27]

A common premenstrual feeling women describe is anger, and the way this anger is felt by women and described by the medical profession tells a lot about the niche women are expected to occupy in society. An ad in a local paper for psychotherapeutic support groups asks: "Do you have PMS? Depression—irritability—panic attacks—food cravings—lethargy—dizziness—headache—backache—anger. How are other women coping with this syndrome? Learn new coping mechanisms; get support from others who are managing their lives."[28] Anger is listed as a symptom in a syndrome, or illness, that afflicts only women. In fuller accounts we find that the reason anger expressed by women is problematic in our society is that anger (with allied feelings such as irritability) makes it hard for a woman to carry out her expected role of maintaining harmonious relationships within the family: "Obviously an anxious and irritable mother is not likely to promote harmony within the family."[29] Her own anger, however substantial the basis for it, must not be allowed to make life hard on those around her. If she has an anger she cannot control she is considered hormonally unbalanced and should seek medical treatment for her malfunction. If she goes on subjecting her family to such feelings, disastrous consequences—construed as a woman's *fault* in the PMS literature—may follow.

Consider this account, in which the woman is truly seen as a mere spark to the man's blaze:

> One night she was screaming at him, pounding his chest with her fists, when in her hysteria she grabbed the collar of his shirt and ripped so hard that the buttons flew, pinging the toaster and the microwave oven. But before Susan could understand what she had done, she was knocked against the kitchen wall. Richard had smacked her across the face with the back of his hand. It was a forceful blow that cracked two teeth and dislocated her jaw. She had also bitten her tongue and blood was flowing from her mouth ... [Richard took her to the emergency room that night and moved out the next morning.] He was afraid he might hit her again because *she was so uncontrollable* when she was in a rage.[30]

In this incident, who was most uncontrollable when in a rage—Richard or Susan? Without condoning Susan's actions, we must see that her violence was not likely to damage her husband bodily. She could have kicked him in the groin or stabbed him with a knife. The point is, she chose relatively symbolic means of expressing her anger; he did not. Yet in the PMS literature *she* is the one cited as uncontrollable, and responsible for *his* actions. The problems of men in these accounts are caused by outside circumstances and other people (women). The problems of women are caused by their own internal failure, a biological "malfunction." What is missing in these accounts is any consideration of why, in Anglo and American societies, women might feel extreme rage at a time when their usual emotional controls are reduced.

That their rage is extreme cannot be doubted. Many women in fact describe their premenstrual selves as being "possessed." One's self-image as a woman (and behind this the cultural construction of what it is to be a woman) simply does not allow a woman to recognize herself in the angry, loud, sometimes violent "creature" she becomes once a month.

> Something seems to snap in my head. I go from a normal state of mind to anger, when I'm really nasty. Usually I'm very even tempered, but in these times it is as if someone else, not me, is doing all this, and it is very frightening.[31]

> It is something that is wound up inside, you know, like a great spring. And as soon as anything triggers it off, I'm away. It is very frightening. Like being possessed, I suppose.[32]

It is an anthropological commonplace that spirit possession in traditional societies can be a means for those who are subordinated by formal political institutions (often women) to express discontent and manipulate their superiors.[33] But in these societies it is clear that propitiation of the possessing spirit or accusation of the living person who is behind the affliction involves the women and their social groups in setting social relations right. In our own topsy-turvy version of these elements, women say they feel "possessed," but what the society sees behind their trouble is really their own malfunctioning *bodies.*

What are the sources of women's anger, so powerful that women think of it as a kind of possessing spirit? A common characteristic of premenstrual anger is that women often feel it has no immediate identifiable cause: "It never occurred to me or my husband that my totally unreasonable behavior toward my husband and family over the years could have been caused by anything but basic viciousness in me."[34]

Anger experienced in this way (as a result solely of a woman's intrinsic badness) cannot help but lead to guilt. And it seems possible that the sources of this diffuse anger could well come from women's perception, however inarticulate, of their oppression in society—of their lower wage scales, lesser opportunities for advancement into high ranks, tacit omission from the language, coercion into roles inside the family and out that demand constant nurturance and self-denial, and many other ills. Adrienne Rich asks:

> What woman, in the solitary confinement of a life at home enclosed with young children, or in the struggle to mother them while providing for them single-handedly, or in the conflict of weighing her own personhood against the dogma that says she is a mother, first, last, and always—what woman has not dreamed of "going over the edge," of simply letting go, relinquishing what is termed her sanity, so that she can be taken care of for once, or can simply find a way to take care of herself?[35]

Rich acknowledges the "embodiment of rage" in women's fantasies and daydreams. Perhaps premenstrually many women's fantasies become reality, as they experience their own violence wrenching at all of society's institutions, not just motherhood, as in Rich's discussion.

To see anger as a blessing instead of as an illness, it may be necessary for women to feel that their rage is legitimate. To feel that their rage is legitimate, it may be necessary for women to understand their structural position in society, and this in turn may entail consciousness of themselves as members of a group that is denied full membership in society simply on the basis of gender.

It is well known that the oppression resulting from racism and colonialism engenders a diffused and steady rage in the oppressed population.[36] Can it be accidental that women ascribing their premenstrual moods often speak of rebelling, resisting, or even feeling "at war"?[37]

Credence for the medical tactic of treating women's bodies with drugs comes, of course, out of the finding that premenstrual moods and discomfort are regular, predictable, and in accord with a woman's menstrual cycle. Therefore, it is supposed, they must be at least partially caused by the changing hormonal levels known to be a part of the cycle. The next step, according to the logic of scientific medicine, is to try to find a drug that alleviates the unpleasant aspects of premenstrual syndrome for the millions of women that suffer them.

Yet if this were to happen, if women's monthly cycle were to be smoothed out, so to speak, we would do well to at least notice what would have been lost. Men and women alike in our society are familiar with one cycle, dictated by a complex interaction of biological and psychological factors, that happens in accord with cycles in the natural world: we all need to sleep part of every solar revolution, and we all recognize the disastrous consequences of being unable to sleep as well as the rejuvenating results of being able to do so. We also recognize and behave in accord with the socially determined cycle of the week, constructed around the demands of work-discipline in industrial capitalism.[38] It has even been found that men structure their moods more strongly in accord with the week than do women.[39] And absenteeism in accord with the weekly cycle (reaching as high as 10 percent at General Motors on Mondays and Fridays)[40] is a cause of dismay in American industry but does not lead anyone to think that workers need medication for this problem.

Gloria Steinem wonders sardonically "what would happen if suddenly, magically, men could menstruate and women could not? Clearly, menstruation would become an enviable, boast-worthy, masculine event":

> Men would brag about how long and how much. Young boys would talk about it as the envied beginning of manhood. Gifts, religious ceremonies, family dinners, and stag parties would mark the day. To prevent monthly work loss among the powerful, Congress would fund a National Institute of Dysmenorrhea.[41]

Perhaps we might add to her list that if men menstruated, we would all be expected to alter our activities monthly as well as daily and weekly and enter a time and space organized to maximize the special powers released around the time of menstruation while minimizing the discomforts.

PMS adds another facet to the complex round of women's consciousness. Here we find some explicit challenge to the existing structure of work and time, based on women's own experience and awareness of capacities that are stifled by the way work is organized. Here we also find a kind of inchoate rage which women, because of the power of the argument that reduces this rage to biological malfunction, often do not allow to become wrath. In the whole history of PMS there are the makings of a debate whose questions have not been recognized for what they are: Are women, as in the terms of our cultural ideology, relegated by the functions of their bodies to home and family, except when, as second best, they struggle into wartime vacancies? Or are women, drawing on the different concepts of time and human capacities they experience, not only able to function in the world of work but able to mount a challenge that will transform it?

NOTES

1. Judy Lever with Michael G. Brush, *Pre-menstrual Tension* (New York: Bantam, 1981), 2, 1.

2. Robert T. Frank, "The Hormonal Causes of Premenstrual Tension," *Archives of Neurology and Psychiatry* 26 (1931).

3. Karen E. Paige, "Effects of Oral Contraceptives on Affective Fluctuations Associated with the Menstrual Cycle," *Psychosomatic Medicine* 33, no. 6 (1971): 533–34.

4. Frank, "The Hormonal Causes of Premenstrual Tension," 1053.

5. Alice Kessler-Harris, *Out to Work: A History of Wage-earning Women in the United States* (New York: Oxford University Press, 1982), 219, 259, 254–55.

6. G. H. Seward, "The Female Sex Rhythm," *Psychological Bulletin* 31 (1934); R. A. McCance, M. C. Luff, and E. E. Widdowson, "Physical and Emotional Periodicity in Women," *Journal of Hygiene* 37 (1937); Edward G. Billings, "The Occurrence of Cyclic Variations in Motor Activity in Relation to the Menstrual Cycle in the Human Female," *Bulletin of Johns Hopkins Hospital* 54 (1933); A. L. Brush, "Attitudes, Emotional and Physical Symptoms Commonly Associated with Menstruation in 100 Women," *American Journal of Orthopsychiatry* 8 (1938).

7. M. Altmann, "A Psychosomatic Study of the Sex Cycle in Women," *Psychosomatic Medicine* 3 (1941); M. Anderson, "Some Health Aspects of Putting Women to Work in War Industries," *Industrial Hygiene Foundation 7th Annual Meeting* (1941); Emil Novak, "Gynecologic Problems of Adolescence," *Journal of the American Medical Association* 117 (1941); Hugh P. Brinton, "Women in Industry," in *Manual of Industrial Hygiene and Medical Service in War Industries*, National Institutes of Health, Division of Industrial Hygiene (Philadelphia: W. B. Saunders, 1943); Eleanor Percival, "Menstrual Disturbances as They May Affect Women in Industry," *The Canadian Nurse* 39 (1943).

8. Kessler-Harris, *Out to Work*, 292.

9. Katharina Dalton and Raymond Greene, "The Premenstrual Syndrome," *British Medical Journal*, May 1953.

10. Sophie Laws, "The Sexual Politics of Pre-menstrual Tension," *Women's Studies International Forum* 6, no. 1 (1983).

11. Harry Braverman, *Labor and Monopoly Capital* (New York: Monthly Review Press, 1974); Seymour Melman, *Profits without Production* (New York: Knopf, 1983). See Richard Edwards, *Contested Terrain: The Transformation of the Workplace in the Twentieth Century* (New York: Basic Books, 1979) for the factors that limited the impact of scientific management in industry.

12. Braverman, *Labor and Monopoly Capital* , Part 4.

13. Michel Foucault, *Discipline and Punish: The Birth of the Prison* (New York: Vintage, 1979), 139.

14. Leith Mullings, "Minority Women, Work, and Health," in Wendy Chavkin, ed., *Women's Health Hazards on the Job and at Home* (New York: Monthly Review Press, 1984), 131, points to the higher frequency of these hazards among minority and working-class women.

15. Reni L. Witt, *PMS: What Every Woman Should Know about Premenstrual Syndrome* (New York: Stein & Day, 1984).

16. Simone de Beauvior, *The Second Sex* (New York: Knopf, 1952), 425.

17. Ann Oakley, *The Sociology of Housework* (New York: Pantheon, 1974), 45.

18. Sheila Ballantyne, *Norma Jean the Termite Queen* (New York: Penguin, 1975), 114.

19. Dalton and Greene, "The Premenstrual Syndrome," 80.

20. Alma Gottlieb, "Sex, Fertility and Menstruation among the Beng of the Ivory Coast: A Symbolic Analysis," *Africa* 52, no. 4 (1982): 44.

21. Mary Parlee, "The Premenstrual Syndrome," *Psychological Bulletin* 80, no. 6 (1973): 461–62.

22. Sharon Golub, "The Effect of Premenstrual Anxiety and Depression on Cognitive Function," *Journal of Personality and Social Psychology* 34, no. 1 (1976); Barbara Sommer, "The Effect of Menstruation on Cognitive and Perceptual–Motor Behavior: A Review," *Psychosomatic Medicine* 35, no. 6 (1973); Witt, *PMS*, 160–62.

23. Lynda Birke and Katy Gardner, *Why Suffer? Periods and their Problems* (London: Virago, 1982), 23.

24. Michelle Harrison, *Self-Help for Premenstrual Syndrome* (Cambridge, MA: Matrix Press, 1984), 16–17.

25. Witt, *PMS*, 151.

26. Marla N. Powers, "Menstruation and Reproduction: An Oglala Case," *Signs* 6 (1980), suggests that the association generally made between menstruation and negative conditions such as defilement may be a result of *a priori* Western notions held by the investigator. She argues that the Oglala Plains Indians have no such association. This does not mean that menstruation is never regarded negatively, of course – see Sally Price, *Co-wives and Calabashes* (Ann Arbor: University of Michigan Press, 1984).

27. See Thomas Buckley, "Menstruation and the Power of Yurok Women: Methods in Cultural Reconstruction," *American Ethnologist* 9, no. 1 (1982): 49.

28. *Baltimore City Paper*, 20 April 1984: 37.

29. Birke and Katy Gardner, *Why Suffer?* 25.

30. Niels H. Lauersen and Eileen Stukane, *PMS Premenstrual Syndrome and You: Next Month Can Be Different* (New York: Simon & Schuster, 1983), 18 (emphasis added).

31. Lever and Brush, *Pre-menstrual Tension*, 28.

32. Ibid., 68.

33. I. M. Lewis, *Ecstatic Religion* (Harmondsworth: Penguin, 1971), 116.

34. Lever and Brush, *Pre-menstrual Tension*, 61.

35. Adrienne Rich, *Of Woman Born* (New York: Bantam, 1976), 285.

36. Frantz Fanon, *The Wretched of the Earth* (New York: Grove Press, 1963); Eugene D. Genovese, *Roll, Jordan, Roll: The World the Slaves Made* (New York: Vintage, 1974), 647.

37. Dalton and Greene, "The Premenstrual Syndrome," 80; Harrison, *Self-Help for Premenstrual Syndrome*, 17; Uriel Halbreich and Jean Endicott, "Classification of Premenstrual Syndromes," in Richard C. Friedman, ed., *Behavior and the Menstrual Cycle* (New York: Marcel Dekker, 1982), 251, 255, 256.

38. E. P. Thompson, "Time, Work-discipline, and Industrial Capitalism," *Past and Present* 38 (1967).

39. Alice S. Rossi and Peter E. Rissi, "Body Time and Social Time: Mood Patterns by Menstrual Cycle Phase and Day of the Week," *Social Science Research* 6 (1977), 32.

40. Braverman, *Labor and Monopoly Capital*, 32.

41. Gloria Steinem, *Outrageous Acts and Everyday Rebellions* (New York: Holt, Rinehart & Winston, 1981), 338.

HUMAN RIGHTS, REPRODUCTIVE HEALTH, AND ECONOMIC JUSTICE: WHY THEY ARE INDIVISIBLE

ROSALIND P. PETCHESKY

The public hospital system in South Africa is so short of cash that it lacks enough workers, medical equipment, ambulances, linens and medicine to provide proper care to the poor, a government commission has found ... Outdated medicine routinely appears in wards. And at two hospitals, several patients died because the equipment they needed was broken or unavailable.'[1]

Due to the nonavailability or poor quality of medication [including contraceptives], patients utilizing services at mostly all PHCs [primary health centres] surveyed in both Gujarat and Rajasthan [India] were required to purchase drugs from the market. Disposable syringes were also purchased by patients as these were usually not available.[2]

A study [in Dhaka, Bangladesh] looked at people's ability to pay for [maternity] services to determine whether cost is a factor contributing to low utilisation. The mean cost of a normal delivery was 25 percent of average monthly household income; the cost of a caesarean section was 95 percent ... 51 percent of the families did not have enough money to pay for maternity care. Among these families, 79 percent had to borrow from a relative or money lender. A quarter of families were spending two to eight times their monthly income for maternity care.[3]

Both the Cairo and the Beijing conference documents affirmed that reproductive and sexual health are part of fundamental human rights. Those documents base reproductive and sexual health in the personal rights of bodily integrity and security of the person as well as the social right to the highest attainable standard of health care, and the information and means to access it.[4] Yet as globalization and market forces trample older notions of social ethics in most countries, it is becoming all too evident that reproductive and sexual rights for women will remain unachievable if they are not connected to a strong campaign for economic justice and an end to poverty. That is the crucial link in the syllogism that is still weakest in international documents and policies and national efforts to implement them.

It is no longer necessary to plead the case in United Nations forums that basic human needs such as health, education, environmental protection, social development, and gender equality must be placed within a "human rights framework." More than a decade of NGO advocacy and grassroots activism has given this framework greater legitimacy in UN debates, so that today "human rights" covers a much broader swathe of issues than egregious state crimes (e.g. torture of prisoners and genocide), to which it was typically limited in the past. Furthermore, "gender" and "gender equality" concepts that only a few years ago were highly disputed by many government delegates and the Holy See as linguistically and culturally "alien" seem likewise to have gained a grudging international acceptance, at least at the rhetorical level. This, too, is the result of relentless, determined effort by feminist NGOs, especially from the global South.

Nonetheless, a stubborn kind of fragmentation seems to persist, not only among international organizations and national policymakers but also among women's movement groups. It is a fragmentation born of professionalization, donor-driven agendas, and a number of other forces. One result is a compartmentalization of women's movement work into discrete "issues"— violence, reproductive rights, sexuality, girls and adolescents, women in development (economics, work)—without sufficient attention to the vital points where these intersect. Such compartmentalization obliterates the most important operational principle of a human rights framework: the principle of *indivisibility*.[5]

In technical terms, the indivisibility principle refers to the necessary integration among the different "generations" of human rights—that is, among civil and political, economic, social and cultural and so-called solidarity rights (such as sustainable human development and environmental safety). More practically speaking, it has to do with the real-life fact that a woman cannot avail herself of her right "to decide freely and responsibly the number, spacing and timing of her children" (ICPD Programme of Action, 7.3) if she lacks the financial resources to pay for reproductive health services or the transport to reach them; if she cannot read package inserts or clinic wall posters; if her workplace is contaminated with pesticides or pollutants that have an adverse effect on pregnancy; or if she is harassed by a husband or in-laws who will scorn her or beat her up if she uses birth control.

AN INTEGRATIVE APPROACH TO HUMAN RIGHTS AND HEALTH

The view that "health is a cross-sectoral issue" and can only be addressed effectively through a broad gender and development lens goes back at least twenty-two years.[6] In 1978 the International Conference on Primary Health Care adopted the WHO Charter's definition of health as "a state of complete physical, mental and social wellbeing, and not merely the absence of infirmity" and as "a fundamental human right." The Alma Ata Declaration not only emphasized "health for all people of the world" but also asserted that primary health care

Includes at least: education concerning prevailing health problems and the methods of preventing and controlling them; promotion of food supply and proper nutrition; an adequate supply of safe water and basic sanitation; maternal and child health care, including family planning; immunization against the major infectious diseases; prevention and control of locally endemic diseases; appropriate treatment of common diseases and injuries; and provision of essential drugs. ...

Involves, in addition to the health sector, all related sectors and aspects of national and community development, in particular agriculture, animal husbandry, food, industry, education, housing, public works, communications and other sectors; and demands the coordinated efforts of all those sectors.

Feminist advocates have written about the theoretical importance of the indivisibility principle as it relates to reproductive and sexual rights and of the various economic and social enabling conditions that must be realized for those rights to become effective.[7] The practical, daily reality of this principle came home to me sharply, however, during a recent trip to South India. Health indicators are widely thought to be relatively high on the scale in Kerala, Andhra Pradesh and Tamil Nadu compared with other developing countries and other Indian states. But the ways in which poverty creates barriers to reproductive and sexual rights remain daunting, even in these "healthier" states.

One example is Kerala, where Vanita Nayak Mukherjee has conducted qualitative research among women in fishing communities on the possible links between reproductive tract infections (RTIs) and menstrual and toilet practices. Her findings tell a grim story in which the combination of lack of sanitary and toilet facilities and culturally embedded gender discrimination seem to exacerbate reproductive, urinary, and gastric morbidity among poor women. Poverty and the absence of toilets affect both sexes. But women alone are condemned by the norms of modesty and shame to suffer bladder retention and postponed defecation until they can sneak outdoors in the dark of night; whereas men apparently feel free any time of day to defecate on the beach and urinate by the roadside. In addition, because of the lack of sanitary pads and private places to use them during menstruation, women feel compelled to go about their lives with unhygienic layers of soiled garments underneath their skirts.[8] What could be more graphic evidence that access to clean water and sanitation—commonly associated with "economic infrastructure"—is essential, not only for health in general but also for reproductive health and gender equality?

In Andhra Pradesh, for *dalit* women (women in "scheduled castes"), issues of health and reproductive and sexual rights form a seamless web with land issues, indebtedness, and caste discrimination. One of the biggest concerns for activists is to organize and politicize dispossessed agricultural labourers, many of whom have lost the small plots allocated to them through land reform measures because of debt. But debt itself is inextricable from the unjust economics of the healthcare system. As a recent survey confirms, "the second most common cause of rural indebtedness" in India is "the increased cost of medical care" due to cost recovery and privatization trends in the health sector.[9] The new "target free approach" (TFA), instituted by India's family planning program to implement Cairo's provisions on reproductive rights, which has had limited effects at best on quality and access to services for poor women in most states, has not really touched the more endemic violations of health and reproductive rights that *dalits* face as a result of poverty and discrimination.[10] These include no water or sanitation in rural villages, persistently high infant and maternal mortality, and a growing incidence of not only RTIs but now HIV, as more and more *dalit* women have become migrant workers and been recruited into the international sex trade.[11]

WHAT'S TRADE GOT TO DO WITH IT?

As HIV/AIDS proliferates in South Asia, India is likely to be confronted with the same dilemma that has plagued sub-Saharan African countries: lack of access to life-prolonging drugs (including anti-retroviral therapy) because of their exorbitant cost on the world market and the corporate bias of the TRIPS (Trade-Related Intellectual Property Rights) Agreement. The TRIPS Agreement was enacted by the World Trade Organization (WTO) in order to safeguard the intellectual property claims and exclusive patents of transnational corporations, thus preventing their products from being "developed, sold or priced by anyone else, anywhere in the world'.[12] While the intricacies of global trade may seem remote from reproductive and sexual rights, in fact they stand precisely at the nexus where health, human rights, and macroeconomics meet. Not only do WTO actions enforcing TRIPS have the power to override national laws and international conventions on health (for example, prohibitions of trade in hazardous wastes and other environmental toxins); they also make it difficult if not impossible, for poor countries to manufacture their own generic brands of patented drugs or to purchase such drugs from cheaper, nonpatent-holding suppliers, without facing trade sanctions or other punitive actions.[13]

An integrative, human rights-based approach to health would recognize that

> [I]ntellectual property rights under the TRIPS agreements must not take precedence over the fundamental human right to the highest attainable standard of health care nor the ethical responsibility to provide lifesaving medications at affordable cost to developing countries and people living in poverty.[14]

This implies that the human right of people in all countries to have access to lifesaving and life-prolonging drugs must take precedence over transnational corporate profits or the presumed right on the part of industry (implicit in intellectual property rights as currently defined) to establish prices based on what the wealthiest markets will bear.

The announcement by the World Bank that it would commit large amounts of money to fighting HIV/AIDS, especially in sub-Saharan Africa, acknowledges a moral obligation on the part of the global economic system to make health care more widely accessible.[15] But it falls short of a human rights-based commitment insofar as it continues to take for granted the absolute control by private companies over prices, even of vital drugs. And it maintains intact the underlying structure of loans and private markets that sinks poor countries at the macro-level and poor women and their families at the micro-level further into debt. In other words, humanitarian gestures like those of the World Bank and other donors (whether Northern governments or private philanthropic foundations) will help to alleviate crises, but do not challenge the fact that health is treated as a commodity rather than as a basic human right.

Viewing the intersections of health, trade, and human rights also raises questions about the devastating health impact on innocent civilians, especially women and children, of economic sanctions against so-called rogue states. The unilaterally imposed U.S. embargo of Cuba, for example—extended in 1996 through the Helms–Burton Act to foreign companies that seek to trade with Cuba—has contributed to increases in maternal malnutrition, low birthweight babies, and premature births. This in a country whose public healthcare provision has until recently been among the best, and whose infant and maternal mortality rates among the lowest, in the world. Because of blocked access to imported parts, the embargo has impaired the ability of Cuba's domestic pharmaceutical industry to release millions of contraceptive pills, so that Cuban women are reliant on donated pills. The embargo's restriction on exports of X-ray film to Cuba has curtailed the availability of mammograms, formerly routine for all Cuban women over thirty-five, to those considered at high risk, with all the implications of increased risk of breast cancer deaths.[16] In other words, the human rights aspects of trade policies are fully gender-specific.

SEEKING ALTERNATIVES: COMMUNITY ORGANIZING FOR HEALTH AND HUMAN RIGHTS

What can women's health activists do to advance a vision that links the principles of human rights, health rights, and economic justice? While efforts to promote this linkage at the level of international conferences and national policies are necessary, such efforts are useless if they are not sustained through community organizing to build popular support at the grassroots level. In Tamil Nadu, the Rural Women's Social and Education Centre (RUWSEC) seeks to implement women's and adolescents' reproductive and sexual rights through community organizing, self-help, and local empowerment. RUWSEC defines reproductive health broadly in terms of community health and women's well-being and operates through a democratic, nonhierarchical structure that employs local villagers (mainly *dalits*) and trains them in computer, administrative, and other skills. Its many varied programs include a clinic—run by community workers, not doctors—that provides a full range of inpatient and outpatient reproductive and primary health services. The clinic functions alongside literacy training; popular health education materials written in Tamil; domestic violence interventions at the village level; and workshops on gender equality and sexuality for *panchayat* (local council) members, women workers in export-processing zones, and adolescent girls and boys in the villages.[17]

RUWSEC's daily work in some 100 villages over more than twenty years contributes to building a popular culture of rights and a sense of entitlement among women and girls as regards their bodies and health and economic opportunities. Local organizers and program coordinators report that, unlike a decade ago, today the women and girls they work with readily assert: "Nobody can take control over my body but me; nobody can claim a right over it."

This translates into gender and generational changes: women no longer wait for men to accompany them to the hospital but go on their own; adolescent girls expect more from life than just marriage and are refusing to marry early or sometimes at all; and children of both sexes are "thinking more for themselves" and thinking in terms of justice, rights, and wrongs. The organization's coordinator of adolescent programs says that the most important reason for this change—even more important than the impact of television and the increase of jobs for women outside the village—is that a whole generation of mothers (and fathers) has now gone through RUWSEC's training program and strongly supports a rights-based vision of gender equality, reproductive/sexual health, and economic independence for its daughters.

The Asmita Resource Centre for Women in Secunderabad is another grassroots organization that is working to embed reproductive health in the larger context of human rights and economic justice. Like RUWSEC, Asmita works mainly among *dalit*, tribal, and other marginalized groups. Its networks extend throughout the state of Andhra Pradesh, promoting a holistic program and popular education across a wide range of sectors: gender violence, economic development and workers' rights, legal and cultural literacy, bridging communal and language divisions, promoting the work of women writers and artists from both Muslim and Hindu communities, and strengthening the access of women and girls to health services, including reproductive and sexual health services. Asmita's "Self-Help in Health" program culminated in the publication of *Nâ Shariram Nâdhi* (India's version of *Our Bodies, Ourselves*) and a program to train rural traditional birth attendants. The group's campaign against sexual harassment in the workplace helped to influence an important judgment and guidelines for employers on sexual harassment issued by the Indian Supreme Court in 1997.[18]

Asmita connects the principle of "my body is mine" to a critique of dominant population and macroeconomic policies and a vision of a more equitable distribution of power, resources, and information across the sexes, castes, classes, and age groups. Its core team systematically invokes the provisions of the Beijing Platform, the Cairo Program and the Women's Convention (CEDAW) in its work with grassroots urban and rural women, seeing these documents as sources of legitimacy for Asmita's empowerment agenda. As the principal NGO responsible for disseminating the Beijing Platform in South India, Asmita has distributed thousands of posters and documents and created a cloth scroll, emphasizing the intersection between women's right to livelihoods, literacy, control over their bodies, political participation and health, and the link between all these and debt cancellation, full employment, a minimum wage, equal wages for women, enhanced social sector budgets, and land reform.[19]

Significantly, the 13th International Day of Action for Women's Health (May 28, 2000) is dedicated to reviving the Alma Ata vision through a campaign for "Health for Women, Health for All NOW!" This campaign involves a critique of the gross inequities in resources for health between rich and poor countries as well as among classes and between men and women within countries (including the highly industrialized countries of the North). It questions the renewed emphasis on user fees and cost recovery schemes that seem to have made health care even further out of reach for millions of poor, elderly, and marginalized people (especially women and children). It condemns World Bank and other "health sector reform" economists for abandoning Alma Ata's principle of universal access ("health care for all") in favor of "targeted approaches" (a euphemism for reduced public sector expenditures).

Above all, this campaign grounds its usual calls for enforcement of women's reproductive rights, gender equity in health care, access to comprehensive services, and actions against gender-based violence in a number of critical demands for structural and economic change, including:

- that national budgets reallocate funds away from militarism and toward "health and other human development priorities";
- that "rich countries and international financial institutions ... substantially reduce the debt burden of poor countries";
- that fair trade should replace protectionist policies as well as the loans and foreign aid that perpetuate dependency;
- that "transnational corporations that profit from health" be subjected to international human rights standards to assure that "profit-maximizing practices" such as patent monopolies do not override "the life-and-death concerns of people."[20]

The statement for the International Day of Action for Women's Health 2000 recognizes that enforcement of these demands will require new mechanisms for international accountability, ones that are far more democratic and responsive to human needs than those followed by the international agencies that currently govern global health and development policies.

The "Health for Women, Health for All NOW" campaign signals a growing attention among transnational women's health movements to the kinds of broad structural transformations that will be necessary to achieve women's reproductive and sexual rights in reality, not just in words. Of course, this is not happening in a vacuum. It is occurring in the context of recent mass protests in Seattle and Washington, D.C., and outside the U.S., against the inequitable impact of globalization and prevailing trade policies. At the same time, women's groups have brought to these protests an awareness of the links between a gender perspective and a human rights perspective and the relevance of both to international trade. The International Day of Action campaign—and, like it, the World March of Women Against Poverty and Violence of October 2000— signals a moving away from "issue compartments" toward a more unified vision. It is the vision that groups like Asmita and RUWSEC have been trying, against formidable odds, to implement in their work with grassroots communities. And it suggests the revolutionary potential of a human rights framework that is linked both to economic justice and to gender justice.

NOTES

1. R. L. Swarns, "Health Care for South Africa's Poor Imperiled by Lack of Funds," *New York Times*, 16 November 1999, A9.
2. I. Capoor et al., "Survey of 10 PHCs in Gujarat and Rajasthan," in V. Ramachandran and L. Visaria, eds., *The Community Needs Based Reproductive and Child Health in India: Progress and Constraints* (Jaipur: Health Watch Trust, 1999), 49.
3. "Poor Health and Expensive Health Services in Dhaka, 1999," RoundUp, *Reproductive Health Matters* 7, no. 14 (1999): 179–80, summarizing S. Nahar and A. Costello, "The Hidden Cost of 'Free' Maternity Care in Dhaka, Bangladesh," *Health Policy and Planning* 13, no. 4 (1998): 417–22.
4. See United Nations, "Programme of Action Adopted at the International Conference on Population and Development," Cairo, 1994, paras. 7.2, 7.3; United Nations, "Platform for Action," Fourth World Conference on Women, Beijing, 1995, paras. 92, 95.
5. R. Copelon and R. Petchesky, "Toward an Interdependent Approach to Reproductive and Sexual Rights as Human Rights: Reflections on the ICPD and Beyond," and F. Butegwa, "International Human Rights Law and Practice: Implications for Women," both in M. Schuler, ed., *From Basic Needs to Basic Rights* (Washington, D.C.: Women in Law and Development International, 1994).
6. See M. Koivusalo and E. Ollila, *Making a Healthy World: Agencies, Actors and Policies in International Health* (London: Zed Books, 1997). See also D. Elson and B. Evers, "Sector Programme Support: The Health Sector—A Gender-aware Analysis" (Graduate School of Social Sciences, University of Manchester, 1998), unpublished, 5.
7. S. Correa and R. P. Petchesky, "Reproductive and Sexual Rights: A Feminist Revision," in G. Sen, A. Germain, and L. C. Chen, eds., *Population Policies Reconsidered.* (Cambridge, MA: Harvard University Press, 1994); S. Correa, *Population and Reproductive Rights* (London: Zed Books, 1994); R. Petchesky and K. Judd, *Negotiating Reproductive Rights* (London: Zed Books, 1998).
8. V. N. Mukherjee, "Gender Dimension of Basic Needs: Women's Access to Menstrual Hygiene and RTIs" (MacArthur Foundation Fellowship for Population Innovation, 1999), unpublished.
9. Women's Environment and Development Organization, *Risks Rights and Reforms: A 50-Country Survey Assessing Government Actions Five Years After the International Conference on Population and Development* (New York: WEDO, 1999), 11.
10. See V. Ramachandran and L. Visaria, eds., *The Community Needs-Based Reproductive and Child Health in India: Progress and Constraints* (Jaipur: Health Watch Trust, 1999).
11. Interview with D. L. Jaya of VEDIKA, Amal Charles of the Society to Train and Educate People's Participation in Development, and R. Girija of SHARADA Women's Organization.

12. Women's Environment and Development Organization, *Primer: Women and Trade—A Gender Agenda for the World Trade Organization* (New York: WEDO, 1999), 10.

13. See K. Silverstein, "Millions for Viagra, Pennies for Diseases of the Poor, *Nation*, 19 July 1999: 13–19. The South African government briefly tried to get around such sanctions by allowing the import of less costly drugs or "compulsory licensing" of local manufacturers to produce their own version of drugs such as AZT. But hostile threats by U.S.-based pharmaceutical companies quickly squelched this rights-minded policy. Global economic inequities make such resistance highly problematic for most developing countries—they would risk the loss of foreign investment and export markets for the sake of their citizens' health.

14. This language was proposed by the NGO Women's Caucus in its efforts to influence government delegations negotiating the World Summit for Social Development +5 "Further Initiatives" document at the United Nations in April, May, and June 2000.

15. This commitment and more recent suggestions by transnational pharmaceutical companies that they might lower the price of AIDS drugs for Africa came in response to pressure from AIDS activists, the UN Secretary-General, UNAIDS and others. See *New York Times*, 24 April 2000: 10; and 12 May 2000: A1. See also J. D. Wolfensohn, "Free from Poverty, Free from AIDS," speech at UN Security Council, 10 January 2000, www.worldbank.org.

16. American Association for World Health, "Denial of Food and Medicine: The Impact of the U.S. Embargo on Health and Nutrition," www.madre.org, 1999.

17. Sokhi S. Subramanian, *Rural Women Take Reproductive Health Matters into Their Own Hands: Rural Women's Social Education Centre* (Selangor, Malaysia: International Council on Management of Population Programmes, 1998). Interviews with T. K. Sundari Ravindran, RUWSEC's honorary executive director, and its field organizers and staff, March 2000.

18. Sabala and Kranti, *Nâ Shariram Nâdhi is Telegu for My Body is Mine* (Puni, 1995). See also National Alliance of Women, *Supreme Court Judgment on Sexual Harassment at Workplace*, Landmark Judgment Series 1 (New Delhi: NAWO, 1997).

19. Interview with Kalpana and Vasant Kannabiran, 26 March 2000. Asmita Resource Centre for Women, *Towards Building a Gender Just Society: Review of Activity 1991–1998* (Hyderabad: Asmita, n.d.), 23–24.

20. *Health for Women, Health for All NOW!* Pamphlet prepared by Likhaan, Philippines (Amsterdam: Women's Global Network for Reproductive Rights, 2000).

RECLAIMING MARXIST FEMINISM
FOR A NEED-BASED SEXUAL POLITICS

ROSEMARY HENNESSY

While the phrase "materialist feminism" has begun to circulate more widely in academic feminism, it has seemed to me that the "materialism" in this signature has become quite narrow, pertaining to matters of discourse and culture while ignoring the rest of social life. This "cultural materialism" is quite different from the historical materialism that provided the basis for socialist feminism. Indeed, recent developments in "materialist feminism" have had the effect of obscuring Marxist feminism as another possible way of understanding and explaining culture. As a result, I would argue that we need boldly to reclaim the banner of "Marxist feminism" (against the repressive tactics of redbaiting and the contention that "there is no alternative" to the dominant regime) in order to signal the value of the historical materialist critique of capital it promotes. Drawing upon the analysis of capitalism developed in historical materialism, as well as the rich archive of work by other Marxists and feminists from the past century, Marxist feminism offers an explanation of society that enables us to think through the systemic relationship of cultural formations to capital and in the process forge a stronger united front in the struggle to transform it.[1]

One of the issues in the debate over cultural versus historical (or Marxist) materialism is how to explain the relationship of changing cultural forms (of gender, sexuality, nationality, race—to name a few) to capitalist political economy—the basic social relations of labor that allow capitalism to be capitalism. Arguing that a Marxist feminist class analysis is not only still pertinent but more needed now than ever means, at the very least, putting capitalism on the agenda as the starting point for theory and practice precisely because it is the prevailing means by which people produce to meet their needs and because the human costs of its "globalization" are growing ever more colossal.

Despite the advances of capitalism—or perhaps as one index of its neoliberal advances—among the most significant developments in feminist theory and politics in the later part of the twentieth century was the retreat from concepts and critical frameworks that explain and combat the ravages of capitalism and the promotion instead of various versions of postmodern analytics and identity politics. In *Profit and Pleasure: Sexual Identities in Late Capitalism*,[2] I question the assumption in much recent work in cultural theory that historical materialism has little or nothing to offer either theories or the politics of sexuality. Against this trend, I argue that the history of identity, and sexual identity in particular, in all of the ways it has been culturally differentiated and lived, has been fundamentally though never simply organized by the social relationships of capitalist wage and domestic labor, commodity production, and consumption. In the book's concluding chapter I consider what might be required to reorient sexual politics in order to take these social relations into account, and propose that we begin from the starting point of human need.

Are sexuality and the larger domain of human sensations and affects it is part of ever completely removed from a more basic set of vital human needs? If we did not ignore the human capacity for sensation and affect in the calculus of human needs, then in forging a collective standpoint for oppositional—even revolutionary—forms of consciousness perhaps we would need to acknowledge how political agency, practice, and commitment are motivated, complicated, and undermined by this capacity. What would it mean to redirect a sexual politics that has been so focused on identity to this relation between affect and need?

Historical materialism begins with the premiss that meeting human needs is the baseline of history. Needs are corporeal—because they involve keeping the body alive—but they are not "natural," because meeting them always takes place through social relationships. In this sense social interaction itself translates into a vital need. Human needs also include the ability to exercise certain human potentials. As a species, humans have many capacities—for intellect, invention, communication, as well as for sensation and affect and for affective social relations. Many human affective capacities are integrated in the satisfaction of vital human needs in that they mediate the social relations through which these needs are provided for. Affective needs are inseparable from the social component of most need satisfaction, then, but they also constitute human needs in themselves in the sense that all people deserve to have the conditions available that will allow them to exercise and develop their affective capacities.

Affective capacities are tied to cognition and to the traces of social contexts that register in them. As only one of a host of human potentials, they also have a relationship to the body's other material needs—its dependence on sustenance, shelter, recovery from illness or injury—all of which require some form of social cooperation in order to be met. Like hunger, the need for affective relations is historically satisfied and takes different forms in various social formations. This affective potential is included in what Marx means by labor—that is, the capacity to satisfy and freely develop vital human needs. Though he does not explicitly name them as such, affective needs are part of the human potential for "self-realization" that Marx often refers to when he contends that the development of needs is historically contingent on the development of human potential.

Under capitalism workers do not retain control of very much of their human potential. The outlawing of so much human potential is, in fact, one of the sites of struggle between capital and labor. Under capitalism's wage-labor system, the worker trades away the potential for self-realization inherent within his or her labor power when he commodifies it on the wage market. We might even say that outlawing the development of full human potential comprises the very scaffolding of human relationships in commodity exchange. In the exchange of labor power for wages the worker is forced to forfeit certain needs—aspects of his or her human potential—embodied in what Marx calls labor. In order to survive within the minimum standard, the worker is forced to give up "time for education, for intellectual development, for the fulfilling of social functions and for social intercourse, for the free play of his bodily and mental activity, even the rest time of Sunday."[3]

The companion to the production of surplus value, then, is the production of "outlawed need." Outlawed need is a very useful concept, which Deborah Kelsh has proposed as a way of understanding a very important consequence of the commodification of labor under capitalism.[4] When the worker meets the capitalist in the marketplace and exchanges his labor power for a wage, many of his human potentials and needs are excluded as the unnamed price of the exchange. Outlawed need is also embedded in the production of labor power outside the workplace. Because the need to reproduce labor power is not part of the calculus of socially necessary labor covered by wages, the domestic labor of feeding, clothing, and caring constitutes an outlawed set of needs. The labor to satisfy these needs is either underpaid or not paid, invariably not valued, and often made invisible as labor by being understood as a woman's natural role.

Another way that needs are outlawed is in the commodification of con-sciousness that occurs as a necessary accompaniment to the production of commodities, the process that Marx describes in his section of *Capital* on the commodity fetish. In commodity capitalism, people lose sight of the social relationships that make possible the marketable goods they consume, and this process requires a fracturing of our human capacities as affective, sensuous, social beings. It is only by severing her human potential to labor from her needs that the worker can present herself as "owner" of her labor power. It is only in this way that she can commodify her capacities and even her personality into a thing that she can sell.

Certainly human needs cannot, do not, speak for themselves—they have to be, *are*, made "sensible." Under capitalism, human affective and sensate capaci-ties have been historically produced such that some ways of organizing them are consolidated into legitimate "experiences" and social relations while others have been outlawed. In constructing sexual identity, for example, the discourses of sexuality produce the meanings of certain human affects and sensations in terms of normative and perverse sexual identifications and desires. "Outlawed affective needs" are not just those organizations of identification and desire that the normative discourses shame. They are also those unspeakable sensations and affects that do not fall easily into any prescribed categories. It may be that the relationship between affect and the "social context" that organizes it and that makes it intelligible is always incomplete. The human potential for sensation and affect which comprises what we call "experience" is always much richer than sanctioned identity categories capture. What is left over are tendencies or human potentials for sensation, affect, and action that normative discourses do not, cannot, name.

Many of these human potentials lie in the domain of outlawed needs that are the "unassimilable outside of capitalism." They cannot be brought back into capitalism without abolishing the very terms of the extraction of surplus value. This domain of outlawed need must continually be reckoned with because it poses a constant and growing threat to capitalist interests; it is the "monstrous necessity" to capitalism that haunts it.[5] Claiming outlawed needs as the stand-point for political action can reorient social movement onto the new ground of this monstrous necessity.

Of course, this task of reorienting would also have to speak to the persist-ence and short-term political uses of identities with all of their affective bag-gage. The reorientation I am suggesting would not deny the ways capitalism exercises its violence through state-supported institutions that regulate and dis-cipline identities. Social movement cannot dismiss people's experiences of these identities but has to work on the ways they are organized through reified cat-egories. This work and the new consciousness it produces arise out of people's collective activity as they measure their outlawed needs against the ways of making sense of them offered by the dominant culture.

The process of organizing collective subjects for social transformation is not merely cognitive and rational—though it is that, too; it also works on the affec-tive investments people have in the identities they claim. One of the ways this work can proceed is through a practice of "disidentification." Disidentification involves working on existing ways of identifying that we embrace and live by. This "work" opens up the identities we take for granted to the historical con-ditions that make them possible. It involves uprooting these identities from stories of a history of suffering—the fertile ground for resentment to grow—and transplanting them into a different conceptual frame, one that allows us to see how this suffering is the product of social relations that outlaw a whole array of human needs. Disidentification entails replacing the narrow resentment of identity politics with the power and passion of the broad collective agency from which capital itself derives.

The work of disidentification arises from a standpoint that counters the dominant knowledges from a position whose empirical reality lies in capitalism's monstrous outside. It is a standpoint that does not claim any single group identity but rather the collectivity of those whose surplus human needs are outlawed. One way to begin this work is to highlight the gap between the identities promoted by the dominant culture and the lived "experience" of social relations that is not summoned by these terms. This is the "excess" that is often "experienced" as an inchoate affect of not belonging, of not fitting in or not feeling at home within the terms that are offered for identity. The process of disidentification can zero-in on this affective component of misrecognition and invite consideration of the ways it is named and routed into emotions that naturalize the existing categories. Disidentification invites the re-narration of this affective excess in relation to capitalism's systemic production of unmet need. At the same time that it works on forms of misrecognition, disidentification also makes visible the ways the dominant organizations of desire and identity are sites of affective investment, and through this critical awareness invites a process of unlearning. Unlearning these investments is always an incomplete, unfinished business, and recognizing this is an important lesson on the limits of one's historical position. This ongoing lesson in historical limits does not have to be dismissive or belittling; it can also fold the forms of affective identification we historically and critically inhabit into a more ambitious political project that claims the radical outside of unmet human needs as the starting point for anti-capitalist mobilizing.

Considering the formation of identities, and sexual identities in particular, in relation to human need, as I am suggesting we might do, opens a way to imagine a collective class agency that does not reify "the proletariat," foreclose sexuality, or relegate it to a secondary status. Resituating sexual politics on the ground of human needs links the human potential for sensation and affect that the discourses of sexual identity organize to the meeting of other vital human needs and calls for a movement for full democracy to begin there. Above all, this reorientation requires that eliminating the social structures of exploitation that capitalism absolutely requires and so violently enacts at the expense of human needs must be on the political agenda, at the very least as the horizon that sets the terms for imagining change.

NOTES

1. In addition to the essays in Part I of this collection, see Rosemary Hennessy and Chrys Ingraham, eds., *Materialist Feminism: A Reader in Class, Difference, and Women's Lives* (New York: Routledge, 1997).
2. Rosemary Hennessy, *Profit and Pleasure: Sexual Identities in Late Capitalism* (New York: Routledge, 2000).
3. Karl Marx *Capital*, vol. 1 (Moscow: Progress Publishers, 1959), 264.
4. Deborah Kelsh, "Desire and Class: The Knowledge Industry in the Wake of Post-structuralism" (Ph.D. dissertation, State University of New York at Albany, 2000).
5. Ibid., 76–77.

PART II

FAMILY: LOVE, LABOR, AND POWER

THE FAMILY IS DEAD, LONG LIVE OUR FAMILIES

JUDITH STACEY

The United Nations proclaimed 1994 the International Year of the Family. However, *the family* is a peculiarly Western and modern concept. Some cultures do not employ the category "family" at all. Many societies that do use the term do so to depict diverse relationships and to convey diverse meanings. By the time the United Nations chose to commemorate the family, both the term and the kinship system it has come to signify had reached a state of intense transformation and political contest, particularly in the United States, but with reverberations worldwide. By proclaiming a global year of the family, the UN imposed deceptive unity on a contested term. Its use of the term also unwittingly derives from a declining theory of modernization that has been criticized as ethnocentric.

MODERNIZATION AND THE FAMILY

In most of Europe and North America the family has become nearly synonymous with the nuclear household unit made up of a married, heterosexual couple and their biological or adopted children. Although popular usage more fluidly adapts the concept to refer to all people related through blood, marriage, or adoption, most Westerners do erroneously associate the family with nature and project it backward into a timeless past. However, historians have demonstrated that in the ancient world the "Roman *familia* referred to all that which belonged to the *paterfamilias*, including slaves and servants, as well as relatives by blood or marriage."[1] Thus, the *Oxford English Dictionary* (*OED*) dates the first entry of the world "family" into the English language to just before the Renaissance, approximately in the year 1400, when it was used to indicate the servants of a house or household.[2] Historians estimate that during the fifteenth century, the vast majority of families (between two-thirds and three-quarters of all families) could not afford to rear their own children to adulthood.[3]

The *OED* places the contemporary popular meaning of family, "the group of persons consisting of the parents and their children, whether actually living together or not," as the *third* of eleven definitions it offers and places its earliest recorded usage in the late seventeenth century.[4] Only during the nineteenth century, in the Victorian era, did our present common meaning of family come to dominance. Until the mid-nineteenth century, historian John Gillis reminds us, "it was accepted that marriage was beyond the reach of many, and that most people would not grow up in the bosom of their families of origin."[5]

It is important to recognize, therefore, that the family is a product of those long historical transformations generally referred to as modernization. Indeed, many historians employ the concept of the modern family to describe the particular domestic arrangements which the family has come to designate. The modern family in the West developed historically out of a patriarchal, pre-modern family economy in which work and family life were thoroughly integrated. In the United States, the modern family system arose in the nineteenth century when industrialization turned men into breadwinners and women into homemakers by separating paid work from households. Beginning first among white, middle-class people, this family pattern came to represent modernity and success. Indeed, the American way of life came to be so identified with this family form that the trade-union movement struggled for nearly a century to secure for male workers the material condition upon which it was based—the male breadwinner wage. However, not until the mid-twentieth century did significant percentages of industrial workers achieve this access to the male breadwinner nuclear family, and it has always exceeded the reach of the vast majority of African Americans. Slaves were not allowed to marry and had no parental rights at all, and few African-American households have ever been able to afford a full-time homemaker. In fact, many African-American mothers have worked as domestic workers in the modern family homes of relatively privileged whites.[6]

The rise of the modern family system spelled the demise of the premodern, family economy, which was explicitly patriarchal. Thus, it represented a shift in what sociologist Deniz Kandiyoti has called "patriarchal bargains."[7] In the classical patriarchal bargain, women accept overt subordination in exchange for protection and secure social status. The modern patriarchal bargain sugarcoats this exchange by wrapping it in an ideology of separate spheres and romantic love. In place of premodern marriages, which were arranged, in whole or in part, by parents and kin for economic, political, and social purposes, modern men and women, seeking love and companionship, voluntarily bind themselves for life to the complementary object of their individual desires. Under the guise of a separate but equal division of labor between male breadwinners and female homemakers, women and children became increasingly dependent upon the earnings of men. The nineteenth century gave rise to cults of "true womanhood," celebrating domesticity and maternalism. This generated conceptions of femininity that continue to infuse Western family ideology.[8] The development of analogous doctrines about the "tender years" of young children who need a specifically maternal form of love and care began to undermine earlier legal doctrines, which had treated children as patriarchal property.[9] U.S. family patterns became more predictable and homogeneous as the modern family system evolved in the nineteenth and twentieth centuries. High mortality and remarriage rates had kept premodern family patterns diverse and complex, but declines in mortality enabled increasing numbers of people to anticipate a normal family life course. By the mid-twentieth century, modern family life patterns, from birth through courtship, marriage, work, childrearing, and death had become so homogeneous, normative, and predictable that the family began to appear natural, universal, and self-evident.

Social scientists are rarely impervious to the tacit cultural understandings of their times. During the post-Second World War period, family sociologists in the United States developed a theory of family modernization that was rooted in the conviction that U.S. family history would prove to be a global model. Arguing that the modern nuclear family was ideally suited to support the functioning of industrial society, and that it was both a product of and handmaiden to Enlightenment progress and democracy, social scientists predicted that it would spread throughout the modernizing world. A product of Western cultural imperialism, the family modernization thesis presumed that the superiority of Western cultural forms would insure their eventual triumph over the "backward" nations and peoples of the globe.[10] Indeed some family scholars came to argue that the early development of the modern nuclear family in the West facilitated Western supremacy in developing capitalism.[11]

So convinced have Western governments been of the superiority of their family patterns that they have often imposed their gender and family patterns on conquered peoples. The United States, for example, disrupted matrilineal and extended kin systems among several indigenous New World cultures by awarding land titles exclusively to male-headed, nuclear household units.[12] In a similar fashion, Europeans have destructively imposed nuclear family principles on very different African kinship systems. In the Zambian copper belt, for example, mineowners ignored and disrupted the actual extended kinship patterns of their workers by distributing benefits only to a worker's wife and children.[13] More often, however, Westerners presumed that the global diffusion of the modern nuclear family system would come about automatically. These rather contradictory ideas about the family—that it is natural and universal, on the one hand, and that it is a sign and agent of Western superiority, on the other—continue to collide in popular and scholarly discourse.

CONTRADICTIONS OF THE FAMILY

We can gain some perspective on contemporary family turmoil by recognizing contradictions inherent in the ideology, principles, and practices of the modern family system, the most glaring of which is the tension between volition and coercion. The ideology of the modern family construes marital commitment as a product of the free will and passions of two equal individuals who are drawn to each other by romantic attraction and complementary emotional needs. However, the domestic division of labor of the modern family system, which made women economically dependent upon male earners, and the subordination of women, both de jure and de facto, provided potent incentives for women to choose to enter and remain in marriages, quite apart from their individual desires. And while men certainly have always enjoyed greater opportunities to pursue their emotional and sexual interests inside and outside of marriage, until quite recently cultural codes and material sanctions led most men to depend upon the personal, emotional, and social services of a full-time homemaker. Political satirist Barbara Ehrenreich has observed that the white middle classes in the United States are likely the only bourgeoisie in history to employ members of their own class as personal servants.[14]

The relative acceptability of the contradiction between egalitarian principles of free love and companionship and inegalitarian forms of material and cultural coercion depended upon the availability and accessibility of a male breadwinner wage. Feminist historians have debated the degree to which working-class wives supported, resisted, or benefited from the trade-union struggle that men conducted to earn wages sufficient to support full-time homemakers and mothers.[15] However, no matter who achieved this arrangement, which Heidi Hartmann has called a patriarchal–capitalist bargain negotiated between male factory owners and laborers, it has proven to be quite ephemeral. The majority of industrial workers did not earn enough to support a full-time housewife until the 1950s or 1960s, and soon after they did so, deindustrialization and post-industrialization conspired to eliminate their jobs and erode their earnings.[16]

Thus, instability was written into the genetic code of the modern family system (on the "Y" chromosome), because its sustenance depended upon the wide availability of stable, livable-wage jobs for men. As that strand of the bargain began to unravel during the 1970s and 1980s, the fragility of the entire gender and family order moved into full view, provoking widespread consternation over "family crisis" throughout the advanced industrial societies.

During the past few decades, every developed industrial nation has experienced soaring divorce rates, falling birth rates, and rising rates of unmarried domestic partners, of step and blended families, and of non-family households. Alarmists who decry family decline in the United States often overlook the transnational character of these demographic trends. A 1977 Viennese study warned that if the rate of increase in European divorce rates during the 1970s were to continue until the year 2000, at that point 85 percent of all European marriages would end in divorce.[17]

During this same period, the employment rates of women and men, formerly quite distinct, began to converge worldwide. Women, especially mothers of young children, now find it necessary to work for pay to support or contribute to the support of families that have been undermined by the loss of jobs and real earnings by men. The loss of steady work, or any work, for men at lower educational levels has been quite dramatic. While more than two-thirds of men with less than a high school education worked full time, year round during the 1970s, a decade later only half could find such steady work.[18] A significant wage gap between men and women persists, but the normalization of female employment and the decline in jobs for men has reduced some of women's economic dependency on men, and thus has weakened one coercive buttress of marriage.

That is one major reason why single motherhood is rising around the globe, and why increasing percentages of single mothers have never been married. Sitcom heroine Murphy Brown has become a controversial symbol of the family circumstances of a small but rising number of affluent, professional women in the U.S. who are choosing to become single mothers rather than to forgo motherhood entirely. In reality, the vast majority of single-mother families confront dire economic circumstances.[19] At the same time that many women began choosing to become mothers alone, and for related reasons, birth rates were falling below replacement levels throughout the postindustrial world. It is particularly striking that women in Italy, an overwhelmingly Catholic country, now give birth to the smallest national average number of children in the advanced industrial world.[20] On the other hand, birth rates have begun to rise in Sweden, despite its reputation as the leading country for family decline.[21] The comparative level of security and confidence that prospective Swedish parents, particularly would-be mothers, derive from their nation's exceptionally progressive tax structure and social welfare provisions is the most likely explanation for this paradox. Meanwhile, the *New York Times* reports that "Eastern Germany's adults appear to have come as close to a temporary suspension of childbearing as any large population in the human experience," a response to the region's dire economic conditions since reunification. The state of Brandenburg has voted to offer parents a cash incentive of $650 per new child born.[22]

Because global capitalism is governed by the endless search for profits through increased productivity and technological development, we can be certain that our only social constant is change. Social change is a permanent and endless feature of our world, and all we can know about the future of family life is that it too will continue to change. Recent developments in reproductive technology and genetic engineering offer glimpses of some of the most dramatic and radical implications of future family scenarios. *Junior*, a 1994 Christmas season family movie starring Arnold Schwarzenegger as a pregnant experimental scientist (a movie which proved to be more popular with women than with men), presages some of the redefinitions of family life in store as science completes its Faustian gift of separating sexuality, conception, gestation, procreation, marriage, child-rearing, and parenting. Pregnant men and test-tube babies, once the standard fare of science fiction, now appear inevitable. We have already reached the point at which a man's sperm can fertilize one woman's ovum, which gestates in the uterus of a second woman, who, in turn, serves as a "surrogate" for yet a third woman, who plans to adopt and rear the offspring, with or without a second man or a fourth woman as co-parent. What and who is the mother, the father, or the family in such a world?

THE POSTMODERN FAMILY CONDITION

The astonishing transformations sketched above indicate that the particular patriarchal bargain of the modern family system has collapsed. Instead, we now forge our intimate lives within the terms of the postmodern family condition described earlier. At the current moment in Western family history, no single family pattern is statistically dominant, and our domestic arrangements have become increasingly diverse. Only a minority of U.S. households still contain married couples with children; and many of these include divorced and remarried adults. More children live with single mothers than in modern families containing a breadwinner dad and a full-time homemaker mom.[23] Most features of the postmodern family condition are most prominent in the United States and Scandinavia. But demographic trends are similar throughout the highly industrialized world, with variations only in the degree, timing, and pace of the changes, but not in their direction. Once the family modernization thesis predicted that all the societies of the globe would converge toward a singular family system—the modern Western family system. Ironically, instead we are converging internationally toward the postmodern family condition of diversity, flux, and instability.

Under postmodern conditions, the social character of practices of gender, sexuality, parenting, and family life, which once appeared to be natural and immutable, become visible and politically charged. While similar demographic trends are dissolving the modern family system throughout the capitalist, industrialized world, national responses to the modern family crisis differ widely. Some societies have adapted to the decline of the male breadwinner family by devising generous social welfare policies that attempt to mitigate some of the destructive impact that marital fragility too often inflicts on children and the unequal burden it places on women. Again the Scandinavian countries, with Sweden and Norway in the lead, set the standards for innovative family support policies of this sort. In both nations, parents of either gender are entitled to apportion a full year's leave with 90 percent pay to take care of a newborn. Because so few fathers availed themselves of this benefit, both Sweden and Norway recently offered them added incentive to do so. Both countries now allow men, and only men, to receive an additional month of paid parental leave beyond the original twelve months, which men and women can allot as they choose. Moreover, Scandinavian workers enjoy paid leave to care for sick children and relatives, as well as universal family allowances, health care, including sex education, contraception, and abortion services, and subsidized high-quality daycare. There are few deadbeat dads in these Nordic nations, because the state assumes responsibility for collecting and distributing childcare payments. As a result, while more than half of single-parent families in the United States live below the official poverty line, in Sweden only 2 percent do so.[24] Most likely this is why Swedish women have been willing to bear more children in recent years. Likewise, Sweden and Norway also followed Denmark's lead in legalizing a form of marriage for same-sex couples before this became a visible political issue in the United States.[25]

Other affluent societies, however, have proven far more hostile to post-modern demographic and cultural changes. They are far less willing to assume public responsibility for addressing the unjust and disruptive effects caused by these changes. The United States is far and away the most extreme in this regard. Reflecting an exceptionally privatized economy, an individualistic culture, and racial antagonisms, social welfare for the poor in the United States has always been comparatively stingy, punitive, and unpopular. Yet even this meager system is currently being dismantled. The United States alone, among eighteen advanced industrial nations, does not provide its citizens with universal health coverage, family allowances, or paid parental leaves.[26] In fact, it was not until the Family Leave Act of 1993 that the right to take an unpaid three-month maternity leave, which few families can afford to use, was mandated for workers in firms with at least fifty employees. Welfare provisions in the United States have always been means-tested, stigmatized, and niggardly.[27] As a result, a higher percentage of single-mother families in the United States, as well as a higher percentage of children in general, live in poverty than in any advanced industrial nation.[28] Conservative estimates of the numbers that current welfare reform legislation will add to this disturbing record have even frightened Senator Moynihan, one of the original advocates of revising the welfare system.[29]

While family support policies in the United States are the weakest in the industrial world, no society has yet to come close to the country's expenditure of politicized rhetoric over family crisis. The politics of gender, sexuality, repro-duction, and family in the U.S. are the most polarized, militant, and socially divisive in the world, precisely because social structural responses to the decline of the modern family system have been so weak. This is an important reason why feminism, gay liberation, and backlash "pro-family" movements are so vocal and influential across the political spectrum.

Rampant nostalgia for the modern family system, or, more precisely, for an idealized version of a 1950s, Ozzie and Harriet image of the family, has become an increasingly potent ideological force in the United States, with milder ver-sions evident in Canada and England.[30] Fundamentalist Christians and right-wing Republicans spearheaded the pro-family movement that abetted the Reagan "revolution" of the 1980s. By the 1994 electoral season, however, even Presi-dent Clinton had embraced the ideology of an explicitly centrist campaign for family values led by a small group of social scientists. This ongoing campaign portrays family breakdown as the primary source of social malaise in the United States, blaming the decline of the married-couple family for everything from crime, violence, and declining educational standards to poverty, drug abuse, and sexually transmitted disease.[31]

There seems to be nearly an inverse relationship between a nation's rhetorical concern over the plight of children in declining families and its willingness to implement policies to ease their suffering. This may appear paradoxical, if not hypocritical, but family support policies are consistent with the historical development of public responsibility for social welfare in each nation. They are strongest in parliamentary governments in which labor movements have achieved a significant voice.[32] Lip service to the family, on the other hand, serves as a proxy for the private sphere and as a rationale for abdicating public responsibility for social welfare. Unfortunately, the more individualistic and market-oriented a society becomes, the more difficult it becomes to sustain family bonds.

LET'S BURY "THE FAMILY"

The decision of the United Nations to proclaim an International Year of the Family represents a tacit acknowledgment that family systems are in crisis around the world. This choice of language, however, proclaims an oxymoronic project, because it begs the question of a universally shared definition of the family. Indeed, the UN Committee on the Family that was responsible for organizing the family year recognized, but tried to evade, this dilemma. First, it prefaced its official set of guiding principles on the family with the claim that "no definition of the family is given because of the great variety of types, cultures, and customs existing in families throughout the world." Yet it also issued a report entitled "Family in Crisis," which began by acknowledging that, "to identify crises which beset families today is not feasible without clarifying what we mean by family." Finally, the same document concluded with the astonishing admission that, "we are aware that the family does not exist."[33]

The family indeed is dead, if what we mean by it is the modern family *system* in which units comprising male breadwinner and female homemaker, married couples, and their offspring dominate the land. But its ghost, the ideology of the family, survives to haunt the consciousness of all those who refuse to confront it. It is time to perform a social autopsy on the corpse of the modern family system so that we may try to lay its troublesome spirit to rest. Perhaps a proper memorial service for the family system we have lost can free us to address the diverse needs of people struggling to sustain intimate relationships under very difficult postmodern family conditions.

Adopting the pathologist's stance of hardhearted, clinical detachment in this case can lead to an uncomfortable conclusion. Historically, all stable systems of marriage and family life have rested upon diverse measures of coercion and inequality. Family *systems* appear to have been most stable when women and men have been economically interdependent, when households served as units of production with sufficient resources to reproduce themselves, and when individuals lacked alternative means of economic, sexual, and social life. Family units of this sort have always been embedded in, supported, and sanctioned by wider sets of kinship, community, and religious ties. Disturbingly, all such family systems have been patriarchal. The stability of the modern family system, which represented a significant departure from several of these principles, depended upon the adequacy and reliability of the male family wage. However, the ceaseless development of capitalist industrialization, which disrupted the premodern patriarchal bargain, has now disrupted the modern one as well, and it will continue to disrupt postmodern familial regimes of any sort.

It is sobering to recognize that throughout history, family crises have been resolved by replacing one male-dominant form of domestic life with another. The Chinese Revolution, for example, supplanted Confucian patriarchy with patriarchal socialism.[34] In the West, The Family resolved the crisis industrialization had induced in the premodern family economy. The modern family system offered women both gains and losses over the prior patriarchal bargain, but now it too has outlived its historic role.

Patriarchal crises are always moments of intense danger and opportunity. Under postmodern family conditions throughout the postindustrial world, women enjoy greater access to education and employment, and a greater need for both, than ever before. As women become less dependent upon male earnings, they are freer to leave or avoid abusive or hostile relationships. At the same time, however, men seem to feel less obliged to commit themselves to familial or parental responsibilities, and more and more women confront the added burdens of the double day. In Eastern Europe, on the other hand, the collapse of the communist patriarchal bargain has unleashed a different kind of patriarchal crisis. Although many women have been freed from mandatory second shifts and ration queues, many have also lost their access to employment, abortion, and childcare, not to speak of food and life itself. Little wonder that as women struggle to survive diverse patriarchal crises, they too can become nostalgic for the relative security provided by prior, more stable, patriarchal forms.

THE FAMILY OF WOMAN

During the late 1950s, just when the modern family system was about to unravel, a humanist book of photographs, *The Family of Man*, enjoyed immense popularity in the U.S.[35] The postmodern family condition that has emerged since then could more aptly be called "the family of woman." Public discourse is preoccupied with the growing ranks of single mothers and fatherless children. The frequently noted feminization of poverty around the globe is a direct product of the feminization of family life that has been taking place since the collapse of the modern industrial order upon which the modern family system depended.

Under conditions of postindustrial, global capitalism, marital instability and woman-centered kin ties are becoming endemic facts of life. This presents postindustrial societies with only two real, and imperfect, options. A nation can choose to recognize and adapt to the new realities, however unwelcome, by assuming greater social responsibility for the welfare of children and citizens, as

Scandinavian societies have tried to do; or societies can resist, deny, and rail against the facts of postmodern family life, resorting to the rhetoric of moral panic and the politics of backlash, so popular in the United States.

Perhaps the postmodern "family of woman" will take the lead in burying The Family at long last. The Family is a concept derived from faulty theoretical premisses and an imperialist logic, which even at its height never served the best interests of women, of their children, or even of many men. We should not be misled by its false gender neutrality. The International Year of The Family was a year like most years, when women often suffered the brunt of family crises and struggled, against increasingly difficult odds, to sustain their kin and spirits. Women, in particular, should be resisting the forces of denial and the backlash against family change. Attacks against welfare are attacks on mothers struggling to sustain vulnerable families. To resist the campaign for family values is by no means to be anti-family. Instead, women should lead efforts to expand public support for an expanded definition of family, one that is honest and tolerant enough to acknowledge and support the diversity of family patterns, preferences, and relationships in which we actually live. It is time to lay to rest the ghost of The Family so that we may begin to build a safe world for living families. The family is dead. Long live our families!

NOTES

1. John Gillis, "Families of Strangers," in *A World of Their Own Making: Myth, Ritual, and the Quest for Family Values* (New York: Basic Books, 1996).
2. *The Compact Edition of the Oxford English Dictionary* (Oxford: Oxford University Press, 1971).
3. Gillis, *A World of Their Own Making*, 7.
4. *The Compact Edition of the Oxford English Dictionary.*
5. Gillis, *A World of Their Own Making*, 6.
6. See, for example, Jacqueline Jones, *Labor of Love, Labor of Sorrow: Black Women, Work and the Family, From Slavery to the Present* (New York: Basic Books, 1985); Paula Giddings, *When and Where I Enter: The Impact of Black Women on Race and Sex in America* (New York: William Morrow, 1984); and Deborah Gray White, *Ar'n't I a Woman? Female Slaves in the Plantation South* (New York: W. W. Norton, 1985).
7. Deniz Kandiyoti, "Bargaining With Patriarchy," *Gender & Society* 2, no. 3 (September 1988), 274–90.
8. See Barbara Welter, "The Cult of True Womanhood, 1820–1860," *American Quarterly* 18 (1996), 151–74; Mary Ryan, "The Empire of the Mother: American Writing about Domesticity 1830–1860," *Women & History* 2/3 (Summer/Fall 1982); and Barbara Epstein, *The Politics of Domesticity: Women, Evangelism and Temperance in Nineteenth-Century America* (New York: Wesleyan University Press, 1977).
9. Michael Grossberg, "Who Gets the Child? Custody, Guardianship, and The Rise of A Judicial Patriarchy in Nineteenth-Century America," *Feminist Studies* 9, no. 2 (Summer 1983), 235–60.
10. The classic formulation of this thesis appears in William J. Goode, *World Revolution and Family Patterns* (New York: Free Press, 1963).
11. This perspective is identified with the Cambridge Group for the History of Population

and Social Structure. See, for example, Peter Laslett, *The World We Have Lost: England Before the Industrial Age* (New York: Charles Scribner's Sons, 1965).

12. For example, the Mashpee of Cape Cod, Massachusetts, suffered this disruption. See James Clifford, "Identity in Mashpee," in his *The Predicament of Culture* (Cambridge, MA: Harvard University Press, 1988). See also Michael Yellowbird and C. Matthew Snipp, "American Indian Families," in Ronald Taylor, ed., *Minority Families in the United States: A Multicultural Perspective* (Englewood Cliffs, NJ: Prentice Hall, 1994).

13. James Ferguson, "Migration, Mineworkers, and 'the Modern Family' on the Zambian Copperbelt," paper presented at American Anthropological Association Meeting, San Francisco, December 1992.

14. Barbara Ehrenreich, *Fear of Falling: The Inner Life of the Middle Class* (New York: Pantheon, 1989).

15. For the initial argument that the struggle for the male breadwinner wage represented collusion between male workers and bosses, and thus between patriarchy and capitalism, see Heidi Hartmann, "Capitalism, Patriarchy and Job Segregation by Sex," in Zillah Eisenstein, ed., *Capitalist Patriarchy and the Case for Socialist-Feminism* (New York: Monthly Review Press, 1979). Jane Humphries challenged this analysis with the claim that working-class wives supported their husbands' *class* struggle for the family wage, in "The Working-Class Family, Women's Liberation and Class Struggle: The Case of Nineteenth-Century British History," *Review of Radical Political Economics* 9 (Fall 1977), 25–41. More recent work has refined and complicated this analysis. See, for example, Martha May, "Bread Before Roses: American Workingmen, Labor Unions and The Family Wage," in Ruth Milkman, ed., *Women, Work and Protest: A Century of U.S. Women's Labor History* (Boston: Routledge & Kegan Paul, 1985).

16. For data and fuller analyses of these processes, see Robert Griswold, *Fatherhood in America* (New York: Basic Books, 1993); and Judith Stacey, *Brave New Families: Stories of Domestic Upheaval in Late Twentieth Century America* (New York: Basic Books, 1990).

17. Katja Boh, "European Family Life Patterns—A Reappraisal," in Katja Boh et. al., eds., *Changing Patterns of European Family Life: A Comparative Analysis of 14 European Countries* (London: Routledge, 1989), 280.

18. Moreover, since 1990 almost twice as many women as men have been added to the paid workforce. "Working Wives Keep America's Families Out of Red," *San Francisco Chronicle,* 14 March 1994.

19. A 1992 study found that the rate of unwed motherhood among women who had attended at least a year of college rose from 5.5 percent in 1982 to 11.3 percent in 1992. The rate for women with professional or managerial jobs, like Murphy Brown, rose from 3.1 percent to 8.3 percent. However, in 1993, 47 percent of families headed by single mothers lived in poverty, compared with 8.3 percent of two-parent families. Jason DeParle, "Census Reports a Sharp Increase Among Never-Married Mothers," *New York Times,* 14 July 1993.

20. United Nations, *The World's Women 1970–1990: Trends and Statistics* (New York: United Nations, 1991).

21. Two of the most alarming interpretations of family decline in Sweden are David Popenoe, *Disturbing the Nest: Family Change and Decline in Modern Societies* (New York: Aldine de Gruyter, 1988), and Allan Carlson, *The Swedish Experiment in Family Politics: The Myrdals and the Interwar Population Crisis* (New Brunswick: Transaction, 1990).

22. Stephen Kinzer, "$650 a Baby: Germany to Pay to Stem Decline in Births," *New York Times,* 25 November 1994.

23. In 1988, approximately 22 percent of children lived in single parent families, 47 percent lived in dual worker families, and 29 percent lived in male breadwinner, female homemaker families. Griswold, *Fatherhood in America,* 220. However, by 1993, 30 per-

cent of births in the United States were to unwed mothers. Kristin A. Moore, "Report to Congress on Out-Of-Wedlock Childbearing," (Washington, D.C.: Child Trends, 1994).

24. Timothy M. Smeeding, "Why the U.S. Antipoverty System Doesn't Work Very Well," *Challenge* (January–February 1992): 33.

25. Same-sex partners who choose to legalize their relationship are entitled to most of the rights and benefits of heterosexual marriage. However, they are not entitled to a church marriage or to adopt children.

26. For comparative data, see Smeeding, "Why the U.S. Antipoverty System Doesn't Work Very Well;" and Irene Wennemo, *Sharing the Costs of Children* (Stockholm: Swedish Institute for Social Research, 1994).

27. Linda Gordon, *Pitied but Not Entitled: Single Mothers and the History of Welfare* (New York: Free Press, 1994).

28. Smeeding, "Why the U.S. Antipoverty System Doesn't Work Very Well."

29. See Daniel Patrick Moynihan, "Congress Builds a Coffin," *New York Review of Books* 43, no. 1 (11 January 1996), 33–36.

30. See Susan Reinhold, "Through The Parliamentary Looking Glass: 'Real' and 'Pretend' Families in Contemporary British Politics," *Feminist Review* 48 (Autumn 1994), 61–78.

31. Perhaps the best-known essay of the centrist family-values campaign is Barbara Defoe Whitehead, "Dan Quayle Was Right," *The Atlantic* 271 (April 1993), 47–84.

32. Harold Wilensky, "Common Problems, Divergent Policies: An 18-Nation Study of Family Policy," *Public Affairs Reporter* 31, no. 3 (May 1990), 1–3.

33. Quotations taken from the United Nations Committee on the Family, "Guiding Principles on the Family," and "Family in Crisis," (Vienna: United Nations International Centre, 1994).

34. Judith Stacey, *Patriarchy and Socialist Revolution in China* (Berkeley: University of California Press, 1983).

35. New York, Museum of Modern Art.

STORIES OF SURVIVAL: CLASS, RACE, AND DOMESTIC VIOLENCE

JANICE HAAKEN

Every Saturday night he beat her, trying to pin the blame for his failure on her by imprinting it on her face.

Alice Walker, *The Third Life of Grange Copeland*

At a fall 2000 conference on domestic violence and the African-American community, Captain Toni Malliet, a black woman and head of the Division of Domestic Violence and Sexual Assault of the Seattle Police Department, began her presentation with a story. She described a nervous young girl with chronic stomachaches, a girl who watched helplessly as her mother was routinely beaten by her father. In a quasi-biblical tone, Malliet told of how this girl grew older and rose up against her father, driving him from the house. "That girl was me.... But now," she continued with a wry smile, "I don't have to take abuse from nobody. I've got a gun, a license to carry it, and I know how to use it."[1] Malliet went on to acknowledge periods of agonizing doubt over working in an institution that often brutalizes her own community. And she expressed unease over arresting men who have little sense of power or control, other than over the women they are terrorizing. After belting out a few lines of "What's Love Got to Do with It?" the Tina Turner song that has become an anthem in the domestic violence field, Malliet concluded by saying that "love's got a lot to do with it." Until those in the community learn to love each other, Malliet insisted, the tragedy of domestic violence will continue. During the question-and-answer period, a woman from the audience asked Malliet what she was doing about a recent incident where police killed two young black men in the Central District of Seattle. This question prompted a discussion of the dangers in relying on the police, and of how domestic violence can't be separated from the broader problem of violence in African-American communities.

As a white feminist academic and activist, I have been interested in how cultural contexts and social identity shape understandings of family violence. In contrast to many conferences I have attended organized by white feminists, presenters and participants at the conference where Toni Malliet spoke were able to hold a complex range of stories and explanations for domestic violence. Introducing the topic of female aggression—whether whipping kids or lashing out against partners—did not elicit a wave of defensive outrage. Discussing the importance of incorporating men into the movement, even those with a history of violence, was not felt to be a threat to female solidarity. Talk of poverty, racism, and alienation did not provoke the rejoinder, which is now reflexive in many domestic violence conferences, that focusing on economic conditions is tantamount to making "excuses" for men. Participants were able to explore myriad determinants of violence, including forms of violence where women play an active part, while still "holding men accountable."

This essay has three primary aims. The first is to contribute to an emerging dialogue on race and class in the domestic violence field. Much of what is underway in the field is limited to providing culturally sensitive services for women in crisis, and including in training procedures an emphasis on the multiple forms of women's oppression. While it is important to address the needs of women of color as victims of domestic violence, my emphasis is on the contributions of women of color at the level of critical social *analysis*. A second aim of the essay is to explore the relationship between race, class, and domestic violence through the lens of a socialist-feminist analysis. I argue that a socialist-feminist perspective, which has been largely absent from feminist discourse on domestic violence in the U.S., allows us to understand a more complex matrix of social factors operating in family violence than does an analysis limited to gender influences. A third aim is to suggest the relevance of psychoanalytic cultural theory to organizing around domestic violence. Although my background as a clinician does inform this project, psychoanalytic cultural theory is a more vital influence in my political work. This perspective brings together social structural and historical factors, on the one hand, and psychological dynamics—particularly unconscious fantasy and defenses—on the other. Psychoanalytic feminism is enlisted to explore collective fantasies and defenses that emerge in framing violence, particularly in negotiating the boundaries of similarity and difference in women's experiences (see Haaken 1998, 1999).

UNITY AND DIFFERENCE

In the early period of mobilization around battering, unity was based on a shared critique of the patriarchal family.[2] Whether having been beaten or not, many women could identify with stories of battered women because they vivified the tragic costs of female economic dependency. Exposing the problem of woman battering dramatically conveyed the idea that the family—the culturally idealized domain allotted to women—could be a living hell. As women were entering the paid workforce in historically unprecedented numbers, the argument that more women are killed in their homes than on the streets underscored the rightfulness and necessity of the exodus.

Over the past decade, the field of domestic violence has shifted toward adoption of the "power and control" model of battering (Pence and Paymar 1993). Based on a radical-feminist critique of patriarchal authority, the power and control model asserts that male desire for dominance is the primary motivation behind woman battering. Male violence is interpreted as a direct by-product of male power and privilege, rather than as a form of male pathology or poor impulse control. The companion argument is that all women are equally vulnerable to male violence, although women differ in the resources available to them in dealing with it.

What is problematic about the model is that power and control motives take on the character of a prime mover, represented as a deeply ingrained male trait that operates independently of contexts or contingencies, such as unemployment, poverty, addiction, or other material conditions. At crosscurrents with this emphasis on battering as a uniform gender problem is the growing presence of women of color in the DV field, insisting on more discussion of differences in women's experiences with violence. Kimberle Williams Crenshaw calls for analyses of the "intersectionality of race, class and gender" and suggests that the "gag order on discussing higher rates of domestic violence in poor communities" has had a conservative effect on the movement (1994: 100). Beth Richie argues that however well intended the initial strategy of downplaying differences in the impact of gender violence in women's lives may have been, it has proven to be a costly one, particularly for women of color.

> I would even argue that the notion that every woman is at risk—one of the hallmarks of our movement's rhetorical paradigm—is in fact a dangerous one in that it has structured a national advocacy response based on a false sense of unity around the experience of gender oppression... In the end, the assumed race and class neutrality of gender violence led to the erasure of low-income women and women of color from the dominant view. (Richie 2000: 1134–35)

Taking seriously the intersectionality of race, class, and gender raises complex questions about the aims and strategies of the movement and the costs of various victories. To what extent *is* domestic violence a similar experience for all women? What are the implications of invoking domestic violence as the primary category through which we understand women's oppression? Can we restore compassion to our portraits of male violence without letting men off the hook? These are among the questions taken up in the following sections.

FEMINIST PERSPECTIVES ON BATTERING

Much like sexual politics, the politics of violence opens up a cultural minefield of emotional reactions and conflicting ideas. Since public discourse on sex and violence wavers between denial and hysteria, feminist engagement with the issue of male violence is perennially overdetermined by more diffuse social anxieties.

It is possible vastly to exaggerate the extent of "rampant" violence in poor communities, just as it is possible to minimize it. But a more important difference in perceptions of violence concerns how it is interpreted or understood. While conservatives emphasize myriad forms of moral laxity, many of which reduce to individual moral choice, progressives are more apt to focus on social and economic determinants of violence. Whereas conservatives decry the "breakdown" of the family, exalt "personal responsibility," and blame working mothers, progressives point to unemployment and income disparities as the primary predictors of violence (see Weiner et al. 1990).

Radical feminism has been the anima behind domestic violence work, although liberal and socialist feminists also have been active in the movement.[3] While socialist feminists emphasize the cross-cultural variability in women's oppression and the historically shifting nature of gender inequality, radical feminists tend to stress universals. They argue that male violence is rooted in the patriarchal system of domination, a system that is the basis of economies and cultures throughout much, if not most, of human history. Whether feudal, capitalist, or socialist, societies throughout history have sanctioned male violence as a means of maintaining a patriarchal social order. Men benefit materially and psychologically from the subordination of women. Further, the threat of violence keeps women from actively resisting. Organizing around domestic violence allows women to expose the grisly reality behind the facade of patriarchal protection, and to dramatize the state of crisis this creates for women. Social movements against racism, homophobia, and class oppression are understood as related struggles but sexism is the basic prototype. While women are acknowledged to be oppressors in the context of class and racial domination, radical feminism tends to cast women as captives to men rather than as subjects acting in their own interests.

Liberal feminists believe that progress is achieved through incremental reforms in the existing political and economic system. Implicit in this strategy of social change is the assumption that male violence is not a structural problem and, further, that it may be alleviated through various corrective measures. These measures include legal protections for victims, but extend as well to ideas about prevention: raising boys to be more sensitive, nurturing, and nonviolent, and raising girls to be more assertive. Liberals also are more apt to adopt a therapeutic/reformist approach to batterers, over against punitive measures, and to stress the connection between alleviating poverty and preventing violence. An extension of this argument is that violence is symptomatic of deeper problems affecting marginalized communities: it is a response to economic deprivations that require state intervention, particularly in ameliorating the effects of poverty.

Both radical feminism and liberal feminism have their insights, and each may crystallize some of the underlying dynamics operating in women's experiences with abusive men. Further, these frameworks often overlap and merge, with feminists finding common ground on many issues. Nonetheless, radical feminists have had a particular interest in organizing around issues such as domestic violence, incest, rape, and prostitution because they sensitize us to the sheer pervasiveness of patriarchal violence. These issues awaken us to the horrifying totality of it all, and arouse a sense of the unifying strength of our oppositional voices. If the enemy is united, then we, too, must be united in our refusal to tolerate threats to women's lives.

Feminist politics converge on some points but differ in their views of the "depth" of the problem of male violence, its primary causes, and strategies for eliminating it. Radical feminists "maximize" whereas liberal feminists "minimize" the problem of male violence. Socialist feminists share with radical feminism the view that male supremacy is a structural problem requiring a transformation of society and its institutions. Violence against women is a worldwide problem that occurs in a broad range of societies—and it requires the mass mobilization of women worldwide in resisting it.

Despite this universality, however, it is important to attend to differences in the meaning and form of male violence, even within a particular country. As Carol Hagemann-White notes in her analysis of feminist organizing in Germany, "the phrase, 'violence against women,' while still widely used, has come to seem inadequate" in capturing the complex political terrain of the movement (1998: 181). The phrase fails to capture, for example, distinctions between wife beating as a response to female challenges to male supremacy and situations where violence against women is an extension of codified patriarchal practices (see Levinson 1989).

For socialist feminists, social class shapes alliances among people, including those within the family, as much as does gender. Domestic violence must be understood within the wider context of social and economic forces impinging upon families and communities. Further, in advanced capitalist societies, power does not rely primarily on the exercise of direct violence. As a means of social control, violence is ill-suited to a system based on creating highly motivated workers and on extracting maximum value from human productive activity. At the same time, physical violence through police powers, as well as economic violence in the form of inadequate food, housing, healthcare, or employment, are endemic in many communities.

WIDENING THE LENS

When we tell the story of male violence through the lens of a socialist-feminist analysis, with social class as the lens on injustice, we are able to see areas of alliance between men and women in coping with social forces that determine their common fate. Both men and women experience the harshness of life and pathologies born of alienation and despair. If the battered wife suffers from what Lenore Walker (1984) terms "learned helplessness," so too does her batterer. This helplessness results from blunted opportunities and bitter disappointments. Whereas affluent men are more consistently reinforced in their sense of entitlement to power over others, working-class men are more apt to experience the unstable, shifting dimensions of manhood. For the affluent, the home is a place of calm refuge from competitive striving; for the oppressed, home is where spirits are revived, and often this takes the form of aggressive outbursts. When work involves self-monitoring and submission to hierarchical control, home is the one place where self-control may be more safely suspended (see Barrett and McIntosh 1991; Stacey, 1990).

Feminists who work with multiple axes of oppression are more apt to recognize the wide continuum of meanings and behaviors subsumed under terms such as "violence" and "aggression." In bourgeois society, many forms of aggressively charged behavior, particularly those of dark-skinned people, are interpreted as "violent." Talking loud, swearing, moving fast, arguing—all of these behaviors may be viewed through a racist, paranoid lens as disturbing indicators of a threatening proneness to aggression. The movement against domestic violence is not immune from this readiness on the part of whites to perceive people of color, particularly black people, as threatening. While cultural interpretations of aggressive behavior do differ, these interpretations are shaped by irrational anxieties and paranoia over those positioned as the "other." In Portland, Oregon, for example, African-American women are more apt to leave shelter—or be asked to leave—for behavior that is perceived by white staff and residents as violent. While this sometimes includes hitting, it also includes more subtle forms of expressive behaviors, for example talking loud or yelling.[4]

bell hooks (1997) argues that even the term "battered woman" collapses too many of the experiences of women under a one-dimensional rubric. The lines separating battered women from women suffering everyday hardships in oppressed communities, including economic violence, are not so easily drawn. By mobilizing around extreme incidents of assault, the domestic violence movement may contribute to the marginalizing of these less dramatic, everyday assaults on women's bodies and spirits. Other critics also point to the limitations of existing categories in the domestic violence field. In distinguishing between what he terms "patriarchal terrorism" and "common couple violence," Michael Johnson (1995) argues that the domestic violence prototype does not adequately bridge the various expressions of physical aggression in families. Many women engage in controlled outbursts of minor violence, as do many men. Episodes of slapping, throwing things, or yelling may dissipate as quickly as they erupt. These forms of aggression must be distinguished from what Johnson terms *patriarchal terrorism*—ritualized physical and emotional assaults intended to break down the woman's sense of self and achieve psychological control over her.

Contrary to claims in the domestic violence movement, poor and working-class women are more apt to be assaulted by their partners than are more affluent women (see Carrillo and Tello 1998). They also are more apt to challenge male authority openly. Indeed, many episodes of domestic violence center on women's contestation of male power within the family (see Gordon 1988). The rage that results from a history of oppression is easily mobilized against displaced targets, acted out against those who are close at hand rather than against more remote rulers. Men are given more cultural latitude than are women to act on their rage, as well as other impulses. Yet for women and men alike, abusive experiences in the past may be re-enacted in the present, particularly as current relational binds evoke earlier disturbing experiences.

While female violence is far less common or destructive than is male violence, it also tends to be presented in the feminist literature as a patina, as not a genuine part of the "core" feminine self. Feminists also tend to insist that female violence is usually defensive, whereas male violence is more often offensive and a means of establishing domination over a woman (Johnson 1995). This position overlooks the deep and varied sources of female outrage. Indeed, the *passivity* of men within the household is a more chronic problem and source of outrage for women than are overt acts of violence.

It is possible to advance a feminist analysis of male violence without totalizing gender differences (e.g. men are bad, women are good; women are the givers of life, men are the destroyers). Critique of gender dichotomies is an essential part of the feminist project, as is theorizing the complex relationship between gender and aggression, on the one hand, and social power, on the other. A toddler may kick his mother, but this does not mean he has power and control over her. A woman may throw a pan at her husband, but this does not mean she is able to get him to do the dishes.

Social class further mediates the relationship between gender, power, and aggression. In her study of girl gangs, Anne Campbell (1991) found that toughness and fighting were not viewed as inimical to femininity. The girls in her study spoke with pride of their street skills, and the importance of having a "reputation for violence." While girls were more apt than boys to avoid causing serious injury or death, Campbell also points out that for both male and female gangs the majority of aggression was in the from of *display*, rather than overt acts of violence.

A singular focus on male tendencies toward violence as a universal proclivity runs the risk of losing sight of material causes of gender violence. While the early battered women's movement stressed forms of economic dependency that made women vulnerable to male violence (Dobash and Dobash 1979; Schechter 1982), more recent feminist discourse stresses the power motives of men, dissociated from their material basis in economic life. Yet cross-cultural research on wife beating continues to stress links between women's access to and control over economic resources and their ability to resist male violence. In one of the most comprehensive cross-cultural studies of family violence, Levinson found that rates of wife beating were lowest in those societies where women organized their own work groups, whether in the form of working side by side in the fields, trading as a group in local markets, or establishing their own economic associations. He concludes that "the presence of exclusively female work groups, whether an indicator of female solidarity or of female economic power, or both, serves to control or prevent wife-beating" (Levinson 1989: 58).

There are real costs in basing victim claims on a highly virtuous portrait of womanhood, and particularly for women who do not conform to this white, middle-class standard. Whereas the cultural melodrama for white women centers on the Good Man entering the stage to rescue the maiden in distress from the smarmy Brute, black women are less apt to be cast in dominant cultural scripts as in need of protection (Hall 1983; Hurtado 1998). The super-strong black woman is represented as lacking in feminine vulnerability, as utterly stoical in the face of hardship (Collins 1990; West 1999). In this same narrative, the African-American woman as "matriarch" is perversely strong, castrating in her capacity to weaken the men within the reach of her influence.

These racist stereotypes also shape the self-representations of many black women, although through a more complex matrix of self-imagery than the stereotype would permit. Domestic violence is a recurrent motif in the writings of many women of color, writings that center on the alloy of pain and pleasure, heartbreak and joy, that binds family members in oppressed communities. Set against a landscape of brutal hardship, stories of family violence in oppressed communities often undermine the stability of our moral categories. And, as the "power and control" model displaces an earlier focus on cycles of violence and family trauma, women of color are more apt to preserve the idea that abusers are acting out histories not of their own making. In their study of domestic violence in Canadian Aboriginal communities, Anne McGillivray and Brenda Comaskey observe that

> If we are to explain the heightened rate of intimate violence in Aboriginal communities in terms of intergenerational patterns of violence, violence as learned behavior, and the normalization and internalization of violence, then the investigation of childhood is central to understanding partner violence. (McGillivray and Comaskey 1999: 57)

So, too, investigating intergenerational patterns of violence takes us into the history of colonized peoples and the destruction of their communities and their culture. In *The Third Life of Grange Copeland*, Alice Walker (1970) gives narrative force to this theme by casting the protagonist's sadistic assaults on his wife as an expression of his social disintegration. While the novel vividly portrays the brutality of Brownfield, the main character in the story, his violence emerges out of the dehumanizing conditions that trap him as a Southern sharecropper, compounded by an early history of neglect. As his father and relatives head North, Brownfield's world as an infant narrows to the presence of his mother, who is forced to leave him alone on the porch as she goes to work gutting fish for making bait. "His mother left him each morning with a hasty hug and a sugartit, on which he sucked through wet weather and dry, across the dusty clearing or miry, until she returned" (p. 6). Brownfield grows up to suck on women as the one source of sustenance in a barren world. As this deprivation is elaborated through the codes of manhood, his emotional life becomes increasingly split between his wife, who is the displaced maternal object and focus of his bitter resentment, and his lover, Josie, heir to the split-off "pleasurable" mother.

His crushed pride, his battered ego, made him drag Mem away from schoolteaching. Her knowledge reflected badly on a husband who could scarcely read and write.... It was his rage at himself, and his life and world that made him beat her for an imaginary attraction she aroused in other men, crackers, although she was no party to any of it. His rage and his anger and his frustration ruled. His rage could and did blame everything, everything on her. (p. 55)

Much of the work of the battered women's movement has been to interrupt this deathly romance, and to warn women about the seductions of emotionally injured men. Indeed, any effort to probe the pain underlying male violence seems to carry women back into its pernicious vortex. Men who batter are often deeply dependent on their wives or girlfriends, even as this dependency is mediated by an equally intense masculine entitlement. Many women both consciously and unconsciously sense the infantile anxieties underlying male rage. And this desperate need can be as important a part of the holding power of abusive relationships for women as is "learned helplessness." While they may put up with a man's abusiveness at times, implicitly accepting his right to restore a sense of masculine potency, abused women also sometimes make claims on men during the "honeymoon" periods following outbreaks of violence. As one client of mine described the dynamic, "He goes off sometimes, and I put up with it. But then he comes around and helps me out when he is trying to make up. It's like he's had his tantrum and now he owes me."

DIVERSE PATHS OF RESISTANCE

For many women of color, escaping the binding ties of family confronts more complex countervailing pressures and ideals than it does for many white women. While women share a common cultural position in maintaining and preserving kinship ties, the project of emancipation from the patriarchal family is a more ambivalent one for women of color than it is for white women. The source of hardships is less readily located within the family structure, and broader contingencies controlling the fates of family members impose themselves more forcefully on daily life. The cultural ideal of the autonomous nuclear family, like that of the autonomous individual, is more apt to be recognized as an illusion.

But just as African-American women's experiences with violence are more complex than the stereotypical drama would suggest, so too are the experiences of other women of color. A common theme in the literature of women of color concerns the difficulty in drawing the boundary between daily hardships and domestic abuse, on the one hand, and in locating a single source of villainy, on the other (Lockhart and White 1989; Davis 2000). Women of color are more apt to live in economically vulnerable communities where bad treatment comes in many forms. In such communities, the capacity to fight back is vital for survival, even though battles are often waged against displaced enemies. Women are the shock absorbers in capitalist society, but there are more shocks to absorb when resources are meager and tensions run high. Many women stake their survival with the tough men, even though these same defensively armored men may turn on them at some point.

In addressing cultural dimensions of domestic violence, Evelyn White (1994) emphasizes the difficulties black women face in acknowledging their own vulnerabilities and in extricating themselves from the pain of men. While this is a consistent refrain in popular literature on the psychology of women, White does not lose sight of the social forces impinging on women's ambivalence about leaving abusive situations. She makes a distinction between empathizing with the oppression black men face and taking responsibility for it.

> You don't have to become your partner's target because the bank didn't give him a loan. You do not have to become the scapegoat when the landlord raises the rent. And you do not have to become the punching bag because he can't afford to take the children to Disneyland. Physical and emotional abuse are not acceptable demonstrations of Black manhood. Black men will not heal their wounded pride or regain a sense of dignity by abusing Black women. (p. 26)

In the battered women's movement, it has been difficult to acknowledge the damaged humanity of men without yielding to the seductive pull of another stereotypical drama, where woman is cast as perpetual nursemaid to an injured manhood. The ideology of romantic love, realized in the context of the nuclear family, intensifies these emotional demands placed on women. But finding a new denouement need not require us to demonize batterers. By focusing on group interventions with abusive men, battered women—as individual partners of abusive men—bear less of the load.

Women of color have been at the forefront of addressing these lacunae in the movement. Theologian Delores Williams (1994) argues that strategies for addressing domestic violence need to take into account influences on multiple levels. First, they must address the national history of violence against women and men in the black community. Second, they must include the workplace, including the abuse and exploitation black domestics suffer in the homes of white employers. And third, strategies must address the violence women face in their own homes and communities.

In laying out a framework for 'justice-making,' Traci West also goes beyond the idea of individual accountability for batterers to include the community's responsibility for gender violence and for supporting women's resistance to it.

> Because of the potent relationship between social and intimate violence this formula must not rely upon an individualistic understanding that isolates "incidents" of sexual and physical assault for redress. Justice-making action calls for a continuous struggle with the manifold cultural assaults that reproduce the conditions of male violence.... Those who benefit from and perpetuate the ongoing social subjugation of African-American women must be held accountable in the justice-making process for women. (West 1999: 197)

West calls for local tribunals, similar to international tribunals for war crimes, which would place on trial those who benefit from violence against women.

This strategy is meant to raise consciousness about how dominant institutions—for example, the banks, the local Housing Authority companies that close operations in poor communities—are deeply implicated in violence against women in poor communities. Domestic violence programs must include anti-poverty measures that would give women meaningful alternatives to abusive situations and resources to rebuild communities devastated by capital flight and underemployment.

In contrast, based on their extensive experience with tribal councils, Native American women assume a more ambivalent stance toward community-based interventions in domestic violence. In Canada, women in First Nations organizations emphasize that "there is 'good medicine' and 'bad medicine' in Aboriginal communities" (McGillivray and Comaskey 1999: 51). While tribal councils sometimes intervene on women's behalf, they as readily rule in favor of abusive men. Even though Aboriginal women tend to favor mediation and alternative remedies to the criminal justice system, researchers Anne McGillivray and Brenda Comaskey found that others preferred outside police intervention to the local councils. This conflict is not surprising, however, in that many of these councils continue to be patriarchal. In spite of revitalized traditional practices, Native American/aboriginal peoples continue to have the highest poverty and unemployment rates in North America.

Coalitions of women of color have begun organizing to address their common and differing experiences with domestic violence. A central aim is to develop a critique of the criminal justice system, while still intervening with batterers. In my own city of Portland, Oregon, LANA, a multi-ethnic group of activist women, formed in 1999 to develop community-based interventions and culturally specific services for women and families (see also Rojas 2000). While the experiences of Latina, Asian, African-American, and Native American women in this group differ, they share a common wariness over relying too heavily on the criminal justice system.

LAW AND ORDER FEMINISM

The history of practices in the United States concerning "chastisement" of women and children within the family are interwoven, bound through the shifting borders of patriarchal authority. Just as child abuse is a historically changing category, so too is domestic violence (see Gordon 1988). As an institution based on reciprocal claims and mutual dependency, the family is recognized as operating according to rules different from those that govern civil society. The instituting of family courts for cases of child abuse and wife battering grew out of an interest in separating domestic assaults from the judicial process of criminal prosecution. An act committed in the family was not judged to be criminal in the same sense that the act would be judged in civil society. The common refrain in the domestic violence movement that the "marriage license is a hitting license" encompasses more than wife abuse. Physical assaults on children remain protected by law, even as the movement for children's rights has gained ground over the past century.

The feminist critique of the criminal justice system that emerged in the battered women's movement focused almost exclusively on the failure of the state to intervene on behalf of women. In confronting rape and battering, activists charged that the police both covertly and overtly supported male violence by refusing to take the complaints of women seriously. Feminists have shown how patriarchy benefits from a legal history of permissiveness toward male battering, expressed in its systematic tendency to "empathize" with men who lose control, who are overtaken in the heat of an argument.

There is controversy among feminists over family courts and other dispute mediation practices, even as there is near unanimity over the importance of criminalizing battering. The term "woman battering" replaced "wife beating" because it foregrounded the status of the victim—as a woman—and forged a linguistic connection with battery, a felony. The criminalizing of this form of abuse was part of a larger strategy of de-privatizing the family and framing domestic violence as a violation of women's civil rights (Siegel 1996; Goldfarb 2000). Mandatory arrest of batterers is now standard law enforcement practice in the United States, as is stricter enforcement of restraining orders (Mullender 1996).

While legal and legislative reforms have remedied some of the more blatant injustices women suffer under patriarchy, they also carry unanticipated freight for women and for feminism. Women of color are the most vocal in registering caveats over measures that summon the power of the state to protect women. One concern centers on the impact of police interventions in poor communities, where arrests and incarceration of males is already staggeringly high. Indeed, these are the very communities where arrest rates for domestic violence are highest and where arresting men is least likely to function as a deterrent (see Davis 2000). Although criminalization remains a cornerstone of the movement, women in communities of color feel most directly the repressive effects of broadening police powers. As McGillivray and Comaskey describe it,

> In discourses on First Nations self-government, the direction is the other way—by-passing the criminal justice system in favor of local policing, circle sentencing, diversion, and ultimately a separate justice system. Aboriginal women subjected to intimate violence are caught between competing discourses. (McGillivray and Comaskey 1999: 92)

Crenshaw suggests that the insistence in the domestic violence field that battering cuts across race and class lines has inhibited feminist analysis of the differential impact of state interventions around domestic violence. Poor women, who are more likely to be women of color, are "erased" from the picture, "pushing them aside to focus on victims for whom politicians and media are more likely to express concern" (1994: 105)

As domestic violence gains legitimacy as an area where women can "reasonably" expect protection from the state, advocates for the poor find that framing poverty as an effect of domestic violence has greater political currency than does addressing structural sources of poverty. Indeed, as the ink was drying on the Violence Against Women Act of 1994, one of the most devastating assaults on poor women was being drafted in the United States Congress. Activists struggling to ameliorate the harsh impact of welfare reform rushed to insist that domestic violence was a leading cause of women seeking public assistance. Congress finally passed a ruling allowing states to adopt waivers that stopped the clock on time limits for public assistance if women could demonstrate that they were victims of domestic violence (Brandwein 1999; *Chicago Daily Herald* 1999).

The joining of domestic violence and poverty did open up political space for talking about the vulnerabilities of poor women. However, discussion centered on domestic violence as the primary cause of female poverty, rather than poverty as a cause of family violence. Advocates argued that the major barrier a woman faces in moving from welfare to work is her male partner, often an abuser (Brandwein 1999). Stories began to appear regularly in the press featuring women who were desperate to get off welfare, but whose male partners defeated them at every turn.

> Doris Robertson can tell you all about how black eyes, uncontrollable crying fits and fear of embarrassment can keep a woman on welfare. She says that's what her husband wanted. "He wanted me to be too down and out of control to go out and get a job," said Robertson, who claims her husband's abuse caused her to lose two jobs during their 14 years together. "He wanted me to live on public aid forever." (Chicago Daily Herald, 1999: 6)

In both poor and affluent communities, women are routinely undermined by the men in their lives. But the line of argument adopted by many welfare activists lays responsibility for female poverty at the feet of poor men. Further, the subtext of this discourse centers on fortifying the boundary between "deserving" and "undeserving" poor women. If poverty requires a redemptive banner of moral justification, women who can display their broken bones and bruises make more compelling victims than do "ordinary" poor women.

As shelters become an avenue for access to public housing and other forms of public assistance, and screening for domestic violence part of the triaging of poor women, it is not surprising that poor women increasingly frame their experiences through a discourse of domestic violence. This is not to suggest that poor women invent stories of abuse. Rather, it is to suggest that if there is only one exit door from a burning building, it will get a great deal of traffic. Since abuse and bad treatment permeate the lives of marginalized communities, assaults by a partner may readily become the primary mode of "giving story" to life's difficulties. The problem isn't that the story is fabricated. Rather, it is that women have so few culturally sanctioned accounts of oppression, particularly in making claims on a system that has a very high threshold for noticing the suffering of women.

WOMEN'S REFUGE AS SOCIAL SYMBOLIC SPACE

There is a long history in patriarchal societies of granting some legitimacy to women who seek refuge from violent men. Even the "rule of thumb"—a provision in nineteenth-century chastisement laws that allowed husbands to discipline their wives with objects no wider than a thumb—introduced limits on the exercise of male power. These limits suggest that the provision of sanctuary for women may as readily reinscribe patriarchal power as it does undermine it. Whereas a "good man" intervenes to rescue the distressed maiden in the patriarchal tale of female bondage, feminism creates a new denouement to the story. It is the power of sisterhood that breaks the grip of the Gothic romance by creating places of sanctuary run by and for women.

Much like the cloistered life of convents in previous eras, battered women's shelters occupy a revered place within feminism. When students in my classes speak of their work in the shelters, they often assume a sacral tone. This work has become a rite of passage for many young women, who demonstrate their commitment to the cause by doing crisis work. Shelter work is powerful because it breaks from the *feminine* position of nursemaid to an injured manhood, turning instead to the care of women brutalized by the fascist elements of patriarchy. Just as *home* elicits associations of protection and nurture, *shelter* evokes similarly maternal associations.

Through the lens of a feminist analysis, the appropriation of maternal imagery is a means of reclaiming the value of female role of caretaker. Further, feminism shifts the object of maternal attention from the exclusive claims of the nuclear family—specifically, children and male partners—to a broader nexus of social relations and sustaining bonds of sisterhood.

At the same time, these idealized spaces within the movement can serve multiple functions, including defensive ones. Idealization—which is vital to many human capacities—becomes pathological when it serves a primarily defensive function in externalizing disturbing psychological states by projecting them onto the "bad object." In social movements, it is important to recognize how groups may come to depend upon their enemies, including real ones, to sustain group well-being. Male violence may become a heightened focus when avoiding conflicts or sources of aggression within the group.

Symptomatic of the defensive idealization of shelter space is the insistence in the field that victimized women play no active part in the dynamic of violence. To some extent, this insistence on the victim's noncomplicity in family violence is an effort to withhold anything that might fuel the flames of victim-blaming. It seems that any female *movement* in situations of family violence registers in the patriarchal imagination as a sign of female *control.* In response, many feminists have insisted on the absolute virtue and nonculpability of abused women.

Countering paranoid and demonized representations of women with highly romanticized ones reinforces, however, the very dichotomized representations of gender that feminism seeks to transcend. During shelter trainings, considerable effort is taken to protect victims from predictable distancing responses—for example, "She must have done something to deserve it." There is a notable gap, however, between the idealized portraits of survivors presented in the trainings and the complex realities of shelter life. Women are intensively case-managed in many shelters. Confrontations between staff and residents are quite common—conflicts over, for example, treatment of children, use of drugs and alcohol, and failure to follow the rules.

Women of color are at the forefront of addressing cultural dimensions of refuge services and of questioning longstanding practices within the battered women's movement. One of the contested practices concerns the confidentiality of the shelter location. The addresses of most shelters are carefully protected, and women residents must sign an agreement that they will not reveal the address to anyone. When she is accepted as a resident, she is dropped off several blocks from the site, which is typically far from her own community. The rationale for these elaborate provisions is that the threat of violence posed by batterers requires security measures and continual vigilance in maintaining the concealed location. Yet in our study of national practices, shelters with published addresses did not report higher incidences of violence than did those that kept the location confidential (Haaken and Yragui, in press). Many advocates claim that open shelters make the problem of male violence less hidden and, further, place more responsibility on the community to secure their safety.

Most defensive operations—individual and collective, pathological and healthy—have some grounding in experience, either present or past. The concealment of crisis facilities may have the same costs as other psychological defenses: they are initially adaptive but come to generate the very anxieties from which they originally sought relief. By enlisting women in the maintenance of the shelter as a "concealed" space of protection, anxieties are introduced concerning the adequacy of maternal protectors. The group reproduces a cultural fantasy that women are collectively impotent and helpless in the face of boundless masculine powers. Women are unable to resist effectively the overpowering influence of even an individual man.

The practice of keeping the shelter secret also may reproduce some of the dynamics operating in situations of abuse. In both the family and refuge settings, women are isolated from friends and community and enlisted by an idealized protector to keep a secret. The base of dependency is narrowed and women are intensively monitored. A vitally important difference, of course, is that the shelter creates a provisional space of safety that supports women in moving beyond this form of dependency. The power asymmetry of the heterosexual pair is displaced by the unity of sisterhood.

Further distinctions are important to recognize as well. While typically confidential, feminist shelters tend to be more "public" than non-feminist ones in that they go beyond providing women sanctuary to engaging in political work. Feminist shelters mobilize women around gender violence, and actively participate in events such as "Take Back the Night." Volunteers and staff are acutely aware of the conflict between their role as service providers, on the one hand, and that of political activists, on the other. Refugees from the patriarchal family, like other political refugees, have immediate and immense needs that can overwhelm service providers.

But the isolation of the shelters from the communities in which women live and the secrecy surrounding the shelters may intensify the burdensomeness of crisis work. The shelter may become the "good protector" in a world of diffusely felt masculine threats that battered women both endure and flee. Just as abused women often experience their mothers as useless and may be unable to draw on a sustaining, internal maternal object, battered women may similarly waver between seeking shelter and finding it useless. But the isolation of shelters as community institutions may contribute to this dynamic. Victimized women may not be able to internalize or hold on to the functions of the shelter as they re-enter their communities, even with transitional housing as a resource.

Women who live in economically marginalized communities are challenging the boundary between the private and public, both in relation to gendered domains of authority and in relation to the shelter's place in the community. In Portland, Oregon, challenging this boundary includes working more closely with confidential shelters to make them more responsive to cultural differences—for example, in the hygiene products available—and in addressing cultural differences in the management of children. But these efforts also involve bringing places of refuge closer to home and making them public. In the fall of 2000, Casa Esperanza (House of Hope) was established by Latina women as an open shelter with a published address. At the dedication of the shelter, those present— an ethnically mixed group of women's advocates, clergy, and neighborhood supporters—were collectively enlisted in the protection of women residents and staff of Casa Esperanza.

CONCLUSIONS

Domestic violence has moved from a radical-feminist to a mainstream political issue in the United States over the past decade, in part because of the important work of activists in the antiviolence movement. The victories of the movement have been costly, however, particularly for women of color and poor women. Since many advocates in the field insist that poverty and unemployment are unrelated to the problem of male violence in the family, this same argument may readily extend into conservative rhetoric concerning the causes of criminal behavior. If the root of the problem is in an intransigent male proclivity for brutality, which good men nobly resist in their nature, the problem of violence is readily reduced to some bedrock of biology or brute state of the masculine psyche.

While men—as husbands, fathers, sexual partners—do continue to oppress and abuse women in the context of domestic life, a singular focus on intimate male partners relieves powerful patriarchal institutions (the state and corporate capitalism) of responsibility. Increasingly, the problems of homeless and poor women, jobless women, and female immigrants are framed through a discourse of battering. It is the man standing at the threshold, blocking her exit from captivity, who is held singularly responsible for her impoverished state, rather than a society organized around obscenely vast differences in wealth and opportunity.

While feminist insistence that men "choose" violence has been an important historical corrective to earlier models, this approach has carried unanticipated freight for women. Even though feminists typically differ from conservatives by stressing cultural determinants of individual actions, the idea that battering is an individual "choice" men make adds fuel to conservative law-and-order campaigns. These campaigns mobilize public outrage by casting criminal behavior as a product of a deviant mind, a perverse and willful dedication to a life of transgressive behavior. And by casting male perpetrators of domestic violence as autonomous agents, we occlude the broader dynamics of power and control that maintain a hold over the drama.

The feminist antiviolence movement has a vital role in deprivatizing gender violence and in raising public consciousness over the abuses women suffer at the hands of men. But the challenge of the movement is in going beyond the domestic sphere and in showing how violence is rooted in the structures of public life, whether they take the brute form of a man's fist or the more "civilized" forms of ruthless economic competition. By expanding the frontiers of the movement to include these normative forms of violence and by showing how poor women and women of color bear a particular burden as the shock absorbers in traumatized communities, the antiviolence movement stands a real chance of creating a new denouement to the Gothic horror of family violence.

NOTES

1. "Health and Mental Health Consequences of Domestic Violence in the African American Community," paper presented at the meetings of the Institute on Domestic Violence in the African American Community, Seattle, WA, 2 December 2000.
2. For an overview of the history of the battered women's movement, see Schecter 1982 and Pleck 1987.
3. For a review of feminist perspectives and discussion of their political implications, see Donovan 1991.
4. This is one of the most recurring conflicts for black women in shelter according to Bridgette Fawnbulleh, director of the African-American Providers Network and staff member of Bradley-Angle House in Portland, Oregon. Fawnbulleh also claims that in Portland, African-American women average two to three days in shelter, while white women average over a month.

REFERENCES

Allard, S. A. 1991. "Rethinking the Batttered Woman Syndrome: A Black Feminist Perspective," *UCLA Women's Law Journal* 1, no. 1: 191–208.

Barrett, M. and M. McIntosh. 1991. *The Anti-Social Family.* New York: W. W. Norton.

Brandwein, R. A., ed. 1999. *Battered Women, Children, and Welfare Reform: The Ties That Bind.* Thousand Oaks: Sage Publications.

Campbell, A. 1991. *Men, Women and Aggression.* New York: Basic Books.

Carillo, R. and J. Tello. 1998. *Family Violence and Men of Color: Healing the Wounded Male Spirit.* New York: Springer.

Chicago Daily Herald. 1999. "State Considering Welfare Waivers," 17 April, section I, 6.

Collins, P. H. 1990. *Black Feminist Thought.* New York: Routledge.

Counts, D. A., J. K. Brown, and J. C. Campbell, eds. 1999. *To Have and To Hit: Cultural Perspectives on Wife Beating.* Urbana: University of Illinois Press.

Crenshaw, K. W. 1994. "Mapping the Margins: Intersectionality, Identity Politics, and Violence against Women of Color," in M. A. Fineman and R. Mykitiuk, eds., *The Public Nature of Private Violence*, 93–118. New York: Routledge.

Davis, A. 2000. "The Color of Violence against Women," *Color Lines: Race, Culture Action*, 3, no. 3, 4–9.

Dobash, E. R. and R. P. Dobash. 1979. *Violence against Wives: A Case against Patriarchy.* New York: Free Press.

Donovan, J. 1991. *Feminist Theory: The Intellectual Traditions of American Feminism.* New York: Continuum.

French, S. G., W. Teays, and L. M. Purdy, eds. 1998. *Violence Against Women: Philosophical Perspectives.* Ithaca: Cornell University Press.

Goldfarb, S. F. 2000. "Violence against Women and the Persistence of Privacy," *Ohio State Law Journal* 61, no. 1: 1–87.

Goldner, V. P., M. Sheinberg, and G. Walker 1998. "Love and Violence: Gender Paradoxes in Volatile Attachments," in B. M. Clinchy and J. K. Norem, eds., *The Gender and Psychology Reader*, 549–71. New York: New York University Press.

Gordon, L. 1988. *Heroes of their Own Lives: The Politics and History of Family Violence.* New York: Viking Press.

Haaken, J. 1998. *Pillar of Salt: Gender, Memory, and the Perils of Looking Back.* New Brunswick: Rutgers University Press.

Haaken, J. 1999. "Women's Refuge as Social Symbolic Space," *Journal for the Psychoanalysis of Culture and Society* 4, no. 2: 315–18.

Haaken, J. 2002. "Bitch and Femme Psychology: Women, Aggression, and Psychoanalytic Social Theory," *Journal for the Psychoanalysis of Culture and Society* 7, no. 2: 202–15.

Haaken, J. and Yragui, N. In press. "Going Underground: Conflicts and Differences in the Domestic Violence Shelter Movement," *Feminism and Psychology.*

Hagemann-White, C. 1998. "Violence without End? Some Reflections on Achievements, Contradictions, and Perspectives of the Feminist Movement in Germany," in R. C. A. Klein, ed., *Multidisciplinary Perspectives on Family Violence.* New York: Routledge.

Hall, J. D. 1983. "'The Mind that Burns in Each Body': Women, Rape and Racial Violence," in A. B. Snitow, C. Stansell, and S. Thompson, eds., *Powers of Desire.* New York: Monthly Review Press.

Herman, J. L. 1992. *Trauma and Recovery.* New York: Basic Books.

hooks, b. 1997. "Violence in Intimate Relationships: A Feminist Perspective," in L. L. O'Toole and J. R. Schiffman, eds., *Gender Violence: An Interdisciplinary Perspective.* New York: New York University Press.

Horley, S. 1991. *The Charm Syndrome.* London: Papermac.

Hurtado, A. 1998. "Relating to Privilege: Seduction and Rejection in the Subordination of White Women and Women of Color," in B. M. Clinchy and J. K. Norem, eds., *The Gender and Psychology Reader,* 698–716. New York: New York University Press.

Johnson, M. P. 1995. "Patriarchal Terrorism and Common Couple Violence: Two Forms of Violence against Women," *Journal of Marriage and the Family* 57, no. 2: 283–94.

Klein, R. C. A., ed. 1998. *Multidisciplinary Perspectives on Family Violence.* New York: Routledge.

Levinson, D. 1989. *Family Violence in Cross-cultural Perspectives.* Newbury Park: Sage.

Lockhart, L. and B. W. White. 1989. "Understanding Marital Violence in the Black Community," *Journal of Interpersonal Violence* 4, no. 4: 421–36.

McGillivray, A. and B. Comaskey. 1999. *Black Eyes All of the Time: Intimate Violence, Aboriginal Women, and the Justice System.* Toronto: University of Toronto Press.

Moore, H. 2000. "Difference and Recognition: Postmillennial Identities and Social Justice," *Signs: Journal of Women in Culture and Society* 25, no. 4: 1129–32.

Mullender, A. 1996. *Rethinking Domestic Violence: The Social Work and Probation Response.* New York: Routledge.

O'Toole, L. L. and J. R. Schiffman, eds. 1997. *Gender Violence: Interdisciplinary Perspectives.* New York: New York University Press.

Pence, E. and M. Paymar. 1993. *Education Groups for Men Who Batter: The Duluth Model.* New York: Springer.

Pleck, E. 1987. *Domestic Tyranny.* New York: Oxford University Press.

Richie, B. E. 2000. "A Black Feminist Reflection on the Antiviolence Movement," *Journal of Women in Culture and Society* 25, no. 4: 1133–37.

Roberts, A. R., ed. 1996. *Helping Battered Women: New Perspectives and Remedies.* New York: Oxford University Press.

Rojas, P. M. 2000. "Rebuilding the Anti-violence Movement," *Color Lines: Race, Culture, Action* 3, no. 3: 4–7.

Schecter, S. 1982. *Women and Male Violence: The Visions and Strengths of the Battered Women's Movement.* Boston: South End Press.

Siegel, R. B. 1996. "'The Rule of Love': Wife Beating as Prerogative and Privacy," *Yale Law Journal* 105: 2117–207.

Stacey, J. 1990. *Brave New Families: Stories of Domestic Upheaval in Late Twentieth Century America.* New York: Basic Books.

Stanley, A. D. 1998. *From Bondage to Contract: Wage Labor, Marriage, and the Market in the Age of Slave Emancipation.* Cambridge: Cambridge University Press.

Walker, A. 1970. *The Third Life of Grange Copeland.* San Diego: Harcourt Brace Jovanovich.

Walker, L. 1984. *The Battered Woman Syndrome.* New York: Springer.

Weiner, N. A., M. A. Zahn, and R. J. Sagi. 1990. *Violence: Patterns, Causes, and Public Policy.* New York: Harcourt Brace Jovanovich.

West, T. C. 1999. *Wounds of the Spirit: Black Women, Violence, and Resistance Ethics.* New York: New York University Press.

White, E. C. 1994. *Chain, Chain, Change: For Black Women in Abusive Relationships.* Seattle: Seal Press.

Williams, D. 1994. "African American Women in Three Contexts of Domestic Violence," in E. S. Fiorenza and M. S. Copeland, eds., *Violence Against Women: Concilium,* 34–43. Maryknoll, NY: Orbis Books.

REDEFINING THE HOME

PURVI SHAH

I sit in my uncle's living room, flanked by four of his male friends, and in their expressions I see how ridiculous I sound. *Marriage is a political and not just a social act.* While my statement is far from revolutionary, inside this home I am a heretic. Convinced that marriage is solely a cultural event, the idea of such an institution being "political" is practically blasphemous. Politics is a presidential race, the latest legislative or court decision. Politics does not include all the ways in which power is maintained. In this house, the "private" ceremony of marriage is considered part of "culture," rather than the "public" realm of "politics." Why? Because it involves "tradition," social customs, and intimacy (real or otherwise) between people.

Such dichotomies as politics/culture and public/private make it nearly impossible to show how family structures and institutions such as marriage can perpetuate or promote violence against women. The idea that the home is private, its affairs governed by culture, makes it possible to justify male superiority and domestic violence—they are simply the result of "tradition," "heritage," and culture. The separation of politics from culture is similarly used to silence activist messages, by barring progressive groups from participating in community events and constructing a sanitized version of culture that suits elite interests and power.

One of the first conceptual revolutions we need to enact is the belief that a home in which violence occurs is a public space. Domestic violence must be seen not as a personal (private) problem within the closed arena of a home, but as a political (public) problem influence by cultural, social, and environmental factors. Through the home and the institutions that embody the home, such as marriage, we must show how the unstated assumptions regarding culture contribute to the perpetuation of violence. Challenging these premises allows domestic violence to be viewed not as a closed family problem, but as a larger social problem.

In the South Asian fight against domestic violence, we must recognize that our resistance transgresses not only personal boundaries but also cultural boundaries. By making domestic violence a cultural-political problem, we counter the ways in which batterers use "tradition" and "history" to justify their behavior. By moving beyond identity politics, beyond the questions of home and homeland, through remaining dedicated to transnational social change, activists can focus on the ideologies behind domestic violence (or heteronormativity or economic exploitation, etc.) rather than individual incidents to build a framework that allows for community participation and intervention.

MY BROTHER'S SEX WAS WHITE, MINE BROWN

CHERRÍE MORAGA

If somebody had asked me when I was a teenager what it means to be Chicana, I would probably have listed the grievances done me. When my sister and I were fifteen and fourteen, respectively, and my brother a few years older, we were still waiting on him. I write "were" as if now, nearly two decades later, it were over. But that would be a lie. To this day in my mother's home, my brother and father are waited on, including by me. I do this now out of respect for my mother and her wishes. In those early years, however, it was mainly in relation to my brother that I resented providing such service. For, unlike my father, who sometimes worked as much as seventy hours a week to feed my face every day, the only thing that earned my brother my servitude was his maleness.

It was Saturday afternoon. My brother, then seventeen years old, came into the house with a pile of friends. I remember Fernie, the two Steves, and Roberto. They were hot, sweaty, and exhausted from an afternoon's basketball and plopped themselves down in the front room, my brother demanding, "Girls, bring us something to drink."

"Get it yourself, pig," I thought, but held those words from ever forming inside my mouth. My brother had the disgusting habit on these occasions of collapsing my sister JoAnn's and my name when referring to us as a unit: his sisters. "Cher'ann," he would say. "We're really thirsty." I'm sure it took everything in his power not to snap his fingers. But my mother was out in the yard working and to refuse him would have brought her into the house with a scene before these boys' eyes which would have made it impossible for us to show our faces at school that following Monday. We had been through that before.

When my mother had been our age, over forty years earlier, she had waited on her brothers and their friends. And it was no mere lemonade. They'd come in from work or a day's drinking. And *las mujeres*, often just in from the fields themselves, would already be in the kitchen making tortillas, warming frijoles or pigs feet, albondigas soup, what-have-you. And the men would get a clean white tablecloth and a spread of food laid out before their eyes and not a word of resentment from the women.

As I stopped to wait on their yearning throats, "jock itch" was all that came to my mind. Their cocks became animated in my head, for that was all that arbitrarily seemed to set us apart from each other and put me in the position of the servant and them the served.

I wanted to machine-gun them all down, but swallowed that fantasy as I swallowed making the boy's bed every day, cleaning his room each week, shining his shoes and ironing his shirts before dates with girls, some of whom I had crushes on. I would lend him the money I had earned housecleaning for twelve hours, so he could blow it on one night with a girl because he seldom had enough money, because he seldom had a job, because there was always some kind of ball practice to go to. As I pressed the bills into his hand, the car honking outside in the driveway, his double-date waiting, I knew I would never see that money again.

Years later, after I began to make political the fact of my being a Chicana, I remember my brother saying to me, "*I've* never felt culturally 'deprived'," which I guess is the term "white" people use to describe Third World people being denied access to *their* culture. At the time, I wasn't exactly sure what he meant, but I remember when retelling the story to my sister, she responded, "Of course, he didn't. He grew up male in our house. He got the best of both worlds." And yes, I can see now that that's true. *Male in a man's world. Light-skinned in a white world. Why change?*

The pull to identify with the oppressor was never as great in me as it was in my brother. For, unlike him, I could never have *become* the white man, only the white man's *woman.*

REVISITING MARX AND ENGELS

ON THE FAMILY

STEPHANIE COONTZ

On what foundation is the present family, the bourgeois family, based? On capital, on private gain.... The bourgeois family will vanish as a matter of course when its complement vanishes, and both will vanish with the vanishing of capital.

If Marx and Engels had bequeathed a set of cut-and-dried answers to theorists and activists rather than a set of useful questions, their writings on the family would be of little interest today. Working with scanty anthropological data and bound by the assumptions of their time, Marx and Engels compressed the complexity of family history, including the range of families normally found *within* any particular society, into a three-stage evolutionary schema of group marriage, followed by pairing marriage and then by monogamy.

While they saw beyond their contemporaries in noting the historical specificity and class origins of the nineteenth-century bourgeois family, their discussion of the family as a mechanism for concentrating private wealth failed to consider transformative tendencies within bourgeois families, including the impact of the women's movement. Nor did they explore the differing origins and dynamics of working-class families.

Engels correctly recognized that the subordination of wives and the growing independence of the nuclear family from larger kin networks were associated with the development of private property, but he had an idealist interpretation of the reason for this "world historical defeat of the female sex"—men's desire to pass wealth onto their own biological sons. As Plekhanov later pointed out in *The Role of the Individual in History*, an economic interpretation of history is not the same as a materialist interpretation of history, because analysis remains at the level of people's motive and ideas, merely substituting a cynical assessment of intentions for a utopian one.

The early writings of Marx also showed traces of idealism, as when he attributed the root of private property to "filthy self-interest." Later, however, Marx recognized that it was the predominance of "self-interest"—indeed its very definition—that needed to be explained. From that point on he sought the source of phenomena and events not in people's desires and motives, whether altruistic or selfish, but in the social relations of production and exchange, as well as the unintended consequences of the cooperation, coercion, and conflict that people entered into in any particular mode of production. Although Marx and Engels transcended their early Hegelian idealism in explaining class relations and alienation, they never applied their new insights to the analysis of gender relations and male dominance.

Further, Marx and Engels accepted the Victorian assumption that most sexual and gender interactions were part of nature, and that nature was of a lower order than culture. They correctly noted that the first social division of labor was between men and women, but wrongly equated this with sexual intercourse, suggesting that the division of labor in the family was "natural." Accordingly, they concluded that the division of labor became "truly" significant only when a split between mental and manual labor appeared. They thus failed to incorporate gender relations and sexual systems into their theory of productive forces and social conflict.

Yet two elements in the methodology of Engels and Marx have always pointed the way to a richer understanding of family life and family change. The first was their materialist insight that reproduction is both a product of historical forces and a historical force of its own. Connected to this was their recognition that the nature of productive work and the source of value are both historically specific. Marx's labor theory of value differed from that of his contemporaries not only in that he defined "value" as a uniquely capitalist phenomenon but also because he made his analysis of value a *critique* of capitalist social relations.

Under capitalism, Marx and Engels argued, only labor that is exchanged against capital is productive labor and produces value. If the good is not sold, however, its value cannot be realized, or even be said to exist. The social labor that went into making the good becomes trapped in the unsold commodity. In consequence, human cooperative endeavors are disguised and controlled by the exchange of *things*.

Meanwhile, the most important kinds of work that humans do—nurturing, for example, and many other "family"-type activities—produce no value under capitalism and are therefore marginalized and denigrated. The implications of this theoretical breakthrough for family analysis are profound.

The second contribution of Marx and Engels to the study of families was their dialectical insistence that social relationships, not just technological forces, lie at the heart of class analysis. In *The German Ideology* Marx suggests that "a certain mode of production, or industrial stage, is always combined with a certain mode of cooperation, or social stage, and this mode of cooperation is itself a 'productive force'."

Modes of cooperation—or coercion—are critical in defining class and understanding social change. And families, along with other socially constructed relationships such as race and gender, are central mechanisms for organizing cooperation and coercion. They are also sites of contradiction in the Marxist sense—places where inherent oppositions occur that are necessary to perpetuate a particular process or social system, and yet also undermine that process or social system.

These insights point the way toward a deeper and richer understanding of families and their meaning in the lives of working people today. Male privilege within the family is real, for example, but men support women and children at a level beyond which the latter could reproduce themselves in this society (as post-divorce statistics on poverty show) *at the same time* as they appropriate work and deference from them. An adequate theoretical account of the family must incorporate the tension between the family's role in maximizing the use of material resources for all its members and in legitimizing the unequal distribution of power and rewards, both internally and externally.

Such a theory must explore both the struggles *within* families over resources, power, and autonomy and the ways in which families advance their members' interests or protect them against other groups. It must, in other words, explain the dualities of family life, as well as encompass the variations in family form and function among different classes and ethnic groups. Only such an approach will help us grasp the complex and contradictory processes that comprise the current "family crisis" in America.

Over the past thirty years, long-term changes in gender and age roles, cultural norms, and technology have interacted with the breakdown of the postwar wage and family bargain to erode the centrality of marriage as the main place where children are raised and intergenerational redistribution takes place. These changes have freed many individuals from repressive or toxic family situations.

At the same time, though, they are part of a general crisis in modern capitalism over how to care for dependencies and foster interpersonal obligations. People tend to feel that crisis first in their families and their personal life. Often, they mistakenly but understandably attribute the pain associated with these changes to the breakdown of "traditional" family ties.

We cannot dismiss their feelings as "false consciousness." In the current economic and social climate, the bourgeois family, especially as it has been democratized by the women's movement, may seem like the highest quality of life to which many working people can aspire. At the same time, most working people live with tensions in their work and family lives that make it important for them to have the option to leave a family that cannot meet their needs. The intricate emotional and political ambivalence this creates cannot be solved by sloganeering. Family debates and struggles need the same nuanced attention to contradiction and contingency that Marx gave to analyzing a similarly complex political situation in *The Eighteenth Brumaire of Louis Bonaparte*.

ON CONCEIVING
MOTHERHOOD AND SEXUALITY:
A FEMINIST-MATERIALIST APPROACH

ANN FERGUSON

> The cathexis between mother and daughter—essential, distorted, misused—is the great unwritten story. Probably there is nothing in human nature more resonant with charges than the flow of energy between two biologically alike bodies, one of which has lain in amniotic bliss inside the other, one of which has labored to give birth to the other.
>
> The "childless woman" and the "mother" are a false polarity which has served the institutions of both motherhood and heterosexuality.... We are, none of us, "either" mothers or daughters; to our amazement, confusion, and greater complexity, we are both.
>
> Adrienne Rich, *Of Woman Born*

A MULTISYSTEMS APPROACH TO
DOMINATION RELATIONS

My approach to understanding motherhood and sexuality is a multisystems feminist-materialist (or socialist-feminist) approach. By "multisystems," I mean an approach that is not reductive; that is, one that does not attempt to reduce male domination to a function of capitalist or commodity production economic systems (classic Marxism), or to reduce race and class domination to a function of patriarchy (classic radical feminism). Rather, I assume that much of human history can be understood only by conceiving societies in terms of interacting but semi-autonomous systems of human domination, three important ones having been class, race/ethnic, and sex/gender. These domination systems may not always support each other, particularly in periods of rapid change or social crisis. One way to understand the social movements of a particular historical period, such as the black civil rights movement of the 1960s or the women's movement of the 1970s in the United States, is to conjecture that a dialectical undermining of one domination system by the historical development of another—for example, race and sex domination undermined by capitalist development—has provoked a social crisis. A multisystems theory, unlike a reductivist approach, does not posit that social crises are automatically resolved by the development of a new social "equilibrium" that guarantees the same level of class, race, or male domination.

What distinguishes my particular multisystems socialist-feminist theory of male domination from others is the concept of "sex/affective production." The concept of sex/affective production develops Gayle Rubin's point (Rubin 1975) that every society has a "sex/gender system" that arranges a sexual division of labor, organizes sexuality and kinship interactions, and teaches sex/gender. It also is connected to Habermas's insight (Habermas 1979) that what is distinctive about humans as a species is the way human societies construct human nature through different types of family and kinship networks. My theory, unlike one tendency within classic Marxist theory, does not privilege the economic realm (the production of *things* to meet human material needs and the manner in which the social surplus gets appropriated) as the material base for all human domination relations. Rather, I conceptualize the production and reproduction of *people* in family and kinship networks as a production process that may take different *forms* or *modes*, depending on the historical relations among parenting, kinship, and sexual structures and economic modes of production. Just as Marxism postulates distinctive "logics" (structural rules) that are characteristic of different modes of class production, so I suggest that each mode of sex/affective production will have its own distinctive logic of exchange of the human services of sexuality, nurturance, and affection, and will therefore differently constitute the human nature of its special product: human children. Because I think that infancy and early childhood form a crucial period in the formation of gender identity and attendant masculine and feminine personality structure, I privilege family and kin networks as an important material base for sex/affective production. It does not follow, however, that sex/affective production is limited to family and kin networks. On the contrary, I argue that modes of sex/affective production specific to capitalist economic development create problematic and contradictory gender identities in both boys and girls in childhood, identities which then make subsequent experiences in peer interaction in schools and communities, and later in workplaces, very important in determining sexual preference, sexual practices, and the ultimate content of one's gender identity.

The separation between the public and the private, the realm of economic production and the realm of domestic life specific to capitalist society, should not lead us to the error of conceptualizing sex/affective production, or the production of people, as a process occurring in a place or realm different from that where the production of things takes place. The sexual division of wage labor, sexual harassment in the workplace, male decision-making and female obedience roles, and high-status male work versus low-status female work are all specific aspects of the capitalist production process which are its sex/affective production component. In the same way the power of the male wage earner versus the nonpaid housewife and class differences in women's ability to pay for childcare and thus obtain leisure time for themselves as mothers are specific examples of the capitalist aspect of sex/affective production. The production of things and the production of people thus interpenetrate. The point of conceptualizing them as separate production systems is that they have different logics, logics which must be understood historically and specifically if we are to understand possibilities for change and strategies of resistance to domination relations embedded in both sorts of production.

Before the specific types of sex/affective production are analyzed, the concepts involved and the underlying assumptions about affection, parenting, and sexuality need to be examined.

THE CONCEPT OF SEX/AFFECTIVE PRODUCTION

The conceptual category of *sex/affective production* is a way of understanding the social organization of labor and the exchange of services that occur between men and women in the production of children, affection, and sexuality. Every human society has its particular mode or modes of organizing and controlling sexuality, affectionate interactions (e.g. friendships, social bonding, alliances), and parenting relationships. Complex class- and race/ethnic-divided societies like our own may have a number of different modes centered in different organizations of family households and kin networks.

Central to all previous modes of organization of this work and service has been a sexual division of labor in the performance of the tasks and the distribution of the services involved. The sexual division of labor in the production and exchange of these sex/affective services (sexuality, affection, parenting) is a key to the social production of people as gendered—that is, as having the consciousness of self as male or female. This consciousness is always relational (i.e. what is male is not-female, and what is female is not-male), thus connecting one to a social sex class which is expected to have certain ideal masculine or feminine characteristics. One of these ideal characteristics is, usually, a sexual attraction for the opposite sex. It is important to note, however, that there is no automatic (merely a strong contingent) connection between gender identity and sexual identity (i.e. sexual preference): one is a deviant male if one is sexually attracted only to men, but one is still a male (and similarly for females who are attracted to females).

In stratified class and caste societies, different economic classes and racial/ethnic groups may hold different sex/gender ideals, although when this happens the lower classes are usually categorized as inferior male and female types "by nature." Often, split categories stereotype the good and bad woman—for example, the Madonna (mother)/whore—exemplifying the hegemony of dominant classes' ideals for men and women, which allows their members (but not those of subordinate classes) to fulfill those preferred ideals.

Many different modes of sex/affective production are male dominant (or patriarchal). In general, they all have in common an unequal and exploitative production and exchange of sexuality, affection, and parenting between men and women; that is, women have less control over the process of production (e.g. control of human reproductive decisions) and the exchange of services, and men characteristically get more than they give in the exchange of these services. They differ in the specific sexual division of labor and the social mechanisms by which men dominate and exploit women, as well as in the female strategies of resistance, escape, and sabotage of male power in parenting, sexuality, and affectional bonding.

In order to understand the "unity" of sex/affective production, we need to explore further its philosophical underpinnings. Why, for example, is it assumed that sexuality, affection, and parenting are intertwined in a way that the production of goods to meet material survival needs are not? What underlying theories of sexuality, affection, and production are assumed? What implications are there for the concepts of human agency, domination, and exploitation that are used in the classification of different modes of sex/affective production? Why link *sexuality* and *affection* in sex/affective production? The underlying assumption is that both sexuality and affection are *bodily* as well as *social* energies, and that they are each specific manifestations of a general type of physical/social energy we can call "sex/affective" energy. We tend to think of affectional bonds as emotional rather than bodily and of sexual bonds as bodily rather than emotional or social. In fact, I would claim, this is a distortion that comes about because of Western dualistic thought patterns. It may be more helpful to conceive of sex/affective energy as a spectrum ranging from the affectional/spiritual/not-specifically-physical interactions, at one pole, to genital sexual exchanges that are physical but not specifically affectional, at the other. A second way to conceive of sex/affective energy is as presenting two different dimensions or aspects which can admit of degree: a dimension of *physical* involvement, attraction, and interconnection of a human being with (an)other human being(s) or objects symbolizing human beings, and a social/*emotional dimension* of involvement, attraction, and interdefinition of self with (an)other human being(s).

We need now to consider some of the insights and problems of the sex/affective production paradigm.

First, a thesis about human nature: humans do not reproduce themselves (i.e. have children) merely as a means to guarantee that their material needs for physical survival will be met (e.g. that they will have children to care for them in old age). Rather, humans are a social species whose needs to connect to one another in some form of sexual and/or affectional interaction are as basic as their material needs as an animal species to produce a material livelihood. Heterosexual mating leads, intentionally or inadvertently, to human procreation, which leads to parenting. Thus, the sexuality and affection that heterosexual mates give each other require the social development of parenting systems in which nurturance/affection, socialization, and physical maintenance of the young are organized. Since patriarchal parenting systems also organize adult sexuality (most often by compulsory heterosexuality in marriage arrangements which impose double-standard monogamy), an interaction exists between the type of sexual exchanges engaged in by adults and the nature, amount, and control of parenting work engaged in by each sex/gender.

A second thesis is that the position of sex/affective production systems as a base for male dominance is a feminist-*materialist* approach in two specific senses. First, we know that human babies require affection and nurturance in order to survive. Thus, mothering or caretaking that involves more than simply feeding and clothing is a material requirement for the reproduction of the human species. Second, human young, unlike other animal species, have bodily energies (e.g. affectional, sexual, nutritional) that are initially without specific objects. The fact that humans are without instincts with fixed goals requires a period of care and socialization of the young that make some system of parenting, and the organization of sexuality and affection around these tasks, a material necessity for the human species.

We need thus to widen the concept of production as socially necessary labor to satisfy basic human material needs, which Marx and Engels introduced in *The German Ideology*, to include not merely a transformation of nature to meet human needs, but also the production and reproduction of new life—that is, the production and transformation of *people* via various historical parenting and sexual systems embedded in family and kin networks.

Let me take a moment to contrast the concept of sex/affective production with other feminist revisions of classical Marxist categories. Some Marxist feminists attempt to revise the classical Marxist emphasis on the primacy of the economic sphere in human social organization (particularly in systems where the production of things involves the creation and distribution of a social surplus). They argue that every economic system involves both production and reproduction, and therefore that modes of reproduction of a system (including the reproduction of labor power and thus modes of procreation) are just as important to the total operation of the system as the production of things. They argue either that we should reject the concept of the social primacy of the economic (the base/superstructure distinction), or that modes of reproduction in family and kin networks are just as much a part of the economic base of a social formation as is the production of things.

The problem with the concepts of modes of reproduction (Brown 1981) and modes of procreation (McDonough and Harrison 1978) is that either (a) they ambiguously mean both human biological and human social reproduction, or (b) they emphasize the production of children as the goal and aim of this form of social relations. Neither approach is satisfactory. The former case allows confusion with the Marxist categories of production/reproduction (Barrett 1980), where the mode of social reproduction of an economic system can be said to occur simultaneously at every site of social relations—for example, in the factory, state, and schools as well as in the family. This concept of social reproduction does not give us any nonfunctional way to conceive of, for example, the relationship between capitalism and patriarchy.

In the second alternative (modes of procreation), human biological reproduction and the regulation of fertility rates would be seen as the goal of these systems. Such an emphasis marginalizes the human incentives to experience the pleasures of sexuality not as reproductive instruments but as intrinsic energizers. We would also miss the ways that affectional and sexual same-sex relations, which develop for their own sake in sexual divisions of labor, are used as mechanisms both to cement (if dominant male) or to resist (if subordinate or deviant male or female) patriarchal sex/affective production processes (Hartmann 1981b).

The sex/affective production paradigm is superior to these other approaches because conceiving of a semi-autonomous system of the organization of sexuality, affection, and the production of children in family and kin networks can allow us to understand how patriarchal relations can persist (since embedded and reproduced in family and kin networks) through changes in modes of production of things (feudalism, capitalism, state socialism). It can conceptualize how changes in family structure due to capitalist development might weaken certain forms of patriarchal sex/affective production while allowing for the possibility that other adaptive forms are developing.

A serious philosophical problem that the concept of sex/affective production raises is how we can distinguish between childcare and sexual or nurturant activities that are work or labor and those that are leisure activities. Using the concept of production assumes one can empirically distinguish between labor (activity socially necessary to meet human material needs) and activity which may be work (not thought of as leisure by its agent) but not labor per se, and activity which is play. Childcare is an aspect of housework that mothers perform at home while caring for infants and small children, yet we know that the very idea that childcare and housework are separate work activities is a historical development caused by the separation of the home from economic production with the development of capitalist production. Ehrenreich and English (1975, 1978) have documented how the combined effect of the domestic science movement, the development of the medical establishment, child development experts, and consumer capitalism in the early twentieth century expanded rather than reduced the tasks thought socially necessary in parenting work.

A parallel historical argument would challenge the view of some feminists that sexual exchanges between men and women in patriarchal societies involve work on the part of women that is not repaid, since the control and sexual satisfaction involved are not equal for both male and female partners. How can we make this argument if we accept recent historical arguments (Foucault 1978; Weeks 1979, 1981) that our very conception of sexuality, its exchange and deployment, as at the center of bodily and mental health, is a recent social construction of discourses developed by bourgeois sexologists and therapists? And if the conception of sexual health itself is historically relative, how can we defend the claim that there is an exchange of socially necessary labor in parenting, sexuality, and affection? Or the claim that patriarchal parenting and sexual systems allow men to control and exploit the productive process of parenting and sexual exchange by contributing less (labor or services) and receiving more (leisure, services, pleasures)?

Even if one admits that there are no ahistorical universal requirements for good parenting, sexuality, or friendship, it does not follow that there is no empirical and historical way to compare male and female inputs, rewards from, and control of these production processes. Marx's concept of socially necessary labor has a "historical and moral element" which in part depends on what has come to be accepted as a decent minimal standard of living, given the available resources and expectations of a society at a particular historical period. Similarly, women's expectations of acceptable sexual satisfaction have changed since the nineteenth century, in part because of the writings of sexologists and in part because of the second-wave women's movement.

The inequality of patriarchal forms of sexual exchange lies not simply in the fact that men characteristically experience more orgasms and sexual satisfaction than women, although this is certainly relevant and can be empirically measured. It is the aspect of domination, the fact that men usually control the nature of the interaction itself as the sexual initiators, that perpetuates the image of women as the sexual objects of men, and women's bodies as the instruments of men's pleasure. In such a situation it would seem that a woman has less agency in the sexual encounter, even though she may experience more orgasms than the man she relates to.

We will not really be able to measure the relative equality or inequality of sexual exchanges until we have a physical model of sexual satisfaction and sexual agency that allows us to make connections between certain bodily states such as body blocks, orgasms, complete orgiastic release (Reich 1970), and the experience of sexual agency versus sexual passivity. But that we have no complete theory suggests merely the need for further empirical sexual research rather than a dead end for the sex/affective production paradigm. No matter how we ultimately measure equality in sexual exchange, we do have some intuitive criteria we can use in the meantime—for example, most would agree that any sexual exchange in which one partner but not the other enjoys orgasms regularly and in which the enjoying partner also controls the sexual process is an unequal exchange.

Finally, the question of one's power or control/agency in sexual and parenting exchanges cannot be separated from the economic, political/legal, and cultural constraints that may limit women's freedom of choice more than men's. Such constraints as economic dependence, legal restrictions on reproductive control, lack of strong female bonding networks that support sexual freedom for women or parental responsibilities for men, and physical violence by one's partner are all empirical factors that make women less free in parenting and sexuality than men. This shows the way in which sex/affective production systems are not autonomous from the economic mode of production, the nature of the state, and so on.

In determining which parental interactions with children are labor and which are leisure, we can agree that this is historically relative to social (and perhaps class and ethnic) expectations of parents and still find a way to compare the equality or inequality of the exchange between women and men in parenting work. No matter how the line between parenting labor and leisure is culturally drawn, it remains clear that most mothers in patriarchal modes of sex/affective production do more direct and indirect parenting work than men in terms of total labor hours spent (where "indirect parenting work" would include wage earning as well as unpaid productive work which produces, or exchanges for, goods necessary to the physical maintenance of infants and children). Folbre (1982) is developing an economic model to compare the waged and nonwaged work (parenting and housework) in the family economy so as to develop a way to measure the relative exploitation of women versus men, and parents versus children. Delphy (1984) argues that the male-dominated family economy continues after divorce, since mothers are saddled with much more direct and indirect parenting work and few fathers provide much in child support funds. Thus, in this sense male exploitation of women who are mothers increases with divorce, which suggests that the rise of single-mother families should be seen not simply as a decline in husband-patriarchy, but rather as the rise of a new patriarchal sex/affective form, which we might call "single mother patriarchy" and which is connected to the shift from family-centered patriarchal forms to more impersonal forms of state patriarchy (hooks 1981; and see below).

A final question concerns the relativity versus universality of the connections between affection, sexuality, and parenting. The analytic categories of sex/affective production would seem to suggest a universal mate–self–child sex/affective triangle which has historically specific forms. Nevertheless, Ariès (1962) and Shorter (1975) argue that affectionate interactions among children, kin, and spouses is characteristic neither of peasant nor of aristocratic families in the medieval period. Rather, it develops as a part of the bourgeois sentimental family, which develops a new conception of childhood and an increased emphasis on affection.

I would agree that we need to conceptualize a different form of patriarchial sex/affective production for aristocratic and peasant families than for bourgeois families. The interpersonal dynamic among parents, children, and mates will obviously be different when affectionate connections are present, or absent, or not exclusive (as when children are cared for by wet nurses, nannies, or extended kin networks). It is obvious that sexual intercourse to produce heirs has a different dynamic than when the resulting children and sexual energy are valued for their own sake.

Despite the relativity of who performs nurturant/affectionate services to children, a caretaker must provide a minimal affection quotient for the child to survive. Thus, the procuring of someone to perform these services is a necessary part of sex/affective production even in aristocratic families. Furthermore, it may be argued that courtly love ideals for extramarital relationships among the medieval aristocracy, idealized homosexual love relationships among ancient Greek male aristocracy, and close same-sex bonding among peasants are evidence that affectionate interactions will come to be institutionalized in some form in human societies where they are lacking in parenting and marriage interactions.

REFERENCES

Ariès, P. 1962. *Centuries of Childhood*. New York: Knopf.

Barrett, M. 1980. *Woman's Oppression Today*. London: Verso.

Brown, C. 1981. "Mothers, Fathers and Children: From Private to Public Patriarchy," in L. Sargent (ed.) *Women and Revolution*. Boston: South End Press.

Delphy, C. 1984. *Close to Home: A Materialist Analysis of Women's Oppression*. Amherst: University of Massachusetts Press.

Ehrenreich, B. and D. English. 1975. "The Manufacture of Housework," *Socialist Revolution* 5, no. 4 (October–December 1975): 5–40.

Ehrenreich, B. and D. English. 1978. *For Her Own Good: One Hundred Fifty Years of the Experts' Advice to Women*. Garden City, NY: Anchor/Doubleday.

Folbre, N. 1982. "Exploitation Comes Home: A Critique of the Marxian Theory of Family Labor," *Cambridge Journal of Economics* 6: 317–29.

Foucault, M. 1978. *The History of Sexuality, Volume 1: An Introduction*. New York: Random House.

Habermas, J. 1979. *Communication and the Evolution of Society*. Boston: Beacon Press.

Hartmann, N. 1981. "The Unhappy Marriage of Marxism and Feminism," in L. Sargent (ed.) *Women and Revolution*. Boston: South End Press.

hooks, b. 1981. *Ain't I a Woman: Black Women and Feminism*. Boston: South End Press.

McDonough, R. and R. Harrison. 1978. "Patriarchy and Relations of Production," in A. Kuhn and A. M. Wolpe, eds., *Feminism and Materialism*. London: Routledge & Kegan Paul.

Marx, K. and F. Engels. 1850. *The German Ideology*. New York: International Publishers.

Reich, W. 1970. *Mass Psychology of Fascism*. New York: Farrar, Strauss & Giroux.

Rich, A. 1995. *Of Woman Born: Motherhood as Experience and Institution*. New York: W. W. Norton.

Rubin, G. 1975. "The Traffic in Women: Notes on the 'Political Economy' of Sex," in R. Reiter, ed., *Toward a New Anthropology of Women*. New York: Monthly Review Press.

Shorter, E. 1975. *The Making of the Modern Family*. New York: Basic Books.

Weeks, J. 1979. *Coming Out: A History of Homosexuality from the Nineteenth Century to the Present*. London: Quartet.

Weeks, J. 1981. *Sex, Politics and Society*. New York: Longman.

BARGAINING WITH PATRIARCHY

DENIZ KANDIYOTI

Of all the concepts generated by contemporary feminist theory, patriarchy is probably the most overused and, in some respects, the most undertheorized. This state of affairs is not due to neglect, since there is a substantial volume of writing on the question, but rather to the specific conditions of development of contemporary feminist usages of the term. While radical feminists encouraged a very liberal usage, to apply to virtually any form or instance of male domination, socialist feminists have mainly restricted themselves to analyzing the relationships between patriarchy and class under capitalism. As a result, the term "patriarchy" often evokes an overly monolithic conception of male dominance, which is treated at a level of abstraction that obfuscates rather than reveals the intimate inner workings of culturally and historically distinct arrangements between the genders.

It is not my intention to provide a review of the theoretical debates around patriarchy (Barrett 1980; Beechey 1979; Delphy 1977; Eisenstein 1978; Hartmann 1981; McDonough and Harrison 1978; Mies 1986; Mitchell 1973; I. Young 1981). Instead, I would like to propose an important and relatively neglected point of entry for the identification of different forms of patriarchy through an analysis of women's strategies in dealing with them. I will argue that women strategize within a set of concrete constraints that reveal and define the blueprint of what I will term the *patriarchal bargain*[1] of any given society, which may exhibit variations according to class, caste, and ethnicity. These patriarchal bargains exert a powerful influence on the shaping of women's gendered subjectivity and determine the nature of gender ideology in different contexts. They also influence both the potential for and the specific forms of women's active or passive resistance in the face of their oppression. Moreover, patriarchal bargains are not timeless or immutable entities, but are susceptible to historical transformations that open up new areas of struggle and renegotiation of the relations between genders.

By way of illustration, I will contrast two systems of male dominance, rendered ideal-typical for the purposes of discussing their implications for women. I use these ideal types as heuristic devices that have the potential of being expanded and fleshed out with systematic, comparative, empirical content, although this essay makes no pretense at providing anything beyond a mere sketch of possible variations. The two types are based on examples from sub-Saharan Africa, on the one hand, and the Middle East, South Asia, and East Asia, on the other. My aim is to highlight a continuum ranging from less corporate forms of householding, involving the relative autonomy of mother–child units evidenced in sub-Saharan polygyny, to the more corporate male-headed entities prevalent in the regions identified by Caldwell (1978) as the "patriarchal belt." In the final section, I analyze the breakdown and transformation of patriarchal bargains and their relationship to women's consciousness and struggles.

AUTONOMY AND PROTEST: SOME EXAMPLES FROM SUB-SAHARAN AFRICA

I had one of my purest experiences of culture shock in the process of reviewing the literature on women in agricultural development projects in sub-Saharan Africa (Kandiyoti 1985). Accustomed as I was to only one type of patriarchy (which I shall describe in some detail later, under the rubric of classic patriarchy), I was ill prepared for what I found. The literature was rife with instances of women's resistance to attempts to lower the value of their labor and, more important, women's refusal to allow the total appropriation of their production by their husbands. Let me give some examples.

Wherever new agricultural schemes provided men with inputs and credit, and the assumption was made that as heads of household they would have access to their wives' unremunerated labor, problems seemed to develop. In the Mwea irrigated rice settlement in Kenya, where women were deprived of access to their own plots, their lack of alternatives and their total lack of control over men's earnings made life so intolerable to them that wives commonly deserted their husbands (Hanger and Moris 1973). In Gambia, in yet another rice-growing scheme, the irrigated land and credit were made available to men only, even though it was the women who traditionally grew rice in tidal swamps, and there was a longstanding practice of men and women cultivating their own crops and controlling the produce. Women's customary duties with respect to labor allocation to common and individual plots protected them from demands by their husbands that they provide free labor on men's irrigated rice fields. Men had to pay their wives wages or lend them an irrigated plot to have access to their labor. In the rainy season, when women had the alternative of growing their own swamp rice, they created a labor bottleneck for the men, who simply had to wait for the days women did not go to their own fields (Dey 1981).

In Conti's (1979) account of a supervised smallholder settlement project in Upper Volta, again the men were provided with land and credit, leaving the women no independent resource base and a very inadequate infrastructure to carry out their daily household chores. The result was vocal protest and refusal to cooperate. Roberts (1989) similarly illustrates the strategies used by women to maximize their autonomy in the African context. Yoruba women in Nigeria, for instance, negotiate the terms of their farm-labor services to their husbands while they aim to devote more time and energy to the trading activities that will enable them to support themselves and ultimately give up such services. Hausa women, whose observance of Islamic seclusion reduces the demands husbands can make for their services, allocate their labor to trade, mainly the sale of ready-cooked foodstuffs.

In short, the insecurities of African polygyny for women are matched by areas of relative autonomy that they clearly strive to maximize. Men's responsibility for their wives' support, while normative in some instances, is in fact relatively low. Typically, it is the woman who is primarily responsible for her own and her children's upkeep, including meeting the costs of their education, with variable degrees of assistance from her husband. Women have very little to gain and a lot to lose by becoming totally dependent on husbands, and hence they quite rightly resist projects that tilt the delicate balance they strive to maintain. In their protests, wives are safeguarding already existing spheres of autonomy.

Documentation of a genuine trade-off between women's autonomy and men's responsibility for their wives can be found in some historical examples. Mann (1985) suggests that despite the wifely dependence entailed by Christian marriage, Yoruba women in Lagos accepted it with enthusiasm because of the greater protection they thought they would receive. Conversely, men in contemporary Zambia resist the more modern ordinance marriage, as opposed to customary marriage, because it burdens them with greater obligations for their wives and children (Munachonga 1982). A form of conjugal union in which the partners may openly negotiate the exchange of sexual and labor services seems to lay the groundwork for more explicit forms of bargaining. Commenting on Ashanti marriage, Abu (1983: 156) singles out as its most striking feature "the separateness of spouses' resources and activities and the overtness of the bargaining element in the relationship." Polygyny and, in this case, the continuing obligations of both men and women to their own kin do not foster a notion of the family or household as a corporate entity.

Clearly, there are important variations in African kinship systems with respect to marriage forms, residence, descent, and inheritance rules (Guyer and Peters 1987). These variations are grounded in complete cultural and historical processes, including different modes of incorporation of African societies into the world economy (Mbilinyi 1982; Murray 1987; S. Young 1977). Nonetheless, it is within a broadly defined Afro-Caribbean pattern that we find some of the clearest instances of noncorporateness of the conjugal family both in ideology and practice, a fact that informs marital and marketplace strategies for women. Works on historical transformations (for example, Etienne and Leacock 1980)

suggest that colonization eroded the material basis for women's relative autonomy (such as usufructary access to communal land or traditional craft production) without offering attenuating modifications in either marketplace or
marital options. The more contemporary development projects discussed above
also tend to assume or impose a male-headed corporate family model, which
curtails women's options without opening up other avenues to security and well-
being. The women perceive these changes, especially if they occur abruptly, as
infractions that constitute a breach of their existing accommodations with the
male-dominated order. Consequently, they openly resist them.

SUBSERVIENCE AND MANIPULATION: WOMEN UNDER CLASSIC PATRIARCHY

These examples of women's open resistance stand in stark contrast to women's
accommodations to the system I will call *classic patriarchy*. The clearest instance
of classic patriarchy may be found in a geographical area that includes North
Africa, the Muslim Middle East (including Turkey, Pakistan, and Iran), and South
and East Asia (specifically, India and China).[2]

The key to the reproduction of classic patriarchy lies in the operations of the
patrilocally extended household, which is also commonly associated with the
reproduction of the peasantry in agrarian societies (E. Wolf 1966). Even though
demographic and other constraints may have curtailed the numerical predominance of three-generational patrilocal households, there is little doubt that they
represent a powerful cultural ideal. It is plausible that the emergence of the
patriarchal extended family, which gives the senior man authority over everyone
else, including younger men, is bound up in the incorporation and control of
the family by the state (Ortner 1978), and in the transition from kin-based to
tributary modes of surplus control (E. Wolf 1982). The implications of the
patrilineal–patrilocal complex for women not only are remarkably uniform but
also entail forms of control and subordination that cut across cultural and
religious boundaries, such as those of Hinduism, Confucianism, and Islam.

Under classic patriarchy, girls are given away in marriage at a very young age
into households headed by their husband's father. There, they are subordinate
not only to all the men but also to the more senior women, especially their
mother-in-law. The extent to which this represents a total break with their own
kin group varies in relation to the degree of endogamy in marriage practices and
different conceptions of honor. Among the Turks, there are lower rates of
endogamy, and a husband is principally responsible for a woman's honor. Among
the Arabs, there is much greater mutuality among affines, and a women's natal
family retains both an interest and a say in protecting their married daughter's
honor (Meeker 1976). As a result, a Turkish woman's traditional position more
closely resembles the status of the "stranger-bride" typical of prerevolutionary
China than that of an Arab woman whose position in the patriarchal household
may be somewhat attenuated by endogamy and recourse to her natal kin.

Whether the prevalent marriage payment is dowry or bride-price, in classic patriarchy women do not normally have any claim on their father's patrimony. Their dowries do not qualify as a form of premortem inheritance since they are transferred directly to the bridegroom's kin and do not take the form of productive property, such as land (Agarwal 1987; Sharma 1980). In Muslim communities, for a woman to press for her inheritance rights would be tantamount to losing her brothers' favor, her only recourse in case of severe ill-treatment by her husband or divorce. The young bride enters her husband's household as an effectively dispossessed individual who can establish her place in the patriliny only by producing male offspring.

The patrilineage totally appropriates both women's labor and progeny and renders their work and contribution to production invisible. Woman's life cycle in the patriarchally extended family is such that the deprivation and hardship she experiences as a young bride is eventually superseded by the control and authority she will have over her own subservient daughters-in-law. The cyclical nature of women's power in the household and their anticipation of inheriting the authority of senior women encourages a thorough internalization of this form of patriarchy by the women themselves.

In classic patriarchy, subordination to men is offset by the control older women attain over younger women. However, women have access to the only type of labor power they can control, and to old-age security, through their married sons. Since sons are a woman's most critical resource, ensuring their lifelong loyalty is an enduring preoccupation. Older women have a vested interest in the suppression of romantic love between youngsters to keep the conjugal bond secondary and to claim sons' primary allegiance. Young women have an interest in circumventing and possibly evading their mother-in-law's control. There are culturally specific examples of how this struggle works to the detriment of the heterosexual bond (Boudhiba 1985; Johnson 1983; Mernissi 1975; M. Wolf 1972), but the overall pattern is quite similar.

The class or caste impact on classic patriarchy creates additional complications. Among the wealthier strata, the withdrawal of women from nondomestic work is frequently a mark of status institutionalized in various seclusion and exclusion practices, such as the purdah system and veiling. The institution of purdah, and other similar status markers, further reinforces women's subordination and their economic dependence on men. However, the observance of restrictive practices is such a crucial element in the reproduction of family status that women will resist breaking the rules, even if observing them produces economic hardship. They forgo economically advantageous options, such as the trading activities engaged in by women in parts of Africa, for alternatives that are perceived as in keeping with their respectable and protected domestic roles, and so they become more exploitable. In her study of Indian lacemakers in Narsapur, Mies (1982: 13) comments:

> Although domestication of women may be justified by the older forms of seclusion, it has definitely changed its character. The Kapu women are no longer *gosha*—women of

a feudal warrior caste—but domesticated housewives and workers who produce for the world market. In the case of the lacemakers this ideology has become almost a material force. The whole system is built on the ideology that these women cannot work outside the house.

Thus, unlike women in sub-Saharan Africa who attempt to resist unfavorable labor relations in the household, women in areas of classic patriarchy often adhere as far and as long as they possibly can to rules that result in the unfailing devaluation of their labor. The cyclical fluctuations of their power position, combined with status considerations, result in their active collusion in the reproduction of their own subordination. They would rather adopt interpersonal strategies that maximize their security through manipulation of the affections of their sons and husband. As M. Wolf's (1972) insightful discussion of the Chinese uterine family suggests, this strategy can even result in the aging male patriarch losing power to his wife. Even though these individual power tactics do little to alter the structurally unfavorable terms of the overall patriarchal script, women become experts in maximizing their own life chances.

Commenting on "female conservatism" in China, Johnson (1983: 21) remarks: "Ironically, women through their actions to resist passivity and total male control, became participants with vested interests in the system that oppressed them." M. Wolf (1974) comments similarly on Chinese women's resistance to the 1950 Marriage Law, of which they were supposed to be the primary beneficiaries. She concludes, however, that despite their reluctance to transform the old family system totally, Chinese women will no longer be content with the limited security their manipulation of family relationships can provide.

In other areas of classic patriarchy, changes in material conditions have seriously undermined the normative order. As expressed succinctly by Cain et al. (1979: 410), the key to and the irony of this system reside in the fact that "male authority has a material base, while male responsibility is normatively controlled." Their study of a village in Bangladesh offers an excellent example of the strains placed by poverty on bonds of obligation between kin and, more specifically, on men's fulfillment of their normative obligations toward women. Almost a third of the widows in the villages were the heads of their own households, struggling to make a living through waged work. However, the labor market segmentation created and bolstered by patriarchy meant that their options for work were extremely restricted, and they had to accept very low and uncertain wages.

Paradoxically, the risks and uncertainties that women are exposed to in classic patriarchy create a powerful incentive for higher fertility, which under conditions of deepening poverty will almost certainly fail to provide them with an economic shelter. Greeley (1983) also documents the growing dependence of landless households in Bangladesh on women's wage labor, including that of married women, and discusses the ways in which the stability of the patriarchal family is thereby undermined. Stacey's (1983) discussion of the crisis in the Chinese family before the revolution constitutes a classic account of the erosion of the material and ideological foundations of the traditional system. She goes on to explore how Confucian patriarchy was superseded by and transformed into new democratic and socialist forms. In the next section, I will analyze some of the implications of such processes of transformation.

THE DEMISE OF PATRIARCHAL BARGAINS: RETREAT INTO CONSERVATISM OR RADICAL PROTEST?

The material bases of classic patriarchy crumble under the impact of new market forces, capital penetration in rural areas (Kandiyoti 1984), or processes of chronic immiseration. While there is no single path leading to the breakdown of this system, its consequences are fairly uniform. The domination of younger men by older men and the shelter of women in the domestic sphere were the hallmarks of a system in which men controlled some form of viable joint patrimony in land, animals, or commercial capital. Among the propertyless and the dispossessed, the necessity of every household member's contribution to survival turns men's economic protection of women into a myth.

The breakdown of classic patriarchy results in the earlier emancipation of younger men from their fathers and their earlier separation from the paternal household. While this process implies that women escape the control of mothers-in-law and head their own households at a much younger age, it also means that they themselves can no longer look forward to a future surrounded by subservient daughters-in-law. For the generation of women caught in between, this transformation may represent genuine personal tragedy, since they have paid the heavy price of an earlier patriarchal bargain, but are not able to cash in on its promised benefits. M. Wolf's (1975) statistics on suicide among women in China suggest a clear change in the trend since the 1930s, with a sharp increase in the suicide rates of women who are over 45, whereas previously the rates were highest among young women, especially new brides. She relates this change explicitly to the emancipation of sons and their new possibility of escaping familial control in the choice of their spouse, which robs the older woman of her power and respectability as mother-in-law.

Despite the obstacles that classic patriarchy puts in women's way, which may far outweigh any actual economic and emotional security, women often resist the process of transition because they see the old normative order slipping away from them without any empowering alternatives. In a broader discussion of women's interest, Molyneux (1985: 234) remarks:

> This is not just because of "false consciousness" as is frequently supposed—although this can be a factor—but because such changes realized in a piecemeal fashion could threaten the short-term practical interests of some women, or entail a cost in the loss of forms of protection that are not then compensated for in some way.

Thus, when classic patriarchy enters a crisis, many women may continue to use all the pressure they can muster to make men live up to their obligations and will not, except under the most extreme pressure, compromise the basis for their claims by stepping out of line and losing their respectability. Their passive resistance takes the form of claiming their half of this particular patriarchal bargain—protection in exchange for submissiveness and propriety.

The response of many women who have to work for wages in this context may be an intensification of traditional modesty markers, such as veiling. Often, through no choice of their own, they are working outside their home and are thus "exposed"; they must now use every symbolic means at their disposal to signify that they continue to be worthy of protection. It is significant that Khomeini's exhortations to keep women at home found enthusiastic support among many Iranian women despite the obvious elements of repression. The implicit promise of increased male responsibility restores the integrity of their original patriarchal bargain in an environment where the range of options available to women is extremely restricted. Younger women adopt the veil, Azari (1983: 68) suggests, because "the restriction imposed on them by an Islamic order was therefore a small price that had to be paid in exchange for the security, stability and presumed respect this order promised them."

This analysis of female conservatism as a reaction to the breakdown of classic patriarchy does not by any means exhaust the range of possible responses available to women. It is merely intended to demonstrate the place of a particular strategy within the internal logic of a given system, parallels to which may be found in very different contexts, such as the industrialized societies of Western Europe and the United States. Historical and contemporary analyses of the transformation of the facts and ideologies of Western domesticity imply changes in patriarchal bargains. Gordon's (1982) study of changing feminist attitudes to birth control in the nineteenth and twentieth centuries describes the strategy of voluntary motherhood as part of a broader calculus to improve women's situation. Cott's (1978) analysis of the ideology of passionlessness among Victorian women also indicates the strategic nature of women's choices.

For the modern era, Ehrenreich (1983) provides an analysis of the breakdown of the white middle-class patriarchal bargain in the United States. She traces the progressive opting out of men from the breadwinner role, starting in the 1950s, and suggests that women's demands for greater autonomy came at a time when men's conjugal responsibility was already much diminished and alternatives for men outside the conjugal union had gained considerable cultural legitimacy. Despite intense ideological mobilization, involving experts such as doctors, counselors, and psychologists who tried to reinforce the idea of the responsible male breadwinner and the domesticated housewife, alternative trends started to emerge and to challenge the dominant normative order. Against this background, Ehrenreich evaluates the feminist and the antifeminist movements and says, "It is as if, facing the age-old insecurity of the family wage system, women chose opposite strategies: either to get out (figuratively speaking) and fight for equality of income and opportunity, or to stay home and attempt to bind men more tightly to them" (1983: 151). The familism of the antifeminist movement could therefore be interpreted as an attempt to reinstate an older patriarchal bargain, with feminists providing a convenient scapegoat on whom to blame current disaffection and alienation among men (Chafetz and Dworkin 1987). Indeed, Stacey (1987: 11) suggests that "feminism serves as a symbolic lightning rod for the widespread nostalgia and longing for lost intimacy and security that presently pervade social and political culture in the United States."

However, the forms of consciousness and struggle that emerge in times of rapid social change require sympathetic and open-minded examination, rather than hasty categorization. Thus Ginsburg (1984) evaluates anti-abortion activism among women in the United States as strategic rather than necessarily reactionary. She points out that disengaging sexuality from reproduction and domesticity is perceived by many women as inimical to their best interests, since, among other things, it weakens the social pressure on men to take responsibility for the reproductive consequences of sexual activity. This concern and the general anxiety it expresses are by no means unfounded (English 1984) and speak to the current lack of viable alternatives for the emotional and material support of women with children. Similarly, Stacey (1987) identifies diverse forms of "post-feminist" consciousness of the postindustrial era. She suggests that a complex and often contradictory merging of depoliticized feminist attitudes to work and family and of personal strategies to enhance stability and intimacy in marriage are currently taking place.

At the ideological level, broken bargains seem to instigate a search for culprits, a hankering for the certainties of a more traditional order, or a more diffuse feeling that change might have gone either too far or badly wrong. Rosenfelt and Stacey's (1987) reflections on postfeminism and Stacey's (1986) discussion of conservative pro-family feminism, although they criticize the alarmist premisses of neoconservative discourse, take some of the legitimate concerns it expresses seriously.

CONCLUSION

Systematic analyses of women's strategies and coping mechanisms can help to capture the nature of patriarchal systems in their cultural, class-specific, and temporal concreteness and reveal how men and women resist, accommodate, adapt, and conflict with each other over resources, rights, and responsibilities. Such analyses dissolve some of the artificial divisions apparent in theoretical discussions of the relationships among class, race, and gender, since participants' strategies are shaped by several levels of constraints. Women's strategies are always played out in the context of identifiable patriarchal bargains that act as implicit scripts that define, limit, and inflect their market and domestic options. The two ideal-typical systems of male dominance discussed in this essay provide different baselines from which women negotiate and strategize, and each affects the forms and potentialities of their resistance and struggles. Patriarchal bargains do not merely inform women's rational choices but also shape the more unconscious aspects of their gendered subjectivity, since they permeate the context of their early socialization, as well as their adult cultural milieu (Kandiyoti 1987a, 1987b).

A focus on more narrowly defined patriarchal bargains, rather than on an unqualified notion of patriarchy, offers better prospects for the detailed analysis of processes of transformation. In her analysis of changes in sexual imagery and mores in Western societies, Janeway (1980) borrows Thomas Kuhn's (1970) terminology of scientific paradigms. She suggests, by analogy, that widely shared ideas and practices in the realm of sexuality may act as sexual paradigms, establishing the rules of normalcy at any given time, but also vulnerable to change when "existing rules fail to operate, when anomalies can no longer be evaded, when the real world of everyday experience challenges accepted causality" (1980: 582). However, sexual paradigms cannot be fully comprehended unless they are inscribed in the rules of more specifically defined patriarchal bargains, as Janeway herself demonstrates in her discussion of the connection between the ideal of female chastity in Western societies and the transmission of property to legitimate heirs before the advent of a generalized cash economy.

To stretch the Kuhnian analogy even further, patriarchal bargains can be shown to have a normal phase and a crisis phase, a concept that modifies our very interpretation of what is going on in the world. Thus, during the normal phase of classic patriarchy, there were large numbers of women who were in fact exposed to economic hardship and insecurity. They were infertile and had to be divorced, or orphaned and without recourse to their own natal family, or unprotected because they had no surviving sons or—even worse—had "ungrateful" sons. However, they were merely considered "unlucky," anomalies and accidental casualties of a system that made sense otherwise. It is only at the point of breakdown that every order reveals its systemic contradictions. The impact of contemporary socioeconomic transformations upon marriage and divorce, on household formation, and on the gendered division of labor inevitably lead to a questioning of the fundamental, implicit assumptions behind arrangements between women and men.

However, new strategies and forms of consciousness do not simply emerge from the ruins of the old and smoothly produce a new consensus, but are created through personal and political struggles, which are often complex and contradictory (Strathern 1987). The breakdown of a particular patriarchal system may, in the short run, generate instances of passive resistance among women that take the paradoxical form of bids for increased responsibility and control by men. A better understanding of the short- and medium-term strategies of women in different social locations could provide a corrective influence to ethnocentric or class-bound definitions of what constitutes a feminist consciousness.

AFTERWORD

More than a decade after the publication of "Bargaining with Patriarchy," I was invited to revisit the arguments I outlined in it.[3] In the intervening period, attempts to analyze bargaining power both within and beyond the household became more numerous and increasingly sophisticated. "Bargaining with Patriarchy" represents one of the early attempts to come to grips with these issues. I argued that bargaining always takes place in the context of "rules of the game" implicit in different systems of male dominance. These rules, whilst subject to change and redefinition, may nonetheless provide a relatively enduring framework for human transactions informing both women's rational choices and the less conscious aspects of their gendered subjectivities. These, in turn, predispose them to favour differing strategies of resistance and/or collusion in different contexts. Thus, I was both presenting women as rational actors deploying a range of strategies intelligible within their normative universe and pointing to the essentially circumscribed nature of the same strategies; in other words, whilst endorsing James Scott's version of resistance I was attempting to eat my Gramscian cake at the same time by arguing that women were nonetheless operating within the parameters of dominant gender ideologies.

In "Gender, Power and Contestation" I examined several frameworks (Scott, Gramsci and Bourdieu) attempting to explain resistance/acquiescence and came to the conclusion that approaches that are primarily geared to elucidating how class dominance works fall short of fully capturing forms of subordination based on gender. Scott's approach implied that both the powerful and the dominated are, up to a point, bound by the same normative constraints. This was also behind my own suggestion that gender orders involve mutually binding constraints that I had labelled, for want of a better term, as "patriarchal bargains." However, the powerful are much better placed to change the rules of the game unilaterally, at which point attempts by subordinates to call their bluff may emerge as rather pitiful and ineffectual forms of rearguard action. Invoking subordinates' rational decision to conform rather than rebel with reference to their recognition that any other course of action is blocked in fact conceals the evidence of hegemony. This also corresponds to one of the central weaknesses of my earlier work.

I, nonetheless, wish to retain my original emphasis on the material basis of patriarchal bargains. However entrenched the nature of dominant ideologies that "naturalize" existing gender arrangements (as in Bourdieu's notion of doxa), they are ultimately unable to withstand the onslaughts of fundamentally transformed material circumstances and have constantly to reinvent themselves (in the manner of Bourdieu's orthodoxy). Moreover, women's attachment to and stake in certain forms of patriarchal arrangements may derive neither from false consciousness, nor from conscious collusion, but from an actual stake in certain positions of power available to them. Experiences of gendered power are not merely fractured by class, race, and ethnicity but by the complicated emotional (and material) calculus implied by different organizations of the domestic realm through women's and men's unfolding life cycles, making analogies with any other form of domination problematic.

At any rate, talking about hegemony in the case of gender relations is helpful only up to a point and mainly by way of analogy. True, the constriction of discursive universe produced by the equation of masculinity or femininity with some of its socially dominant variants and of sexual relations with heterosexuality bespeaks a powerful dominant ideology. Poststructuralist feminists go furthest by arguing that it is the gender division itself which is generative of oppression, by marking out certain gendered identities as subordinate, rather than the institutionalized privileges of men over women per se. The principal form of false consciousness, in this case, would reside in taking these divisions at face value (as "foundational") rather than seeing through them as the effects of a particular kind of discursive formation. However, analyses that problematize the gender division itself (and treat it as an originary act of discursive violence) do not automatically further our intimate understandings of the specific social relations or institutional frameworks that reproduce gendered inequalities; hence some of the difficulties in letting go of concepts such as male dominance and patriarchy in favour of gender, especially if this latter is not grounded in a theory of social relations. There seems to be no obvious way of bridging the gap between theories of gender and feminist social practice, which is why I feel that the concept of "patriarchal bargain" may still have some utility.

NOTES

1. Like all terms coined to convey a complex concept, the term *patriarchal bargain* represents a difficult compromise. It is intended to indicate the existence of set rules and scripts regulating gender relations, to which both genders accommodate and acquiesce, yet which may nonetheless be contested, redefined, and renegotiated. Some suggested alternatives were the terms "contract," "deal," or "scenario"; however, none of these fully captured the fluidity and tension implied by *bargain*. I am grateful to Cynthia Cockburn and Nels Johnson for pointing out that the term "bargain" commonly denotes a deal between more or less equal participants, so it does not accurately apply to my usage, which clearly indicates an asymmetrical exchange. However, women as a rule bargain from a weaker position.

2. I am excluding not only Southeast Asia but also the Northern Mediterranean, despite important similarities in the latter regarding codes of honor and the overall importance attached to the sexual purity of women, because I want to restrict myself to areas where the patrilocal–patrilineal complex is dominant. Thus societies with bilateral kinship systems, such as Greece, in which women do inherit and control property and receive dowries that constitute productive property, do not qualify despite important similarities in other ideological respects. This is not, however, to suggest that an unqualified homogeneity of ideology and practice exists within the geographical boundaries indicated. For example, there are critical variations within the Indian subcontinent that have demonstrably different implications for women (Dyson and Moore 1983). Conversely, even in areas of bilateral kinship, there may be instances in which all the facets of classic patriarchy—namely property, residence, and descent through

the male line—may coalesce under specified circumstances (Denich 1974). What I am suggesting is that the most clear-cut and easily identifiable examples of classic patriarchy may be found within the boundaries indicated in the text.

3. See "Gender, Power and Contestation: Rethinking "Bargaining with Patriarchy'," in Jackson and Pearson 1998.

REFERENCES

Abu, K. 1983. "The Separateness of Spouses: Conjugal Resources in an Ashanti Town," in C. Oppong, ed., *Female and Male in West Africa*, 156–68. London: George Allen & Unwin.

Agarwal, B. 1987. "Women and Land Rights in India." Unpublished manuscript.

Azari, F. 1983. "Islam's Appeal to Women in Iran: Illusion and Reality," in F. Azari, ed., *Women of Iran: The Conflict with Fundamentalist Islam*. London: Ithaca Press.

Barrett, M. 1980. *Woman's Oppression Today*. London: Verso.

Beechey, V. 1979. "On Patriarchy," *Feminist Review* 3: 66–82.

Boudhiba, A. 1985. *Sexuality in Islam*. London: Routledge & Kegan Paul.

Cain, M., S. R. Khanan, and S. Nahar. 1979. "Class, Patriarchy, and Women's Work in Bangladesh," *Population and Development Review* 5: 408–16.

Caldwell, J. C. 1978. "A Theory of Fertility: From High Plateau to Destabilization," *Population and Development Review* 4: 553–77.

Chafetz, J. S. and A. G. Dworkin. 1987. "In Face of Threat: Organized Antifeminism in Comparative Perspective," *Gender & Society* 1: 33–60.

Conti, A. 1979. "Capitalist Organization of Production through Noncapitalist Relations: Women's Role in a Pilot Resettlement Project in Upper Volta," *Review of African Political Economy* 15/16: 75–91.

Cott, N. F. 1978. "Passionlessness: An Interpretation of Victorian Sexual Ideology, 1790–1850," *Signs: Journal of Women in Culture and Society* 4: 219–36.

Delphy, C. 1977. *The Main Enemy*. London: Women's Research and Resource Centre.

Denich, B. S. 1974. "Sex and Power in the Balkans," in M. Z. Rosaldo and L. Lamphere, eds., *Women, Culture and Society*, 243–62. Palo Alto: Stanford University Press.

Dey, J. 1981. "Gambian Women: Unequal Partners in Rice Development Projects," in N. Nelson, ed., *African Women in the Development Process*, 109–22. London: Frank Cass.

Dyson, T. and M. Moore. 1983. "On Kinship Structures, Female Autonomy and Demographic Behavior," *Population and Development Review* 9: 35–60.

Ehrenreich, B. 1983. *The Hearts of Men*. London: Pluto Press.

Eisenstein, Z. 1978. "Developing a Theory of Capitalist Patriarchy and Socialist Feminism," in Z. Eisenstein, ed., *Capitalist Patriarchy and the Case for Socialist Feminism*, 5–40. New York: Monthly Review Press.

English, D. 1984. "The Fear That Feminism Will Free Men First," in A. B. Snitow, C. Stansell, and S. Thompson, eds., *Powers of Desire: The Politics of Sexuality*, 97–102. New York: Monthly Review Press.

Etienne, M. and E. Leacock, eds. 1980. *Women and Colonization*. New York: Praeger.

Ginsburg, F. 1984. "The Body Politic: The Defense of Sexual Restriction by Anti-Abortion Activists," in C. S. Vance, ed., *Pleasure and Danger: Exploring Female Sexuality*, 173–88. London: Routledge & Kegan Paul.

Gordon, L. 1982. "Why Nineteenth-Century Feminists Did Not Support 'Birth Control' and Twentieth-Century Feminists Do: Feminism, Reproduction, and the Family," in B. Thorne and M. Yalom, eds, *Rethinking the Family: Some Feminist Questions*, 40–53. New York: Longman.

Greeley, M. 1983. "Patriarchy and Poverty: A Bangladesh Case Study," *South Asia Research* 3: 35–55.

Guyer, J. I. and P. E. Peters. 1987. "'Introduction' to Conceptualizing the Household: Issues of Theory and Policy in Africa," *Development and Change* 18: 197–213.

Hanger, J. and J. Moris. 1973. "Women and the Household Economy," in R. Chambers and J. Mons, eds., *Mwea: An Irrigated Rice Settlement in Kenya*, 209–44. Munich: Weltforum Verlag.

Hartmann, H. 1981. "The Unhappy Marriage of Marxism and Feminism: Towards a More Progressive Union," in I. Sargent, ed., *Women and Revolution*, 40–53. London: Pluto Press.

Jackson, C. and R. Pearson, eds. 1998. *Feminist Visions of Development*. London: Routledge.

Janeway, E. 1980. "Who Is Sylvia? On the Loss of Sexual Paradigms," *Signs: Journal of Women in Culture and Society* 5: 573–89.

Johnson, K. A. 1983. *Women, the Family and Peasant Revolution in China*. Chicago: Chicago University Press.

Kandiyoti, D. 1984. "Rural Transformation in Turkey and Its Implications for Women's Studies," in *Women on the Move: Contemporary Transformations in Family and Society*, 17–29. Paris: UNESCO.

Kandiyoti, D. 1985. *Women in Rural Production Systems: Problems and Policies*. Park: UNESCO.

Kandiyoti, D. 1987a. "Emancipated but Unliberated? Reflections on the Turkish Case." *Feminist Studies* 13: 317–38.

Kandiyoti, D. 1987b. "The Problem of Subjectivity in Western Feminist Theory." Paper presented at the American Sociological Association Annual Meeting, Chicago.

Kuhn, T. 1970. *The Structure of Scientific Revolutions*, 2d ed. Chicago: Chicago University Press.

McDonough, R. and R. Harrison. 1978. "Patriarchy and Relations of Production," in A. Kuhn and A. M. Wolpe, eds., *Feminism and Materialism*, 11–14. London: Routledge & Kegan Paul.

Mann, K. 1985. *Marrying Well: Marriage, Status and Social Change among the Educated Elite in Colonial Lagos*. Cambridge: Cambridge University Press.

Mbilinyi, M. J. 1982. "Wife, Slave and Subject of the King: The Oppression of Women in the Shambala Kingdom," *Tanzania Notes and Records* 88/89: 113.

Meeker, M. 1976. "Meaning and Society in the Near East: Examples from the Black Sea Turks and the Levantine Arabs," *International Journal of Middle East Studies* 7: 383–422.

Mernissi, F. 1975. *Beyond the Veil: Male–Female Dynamics in a Muslim Society*. New York: Wiley.

Mies, M. 1982. "The Dynamics of Sexual Division of Labour and the Integration of Women into the World Market," in L. Beneria, ed., *Women and Development: The Sexual Division of Labour in Rural Societies*, 1–28. New York: Praeger.

Mies, M. 1986. *Patriarchy and Accumulation on a World Scale: Women in the International Division of Labour*. London: Zed Books.

Mitchell, J. 1973. *Women's Estate*. New York: Vintage.

Mitchell, J. 1986. "Reflections on Twenty Years of Feminism," in J. Mitchell and A. Oakley, eds., *What is Feminism?* 34–48. Oxford: Basil Blackwell.

Molyneux, M. 1985. "Mobilization Without Emancipation? Women's Interests, the State and Revolution in Nicaragua," *Feminist Studies* 11: 227–54.

Munachonga, M. L. 1982. "Income Allocation and Marriage Options in Urban Zambia: Wives Versus Extended Kin." Paper presented at conference on Women and Income Control in the Third World, New York.

Murray, C. 1987. "Class, Gender and the Household: The Developmental Cycle in Southern Africa," *Development and Change* 18: 235–50.

Ortner, S. 1978 "The Virgin and the State," *Feminist Studies* 4: 19–36.

Roberts, P. 1989. "Rural Women in Western Nigeria and Hausa Niger: A Comparative Analysis," in K. Young, ed., *Serving Two Masters: Third World Women in Development.* New Delhi: Allied Publishers.

Rosenfelt, D. and J. Stacey. 1987. "Second Thoughts on the Second Wave," *Feminist Studies* 13: 341–61.

Sharma, U. 1980. *Women, Work and Property in North West India.* London: Tavistock.

Stacey, J. 1983. *Patriarchy and Socialist Revolution in China.* Berkeley: University of California Press.

Stacey, J. 1986. "Are Feminists Afraid to Leave Home? The Challenge of Conservative Pro-Family Feminism," in J. Mitchell and A. Oakley, eds., *What is Feminism?* 219–48. Oxford: Basil Blackwell.

Stacey, J. 1987. "Sexism by a Subtler Name? Postindustrial Conditions and Postfeminist Consciousness in the Silicon Valley," *Socialist Review*, November: 728.

Strathern, M. 1987. "An Awkward Relationship: The Case of Feminism and Anthropology," *Signs: Journal of Women in Culture and Society* 12: 276–92.

Wolf, E. 1966. *Peasants.* Englewood Cliffs, NJ: Prentice-Hall.

Wolf, E. 1982. *Europe and the People Without History.* Berkeley: University of California Press.

Wolf, M. 1972. *Women and the Family in Rural Taiwan.* Palo Alto: Stanford University Press.

Wolf, M. 1974. "Chinese Women: Old Skills in a New Context," in M. Z. Rosaldo and L. Lamphere, eds., *Women, Culture and Society*, 157–72. Palo Alto: Stanford University Press.

Wolf, M. 1975. "Woman and Suicide in China," in M. Wolf and R. Witke, eds., *Women in Chinese Society*, 111–41. Palo Alto: Stanford University Press.

Young, I. 1981. "Beyond the Unhappy Marriage: A Critique of the Dual Systems Theory," in L. Sargen, ed., *Women and Revolution*, 43–69. London: Pluto Press.

Young, S. 1977. "Fertility and Famine: Women's Agricultural History in Southern Mozambique," in R. Palmer and N. Parsons, eds., *The Roots of Rural Poverty in Central and Southern Africa*, 66–81. London: Heinemann.

THE DISAPPEARING FATHERS
UNDER GLOBAL CAPITALISM

TEMMA KAPLAN

As fathers and governments throughout the world flee paternal responsibilities, patriarchy needs to be discussed comparatively in class and historical terms. Today's problems, the absence of fathers and the continued subordination of women, are nothing new among the poorest people, dating back at least to the sixteenth century. What is new is the extension of this pattern as more and more people arrive in towns and cities without any means of support. What was once called urbanization without industrialization has turned into the feminization of poverty, with the condition of women and children becoming more and more precarious.

Considering patriarchy as the rule of fathers and potential fathers according to a generational, hierarchical system presumes the existence of households governed by men, beginning with grandfathers and running through fathers, brothers, husbands, and sometimes sons, and culminating in the supreme authority of the state. Linda Gordon and Allen Hunter, Judith Stacey, and Steve Stern have all remarked that the problem women and society now confront is a system of male domination accompanied by the *absence* of fathers and grandfathers, and the existence of governments that increasingly wish to privatize all social services. Unlike stereotypical patriarchy, the current system of subordinating women and controlling their sexuality, their reproductive capacities, their labor, and their well-being seems to depend on an invisible hand, the invisible hand of absent generations of fathers who have no interest in supporting the well-being of the poorest women and children.

Those who presume that some bond has been broken may confuse patriarchy with a contract between men and women according to which related men in several generations can do as they wish—beat and sexually abuse women, rule over them and their children, and define and interpret all religious and secular laws—in return for economic support. But, just as feudalism is primarily a system of extracting labor from people who defer because they are powerless, so patriarchy has always been nothing more than a system of male domination. The apparent changes in how power is wielded may be related to the increasing consolidation of private property in the hands of a smaller and smaller number of men, and to the globalization of labor, inasmuch as capitalists are no longer concerned with reproducing the labor force.

Focusing on capitalism and exploitation does not alone explain male domination or its attendant brutalization of women and children, but frequently overlooked patterns do appear. In surges beginning with the first European imperialism of the fifteenth century and occurring in certain places up to our own time, people freed from servitude on the land also suffered from being pushed off the land without any means of employment in the cities. With the destruction of feudalism in parts of western Europe, the colonial reorganization of land in Asia, Africa, Latin America, and the Middle East, the end of slavery in the United States and Brazil in the nineteenth century, and the increased mechanization of agriculture around the globe since the Second World War, peasants have lost access to land. Male laborers have frequently been forced to migrate to find work. They have usually tramped to a nearby town; then, those lacking steady employment have moved further and further away from their original homes and families. The largely young, European, male labor force which formed the mass base of the first imperialist ventures into Latin America, Asia, and Africa often went in search of riches, but lacked other employment when they stayed.

While exploiting other continents, the European foot soldiers left behind wives and children, especially in port cities such as Seville and Genoa. The women of the colonies fared no better; they were frequently seduced and abandoned in Peru and Mexico, India and Kenya.[1]

Nineteenth-century Spanish and Italian landless day laborers, who the Argentines called *las golondrinas* (the swallows), followed the harvests from the northern to the southern hemisphere. Often they found collateral work in the new place and stopped sending money home. Miners from Cornwall and Scotland sought work in the United States when the mines at home ran out, in the nineteenth century. They too left wives and children behind. The women became single women heads of households, and attempted to raise their children as they might. Single women raising children alone or with other women who were not necessarily blood relatives became one of the possible working-class family forms, back to the sixteenth century.

The pattern that Daniel Patrick Moynihan identified as the "black family," or the "black matriarchy," of poor women raising children alone or with kin and friends has been the model for one kind of proletarian family in certain places around the globe for centuries. It has been the family structure of poverty under capitalism. The heroism of ordinary women did not win them recognition in the past any more than it provides them with respect in the present. Nor did the absence of fathers free single mothers from the domination of men. Liberation from the most oppressive conditions on the land have often come with the freedom of poor families to starve. To survive, mothers and daughters also went in search of work. Women who had borne children served as wet nurses in early modern Italy, France, and Spain, or they took in laundry or sewing to sustain their families when men were gone from home or unable to contribute their share to the common good. Young girls from countries such as Belgium and Austria in the eighteenth century, Ireland, Mexico, and Guatemala in the nineteenth and twentieth centuries, and Japan and China in the early twentieth century were sent out to be servants or prostitutes, first in nearby towns and cities, and then in places as far away as the United States.[2] Not only were the women themselves not freed from ties to their families; they, like the women textile workers of Lowell and Lawrence, Massachusetts, and Korea, were frequently sources of revenue for their fathers, inadvertently subsidizing patriarchy.

Patriarchy as an economic relationship under capitalism may always have depended on property and community control of reproduction. Those men who had no access to property merely needed prepared food, clothing, shelter, and sex. Men alone could be rowdy, and drinking and cavorting frequently interfered with their ability to perform disciplined work. According to George Chauncey, writing about the first part of the twentieth century in Zambia (formerly Northern Rhodesia), and Thomas Klubock, writing about Chile in the same period, mine owners built workers' housing to promote stable family life, to reduce drunkenness, and to create a more docile workforce.[3] Women in mining communities, however, suffered both from the bad living conditions and the low wages of their fathers and husbands, and from battering by male relatives, as Agnes Smedley sadly recalled about her early days in Colorado in *Daughter of Earth* and Domitila Barros de Chungara remembered in *Let Me Speak!*, which tells about her life in the Bolivian mining community of Siglo XX.[4] The direct exploitation of men and women who worked for wages, and the abuse of women by oppressed men, polluted the sexual and social relationships between them and between fathers and children in the household.

What has changed in the past forty years in the industrialized countries is that governments are no longer preoccupied with the condition of children and with reproducing the labor force. Margaret Hewitt in *Wives and Mothers in Victorian Industry* (a book that deserves reprinting) wrote that Tories in mid-nineteenth-century Great Britain were largely afraid that the working class would not reproduce itself because a certain (though small) percentage of female factory workers were mothers.[5] They were forced to place their children with impoverished old women, who took in as many as ten infants at a time. Without baby formula—not widely available until the twentieth century—they fed infants breadcrumbs dissolved in watered milk, and drugged them to keep them quiet. Such children, like the French foundlings of whom Olwen Hufton has written, died in large numbers.[6] According to Hewitt, paternalism and fears about future labor shortages caused Tory Radicals to impose protective legislation, preventing pregnant women and mothers from performing most factory work. What we are seeing today is the collapse of fears about labor shortages in the global economy where moving operations to countries with vast labor supplies in East and Southeast Asia, and in Central and South America, and, increasingly, in Africa, no longer makes it necessary to worry about who will serve in the factories.

Women around the world, nevertheless, still provide the main support for their children, as men move from family to family or find no need to be in families at all. Steve Stern suggests that women shantytown dwellers in Mexico and elsewhere in Latin America (and I would add Africa) have been attempting to gain free or nearly free housing by securing land rights to substantial houses they build from shacks they construct in squatter communities. As Stern says, even if poor men reside with their wives and children, they seldom can afford to pay rent from their meager wages. And once a woman has a house, she can afford to leave an abusive relationship. Paule Marshall describes an earlier version of this pattern in *Brown Girl, Brown Stone*, where the Barbadian immigrant women in Brooklyn in the 1930s scrimp and save to provide a house for their children even if their husbands leave home.[7] Ruth Behar's *Translated Woman: Crossing the Border with Esperanza's Story*, Elsa Joubert's *The Long Journey of Poppie Nongena*, and Carolina de Jesus's *Child of the Dark*[8] use different genres to tell about how single mothers in Mexico, South Africa, and Brazil secure housing and fight to survive against the brutality of fathers, husbands, and governments who not only fail to support the women and their children, but are responsible for the family's desperate straits.

South Africa under apartheid epitomized the connection between declining patriarchal relations and the expansion of capitalism unaffected by labor shortages. Apartheid was a system for regulating land and labor and for keeping the races apart from one another. As whites mechanized land they had stolen from people of color, and as cattle-rearing developed, there was less and less need for agricultural laborers. The government expelled people of color to the wastelands outside the fertile areas. Blacks were driven to take whatever jobs they could get. Except for nannies, who had to leave their own children in the countryside to fend for themselves, there was little demand for female workers. Black men could sometimes find jobs as contract laborers in the mines and industries of South Africa, but they could only take up this work if they left their wives and children behind in the desolate lands called Bantustans, where there was little in the way of water, food, educational opportunities, or health facilities. Sometimes the men sent money home; frequently, the little the men earned went for their own upkeep and entertainment.

Many women, rather than watch their children starve and die for lack of medical care, tried illegally to join husbands in cities such as Cape Town where they could secure employment. Sociologist Linzi Manicom has gone so far as to call apartheid a system of gender as well as racial discrimination.[9] The government, inadvertently echoing Marx's view about surplus labor, called women and children "surplus people," because they could not produce profits.

The South African government refused to concern itself with providing social support that would have assured the perpetuation of the labor force largely made up of men of color. These white patriarchs mirrored other global capitalists' lack of concern about reproducing the labor force, so confident were they of endless supplies of poorer and more desperate laborers in the next port or the next country.

Regina N'tongana, a leader of the women's committee in the squatter community called Crossroads at the edge of Cape Town, strove from 1978 to 1985 to protect her three surviving children from the government, which sought to return them to the Bantustans to die. She fought her way back to Cape Town, and, with the help of others, carved out a new community where none had existed before. The women built shanties, established schools and childcare centers, and forged committees to administer their settlement. When the government sent in the bulldozers to tear down their houses, the women resisted and rebuilt. They chained themselves to the gates of parliament. They worked with church organizations to shame the government before national and international public opinion. When the government finally allied with male gang leaders from the squatter community and succeeded in driving out many of the original people, the women with some male aid rebuilt and formed organizations to help other women like them.[10]

Although the poorest women under capitalism, since the sixteenth century, have experienced male domination according to similar patterns, the international feminization of poverty is due to declining concern with reproducing the labor force. Nostalgia for the family has paradoxically accompanied lack of interest in children and contempt for their mothers. Fathers and states no longer even claim to protect the interests of the poorest women in society. But, as the movements in the shantytowns of Latin America and Africa amply demonstrate, certain women have been able to fight back. Our task is to reveal the cynicism of the ideologues who call for the strengthening of "the family" while cutting support for the poorest single mothers and their children, and to support what women's movements are trying to do all over the globe: to win resources they themselves control.

From confronting abusers to winning housing and reproductive rights, women of all classes are demanding new rights to live and support their children whether or not their existence serves the interests of global capitalism, whether or not authorities hate them for merely trying to survive.

NOTES

1. For a consideration of the condition of poor women in early modern Spain and Peru, see Mary Elizabeth Perry, *Crime and Society in Early Modern Seville* (Hanover, NH: University Press of New England, 1980); *Gender and Disorder in Early Modern Seville* (Princeton, NJ: Princeton University Press, 1990); and Alejandra Osorio, "Witches and Witchcraft Under Colonial Rule; Female Forms of Social Control in Seventeenth Century Lima. Paper presented at the Berkshire Conference on the History of Women, University of North Carolina, Chapel Hill, 9 June 1996.

2. An especially vivid account of the transportation of a Japanese peasant girl to serve

as a prostitute can be found in the film *Sandakan, No. 8* (1974), directed by Kumai Kei.

3. George Chauncey, Jr., "The Locus of Reproduction: Women's Labour in the Zambian Copperbelt, 1927–1953," *Journal of South African Studies* 7, no. 2 (1981): 135–64; and Thomas Miller Klubock, "Morality and Good Habits: The Construction of Gender and Class in the Chilean Copper Mines, 1904–1951," in John D. French and Daniel James, eds., *The Gendered World of Latin American Women Workers: From Household and Factory to the Union Hall and Ballot Box* (Durham, NC: Duke University Press, 1997), 232–3.

4. Agnes Smedley, *Daughter of Earth: A Novel* (Old Westbury, NY: Feminist Press, 1976); Domitila Barros de Chungara, *Let Me Speak! Testimony of Domitila, A Woman of the Bolivian Mines* (New York: Monthly Review Press, 1978).

5. Margaret Hewitt, *Wives and Mothers in Victorian Industry* (London: Rockliff, 1958).

6. Olwen H. Hufton, *Bayeux in the Eighteenth Century: A Social Study* (Oxford: Clarendon Press, 1967); *The Poor of Eighteenth-Century France 1750–1789* (Oxford: Oxford University Press, 1974).

7. Paule Marshall, *Brown Girl, Brownstones* (Old Westbury, NY: Feminist Press, 1981).

8. Ruth Behar, *Translated Woman: Crossing the Border with Esperanza's Story* (Boston: Beacon Press, 1993); Elsa Joubert, *The Long Journey of Poppie Nongena* (Johannesburg: Jonathan Ball, 1980); and Carolina Maria de Jesus, *Child of the Dark* (New York: Dutton, 1962).

9. Linzi Manicom, "Ruling Relations: Rethinking State and Gender in South African History," *Journal of African History* 33 (1992): 441–65.

10. See Josette Cole, *Crossroads: The Politics of Reform and Repression 1976–1986* (Johannesburg: Ravan Press, 1987) for a remarkable description and analysis of the events at Crossroads as they were unfolding; and Temma Kaplan, *Crazy for Democracy: Women in Grassroots Movements* (New York: Routledge, 1997), where I studied Mrs. N'tongana and her associates in the Surplus People's Project as they tried to support other movements of women who were trying to secure land and housing rights in the Western Cape.

PART III

WAGE LABOR AND STRUGGLES

WOMEN WORKERS AND CAPITALIST SCRIPTS: IDEOLOGIES OF DOMINATION, COMMON INTERESTS, AND THE POLITICS OF SOLIDARITY

CHANDRA TALPADE MOHANTY

We dream that when we work hard, we'll be able to clothe our children decently, and still have a little time and money left for ourselves. And we dream that when we do as good as other people, we get treated the same, and that nobody puts us down because we are not like them.... Then we ask ourselves, "How could we make these things come true?" And so far we've come up with only two possible answers: win the lottery, or organize. What can I say, except I have never been lucky with numbers. So tell this in your book: tell them it may take time that people think they don't have, but they have to organize! ... Because the only way to get a little measure of power over your own life is to do it collectively, with the support of other people who share your needs.

Irma, a Filipina worker in the Silicon Valley, California[1]

Irma's dreams of a decent life for her children and herself, her desire for equal treatment and dignity on the basis of the quality and merit of her work, her conviction that collective struggle is the means to "get a little measure of power over your own life," succinctly capture the struggles of poor women workers in the global capitalist arena. In this essay I want to focus on the exploitation of poor Third World women, on their agency as workers, on the common interests of women workers based on an understanding of shared location and needs, and on the strategies/practices of organizing that are anchored in and lead to the transformation of the daily lives of women workers.

GENDER AND WORK: HISTORICAL AND IDEOLOGICAL TRANSFORMATIONS

"Work makes life sweet," says Lola Weixel, a working-class Jewish woman in Connie Field's film *The Life and Times of Rosie the Riveter*. Weixel is reflecting on her experience of working in a welding factory during the Second World War, at a time when large numbers of U.S. women were incorporated into the labor force to replace men who were fighting the war. In one of the most moving moments in the film, she draws attention to what it meant to her and to other women to work side by side, to learn skills and craft products, and to be paid for the work they did, only to be told at the end of the war that they were no longer needed and should go back to being girlfriends, housewives, and mothers. While the U.S. state propaganda machine was especially explicit on matters of work for men and women, and the corresponding expectations of masculinity/femininity and domesticity in the late 1940s and 1950s, this is no longer the case in the 1990s. Shifting definitions of public and private, and of workers, consumers and citizens, no longer define wage-work in visibly masculine terms. However, the dynamics of job competition, loss, and profit-making in the 1990s are still part of the dynamic process that spelled the decline of the mill towns of New England in the early 1900s and that now pits "American" against "immigrant" and "Third World" workers along the U.S./Mexico border or in Silicon Valley in California. Similarly, there are continuities between the women-led New York garment-workers strike of 1909, the Bread and Roses (Lawrence textile) strike of 1912, Lola Weixel's role in union organizing during the Second World War, and the frequent strikes in the 1980s and 1990s of Korean textile and electronics workers, most of whom are young, single women.[2] While the global division of labor in 1995 looks quite different from what it was in the 1950s, ideologies of women's work, the meaning and value of work for women, and women workers' struggles against exploitation remain central issues for feminists around the world. After all, women's labor has always been central to the development, consolidation, and reproduction of capitalism in the U.S. and elsewhere.

In the United States, histories of slavery, indentured servitude, contract labor, self-employment, and wage-work are also simultaneously histories of gender, race, and (hetero)sexuality, nested within the context of the development of capitalism. Thus, women of different races, ethnicities, and social classes had profoundly different, though interconnected, experiences of work in the economic development from nineteenth-century economic and social practices (slave agriculture in the South, emergent industrial capitalism in the Northeast, the hacienda system in the Southwest, independent family farms in the rural Midwest, Native American hunting/gathering and agriculture) to wage-labor and self-employment (including family businesses) in the late twentieth century. In 1995, almost a century after the Lowell girls lost their jobs when textile mills moved South to attract nonunionized labor, feminists are faced with a number of profound analytical and organizational challenges in different regions of the world. The material, cultural, and political effects of the processes of domination and exploitation which sustain what is called the New World Order[3] are devastating for the vast majority of people in the world—and most especially for impoverished and Third World women. Maria Mies argues that the increasing division of the world into consumers and producers has a profound effect on Third World women workers, who are drawn into the international division of labor as workers in agriculture; in large-scale manufacturing industries like textiles, electronics, garments, and toys; in small-scale manufacturing of consumer goods like handicrafts and food processing (the informal sector); and as workers in the sex and tourist industries.[4]

The values, power, and meanings attached to being either a consumer or a producer/worker vary enormously depending on where and who we happen to be in an unequal global system. In the 1990s, it is, after all, multinational corporations that are the hallmark of global capitalism. In an analysis of the effects of these corporations on the new world order, Richard Barnet and John Cavanagh characterize the global commercial arena in terms of four intersecting webs: the Global Cultural Bazaar (which creates and disseminates images and dreams through films, television, radio, music, and other media), the Global Shopping Mall (a planetary supermarket which sells things to eat, drink, wear, and enjoy through advertising, distribution, and marketing networks), the Global Workplace (a network of factories and workplaces where goods are produced, information processed, and services rendered), and, finally, the Global Financial Network (the international traffic in currency transactions, global securities, etc.).[5] In each of these webs, racialized ideologies of masculinity, femininity, and sexuality play a role in constructing the legitimate consumer, worker, and manager. Meanwhile, the psychic and social disenfranchisement and impoverishment of women continues. Women's bodies and labor are used to consolidate global dreams, desires, and ideologies of success and the good life in unprecedented ways.

Feminists have responded directly to the challenges of globalization and capitalist modes of recolonization by addressing the sexual politics and effects on women of (a) religious fundamentalist movements within and across the boundaries of the nation-state; (b) structural adjustment policies (SAPs); (c) militarism, demilitarization, and violence against women; (d) environmental degradation and land/sovereignty struggles of indigenous and native peoples; and (e) population control, health, and reproductive policies and practices.[6] In each of these cases, feminists have analyzed the effects on women as workers, sexual partners, mothers and caretakers, consumers, and transmitters and transformers of culture and tradition. Analysis of the ideologies of masculinity and femininity, of motherhood and (hetero)sexuality and the understanding and mapping of agency, access, and choice are central to this analysis and organizing. Thus, while my characterization of capitalist processes of domination and recolonization may appear somewhat overwhelming, I want to draw attention to the numerous forms of resistance and struggle that have also always been constitutive of the script of colonialism/capitalism. Capitalist patriarchies and racialized, class/caste-specific hierarchies are a key part of the long history of domination and exploitation of women, but struggles against these practices and vibrant, creative, collective forms of mobilization and organizing have also always been a part of our histories.

Teresa Amott and Julie Matthaei, in analyzing the U.S. labor market, argue that the intersection of gender, class, and racial-ethnic hierarchies of power has had two major effects:

> First, disempowered groups have been concentrated in jobs with lower pay, less job security, and more difficult working conditions. Second, workplaces have been places of extreme segregation, in which workers have worked in jobs only with members of their same racial-ethnic, gender, and class group, even though the particular racial-ethnic group and gender assigned to a job may have varied across firms and regions.[7]

While Amott and Matthaei draw attention to the sex-and-race typing of jobs, they do not *theorize* the relationship between this job typing and the social identity of the workers concentrated in these low-paying, segregated, often unsafe sectors of the labor market. While the economic history they chart is crucial to any understanding of the race-and-gender basis of U.S. capitalist processes, their analysis begs the question of whether there is a connection (other than the common history of domination of people of color) between *how* these jobs are defined and *who* is sought after for the jobs.

By examining two instances of the incorporation of women into the global economy (women lacemakers in Narsapur, India, and women in the electronics industry in the Silicon Valley) I want to delineate the interconnections between gender, race, and ethnicity, and the ideologies of work which locate women in particular exploitative contexts. The contradictory positioning of women along class, race, and ethnic lines in these two cases suggests that, in spite of the obvious geographical and sociocultural differences between the two contexts, the organization of the global economy by contemporary capital positions these workers in very similar ways, effectively reproducing and transforming locally specific hierarchies. There are also some significant continuities between home-work and factory work in these contexts, in terms of both the inherent ideologies of work as well as the experiences and social identities of women as workers. This tendency can also be seen in the case studies of black women workers (of Afro-Caribbean, Asian, and African origin) in Britain, especially women engaged in homework, factory work, and family businesses.[8]

HOUSEWIVES AND HOMEWORK: THE LACEMAKERS OF NARSAPUR

Maria Mies's 1982 study of the lacemakers of Narsapur, India, is a graphic illustration of how women bear the impact of development processes in countries where poor peasant and tribal societies are being "integrated" into an international division of labor under the dictates of capital accumulation. Mies's study illustrates how capitalist production relations are built upon the backs of women workers defined as *housewives*. Ideologies of gender and work and their historical transformation provide the necessary ground for the exploitation of the lacemakers. But the definition of women as housewives also suggests the heterosexualization of women's work—women are always defined in relation to men and conjugal marriage. Mies's account of the development of the lace industry and the corresponding relations of production illustrates fundamental transformations of gender, caste, and ethnic relations. The original caste distinctions between the feudal warrior castes (the landowners) and the Narsapur (poor Christians) and Serepalam (poor Kapus/Hindu agriculturalists) women are totally transformed through the development of the lace industry, and a new caste hierarchy is effected.

At the time of Mies's study, there were sixty lace manufacturers, with some 200,000 women in Narsapur and Serepalam constituting the workforce. Lace-making women worked six to eight hours a day, and ranged in age from six to eighty. Mies argues that the expansion of the lace industry between 1970 and 1978 and its integration into the world market led to class/caste differentiation within particular communities, with a masculinization of all nonproduction jobs (trade) and a total feminization of the production process. Thus, men sold women's products and lived on profits from women's labor. The polarization between men's and women's work, where men actually defined themselves as exporters and businessmen who invested in women's labor, bolstered the social and ideological definition of women as housewives and their work as "leisure time activity." In other words, work, in this context, was grounded in sexual identity, in concrete definitions of femininity, masculinity, and heterosexuality.

Two particular indigenous hierarchies, those of caste and gender, interacted to produce normative definitions of "women's work." Where, at the onset of the lace industry, Kapu men and women were agricultural laborers and it was the lower-caste Harijan women who were lacemakers, with the development of capitalist relations of production and the possibility of caste/class mobility it was the Harijan women who were agricultural laborers while the Kapu women undertook the "leisure time" activity of lacemaking. The caste-based ideology of seclusion and purdah was essential to the extraction of surplus value. Since purdah and the seclusion of women are a sign of higher caste status, the domestication of Kapu laborer women—where their (lacemaking) activity was tied to the concept of the "women sitting in the house"—was entirely within the logic of capital accumulation and profit. Now, Kapu women, not just the women of feudal, landowning castes, are in purdah as housewives producing for the world market.

Ideologies of seclusion and the domestication of women are clearly sexual, drawing as they do on masculine and feminine notions of protection and property. They are also heterosexual ideologies, based on the normative definition of women as wives, sisters, and mothers—always in relation to conjugal marriage and the "family." Thus, the caste transformation and separation of women along lines of domestication and nondomestication (Kapu housewives versus Harijan laborers) effectively link the work that women do with their sexual and caste/class identities. Domestication works, in this case, because of the persistence and legitimacy of the ideology of the housewife, which defines women in terms of their place within the home, conjugal marriage, and heterosexuality. The opposition between definitions of the "laborer" and of the "housewife" anchors the invisibility (and caste-related status) of work; in effect, it defines women as *non-workers*. By definition, housewives cannot be workers or laborers; housewives make male breadwinners and consumers possible. Clearly, ideologies of "women's place and work" have real material force in this instance, where spatial parameters construct and maintain gendered and caste-specific hierarchies. Thus, Mies's study illustrates the concrete effects of the social definition of women as housewives. Not only are the lacemakers invisible in census figures (after all, their work is leisure), but their definition as housewives makes possible the definition of men as "breadwinners." Here, class and gender proletarianization, through the development of capitalist relations of production and the integration of women into the world market, is possible because of the history and transformation of indigenous caste and sexual ideologies.

Reading the operation of capitalist processes from the position of the housewife/worker who produces for the world market makes the specifically gendered and caste/class opposition between laborer and the nonworker (housewife) visible. Moreover, it makes it possible to acknowledge and account for the hidden costs of women's labor. And, finally, it illuminates the fundamentally *masculine* definition of laborer/worker in a context where, as Mies says, men live off women who are the producers. Analyzing and transforming this masculine definition of labor, which is the mainstay of capitalist patriarchal cultures, is one of the most significant challenges we face. The effect of this definition of labor is not only that it makes women's labor and its costs invisible, but that it undercuts women's agency by defining them as victims of a process of pauperization or of "tradition" or "patriarchy," rather than as agents capable of making their own choices.

In fact, the contradictions raised by these choices are evident in the lacemakers' responses to characterizations of their own work as "leisure activity." While the fact that they did "work" was clear to them and while they had a sense of the history of their own pauperization (with a rise in prices for goods but no corresponding rise in wages), they were unable to explain how they came to be in the situation they found themselves. Thus, while some of the contradictions between their work and their roles as housewives and mothers were evident to them, they did not have access to an analysis of these contradictions which could lead to (a) seeing the complete picture in terms of their exploitation; (b) strategizing and organizing to transform their material situations; or (c) recognizing their common interests as women workers across caste/class lines. As a matter of fact, the Serepalam women defined their lacemaking in terms of "housework" rather than wage-work, and women who had managed to establish themselves as petty commodity producers saw what they did as entrepreneurial: they saw themselves as selling *products* rather than *labor*. Thus, in both cases, women internalized the ideologies that defined them as nonworkers. The isolation of the work context (work done in the house rather than in a public setting) as well as the internalization of caste and patriarchal ideologies thus militated against organizing as *workers*, or as *women*. However, Mies suggests that there were cracks in this ideology: the women expressed some envy toward agricultural laborers, whom the lacemakers saw as enjoying working together in the fields. What seems necessary in such a context, in terms of feminist mobilization, is a recognition of the fact that the identity of the housewife needs to be transformed into the identity of a "woman worker or working woman." Recognition of common interests as housewives is very different from recognition of common interests as women and as workers.

IMMIGRANT WIVES, MOTHERS, AND FACTORY WORK: ELECTRONICS WORKERS IN THE SILICON VALLEY

My discussion of the U.S. end of the global assembly line is based on studies by Naomi Katz and David Kemnitzer (1983) and Karen Hossfeld (1990) of electronics workers in the so-called Silicon Valley in California. An analysis of production strategies and processes indicates a significant ideological redefinition of normative ideas of factory work in terms of the Third World, immigrant women who constitute the primary workforce. While the lacemakers of Narsapur were located as *housewives* and their work defined as *leisure time activity* in a very complex international world market, Third World women in the electronics industry in the Silicon Valley are located as *mothers*, *wives*, and *supplementary* workers. Unlike the search for the "single" woman assembly worker in Third World countries, it is in part the ideology of the "married woman" which defines job parameters in the Valley, according to Katz and Kemnitzer's data.

Hossfeld also documents how existing ideologies of femininity cement the exploitation of the immigrant women workers in the Valley, and how the women often use this patriarchal logic against management. Assumptions of "single" and "married" women as the ideal workforce at the two geographical ends of the electronics global assembly line (which includes South Korea, Hong Kong, China, Taiwan, Thailand, Malaysia, Japan, India, Pakistan, the Philippines, and the United States, Scotland, and Italy) are anchored in normative understandings of femininity, womanhood, and sexual identity. The labels are predicated on sexual difference and the institution of heterosexual marriage and carry connotations of a "manageable" (docile?) labor force.[9]

Katz and Kemnitzer's data indicates a definition and transformation of women's work which relies on gender, race, and ethnic hierarchies already historically anchored in the U.S. Further, their data illustrates that the construction of "job labels" pertaining to Third World women's work is closely allied with their sexual and racial identities. While Hossfeld's more recent study reinforces some of Katz and Kemnitzer's conclusions, she focuses more specifically on how "contradictory ideologies about sex, race, class, and nationality are used as forms of both labor control and labor resistance in the capitalist workplace today."[10] Her contribution lies in charting the operation of gendered ideologies in the structuring of the industry and in analyzing what she calls "refeminization strategies" in the workplace.

Although the primary workforce in the Valley consists of Third World and newly immigrant women, substantial numbers of Third World and immigrant men are also employed by the electronics industry. In the early 1980s, 70,000 women held 80 to 90 percent of the operative or laborer jobs on the shop floor. Of these, 45 to 50 percent were Third World, especially Asian, immigrants. White men held either technician or supervisory jobs. Hossfeld's study was conducted between 1983 and 1986, at which time she estimates that up to 80 percent of the operative jobs were held by people of color, with women constituting up to 90 percent of the assembly workers. Katz and Kemnitzer maintain that the industry actively seeks sources of cheap labor by deskilling production and by using race, gender, and ethnic stereotypes to "attract" groups of workers who are "more suited" to perform tedious, unrewarding, poorly paid work. When interviewed, management personnel described the jobs as (a) un-skilled (as easy as a recipe); (b) requiring tolerance for tedious work (Asian women are therefore more suited); and (c) supplementary activity for women whose main tasks were mothering and housework.

It may be instructive to unpack these job labels in relation to the immigrant and Third World (married) women who perform the jobs. The job labels recorded by Katz and Kemnitzer need to be analyzed as definitions of *women's work*, specifically as definitions of *Third World/immigrant women's work*. First, the notion of "unskilled" as easy (like following a recipe) and the idea of tolerance for tedious work both have racial and gendered dimensions. Both draw upon stereotypes which infantilize Third World women and initiate a nativist discourse of "tedium" and "tolerance" as characteristics of non-Western, primarily agricultural, premodern (Asian) cultures. Second, defining jobs as sup-plementary activity for mothers and housewives adds a further dimension: sexual identity and appropriate notions of heterosexual femininity as marital domesticity. These are not part-time jobs, but they are defined as supplemen-tary. Thus, in this particular context (Third World) women's work needs are defined as temporary.

While Hossfeld's analysis of management logic follows similar lines, she offers a much more nuanced understanding of how the gender and racial stereotypes prevalent in the larger culture infuse worker consciousness and resistance. For instance, she draws attention to the ways in which factory jobs are seen by the workers as "unfeminine" or not "ladylike." Management exploits and reinforces these ideologies by encouraging women to view femininity as contradictory to factory work, by defining their jobs as secondary and temporary, and by asking women to choose between defining themselves as women or as workers. Woman-hood and femininity are thus defined along a domestic, familial model, with work seen as supplemental to this primary identity. Significantly, although 80 percent of the immigrant women in Hossfeld's study were the main income producers in their families, they still considered men to be the breadwinners.

Thus, as with the exploitation of Indian lacemakers as "housewives," Third World/immigrant women in the Silicon Valley are located as "mothers and homemakers" and only secondarily as workers. In both cases, men are seen as the real breadwinners. While (women's) work is usually defined as something that takes place in the "public" or production sphere, these ideologies clearly draw on stereotypes of women as home-bound. In addition, the *invisibility* of work in the Indian context can be compared to the *temporary/secondary* nature of work in the Valley. Like the Mies study, the data compiled by Hossfeld and Katz and Kemnitzer indicates the presence of local ideologies and hierarchies of gender and race as the basis for the exploitation of the electronics workers. The question that arises is: how do women understand their own positions and construct meanings in an exploitative job situation?

Interviews with electronics workers indicate that, contrary to the views of management, women do not see their jobs as temporary but as part of a lifetime strategy of upward mobility. Conscious of their racial, class, and gender status, they combat their devaluation as workers by increasing their income: by job-hopping, overtime, and moonlighting as pieceworkers. Note that, in effect, the "homework" that Silicon Valley workers do is performed under conditions very similar to the lacemaking of Narsapur women. Both kinds of work are done in the home, in isolation, with the worker paying her own overhead costs (like electricity and cleaning), with no legally mandated protections (such as a minimum wage, paid leave, health benefits, etc.). However, clearly the meanings attached to the work differ in both contexts, as does the way we understand them.

For Katz and Kemnitzer the commitment of electronics workers to class mobility is an important assertion of self. Thus, unlike in Narsapur, in the Silicon Valley homework has an entrepreneurial aspect for the women themselves. In fact, in Narsapur women's work turns the men into entrepreneurs! In the Valley, women take advantage of the contradictions of the situations they face as *individual workers*. While in Narsapur it is purdah and caste/class mobility which provide the necessary self-definition required to anchor women's work in the home as leisure activity, in the Silicon Valley it is a specifically *American* notion of individual ambition and entrepreneurship which provides the necessary ideological anchor for Third World women.

Katz and Kemnitzer maintain that this underground economy produces an *ideological* redefinition of jobs, allowing them to be defined as other than the basis of support of the historically stable, "comfortable," white, metropolitan working class. In other words, there is a clear connection between low wages and the definition of the job as supplementary, and the fact that the lifestyles of people of color are defined as different and cheaper. Thus, according to Katz and Kemnitzer, women and people of color continue to be "defined out" of the old industrial system and become targets and/or instruments of the ideological shift away from class toward national/ethnic/gender lines.[11] In this context, ideology and popular culture emphasize the individual maximization of options for personal success. Individual success is thus severed from union activity, political struggle, and collective relations. Similarly, Hossfeld suggests that it is the racist and sexist management logic of the needs of "immigrants" that allows the kind of exploitative labor processes that she documents.[12] However, in spite of Katz and Kemnitzer's complex analysis of the relationship of modes of production, social relations of production, culture, and ideology in the context of the Silicon Valley workers, they do not specify why it is Third World women who constitute the primary labor force. Similarly, while Hossfeld provides a nuanced analysis of the gendering of the workplace and the use of racial and gendered logic to consolidate capitalist accumulation, she also sometimes separates "women" and "minority workers,"[13] and does not specify why it is women of color who constitute the major labor force on the assembly lines in the Valley. In distinguishing between women and people of color, Katz and Kemnitzer tend to reproduce the old conceptual divisions of gender and race, where women are defined primarily in terms of their gender and people of color in terms of race. What is excluded is an *interactive* notion of gender and race, whereby women's gendered identity is grounded in race and people of color's racial identities are gendered.

I would argue that the data compiled by Katz and Kemnitzer and Hossfeld does, in fact, explain why Third World women are targeted for jobs in electronics factories. The explanation lies in the redefinition of work as temporary, supplementary, and unskilled, in the construction of women as mothers and homemakers, and in the positioning of femininity as contradictory to factory work. In addition, the explanation also lies in the specific definition of Third World, immigrant women as docile, tolerant, and satisfied with substandard wages. It is the ideological redefinition of women's work that provides the necessary understanding of this phenomenon. Hossfeld describes some strategies of resistance in which the workers utilize against management the very gendered and racialized logic that management uses against them. However, while these tactics may provide some temporary relief on the job, they build on racial and gender stereotypes which, in the long run, can be and are used against Third World women.

DAUGHTERS, WIVES, AND MOTHERS: MIGRANT WOMEN WORKERS IN BRITAIN

> Family businesses have been able to access minority women's labor power through mediations of kinship and an appeal to ideologies which emphasize the role of women in the home as wives and mothers and as keepers of family honor.[14]

In a collection of essays exploring the working lives of black and minority women inside and outside the home, Sallie Westwood and Parminder Bhachu focus on the benefits afforded the British capitalist state by the racial and gendered aspects of migrant women's labor. They point to the fact that what has been called the "ethnic economy" (the way migrants draw on resources to survive in situations where the combined effects of a hostile, racist environment and economic decline serve to oppress them) is also fundamentally a gendered economy. Statistics indicate that Afro-Caribbean and non-Muslim Asian women have a higher full-time labor participation rate than white women in the U.K. Thus, while the perception that black women (defined, in this case, as women of Afro-Caribbean, Asian, and African origin) are mostly concentrated in part-time jobs is untrue, the *forms* and *patterns* of their work lives within the context of homework and family firms, businesses where the entire family is involved in earning a living, either inside or outside the home, bears examination. Work by British feminist scholars[15] suggests that familial ideologies of domesticity and heterosexual marriage cement the economic and social exploitation of black women's labor within family firms. Repressive patriarchal ideologies, which fix the woman's role in the family, are grounded in inherited systems of inequality and oppression in black women's cultures of origin. And these very ideologies are reproduced and consolidated in order to provide the glue for profit-making in the context of the racialized British capitalist state.

For instance, Annie Phizacklea's work on Bangladeshi homeworkers in the British clothing industry in the West Midlands illuminates the extent to which family and community ties, maintained by women, are crucial in allowing this domestic subcontracting in the clothing industry to undercut the competition in terms of wages and long workdays and its cost to women workers. In addition, Sallie Westwood's work on Gujarati women factory workers in the East Midlands hosiery industry suggests that the power and creativity of the shop-floor culture—which draws on cultural norms of femininity, masculinity, and domesticity while simultaneously generating resistance and solidarity among the Indian and white women workers—is, in fact, anchored in Gujarati cultural inheritances. Discussing the contradictions in the lives of Gujarati women within the home and the perception that male family members have of their work as an extension of their family roles (not as a path to financial independence), Westwood elaborates on the continuities between the ideologies of domesticity within the household, which are the result of (often repressive) indigenous cultural values and practices, and the culture of the shop floor. Celebrating each other as daughters, wives, and mothers is one form of generating solidarity on the shop floor—but it is also a powerful refeminization strategy, in Hossfeld's terms.

Finally, family businesses, which depend on the cultural and ideological resources and loyalties within the family to transform ethnic "minority" women into workers committed to common familial goals, are also anchored in women's roles as daughters, wives, mothers, and keepers of family honor.[16] Women's work in family business is unpaid and produces dependencies that are similar to those of homeworkers whose labor, although paid, is invisible. Both are predicated on ideologies of domesticity and womanhood which infuse the spheres of production and reproduction. In discussing Cypriot women in family firms, Sasha Josephides cites the use of familial ideologies of "honor" and the construction of a "safe" environment outside the public sphere as the bases for a definition of femininity and womanhood (the perfect corollary to a paternal, protective definition of masculinity) that allows Cypriot women to see themselves as workers for their family, rather than as workers for themselves. All conflict around the question of work is thus accommodated within the context of the family. This is an important instance of the privatization of work, and of the redefinition of the identity of women workers in family firms as doing work that is a "natural extension" of their familial duties (not unlike the lacemakers). It is their identity as mothers, wives, and family members that stands in for their identity as workers.[17] Parminder Bhachu's work with Punjabi Sikhs also illustrates this fact. Citing the growth of small-scale entrepreneurship among South Asians as a relatively new trend in the British economy, Bhachu states that women workers in family businesses often end up losing autonomy and re-enter more traditional forms of patriarchal dominance where men control all or most of the economic resources within the family: "By giving up work, these women not only lose an independent source of income, and a large network of often female colleagues, but they also find themselves sucked back into the kinship system which emphasizes patrilaterality." Women thus lose a "direct relationship with the productive process," thereby raising the issue of the invisibility (even to themselves) of their identity as workers.[18]

This analysis of migrant women's work in Britain illustrates the parallel trajectory of their exploitation as workers within a different metropolitan context than the U.S. To summarize, all these case studies indicate ways in which ideologies of domesticity, femininity, and race form the basis of the construction of the notion of "women's work" for Third World women in the contemporary economy. In the case of the lacemakers, this is done through the definition of homework as leisure time activity and of the workers themselves as housewives. As discussed earlier, indigenous hierarchies of gender and caste/class make this definition possible. In the case of the electronics workers, women's work is defined as unskilled, tedious, and supplementary activity for mothers and homemakers. It is a specifically American ideology of individual success, as well as local histories of race and ethnicity, that constitute this definition. We can thus contrast the *invisibility* of the lacemakers as workers to the *temporary* nature of the work of Third World women in Silicon Valley. In the case of migrant women workers in family firms in Britain, work becomes an extension of familial roles and loyalties, and draws upon cultural and ethnic/racial ideologies of womanhood, domesticity, and entrepreneurship to consolidate patriarchal dependencies. In all these cases, ideas of flexibility, temporality, invisibility, and domesticity in the naturalization of categories of work are crucial in the construction of Third World women as an appropriate and cheap labor force. All of the above ideas rest on stereotypes about gender, race, and poverty, which in turn characterize Third World women as workers in the contemporary global arena.

Eileen Boris and Cynthia Daniels claim that "homework belongs to the decentralization of production that seems to be a central strategy of some sectors and firms for coping with the international restructuring of production, consumption, and capital accumulation."[19] Homework assumes a significant role in the contemporary capitalist global economy. The discussion of homework performed by Third World women in the three geographical spaces discussed above—India, the U.S., and Britain—suggests something specific about capitalist strategies of recolonization at this historical juncture.

Homework emerged at the same time as factory work in the early nineteenth century in the U.S., and, as a system, has always reinforced the conjoining of capitalism and patriarchy. Analyzing the homeworker as a wage laborer (rather than an entrepreneur who controls both her labor and the market for it) dependent on the employer for work, which is carried out usually in the "home" or domestic premises, makes it possible to understand the *systematic* invisibility of this form of work. What allows this work to be so fundamentally exploitative as to be invisible as a form of work are ideologies of domesticity, dependency, and (hereto)sexuality, which designate women—in this case, Third World women—as primarily housewives/mothers and men as economic supporters/ breadwinners. Homework capitalizes on the equation of home, family, and patriarchial and racial/cultural ideologies of femininity/masculinity with work. This is work done at home, in the midst of doing housework, childcare, and other tasks related to "homemaking," often work that never ceases. Characterizations of "housewives," "mothers," and "homemakers" make it impossible to see homeworkers as workers earning regular wages and entitled to the rights of workers. Thus, not just their *production*, but homeworkers' *exploitation* as workers, can, in fact, also remain invisible, contained within domestic, patriarchal relations in the family. This is a form of work that often falls outside accounts of wage labor, as well as accounts of household dynamics.[20]

Family firms in Britain represent a similar ideological pattern, within a different class dynamic. Black women imagine themselves as entrepreneurs (rather than as wage laborers) working for the prosperity of their families in a racist society. However, the work they do is still seen as an extension of their familial roles and often creates economic and social dependencies. This does not mean that women in family firms never attain a sense of autonomy, but that, as a system, the operation of family business exploits Third World women's labor by drawing on and reinforcing indigenous hierarchies in the search for upward mobility in the (racist) British capitalist economy. What makes this form of work in the contemporary global capitalist arena so profoundly exploitative is that its invisibility (both to the market, and sometimes to the workers themselves) is premissed on deeply ingrained sexist and racist relationships within and outside heterosexual kinship systems. This is also the reason why changing the gendered relationships that anchor homework and organizing homeworkers become such challenges for feminists.

The analysis of factory work and family business in Britain and of homework in all three geographical locations raises the question of whether homework and factory work would be defined in these particular ways if the workers were single women. In this case, the construct of the worker is dependent on gender ideologies. In fact, the idea of work or labor as necessary for the psychic, material, and spiritual survival and development of women workers is absent. Instead, it is the identity of women as housewives, wives, and mothers (identities also defined outside the parameters of work) that is assumed to provide the basis for women's survival and growth. These Third World women are defined out of the labor/capital process as if work in their case isn't necessary for economic, social, psychic autonomy, independence, and self-determination—a nonalienated relation to work is a conceptual and practical impossibility in this situation.

COMMON INTERESTS/DIFFERENT NEEDS: COLLECTIVE STRUGGLES OF POOR WOMEN WORKERS

Thus far, this essay has charted the ideological commonalities of the exploitation of (mostly) poor Third World women workers by global capitalist economic processes in different geographical locations. How do we conceptualize the question of "common interests" based in a "common context of struggle," such that women are agents who make choices and decisions that lead to the transformation of consciousness and of their daily lives as workers?

As discussed earlier, with the current domination in the global arena of the arbitrary interests of the market and of transnational capital, older signposts and definitions of capital/labor or of "the worker" or even of "class struggle" are no longer totally accurate or viable conceptual or organizational categories. It is, in fact, the predicament of poor working women and their experiences of survival and resistance in the creation of new organizational forms to earn a living and improve their daily lives that offers new possibilities for struggle and action.[21] In this instance, then, the experiences of Third World women workers are relevant for understanding and transforming the work experiences and daily lives of poor women everywhere. The rest of this essay explores these questions by suggesting a working definition of the question of the common interests of Third World women workers in the contemporary global capitalist economy, drawing on the work of feminist political theorist Anna G. Jonasdottir.

Jonasdottir explores the concept of women's interests in participatory democratic political theory. She emphasizes both the formal and the content aspects of a theory of social and political interests that refers to "different layers of social existence: agency and the needs/desires that give strength and meaning to agency."[22] Adjudicating between political analysts who theorize common interests in formal terms (i.e. the claim to actively "be among," to choose to participate in defining the terms of one's own existence, or acquiring the conditions for choice) and those who reject the concept of interests in favor of the concept of (subjective) individualized, and group-based "needs and desires" (the consequences of choice), Jonasdottir formulates a concept of the common interests of women that emphasizes the former, but is a combination of both perspectives. She argues that the formal aspect of interest (an active "being among") is crucial: "Understood historically, and seen as emerging from people's lived

experiences, interests about basic processes of social life are divided systematically between groups of people insofar as their living conditions are systematically different. Thus, historically and socially defined, interests can be
characterized as 'objective.'"[23] In other words, there are systematic material and
historical bases for claiming Third World women workers have common interests.
However, Jonasdottir suggests that the second aspect of theorizing interest, the
satisfaction of needs and desires (she distinguishes between agency and the result
of agency), remains an open question. Thus, the *content* of needs and desires from
the point of view of interest remains open for subjective interpretation.

How does this theorization relate to conceptualizations of the common interests of Third World women workers? Jonasdottir's distinction between agency
and the result of agency is a very useful one in this instance. The challenges for
feminists in this arena are (a) understanding Third World women workers as
having objective interests in common as workers (they are thus agents and make
choices as workers); and (b) recognizing the contradictions and dislocations in
women's own consciousness of themselves as workers, and thus of their needs
and desires—which sometimes militate against organizing on the basis of their
common interests (the results of agency).

In the case of women workers in the free-trade zones in a number of
countries, trade unions have been the most visible forum for expressing the
needs and demands of poor women. The sexism of trade unions, however, has
led women to recognize the need for alternative, more democratic organizational structures, and to form women's unions (as in Korea, China, Italy, and
Malaysia)[24] or to turn to community groups, church committees, or feminist
organizations. In the U.S., Third World immigrant women in electronics factories
have often been hostile to unions, which they recognize as clearly modeled in
the image of the white, male, working-class American worker. Thus, church
involvement in immigrant women workers' struggles has been an important
form of collective struggle in the U.S.[25]

Women workers have developed innovative strategies of struggle in women's
unions. For instance, in 1989 the Korean Women Workers Association staged an
occupation of the factory in Masan. They moved into the factory and lived
there, cooked meals, guarded the machines and premises, and effectively stopped
production.[26] In this form of occupation of the work premises, the processes of
daily life become constitutive of resistance (also evident in the welfare rights
struggles in the U.S.) and opposition is anchored in the systematic realities of
the lives of poor women. It expresses not only their common interests as
workers, but acknowledges their social circumstance as *women* for whom the
artificial separation of work and home has little meaning. This "occupation" is
a strategy of collective resistance that draws attention to poor women workers
building community as a form of survival.

Kumudhini Rosa makes a similar argument in her analysis of the "habits of
resistance" of women workers in Free Trade Zones (FTZs) in Sri Lanka,
Malaysia, and the Philippines.[27] The fact that women live and work together in

these FTZs is crucial in analyzing the ways in which they build community life, share resources and dreams, provide mutual support and aid on the assembly line and in the street, and develop individual and collective habits of resistance. Rosa claims that these forms of resistance and mutual aid are anchored in a "culture of subversion" in which women living in patriarchal, authoritarian households, where they are required to be obedient and disciplined, acquire practice in "concealed forms of rebelling."[28] Thus, women workers engage in "spontaneous" strikes in Sri Lanka, "wildcat" strikes in Malaysia, and "sympathy" strikes in the Philippines. They also support each other by systematically lowering the production target, or helping slow workers to meet the production targets on assembly lines. Rosa's analysis illustrates recognition of the common interests of women workers at a formal "being among" level. While women are conscious of the contradictions of their daily lives as women and as workers, and enact their resistance, they have not organized actively to identify their collective needs and to transform the conditions of their daily lives.

While the earlier section on the ideological construction of work in terms of gender and racial/ethnic hierarchies discussed homework as one of the most acute forms of exploitation of poor Third World women, it is also the area in which some of the most creative and transformative collective organizing has occurred. The two most visibly successful organizational efforts in this arena are the Working Women's Forum (WWF) and SEWA (Self-Employed Women's Association) in India, both registered as independent trade unions, and focusing on incorporating homeworkers, as well as petty traders, hawkers, and laborers in the informal economy into their membership.[29]

There has also been a long history of organizing homeworkers in Britain. Discussing the experience of the West Yorkshire Homeworking Group in the late 1980s, Jane Tate states that

> a homework campaign has to work at a number of levels, in which the personal inter-connects with the political, the family situation with work, lobbying Parliament with small local meetings. In practical terms, the homeworking campaigns have adopted a way of organizing that reflects the practice of many women's groups, as well as being influenced by the theory and practice of community work. It aims to bring out the strength of women, more often in small groups with a less formal structure and organization than in a body such as a union.[30]

Issues of race, ethnicity, and class are central in this effort since most of the homeworkers are of Asian or Third World origin. Tate identifies a number of simultaneous strategies used by the West Yorkshire Group to organize homeworkers: pinpointing and making visible the "real" employer (or the real enemy), rather than directing organizational efforts only against local subsidiaries; consumer education and pressure, which links the buying of goods to homeworker struggles; fighting for a code of work practice for suppliers by forming alliances between trade unions, women's organizations, and consumer groups; linking campaigns to the development of alternative trade organizations (for instance,

SEWA); fighting for visibility in international bodies like the ILO; and, finally, developing transnational links between local grassroots homeworker organizations—thus sharing resources and strategies, and working toward empowerment. The common interests of homeworkers are acknowledged in terms of their daily lives as workers and as women—there is no artificial separation of the "worker" and the "homemaker" or the "housewife" in this context.

Swasti Mitter discusses the success of SEWA and WWF in terms of (a) their representing the potential for organizing powerful women workers' organizations (the membership of WWF is 85,000 and that of SEWA is 46,000 workers) when effective strategies are used; and (b) making these "hidden" workers visible as *workers* to national and international policymakers. Both WWF and SEWA address the demands of poor women workers, and both include a development plan for women which includes leadership training, childcare, women's banks, and producer's cooperatives which offer alternative trading opportunities. Renana Jhabvala, SEWA's secretary, explains that, while SEWA was born in 1972 in the Indian labor movement and drew inspiration from the women's movement, it always saw itself as a part of the cooperative movement as well. Thus, struggling for poor women workers' rights always went hand in hand with strategies to develop alternative economic systems.

This emphasis on the extension of cooperative (or democratic) principles to poor women, the focus on political and legal literacy, education for critical and collective consciousness, and developing strategies for collective (and sometimes militant) struggle *and* for economic, social, and psychic development, makes SEWA's project a deeply feminist, democratic, and transformative one. Self-employed women are some of the most disenfranchised in Indian society—they are vulnerable economically, in caste terms, physically, sexually, and in terms of their health, and of course they are socially and politically invisible. Thus, they are also one of the most difficult constituencies to organize. The simultaneous focus on collective struggle for equal rights and justice (struggle against), coupled with economic development on the basis of cooperative, democratic principles of sharing, education, self-reliance, and autonomy (struggle for), is what is responsible for SEWA's success at organizing poor, home-based, women workers. Jhabvala summarizes this when she says,

> The combination of trade union and cooperative power makes it possible not only to defend members but to present an ideological alternative. Poor women's cooperatives are a new phenomenon. SEWA has a vision of the cooperative as a form of society which will bring about more equal relationships and lead to a new type of society.[31]

SEWA appears to come closest to articulating the common interests and needs of Third World women workers in the terms that Jonasdottir elaborates. SEWA organizes on the basis of the objective interests of poor women workers; both the trade-union and cooperative development aspects of the organizational strategies illustrate this. The status of poor women workers as workers and as citizens entitled to rights and justice is primary. But SEWA also approaches the deeper level of the articulation of needs and desires based on recognition of subjective, collective interests. As discussed earlier, it is this level of the recognition and articulation of common interest that is the challenge for women workers globally. While the common interests of women workers *as workers* have been variously articulated in the forms of struggles and organization reviewed above, the transition to identifying common needs and desires (the *content* aspect of interest) of Third World women workers, which leads potentially to the construction of the *identity* of Third World women workers, is what remains a challenge—a challenge that perhaps SEWA comes closest to identifying and addressing.

I have argued that the particular location of Third World women workers at this moment in the development of global capitalism provides a vantage point from which to (a) make particular practices of domination and recolonization visible and transparent, thus illuminating the minute and global processes of capitalist recolonization of women workers, and (b) understand the commonalities of experiences, histories, and identity as the basis for solidarity and in organizing Third World women workers transnationally. My claim here is that the definition of the social identity of women as workers is not only class-based but, in this case, must be grounded in understandings of race, gender, and caste histories and experiences of work. In effect, I suggest that homework is one of the most significant and repressive forms of "women's work" in contemporary global capitalism. In pointing to the ideology of the "Third World woman worker" created in the context of a global division of labor, I am articulating differences located in specific histories of inequality: histories of gender and caste/class in the Narsapur context, and histories of gender, race, and liberal individualism in the Silicon Valley and in Britain.

However, my argument does not suggest that these are discrete and separate histories. In focusing on women's work as a particular form of Third World women's exploitation in the contemporary economy, I also want to foreground a particular history that Third and First World women seem to have in common: the logic and operation of capital in the contemporary global arena. I maintain that the interests of contemporary transnational capital and the strategies employed enable it to draw upon indigenous social hierarchies and to construct, reproduce, and maintain ideologies of masculinity/femininity, technological superiority, appropriate development, skilled/unskilled labor, and so on. Here I have argued this in terms of the category of "women's work," which I have shown to be grounded in an ideology of the Third World women worker. Thus, analysis of the location of Third World women in the new international division of labor must draw upon the histories of colonialism and race, class and capitalism, gender and patriarchy, and sexual and familial figurations. Analysis of the ideological definition and redefinition of women's work thus indicates a political basis for common struggles, and it is this particular forging of the political unity of Third World women workers that I would like to endorse. This is in opposition to ahistorical notions of the common experience, exploitation, or strength of Third World women or between Third and First World women, which serve to naturalize normative Western feminist categories of self and other. If Third World women are to be seen as the *subjects of theory and of struggle*, we must pay attention to the specificities of their/our common *and* different histories.

In summary, this essay highlights the following analytic and political issues pertaining to Third World women workers in the global arena: (1) it writes a particular group of women workers into history and into the operation of contemporary capitalist hegemony; (2) it charts the links and potential for solidarity between women workers across the borders of nation-states, based on demystifying the ideology of the masculinized worker; (3) it exposes a domesticated definition of Third World women's work to be in actuality a strategy of global capitalist recolonization; (4) it suggests that women have common interests as workers, not just in transforming their work lives and environments, but in redefining home spaces so that homework is recognized as work to earn a living rather than as leisure of supplemental activity; (5) it foregrounds the need for feminist liberatory knowledge as the basis of feminist organizing and collective struggles for economic and political justice; (6) it provides a working definition of the common interests of Third World women workers based on theorizing the common social identity of Third World women as women/workers; and, finally, (7) it reviews the habits of resistance, forms of collective struggle, and strategies of organizing of poor, Third World women workers. Irma is right when she says that "the only way to get a little measure of power over your own life is to do it collectively, with the support of other people who share your needs." The question of defining common interests and needs such that the identity of Third World women workers forms a potentially revolutionary basis for struggles against capitalist recolonization, and for feminist self-determination and autonomy, is a complex one. However, as maquiladora worker Veronica Vasquez and the women in SEWA demonstrate, women are already waging such struggles. The end of the twentieth century may be characterized by the exacerbation of the sexual politics of global capitalist domination and exploitation, but it is also suggestive of the dawning of a renewed politics of hope and solidarity.

NOTES

1. See Karen Hossfeld, "United States: Why Aren't High-Tech Workers Organised?" in Women Working Worldwide, eds., *Common Interests: Women Organizing in Global Electronics* (London: Black Rose Press, 1991), 33–52, esp. 50–51.
2. Karen Brodkin Sacks, "Introduction," in Karen Brodkin Sacks and D. Remy, eds., *My Troubles Are Going to Have Trouble with Me: Everyday Trials and Triumphs of Women Workers* (New Brunswick: Rutgers University Press, 1984), esp. 10–11.
3. Jeremy Brecher, "The Hierarch's New World Order—and Ours," in Jeremy S. Brecher et al., eds., *Global Visions, Beyond the New World Order* (Boston: South End Press, 1993), 3–12.

4. See Maria Mies, *Patriarchy and Accumulation on a World Scale: Women in the International Division of Labor* (London: Zed Books, 1986), 114–15.

5. Richard J. Barnet and John Cavanagh, *Global Dreams: Imperial Corporations and the New World Order* (New York: Simon & Schuster, 1994), esp. 25–41.

6. For examples of cross-national feminist organizing around these issues, see the following texts: Gita Sahgal and Nira Yuval Davis, eds., *Refusing Holy Orders, Women and Fundamentalism in Britain* (London: Virago, 1992); Valentine M. Moghadam, *Identity Politics and Women, Cultural Reassertions and Feminisms in International Perspective* (Boulder: Westview Press, 1994); *Claiming Our Place, Working the Human Rights System to Women's Advantage* (Washington, D.C.: Institute for Women, Law and Development, 1993); Sheila Rowbotham and Swasti Mitter, eds., *Dignity and Daily Bread: New Forms of Economic Organizing among Poor Women in the Third World and the First* (New York: Routledge, 1994); and Julie Peters and Andrea Wolper, eds., *Women's Rights, Human Rights: International Feminist Perspectives* (New York: Routledge, 1995).

7. Teresa L. Amott and Julie A. Matthaei, *Race, Gender and Work: A Multicultural Economic History of Women in the United States* (Boston: South End Press, 1991), 316–17.

8. The case studies I analyze are: Maria Mies, *The Lacemakers of Narsapur, Indian Housewives Produce for the World Market* (London: Zed Books, 1982); Naomi Katz and David Kemnitzer, "Fast Forward: The Internationalization of the Silicon Valley," in June Nash and M. P. Fernandez-Kelly, *Women, Men, and the International Division of Labor* (Albany: SUNY Press, 1983), 273–331; Naomi Katz and David Kemnitzer, "Women and Work in the Silicon Valley," in Sacks and Remy, eds., *My Troubles Are Going to Have Trouble with Me*, 193–208; and Karen J. Hossfeld, "Their Logic Against Them: Contradictions in Sex, Race, and Class in the Silicon Valley," in Kathryn Ward, ed., *Women Workers and Global Restructuring* (Ithaca: Cornell University Press, 1990), 149–78. I also draw on case studies of black women workers in the British context in Sallie Westwood and Parminder Bhachu, eds., *Enterprising Women* (New York: Routledge, 1988).

9. Hossfeld, "United States." Aihwa Ong's discussion of the various modes of surveillance of young Malaysian factory women as a way of discursively producing and constructing notions of feminine sexuality is also applicable in this context where "single" and "married" assume powerful connotations of sexual control. See Aihwa Ong, *Spirits of Resistance and Capitalist Discipline: Factory Women in Malaysia* (Albany: SUNY Press, 1987).

10. Hossfeld, "Their Logic Against Them," 149. Hossfeld states that she spoke to workers from at least thirty Third World nations (including Mexico, Vietnam, the Philippines, Korea, China, Cambodia, Laos, Thailand, Malaysia, Indonesia, India, Pakistan, Iran, Ethiopia, Haiti, Cuba, El Salvador, Nicaragua, Guatemala, Venezuela, as well as southern Europe, especially Portugal and Greece). It may be instructive to pause and reflect on the implications of this level of racial and national diversity on the shop floor in the Silicon Valley. While all these workers are defined as "immigrants," a number of them as recent immigrants, the racial, ethnic, and gender logic of capitalist strategies of recolonization in this situation locate all the workers in similar relationships to the management, as well as to the U.S. state.

11. Assembly lines in the Silicon Valley are often divided along race, ethnic, and gender lines, with workers competing against each other for greater productivity. Individual worker choices, however imaginative or ambitious, do not transform the system. Often they merely undercut the historically won benefits of the metropolitan working class. Thus, while moonlighting, overtime, and job-hopping are indications of individual modes of resistance and of an overall strategy of class mobility, it is these

very aspects of worker's choices which support an underground domestic economy that evades or circumvents legal, institutionalized, or contractual arrangements that add to the indirect wages of workers.

12. Hossfeld, "Their Logic Against Them," 149: "You're paid less because women are different than men" or "Immigrants need less to get by."

13. Ibid., 176.

14. Westwood and Bhachu, "Introduction," *Enterprising Women*, 5. See also, in the same collection, Annie Phizacklea, "Entrepreneurship, Ethnicity and Gender," 20–33; Parminder Bhachu, "Apni Marzi Kardhi Home and Work: Sikh Women in Britain," 76–102; Sallie Westwood, "Workers and Wives: Continuities and Discontinuities in the Lives of Gujarati Women," 103–31; and Sasha Josephides, "Honor, Family, and Work: Greek Cypriot Women Before and After Migration," 34–57.

15. Phizacklea, "Entrepreneurship, Ethnicity and Gender"; Westwood, "Workers and Wives"; Josephides, "Honor, Family, and Work"; and others.

16. See Josephides, "Honor, Family, and Work"; Bhachu, "Apni Marzi Kardhi."

17. Josephides, "Honor, Family, and Work."

18. Bhachu, "Apni Marzi Kardhi"; quotation at 85.

19. For a thorough discussion of the history and contemporary configurations of home-work in the U.S., see Eileen Boris and Cynthia R. Daniels, eds., *Homework, Historical and Contemporary Perspectives on Paid Labor at Home* (Urbana: University of Illinois Press, 1989). See especially "Introduction," 1–12; M. Patricia Femandez-Kelly and Anna Garcia, "Hispanic Women and Homework: Women in the Informal Economy of Miami Los Angeles," 165–82; and Sheila Allen, "Locating Homework in an Analysis of the Ideological and Material Constraints on Women's Paid Work," 272–91.

20. Allen, "Locating Homework."

21. See Rowbotham and Mitter, "Introduction," in Rowbotham and Mitter, eds., *Dignity and Daily Bread*.

22. Anna G. Jonasdottir, "On the Concept of Interest Women's Interests, and the Limitations of Interest Theory," in Kathleen Jones and Anna G. Jonasdottir, eds., *The Political Interests of Gender* (London: Sage Publications, 1988), 33–65, esp. 57.

23. Ibid., 41.

24. See Women Working Worldwide, eds., *Common Interests*.

25. Ibid., 38.

26. Ibid., 31.

27. Kumudhini Rosa, "The Conditions and Organisational Activities of Women in Free Trade Zones: Malaysia, Philippines and Sri Lanka, 1970–1990," in Rowbotham and Mitter, eds., *Dignity and Daily Bread*, 73–99, esp. 86.

28. Ibid., 86.

29. Swasti Mitter, "On Organising Women in Causalized Work: A Global Overview," in Rowbotham and Mitter, eds., *Dignity and Daily Bread*, 14–52, esp. 33.

30. Jane Tate, "Homework in West Yorkshire," in Rowbotham and Mitter, eds., *Dignity and Daily Bread*, 193–217, esp. 203.

31. Renana Jhabvala, "Self-Employed Women's Association: Organising Women by Struggle and Development," in Rowbotham and Mitter, eds., *Dignity and Daily Bread*, 114-38, 135.

THE HIDDEN HISTORY OF AFFIRMATIVE ACTION: WORKING WOMEN'S STRUGGLES IN THE 1970s AND THE GENDER OF CLASS

NANCY MACLEAN

> If feminism is taken to be a recognition that women as a sex suffer inequalities and a commitment to the elimination of these sex-based hierarchies, then the struggles of union women for pay equity and for mechanisms to lessen the double burden of home and work should be as central to the history of twentieth-century feminism as the battle for the enactment of the Equal Rights Amendment.[1]

In 1993, the New York City Fire Department issued a curious order: no pictures could be taken of Brenda Berkman, on or off duty, inside or outside of a firehouse. Berkman was a firefighter, a fifteen-year veteran of the force. The order was the latest shot in a protracted battle against her and others like her: women claiming the ability to do a job that had been a men's preserve for all of the Fire Department's 117-year, tradition-conscious history. The struggle began in 1977, when the City first allowed women to take the Firefighter Exam—and then promptly changed the rules on the physical agility section when four hundred women passed the written portion of the test. Five years and a victorious class-action suit for sex discrimination later, forty-two women passed the new, court-supervised tests and training and went on to become the first female firefighters in New York's history. Among them was Berkman, founding president of the United Women Firefighters, and the most visible and outspoken of the group.[2]

Frozen out by white male co-workers and betrayed by the firefighters' union, the women found their only dependable internal allies in the Vulcan Society, the organization of black male firefighters, who had themselves fought a long battle against discrimination in the Fire Department. They now stood by the women, even to the point of testifying in support of their class-action suit, despite "enormous pressure to remain silent." The tensions surrounding the entrance of women into the fire department were explosive, though women constituted a mere 0.3 percent of the City's 13,000-member uniformed fire force. Like the no-photographs order from the top, the uncoordinated acts of hostility from would-be peers, alongside the support of the Vulcan Society, signal us that a great deal was at stake. Even in cases less egregious than the New York firefighters, the boundary crossing backed by affirmative action affected something that mattered deeply to many men, especially many white men, in a way that often transcended logic.[3]

Yet, historians of the modern U.S. have only begun to examine workplace-based sex discrimination and affirmative action struggles such as those of the United Women Firefighters. More attention is in order. On the one hand, disgust with discrimination and low-paying, dead-end jobs moved large numbers of working women to collective action in the last quarter century. On the other hand, these struggles produced an unprecedented assault not just on previously unyielding patterns of occupational sex and race segregation and the economic inequality stemming from them, but also on the gender system that sustained men's power and women's disadvantage and marked some women as more appropriate for certain types of work than others. In challenging discrimination and demanding affirmative action, in fact, the struggles described here redefined gender, race, and class, by undermining associations built up over more than a century (some historians would say far longer in the case of gender and class). These associations led men and women to have some sharply different experiences of what it meant to be working class. And though my focus here is on the transformation in class and gender specifically, race is deeply embedded in both of these categories and in the associations they carry, if not always accessible in the extant sources.

Anti-discrimination and affirmative action struggles challenged this system of expectations and the patterns of inequality it perpetuated. Time and again, the system-recasting properties of affirmative action proved necessary to ensure equal treatment. Breaking down job ghettos and the habits that kept them in place required new practices such as wide advertising of job openings, recruitment from new sources, the analysis of jobs to determine skill requirements, the setting up of training programs to teach those skills, and in some cases the setting of specific numerical goals and timetables for recruiting and promoting women (impugned misleadingly by critics as "quotas"). By performing old work in new ways and by breaking into new jobs formerly closed to them, the women involved in these efforts began, in effect, to reconstitute gender, and with it class, permanently destabilizing the once-hegemonic distinction between "women's work" and "men's work." To reconstitute is not to root out, of course: class inequality is if anything more shamelessly robust today than it was a quarter-century ago. Yet the *meaning* of particular class positions and experiences of them have shifted with the entrance of minority men and women of all groups in ways that invite attention. That we have forgotten how dramatic and radical a departure this was is a tribute to the success of their efforts.

In what follows, I will sketch out a preliminary reading of the story of women and affirmative action, focusing on three types of collective action that became widespread in the 1970s. In the first type, a decentralized mass movement arose as working women across the country took hold of the new ideas in circulation about gender, applied them to their own situations, and agitated for change, typically through the vehicle of ad hoc women's caucuses that involved women in a range of job categories. In the second type, full-time organizers sought to expand these caucus efforts into city-wide organizations for working women in clerical jobs. And in the third variant, individual low-income women and advocates for them turned to affirmative action as an anti-poverty strategy for women, particularly female household heads, and began a concerted push for access to "nontraditional" blue-collar jobs for women. Those involved in all three efforts worked to mobilize working women across racial and race and ethnic lines. Although smaller numbers of women of color became involved in the first two forms of collective action, they became especially visible in campaigns for "nontraditional" employment.

WOMEN'S CAUCUSES

To appreciate what has changed in the last quarter-century and why struggles such as the New York City firefighters became so pitched, it helps to consider some of the associations between gender and class that workers of this era— male and female—inherited. The most relevant cases are secretarial work and construction, both of which would become sites of contestation in the 1970s. Interestingly, however, the first big challenges to sex discrimination in the 1960s did not come from either of these poles on the spectrum of gendered employment. Rather, the challenges came from wage-earning women in factory jobs, who discovered a new resource in legislation won by the civil rights movement in 1964.

Alice Peurala, for example, who had been stymied each time she tried for promotion since she was first hired at U.S. Steel Corporation in 1953, said that when the Civil Rights Act came along "I thought, here's my chance." The protests of women such as Peurala, we can see now, prompted the development of an organized feminist movement. It was, after all, the Equal Employment Opportunities Commission's (EEOC) negligence in handling these charges of sex discrimination that led to the formation of the National Organization for Women (NOW), whose founders included labor organizers and women of color as well as their more well-known, affluent, white counterparts. In other words, noted the labor historian Dennis Deslippe, "women unionists did not merely complement the efforts of middle-class feminists; they helped construct second-wave feminism."[4]

Such efforts were brought to the attention of a broad audience by the mass media. By the early 1970s, television news, magazines, and newspapers all carried stories about sex discrimination in employment and women's struggles against it, as well as reports of the wider women's movement. The gender consciousness promoted by such stories stimulated women to look at their jobs afresh, and to imagine class itself in new ways. By 1970, large numbers of American women began to act on this new thinking at work. Borrowing a tactic from mostly male, blue-collar African Americans, and taking strength from the general ferment among rank-and-file workers in the early 1970s, symbolized by the famed Lordstown wildcat strike, these women joined together with like-minded co-workers to build women's caucuses as their characteristic vehicle of struggle. The caucuses embodied, in effect, a new social theory: blacks of both sexes and women of all races who joined together implicitly announced that traditional class tools were ill-suited to the issues that concerned them. In form, the caucuses crossed divisions of occupation in order to overcome the isolation and competition that allowed their members to be pitted against one another. Using separate structures, they fought not simply to achieve racial and gender integration at work but to redefine it.

The caucuses spread rapidly within a few years, one sparking the next like firecrackers on a string. Women were organizing in steel plants and auto factories, in banks and large corporations, in federal and university employment, in trade unions and professional associations, and in newspaper offices and television networks. Few sites remained undisturbed.[5] While women's historians have shown how consciousness-raising groups—mainly white and middle class—broadened and deepened the women's movement, the importance of these caucuses—working class and sometimes mixed race—has been overlooked. Caucuses not only developed a critical consciousness among working women but also won tangible improvements. Without their efforts, Title VII would have been a dead letter for women.[6]

These early women's caucuses nearly always came about because some women suddenly rejected some expectation arising from contemporary constructions of gender and class. "*Without exception*," a contemporary news story reported (using italics to drive home the point), "*a principal demand of the women's caucuses is for respect*." Often a small slight triggered a sense among the women that a broader pattern of discrimination had been just been revealed.

In virtually every case where women's caucuses came together, demands for affirmative action emerged logically out of the struggle against discrimination. So striking is this pattern that I have yet to come across a case in which participants *did not* see affirmative action as critical to the solution. Examples are legion: they range from the *New York Times* group, to steel workers, telephone operators, and NBC female employees, 600 of 900 of whom were secretaries when they began organizing in 1971. Even the Coalition of Labor Union Women (CLUW), loyal to a trade-union officialdom skeptical about affirmative action, came out strongly in its favor. Successful efforts by African-American men to wield affirmative action as a battering ram against discrimination only reinforced women's resolve.

Time and again, it was affirmative action that women embraced to open the advertising of jobs, broaden outreach for recruitment, introduce job analysis and training, set specific numerical goals for recruiting and promoting women, and mandate timetables for achieving these changes, all commitments for which management would be held accountable. As early as 1971, NOW literature was thus proclaiming affirmative action as "the key to ending job discrimination," and numerical goals and timetables as "the heart of affirmative action." Typically, and contrary to the notion that affirmative action benefitted only privileged women, these plans covered the gamut of female employees. No longer restricted to clerical and cleaning work, women in lower-paying positions—black and white—could now get more lucrative jobs as, for example, security guards, machine operators, mail carriers, and commissioned salespeople.[7]

CLERICALS

Yet, the largest single number of wage-earning women—one in three—remained in clerical jobs, and they became the target of the second kind of organizing initiative. These jobs were among the most sex-segregated: in 1976, for example, women made up 91.1 percent of bank tellers and 98.5 percent of secretaries and typists. The income of clerical workers fell below that of male wage earners in every category except farming.[8] Seeking to make the women's movement more relevant to working-class women, some feminists set out in 1973 to develop an organizing form geared to women office workers and to build a network that could spread the new consciousness. "The women's movement was not speaking to large numbers of working women," remembered Karen Nussbaum, one of the national leaders of the effort; "we narrowed the focus of our concerns, in order to broaden our base." Among the groups thus created were 9 to 5 (Boston), Women Employed (Chicago), Women Office Workers (New York), Cleveland Women Working, Women Organized for Employment (San Francisco), and Baltimore Working Women. By the end of the 1970s, a dozen such groups existed and had affiliated with an umbrella network called Working Women; together they claimed a membership of eight thousand. The racial composition of the groups varied by locality, but black women appeared to participate in larger numbers in these than in the women's caucuses, sometimes making up as much as one-third of the membership.[9]

What linked them all together was a categorical rejection of the peculiar gender burdens of their work: above all, the low pay and demands for personal service. Appropriating National Secretaries' Day for their own purposes, the groups demonstrated for "Raises, Not Roses!" and a "Bill of Rights" for office workers. "What we're saying," as one 9 to 5 speaker explained in 1974, "is that an office worker is not a personal servant, and she deserves to be treated with respect and to be compensated adequately for her work."

These collective efforts were tackling something more insidious and more pervasive than the culture of office work. Writing about the emerging movement, Jean Tepperman perceived this at the time: "The stereotypes of clerical workers—stupid, frivolous, weak, useful only to help men do the *real* work—are just stereotypes of all women, translated into an office setting." Yet these stereotypes had a particular class content.

It's possible to convince someone that a woman lawyer or college professor is a serious, intelligent person. But many people see those women as exceptions—they're not "just" secretaries, or waitresses, or housewives, like most women. So when clerical workers begin to organize and assert themselves, it is a much more basic challenge to stereotypes of women, and very important to *all* women who want real change.[10]

A lot was at stake for both sides.

Neither professional associations nor unions, these office worker organizations constituted a new model, one that used research, creative publicity, and media-savvy direct action to develop a mass membership and power base. Increasing wages and respect for office workers were their top concerns, but not far behind were securing and monitoring affirmative action programs. Perhaps the most famous instance of such efforts involved female bank employees in Willmar, Minnesota, in 1997. When their bank hired a man to do the same work as they were for $300 more a month, and then asked long-time female employees to train him for a management position, they balked. After filing charges with the EEOC, the women went on strike for a list of demands including an affirmative action program. For months they braved the Minnesota winter on the picket lines to win their demands, a fight immortalized in the documentary *The Willmar 8*.[11]

The Working Women network was distinct from but thus connected to another vehicle used by some contemporary wage-earning women to fight sex discrimination: the labor movement. Prompted by their female members and leaders, who sometimes organized in women's committees or caucuses, the more progressive unions in these years provided growing support to affirmative action in particular and feminist policies more generally.[12] Black women in particular found in collective bargaining contracts effective tools for attacking inequality; they were almost twice as likely as white women to belong to unions. Black women such as Addie Wyatt, Ola Kennedy, and Clara Day—who called her union "one of the greatest civil rights workers"—also played leading roles in CLUW and, to a lesser degree, the Coalition of Black Trade Unionists.[13] Thus, while many unionists—probably most of those in craft occupations and the uniform trades—opposed affirmative action, some parts of the labor movement—prodded by women and African-American men—welcomed the remaking of class that was taking place through the reconstitution of gender and race.

NON-TRADITIONAL JOBS

As women's caucuses and office worker groups continued into the late 1970s, a new form of organizing for affirmative action spread: training and placement of women in so-called "nontraditional" blue-collar jobs, particularly in construction. Here, advocates of gender equity came up more directly against sex-typed class consciousness among craftsmen who by long tradition equated working-class pride and "defiant egalitarianism" vis-à-vis bosses with, as the labor historian David Montgomery once observed, "patriarchal male supremacy."[14] Feminists turned to the nontraditional work strategy in the belief that as women got access to these jobs and the higher wages they offered, their movement out of the female job ghetto would also relieve the overcrowding that pulled down women's wages.[15] Men without a college education had long found in these jobs both good wages and personal pride; that women were steered away from even considering them was itself a mark of gender discrimination. Building on the reforms wrested by civil rights workers and women's caucuses, the new initiatives marked both a more self-conscious attempt to relieve female poverty and a more frontal challenge to the sexual division of labor in working-class jobs. Two groups came together to make them work. On the one side, emboldened by the ideas of the times and the start of affirmative action, some wage-earning women defied custom and criticism by entering "men's" trades in the hopes of bettering their incomes.[16] On the other side, stirred by the Poor People's Campaign and the National Welfare Rights Organization, some female organizers set out to alleviate women's poverty and change the gender system that enforced it. In both groups, white women and women of color found themselves addressing racial issues in order to build class-based women's coalitions.

One of the pioneer organizations was Advocates for Women, founded in San Francisco in 1972. Its founders self-consciously broke ranks with women's movement organizations such as NOW that seemed ever more single-mindedly focused on the Equal Rights Amendment and the concerns of better-off women. Taking advantage of newly available federal funds, Advocates for Women began recruiting and training women for nontraditional jobs. Directed by a Latina, Dorothea Hernandez, the organization aimed to reach "women of all races and cultures with emphasis on low-income women who must support themselves and their families." The rationale for the effort was to the point: "Poverty is a woman's problem"; hence, "women need money." The best way to ensure their access to it was through their own earnings.

Over the next few years, variations on the basic nontraditional jobs model sprang up in locations across the country. By mid-decade, 140 women's employment programs were in operation, from San Francisco, New York, Chicago, and Washington, D.C., to Atlanta, Dayton, Louisville, Raleigh, San Antonio, and Wichita. In an initiative launched in 1979, over ninety of them, from twenty-seven states, joined together to form the Women's Work Force Network, which soon created a Construction Compliance Task Force to facilitate women's entrance into the building trades.[17] Women of color tended to be prominently involved, both as workers and as leaders. In New York, for example, black women and Latinas helped run United Tradeswomen, and their concerns prompted discussions about how racism and sexism worked together in the construction industry. One result was special attention to the exclusion of black women from the trades and pressure for their inclusion, such as the 1981 demand that at the Convention Center construction site "at least one half of women hired be women of color."[18]

Even in the Appalachian South, often thought of as a bulwark of tradition, women began to organize for access to the better-paying work long monopolized by men. In 1977, several women who had grown up in the region's coalfields set up the Coal Employment Project "to help women get and keep mining jobs." The number of female underground coal miners grew from zero in 1973 to over 3,500 by the end of 1981, when they comprised 2 percent of the workforce. Often widowed or divorced and raising children on their own, coalmining women took these jobs for the same reasons that led other women to construction sites: the work paid more than three times as much as they could get elsewhere. Mining also held more interest and prestige. To women who had grown up in the area coal was, as one put it, "part of our heritage."[19]

These endeavors marked an explicit feminist challenge not only to prevailing ideas of class as something that fitted men for self-reliance and women for dependence on and service to men, but also to the model of anti-poverty policy enshrined in the War on Poverty. Constructed on the premises set forth in the Moynihan Report, which explicitly argued that the problem for poor black families was that so many were female-headed, this approach assumed that the key task was to generate jobs for poor men, particularly black men, that would enable them to support families. Women's employment at best signaled family pathology; at worst, it created it, by depriving men of rightful dominance. Disparaged today, this thinking exerted a powerful influence through the 1970s, not just in government but in civil rights and black nationalist circles as well.[20] Participants in women's nontraditional employment programs, black and white, argued a very different case. Not only were large numbers of women likely to continue heading families: they had a right to do so in comfort and dignity. Poor men needed good jobs, to be sure, but so did poor women. "Money meant independence," a divorced electrician explained; "a trade meant ... being able to support my family without having a man around, if I couldn't find a decent man to relate to the family."[21]

If we look at these initiatives in light of theories that gender is constituted through performance and see these women as engaged in performances that revised existing notions of womanhood and manhood alike, richer, subtler meanings emerge. Performing nontraditional work changed many of the women who did it, as did receiving the higher wages once reserved for men. "As I grow stronger," wrote one woman miner, "as I learn to read the roof [of the mine] like the palm of a hand, the confidence grows that I can do this work.... To survive, you learn to stand up for yourself. And that is a lesson worth the effort to learn."[22] Bordering on conversion narratives, such expressions of personal growth from both black and white women pervade the sources on nontraditional work. (They also help to make sense of some men's intense resistance to women's entry into their trades, a resistance which seemed to be directed against precisely such feelings of equivalence and efficacy.)

One need not romanticize these changes to realize that cumulatively they could not help but alter meanings of womanhood and manhood in the wider culture. When members of the United Mine Workers of America (UMWA) began getting pregnant, surely it signified a sea change in the relationship between gender and class. For generations, the miner had symbolized male working-class fortitude in American culture; now it seemed that character of exemplary mettle might happen to be a mother. When female union members lobbied so effectively that they won unanimous support from the 1983 UMWA convention for the inclusion of parental leave as a contract demand in upcoming coal negotiations, surely it also marked a sea change in the labor movement. By pushing not simply for maternity leave but for paternity leave as well, they opened the possibility that the icon of working-class manhood—immortalized in America's finest labor ballads—might choose to be a stay-at-home dad.[23]

As women in these struggles remade class and gender, they often found themselves tackling race as well: struggle led to deeper learning. Even when women's caucuses arose in predominately white offices, for example, at least one or a few black women were usually actively involved. Inquiries into sex discrimination uncovered racial discrimination as well, as in a landmark suit by Women Employed against the Harris Trust and Savings Bank in Chicago. Many women's groups quickly realized the need to establish ties with black workers' caucuses or informal groups. The resulting coalitions were rarely tension-free—particularly for black women, who likely felt keenly the need for both groups and the limitations of each—but they were certainly educational, and often effective at bringing greater rewards to the partners than they could have achieved alone. When full-time organizations developed, white women sometimes occupied all or most of the staff positions initially. This became a particular problem in the construction industry drive, because women of color made up a large proportion of the low-income constituency the organizations aimed to serve. Recognizing this, some of these groups consciously set out to reconstruct themselves by applying affirmative action internally.[24]

At the same time, the nontraditional jobs effort enabled even predominately white women's organizations to develop alliances with black and Chicano rights organizations fighting for fair employment. One case in point is the United Women Firefighters with whom this story began, who won support from the black male firefighters of the Vulcan Society. Another example is the *New York Times* Women's Caucus, which coordinated its efforts with those of the black workers' caucus throughout the struggle. Women telephone workers and steel workers engaged in class-action suits did the same. For its part, Women Employed combined with other civil rights organizations to sue the Chicago District Office of the EEOC for negligence in 1977, and continued to cultivate collaborative relationships thereafter. Alliances such as this could alter both parties, making the women's groups more antiracist and making the civil rights groups more feminist in their thinking and programs. Although much more research needs to be done before we can draw sound conclusions about the ways that race operated in these women's struggles, it is clear that working-class women's groups provide important models for feminist multiracial coalition building.

I do not want to overstate the changes that occurred. If women tried to rewrite the script, so could men. Resistance was common, and sometimes fierce, as the example of the New York City firefighters illustrates. To take one obvious case: as if to certify their own now-uncertain masculinity and remind women of their place, some men turned to sexual harassment. While hardly new, this tactic seemed to be used more aggressively and self-consciously where men found treasured gender privileges and practices in question—as in the case of the New York firefighters. It was almost as though the men involved were marking the workplace as their territory, as indeed they were when they posted up pornography—a common practice in these situations. As one observer grasped: "By forcing sexual identities into high relief, men submerge the equality inherent in the work and superimpose traditional dominant and subordinate definitions of the sexes."[25] The support of black firemen complicated, but did not forestall, this development.

Putting face-to-face resistance to the side for the moment—which may in any case distract us from the variety and complexity in male responses—it is plain to see that the struggles described here have left much undone.[26] By and large, working women still face serious obstacles in trying to support themselves and their families. As much as it has diminished, occupational sex and race segregation has hardly disappeared, as any glance at a busy office or construction site will show. For men and women to be equally represented throughout all occupations in the economy today, 53 out of every 100 workers would have to change jobs. While the absolute number of women in the skilled trades has grown, moreover, they hold only 2 percent of the well-paying skilled jobs. In any case, these good jobs for people without higher education, as each day's newspaper seems to announce, are themselves an endangered species. In fact, while the wage gap between the sexes has narrowed, only about 40 percent of the change is due to improvement in women's earnings; 60 percent results from the decline in men's real wages. The persistent disadvantage in jobs and incomes contributes to another problem that has grown more apparent over the last two decades: the impoverishment of large numbers of women and their children, particularly women of color. Many of these poor women, moreover, are already employed. In 1988, more than two in five women in the workforce held jobs that paid wages below the federal poverty level.[27] So I am not arguing that some kind of linear progress has occurred and all is well.

Still, affirmative action was never intended as a stand-alone measure or panacea. From the outset, advocates were nearly unanimous in their insistence that it would work best in conjunction with full employment above all, but also with such measures as pay equity, unionization, and improvements in education and training. Affirmative action's mission was not to end poverty, in any case, but to fight occupational segregation. And there it has enjoyed unprecedented, if modest, success. The best indicator is the index of occupational segregation by sex: it declined more in the decade from 1970 to 1980, the peak years of affirmative action enforcement, than in any other comparable period in American history. As of 1994, women made up over 47 percent of bus drivers, 34 percent of mail carriers, and 16 percent of police—all jobs with better pay and benefits than most "women's work." This lags slightly behind nontraditional jobs requiring post-secondary training: women now account for nearly 40 percent of medical school students (20 percent of practicing physicians), nearly 50 percent of law school students (24 percent of practicing lawyers), and almost half of all professionals and managers.[28] The ways that white women and women of color fit into these patterns again complicate analyses based on sex alone. Yet whether in blue-collar, pink-collar, or professional jobs, white and black women have gained benefits from breaking down sex barriers.

It would be absurd, of course, to give affirmative action exclusive credit for these changes. The policies described here came to life as the result of a broader history involving women's own determination to close the gap between the sexes in education and labor force participation, institutional fears of lawsuits for discrimination, new developments in technology and labor demand, and changes that feminism and civil rights brought about in American culture. The mass entry of women into hitherto "men's work" in particular is deeply rooted in the breakdown of the family-wage-based gender system. It is both result and reinforcement of a host of other changes: new expectations of lifelong labor force participation among a majority of women, the spread of birth control, the growing unreliability of marriage, the convergence in women's and men's patterns of education, the demise of associational patterns and sensibilities based on stark divisions between the sexes—even the growing participation of women in sports. But if it would be foolish to exaggerate the causative role of affirmative action, it would also be sophistry to deny or underrate that role. It has furthered as well as been fostered by these other developments.[29] Women simply could not have effected the changes described here without its tools and the legal framework that sustained them. There are sound reasons why by 1975 virtually every national women's organization from the Girl Scouts to the Gray Panthers supported affirmative action, and why today that support persists from the African American Women's Clergy Association at one end of the alphabet to the YWCA at the other.[30]

Yet there is a curious disjuncture between these organizations and the female constituency they claim to represent: repeated polls have found that white women in particular oppose affirmative action by margins nearly matching those among white men (which vary depending on how the questions are worded).[31] No doubt several factors help to explain this paradox, not least of them the racial framing of the issue, which encourages white women to identify with white men against a perceived threat from non-whites. The preference for personal politics over political economy at the grassroots has also led many women to interpret feminism in terms of lifestyle choices rather than active engagement in public life. Struggles for the ERA and reproductive rights ultimately eclipsed employment struggles on the agenda of the women's movement in the 1970s. And most major women's organizations have come to emphasize service or electoral politics over grassroots organizing, and staff work over participation of active members. All of these developments help to explain why today there is so little in the way of a well-informed, mobilized, grassroots female constituency for affirmative action—a vacuum that, in turn, has made the whole policy more vulnerable to attack.

Surely another reason, however, for the paradoxical gulf between feminist national offices and grassroots sentiment on this issue is the historical amnesia that has obliterated the workplace-based struggles of the modern era from the collective memory of modern feminism—whether women's caucuses, clerical worker organizing, the fight for access to nontraditional jobs, or union-based struggles. If not entirely forgotten, these efforts on the part of working women are so taken for granted that they rarely figure prominently in narratives—much less interpretations—of the resurgence of women's activism. This disregard is especially ironic in that such struggles likely contributed more than we realize to our own era's heightened consciousness concerning the social construction and instability of the categories of gender, race, and class. Activists, that is, had begun the task of denaturalizing these categories and their associated hierarchies well before academics took up the challenge. Historical scholarship has begun excavating the buried traditions of working-class women that can help us re-think the trajectories of modern feminism; many, many more stories remain to be uncovered.

These stories have implications for how we approach the future as well as the past. As a recent gathering of feminist practitioners and scholars concluded, "we need to enlarge [our idea of] what counts as theory." Convened by the pioneering feminist economist Heidi Hartmann, those who took part in the discussion all expressed frustration at how theory has come to be equated ex-clusively with deconstruction, and how that constricted definition, in turn, has steered many people—especially but not only non-academic feminists—"away from theory."[32] It need not be this way. Practical struggles such as those over employment discrimination and affirmative action can advance the project of enlarging the purview of feminist theory, for they raise a host of questions for it: questions about the meaning and effects of different sexual divisions of labor, about the sources of collective consciousness and action among working women in the postwar period, about the relationships among sex discrimination and class and racial oppression, about how workplace-based performance affects consciousness and social relations, and about the connections between capital-ism, labor, and state policy in the shaping of our lives. Above all, they remind us to think about change, and the agency and power needed for it. A feminist theory that began to tackle such issues might find that it had more to say to the majority of American women, whose foremost concerns, they repeat over and over again, are economic (defining economic expansively). This is not an argu-ment to suppress sexual politics, ignore reproductive rights, or avoid questions of culture and subjectivity; new thinking on all these fronts contributed much to the struggles described here. It is to say that attention to other, neglected issues—issues of economic inequality, employment, and class foremost among them—could enrich historical scholarship on the women's movement and invigorate feminist theory and practice. Attention to employment issues could also focus the current interest in difference on the arena where it ultimately matters most: the search for solid ground for alliances across differences to win changes that would enhance all of our lives.[33]

NOTES

1. Dorothy Sue Cobble, "Recapturing Working-Class Feminism: Union Women in the Postwar Era," in Joanne Meyerowitz, ed., *Not June Cleaver: Women and Gender in Postwar America, 1945–1960* (Philadelphia: Temple University Press, 1994).

2. The information in this and the two subsequent paragraphs is compiled from multiple documents, too numerous for individual citation, all found in the United Women Firefighters Papers, box 4, First Women Firefighters of New York City Collection, Robert F. Wagner Labor Archives, New York University, New York.

3. Brenda Berkman to David J. Floyd, December 23, 1983, box 4, United Women Firefighters Papers. Of course, some individual white men supported women in these struggles and some individual black men proved hostile.

4. Interview with Alice Peurala in Brigid O'Farrell and Joyce L. Kornbluh, *Rocking the Boat: Union Women's Voices, 1915–1975* (New Brunswick, NJ: Rutgers University Press, 1996), 268; Dennis A. Deslippe, "Organized Labor, National Politics, and Second-Wave Feminism in the United States, 1965–1975," *International Labor and Working-Class History* 49 (Spring 1996), quotation on 161; also 147, 150.

5. Susan Davis, "Organizing from Within," *Ms.*, August 1972, 92; Mary Scott Welch, "How Women Just Like You Are Getting Better Jobs," *Redbook*, September 1977. See also Philip Foner, *Women and the American Labor Movement*, vol. 2 (New York: Free Press, 1980), 542–43; O'Farrell and Kornbluh, *Rocking the Boat*, 274–76. On Black workers' caucuses and rank-and-file unrest in the period, see Burton H. Hall, ed., *Autocracy and Insurgency in Organized Labor* (New Brunswick, NJ: Transaction Books, 1972); Dan Georgakas and Marvin Surkin, *Detroit: I Do Mind Dying—A Study in Urban Revolution* (New York: St. Martin's Press, 1975); Staughton Lynd and Alice Lynd, *Rank and File: Personal Histories by Working-Class Organizers* (Boston: Beacon Press, 1973).

6. One recent study has found in such caucuses the predominant form of gender-conscious activism among women in the 1980s. See Mary Fainsod Katzenstein, "Feminism within American Institutions: Unobtrusive Mobilization in the 1980s," *Signs: Journal of Women in Culture and Society* 16 (Fall 1990), 27–54. Women involved in such efforts not infrequently developed international connections, helping women in other countries to start their own caucuses and sharing information thereafter. For an example, see Mary Stott to Betsy Wade, March 18 [*c.* 1975], box 1, *New York Times* Women's Caucus Papers, Schlesinger Library, Radcliffe College, Cambridge (hereafter NYTWC).

7. See "Fact Sheet: *Boylan* v. *New York Times*," box 1, NYTWC; press release, 6 Oct. 1978, ibid.; Welch, "How Women Just Like You"; NOW, "Affirmative Action: The Key to Ending Job Discrimination," 28 Apr. 1971, box 44, National Organization for Women (NOW) Papers, Schlesinger Library Radcliffe College, Cambridge MA; Lucy Komisar, in *NOW York Woman*, July 1971.

8. Roberta Goldberg, *Organizing Women Office Workers: Dissatisfaction, Consciousness, and*

Action (New York: Praeger, 1983), 22. See also the popular Louise Kapp Howe, *Pink Color Workers: Inside the World of Women's Work* (New York: Avon, 1977).

9. Quotation from David Plotke, "Women Clerical Workers and Trade Unionism: Interview with Karen Nussbaum," *Socialist Review* 49 (January–February 1980): 151.

10. Jean Tepperman, *Not Servants, Not Machines: Office Workers Speak Out* (Boston: Beacon Press, 1976), 66, 80.

11. See, for example, Women Employed, *The Status of Equal Employment Opportunity Enforcement: An Assessment of Federal Agency Enforcement Performance—OFCCP and EEOC* (Chicago: Women Employed, 1980). On the Willmar events, see Foner, *Women and the American Labor Movement*, 491–92.

12. On the way that office worker organizations sometimes spun off union locals, such as the Service Employees International Union Local 925 in Boston, see Nussbaum interview. For the story of one longstanding women's committee in an IUE factory local, see Alex Brown and Laurie Sheridan, "Pioneering Women's Committee Struggles with Hard Times," *Labor Research Review* 11 (Spring 1988): 63–77. See also Deborah E. Bell, "Unionized Women in State and Local Government," in Ruth Milkman, ed., *Women, Work and Protest* (New York: Routledge & Kegan Paul, 1985); Ruth Milkman, "Women Workers, Feminism, and the Labor Movement since the 1960s," in ibid.; Union WAGE, *Organize! A Working Women's Handbook* (Berkeley: Union WAGE Educational Committee, September 1975).

13. See, for example. "Black Women in the Labor Movement: Interviews with Clara Day and Johnnie Jackson," *Labor Research Review* 11 (Spring 1988): 80, 82. The best single reference on CLUW, the Coalition of Black Trade Unionists, and Union WAGE, another labor women's group is Foner, *Women and the American Labor Movement*, 506, 497–501. On the latter's support for affirmative action, see "Purpose and Goals," *Organize! A Working Women's Handbook*, 21.

14. David Montgomery, *Workers Control in America: Studies in the History of Work, Technology, and Labor Struggles* (New York: Cambridge University Press, 1979), 13. See also Freeman. Although the focus here is on wage-earning jobs, working-class men were by no means alone or singular in their resistance to women's entry into their occupations. For the hostility of male lawyers, which the authors attribute to "a distinctive professional ethos," see Bradley Soule and Kay Standley, "Perceptions of Sex Discrimination in Law," *American Bar Association Journal* 59 (October 1973): 1144–47, quotation on 1147.

15. "The Best Jobs for Women in the Eighties," *Women's Day*, 15 Jan. 1980, box 1, United Tradeswoman Records, Robert F. Wagner Labor Archives, New York University, New York; Judy Heffner, "A Conversation with Barbara Bergmann," *Women's Work*, March–April 1977, 12. For elaboration of the economic argument for affirmative action for women, see Barbara R. Bergmann, *The Economic Emergence of Women* (New York: Basic Books, 1986), 146–72.

16. An example with major ramifications was the case of Lorean Weeks, who, after almost twenty years of "exemplary" service as a telephone operator, applied for the position of "switchman" in 1966, only to be denied it because she was a woman and then harassed for protesting her exclusion. Weeks went on to sue Southern Bell and assist the EEOC's landmark action against AT&T. See New York NOW, press release, 29 Mar. 1971, box 627, Bella Abzug Papers, Rare Book and Manuscript Library, Columbia University, New York.

17. For details of their efforts, see Wider Opportunities for Women, *National Directory of Women's Employment Programs: Who They Are, What They Do*, box 2, WOW Papers; Women's Work Force, "New Connections," Network Conference Report (Washington

DC., 21–23 May 1979), box 2, ibid.; Betsy Cooley et al. to Weldon J. Rougeau, November 16, 1979, box 1, ibid., November 1, 1979, box 18, ibid.

18. "Demonstrate to Demand Construction Jobs for Women!" box 1, United Trades-women Records, 5 Aug. 1981; *United Trades Newsletter* 1 (Fall 1980): 2, ibid.; February 1983: 1–9, ibid.; Bernice Fisher, "United Tradeswomen Going Beyond Affirmative Action" *Womanews* (March [1981]), ibid. Such efforts notwithstanding, white women ended up with a disproportionate share of skilled construction jobs, a pattern that needs explanation. See Deborah M. Figart and Ellen Mutari, "Gender Segmentation of Craft Workers by Race in the 1970s and 1980s," *Review of Radical Political Economics* 25, no. 1 (1993), 50–66.

19. Coal Employment Project, brochure from Fifth National Conference of Women Coal Miners, 24–25 June 1983, Dawson, Pennsylvania (materials in author's posses-sion); *Coal Mining Women's Support Team News* 1 (September–October 1978): 4, box 76, CLUW Papers; Christine Doudna, "Blue Collar Women," *Foundation News*, March/April 1983, 40–44, box 25, WOW Papers; quotations from Dorothy Gallagher, "The Women Who Work in the Mines," *Redbook*, June 1980: 29, 139. Similar reports came from Chicana copper miners in Arizona, suggesting commonalities across race and region in the ways women experienced the move in "men's work." See Barbara Kingsolver, *Holding the Line: Women in the Great Arizona Mine Strike of 1983* (Ithaca, NY: ILR Press, 1989), 73–96.

20. For explicit criticism of "the Moynihan Effect" on women's employment opportuni-ties, see Ann Scott and Lucy Komisar, *...And Justice For All: Federal Equal Opportunity Effort against Sex Discrimination* (Chicago: NOW, 1971), 14.

21. See, for example, "Preliminary Proposal Jobs 70," 15 Aug. 1972, box 3, WOW Papers; Ann Brickle, quoted in Jean Reith Schroedel, *Alone in a Crowd: Women in the Trades Tell Their Stories* (Philadelphia: Temple University Press, 1985), 191. For related, earlier black women's social thought, see Linda Gordon, "Black and White Visions of Wel-fare: Women's Welfare Activism, 1890–1945," *Journal of American History* 78 (Septem-ber 1991): 559–90.

22. Gallagher, "The Women Who Work in the Mines," 139. See also Laura Berman, "The Struggles of Tradeswoman," *Detroit Free Press*, 26 Aug. 1979, box 9, CLUW Records. Such testimony supports Alice Kessler-Harris's case that "the wage … con-tains within it a set of social messages and a system of meanings that influence the way women and men behave." See Alice Kessler-Harris, *A Women's Wage: Historical Meanings and Social Consequences* (Lexington: University of Kentucky Press, 1990), 7.

23. Doudna, "Blue Collar Women," 43; Cosby Totten, Goldie Totten, and June Rostan, "Women Miners' Fight for Parental Leave," *Labor Research Review* 7 (Spring 1988): 89–95, esp. 93.

24. Women Employed, *Status of Equal Employment Opportunity Enforcement*, 40; Davis, "Organizing from Within," 93–94; "Fighting Sexism on the Job" (document from a women's struggle in the United Steelworkers, with special emphasis on the victimiza-tion of black women at Great Lakes Steel), in Rosalyn Baxandall and Linda Gordon with Susan Reverby, *America's Working Women: A Documentary History, 1600 to the Present* (New York: W. W. Norton, 1995), 373–74. For WOW's internal affirmative action effort, see Affirmative Action Committee, minutes September 22, 1974, box 9, WOW Papers, and ibid., September 19, 1974.

25. Marian Swerdlow, "Men's Accommodations to Women Entering a Nontraditional Occupation: A Case of Rapid Transit Operatives," *Gender and Society* 3 (September 1981), 381. See also Joshua B. Freeman, "Hardhats: Construction Workers, Manlines, and the 1970 Pro-War Demonstrators," *Journal of Social History* 26 (Summer 1993),

726–31; Schroedel, *Alone in a Crowd,* 10, 60–61, 126, 170. For a groundbreaking analysis of sexual harassment as a mechanism of social control, see Mary Bulzarik, "Sexual Harassment at the Workplace: Historical Notes," in James Green, ed., *Workers' Struggles, Past and Present: A Radical American Reader* (Philadelphia: Temple University Press, 1983), 117–35.

26. For salutary correctives to the idea of monolithic male opposition and portrayals instead of a more complex (and politically promising) spectrum of male views on women's entry into nontraditional jobs, see Brigid O'Farrell and Sharon L. Harlan, "Craftworkers and Clerks: The Effect of Male Co-Worker Hostility on Women's Satisfaction with Non-Traditional Jobs," *Social Problems* 29 (February 1982): 252–65.

27. Chicago Women in Trades, *Building Equal Opportunity: Six Affirmative Action Programs for Women Construction Workers* (Chicago: CWIT, 1995), 5; Heidi Hartmann, "The Recent Past and Near Future for Women Workers: Addressing Remaining Barriers" (speech delivered 20 May 1995 at the Women's Bureau, U.S. Department of Labor, Washington, DC, distributed by Institute for Women's Policy Research), 3, 8, 10; "Program and Policy Agenda," WOW Papers, 4.

28. Data from Hartmann, "Recent Past and Near Future," 3, 8 and 10; IWPR, *Affirmative Action in Employment: An Overview* (Washington, D.C.: IWPR, 1996), 3–4. On the value of affirmative action, see Bergmann, *The Economic Emergence of Women,* 146–72.

29. For assessments of affirmative action's contribution to the changes, see "Program and Policy Agenda," WOW Papers, 5; IWPR, *Affirmative Action in Employment.* For the demise of the family-wage-based sex–gender system, see Stephanie Coontz, *The Way We Never Were: American Families and the Nostalgia Trap* (New York: Basic Books, 1992); Judith Stacey, *Brave New Families: Stories of Domestic Upheaval in Late-Twentieth Century America* (New York: Basic Books, 1990).

30. On support for affirmative action, see, for example, the U.S. National Women's Agenda," [1975], box 10, AFSCME Program Development Department Records.

31. For reports that white women oppose affirmative action by nearly as large a margin as white men, particularly when the question is worded as "preferences," see Charles Krauthammer, "Calling for an End to the Affirmative Action Experiment," *Chicago Tribune,* 14 April 1995, section I, 1. Polls taken in the wake of the anti-affirmative action California Proposition 209 in 1996 confirmed the pattern.

32. Heidi Hartmann et al., "Bringing Together Feminist Theory and Practice: A Collective Interview," *Signs: Journal of Women in Culture and Society* 21 (Summer 1996): 946.

33. On the poll data and its implications for feminism, see Martha Burk and Heidi Hartmann, "Beyond the Gender Gap," *Nation,* 10 June 1996: 18–21.

MAKING FANTASIES REAL: PRODUCING WOMEN AND MEN ON THE MAQUILA SHOP FLOOR

LESLIE SALZINGER

In the early 1990s, I went to Mexico's northern border to study the role of gender in global production. In Mexico, the bulk of such production takes place in maquiladoras (or maquilas)—export-processing factories owned by foreign (usually U.S.) capital. First established in 1965 on Mexico's northern border, maquilas employ low-paid Mexican workers to assemble U.S.-produced parts into goods to be sold on the U.S. market.

Panoptimex was the first plant I saw, and its shop floor fulfilled my stereo-typical expectations. The "docile women" of managerial dreams and feminist ethnography, theory, and nightmare were there in the flesh. Rows of them, smiling lips drawn red, darkened lashes lowered to computer boards, male supervisors looking over their shoulders, monitoring finger speed and manicure in a single look. It was visible at a glance: femininity incarnate in the service of capitalism.

But the story would not prove to be so straightforward. Although the femininity enacted at Panoptimex appears to be imported from the women workers' homes and family lives, what is most noticeable over time spent in the plant is the amount of work dedicated to creating appropriately gendered workers. It has become a truism to note that globalization is fueled by the search for docile, dexterous, and cheap labor, and Third World women are understood as "cheap labor" par excellence. Nonetheless, a closer look at an actual, live global factory suggests that this formulation puts the cart before the horse. Women workers are not always and already father-cowed, mother-trained and husband-supported. Rather, productive femininity is a paradigm through which managers view, and therefore structure, assembly work and through which they imagine, describe, and define job applicants and workers. The people we think of as classic "women workers" are formed within these ways of thinking and being. Thus, it is a mistake to think that their presence in the factory makes global production possible. To the contrary, they are global production's finished products. Gender indeed is a significant aspect of globalization, but it is the rhetoric of "femininity," rather than the presence of flesh-and-blood women, that enables low-cost production.

All this is nowhere more apparent than in Mexico's maquila industry, where the image of the "woman worker" persists in shaping shop-floor relations, even in the face of a massive influx of young men into these feminized jobs. A closer look at the history of this paradox, and, more importantly, an exploration of how the image of "femininity" operates on a particular maquila shop floor, make it possible to see the construction of "Third World women workers" in action and thereby to grasp better the role of gender in globalization.

The gendering of the maquila industry has a long and contradictory history. When the industry was first established in 1965, it was already framed in highly publicized, gendered rhetorics. Supposedly, its main purpose was to absorb the large number of Mexican men (*braceros*) who at the time were being expelled from their migrant farm-worker jobs in the western United States. However, like managers of other export-processing factories in free-trade zones around the world, maquila-hiring departments already had an image of "assembly workers," and male farm workers were not part of it. Advertising for *senoritas* and *damitas* throughout the border areas made clear—only young women need apply. These policies were repeatedly, if indirectly, legitimated in public discussions by managers, union bosses, and political commentators, who all persistently invoked the superiority of women workers and the deficiencies of their male counterparts. In a typical article, a manager commented matter-of-factly: "Eighty-five percent of the labor force is made up of women, since they're more disciplined, pay more attention to what they do, and get bored less than men do."

In the early 1980s, the image of the docile young woman began to crack. Inter-union conflicts led to several strikes, bringing anomalous pictures of defiant women workers, sticks in hand, to the front pages of local newspapers. Shortly thereafter, peso devaluations dramatically cut wage costs in dollar terms, and the demand for maquila workers soared. This led to a shortage of young women willing to work at maquila wages and to an increasingly assertive attitude on the part of those already employed. Confronted by young women workers who did not behave like "women" at all, some managers faced by shortages turned to young men. By the end of the decade, men made up close to half the maquila workforce.

As a result of this history, a tour of the industry in the early 1990s revealed an increasingly paradoxical situation. Despite the large numbers of male workers, descriptions of the prototypically malleable female worker emerged again and again. In an interview held more than a decade after men began entering maquila jobs in large numbers, the head of labor relations for the Association of Maquiladoras still advocated hiring women, commenting: "Men are not inclined to sit. Women are calmer about sitting." Despite the increasing scarcity of the women purportedly described, the rhetoric of femininity persisted, shaping the decisions and expectations of managers and workers alike.

It was in this context that I began to ask how this persistent image operated in production, and how it was related to the emblematic, but—as I gradually came to realize—unusual women of Panoptimex. Over eighteen months I studied four maquila shop floors. Three of these, including Panoptimex, were in Ciudad Juárez, the border city containing the largest number of maquila workers in Mexico. One was farther south, having moved in search of the docile women workers who had become increasingly elusive at the border. Managers in three of these maquilas remained committed to the idea that assembly work is necessarily "women's work," and the fourth had let the image go, but only under pressure. Thus, the image had effects across the board. Nonetheless, its impact varied dramatically across the plants, creating different types of shop-floor subjects with differing levels of productivity.

In the Juárez auto parts assembly plant, a group of U.S. managers were deeply wedded to the notion that the work was appropriately "women's work." Yet they could not attract enough female workers and succeeded only in antagonizing most of their male employees and provoking them to interfere with their female co-workers' production. In another auto parts plant located outside Juárez, Mexican managers were intent on showing that they were cosmopolitan: they dismissed the notion that their rural women workers were merely "traditional Mexican women" and organized them into teamwork and leadership training. This training used the rhetoric of assertiveness and self-discipline—all, of course, in the service of work output, and it evoked a distinctive, and highly productive, shop-floor "femininity." And in a Juárez-based hospital-garment assembly factory, responding to a distinctly "unfeminine" strike, Mexican managers deliberately turned to male workers, scrapping completely the image of the "feminine" assembly worker and consciously working outside that framework.

Thus, the rhetoric of productive femininity was always meaningful on these shops floors; yet it had distinctive effects on each of them, depending on the managers' senses of who they themselves were. Such managerial self-concepts set in motion both the rhetoric of femininity and the labor control strategies within which it was communicated. It was only at Panoptimex, though, that I saw women workers who actually resembled the ones described in transnational accounts. At Panoptimex, therefore, we can excavate the construction of the paradigmatic feminine subject—by tracing the multiple forces that come together to bring her into being.

Panoptimex makes televisions, and it is managers' consequent obsession with the visual, in the context of the transnational rhetoric of feminine productivity, that decides what is the appropriate way to be a woman (or a man) in a particular place. At Panoptimex, labor control practices based on the heightened visibility of workers create self-conscious and self-monitoring women on the one hand, and emasculated men on the other. In this process, managerial framing generates, rather than simply takes advantage of, a particular set of gendered subjectivities and in so doing establishes order on the shop floor.

The plant manager is an ash-blond South American who has his sights set on being promoted to the company's metropolitan headquarters. He is obsessed with the aesthetics of "his" factory—repainting the shop floor his trademark colors and insisting on ties for supervisors and uniforms for workers. The plant is the company's showpiece in Mexico: a state-of-the-art facility whose design has been so successful that its blueprint was recently bought by a competitor building a second factory in Juárez.

The factory floor is organized for visibility—a panopticon in which everything is marked. Yellow tape lines the walkways; red arrows point to test sites; green, yellow, and red lights glow above the machines. On the walls hang large, shiny white graphs documenting quality levels in red, yellow, green and black. Just above each worker's head is a chart full of dots: green for one defect, red for three defects, gold stars for perfect days. Workers' bodies, too, are marked: yellow, sleeveless smocks for new workers; light blue smocks for more seasoned women workers; dark blue jackets for male workers and mechanics; orange smocks for (female) "special" workers; red smocks for (female) group chiefs; lipstick, mascara, eyeliner, rouge, high heels, miniskirts, identity badges.... Everything is signaled.

Ringing the top of the production floor are windows. One flight up sit the managers, behind glass, looking—or perhaps not. From on high, they "keep track of the flow of production," calling down to a supervisor to ask about a slowdown, which is easily visible from above in the accumulation of televisions in one part of the line, gaps further along or in a mound of sets in the center of a line that also has technicians clustered nearby. Late afternoons, the plant manager and his assistant descend. Hands clasped behind their backs, they stroll the plant floor, stopping to chat and joke—just as everyone says—with "the young and pretty ones." The personnel department (its staff are titled "social workers") is entirely focused on questions of appropriate appearance and behavior, rather than on the work itself. "That's not manly. A man with trousers wouldn't behave like that!" one of the social workers tells a young male worker who showed his ex-girlfriend's letter to others on the line. "Remember this: it's nice to be important, but more important to be nice," she counsels a young woman who keeps getting into arguments with her co-workers. Behavior, attitude, demeanor—typically in highly gendered form—is evaluated here. Skill, speed, and quality rarely come up.

Managerial focus on the look of things is reflected in the demographics of the workplace as well. Close to 80 percent of the plant's direct line workers are women. They sit in long lines, always observed, repeating the same meticulous gestures a thousand times over the nine-hour day. During the 1980s, when it became difficult to hire women workers and most Juárez maquilas began hiring men, the company went so far as to recruit a bus-load of young women from a rural village 45 minutes away. The company, calmed by the sight of the familiarly populated lines, for years provided the workers with free transportation to and from the factory. This economic decision, one not made by most companies in the area, suggests the way in which Panoptimex managers' visually oriented attentional practices heightened their commitment to the transnational image of the woman worker.

Lines are "operator controlled." The chassis comes to a halt in front of the worker; she inserts her components and pushes a button to send it on. There is no piece rate, no moving assembly line to hurry her along. But in this fishbowl, no one wants to be seen with the clogged line behind her, an empty space ahead of her and managers peering from their offices above. If she does slow momentarily, the supervisor materializes. "Ah, here's the problem. What's wrong, my dear?" For the supervisor is, of course, watching as well as watched. He circles behind seated workers, monitoring efficiency and legs simultaneously—his gaze focused sometimes on "nimble fingers" at work and sometimes on the quality of a hairstyle. Often he will stop by a favorite operator—chatting, checking quality, flirting. His approval marks "good worker" and "desirable woman" in a single gesture.

"Did you see him talking to her?" For the eyes of workers are also at work, quick side-glances registering a new style, making note of wrinkles that betray ironing undone. "Uuf, look how she's dressed!" With barely a second thought, women workers can produce five terms for "give her the once over." A young woman comments that when she started work she used no make-up and only wore dresses below the knee. But then her co-workers started telling her she looked bad, that she should "fix herself up." As she speaks, her best friend affectionately surveys her painted face and nails, and her miniskirted physique. "They say one's appearance reveals a lot," she remarks. Two lines down, another young woman mentions she missed work the day before because she slept too late. Too late, that is, to do her hair and make-up and still make the bus. To come to work is to be seen, to watch, and so to watch and see yourself.

The ultimate arbiter of desirability, of course, is neither one's self nor one's co-workers, but supervisors and managers. Workers gossip constantly about who is or is not chosen. For those (few) who are so anointed, the experience is one of personal power. "If you've got it, flaunt it!" a worker comments gleefully, looking from her lace body-suit to the supervisor hovering nearby. This power is often used more instrumentally as well. On my first day in the plant, a young woman—known as one of the "young and pretty ones" favored by managerial notice—is stopped by guards for lateness. She slips upstairs and convinces the plant manager to intercede for her. She is allowed to work after all. The lines sizzle with gossip.

The few men on the line are not part of these games. Physically segregated from the women workers, they stand rather than sit, attaching screen and chassis to the television cabinet at one end of the line, packing the finished product at the other. They move relatively freely, joking and laughing and calling out— noisy but ignored. The supervisor is glaringly absent from their section of the line, and they comment disdainfully that he's afraid to bother them. Nonetheless, when they get too obviously boastful, he brings their behavior to a halt. Abruptly he moves the loudest of them, placing them in soldering, where they sit in conspicuous discomfort among the "girls," while the men who have not been moved make uneasy jokes about how boring it is "over there."

One young man says he came here intentionally for all the women. "I thought I'd find a girlfriend. I thought it would be fun." "And was it?" I ask. There's a pause. "No one paid any attention to me," he responds finally, a bit embarrassed, laughing and downcast. His experience reminds me of a story told by one of the women workers who returned to the factory after having quit. "It's a good environment here," she says. "In the street they [men] mess with us, but here, we mess with them a little. We make fun of them and they get embarrassed."

In the factory, to be male is to have the right to look, to be a "supervisor." As for the male line worker, standing facing the line, eyes trained on his work, he does not count as a man. In the plant's central game, he is neither subject nor object. As a result, he has no location from which to act—either in his relation to the women in the plant or in relation to factory managers.

What is striking once inside the plant is how much work is involved in the ongoing labor of constructing appropriate "young women"—and "young men"—out of new hires. Gendered meanings are forged within the context of panoptic labor control strategies in which women are constituted as desirable objects and male managers as desiring subjects. Male workers become not-men, with no standing in the game. These identities are defined by management in the structure of the plant, but they are reinforced by workers. Young women workers take pleasure in the experience of being desirable and in their use of this delicious if limited power in attempting to evade the most egregious aspects of managerial control. As male workers attempt to assert masculinity, they become vulnerable to managerial ability to undercut these assertions.

The gendered meanings and subjectivities developed here are familiar. It appears that Panoptimex managers have indeed found their ideal feminine workers, and simply supplemented them with the predictably rebellious young men of international repute. Certainly that is the managers' own understanding. Nonetheless, managers' beliefs are also a product of external rhetorics—in this case, discourses from their own national cultures and from the transnational industry they work for. Closer inspection reveals instead the localized operations of the expectation of femininity, as managers who are committed to the look of things go to unusual lengths to create the subjects they expect to see. Thus, Panoptimex's docile women and emasculated men are local products, created through the self-fulfilling prophecy of management's hiring and labor-control tactics. Here we see the transnational rhetoric of femininity put into local practice.

Panoptimex is a compelling case not because it is typical, but because it is unusual. It stands out for the remarkable accuracy with which its workers in-carnate—literally bring to life—the image of home-grown feminine docility, an image that in fact is generated not in their homes, but in transnational managerial rhetoric and imagination. Panoptimex workers are classic simulacra, embodiments of a fantasized reality.

In focusing on the symbolic practices and formative descriptions of shop-floor life, rather than on gender demographics or managerial portrayals of workers, a distinctive set of social processes come into focus. We can see how subjects are evoked on the shop floor, rather than imported from outside the factory. And we can begin to describe the local conditions necessary for transnational images of docile femininity to be construed and acted upon. The workers of Panoptimex do not enter the factory with a gender identity that is already set, but neither do they automatically reflect managerial fantasy. Rather, managers are located within many discourses—the feminine worker is only one. Panoptimex managers also participate in a work world in which the visual is disproportionately highlighted. It is at the intersection of those two frameworks that the painted, permed and pliant Panoptimex woman emerges—born not of a Mexican father and mother, but of transnational perspectives. Panoptimex workers are as much global products as are the televisions they assemble.

MACHOS AND MACHETES IN
GUATEMALA'S CANE FIELDS

ELIZABETH OGLESBY

Last year, at twenty-four, Sebastián Tol was a "champion" cane cutter on the agro-export plantations of Guatemala's Pacific coast, averaging over ten tons a day.[1] At the end of the harvest season, however, he returned home to the highlands with shoulder pain that made it difficult to do even routine chores. This year, his place on the plantation work crew was taken by his eighteen-year-old brother, Santiago, who also has hopes of becoming a champion. A month before the start of the harvest, Santiago began buying weekly vitamin injections for half a day's wage each, which he believes will increase his endurance in the cane fields.

The Guatemalan sugar industry tripled its production over the last two decades, and Guatemala is now the third largest sugar exporter in Latin America. This expansion is due in large part to a modernization campaign designed to raise the productivity of cane cutters, most of whom are migrant workers from the indigenous highlands. Long infamous for using extreme violence to quell worker unrest, the sugar plantations in Guatemala are now devising alternate means to achieve labor discipline, by combining new technologies with wage incentives, human capital investments, and a refashioning of workers' identities. Central to this strategy is the creation of a subset of "vanguard" cane cutters: young men generally between the ages of eighteen and twenty-five who are pushed to compete with each other to reach productivity goals.

Indeed, productivity has soared across the sector. In 1980, cane workers were paid by the day and would cut between one and two tons per day; last year they were paid by the ton and the daily average among workers had risen to six tons. Productivity increases stem from a combination of technical changes and a social re-engineering of the harvest labor force. Technical changes include heavier, curved machetes, mechanical cane loading, and the Taylorization of cane cutting—that is, the use of time-and-motion studies to break down the labor process into precise, repeatable movements. Taylorist methods control how a worker holds and swings the machete, and how many movements are used to cut and lay the cane. But plantation managers stress that, beyond these techniques, a key component is the effort to transform workers' attitudes toward cane cutting. The plantations' goal is to create new attitudes that they hope will undercut opposition to a labor regime that places increasingly severe demands on the bodies of workers.

One way this is done is through the masculinization of the harvest labor force. Industrial psychologists recruit and train the cane cutters, who are exclusively male and mostly young. Only men are permitted to live in the migrant camps. Food is prepared in industrial kitchens by male cooks, many of whom learned to cook while serving in the army. The new diets are supposed to provide 3,700 calories daily, and they include a careful balance of proteins and carbohydrates to ensure that workers don't lose weight during the harvest. Cane cutters get oral rehydration drinks and health exams. They are weighed periodically, and their muscles are measured. Their bodies and productivity levels are monitored, and all of this information gets recorded in year-by-year databases.

The masculinization of harvest labor is not only about recruiting men; it's also about reinforcing ideas of masculinity among cane cutters. On the one hand, the mills try to create camaraderie in the work camps and a sense that these are spaces where workers can be free from family pressures. Many of the migrant camps have televisions and VCRs, and there are "entertainment nights" with Mexican *vaquero* films or Rambo movies. Exotic dancers are sometimes hired to perform at the camps, and at the end of the harvest workers are taken on excursions to the beach or to a local cantina. The absence of older male relatives in the camps creates a sense of heightened freedom, a sort of extended adolescence, for younger workers, especially in a region like the coast that abounds with bars and brothels.

On the other hand, management appeals to machismo in its attempt to foment competition around production quotas. Top cane cutters are awarded prizes ranging from T-shirts to tape recorders, bicycles, and a grand prize of a motorcycle. Every week management distributes a computer printout of the top individual cane cutters and their scores. The "engineers," as workers call them, visit the housing camps regularly. "They tell us how great we are, and that we're ahead of all the other fronts," a 21-year-old worker told me. Another worker elaborated. "We're macho here. It's like at a fair, when they put a prize on top of a greased pole. Even though you know you can't reach it, you have to try."

In addition to the seemingly universal belief in the power of vitamin B injections, some cane cutters use amphetamines to extend their endurance. But when drugs are used to dull the effects of exhaustion and dehydration, heatstroke becomes a serious danger for workers in the sweltering cane fields. I asked a crew foreman why he thought many cane cutters were working themselves sick. "If you ask them," he said, "they'll probably tell you it's to get the wages, or maybe the prize. But I can tell you that a part of it has to do with the pure competition." The manipulation of masculinity to boost output doesn't erase workers' awareness of exploitation on the plantations, however. Cane cutters complain about the heat, the grueling hours, and the belief that the plantations constantly cheat them out of their fair pay. "The prizes and all that, it's a bunch of crap," protested one worker with five years' experience. "We're the ones who pay for it, with the money they steal from our pay. They give tape recorders, so what? If they would give out a little bit of land, now that would be worth working for!"

There hasn't been a major labor strike in the sugar sector since 1980, at the height of the civil war, and the sugar unions that existed in the 1970s disappeared with the repression. But temporary work stoppages are fairly common at many plantations, and worker turnover is high. Are cane workers "disciplined" by these practices? Many, like Sebastián Tol, pay a high price with broken bodies, but in general, workers' perceptions of the plantations appear to have changed little. The promotion of masculine work identities on the plantations doesn't make workers dislike cutting cane any less, and it doesn't seem to replace class-consciousness. But when this is crosscut by an emphasis on the recruitment of youth, it does create a separate group of workers for whom labor migration to the coast is a sort of multi-year rite of passage and a steppingstone toward aspirations of future U.S.-bound migration.

Sebastián Tol told me that he wasn't thinking of cutting sugar cane any more. But he had heard from other workers from the coast that in Alabama there were many jobs "cutting chickens," and that if his shoulder would just heal he was going to try his luck in *el norte*.

NOTE

1. Sebastián and Santiago are the pseudonyms of two highlands brothers.

AN INTERNATIONAL PERSPECTIVE
ON SLAVERY IN THE SEX INDUSTRY

JO BINDMAN

At Anti-Slavery International, we believe that exclusion from society contributes to the worldwide association of the sex industry with slavery-like practices. The major characteristics of slavery are violence with impunity, sometimes leading to death, loss of freedom of movement, and transfer to another owner/master for money or goods without informed consent. It is associated with a lack of full citizenship rights.

The designation of prostitution as a special human rights issue emphasizes the distinction between sex work and other forms of female, dangerous, and low-status labor, such as domestic or food service work, or work in factories and on the land. It hides the commonality, the shared experience of exploitation, which links people in all such work. The distinction between "the prostitute" and everyone else helps to perpetuate her exclusion from the ordinary rights which society offers to others, such as rights to freedom from violence at work, to a fair share of what she earns, or to leave her employer. An employment or labor perspective, designating prostitution as sex work, can bring this work into the mainstream debate on human, women's, and workers' rights. It also allows us to recognize that the sex industry is not always where the worst conditions are to be found.

Since the Convention for the Suppression of the Traffic in Persons and the Exploitation of the Prostitution of Others was published by the United Nations in 1949, our view on women has changed. We can no longer characterize women as purely passive, and this Convention is no longer appropriate to meeting their needs. Nor has it proved successful. We must fight to ensure that women have the same basic rights as everyone else, so that women can take their own decisions.

Let us look at how slavery finds its way into the sex industry. The sex industry exists all over the world and has a huge variety of forms: sex may be sold as striptease or in go-go bars, pick-up bars, night clubs, massage parlors, saunas, truck stops, restaurants and coffee shops, barber shops, in straight-forward brothels which provide no other service, via escort agencies, or on the street. Most people who work in these establishments lack formal contracts with the owners or managers but are subject to their control. Those who work in the sex industry are commonly excluded from mainstream society. They are thereby denied whatever international, national, or customary protection from abuse is available to others as citizens, women, or workers.

The lack of international and local protection renders sex workers vulnerable to exploitation in the workplace and to violence at the hands of management, customers, law enforcement officials, and the public. The need for worker pro-tection, to include occupational health and safety provisions, is of particular relevance in the context of HIV/AIDS and other sexually transmitted infections. Sex workers, without rights in their place of work, are uniquely vulnerable to disease, routinely lacking the full combination of information, materials, and authority necessary to protect themselves.

In fact, existing human rights and slavery conventions are in theory sufficient to take the slavery out of the sex industry. The existing conventions outlaw slavery in, for example, the carpet industry in India, in the growing of sugar cane in Haiti, and in domestic service in Indonesia and in the United Kingdom. While all of these abuses continue to exist, the existence of conventions means that pressure can be brought to bear on governments to enact them in national law. Once they are part of the law, affected persons, groups and activists can work to ensure the enforcement of the law. This is in essence how Anti-Slavery International works, with our partners on the ground. It can be a slow process, but we believe it can eventually eliminate modern forms of slavery. So in the sex industry, too, conventions can be used. But in the case of the sex industry, the ending of slavery-like practices is held back by the distinction between sex workers, or prostitutes, and other workers.

We want to point to the international conventions that protect the rights of children kept in appalling conditions in the carpet industry or of plantation workers trapped in debt-bondage, and that would allow sex workers to claim their rights as full members of local and world society. To do this we first need to identify prostitution as work, as an occupation susceptible like others to exploitative practices. Then sex workers can be included and protected under the existing instruments which aim to protect all workers from exploitation, and women from discrimination. It is exploitation in every form that Anti-Slavery International exists to fight.

There is undoubtedly a shared abhorrence of the shocking circumstances in which prostitution often takes place. Many women and girls in the industrialized and developing worlds are brought into the sex industry by deception or find themselves forced to stay within it against their will. There is debt-bondage in which the bonded person effectively becomes the property of the creditor until the debt is paid, rendering the bonded person extremely vulnerable to abuse. It is a system in which an initial payment must be worked off indefinitely on terms set by the creditor and rarely made explicit to the bonded person, who may be passed with their debt from owner to owner. This practice is common in different industries the world over—in plantation agriculture, brick manufacture, and carpet weaving. Debt-bonded women in Taiwan's sex industry can be confined in semi-darkness, allowed out rarely and only under armed guard. In Thailand, they may be forced to receive twenty customers per day, powerless to protect themselves with condoms, with the cost of medical treatment and abortion added to their debt, and discarded if they test HIV-positive.

There is trafficking, often combined with debt-bondage, which transports women across national boundaries for various purposes, of which domestic work, "mail-order" marriage, and prostitution are most common. Agents in the sex industry bring women and girls from Nepal to India, from the Dominican Republic to Germany, where they are completely dependent upon their traffickers. They have little knowledge of the local language, customs or law, and may not know how to get home even if they have access to their passports. They are threatened with their unpaid debt. At the mercy of the traffickers, they are forced to work long hours in inhumane surroundings.

There is child labor outside the family, which deprives millions of children of the future that an education can provide. Long working hours, cramped conditions, and lack of care in childhood can damage health for life. Children are often preferred as cheaper and less able to resist poor conditions than adults. They are particularly vulnerable to sexual abuse in the workplace—in the case of child domestic workers, it is almost commonplace. Thousands of girls in their early teens are in brothels or on the streets, their youth rendering them especially vulnerable to intimidation.

Exacerbating these problems and creating others in countries where welfare and education provisions protect citizens from debt-bondage, trafficking, and child labor are laws aimed at suppressing the sex industry, which criminalize women. Criminalization in the United Kingdom deprives women in the sex industry of civil rights. It means that women can be arrested, locked up, and fined on the evidence of the condoms that they must carry to protect their lives. Women can be beaten, raped, or even murdered without recourse to police protection.

The examples I give here are of slavery in the sex industry. However, slavery is not inherent to the sex industry. Many women all over the world go to courageous lengths to enter the sex industry. In our world today, people in general and women in particular are often faced with limited opportunities to provide for themselves and their families. These are women considering all the dangers to which social exclusion will expose them, and the economic exploitation that they may face, and still calculating that this is their best available option.

Can we tell such people what they may or may not do? Do they deserve anything less than the best possible conditions sought for other workers? Can we tell them that we would take away their power to choose this occupation, maybe condemning them to worse conditions in another field? Work, for example, in a glass factory in India, where the heat, fumes, noise, and constant risk of terrifying injuries from the furnaces create a hell for its workers and where life expectancy is said to be reduced by ten to fifteen years. Or back-breaking toil in subsistence agriculture all day, followed by a load of domestic duties, just to scrape together the bare minimum for survival. Closer to home, it can be better than cleaning lavatories or enduring monotonous hours for very low pay on the production line. And it could be the only job available where a mother can be around to collect her children from school.

We in the human rights field must work alongside efforts toward economic justice, toward viable economic alternatives for everyone, ending vulnerability to slavery-like practices. Let us at the same time fight debt-bondage, trafficking, child labor and the inhumane conditions, violence, and intimidation they incorporate. Let us fight laws which exclude women in the sex industry from society and which deprive them of the rights that everyone else enjoys, at least on paper. Let us fight exploitation in every form.

GLOBALIZING SEX WORKERS' RIGHTS

KAMALA KEMPADOO

Besides the location of women in the sex trade as workers, migrants and agents, racism positions Third World sex workers in international relations.

The brown or black woman is regarded as a desirable, tantalizing, erotic subject, suitable for temporary or non-marital sexual intercourse—the ideal "outside" woman—and rarely seen as a candidate for long-term commitment, an equal partner, or as a future mother. She thus represents the unknown or forbidden yet is positioned in dominant discourse as the subordinated "other."

The exoticization of the Third World "other" is as equally important as economic factors in positioning women in sex work. In other words, it is not simply grinding poverty that underpins a woman's involvement in prostitution. Race and ethnicity are equally important factors for any understanding of contemporary sex industries.

As the *New York Times* reports, "Exotic Imports Have Captured Italy's Sex Market," referring to the increased importance of African women in sex work in Rome, and simultaneously illuminating the connection that is still made between Third World women and the exotic (July 9, 1997). However, prostitution is a realm of contradictions. Thus, even with the heightened exoticization of the sexuality of Third World women and men, they are positioned within the global sex industry second to white women. White sex workers invariably work in safer, higher paid, and more comfortable environments; brown women— Mulattas, Asians, Latinas—form a middle class; and black women are still conspicuously overrepresented in the poorest and most dangerous sectors of the trade, particularly street work.

The second dimension of racism is somewhat less obvious, yet concerns the neocolonialism that is evinced in much recent feminist and pro-sex worker writings that have come out of the United States and Western Europe. Kathleen Barry's work on the trafficking of women, *Female Sexual Slavery* (1984), best illustrates this tendency.

In true colonial fashion, Barry's mission is to rescue those whom she considers to be incapable of self-determination. And along with this mission goes a particular cultural definition of sex itself. Subaltern understandings and lived realities of sexuality and sexual-economic relations, such as found in various African or Caribbean countries, for example, where one can speak of a continuum of sexual relations from monogamy to multiple sexual partners and where sex may be considered as a valuable asset for women to trade with, are ignored in favor of specific Western ideologies and moralities regarding sexual relations.

The neocolonialism that surfaces in such representations of the lives and situations of Third World women across the globe does not, however, end with radical feminists or the anti-trafficking lobby. Some prostitutes' rights advocates assume that Western development, capitalist modernization, and industrialization will enable women in developing countries to exercise choice and attain "freedom." Seen to be trapped in underdeveloped states, Third World prostitutes continue to be positioned in this discourse as incapable of making decisions about their own lives, forced by overwhelming external powers completely beyond their control into submission and slavery. Western women's experience is thus made synonymous with assumptions about the inherent superiority of industrialized capitalist development and Third World women are placed in categories of pre-technological "backwardness," inferiority, dependency, and ignorance.

Since the 1970s, sex work has been an organizing basis for women, men, and transgenders in different parts of the world. But while the emergence of prostitutes' rights groups and organizations in Western Europe and North America up to the early 1990s has been well documented, there is little written on the global movement.

Despite this lack of recognition, sex workers in Third World and other non-Western countries have been busy, taking action, demonstrating against injustices they face, and demanding human, civil, political, and social rights. Thus, not only was an Ecuadorian association formed in 1982, but it held a sex workers' strike in 1988. In Brazil, a national prostitutes' conference took place in 1987, giving rise to the establishment of the National Network of Prostitutes, Da Vida. In Montevideo, Uruguay, AMEPU inaugurated its childcare center and new headquarters after making its first public appearance in the annual May Day march in 1988. The Network of Sex Work Projects, founded in 1991, began to make its links with sex workers' rights and healthcare project in the Asian and Pacific region, slowly creating a truly international network, which today includes at least forty different projects and groups in as many different countries around the world.

The year 1992 witnessed the founding of the Venezuelan Association of Women for Welfare and Mutual Support (AMBA), with the Chilean group Association for the Rights of Women, "Angela Lina" (APRODEM), and the Mexican Union Unica following suit in 1993. Two national congresses were held by the Ecuadorian sex workers' rights association in 1993 and 1994. The Maxi Lindner Association in Suriname, the Indian Mahila Samanwaya Committee, and the Colombian Association of Women (Cormujer) were also established by 1994. In the same year around four hundred prostitutes staged a protest against the closing of a brothel in Lima, Peru, with the slogan "We want to work, We want to work"; and in Paramaribo, Suriname, sex workers made a first mass public appearance on AIDS Day, marching through the city with the banner "No Condom, No Pussy," drawing attention to their demands for safe sex. Also, 1994 witnessed the founding of The Sex Worker Education and Advocacy Taskforce (SWEAT) in South Africa. In 1996, groups in Japan and the Dominican Republic—Sex Workers! Encourage, Empower, Trust, and Love Yourselves! (SWEETLY) and Movement of United Women (MODEMU)—were formed, and in the same year the Indian organization held its first congress in Calcutta, as well as organizing several protests and demonstrations against harassment and brutality. In 1997, with the help of AMBAR in Venezuela, the Association for Women in Solidarity (AMAS) became the first Nicaraguan group, comprising mainly street workers. Other sex worker organizations have been reported to exist in Indonesia, Tasmania, Taiwan, and Turkey.

While clearly there is a need for autonomous organizing and consolidation of each group's position, within its own political, economic and cultural context, it is evident that sex workers do not view the struggle as isolated from that of other members of society. As prostitutes, migrant workers, transgenders, family breadwinners, single parents, HIV-positives, or teenagers, many recognize the multiple arenas in which their lives play, and consequently the multiple facets of social life that must be addressed. Gay, lesbian, bisexual, and transgender organizations, legal and human rights activists, healthcare workers, labor unions, and other sex industry workers are potential allies in the struggle to transform sexual labor into work that is associated with dignity, respect, and decent working conditions. The coalitions that are taking shape through everyday resistances of sex workers also bring new meanings to the women's movement and feminism. It is hopefully from this matrix of resistance and coalitions that sex workers' rights will be embraced in the decades to come.

PART IV

ECONOMICS, SOCIAL WELFARE, AND PUBLIC POLICY

STILL UNDER ATTACK:
WOMEN AND WELFARE REFORM

MIMI ABRAMOVITZ

Social programs have always been a double-edged sword for women, regulating their lives on the one hand and providing needed resources on the other. The welfare state has always been an arena of political struggle.

Welfare reform became a hot political issue in the early 1990s. During the 1992 presidential election campaign, Bill Clinton drew frequent and loud applause when he declared that welfare should provide "a second chance, not a way of life." By late 1994, the president's plan to cut welfare had lost ground to the Republicans' Contract With America, which called for ending welfare altogether. In August 1996, Congress passed the Personal Responsibility and Work Opportunity Reconciliation Act of 1996 (PRA), better known as "welfare reform." This historic act, which slashed a wide range of safety-net programs for the poor, ended forty years of direct federal intervention in the nation's social-welfare system and paved the way for an attack on the entire welfare state. For the first time, welfare assistance became a short-term benefit, run by the states, without the guarantee of federal funding.

THE WIDER CONTEXT OF THE ATTACK ON WELFARE

The term "welfare" refers both to social programs and to the promise of well-being. The discrepancy between this promise of well-being and the actual quality of life for many people has led most Western industrial nations, at some point in time, to create a welfare state. Since welfare states determine who benefits from and who pays for government programs, they remain highly controversial. To understand better what happened to the U.S. welfare program for single mothers, we first need to discuss three background issues: the core social welfare programs, the forces behind the latest attack on welfare, and the ideological underpinnings of the campaign to reform the program.

WHAT IS WELFARE? THE CORE PROGRAMS

The United States launched its modern welfare state during the Great Depression of the 1930s, when the collapse of the economy created massive unemployment, major business failures, and mounting social protests. The Depression was supposed to end quickly, the relief programs were supposed to be temporary, and private charities were expected to meet the remaining demand for aid. Instead, the length and severity of the economic crisis forced Congress to acknowledge what it had preferred for so long to ignore: that market economies rarely provide enough jobs or income for everyone and that to prevent chaos and disaffection the federal government must assume major responsibility for social welfare. After considerable partisan debate, in 1935 Congress reluctantly passed the Social Security Act. This landmark legislation transferred responsibility for social welfare from the states to the federal government, replacing temporary and sporadic state-administered programs with a permanent social welfare system—some thirty to fifty years after most other Western industrial nations had taken this step.

The Social Security Act established two types of cash benefit: social insurance and public assistance. The social insurance programs included a pension for retired workers (what we informally call Social Security) and Unemployment Insurance, which replaces the wages of those who face temporary unemployment. Social Security is funded by a payroll tax that is paid half by the worker and half by the employer, while Unemployment Insurance is financed through a tax on the employer alone. These programs, which now cover more than 95 percent of all wage earners, have become so well accepted that most people think of them as rights, not as assistance.

The Social Security Act also included three public assistance programs for the poor: Aid to Dependent Children (ADC), Old Age Assistance (OAA), and Aid to the Blind (AB); Aid to the Permanently and Totally Disabled (APTD) was added in 1956. Welfare is the popular name for ADC, which provides financial assistance to children who are continuously deprived of support due to the death, absence, or incapacity of a parent or caretaker. (ADC became known as AFDC in 1962, when Congress passed a limited program for households with an unemployed father.) In 1965, Medicaid and Medicare were added to the Social Security program, and in 1974 OAA, AB, and APTD were combined into a federalized income-support program called Supplemental Security Income (SSI). It was hoped that this consolidation would standardize these programs and reduce their stigma. The only program to be left out of this important consolidation was AFDC, the program which addressed the needs of poor women and children. In 1996, Congress replaced AFDC with Temporary Aid to Needy Families (TANF), Title I of the PRA, popularly known as welfare reform.

In contrast to the positive notion of rights attached to social insurance, Americans think of the public assistance programs in negative terms such as charity, handouts, or the dole. Until the late 1990s, politicians dared not tamper with the social insurance programs for fear of losing too many votes. In fact, by the early 1990s, nearly 50 percent of all households drew on government benefits—from Food Stamps to Social Security to mortgage-interest tax deductions.[1] But no such fears prevented politicians from repeatedly attacking the welfare program for single mothers.

Fueled by the dictates of the economic recovery plan, conservative analysis of social programs, and a dislike of government programs, the attack on welfare included five targets: the cost and size of AFDC, women's work behavior, women's childbearing choices, the entitlement status of social programs, and the overall role of the federal government in society. In too many cases welfare reform translates into increased stress, hardship, and poverty for poor women, leading many commentators to ask: from welfare to what?

CUTTING THE COST AND SIZE OF WELFARE

The first assault on the welfare state began in the early 1980s and emphasized the cost and size of its programs. The unpopularity of AFDC and its constituents—poor single mothers—made welfare an easy target for Ronald Reagan's economic recovery plan. The administration's budget cutters argued that AFDC wasted funds on undeserving women and bloated bureaucracies; that it drained the treasury and fueled the deficit. They also insisted that women on welfare live "high on the hog." Yet the facts suggest otherwise. The average benefit rose from $178 a month in 1970 to $275 in 1980.[2] During the same time, however, due to inflation, its real purchasing power fell more than 40 percent. In no state did the combined value of the meager AFDC and Food Stamps grant lift a family of three above the official poverty line. Advocates of the poor called for higher AFDC benefits as part of the 1988 Family Support Act, but their proposal did not survive the political process.

While the cost of AFDC had indeed grown over the years, it could hardly be held responsible for the budget deficit or the nation's economic woes. In fact, it amounted to only 1.1 percent of the federal budget; 3.0 percent including the cost of Food Stamps (FS) and Supplemental Security Income (SSI). The state paid additional shares for AFDC. In contrast, a much larger 20.3 percent of the federal budget went to Social Security and 28 percent to military spending.

The federal share of AFDC costs rose to $14 billion in 1995, but fell to 0.9 percent of the federal budget; 4.5 percent including FS and SSI. That year Social Security took 22 percent and defense absorbed 18.5 percent. As for bureaucratic costs, benefits amounted to 88 percent of the $14 billion spent for AFDC in 1995, administration only 12 percent.[3] Overall welfare spending fell far below the approximately $104 billion devoted to subsidies and tax breaks for U.S. corporations—or what some refer to as "corporate welfare."[4] In addition, the beneficiaries of the Food Stamps, Medicaid, and housing programs included some agriculture, medical, and real estate interests.

The myths surrounding welfare's size matched the misperceptions of its cost. By the late 1970s, welfare's critics told us that the rolls had exploded and created an uncontrollable mess. But AFDC's expansion mirrored social forces over which individuals typically have little or no control. The welfare rolls grew steadily during the late 1940s and 1950s, serving from 1 to 2 million individuals a year. The numbers doubled from about 3.0 million in 1960 to 10.2 million in 1971, reflecting high poverty rates but also the demands of the civil rights and welfare rights movements.[5] Even so, AFDC's expansion kept pace with natural population increases, serving a steady 2 to 3 percent of all Americans until 1969, when it jumped to more than 4 percent. From 1971 to 1990, the caseload once again stabilized at 10 to 11 million people per year, or 4 to 5 percent of the U.S. population—except during recessions, when the numbers rose.[6]

Although welfare's growth reflected a normal response to population growth, fluctuating economic conditions, liberalized program rules, and pressure from social movements, critics used the convergence of three other developments to argue that welfare's expansion stemmed from the unacceptable values and behavior of the poor. In the 1970s, in some high-benefit states, the welfare grant began to exceed the minimum wage, making work less economically attractive than welfare for some women. This led critics to depict women on welfare as lazy. When the proportion of women of color, especially black women, peaked at 44 percent of the caseload, the condition of the program became racialized. And as single mothers replaced widows on the rolls, critics said welfare fueled immorality.

Drawing on these negative stereotypes, the newly elected Reagan administration justified its deep cuts in welfare by arguing that denying poor women welfare would force them to mend their ways. Beginning in the 1980s, lawmakers cut welfare by tightening eligibility rules, lowering benefits, and defunding a host of social programs. The changes pushed thousands of women off the rolls into low-paid jobs, but also into dangerous welfare hotels, drug-plagued streets, and unsafe relationships. Congress also encouraged the states to experiment with stiff welfare-to-work programs, which paved the way for the 1988 Family Support Act (FSA). The FSA transformed AFDC from a program to help single mothers stay home with their children into a mandatory work program. Blaming welfare's size and cost on the values and behavior of the poor, lawmakers hid the real agenda of welfare reform: supplying business with more low-paid labor, shrinking the welfare state, and stigmatizing single motherhood.

ENFORCING THE WORK ETHIC

The second attack on welfare trained its sights on women's work behavior. It meshed with efforts of Presidents Reagan, Bush, and Clinton to promote economic growth by lowering labor costs for employers. Indeed, TANF's "work-first" policy flooded the labor market with thousands of workers. The increased competition for jobs pressed wages down and made it harder for unions to negotiate good contracts.

From 1935 until the late 1960s, society expected women, especially mothers of young children, to stay home—although poverty prevented women from following this advice. Official welfare policy, which incorporated this gender norm, penalized recipients if they went to work. Of course, welfare departments regularly skirted the federal guidelines by setting benefits lower than wages, restricting eligibility, and otherwise servicing local employers who wanted poor women to fill low-paying jobs.

By the mid-1970s, social attitudes toward women's work had changed. The feminist movement encouraged women to seek greater independence by earning their own way. At the same time, the demand for female workers grew in response to both the rapid expansion of low-paid service jobs typically reserved for women and the fears of business and industry that labor shortages in the service sector would lower their profits by pushing wages up. Some business experts predicted that by the year 2000 labor markets would be "tighter than at any time in recent history."[7] During this period, rising welfare grants in the higher benefit states made it economically rational for some women to choose welfare over work.

Rather than try to attract women workers by addressing their concerns about unequal pay, health benefits, and family responsibilities, business urged government to consider welfare reform. In 1986, the National Alliance of Business (NAB) concluded, "welfare recipients represent an important source of needed workers" that must be "encouraged to enter the labor market through government-subsidized education, training, and social services."[8]

The dramatic conversion of welfare from a program that allowed single mothers to stay home with their children into a mandatory work program in the late 1980s led most observers to believe that the twenty-year effort to revamp welfare had ended. Thus Clinton surprised nearly everyone when, in 1992, he proposed to transform AFDC into a transitional and temporary work program. If the assault on welfare's size and cost depended on misinformed explanations of welfare's growth, the push for a more intense work program drew on myths about women, welfare, and work—in particular the portrayal of women on welfare as lazy and unmotivated.

Those who accepted these myths ignored massive amounts of contradictory evidence. For years researchers had reported that more than half of all single mothers on welfare had a prior work history, had worked while receiving benefits, and left the rolls within two years in response to the availability of decent paying jobs with adequate transportation, childcare, and health benefits.[9]

As noted above, the stiff work-first rules combined with a strong economy caused a sharp drop in the welfare rolls. The early reports indicated that around 50 percent of the former recipients found work. However, the other 50 percent did not,[10] despite a 4.2 unemployment rate—the lowest since the 1960s. And this does not include those people that the researchers failed to locate. Of the recipients that did find work, many simply joined the ranks of the working poor—earning between $6.00 and $8.00 an hour. The former recipients told researchers that due to low wages they could no longer make ends meet.[11] Their wages exceeded the $5.15 an hour minimum wage, but this did not lift their families out of poverty. Life for many former recipients has, if anything, worsened. A New Jersey women commented: "How are you supposed to survive on the minimum wage—feed the kids, pay the rent, utilities?"[12] In addition to below-poverty wages, welfare reform cost many women access to Food Stamps, Medicaid, and low-rent housing. In some cases, welfare failed to provide the promised transitional medical and childcare services needed by women to get and keep a job. Other women simply lost prior benefits. "I was worse off when I was working than I am now," explained one Massachusetts woman.

Because the studies tracking women who leave welfare rarely reach the jobless women and the most troubled families, the findings barely capture the true hardship of women no longer on welfare. We do know, however, that the number of children living below *one-half the poverty line* for a family of three (or less than $6,401 as a yearly income in 1997) grew by 400,000 between 1995 and 1997. We also know that one out of five children who live in poverty face a greater chance of having stunted growth, less education, and lower projected earnings than children raised above the poverty line. Statisticians trace much of the nationwide rise in poverty directly to the loss of government benefits.[13] Living in the gap between the haves and the have-nots, many families report increased anxiety and stress.

Welfare reform also affects community life adversely. In the absence of jobs and decent pay, welfare dollars kept local merchants afloat in lower income communities. The merchants, in turn, hired local residents, made streets safer, and otherwise sustained the neighborhood's viability. Welfare reform has reduced the amount of cash flowing into poor communities, draining the last bit of money out of places abandoned by business and industry during the last twenty-five years for cheaper labor elsewhere. The nation's cities feel the negative impact of welfare reform in still another way. Already home to most of the nation's poverty and unemployment, they now find themselves serving a larger share of the national and state welfare population—even though the absolute numbers have dropped.[14]

In the past, when the economy failed poor women, they could turn to welfare until their circumstances improved or they could combine work with some welfare aid. But lifetime limits on welfare eligibility effectively eliminates this option. In those states that imposed a two-year time limit, thousands of women have already exhausted their benefits forever. By 2002, the five-year cap will take effect in all states. A former recipient noted, "They should not have a five-year time limit on people who are not able to get on their feet right away. You could get hurt or sick, then what? They should look at each situation. Every situation is different."[15] Time-limited welfare ignores important realities: some women cannot work outside the home due to ill health, low education, lack of skills, disabilities, emotional problems, or other barriers to employment. Another reality is that the labor market rarely has room for all those ready and able to work.

UPHOLDING THE FAMILY ETHIC

A third part of the assault on poor women and welfare aim at women's marital, childbearing, and parenting behavior. This attack enforced the family values agenda pushed by the New Right since the early 1980s, if not before, and included in the ongoing economic recovery plan. Like the work ethic, welfare reform also embodies the "family ethic"—a set of beliefs holding that everyone should marry and live in two-parent, heterosexual households, preferably with one wage earner and one homemaker.[16] With this narrow version of "family" in mind, in the late 1980s the New Right declared that the family, as they defined it, was imperiled by the rise of working wives, single mothers, divorced couples, gay parents, interracial marriages, test-tube babies, legalized abortion, birth control, the sexual revolution—and *government welfare programs*.[17]

Welfare reform's ostensible concern about parenting has not translated into policies that help poor women take care of their kids. Originally designed to enable single mothers to stay home, welfare once represented a partial acknowledgement of the important and time-consuming role of parenting. In contrast, TANF's time limits, stiff work rules, and heavy sanctions devalue women's caretaking work. They also make it harder for poor women to supervise their children effectively, especially in neighborhoods plagued by drugs, crime, and violence.

ATTACKING ENTITLEMENTS

The fourth attack on welfare also meshed well with the economic recovery plan begun in the early 1980s. By undercutting the principle of entitlement—the strongest feature of the U.S. social welfare system—it helped to weaken the welfare state and discredit the regulatory role of the federal government.

The notion of entitlement represents a philosophical commitment and a budgetary mechanism that place the government on the side of people in need. Since the 1930s, the federal government pledged responsibility for the general welfare of its citizens and provided regular and automatic funding for a group of programs called entitlements. In theory, as long as welfare fell into the entitlement category, no one who met the program's eligibility rules went without assistance. While many states historically denied or provided very low benefits to persons of color or otherwise manipulated the rules, the entitlement principle set a standard to be reached and enforced.[18]

When the PRA converted welfare from a federal entitlement program into a block grant administered by the states, it made one of the most far-reaching changes in U.S. social welfare since the passage of the 1935 Social Security Act. Once welfare lost its entitlement status, the federal guarantee of monies disappeared. No longer will federal welfare funding to the states automatically rise when inflation, recession, population growth, or other conditions intensify the demand. If the need for welfare in a state exceeds its resources, its lawmakers must now choose between unpopular options: raising taxes, cutting benefits, denying aid to the poor, creating a waiting list, or simply ending welfare.[19] Moreover, the funding for TANF expires in the year 2002, at which time the program's future funding becomes subject to the highly politicized and uncertain congressional budget process.

By transforming welfare into a state-run block grant, Congress also fragmented an already decentralized system. Prior to TANF, states complied with federal guidelines in exchange for federal support. This created some uniformity while delegating considerable control to the states, including the right to define "need," to set their own benefit levels, and to establish other rules. By honoring states' rights, the program created the space for discriminatory practices, as noted above. It also resulted in interstate benefit differences that exceeded variations in the cost of living. In 1996, benefits ranged from a high of $923 a month in Alaska to a low of $120 a month in Mississippi. Now that states can use some TANF dollars for other than cash assistance, more state to state variation will occur.

Ending welfare as an entitlement poses a real threat to the economic security of poor women and children. But for those who oppose what they refer to as "big government," welfare reform represents the first step in a wider effort to dismantle the more popular social welfare programs serving the middle class as well as the poor. The taboo against tampering with *any* entitlement program has been broken, which makes it that much easier to target others. Indeed, shortly after President Clinton signed the welfare reform bill which stripped AFDC of its entitlement status, the Commission on Social Security Reform recommended several ways to privatize Social Security—the nation's strongest and most universal income support program—previously believed to be politically untouchable. Since then Congress has been debating not *if* but *how and when* to turn Social Security over to Wall Street and Medicare over to the private insurance companies.

The attack on the welfare state also helps to discredit the overall role of the federal government in society, another goal of the economic recovery program. President Clinton himself declared that "the era of big government is over." Once the government comes under this kind of political fire, it becomes that much easier to cut taxes and limit the ability of the government to protect consumers, workers, and the environment; to regulate business practices, and to otherwise limit corporate America's already high profits. In 1999 the Supreme Court ruled in favor of three cases (unrelated to welfare) that "significantly strengthened the power of the states in the Federal system while weakening those of the Federal Government." The editors of the *New York Times* concluded that these "alarming decisions will make it harder to enforce uniform policies on matters of national concern like the environment or health."[20]

THE WAR ON WELFARE CONCERNS ALL WOMEN

Welfare reform harms poor women on public assistance first and foremost. But it also threatens the right of *all* women to decent pay, to control their own sexuality, to live free of abusive relationships, and to survive in families that do not fit the two-parent model. Welfare reform does this by undercutting caretaking supports, reproductive rights, safety from male violence, and economic independence.

CARETAKING SUPPORTS   As with life insurance, women hope that they will never need it, but any woman can fall on hard times. Since welfare reform downplays the value of women's work, it undercuts the need to support women's caretaking activities in the home. By legitimizing social program cuts, welfare reform poses a threat to the economic resources of all families that rely on government dollars to help with the cost of housing, healthcare, childcare, elder care, family leave, and other services. Cutting these programs also shifts the costs of caretaking and homemaking from the government back to women in the home and increases the burden of those trying to balance work and family responsibilities. Depriving women of caretaking supports makes it harder for women to work outside the home, an outcome desired by family-values advocates for women—other than single mothers on welfare.

REPRODUCTIVE RIGHTS   The attack on poor women's reproductive choices also undermines the reproductive rights of all women. The welfare reformers insist that poverty is caused by sex and childbearing rather than lack of skills, poor education, and low-paying jobs. In response, welfare reform tries to control women's reproductive choices. Once the government wins the right to deny aid to women who have children while on welfare and to otherwise limit the reproductive rights of poor women, it becomes that much easier to tamper with the reproductive rights of all women. The pattern already exists. Shortly after 1973, when the Supreme Court (in *Roe* v. *Wade*) granted women the right to an abortion, the right-to-life forces won passage of the Hyde Amendment, which forbids the use of Medicaid dollars for abortions. Since then, abortion foes have successfully limited the reproductive rights of women regardless of their economic class. Welfare reform follows suit.

MALE VIOLENCE   Male violence poses a serious problem for women on and off welfare. Researchers estimate that from 50 to 65 percent of welfare recipients have experienced abuse. Feminists fought for the Family Violence Option in the 1996 welfare law to ensure that the states screen welfare recipients for battering, provide services, and waive work rules that would force women off welfare into abusive situations. Unfortunately, few states actively enforce these safeguards. A woman is battered every fifteen minutes in the United States. Two to four million are battered every year. While not all battered women are poor or on welfare, adequate welfare provision makes it economically possible for any woman to escape dangerous and exploitative relationships.

ECONOMIC INDEPENDENCE   The attack on welfare threatens the economic independence of all women by making it harder to earn a living. First, a smaller welfare state means fewer of the public-sector jobs that enabled many women—both white women and women of color—to enter the middle class. Second, to the extent that time limits, work rules, and punitive sanctions increase the competition for low wage jobs, welfare reform presses wages down for all low-paid workers, both women and men. Finally, shrinking welfare benefits undercuts cash aid, which represents a potential economic backup for any woman. The economic security provided by such a fallback makes it easier for workers to fight exploitation on the job and harder for employers to keep workers in line. The security also permits women to take the risks associated with resisting male domination in the home.

WHY NOW?

We have seen that welfare reform has wreaked havoc on women's lives and the wider welfare state. Drawing on myths about the relationship between welfare and women's work, marital, childbearing, and parenting behavior, today's welfare programs intensify the regulation of women's lives. Ignoring massive research findings, labor-market realities, and the dynamics of family life, welfare reformers attacked the program for single mothers and then interpreted declining welfare rolls as a success. However, welfare rights advocates maintain that welfare reform has failed because it has increased the economic vulnerability of many poor women, threatened the well-being of many of the non-poor, did little or nothing to help poor women and children escape poverty, and undercut the entire welfare state.

Welfare reform was neither accidental nor simply mean-spirited. Rather, it helped to carry out the well-known plan for economic recovery which increased the profits for those at the top by imposing austerity on nearly everyone else. Welfare reform helped lower labor costs, shrink the welfare state, enforce family values, and discredit the role of the federal government in wider society. Forcing women off welfare keeps wages down by expanding the supply of workers who must compete for low-paying jobs. Welfare reforms also threatened the wider welfare state by creating support for social program cuts and undermining the principle of entitlement. This disinvestment in social welfare reflected corporate America's abandonment of U.S. workers and eased its fears that government spending competed for funds with private investment. By attacking social welfare programs, the nation's leaders also helped to discredit the federal government's protective and regulatory functions. In no small way, welfare reform enforced the family values agenda promulgated by the social conservatives who deplore not only single mothers but also homosexuality, sex education, and the right to abortion.

The economic recovery plan initiated in the early 1980s also weakened the power of social movements that tried to resist this austerity plan. Social movements represent the interests of the more powerless members of society. During the years after the Second World War, these movements gained members and influence by, among other things, winning a wide range of government benefits for their members and others. Like a strike fund, the availability of these benefits, especially unemployment insurance, welfare, and health insurance, also increased the movement's bargaining power with employers and with the government.

Ronald Reagan signaled the assault on social movements when he broke the air traffic controllers' strike, attacked the gains of the civil rights movement, and became the first president to speak out against abortion. These actions let business and the wider public know that it was okay to "go after" the trade unions, civil rights, and women's movements, which lost many of their hard-won gains. The losses placed the movements on the defensive, cost them members and deprived them of time, money, and energy needed to fight back, much less progress. However, the effort to silence protest never fully succeeded. Indeed activism, including social welfare activism, has a long history in the United States. Whenever the attacks occurred, poor, working and middle-class women fought back. The current assault on the welfare state is no exception.

NOTES

1. U.S. Congressional Budget Office, *Reducing Entitlement Spending* (Washington, D.C.: U.S. Government Printing Office, 1994), x, Table 1.
2. U.S House of Representatives, Committee on Ways and Means, *Overview of Entitlement Programs, 1998 Green Book* (Washington, D.C.: U.S. Government Printing Office, 1998), 402, Table 7–2.
3. U.S. House of Representatives, Committee on Ways and Means, *Overview of Entitlement Programs, 1998 Green Book* (Washington, D.C.: U.S. Government Printing Office, 1998), 413, Table 6; U.S. Congress, Congressional Budget Office, *The Economic Budget Outlook, 2000–2009* (Washington, D.C.: U.S. Government Printing Office, 1999), 136, Historical Tables; Robert Pear, "Welfare and Food Stamp Rolls Ends Six Years of Increases," *New York Times*, 14 March 1995: 18; Center for Law and Social Policy, "AFDC Caseload Declines: Implications for Block Grant Planning" (Washington, D.C.: 2 October 1995), 1, Factsheet.
4. Labor Institute, *Corporate Power and the American Dream* (New York: Labor Institute, April 1995), 82.
5. Francis Fox Piven and Richard Cloward, *Regulating the Poor: The Functions of Public Assistance* (New York: Pantheon, 1971).
6. U.S. House of Representatives, Committee on Ways and Means, *Overview of Entitlement Programs, 1998 Green Book* (Washington, D.C.: U.S. Government Printing Office, 1998), 413, Table 6.
7. Aaron Bernstein, "Where the Jobs Are The Skills Aren't," *Business Week*, 19 September 1988: 108; U.S. Department of Labor, *Workforce 2000: Work and Workers for the 21st Century* (Washington, D.C.: U.S. Government Printing Office, 1987).

8. National Alliance of Business, *Employment Policies: Looking to the Year 2000*, February 1986, I, 8.

9. See, for example, LaDonna Pavetti, "The Dynamics of Welfare and Work: Exploring the Process by which Young Women Work Their Way off Welfare," cited in U.S. House, Committee on Ways and Means, *Overview of Entitlement Programs, 1994 Green Book* (Washington, D.C.: U.S. Government Printing Office, 1994), 40, 43–44.

10. Sharon Parrott, *Welfare Recipients Who Find Jobs: What Do We Know About Their Employment and Earnings?* (Washington, D.C.: Center on Budget and Policy Priorities, 16 November 1998), 9.

11. Ibid., 5–19.

12. Irene Skricki, *Unheard Voices: Participants Evaluate the JOBS Program* (Washington D.C.: Coalition on Human Needs, January 1993), 13.

13. Joyce Short, "The Great Enemy of Morality is Indifference," *Legal Service of New Jersey Report*, February/March 1999: 9; CBPP on poverty (children living below one-half the poverty line) cited in CDF summary sheet.

14. *The Impact of Welfare Reform in the 30 Largest U.S. Cities: 1999* (Washington, D.C.: Brookings Institution, February 1999).

15. Legal Services of New Jersey, *Assessing Work First: What Happens after Welfare?* (New Brunswick, NJ: June 1999), 74.

16. Mimi Abramovitz, *Regulating the Lives of Women: Social Welfare Policy from Colonial Times to the Present*, 2d ed. (Boston: South End Press, 1996).

17. David Popenoe, "The Family Transformed," *Family Affairs* 2, nos. 2–3 (Summer/Fall 1989): 1, 2.

18. Mimi Abramovitz, *Regulating the Lives of Women*.

19. Center on Budget and Policy Priorities, "Summary Effects of House Bill H.R.4 on Low Income Programs," short brief (Washington, D.C.: 1995), 3.

20. Editors, "Supreme Mischief," *New York Times*, 24 June 1999: A26; Linda Greenhouse, "States Are Given New Legal Shield by Supreme Court," *New York Times*, 24 June 1999: A1, A22.

TOWARD A STRATEGY FOR
WOMEN'S ECONOMIC EQUALITY

CHRIS TILLY AND RANDY ALBELDA

While women's economic advancement over the past four decades has been tremendous, the agenda of equal opportunity remains far from finished in the United States. It is easier for a woman to get elected to office, hold a full-time job, and support herself without having to depend on a man, but women still face enormous barriers to economic equality. For some educated and accomplished women that barrier is the glass ceiling, but for far too many women—and their children—the barrier is a bottomless pit, with few ladders up and out. In fact, U.S. women have suffered serious economic setbacks in the last few years—notably the 1996 welfare "reform" law, which shredded the safety net for single mothers, and average women's wage rates that have fallen further behind men's once more, ending two decades of relative wage gains. Women, including mothers, are now expected to work for wages, but they face sharply unequal opportunities in the labor market, as well as unequal responsibilities in the home.

Fulfilling an agenda for women's economic equality will take more than debunking myths, explaining realities, and proposing new policies, however sensible they may be. Achieving equality is a question of power—of economic and social power, but most decisively of political power. At this point, the power of low-income women and their allies is at a low ebb. But advocates of equality have begun to form new alliances and hatch new strategies, so the coming years may see some surprising power shifts.

POWER SURGE: WHAT IT WILL TAKE
TO REVERSE ECONOMIC INEQUALITY

There is no magic answer for how to repulse the backlash against welfare and women's rights. If there were, the women's rights and welfare rights movements would have figured it out long ago. But from the long history of struggles for economic and social equality in this country—and from the setbacks as well as the triumphs in these struggles—we can outline the elements of a strategy for change.[1] We focus here particularly on a strategy for winning real welfare reform that can actually help end poverty and enhance economic equality for all women. That's because we believe that the best way to achieve women's economic equality is by lifting up the bottom.

To build the power to advance women's economic equality, we need a strategy with four components.[2] To start with, the strategy must target power in the workplace—expanding the voice and bargaining power of women and of low-wage workers in the employment relationship. Another key element is conventional politics, encompassing electoral mobilization, lobbying, and litigation (challenging bad laws, or challenging the failure to implement good laws). The power of protest has always been and remains important for "outsiders" far from the centers of power. Finally, the ultimate battle involves shaping public opinion, by telling the truth in ways that spark people's imagination, sympathy, and solidarity.

These four strategic elements are by no means separate. Changing laws via conventional politics can widen the scope for power in the workplace or for protest. Protest is a tool for influencing workplace power, conventional politics, and public opinion. Public opinion, in turn, exerts enormous leverage on legislative action and on the effectiveness of protest. But it is helpful to look at the four as distinct, though overlapping and interacting, arenas of action. Through this prism, let's look briefly at the past, present, and possible future of battles for women's economic equality.

WORKPLACE POWER STRUGGLES: PAST, PRESENT, FUTURE

If we are to become a "nation of workers" which includes even mothers of young children, then the struggle for workplace equality is a vital component for improving the lives of women and their families. The history of workplace-based efforts to win equality for women is largely, for better or worse, the history of unions. As social historian Ruth Milkman points out, there have been four major cohorts of unionism in the United States, and each cohort's attitude toward women at its inception has continued to color its relationship with women.[3] Dating back to the nineteenth century, the earliest stable unions were male-dominated craft unions, such as those in the building trades and printing, which have historically viewed women with suspicion as low-wage competitors, and to a large extent continue to do so. (Other union movements from that era, such as the Knights of Labor and later the International Workers of the World, welcomed women, but did not survive.) A second wave of unionism in the 1910s, especially in the clothing and textile industries, sought to organize women—who made up a growing portion of the workforce in those industries—but maintained a paternalistic attitude toward them as vulnerable workers in need of particular protection. The reality was more complicated than that attitude would allow: women were particularly subject to employer abuse in the early decades of the century, but also led and took part in militant actions such as the 1909 "Uprising of the 20,000," a hard-fought thirteen-week strike of women shirtwaist workers in New York City.

The tide turned for women in the labor movement in the 1930s with the rise of the CIO. Women were integral to the mass production manufacturing industries in the 1930s and 1940s, and the CIO organized them as equals and took a formal stand against gender discrimination—although CIO unions also took part in the displacement of women workers by returning servicemen at the end of the Second World War. Finally, the service, clerical, and public sector unions that grew after the war have organized occupations that are predominantly female (nurses, teachers, clerical workers), and have been powerfully influenced by the resurgent women's movement of the 1960s. Unions from this wave, such as the Service Employees International Union (SEIU), the American Federation of State, County, and Municipal Employees (AFSCME), the American Nurses Association (ANA), and the National Education Association (NEA), have promoted women leaders and SEIU and AFSCME have actively campaigned for comparable worth since the 1980s.

At present, workplace efforts for gender equality reflect this mixed legacy. At one extreme, women in the building trades continue to battle against outright exclusion (carried out through informal means, since formal bars are now illegal). On the other hand, "fourth-wave" unions representing service and clerical workers are actively seeking to organize women, win pay equity, and establish more work/family flexibility. Enriching the mix is the sprouting, since the 1970s, of new advocacy groups oriented to women workers, but not directly focused on unionization. The Cleveland-based Nine to Five/National Association of Working Women is perhaps the best known, but numerous other groups such as Boston's Office Technology Education Project and San Francisco's New Ways to Work combine education, lobbying, and, in some cases, organizing to confront issues ranging from workplace safety and health, to pay equity, to work/family issues. Meanwhile, within the AFL–CIO itself, new leadership elected in 1995 rode into office on a reform platform. After a century of federation presidents from unions representing male, blue-collar workers, particularly the building trades, the AFL–CIO elected John Sweeney, then president of the Service Employees International Union—a fast-growing, forward-looking fourth-wave union that mainly encompasses white- and pink-collar workers. In a potent bit of symbolism, Sweeney's slate included Linda Chavez-Thompson of AFSCME as executive vice president, another fourth-waver and the first woman to hold a top AFL–CIO office. While the actual change delivered to date by these leaders has been limited, they offer an important opening for new activism. At this point, the main obstacle to unions' contribution to equality for women is no longer hostility or indifference within the labor movement (though those problems certainly remain), but rather the unions' shrinking percentage share of the workforce, which continues to dwindle toward the single digits.

And that sets the stage for the future. In our view—and in the view of many innovators in the labor movement—the strategies most likely to succeed in rebuilding the labor movement are those that will increase their involvement in battles for gender equality. Women make up a growing share of the workforce, particularly the barely unionized service sector, and are on average more supportive of unions than men, so any survival strategy for the AFL–CIO must place a priority on organizing predominantly female occupations and industries. More broadly, in order to succeed, the union movement must reclaim its mantle as the spokesperson for all workers and low-income people, not just the few covered by union contract. From Sweeney down to the local level, much of the labor movement has begun to take on this challenge, championing a higher minimum wage, local living wage ordinances, and other measures that will help the lowest paid. Though they have not made welfare reform a central issue, the AFL–CIO leadership has taken some progressive stands opposing punitive reform—in part due to the displacement threat that workfare poses to their public employee membership base—and local leaders have in some cases gone beyond statements to play an active role in coalitions defending welfare rights.[4]

In addition, the labor movement of the future is likely to make more use of organizing tools that offer new opportunities to mobilize women. Because labor law itself offers so little protection for unions, they will have to rely increasingly on labor–community coalitions. Women have long played a prominent role in community-based organizations, and community action often focuses on "consumption" issues of particular concern to women as mothers and homemakers: housing, healthcare, social services and so on. In building bridges with communities, unions will be compelled to take on more of this agenda. Unions will also have to undertake more city-wide, industry-wide organizing—like the Justice for Janitors campaign that has tried to organize janitors across whole cities—rather than traditional shop-by-shop campaigns. Again, since family responsibilities and limited job opportunities make women more likely than men to move in and out of the workforce, and from one workplace to another, this new organizing approach should be a better fit with women's work lives.

CONVENTIONAL POLITICS: UNCONVENTIONAL APPROACHES?

In some ways, conventional politics has been the "toughest nut to crack" for low-income women and their advocates. Low representation of women and the political establishment's lack of interest in poor women have served to cut out effective anti-poverty, employment, and childcare policies for women and their children. After all, children can't vote, and low-income people usually turn out at the polls only when there are candidates who excite them and address their issues—which occurs all too infrequently.

Historically women have been largely locked out of conventional political activity, but hammered at the door until they got in. Women's suffrage organizations blossomed after the Civil War as part of a broader women-led movement for social improvement, and finally won the vote nationwide in 1920. Even without the vote, the late nineteenth and early twentieth centuries saw middle-class organizations such as the Women's Christian Temperance Union, the General Federation of Women's Clubs, and the National Association of Colored Women combine lobbying with education, charitable work, and in some cases protest. Once the vote was won, the enormous but superficially united women's suffrage movement splintered: the National Woman Party proposed an Equal Rights Amendment in 1923 and pursued it single-mindedly, whereas the League of Women Voters and other women's organizations opposed the amendment on the basis that it would outlaw special protections for women workers, who were particularly vulnerable.[5] Nonetheless, women had found a foothold, and participated in political campaigns and coalitions from the New Deal of the 1930s to the Great Society of the 1960s.

With the second women's movement of the 1960s came a new growth of women's lobbying and electoral organizations—such as the National Organization for Women and the National Women's Political Caucus—and a surge in the number of women elected officials, including governors and senators for the first time. Despite this, the Equal Rights Amendment fell short of ratification in 1982 and electoral progress has been limited. Women are still under-represented as elected officials at virtually all levels, especially in Congress.

And although the New Left began the mobilization of women, the New Right has also been very effective at organizing women's political involvement around conservative backlash issues—opposing abortion, upholding "traditional" family structures, defending white privilege, and cutting taxes. Conservative women claim that not only has equality for women been accomplished, it has gone too far. For the last two decades much of middle-class women's political energies has gone into defending reproductive rights, including supporting pro-choice candidates, regardless of their positions on women's economic equality.

And that's where we stand today—with unprecedented numbers of women involved in conventional politics, but with the legislative agenda for women's equality largely stalled. In 1995, when the Personal Responsibility Act, the harsh, Republican-crafted federal welfare reform, first came up for a vote, all four white women senators—Democrat and Republican alike—voted for it. (The lone African-American woman in the Senate, Carol Moseley Braun—since defeated for re-election—cast a nay vote.) And the most visible woman governor, Christine Todd Whitman of New Jersey, is a tax-cutting, service-slashing conservative. In fact, given the rush by state legislatures and governors to make welfare stingier, welfare advocates have had to rely primarily on the courts to defend welfare rights. Sitting judges still to some extent reflect the more liberal politics of earlier decades—and also take more seriously the constitutional and statutory guarantees that are often ignored by legislators and administrators anxious to cut costs and score political pints. But litigation to defend the rights of poor women can only be a holding action.

Regaining ground for women's equality in conventional politics calls for a four-pronged strategy. First, shifting the balance of power will require registering and mobilizing many who don't vote now, particularly poor people and people of color. Second, any electoral advances will be limited until we reform campaign financing to lessen the influence of rich individuals and corporations. Not surprisingly, corporations and the wealthy have little interest in shifting funding priorities or in empowering low-income people. Progressive candidates rarely can afford to make their way through the electoral process. Third, women in general and low-income women in particular need to consolidate new alliances in the electoral arena. Potential allies include the labor movement (as noted above), communities of color, and churches and religious activists, who have often taken a strongly compassionate stand on issues of poverty and human services, despite more anti-woman positions on issues such as reproductive choice. One possible outcome of the alliance-building process is the growth of third parties, and the progress of new third-party initiatives such as the New Party, the Labor Party, and the 21st Century Party (initiated by the National Organization for Women) bears watching. Finally, new ways must be found to win the hearts and minds of working people, so many of whom are currently swayed by anti-tax, anti-government, and anti-welfare rhetoric.

PROTEST AND SURVIVE

Protest has long been a potent political lever for women, and particularly for poor women.[6] The history of protest overlaps intimately with the history of unionism and of electoral politics: unionists organized and struck, but also demonstrated for causes such as the eight-hour day; suffragists lobbied, but also rallied and marched. But women and their allies also have a long history of protests focused on issues of family, consumption, and unpaid domestic labor— issues that are typically more peripheral to unions and electoral politics. In the first years of the century, women repeatedly organized food boycotts and tenant unions to resist high prices and rents. During the 1920s, women's auxiliaries consisting of the wives of male union members demanded government creation of local health departments and maternal and child health programs. The Communist Party-organized United Council of Working Class Wives mobilized women on issues of cost of living, education, and social welfare, and when the Depression hit joined the newly formed Unemployed Councils in demanding better relief as well as more jobs. The black Housewives' Leagues launched "Don't Buy Where You Can't Work" boycott campaigns in major cities, and also called for job creation during the Depression.

In the decades after the Second World War, the civil rights movement and the second-wave women's movement cross-fertilized with community organizing, giving rise to new protests. Civil rights activists, realizing that formal legal rights did not guarantee economic equality, broadened their focus once the Civil Rights Act was won in 1964. After all, when Martin Luther King was killed in

1968, he was in Memphis to support a sanitation workers' strike. The Lyndon Johnson administration's mid-1960s' War on Poverty offered an opening for a new wave of organizing in low-income communities. One dramatic outgrowth of this ferment was the National Welfare Rights Organization (NWRO), formed in 1967, building on earlier local efforts. NWRO activated poor women to demand AFDC benefits that they were already entitled to, and protested and lobbied to expand welfare recipients' rights. NWRO reached its high-water mark in 1971, with 900 chapters in fifty states, but folded in 1975 as political times changed.

Protests continue up to the present. In 1987 the newly formed National Welfare Rights Union (NWRU) picked up NWRO's torch; in 1992, the Oakland, California-based Women's Economic Agenda Project brought hundreds of women together for a Poor Women's Convention. Advocates for more effective welfare policies have devised creative approaches to protest. NWRU has organized welfare office sit-ins and takeovers of abandoned housing. On Valentine's Day 1995, in response to a call by JEDI Women (Justice, Economic Dignity, and Independence for Women) of Salt Lake City, activists in seventy-six cities carried out actions on the theme "Our Children's Hearts Are in Your Hands," targeting the punitive Personal Responsibility Act then before Congress. Participants in the actions mailed 61,000 postcards to legislators. The JEDI women themselves marched into the Salt Lake City Federal Building to present their legislators with a port-a-crib full of cards colored by children in daycare centers.[7] But in the shadow of the conservative backlash, protests appear less and less effective, and are more likely to mobilize hundreds in a given city than tens of thousands. Ironically, women and men have turned out in hundreds of thousands to defend other rights related to gender equity—reproductive choice, gay and lesbian rights—but have not responded in large numbers to the welfare "reform" that poses perhaps the sharpest current attack on women's rights.

Looking to the future, protest can play two important roles in the push for welfare rights and full equality for women. For one thing, protests constitute an ongoing moral presence that can help to shape public opinion and shame legislators. Though protests may not currently seem to move us much further forward on welfare rights, they are most definitely helping to prevent us from sliding further backwards. But protests serve a second role as well, and one where there is room for growth and experimentation: they make an unfair system harder to govern. The National Welfare Rights Organization strategy started by mobilizing poor women to demand rights that were already on the books, exploiting the margin of administrative discretion that already existed; they backed up these demands with the threat of disruption. We can't apply the same strategy uncritically at a time of cutbacks, but we can apply the same principles. For example, in many states, the executive branch is using administrative discretion to reduce eligibility and benefit levels beyond what's required by law, so they can boast of reduced welfare rolls and decreased spending. These discretionary actions mark a pressure point where protest can potentially win immediate, material gains for poor women, while exposing politicians' dishonesty. In many cases social services staff, whose own jobs are threatened by the anti-welfare assault, may be helpful in identifying and acting on these pressure points.

THE BATTLE FOR PUBLIC OPINION

The history of the tussle over public opinion is completely intertwined with the long history of labor, electoral, and protest strategies we have already outlined. But history does hold some important lessons. For one thing, the mobilization of public opinion has often been a two-edged sword. For example, middle-class female reformers used arguments about morality and the sacredness of the family to win support for Mother's Aid, the state-level predecessor to AFDC. But those same arguments, coupled with class prejudice, convinced the reformers and their allies that Mother's Aid should involve close monitoring of the behavior of recipients, and should only be made available to "morally fit" mothers.[8] As this example points out, U.S. public opinion—and with it U.S. public policy—have always distinguished between the deserving and undeserving poor.[9]

That distinction continues to haunt us. Sympathy for poor people, especially children, coexists with resentment of "freeloaders." An expectation that government should make our lives better clashes with cynicism about the willingness or ability of government to accomplish anything constructive. Consciousness of harder economic times does not displace the deeply held conviction that anyone can make it if she/he really tries. And running through it all, in the minds of most Americans, is the notion that many—perhaps most—of the poor are undeserving. In sociologist Mark Rank's study of welfare in Wisconsin, perhaps his most discouraging finding came when he surveyed welfare recipients about their views of why they and others were on welfare. Rank asked whether recipients believed they were solely responsible for being on welfare, whether it was due to circumstances beyond their control, or some combination of the two. Speaking of themselves, 82 percent of recipients blamed circumstances beyond their control, 12 percent cited a combination, and 6 percent took full responsibility. But, as for other recipients, 90 percent of those welfare recipients stated that "people on welfare" are partially or fully to blame for their situation. In short, even most welfare recipients themselves classify other recipients as undeserving.[10]

The result of this strong streak of blame is that public opinion victories tend to be narrow and fragile. In the fight against the 1995 Personal Responsibility Act, the struggle for public opinion was critical in securing President Clinton's veto of the legislation. But it appears that what tipped the balance was not the National Welfare Rights Union's street actions, not the National Organization for Women's rally in Washington that defined welfare cuts as violence against women, and not the *New York Times* ad by the feminist Committee of One Hundred Women, who declared that "a war against poor women is a war against all women!" Instead, a leak of the Clinton administration's internal estimate that the law would plunge one million children into poverty, and a media push focusing on children, spearheaded by the Children's Defense Fund and the National Association of Social Workers, finally achieved a Clinton veto. Of course, concern with the plight of children is an entirely appropriate response to punitive welfare reform proposals. But focusing on children alone minimizes the assault on the rights of women and of poor people, and leaves the door open for policies that control and punish women "for the sake of the children." As the Welfare Warriors of Milwaukee, Wisconsin, wrote in an angry 1995 open letter, "It is time for our allies to do more than apologize for our existence. It is time to stand up for our right to public support for our children and our right to mother our own children."[11] In any case, the appeal for child welfare was not sufficient to stop the same legislation the following year.

In future attempts to move public opinion, the tools used to date will remain important. There is an ongoing need for publications put out jointly by recipients and advocates, such as Boston's *Survival News* and Milwaukee's *Welfare Mothers' Voice*; op-eds and cable television talk show appearances; *New York Times* ads and speaking tours. But many of these media preach primarily to the already converted, while potential allies turn the page or flip the channel. If we acknowledge that the battle for public opinion is actually more like a war of position, we must find ways to use the equivalent of both artillery and house-to-house combat.

The "big guns" consist of advertising, particularly on television and radio. When New York governor George Pataki announced a budget featuring $4 billion in budget cuts in February 1995, a coalition of unions, students, seniors, and others launched a grassroots campaign of lobbying and protest. But at the same time, unions and various institutional interests such as hospitals and home-care associations spent several million dollars on an advertising blitz. Pataki's ratings went from 38 percent negative to 63 percent; 65 percent of survey respondents said the budget fight made them "think less of the Republican Party of New York generally"[12] Of course, advertising takes money, so poor people can only pursue this strategy if they find allies with deep pockets—unions and churches being two key examples.

As for the "house-to-house combat," it translates into one-to-one and small group discussion and education. The issues surrounding welfare are complex; sound bites cannot adequately capture them. Winning support for a full women's equality agenda means challenging deeply held beliefs about family, work, and government, while tapping into and nurturing other, equally deeply held beliefs—working through the contradictions we presented above. Many forums are possible for this kind of discussion: house meetings, churches and other places of worship, PTAs, unions—wherever people live, work, and socialize. Mobilizing the people-power for this kind of effort is even more difficult than mobilizing the millions for advertising campaigns, but it is certain that without this nitty-gritty educational process any leverage over public opinion will remain weak.

PUTTING IT ALL TOGETHER

Workplace organizing, conventional politics, protest, and campaigns to influence public opinion form a unified package. None will work very well without all the other elements. Furthermore, all of them require the building of new alliances and the strengthening of old ones. As with every major advance for women's economic inequality in the past, broad coalitions uniting disparate interests will make the difference. It can be done. And it has to be done. The costs and the inefficiencies in our current system are keeping many people in this country down. The burden of child rearing is left to individual families, a larger and larger percentage of which cannot find the time or money to do it well. Meanwhile, many families in dire poverty are trapped in unsafe neighborhoods, and a generation of children is growing up with little or no vision of a viable economic future. The costs of poverty, injustice, and inequality corrode the social fabric—sometimes sparking short-term explosions like urban riots, but more important leading to long-term social polarization and decay. Taking into account how costly our current system has become and who is currently bearing those costs, the new costs of fixing the system are a good investment.

We all deserve a better society: one where women and men get equal treatment, where employers and the government recognize family needs, and where poverty is replaced by opportunity. Equality for women and a better life for families of all kinds hang in the balance. It's time to smash those glass ceilings and banish those bottomless pits!

NOTES

1. This discussion of strategy draws greatly on two excellent pieces on political strategy for welfare rights: Mimi Abramovitz, *Under Attack, Fighting Back: Women and Welfare in the United States* (New York: Monthly Review Press, 1996), Part 4; Ann Withorn, "The Politics of Welfare Reform: Knowing the Stakes, Finding the Strategies," *Resist Newsletter* 5, no. 3 (April 1996). In discussions of past political battles, we also draw on the essays in Louise A. Tilly and Patricia Gurin, eds., *Women, Politics, and Change* (New York: Russell Sage Foundation, 1990). We also thank Ann Withorn, Diane Dujon, and members of the Boston area Academics' Working Group on Poverty for very helpful discussions.
2. This four-part approach to strategy borrows from the Detroit-based National Welfare Rights Union, although we have set a somewhat broader agenda (since the target we focus on goes beyond welfare rights to encompass women's economic equality in general). In 1994, NWRU proposed a four-part strategy involving organizing, legislation, public relations, and legal strategy to combat the wave of punitive welfare "reforms" sweeping the country. Abramovitz, *Under Attack, Fighting Back*, 133.
3. Ruth Milkman. "Gender and Trade Unionism in Historical Perspective," in Tilly and Gurin, eds., *Women, Politics, and Change*, 87–107.
4. Withorn, "The Politics of Welfare Reform."
5. Nancy F. Cott, "Across the Great Divide: Women in Politics Before and After 1920," in Tilly and Gurin, eds., *Women, Politics, and Change*, 153–76.

6. This history of protest is based primarily on Abramovitz, *Under Attack, Fighting Back*, which provides much more detail than is presented here.

7. Welfare Mothers' Voice. "Fighting Back: Welfare 'Reform'—JEDI Women Spark Protests in 76 Cities," *Works in Progress* (Applied Research Center, Oakland, CA, April 1995), 6.

8. Barbara J. Nelson, "The Gender, Race, and Class Origins of Early Welfare and the Welfare State: A Comparison of Workmen's Compensation and Mother's Aid," in Tilly and Gurin, eds., *Women, Politics, and Change*, 413–35; and Linda Gordon, *Pitied But Not Entitled: Single Mothers and the History of Welfare* (New York: The Free Press, 1994).

9. Michael B. Katz, *The Undeserving Poor: From the War on Poverty to the War on Welfare* (New York: Pantheon, 1989).

10. Mark R. Rank, *Living on the Edge: The Realities of Welfare in America* (New York: Columbia University Press, 1994), 133, 142.

11. Welfare Warriors, "An Open Letter from Welfare Warriors to Friends of Families who Receive Welfare Child Support," *Works in Progress* (Applied Research Center, Oakland, April 1995), 7.

12. Labor Research Association, "Case Study in the New Politics," *LRA's Economic Notes*, May 1995: 3.

PUBLIC IMPRISONMENT AND PRIVATE VIOLENCE: REFLECTIONS ON THE HIDDEN PUNISHMENT OF WOMEN

ANGELA Y. DAVIS

Over the last twenty-five years, feminist research and activism on sexual assault and domestic violence have generated campaigns and services on local, national, and international levels and an increasingly popular culture of resistance which has helped to unveil the global pandemic of violence against women. At the same time, research and activism have developed on a much smaller scale around women in prison. The work in these two areas has intersected in a number of important ways, including the amnesty campaign for women convicted of killing abusive spouses or partners. Moreover, one of the salient themes in the current literature on women in prison is the centrality of physical abuse in the lives of women subject to state punishment. Even so, the domestic violence and women's prison movements remain largely separate.

Considering the enormous increase in the numbers of imprisoned women during this contemporary era of the U.S. prison industrial complex, we need to examine the potential for establishing deeper and more extensive alliances between the anti-violence movement and the larger women's prison movement. Therefore this essay explores preliminarily some of the historical and philosophical connections between domestic violence and imprisonment as two modes of gendered punishment—one located in the private realm, the other in the public realm. This analysis suggests that the women's anti-violence movement is far more integrally related to the women's prison movement than is generally recognized.

The history of prison reform reveals multiple ironies. While imprisonment is now the dominant mode of public punishment and is associated with egregious human rights abuses, it was once regarded as a promise of enlightened moral restoration, and thus as a significant improvement over forms of punishment that relied on the infliction of corporal pain. In the era of flogging, pillories, and stocks, reformers called for the penitentiary as a more humane alternative to the cruelty of corporal punishment. During the nineteenth century, however, even as (mostly white) men in Europe and the United States convicted of violating the law were increasingly sentenced to prison, as opposed to being subjected to torture and mutilation, (white) women's punishment remained emphatically linked to corporal violence inflicted upon them within domestic spaces. These patriarchal structures of violence affected black women in different ways, primarily through the system of slavery. Today, it is easy to see how gender and race limitations of the nineteenth-century discourse on punishment reform ruled out the possibility of linking domestic torture with public torture, and thus of a related campaign against the gendered violence visited on women's bodies.

Sometimes, however, the boundaries between private and public punishment were blurred. Long before the emergence of the reform movement which succeeded in establishing imprisonment as generalized punishment, there was a prison for women—the first documented prison for women, in fact—in the Netherlands.[1] Amsterdam's Spinhuis, which opened in 1645, contained cells for women who could not "be kept to their duties by parents or husbands."[2] In seventeenth-century Britain, use of the branks—sometimes known as the scold's or gossip's bridle—to punish women who did not respect patriarchal authority[3] also indicates the permeability of borders between public and private. According to Russell Dobash et al.,

> The branks was an iron cage placed over the head, and most examples incorporated a spike or pointed wheel that was inserted into the offender's mouth in order to "pin the tongue and silence the noisiest brawler." This spiked cage was intended to punish women adjudged quarrelsome or not under the proper control of their husbands. The common form of administering this punishment was to fasten the branks to a woman and parade her through the village, sometime [sic] chaining her to a pillar for a period of time after the procession.... Although these were public chastisements they were integrally linked to household domination. In some towns arrangements were made for employing the branks within the home.... [M]en often used the threat of the branks to attempt to silence their wives, "If you don't rest with your tongue, I'll send for the [town jailor] ... to hook you up." In this example, we see how patriarchal domination and state domination were intricately intertwined.[4]

When early reformers like John Howard and Jeremy Bentham called for systems of punishment that would putatively minimize violence against the human body, prevailing ideas about the exclusion of women from public space did not allow for the emergence of a reform movement that also contested the ubiquitous violence against women. Such movements did not develop until the late twentieth century. Ironically, as "private" sexual and physical assaults against women are increasingly constructed as "crimes" and, therefore, subject to "public" sanctions, the "public" imprisonment of women remains as hidden as ever. At the same time, greater numbers of women, especially women of color, are subjected to the public punishment of prison as they simultaneously experience violence in their intimate and family relationships. The two modes of punishment remain as disarticulated in both popular and scholarly discourse as they were over a century ago.

Today, as structural racism becomes more entrenched and simultaneously more hidden, these two forms of punishment together camouflage the impact of racism on poor women of color. Domestic violence as a form of punishment is rarely perceived as integrally connected to the modes of punishment implemented by the state. Many recent studies recognize that large numbers of imprisoned women are survivors of family violence. Joanne Belknap's study, *The Invisible Woman: Gender, Crime and Justice,* which looks at the impact of the criminal justice system on women, insightfully examines both imprisonment and battering.[5] As a criminologist, however, Belknap necessarily frames her study with the categories—rarely problematized in criminological and legal discourses—of "female offender" and "female victim."[6] Her examination of women's imprisonment constructs women prisoners as "female offenders," while her analysis of male violence against women constructs women as "victims" of crime.[7] In the first instance women are perpetrators, and in the second they are victims. Belknap develops a range of important feminist critiques of traditional criminological theories and sheds light on the ways women tend to suffer more from imprisonment practices than do their male counterparts. She also makes valuable observations on the continued invisibility of male violence, even in an era of expanding campaigns, services, and feminist theorizing around these issues. This essay suggests, however, that her work can also encourage us to think more deeply about the patriarchal power circuits from the state to the home, which are disconnected by the ideological division of the "public" and the "private," thus rendering the underlying complexities of women's punishment invisible.

Pat Carlen's 1983 study, *Women's Imprisonment: A Study in Social Control,* highlights the co-constitutive character of women's public and private punishment.[8] This case study on the Scottish women's prison Cornton Vale argues that both violent and nonviolent informal disciplining in the home are as important to the construction of domestic life as the parallel, often similar, and indeed symbiotically related discipline that is the foundation of prison practices.[9]

> In general, the motto of those charged with the penal regulation of deviant women has been 'discipline, medicalise and feminise'! Women's imprisonment both in Great Britain and in the United States has traditionally been characterized by its invisibility, its domesticity and its infantalisation.[10]

In Scotland, the inhabitants of Cornton Vale are largely working-class white women and, as Carlen points out, the intersection of public and private axes of domination is very much class-determined. While Carlen's study does not put into the foreground the influence of race—which is no less important to an understanding of white women's imprisonment than of the imprisonment of women of color—it should be pointed out that throughout the urban areas of Europe and the United States a vastly disproportionate number of women prisoners come from racially marginalized communities. What Carlen refers to as a "fusion of the private and public realms of family discipline with the penological regulation of deviant women [which] has, in fact, received nominal recognition,"[11] then, becomes even more complex when race is taken into consideration.

Sociologist Beth Richie, who has also attempted to link the private and public punishment of women, has studied what she calls the "gender entrapment" of black women, who are, in many instances, "compelled to crime" and subsequently imprisoned by the same conditions that inform their subjection to violence within their personal relationships.[12] She writes about

> African American women from low-income communities who are physically battered, sexually assaulted, emotionally abused, and involved in illegal activity. Their stories vividly contradict the popular impression—perpetuated by mainstream social scientists, human service providers, public policy analysts and legislators—that the escalating rates of violence against women, poverty, addiction and women's participation in crime is because of women's psychological, moral, or social inadequacies.[13]

Richie chose to translate the legal category "entrapment" into the theoretical paradigm "gender entrapment" because it allows her to examine the intersections of gender, race, and violence. This paradigm also facilitates an understanding of the ways in which women who experience poverty and violence in their personal lives end up being punished for a web of social conditions over which they have no control.[14] While Richie presents a provocative analysis of the means by which women can be led to engage in illegal activities, either as a direct result of the violence in their intimate relationships or the threat of it, it is not within the purview of her sociological study to examine the historical continuum between domestic and state-inflicted punishment of women.

In much of the historical literature on women's imprisonment, the emergence of a "domestic model" of imprisonment for women toward the end of the nineteenth century is represented as the advent of a specifically female approach to public punishment. This relocation of domestic punishment regimes to the public sphere did not result in any less punishment in the home. The continued social sanctioning of private violence against women historically has minimized the numbers of women subject to public punishment. Because of the ironclad ideological connection between "crime" and "punishment," women's punishment is seldom disarticulated from the unlawful activities that lead them to prison, which makes it all the more difficult to articulate "private" and "public" punishment. The assumption that women constitute a relatively small portion of the imprisoned population simply because they commit fewer crimes continues to reign over common sense and over criminological discourse. Therefore the fact that women are punished in venues other than prison and in accordance with authority not directly assumed by the state might begin to explain the relatively small numbers of imprisoned women.

State-sanctioned punishment is informed by patriarchal structures and ideologies that have tended to produce historical assumptions of female criminality linked to ideas about the violation of social norms defining a "woman's place." Feminist historians have uncovered evidence of severe corporal punishment inflicted on women accused of adultery, for example, while the behavior of male adulterers has been normalized. At the same time, violence against women inflicted within domestic spaces has only recently begun to be "criminalized." Considering the fact that as many as half of all women are assaulted by their husbands or partners,[15] combined with dramatically rising numbers of women sentenced to prison, it may be argued that women in general are subjected to a far greater magnitude of punishment than men. At the same time, because patriarchal structures are contested in so many arenas, including transnational campaigns challenging domestic violence, women are now subjected to public punishment in greater numbers than ever before. Even though women are still represented as negligible targets of the prison system, the continued pandemic of private punishment, connected with the soaring numbers of women being sent to prison, combine to create a picture of the lives of poor, working-class and racially marginalized women as overdetermined by punishment. This is not to dismiss the extent to which middle-class women are also victims of violence in their families and intimate relationships. They are not, however, "entrapped"—to use Richie's term—in the same web of social conditions that places many poor women of color on the track that leads to prison and thus causes them to experience surplus punishment.

Paradoxically, prison reform movements in general have tended to bolster, rather than diminish, the stronghold of prisons on the lives of the individuals whom they hold captive. Michel Foucault has pointed out that from the beginning reform has always been linked to the evolution of the prison, which, in turn, has become more entrenched due in part precisely to the effectiveness of reforms.[16]

> [T]he movement for reforming the prisons, for controlling their functioning, is not a recent phenomenon. It does not even seem to have originated in a recognition of failure. Prison "reform" is virtually contemporary with the prison itself: it constitutes, as it were, its programme. From the outset, the prison was caught up in a series of accompanying mechanisms, whose purpose was apparently to correct it, but which seem to form part of its very functioning, so closely have they been bound up with its existence throughout its long history.[17]

In other words, prison reform campaigns, focusing on men's as well as women's institutions, generally have called for the improvement of prisons, but rarely have problematized the role of prisons as the dominant mode of punishment. Thus, as reforms have been instituted, prison systems have become more entrenched both structurally and ideologically. Today, when punishment in the United States has become a veritable industry consolidating the linkages between government and transnational corporations in ways that mirror and strengthen the military industrial complex, it is as difficult to question the need for prisons on such a large scale as it is to question the need for such a vast military machine.

When the reform movement calling for separate prisons for women emerged in England and the United States during the nineteenth century, Elizabeth Fry,

Josephine Shaw, and other advocates argued against the prevailing conception that criminal women were beyond the reach of moral rehabilitation. Like male convicts, who presumably could be "corrected" by rigorous prison regimes, female convicts, they suggested, could also be molded into moral beings by differently gendered imprisonment regimes. Architectural changes, domestic regimes, and an all-female custodial staff were implemented in the reformatory program proposed by reformers,[18] and eventually women's prisons became as strongly anchored to the social landscape as men's prisons. Their relative invisibility was as much a reflection of the domestic space reinscribed on women's public punishment, as it was of the relatively small numbers of women incarcerated in these new institutions.

This feminization of public punishment in England and the United States was explicitly designed to reform white women. Twenty-one years after the first reformatory in England was established in London in 1853, the first U.S. reformatory for women was opened in Indiana.[19]

> [The] aim was to train the prisoners in the "important" female role of domesticity. Thus, an important part of the reform movement in women's prisons was to encourage and ingrain "appropriate" gender roles, such as vocational training in cooking, sewing, and cleaning. To accommodate these goals, the reformatory cottages were usually designed with kitchens, living rooms, and even some nurseries for prisoners with infants.[20]

This feminized public punishment, however, did not affect all women in the same way. When black women were imprisoned in reformatories, they often were segregated from white women. Moreover, they tended to be disproportionately sentenced to serve time in men's prisons. In the Southern states in the aftermath of the Civil War, black women endured the cruelties of the convict lease system unmitigated by the feminization of punishment; neither their sentences, nor the labor they were compelled to do, was lessened by virtue of their gender. As the U.S. prison system evolved during the twentieth century, feminized modes of punishment—the cottage system, domestic training, and so on—were designed, ideologically, to reform white women, relegating women of color, in large part, to realms of public punishment that made no pretense of offering them femininity.

Moreover, as Lucia Zedner has pointed out, sentencing practices for women within the reformatory system often required women to do more time than men for similar offenses. "This differential was justified on the basis that women were sent to reformatories not to be punished in proportion to the seriousness of their offense but to be reformed and retrained, a process that, it was argued, required time."[21] At the same time, Zedner points out, this tendency to send women to prison for longer terms than men was accelerated by the eugenics movement, "which sought to have 'genetically inferior' women removed from social circulation for as many of their childbearing years as possible."[22] Although, as Nicole Rafter points out, racism may not be the primary explanatory factor underlying late-nineteenth-century eugenic criminology,[23] the eugenic discourses that presumed to define white normalcy against white deviancy—intellectual impairment, criminality, physical disability, and so on—relied on the same logic of exclusion as racism itself, and therefore could be easily retooled for racist uses.

In the latter twentieth century, women's prisons have begun to look more like their male counterparts, particularly those that have been constructed in the era of the prison industrial complex. As corporate involvement in punishment begins to mirror corporate involvement in military production, rehabilitation is becoming displaced by penal aims of incapacitation. Now that the population of prisons and jails is approaching two million, the rate of increase in the numbers of women prisoners has surpassed that of men. As criminologist Elliot Currie has pointed out,

> [f]or most of the period after World War II, the female incarceration rate hovered at around 8 per 100,000; it did not reach double digits until 1977. Today it is 51 per 100,000.... At current rates of increase, there will be more women in American prisons in the year 2010 than there were inmates of both sexes in 1970. When we combine the effects of race and gender, the nature of these shifts in the prison population is even clearer. The prison incarceration rate for black women today exceeds that for white *men* as recently as 1980.[24]

A quarter-century ago, in the era of the Attica uprising and the murder of George Jackson at San Quentin, radical movements developed against the prison system as a principal site of state violence and repression. In part as a reaction to the invisibility of women prisoners in this movement, and in part as a consequence of the rising women's liberation movement, specific campaigns developed in defense of the rights of women prisoners. While many of these campaigns put forth, and continue to advance, radical critiques of state repression and violence, those taken up within the correctional community have been influenced largely by liberal constructions of gender equality.

In contrast to the nineteenth-century reform movement, which was grounded in an ideology of gender difference, late-twentieth-century "reforms" have relied on a "separate but equal" model. This "separate but equal" approach often has been applied uncritically, ironically resulting in demands for more repressive conditions in order to render women's facilities "equal" to men's. For example, Tekla Dennison Miller, former warden of Huron Valley Women's Prison in Michigan, identifies her crusade for equality during the 1980s as strongly feminist. The problematic character of such an approach is revealed in her discussion of security.

> Staffing was far leaner at Huron Valley Women's than at men's prisons. When it opened ... [t]here were no yard officers at Women's, let alone a yard sergeant to watch prisoner movement and yard activities. The yards are the favorite areas for prisoner on prisoner assaults. There was also only one Assistant Deputy Warden. Men's prisons were allowed two ADWs, one for security and one for housing, but male central office

administration claimed, "Women prisoners pose no security threat. They're just basic pains in the ass and are mostly interested in painting their nails and harassing us for more personal property. They need a housing deputy, not a security deputy."[25]

In her campaign for gender equality, Miller also criticized security practices for the unequal allocation of weapons:

> Arsenals in mens' prisons are large rooms with shelves of shotguns, rifles, hand guns, ammunition, gas canisters, and riot equipment.... Huron Valley Women's arsenal was a small, five feet by two feet closet that held two rifles, eight shotguns, two bull horns, five hand guns, four gas canisters and twenty sets of restraints.[26]

After a prisoner, intent on escaping, successfully climbed over the razor ribbon and was captured after jumping to the ground on the other side, a local news reporter, whom Miller described as "an unexpected ally in the ongoing fight for parity," questioned the policy of not firing warning shots for women escapees.[27] As a result, Miller observed,

> escaping women prisoners in medium or higher [security] prisons are treated the same way as men. A warning shot is fired. If the prisoner fails to halt and is over the fence, an officer is allowed to shoot to injure. If the officer's life is in danger, the officer can shoot to kill.[28]

Paradoxically, demands for parity with men's prisons, instead of creating greater educational, vocational, and health opportunities for women prisoners, often have led to more repressive conditions for women. This is not only a consequence of deploying liberal—that is, formalistic—notions of equality, but, more dangerously, allowing male prisons to function as the punishment norm. Miller points out that she attempted to prevent a prisoner, whom she characterizes as a "murderer" serving a long term, from participating in graduation ceremonies at the University of Michigan.[29] (Of course, she does not indicate the nature of the woman's murder charges—whether, for instance she was convicted of killing an abusive partner, as is the case for a substantial number of women convicted of such charges.) Although Miller did not succeed in preventing the inmate from participating in the commencement ceremony, the prisoner was made to wear leg chains and handcuffs with her cap and gown.[30]

A more widely publicized example of the use of repressive paraphernalia, historically associated with the treatment of male prisoners to create "equality" for female prisoners, was the 1996 decision by Alabama's prison commissioner to establish women's chain gangs.[31] After Alabama became the first state to reinstitute chain gangs in 1995, then State Corrections Commissioner Ron Jones announced the following year that women would be shackled while they cut grass, picked up trash, and worked a vegetable garden at Julia Tutwiler State Prison for Women. This attempt to institute chain gangs for women was in part a response to lawsuits by male prisoners, who charged that male chain gains discriminated against men by virtue of their gender. Immediately after Jones's announcement, however, he was fired by Governor Fob James, who obviously was pressured to prevent Alabama from acquiring the dubious distinction of being the only U.S. state to have equal opportunity chain gangs.

Four months after Alabama's embarrassing flirtation with the possibility of chain gangs for women, Sheriff Joe Arpaio of Maricopa County, Arizona—represented in the media as "the toughest sheriff in America"—held a press conference to announce that because he was "an equal opportunity incarcerator," he was establishing the country's first female chain gang.[32] When the plan was implemented, newspapers throughout the country carried a photograph of chained women cleaning Phoenix's streets. While Sheriff Arpaio's policy regarding women prisoners has been criticized as little more than a publicity stunt, the fact that this women's chain gang emerges against the backdrop of a generalized increase in the repression inflicted on women prisoners—including the proliferation of security housing units, which parallel the development of super maximum security prisons—is cause for alarm. Since the population of women in prison now comprises a majority of women of color, the historical resonances of slavery, colonization, and genocide should not be missed in these images of women in chains and shackles.

As the level of repression in women's prisons increases, and, paradoxically, as the influence of domestic prison regimes recedes, sexual abuse—which, like domestic violence, is yet another dimension of the privatized punishment of women—has become an institutionalized component of punishment behind prison walls. Although guard-on-prisoner sexual abuse is not sanctioned as such, the widespread leniency with which offending officers are treated suggests that for women prison is a space in which the threat of sexualized violence that looms in the larger society is effectively sanctioned as a routine aspect of the landscape of punishment behind prison walls.

According to a recent Human Rights Watch report on the sexual abuse of women in U.S. prisons:

> Our findings indicate that being a woman prisoner in U.S. state prisons can be a terrifying experience. If you are sexually abused, you cannot escape from your abuser. Grievance or investigatory procedures, where they exist, are often ineffectual, and correctional employees continue to engage in abuse because they believe they will rarely be held accountable, administratively or criminally. Few people outside the prison walls know what is going on or care if they do know. Fewer still do anything to address the problem.[33]

The following excerpt from the summary of this report, entitled *All Too Familiar: Sexual Abuse of Women in U.S. State Prisons*, reveals the extent to which women's prison environments are violently sexualized, thus recapitulating the familiar violence that characterizes many women's private lives:

> We found that male correctional employees have vaginally, anally, and orally raped female prisoners and sexually assaulted and abused them. We found that in the course of committing such gross misconduct, male officers have not only used actual or threatened physical force, but have also used their near total authority to provide or

deny goods and privileges to female prisoners to compel them to have sex or, in other cases, to reward them for having done so. In other cases, male officers have violated their most basic professional duty and engaged in sexual contact with female prisoners absent the use or threat of force or any material exchange. In addition to engaging in sexual relations with prisoners, male officers have used mandatory pat-frisks or room searches to grope women's breasts, buttocks, and vaginal areas and to view them inappropriately while in a state of undress in the housing or bathroom areas. Male correctional officers and staff have also engaged in regular verbal degradation and harassment of female prisoners, thus contributing to a custodial environment in the state prisons for women which is often highly sexualized and excessively hostile.[34]

This report argues that the prevalence of sexual abuse in women's prisons is in violation of the U.S. Constitution as well as of international human rights law.[35] The upcoming visit in summer 1998 to a number of U.S. women's prisons by the United Nations Special Rapporteur on Violence Against Women further highlights the importance of framing the conditions of imprisoned women within the context of the anti-violence movement and within a larger human rights context. As Linda Burnham has pointed out,

> [t]he intent of the human rights paradigm is to position women's issues central to human rights discourse; negate the tendency to view women's issues as private matters; provide teeth and a structure of accountability for women's oppression that includes but is not limited to the state; and provide an overarching political framework capable of connecting the full range of women's issues and the full diversity of their social identities and circumstances.[36]

The sexual abuse of women in prison is one of the most heinous state-sanctioned human rights violations within the United States today. Women prisoners represent one of the most disfranchised and invisible adult populations in our society. The absolute power and control the state exercises over their lives both stems from and perpetuates the patriarchal and racist structures that for centuries have resulted in the social domination of women. As the prison industrial complex threatens to transform entire communities into targets of state punishment, the relatively small, but rapidly increasing, percentage of imprisoned women should not be used as a pretext for ignoring the complicated web of women's punishment. The moment may very well be ripe for forging alliances and for establishing links with international movements for human rights.

NOTES

1. See Lucia Zedner, "Wayward Sisters: The Prison for Women," in Norval Morris and David J. Rothman, eds., *The Oxford History of the Prison* (Oxford: Oxford University Press, 1998), 295.
2. Ibid.
3. See Russell P. Dobash et al., *The Imprisonment of Women* (New York: Blackwell, 1986), 19–20.
4. Ibid.
5. See Joanne Belknap, *The Invisible Woman: Gender, Crime, and Justice* (Cincinnati: Wadsworth, 1996).

6. See ibid.
7. See generally ibid.
8. Pat Carlen, *Women's Imprisonment: A Study in Social Control* (London: Routledge & Kegan Paul, 1983).
9. See ibid., p. 18.
10. Ibid.
11. Ibid., p. 86.
12. Beth E. Richie, *Compelled to Crime: The Gender Entrapment of Battered Black Women* (New York: Routledge, 1996).
13. Ibid.
14. "When applied to African American battered women who commit crimes, I used gender entrapment to describe the socially constructed process whereby African American women who are vulnerable to men's violence in their intimate relationship are penalized for behaviors they engage in even when the behaviors are logical extensions of their racialized gender identities, their culturally expected gender roles, and the violence in their intimate relationship. The model illustrates how gender, race/ethnicity, and violence can intersect to create a subtle, yet profoundly effective system of organizing women's behavior into patterns that leave women vulnerable to private and public subordination, to violence in their intimate relationships and, in turn, to participation in illegal activities. As such, the gender-entrapment theory helps to explain how some women who participate in illegal activities do so in response to violence, the threat of violence, or coercion by their male partners." Ibid. 4.
15. Belknap, *The Invisible Woman*, 172.
16. Michel Foucault, *Discipline and Punish: The Birth of the Prison*, trans. Alan Sheridan (New York: Vintage, 1979), 234.
17. Ibid.
18. See Estelle B. Freedman, *Their Sisters' Keepers: Women's Prison Reform in America, 1830–1930* (Ann Arbor: University of Michigan Press, 1991), chaps. 3–4.
19. See Belknap, *The Invisible Woman*, 95.
20. Ibid.
21. Zedner, "Wayward Sisters," 318.
22. Ibid.
23. See Nicole Hahn Rafter, *Creating Born Criminals* (Chicago: University of Illinois Press, 1998), 50.
24. Elliot Currie, *Crime and Punishment in America* (New York: Henry Holt, 1998), 14.
25. Tekla Dennison Miller, *The Warden Wore Pink* (New Haven: Yale University Press, 1996), 97.
26. Ibid., 97–98.
27. Ibid., 100.
28. Ibid.
29. See ibid., 121.
30. See ibid.
31. See Curtis Wilkie, "Weak Links Threaten Chain Gangs: Revised Prison Work Program Facing Voter Disapproval, Inmates' Legal Action," *Boston Globe*, 18 May 1996: 1,1.
32. See "48 Hours, Arizona Sheriff Initiates Equal Opportunity by Starting First Chain Gang for Women," CBS television broadcast, 19 September 1996.
33. Human Rights Watch, *All Too Familiar: Sexual Abuse of Women in U.S. State Prisons*, www.hrw.6rg/hrw/summaries/s.us96d (visited 31 May 1998).
34. Ibid., 2.
35. See ibid.
36. Linda Burnham, "Beijing and Beyond," *Crossroads*, March 1996: 16.

CONCEPTUALIZING
WOMEN'S INTERESTS

MAXINE MOLYNEUX

The political pertinence of the issue of whether states, revolutionary or other-wise, are successful in securing the interests of social groups and classes is generally considered to be twofold. First, it is supposed to enable prediction or at least political calculation about a given government's capacity to maintain the support of the groups it claims to represent. Second, it is assumed that the nature of the state can be deduced from the interests it is seen to be advancing.[1] Thus the proposition that a state is a "worker's state," capitalist state, or even a "patriarchal state' is commonly tested by investigating how a particular class or group has fared under the government in question.

However, when we try to deploy similar criteria in the case of women a number of problems arise. If, for example, we conclude that because revolution-ary governments seem to have done relatively little to remove the means by which gender subordination is reproduced, that women's interests have not been represented in the state and hence women are likely to turn against it, we are making a number of assumptions: that gender interests are the equivalent of "women's interests"; that gender should be privileged as the principal determi-nant of women's interests; and that women's subjectivity, real or potential, is also structured uniquely through gender effects. It is also supposed by extension that women have certain common interests by virtue of their gender, and that these interests are primary for women. It follows, then, that trans-class unity among women is to some degree given by this communality of interests.[2]

Yet while it is true that at a certain level of abstraction women can be said to have some interests in common, there is no consensus over what these are or how they are to be formulated. This is in part because there is no theoreti-cally adequate and universally applicable causal explanation of women's subor-dination from which a general account of women's interests can be derived. Women's oppression is recognized as being multicausal in origin and mediated through a variety of different structures, mechanisms, and levels, which may vary considerably across space and time. There is therefore continuing debate over the appropriate site of feminist struggle and over whether it is more important to focus attempts at change on objective or subjective elements; on structures or on men; on laws and institutions; or on interpersonal power relations—or on all of them simultaneously. Since a general conception of interests (one which has political validity) must be derived from a theory of how the subordination of a determinate social category is secured, and supposes some notion of structural determinacy, it is difficult to see how it would overcome the two most salient and intractable features of women's oppression—its multicausal nature, and the extreme variability of its forms across class and nation. These factors vitiate attempts to speak *without qualification* of a unitary category "women" with a set of already constituted interests that are common to it. A theory of interests that is applicable to the debate about women's capacity to struggle for, and benefit from, social change must begin by recognizing difference rather than assuming homogeneity.

It is clear from the extensive feminist literature on women's oppression that a number of different conceptions prevail of what women's interests are, and that these in turn rest, implicitly or explicitly, upon different theories of the causes of gender inequality. For the purpose of clarifying the issues discussed here, three conceptions of women's interests that are frequently conflated will be delineated. These are (1) "women's interests"; (2) strategic gender interests; and (3) practical gender interests.

Although present in much political and theoretical discourse, the concept of *women's interests* is, for the reasons given above, a highly contentious one. Because women are positioned within their societies through a variety of different means—among them class, ethnicity, and gender—the interests which they have as a group are similarly shaped in complex and sometimes conflicting ways. It is therefore difficult, if not impossible, to generalize about "the interests of women." Instead, we need to specify how the various categories of women might be affected differently, and act differently, on account of the particularities of their social positioning and their chosen identities. However, this is not to deny that women may have certain general interests in common. These can be called gender interests to differentiate them from the false homogeneity imposed by the notion of "women's interests."

Gender interests are those that women (or men, for that matter) may develop by virtue of their social positioning through gender attributes. Gender interests can be either strategic or practical, each being derived in a different way and each involving different implications for women's subjectivity. Strategic interests are derived in the first instance deductively—that is, from the analysis of women's subordination and from the formulation of an alternative, more satisfactory set of arrangements to those that exist. These ethical and theoretical criteria assist in the formulation of strategic objectives to overcome women's subordination, such as the abolition of the sexual division of labor, the alleviation of the burden of domestic labor and childcare, the removal of institutionalized forms of discrimination, the establishment of political equality, freedom of choice over childbearing, and the adoption of adequate measures against male violence and control over women. These constitute what might be called strategic gender interests, and are the ones most frequently considered by feminists as women's "real" interests. The demands that are formulated on this basis are usually termed "feminist," as is the level of consciousness required to struggle effectively for them.[3]

Practical gender interests are given inductively and arise from the concrete conditions of women's positioning by virtue of their gender within the division of labor. In contrast to strategic gender interests, practical gender interests are formulated by the women themselves who are within these positions rather than through external interventions. Practical interests are usually a response to an immediate perceived need and they do not generally entail a strategic goal such as women's emancipation or gender equality. Analyses of female collective action frequently deploy this conception of interests to explain the dynamic and goals of women's participation in social action. For example, it has been argued that by virtue of their place within the sexual division of labor, as those primarily responsible for their households' daily welfare, women have a special interest in domestic provision and public welfare.[4] When governments fail to provide these basic needs women withdraw their support; when the livelihood of their families, especially their children, is threatened, it is women who form the phalanxes of bread rioters, demonstrators, and petitioners. It is clear from this example, however, that gender and class are closely intertwined; it is, for obvious reasons, usually poor women who are so readily mobilized by economic necessity. Practical interests, therefore, cannot be assumed to be innocent of class effects. Moreover, these practical interests do not in themselves challenge the prevailing forms of gender subordination, even though they arise directly out of them. An appreciation of this is vital in understanding the capacity or failure of states or organizations to win the loyalty and support of women.

This raises the question of the pertinence of these ways of conceptualizing interests for an understanding of women's consciousness. This is a complex matter that cannot be explored in detail here, but three initial points can be made. First, the relationship between what we have called strategic gender interests and women's recognition of them and desire to realize them cannot be assumed. Even the "lowest common denominator" of interests that might seem uncontentious and of universal applicability (e.g. complete equality with men, control over reproduction, and greater personal autonomy and independence from men) are not readily accepted by all women. This is not just because of "false consciousness," as is frequently supposed, although this can be a factor, but because such changes realized in a piecemeal fashion could threaten the short-term practical interests of some women, or entail a cost in the form of a loss of forms of protection which is not then compensated for. Thus the formulation of strategic interests can be effective as a form of intervention only when full account is taken of these practical interests. Indeed, it is the politicization of these practical interests and their transformation into strategic interests that women can identify with and support which constitutes a central aspect of feminist political practice.

Second, and following on from the first, the way in which interests are formulated, whether by women or political organizations, will vary considerably across space and time and may be shaped in different ways by prevailing political and discursive influences. This is important to bear in mind when considering the problem of internationalism and the limits and possibilities of cross-cultural solidarity. And finally, since "women's interests" are significantly broader than gender interests, and are shaped to a considerable degree by class factors, women's unity and cohesion on gender issues cannot be assumed. While gender issues can form the basis of unity around a common program, such unity has to be constructed; it is never given. Moreover, even when unity exists, it is always conditional, and the historical record suggests that it tends to collapse under the pressure of acute class conflict. Unity is also threatened by differences of race, ethnicity, and nationality. It is therefore difficult to argue, as some feminists have done, that gender issues are primary for women at all times.[5]

This general problem of the conditionality of women's unity and the fact that gender issues are not necessarily primary is nowhere more clearly illustrated than by the example of revolutionary upheaval. In such situations, gender issues are frequently displaced by class conflict, and this is principally because although women may suffer discrimination on the basis of gender and may be aware that they do, they nonetheless suffer differentially according to their social class. These differences crucially affect attitudes toward revolutionary change, especially if this is in the direction of socialism. This does not mean that because gender interests are an insufficient basis for unity among women in the context of class polarization, they disappear. Rather, they become more specifically attached to, and defined by, social class.

These, then, are the different ways in which the question of women's interests can be addressed. An awareness of the complex issues involved serves to guard against any simple treatment of the question of whether a state is or is not acting in the "interests of women"; that is, whether all or any of these interests are represented within the state.

Before any analysis can be attempted it is first necessary to specify in what sense the term "interest" is being deployed. As suggested earlier, a state may gain the support of women by satisfying either their immediate practical demands or certain class interests, or both. It may do this without advancing their strategic interests at all. However, the claims of such a state to be supporting women's *emancipation* could not be substantiated merely on the evidence that it maintained women's support on the basis of representing some of their more practical or class interests.

SANDINISTA POLICY WITH REGARD TO WOMEN

A detailed analysis of the impact of Sandinista social policies is beyond the scope of this discussion.[6] Instead, I will briefly summarize some of the main conclusions in relation to the issues raised earlier by considering the effects of the reforms in terms of the three categories of interest outlined at the beginning. If we disaggregate the concept of "women's interests" and consider how different categories of women fared since 1979, it is clear that the majority of women in Nicaragua were positively affected by the government's redistribution policies. This is so even though fundamental structures of gender inequality were not dismantled. In keeping with the socialist character of the government, policies were targeted in favor of the poorest sections of the population and focused on basic needs provision in the areas of health, housing, education, and food subsidies. In the short span of only five years the Sandinistas reduced the illiteracy rate from over 50 percent to 13 percent, doubled the number of educational establishments, increased school enrollment, eradicated a number of mortal diseases, provided the population with basic healthcare services, and achieved more in their housing program than Somoza had in his entire period of rule.[7] In addition, the land reform canceled peasants' debts and gave thousands of rural workers secure jobs on the state farms and cooperatives or their own parcels of land.[8] These policies have been of vital importance in gaining the support of poor women. According to government statistics, women form over 60 percent of the poorest Nicaraguans; in the poorest category in Managua (income less than 600 cordobas per month) there are 354 women for each 100 men.[9] It is these women, by virtue of their class position, who have been the direct beneficiaries of Sandinista redistributive efforts, as have their male counterparts. But by the same token, it is obvious that not all women were to benefit from these programs; women whose economic interests lay in areas adversely affected by Sandinista economic policies (imports, luxury goods, etc.) suffered some financial loss, as did most women from the privileged classes as a result of higher taxation. It is also the case that while poor women benefited from the welfare provisions, they were also the most vulnerable to the pressures of economic constraints and especially to shortages in basic provisions.

In terms of practical gender interests these redistributive policies also had gender as well as class effects. By virtue of their place within the sexual division of labor, women are disproportionately responsible for childcare and family health, and they are particularly concerned with housing and food provision. The policy measures directed at alleviating the situation in these areas, not surprisingly, elicited a positive response from the women affected by them, as borne out by the available research into the popularity of the government. Many of the campaigns mounted by the women's organization AMNLAE were directed at resolving some of the practical problems women faced, as exemplified by their mother and child healthcare program, or by their campaign aimed at encouraging women to conserve domestic resources to make the family income stretch further and thus avoid pressure building up over wage demands or shortages.[10] A feature of this kind of campaign is its recognition of women's practical interests, but, in accepting the division of labor and women's subordination within it, it may entail a denial of their strategic interests. This is the problem with many women's organizations in the socialist bloc.

With respect to strategic interests—the acid test of whether women's emancipation was on the political agenda or not—the progress which was made was modest but significant. Legal reform, especially in the area of the family, confronted the issue of relations between the sexes and of male privilege, by attempting to end a situation in which most men were able to evade responsibility for the welfare of their families while retaining sole legal rights to the children. Through the provisions of the new laws, women acquired custody rights and men became liable for a contribution to household and childcare maintenance, in cases where paternity was acknowledged. This contribution could be made in cash, in kind, or in the form of services. The meetings called to discuss these reforms also enabled the issue of domestic labor to be politicized in the discussions of the need to share this work equally among all members of the family. The land reform program tackled the problem of rural women's invisibility by encouraging their participation and leadership in cooperatives and by giving them wages for their work and titles to land. There was also an effort to establish childcare agencies such as nurseries, preschool services, and the like. Some attempts were made to challenge female stereotypes, not just through outlawing the exploitation of women in the media, but also by promoting some women to positions of responsibility and emphasizing the importance of women in the militia and reserve battalions.[11] And finally, there was a sustained effort to mobilize women around their own needs through the women's organization, and there was discussion of some of the questions of strategic interest, although this has been sporadic and controversial. In these respects Nicaragua is fairly typical of other countries in the socialist periphery.

To sum up, we can see that it is difficult to discuss socialist revolutions in terms of an undifferentiated conception of women's interests and even more difficult to conclude that these interests have not been represented in state policymaking. The Sandinista record on women is certainly uneven, and it is as yet too early to make any final assessment of it, especially while it confronts increasing political, economic, and military pressures. Nonetheless, it is clear that the Sandinistas have gone further than most Latin American governments (except Cuba) in recognizing both the strategic and practical interests of women and have brought about substantial improvements in the lives of many of the most deprived. When AMNLAE stated that its priority is defense of the revolution because the latter provides the necessary condition for realizing a program for women's emancipation, it was, with certain qualifications, correct. Yet these qualifications remain important, and they have a significance which goes beyond the Sandinista revolution to the wider question of the relationship between socialism and feminism. Three of these, which are general to socialist states, can be listed here in summary form.

The first is that although strategic gender interests are recognized in the official theory and program of women's emancipation, they nonetheless remain rather narrowly defined because they are based on the privileging of economic criteria. Feminist theories of sexual oppression, or the critique of the family or of male power, have had little impact on official thinking, and indeed are sometimes suppressed as being too radical and too threatening to popular solidarity. There is a need for greater discussion and debate around these questions both among the people and within the organs of political power, so that the issue of women's emancipation remains alive and open, and does not become entombed within official doctrine.

The second issue concerns the relationship that is established by planners between the goal of women's emancipation and other goals, such as economic development, that have priority. It is not the *linkage* itself that constitutes the problem—principles such as social equality and women's emancipation can be realized only within determinate conditions of existence. So linking the program for women's emancipation to these wider goals need not necessarily be a cause for concern because these wider goals may constitute the preconditions for realizing the principles. The question is rather the nature of the links: are gender interests *articulated into* a wider strategy of economic development, for example, or are they irretrievably *subordinated to it?* In the first case we would expect gender interests to be recognized as being specific and irreducible, and requiring something more for their realization than is generally provided for in the pursuit of the wider goals. Thus, when it is not possible to pursue a full program for women's emancipation this can be explained and debated. The goal can be left on the agenda, and every effort made to pursue it within the existing constraints. In the latter case, the specificity of gender interests is likely to be denied or its overall importance minimized. The issues are trivialized or buried; the program for women's emancipation remains one conceived in terms of how functional it is for achieving the wider goals of the state. It is difficult to say how these issues will be resolved in Nicaragua in the long run. For the moment, the intense pressures that the Sandinistas are under make it difficult to resist the pattern which has emerged elsewhere in the socialist bloc of countries, that of subordination rather than linkage or articulation.

And this raises the third general issue, which is that of political guarantees. For if gender interests are to be realized only within the context of wider considerations, it is essential that the political institutions charged with representing these interests have the means to prevent their being submerged altogether and action on them being indefinitely postponed. Women's organizations, the official representatives of women's interests, should not conform to Lenin's conception of mass organizations as mere "transmission belts of the party." Rather, they must enjoy a certain independence and exercise power and influence over party policy, albeit within certain necessary constraints. In other words, the issue of gender interests and their means of representation cannot be resolved in the absence of a discussion of socialist democracy and the forms of the state appropriate to the transition to socialism; it is a question therefore not just of *what* interests are represented in the state but, ultimately and crucially, of *how* they are represented.

NOTES

1. There is a third usage of the term "interest" found in Marxist writing which explains collective action in terms of some intrinsic property of the actors and/or the relations within which they are inscribed. Thus, class struggle is ultimately explained as an effect of the relations of production. This conception has been shown to rest on essentialist assumptions and provides an inadequate account of social action. For a critique of this notion see Edward Benton, "Realism, Power and Objective Interests," in Keith Graham, ed., *New Perspectives in Political Philosophy* (Cambridge: University Press, 1982); and Barry Hindess, "Power, Interests and the Outcome of Struggles," *Sociology* 16, no. 4 (1982).

2. Zillah Eisenstein, editor of *Capitalist Patriarchy* (1979), has produced a sophisticated version of the argument that women constitute a "sexual class," and that for women gender issues are primary. See Zillah Eisenstein, *Feminism and Sexual Equality* (New York: Monthly Review Press, 1984).

3. It is precisely around these issues, which also have an ethical significance, that the theoretical and political debate must focus. The list of strategic gender interests noted here is not exhaustive but is merely exemplary.

4. Temma Kaplan, "Female Consciousness and Collective Action: The Case of Barcelona 1910–1918," *Signs: Journal of Women in Culture and Society* 7, no. 3 (Spring 1982); Olwen Hufton, "Women in Revolution 1789–1796," *Past and Present* 53 (1971).

5. This is the position of some radical feminist groups in Europe.

6. For a fuller account of Sandinista social policies, see Thomas Walker, ed., *Nicaragua: The First Five Years* (New York: Praeger, 1982); for their policies on women see my article in the same volume.

7. Thomas Walker, ed., *Nicaragua in Revolution*, 2d ed. (New York: Praeger, 1985).

8. Carmen Diana Deere, "Cooperative Development and Women's Participation in the Nicaraguan Agrarian Reform," *American Journal of Agricultural Economics*, December 1983; CIERA, *Informe Annual 1983* (Managua: CIERA, 1984); CIERA, *Managua es Nicaragua* (Managua: CIERA, 1984); CIERA, *La Mujer en las Cooperativas Agropecuarias en Nicaragua* (Managua: CIERA, 1984).

9. Unpublished data from the Instituto Nacional de Estadisticas y Censos, Managua, December 1981.

10. AMNLAE argued that the implications of women conserving resources under a socialist government are radically different from those under capitalism because the beneficiaries are the people in the first case and private interests in the second.

11. Although there are no women in the nine-member junta which constitutes the FSLN leadership, the vice president of the Council of State was a woman, and women assumed many key positions in the party at the regional level. On three occasions after 1979 women filled ministerial posts.

PART V

POLITICS AND SOCIAL CHANGE

APPRECIATING OUR BEGINNINGS

SHEILA ROWBOTHAM

In 1970, on the last weekend of February, the first women's liberation conference was held in Britain. Over five hundred people, mainly women, poured into
a trade-union college, Ruskin, at Oxford. They overflowed into the forbidding
splendour of the Oxford Students' Union, which had only recently admitted
women students. Suddenly, in this preserve of ruling-class men, young women
were speaking of liberation and revolution.

Where had they all come from and what had brought them to a women's
liberation conference?

I used to think that if you lived through a historical process you would know
what happened. When you look back as a historian, there are so many frustrat-
ing gaps that can never be filled because trails have been lost. This is especially
the case in attempting to uncover the organizing beneath the surface which
contributes to the eruption of apparently spontaneous movements. When these
involve women, the links are frequently submerged over time because the connections are personal and implicit.

Because I am a historian by trade I have lived a double life, participating in
the women's movement while contributing to its chronicling and preserving
archives, but interpretations shift and as material accumulates patterns become
hard to summarize. My double life has made me realize that living through
events can give you insights; it does not, however, give rise to any easy overview.

An obvious problem is the tension between near sight and long sight. One's
involvement as a participant is necessarily from particular perspectives. But one's
training as a historian is to correct, curb, restrain subjectivity to enter the view-
points of others. These two ways of seeing do not automatically converge. The
historical craft has to tussle with the political polemicist.

There can be no easy resolution for the political struggle, for women's liberation continues even though in differing forms and with the fragmentation of
assumptions. It is not just "history."

However, the passage of time has brought a certain remoteness from the origins of the contemporary movement. This distance has meant that already there are powerful assumptions circulating about what moved us to organize two decades ago. Many of these assumptions present versions of the lived past which are unrecognizable to participants. This would indicate a place for the chronicling of memory. Perhaps for this reason and simply because the passing of time makes reflection possible, several books have begun to appear on the influences and development of the British movement.

Internationally, of course, there are many stories and a shifting timespan since the early groups appeared in the U.S. in the 1960s. The historical explanations get really complicated when one seeks to understand the emergence of a modern feminist movement in, for example, countries as diverse as the United States and India.

However, even Britain and even one's own political home ground can be perplexing. Why did we go to the Ruskin conference in 1970, for example; why not in 1960 or 1965? At this point the chronicler as participant begins to suffer from a bad attack of near view. In one sense too much is known about one's own particularity and the chronicle dissolves into subjectivity.

I still am not really able to comprehend why grievances experienced by women I had known for several years took until 1970 to erupt into a new kind of political force. Why had I identified with Mary Wollstonecraft and Emma Goldman as individuals in the late 1950s and early 1960s, but failed to see a general condition of women? Why was it obvious that the ideas of the ruling class were dominant in society yet not clear to me that culture was male-defined until the late 1960s?

As a student at an Oxford college formed by early feminist campaigners for women's higher education, Miss Buss and Miss Beale, I felt no gratitude for their rather stuffy portraits which hung above the dons' high table. Nor were I and my contemporaries conscious that our arrival at university was part of a sociological shift in capitalist societies in which women from working-class and lower-middle-class uneducated backgrounds were beginning to move into higher education in greater numbers. At eighteen we perceived our new mobility in individual terms. We could not be aware that some future historian would observe our individual sense of choice as a removed sociological process. How could we know that our uprootedness, our existential subjectivity, was going to be caught and labeled "Influences on Re-emergence of Feminism"?

To have been a participant thus increases the tension between the intricacies of biography, which deal with subjectivity, and the broad sociological brush-strokes, which tend to obliterate detail. Nonetheless, the struggle for combination enriches the record.

Historians who seek to probe the transmission of consciousness which always precedes new forms of collective action have to hunt rumor and hearsay. It is this will-o'-the-wisp stuff which grows faint over time. Participants certainly

can contribute to the reconstruction and partially chart their impact and movement. During 1968 several rumors traveled to Britain and several young women
on the left began to prick up their ears.

In the U.S. they protested against the Miss America beauty contest by crown-
ing a sheep and depositing bras, girdles, curlers, and issues of *The Ladies' Home
Journal* in a trash can. The label "bra burners" became the shorthand metaphor
of a new kind of feminist defiance. In those days when we mumbled complaints
to socialist men, they told us to read Lenin's "On the Emancipation of Women."
This was "politics." But Lenin does not mention girdles, curlers, or bras. Nor
has he that much to say on beauty or seem to think sex was as important as it
seemed to young women in their twenties in the late 1960s. Did this "politics"
need certain extensions, then?

From Germany we heard women in the student movement had written a
paper for a conference which men had refused to discuss. At the back of the
hall—so the story goes—a tall, auburn-haired young woman had reached in her
bag, taken out a tomato and thrown it at a leading male Marxist theorist. Now
German Marxist theorists in the student movement twenty years ago had a lot
of weight. They spoke in sentences of elaborate construction, they had access
to texts we could not read, they faced a ferocious police force and tried to teach
us how to form a human wedge to break police lines. They were also intent on
consciously developing a new culture which would break with the fascist past.
Politics for them was not simply about reforms or taking power, they said; they
were developing prototypes of future organization which would contribute to
shaping a completely revolutionized society. But they couldn't discuss the wom-
en's paper because it was not sufficiently important. So how did you get to be
important? Again the rumor was that in retaliation the women at the conference
drew the penises of the leading Marxist theorists and stuck their drawings all
over the wall with comments. What a thing to do, we thought in shocked
admiration.

Young mothers, swept into the continuous activism of the German anti-
authoritarian student movement, wanted collective forms of care. Both men and
women began to argue for more attention to be paid to the upbringing and
education of children. A new society demanded a new psychology and a new
definition of politics.

So the rumors began to meet concepts and in this way ceased to be simply
strange tales.

At a student movement conference at Frankfurt in 1968 Helke Sander demanded
crèches at meetings and said:

> The separation between private and public life always forces the woman into lonely
> endurance of her role.... Women can only find their identity if the problems previ-
> ously hidden in the private sphere are articulated and made into the focus for women's
> political solidarity and struggle.[1]

In the United States similar ideas about the personal as political and the need to prefigure the desired utopia in everyday action had been brewing throughout the 1960s. The ideas were traveling internationally not so much as worked out theory but as a welter of assumptions that challenged the existing concepts of politics which prevailed on the European Marxist and social-democratic left.

The "new politics" thus contributed ways of conceiving identity and action which provoked some of the questions raised by young women radicalized by the student movement and the community organizing of the American New Left.

In Britain we had also seen civil rights demonstrations on television; we had read about black power and thus learned about the struggle which was not simply about formal rights but also raised issues of cultural identity, access to symbolic space, the power to define one's self, a challenge to how one was regarded and represented. Some of us at the Dialectics of Liberation conference in 1967 had puzzled over Stokeley Carmichael's hostile response to a young white woman's question. It seemed the dialectic could run into disturbing blockages.

Equally influential was the anti-imperialist movement against the U.S. role in Vietnam. Vietnamese women's suffering and bravery as fighters made a deep impression on young women supporters in the West. Despite the differences in our circumstances, they gave us inspiration and a political language of colonialism which we could adapt.

The radical movement of the late 1960s in Britain, as in the U.S. and in the French "May Events"—the dramatic student and workers' uprising—held out the promise of a politics of everyday life which touched the individual imagination, which abolished hierarchy and did not repeat the Stalinist error of justifying the means by the end. But the actual reality of political practice differed. The dream of the "beloved community" raised hopes which it did not realize.

Straddled across the gap between hope and experience, some young radical women began to wonder. Why did men split us into comrades and "chicks," for example? The first were tolerated in the public important sphere of politics. The second were to be bedded, in the trivial personal realm of lust and passion. Why, I can remember wondering, couldn't you be a woman and a person doing both?

Already by 1969 I was scouring Trotsky and Kollontai, Sartre and Fanon for answers. We had a few modern articles from the U.S. and Juliet Mitchell's *The Longest Revolution*, published in 1966. It felt as if we literally had to gobble ideas. There was a powerful sense that the world was moving, but we certainly did not see ourselves as consciously theorizing a new women's movement.

The ideas which served us were not then biologically restricted. We borrowed many of the formative political concepts from other contemporary movements. They were transplanted and changed, but feminist concepts are not hermetically sealed from wider politics. They developed both in tune with and because of disharmonies in the practice of the New Left. New ways of thinking raised possibilities and forced young women to challenge why these were exclusive to the male gender. We were from the beginning talking of equality and difference in the same breath. We also shared with the French and Americans an insistence on seeking our own way through oppression and a determination to go beyond our own social and political confines.

It was not all rumors and concepts. There were larger changes at work in capitalist society which meant that many young women responded to the media coverage about bra burners with enthusiasm. News of "women's lib"—which was designed to mock—brought women into the movement who had not taken part in the Marxist student left.

Many of these were young women who through higher education were destined for the expanding administrative and welfare jobs opening up. Sociologically and psychologically, a generation was entering a world which was dramatically different from that of their mothers.

In a collection of essays about girls growing up in the 1950s, *Truth, Dare or Promise*, this thwarted sense of possibility is detailed. Valerie Walkerdine, for instance, says:

> They held out a dream. Come, they told me. It is yours. You are chosen. They didn't tell me, however, that for years I would no longer feel any sense of belonging, nor any sense of safety, that I didn't belong in the new place any more than I now belonged in the old.

She also captures the pain and relief of the break with our mothers' destiny: "My mother in this history has no history. She lurks silently in the kitchen. I cannot find her in my dream because the kitchen is where I am most afraid to look."[2]

Turning our backs on our mothers, we also turned outwards to try and meet them on their own terms. We searched assiduously for historical feminist mothers and were amazed at finding such a host. We even met some of them. As for the kitchen, what did we make there but political economy? Mothering, we were resolved, should be transformed. It was to be abolished, shared, extended throughout society. Later in poems, novels, and therapy we were to seek the courage to face our actual mothers.

For women with young children, new forms of mothering were practical needs, not abstract concepts about personal politics. Again hopes had been raised. We, the newly educated, had been told we were equal. But a prosperous welfare capitalism did not seem to think that meant more nurseries. The contradictions of childcare and housework were thus extremely important influences in bringing women into the women's liberation movement.

Equally explosive was sexuality. Sue O'Sullivan, an American member of one of the first consciousness-raising groups which formed in Tufnell Park, North London, described this in an article in *Spare Rib*:

> During the late 1950s the hold of traditional sexual morals was breaking down. Sex, divorce, motherhood, the family, youth, were all beginning to be seen as problems. No coherent alternative morality emerged, but the cohesion of the old one was weakening.

She goes on:

> Our lives were changing but were filled with confusion and ambivalence, not the least about sleeping with men and using birth control.... Women had not defined their own needs, but they were as always terrified of unwanted pregnancies.[3]

Sexually too, then, we were being presented with a freedom which was not of our making. While permissive sexual attitudes presented new possibilities for young women in the 1960s, they also landed us with new problems. Orgasms, masturbation, and the clitoris swept into political discussion.

In 1970, influenced by the movement in the States, gay liberation formed. Initially men and women were together, but by 1971 lesbian women were seeking to define their differences from men. In the women's issue of the magazine *Come Together* they wrote that while men had been brought up to "organize, talk and dominate," women had been "taught not to believe in ourselves, in our judgment, but to act dumb and wait for a man to make the decisions. As lesbians, 'women without men,' we have always been the lowest of the low."[4]

However, a member of the first lesbian group in Britain also criticized the idea that the "sisterhood" of women's liberation could alone provide the means of change. Relating differently must be a means of change, not an end in itself: "One is not attacking the system by hopping from one oppressed category to another."[5]

The desire for both personal and social transformation traveled beyond the original groups politicized by Marxism and the New Left because there were lived contradictions in which the slogans and assumptions that sprang up like mushrooms in the new movements met.

The transitions were not always so smooth. The small groups which began to form in 1969 tied themselves up in knots about whether they were seeking their own liberation or were evangelically reaching out to working-class women.

There were some stirrings among working-class women, but in quite different contexts and with different concerns than the young women from the radical student left. In 1968 a woman in the Hull fishing community, Lil Bilocca, led a struggle for greater safety on the trawlers after a sea disaster in which forty men died. She faced contempt and derision locally for taking this public stance, not only from the trawler owners but from some of the fishermen, who thought she was stepping out of her place as a woman. A women's rights group formed in her defense.

It is interesting in retrospect to note how the community organization of women in the working class on behalf of kin and community ran parallel with the re-emergence of a feminist movement. Although there have been interactions, the starting point of radicalization is not contesting as an individual woman the way in which society sets one's destiny. Instead Lil Bilocca and many others since, including women in the black communities, have begun to resist because the live of others are threatened and distorted by capitalist exploitation, and by the oppression of class and race. In the process of struggle many women came to envisage and desire new ways of being women.

In the late 1960s the language of rights prevailed in the labor movement rather than the language of liberation, which conceived transformation of all relations.

In 1968 Ford's sewing-machinists went on strike for equal pay, or, more precisely, to be graded at a skilled rate. A trade-union organization was formed, the National Joint Action Committee for Women's Equal Rights, or NJACWER for short. In 1970 the Labour MP Barbara Castle got an Equal Pay bill through parliament designed to come into effect in 1975. The aim of NJACWER was to extend the narrow basis of equal pay, which applied only to those women workers who could be said to do the same work as men. It also wanted to look at wider forms of inequality.

Some women involved in NJACWER were active in forming some of the early women's liberation groups. In Bristol, for example, the meeting on equal pay turned into a women's liberation meeting. Despite the differences of class, there are some interesting signs that women in the trade-union movement were seeking a language which expressed forms of subordination and oppression not easily restricted in terms of "rights."

Again the new political language was coming from the black movement internationally. For example, in 1968 the Trades Union Congress report recorded a Miss J. O'Connell accusing male trade unionists of industrial "apartheid" because of lack of action on equal pay and the concentration of women in low-paid jobs.

The following year Mrs M. Turner told Congress that women had developed "inferiority complexes" from being relegated to low-paid jobs which were classed as unskilled. She said, "James Baldwin once remarked in connection with racial discrimination that the white supremacists had only really succeeded when the oppressed people began to believe they were inherently inferior, in other words they began to accept the discriminators' view of themselves."[6]

This interest in the internal bonds upon consciousness thus was present among trade-union women as well as the radical young, politicized by the New Left.

Audrey Wise, an official in the shop workers' union, USDAW, which organizes many women, argued in the January 1969 issue of the left student paper *Black Dwarf*, which declared 1969 as the "Year of the Militant Woman':

> We must ask ourselves in any case equality with what? Do men have such idyllic lives that we want the same for ourselves? In a world where people are valued as economic units rather than as people, to be an equal economic unit must not be the height of our ambition.[7]

Early in 1969 a few of us took the women's issue of *Black Dwarf* to a students' festival at Essex University. After an explosive and chaotic meeting, a small group met and agreed to meet again in London.

This was to be the start of the Women's Liberation workshop in London. The fragile network of London groups formed a newsletter, *Harpies Bizarre*, later *Shrew*. Meanwhile, groups were formed and produced the Trotskyist magazine *Socialist Woman*. In Coventry young women in International Socialism formed a group which included some local working-class women.

In the autumn of 1969 at a meeting of radical historians at Ruskin College, Oxford, a small group of women met to discuss having a conference on women's history. As we squashed into a small student bedroom, we discussed the need to challenge how history had been presented to us. A young American socialist, Barbara Winslow, pointed out that we had not yet had a meeting on the contemporary situation of women. History should come later.

It was the small group squashed into the bedroom which set about organizing the February 1970 conference. History indeed was a significant strand. There was a talk on women's organization around production and consumption in the early nineteenth century and one on the traditions in the revolutionary movements in France from 1789 to the Paris Commune. Audrey Wise spoke from the trade unions. A group of women in Peckham gave a paper describing how housework affected one's consciousness. Men organized the crèche—an innovative move in 1970.

The origins of the women's movement were then in a period of great optimism about the possibilities of transforming all social relations. Change was not just getting external gains but changing one's self and daily life. The political assumptions which formed the women's movement were part of the general currency of political debate. But they acquired particular meanings for groups of women who found themselves facing new possibilities and new constraints. Decades later, it is useful to regard these not as absolutes, slogans writ in stone, but as historically created. We can appreciate their radical and innovative creativity without accepting them uncritically. For without a reflective process of critical understanding, there can be no strong political tradition to sustain us when the snags appear. It was not to be quite so easy as we imagined to change women, men, and the world.

One of the speakers at the 1970 conference, a child psychologist in the Tufnell Park group active in the antiwar movement, Rochelle Wortis, argued that patterns of childrearing were socially and culturally determined, not biological. Any change in children's upbringing, any transformation of society in order to liberate women as well as men, must incorporate from the beginning more shared responsibility for the care and socialization of children at every stage. She added, "It is hoped that this weekend will provide the opportunity for discussing ways to attempt to change our own lives, so that we determine for ourselves the practical solution and the political solution for our own emancipation."[8]

In the decades since, Rochelle Wortis's children have grown into adulthood and the women's movement has grown internationally. I do not think she realized quite how many weekends it would take, or the complexities which would arise when much wider, diverse groups of women began to think how they could combine changing their own lives with the transformation of society.

NOTES

1. Helke Sander, "Action Committee for the Liberation of Women," SDS Conference, Frankfurt, unpublished MS, 1968.
2. Valerie Walkerdine in Liz Heron, ed., *Truth, Dare or Promise: Girls Growing Up in the 50s* (London: Virago, 1985), 74, 75.
3. Sue O'Sullivan, "Capping the Cervix," *Spare Rib* 105 (April 1981).
4. *Come Together* 3, Gay Women's Liberation issue (1971).
5. Quoted in Sheila Rowbotham, "The Beginnings of Women's Liberation Britain" (1972), in Sheila Rowbotham, *Dreams and Dilemmas: Collected Writings* (London: Virago, 1983).
6. Quoted in Sheila Rowbotham, *Woman's Consciousness, Man's World* (Harmondsworth: Penguin, 1973), 97.
7. Audrey Wise, "Equal Pay is Not Enough," *Black Dwarf* 10 (January 1969).
8. Rochelle Wortis, Women's Liberation Conference, Ruskin College, Oxford, 1970.

LISTEN UP, ANGLO SISTERS

ELIZABETH MARTÍNEZ

COLONIZED WOMEN: LA CHICANA

For the women of a colonized group, even the most politicized, their oppression as women is usually overshadowed by the common oppression of both male and female. Black and brown people in this country often see themselves as fighting for sheer survival against the physical genocide of racism, war, police brutality, hunger and deprivation, and against the cultural genocide of Anglo institutions and values. As a result, most colonized women will feel an impulse toward unity with, rather than enmity toward, their brothers. When the colonized group is in the minority, as in the United States, this becomes even more true.

The woman from a colonized people also recognizes that many times it has been easier for her economically than for the men of her group. Often she can get a job where a man cannot. She can see the damage done to the man as a result, and feels reluctant to risk threatening his self-respect ever further. This may be a short-range viewpoint, involving false definitions of manhood, but it is created by immediate realities whose force cannot merely be wished away. It is also a fact that in many Chicano families, the woman makes many of the important decisions—not just consumer decisions—though the importance of her role will be recognized only privately. This may seem hypocritical or demeaning, but the knowledge of having real influence affects how the Chicana feels.

The family is also seen differently by women from the colonial experience. It often serves as a fortress, a defense against the inimical forces of the dominant society, a source of strength for a people whose identity is constantly under attack. Within that fortress, the woman as mother remains central. She is the principle of life, of survival and endurance. The children survive through her willpower. So the family is a fortress in the face of genocidal forces, a major source of strength for a people whose identity is constantly being whittled away. For young, alienated Anglo women, on the other hand, the family—especially when nuclear—is often seen as an oppressive, patriarchical institution that limits

women to the roles of housewife and mother. Her attitude is almost the opposite of the Chicana's.

The family is but one example of how the culture or lifestyle of a colonized
people becomes a weapon of self-defense in a hostile world—even when that
culture or lifestyle might be oppressive to half of the people. To challenge such
a lifestyle often means to risk being seen as adopting the enemy's position. "We
don't want to become like the dominating Anglo women," you could hear
Chicanas say in the 1960s and 1970s—and in later years as well. The comment
shows a lack of understanding of the Anglo woman's struggle, but it also reveals
how, for a colonized people, cultural integrity is deeply interwoven with survival.
The middle-class Anglo woman must therefore beware of telling her sisters of
color to throw off their chains without at least first understanding the origins
and reasons for those "chains." She should also first ask herself: are there
perhaps some aspects of these other lifestyles from which white women might
still learn?

At the same time, we can hope that women from the colonized populations
will listen with open minds to their Anglo sisters' ideas about women's liberation
and then take another look at their own values. There is, for example, nothing
worth preserving about the tradition of two young Chicano males fighting at a
dance over some girl whom both hardly know, to prove their manhood. There
is also much to be gained by considering the idea that male authoritarianism
does not oppress women only, but also the masses—many being people of
color. In other words, feminism must be antiracist (since vast numbers of women
suffer racism) and antiracism must be feminist (since half of those suffering
racism are women).

Such an open-minded exchange of ideas will often be difficult. But for those
who seek to affirm a revolutionary vision and change the basic system under
which we live, does any other real choice exist? How else can we create a society
based on interdependency and balance instead of hierarchy?

Plagued by Western habits of either/or, dualistic thinking, we all may fail to
understand that race, class, and gender interconnect to sustain a corporate ruling
class. In the language of African-American essayist bell hooks, they are interlocking systems of oppression. Neither Latina nor Anglo women should yield
to the temptation of making a hierarchy of oppressions where battles are fought
over whether racism is "worse" than sexism: or class oppression is "deeper"
than racism, and so on. Instead of hierarchies we need bridges—which, after all,
exist to make two ends meet.

CARAMBA, OUR ANGLO SISTERS JUST DIDN'T GET IT

Today, when a strong defense of reproductive rights by women of all racial and
ethnic origins is urgently needed, what do we find? Too often pro-choice Anglo
women just don't… "get it." The historic April 5, 1992, march in Washington,
D.C., to defend reproductive rights became another occasion when women of

color saw their demands for a front seat denied and their protests against such treatment drowned in a deluge of defensiveness. Once again they heard those familiar claims of good intentions. Once again they heard that patronizing line about how African-American and Latina women are just too busy fighting racism or too constrained by their religion to be concerned with choice.

One begins to wonder: maybe it's wrong to say they just don't get it. Maybe they do "get it" but don't want to yield any degree of control. In any case, the story needs to be told and lessons drawn.

A few days before the Washington march, an ad hoc coalition embracing six organizations of Asian/Pacific Island, Black, Latina and Native American women, together with the International Coalition of Women Physicians, spoke out about the National Organization for Women (NOW). In its public statement the ad hoc coalition—called the Women of Color Reproductive Rights Groups—listed criticisms of NOW actions related to the march. These included failing to contact organizations of women of color in time for them to participate in planning and strategizing for the march; failing to acknowledge the suggestion that a women-of-color delegation be prominently located in the march lineup; and failing to seek their input about rally speakers. Those criticisms reflected long experience of being invited to join an action after plans had been made (by Anglo women), of being relegated to the back of a march, and of being scheduled to speak late in the program when people would already be leaving. The coalition's statement spelled out the heart of the matter:

> Historically, the relationship between women of color and the broader reproductive rights community has suffered due to the uneven power relationship between the long-established reproductive rights organizations and the newly established women of color reproductive rights organizations. In spite of our limited resources, [our activities] have been responsible for the increased awareness and for the educating, organizing, and mobilizing of our communities.... If NOW's leadership is serious about strengthening their relationship with women of color not only our right to reproductive freedom must be respected, but our right to decide who our representatives will be—the right to self-determination—must be respected.

One of the main organizers of this protest was Luz Alvarez Martínez, director of the Organización Nacional de La Salud de La Mujer Latina (National Latina Health Organization) in Oakland, California. According to Alvarez Martínez, NOW president Patricia Ireland originally said she wanted women-of-color organizations to feel included in the march—then failed to implement this beyond contacting three African-American groups in Washington, D.C. (but no other black groups and not any Latinas at first). In the days that followed, Alvarez Martínez said, national NOW leaders responded with inaction and excuses to women-of-color demands for a key role in planning, marching, and speaking.

The ad hoc coalition then urged women going to the march to wear green armbands as a sign of protest, to march together and to write letters of protest to NOW's board. NOW had asked Alvarez Martínez to be a speaker at the Washington rally, but, she said, "after getting no input whatsoever, we were not about to be used as window dressing by speaking at the rally." As it turned out, five other Latinas did speak that day—all of them before the march, and none during the official rally program.

Throughout this struggle, the ad hoc coalition stressed that their protest aimed to strengthen the reproductive-rights movement. Coalition groups were committed to fight for the right "of all women—especially poor women and women of color—to safe, affordable, and quality reproductive services." The National Latina Health Organization and others urged members to march on April 5. But, as Alvarez Martínez told me, "NOW and others like them must change. That's our goal—to achieve real unity so we will be stronger."

"Some in the group would like to meet with NOW," Julia Scott of the National Black Women's Health Project in Washington, D.C., commented to me at the time, "but mostly the top priority is to develop and organize ourselves so that this problem never happens again. So that we come to the table as equal partners. They have to learn to operate differently with us." That is the heart of the matter, Scott said. "It's about doing things differently. Realizing that maybe your way isn't the best way. Right now, when faced with diversity, they resist changing." An urgent need to fight some appalling new piece of anti-choice legislation becomes the justification for not taking the time to resolve this issue. Scott saw a particular need to challenge NOW's rhetoric of inclusion.

The conduct of national NOW in the April 5 series of events was typical of the mainstream feminist movement. As Scott pointed out, "White feminism's biggest mistake was not working with poor, working-class women. The problem isn't just racism on their part, it's also a middle-class perspective. It includes a failure to study the lessons of history about white feminism's mistakes in relating to women of color."

The Conference on Population Control held in Cairo in 1994 showed that those lessons of history still needed to be learned, above all the lesson that issues of class and race can still divide the pro-choice movement if not recognized. According to Alvarez Martínez, the Cairo conference focused heavily on abortion rights, and the document coming out of it did not take seriously the needs of marginalized women and women in poor countries. Still, it was the first time women of color were included in an international conference on those reproductive-rights issues. By the time the United Nations Fourth World Conference on Women and the accompanying conference of non-governmental organizations took place in Beijing in 1995, the old ad hoc grouping had become the Coalition for Reproductive Health Rights. The voices of women of color could no longer be denied.

Back in Oakland, Alvarez Martínez not only criticizes Anglo sisters whose attitudes need to change; she also points to those who *have* grown, including NOW leaders. In San Francisco, women of color for reproductive rights experienced a local struggle similar to the one around the Washington, D.C., march. Out of the resulting dialogue came a good working relationship with NOW leader Elizabeth Toledo, Planned Parenthood, and other predominantly white groups. "They don't always see what they do wrong, but when you tell them, they get it," Alvarez Martínez said after the dialogue. This experience suggests a model for joint pro-choice efforts around the country.

The problem has often been rooted in a racist arrogance underlying the attitude of many Anglo women toward Latina views on reproductive rights. In the guise of understanding our culture, or sympathizing with our daily survival needs, they have characterized Latina feminism as inherently more conservative than the Anglo variety. Much ignorance of Latina views and experience feeds that stereotype.

If we look more closely at Latina views, we find that reproductive freedom is a major concern of Latinas and not some taboo subject or minor matter. In 1977, when Congress ended federal funding of abortions, the first victim was a 27-year-old Chicana—Rosie Jiménez from McAllen, Texas, daughter of migrant workers—who died at the hands of an illegal abortionist after six days of suffering.

The Rosie Jiménez case was one reason for the formation in 1990 of an ad hoc coalition, Latinas pro Derechos Reproductivos (Latinas for Reproductive Choice), by Luz Alvarez Martínez and five other women. The appointment of David Souter to the U.S. Supreme Court, and the increasing likelihood of the court overthrowing *Roe* v. *Wade*, also spurred this action. It is a myth, the group maintains, that Latinas do not have abortions; they just don't talk about them. In fact, the Latina abortion rate in 1994 was 26.1 per thousand, compared with 26.6 per thousand for non-Latinas.[1]

Today, Latina abortions constitute about 13 percent of the total in the United States, which is disproportionate to the Latina percentage of the population. According to a poll of women of color on reproductive-health issues that was conducted by the National Council of Negro Women and the Communications Consortium Media Center (both in Washington, D.C.), only 25 percent of Latinas are opposed to abortion in all circumstances.

It has never been easy for Latinas to advance abortion rights. A Latina in Corpus Christi, Texas, is believed to be the first U.S. Catholic excommunicated for pro-choice activism. In the face of such experiences, one of the goals of Latinas pro Derechos Reproductivos was to break the silence on reproductive-rights issues. At the same time, they considered abortion too narrow a focus. "We are redefining choice," Alvarez Martínez said; choice has to include having all the healthcare services and information that enable a woman to make her own decision freely.

Choice also has to include freedom from sterilization abuse—another form of reproductive oppression. For women of color this is a major concern. While a Medicaid-funded abortion may be hard or impossible to get in some states (it is still legal in California), sterilization services are provided by states under Medicaid, and the federal government reimburses states for 90 percent of those expenses. Some public hospitals have two films they show to women seeking contraceptive information: the English-language film emphasizes conventional contraceptive methods, and the Spanish-language film stresses sterilization. Sometimes a woman must agree to sterilization to get an abortion. Sterilization rates run up to 65 percent for Latinas in some parts of the United States; in New York, for example, the Latina rate is seven times higher than that of white women. Yet too often pro-choice Anglo women ignore or downplay sterilization abuse. Even though there are now laws against it, such abuse continues. Choice also has to mean freedom from the abuse of birth-control methods like Norplant.

The word "choice" has no meaning if women don't first have access to quality healthcare. That means a national health plan, information and education on sexuality that is culturally relevant and in the necessary languages, and affordable birth control. It means adequate prenatal care so healthy babies can be born. It means access to fertility services, which are never considered an issue for poor women. All these needs point to the fact that class differences cut across the choice issue again and again.

In short, Latinas' views on reproductive rights are often more radical than Anglo women's views and not "conservative," as some say, because their definition of choice requires more profound social change than just abortion rights or preventing pregnancy. As Alvarez Martínez told me in early 1998:

> We are for social change. Our focus is on Latinas and health, not just reproductive rights. We are trying to change the way funding is done. It shouldn't just be focused, for example, on preventing teenage pregnancy by preaching abstinence. It has to look at the entire social situation of the women.

There is still a need, she added, to push for more understanding in Anglo women concerned with reproductive rights. "Many are still not aware of Latina women as active in this field." Yet today we have not only the National Latina Health Organization but also the National Latina Institute for Reproductive Health, which in the 1990s came out of Catholics for Free Choice, based in the Washington, D.C. area and does regional organizing; the more grassroots Latina Roundtable on Health and Reproductive Rights, in New York (also founded in the 1990s); and the Mujeres Project in San Antonio, Texas, which focuses on reproductive health.

Differences with Anglo women in the struggle for reproductive rights reflect inter-feminist relations in many arenas. Problems explode periodically and demand constant discussion. Latina, Black, Asian/Pacific Island American, and Native American women are unlikely to unite with the war cry of "Abortion is liberation!" but they can and will work with Anglo women when respect and space are given.

Among women of color, increased communication and coordination are future goals. The coalition that opposed NOW policies in 1992 did not become permanent, as once hoped, for lack of funding, Alvarez Martínez said. Funders forced them to choose between support for their individual projects and for collaborative work; most had to choose the former. But the groups are still in touch and collaborate informally. They can all take the stand that as women of color in the reproductive-freedom movement, "We will no longer be silent or invisible!"

AFTERWORD[2]

Making what we may call a revolution for the century-after-tomorrow demands that we build a unified and therefore powerful force for change. That cannot be done without overcoming racist divisions at the grassroots level.

To overcome those divisions requires white attitudes changing, and more than that. Our exclusively black–white model of racialism must be abandoned in favor of one that includes all peoples of color. We then have a foundation for potential alliances among people of color, which are more critical than ever given today's new divide-and-conquer tactics.

For those alliances to grow, Latinas and Latinos must understand the dangers of nationalism (or its younger brother, identity politics). Nationalism obscures issues of class, often benefits only our access-hungry careerists, and can prevent Raza along with other marginalized folk from uniting around class.

For those alliances to grow, Latinos need to practice a constant, profound honesty about ourselves and our weaknesses, especially racist attitudes within our own community toward other people of color. We also need to be self-critical about how we sometimes let power corrupt.

All this points to the great need for a radical force within each community of color to pursue liberating politics and combat conservative or reactionary tendencies within each community. The good news of 1998 was that the first national Black Radical Congress (with 2,000 people attending), the first Asian American Left Forum, and various meetings to build a New Raza Left all took place within the same six months. There's hope!

To build unity requires recognizing the central role of young activists. They are vigorously fighting the attack on this century's Reconstruction. Their anger at today's ugly society often translates into a passionate drive for unity across color lines.

And the best lesson of all: women are the world's most consistent alliance-builders. When women of color lead the way in a movement, it will almost always be stronger. When any women lead the way in uniting people, let tyrants beware.

All very nice, you say, but get practical. Where and when can alliances be built?

A common agenda for people of color should include, for starters, standing together against hate crimes. Against police abuse, which intensifies as poverty deepens today. Against the denial of adequate healthcare (walk into the emergency room of any big-city public hospital and who's waiting there along with poor whites?).

Surely we should all be able to unite for our children's well-being. Against the drug traffic, gang warfare, and the demonization of youth. Against neglected, underfunded, inequitable education, beginning with the inner-city schools. We need one million parents and teachers of all colors to march on that too-White House calling for the nation to stop wasting millions of minds. We also need to see how dance, music, theater, art, poetry, are major arenas for alliance-building, especially among youth. Culture can usher in new visions.

Education without language rights is impossible. Sometimes bilingual programs have been made a divisive issue between black and brown. But recognition of "Black English" as a lingua franca, with its own structure and norms, can provide a bridge for appreciating why children should not be forced to forget their home language in order to learn English. Let them know both! The June 1997 vote to end bilingual education in California showed that division is not inevitable; a majority of African Americans opposed that measure along with the great majority of Latinos.

Of the many arenas for alliance-building, none is more fundamental than the workplace. In recent years, community organizing has unleashed new forces everywhere. Imagine if that were combined with creative, democratic union organizing that genuinely involves the rank and file. Imagine a new labor movement that incorporates millions of the unorganized—for example, day laborers and domestic workers.

The dream of social transformation from the bottom up then becomes less elusive. Can't you see the Rainbow Warriors smiling, when they win a victory here and there, knowing they fought the good fight? Yes, and they also know more good fights lie ahead.

NOTES

1. "Unintended Pregnancy in the U.S.," *Family Planning Perspectives* (Alan Guttmacher Institute, Washington, D.C., January 1998).
2. Written in 1998.

CAPITALISM AND HUMAN EMANCIPATION: RACE, GENDER, AND DEMOCRACY

ELLEN MEIKSINS WOOD

Speaking to American students at the height of student activism in the 1960s Isaac Deutscher delivered a not altogether welcome message: "You are effervescently active on the margin of social life, and the workers are passive right at the core of it. That is the tragedy of our society. If you do not deal with this contrast, you will be defeated."[1] That warning may be no less apposite today than it was then. There are strong and promising emancipatory impulses at work today, but they may not be active at the core of social life, in the heart of capitalist society.

It is no longer taken for granted on the left that the decisive battle for human emancipation will take place on the "economic" terrain, the home ground of class struggle. For a great many people the emphasis has shifted to struggles for what I shall call extra-economic goods—gender-emancipation, racial equality, peace, ecological health, democratic citizenship. Every socialist ought to be committed to these goals in themselves—in fact, the socialist project of class emancipation always has been, or should have been, a means to the larger end of human emancipation. But these commitments do not settle crucial questions about agencies and modalities of struggle, and they certainly do not settle the question of class politics.

A great deal still needs to be said about the conditions for the achievement of these extra-economic goods. In particular, if our starting point is capitalism, then we need to know exactly what kind of starting point this is. What limits are imposed, and what possibilities created, by the capitalist regime, by its material order and its configuration of social power? What kinds of oppression does capitalism require, and what kinds of emancipation can it tolerate? In particular, what use does capitalism have for extra-economic goods, what encouragement does it give them, and what resistance does it put up to their attainment? I want to make a start on answering these questions, and as the argument develops I shall try to throw them into relief by making some comparisons with precapitalist societies.

CAPITALISM AND EXTRA-ECONOMIC GOODS

Let me begin by saying that certain extra-economic goods are simply not compatible with capitalism, and I do not intend to talk about them. I am convinced, for example, that capitalism cannot deliver world peace. It seems to me axiomatic that the expansionary, competitive, and exploitative logic of capitalist accumulation in the context of the nation-state system must, in the longer or shorter term, be destabilizing, and that capitalism—and at the moment its most aggressive and adventurist organizing force, the government of the United States—is and will for the foreseeable future remain the greatest threat to world peace.[2]

Nor do I think that capitalism can avoid ecological devastation. It may be able to accommodate some degree of ecological care, especially when the technology of environmental protection is itself profitably marketable. But the essential irrationality of the drive for capital accumulation, which subordinates everything to the requirements of the self-expansion of capital and so-called growth, is unavoidably hostile to ecological balance. If destruction of the environment in the Communist world resulted from gross neglect, massive inefficiency, and a reckless urge to catch up with Western industrial development in the shortest possible time, in the capitalist West a far more wide-ranging ecological vandalism is not an index of failure but a token of success, the inevitable by-product of a system whose constitutive principle is the subordination of all human values to the imperatives of accumulation and the requirements of profitability.

It has to be added, though, that the issues of peace and ecology are not very well suited to generating strong anticapitalist forces. In a sense, the problem is their very *universality*. They do not constitute social forces because they simply have no specific social identity—or at least they have none except at the point where they intersect with class relations, as in the case of ecological issues raised by the poisoning of workers in the workplace, or the tendency to concentrate pollution and waste in working-class neighborhoods rather than in privileged suburbs. But, in the final analysis, it is no more in the interests of the capitalist than of the worker to be wiped out by a nuclear bomb or dissolved in acid rain. We might as well say that given the dangers of capitalism, no rational person should support it; but this, needless to say, is not how things work.

The situation with race and gender is almost the reverse. Antiracism and antisexism do have specific social identities, and they can generate strong social forces. But it is not so clear that racial or gender equality are antagonistic to capitalism, or that capitalism cannot tolerate them as it cannot deliver world peace or respect the environment. Each of these extra-economic goods, then, has its own specific relation to capitalism.

The first point about capitalism is that it is uniquely indifferent to the social identities of the people it exploits. This is a classic case of good news and bad news. First, the good news—more or less. Unlike previous modes of production, capitalist exploitation is not inextricably linked with extra-economic, juridical or political identities, inequalities or differences. The extraction of surplus value from wage laborers takes place in a relationship between formally free and equal individuals and does not presuppose differences in juridical or political status. In fact, there is a positive tendency in capitalism to *undermine* such differences, and even to dilute identities like gender or race, as capital strives to absorb people into the labor market and to reduce them to interchangeable units of labor abstracted from any specific identity.

On the other hand, capitalism is very flexible in its ability to make use of, as well as to discard, particular social oppressions. Part of the bad news is that capitalism is likely to co-opt whatever extraeconomic oppressions are historically and culturally available in any given setting. Such cultural legacies can, for example, promote the ideological hegemony of capitalism by disguising its inherent tendency to create underclasses. When the least privileged sectors of the working class coincide with extra-economic identities like gender or race, as they so often do, it may appear that the blame for the existence of these sectors lies with causes other than the necessary logic of the capitalist system.

It is not, of course, a matter of some capitalist conspiracy to deceive. For one thing, racism and sexism function so well in capitalist society partly because they can actually work to the advantage of certain sectors of the working class in the competitive conditions of the labor market. The point, though, is that if capital derives advantages from racism or sexism, it is not because of any structural tendency in capitalism toward racial inequality or gender oppression, but on the contrary because they disguise the structural realities of the capitalist system and because they divide the working class. At any rate, capitalist exploitation can in principle be conducted without any consideration for colour, race, creed, gender, any dependence upon extra-economic inequality or difference; and more than that, the development of capitalism has created ideological pressures *against* such inequalities and differences to a degree with no precedent in precapitalist societies.

RACE AND GENDER

Here we immediately come up against some contradictions. Consider the example of race. Despite the structural indifference of capitalism to extra-economic identities (or in some sense because of it), its history has been marked by probably the most virulent racisms ever known. The widespread and deep-rooted racism directed against blacks in the West, for example, is often attributed to the cultural legacy of colonialism and slavery which accompanied the expansion of capitalism. But on second thought, while this explanation is certainly convincing up to a point, by itself it is not enough.

Take the extreme case of slavery. A comparison with the only other known historical examples of slavery on such a scale will illustrate that there is nothing automatic about the association of slavery with such virulent racism, and may suggest that there is something specific to capitalism in this ideological effect.

In ancient Greece and Rome, despite the almost universal acceptance of slavery, the idea that it was justified by natural inequalities among human beings was not the dominant view. The one notable exception, Aristotle's conception of natural slavery, never gained currency. The more common view seems to have been that slavery was a convention, though a universal one, which was justifiable simply on the grounds of its usefulness. In fact, it was even conceded that this useful institution was *contrary to nature*. Such a view appears not only in Greek philosophy but was even recognized in Roman law. It has even been suggested that slavery was the only case in Roman law where there was an acknowledged conflict between the *ius gentium*, the conventional law of nations, and the *ius naturale*, the law of nature.[3]

This is significant not because it led to the abolition of slavery, which it certainly did not; nor does it in any way mitigate the horrors of ancient slavery. It is worth noting because it suggests that, in contrast to modern slavery, there seemed to be no pressing need to find a justification for this evil institution in the natural, biological inferiority of certain races. Ethnic conflicts are probably as old as civilization; and defences of slavery based, for example, on biblical stories about tainted inheritance have had a long history. There have also been theories of climatic determinism, from Aristotle to Bodin; but the determinants here are environmental rather than racial. Modern racism is something different, a more viciously systematic conception of inherent and natural inferiority, which emerged in the late seventeenth or early eighteenth century and culminated in the nineteenth century when it acquired the pseudo-scientific reinforcement of *biological* theories of race, and continued to serve as an ideological support for colonial oppression even after the abolition of slavery.

It is tempting to ask, then, what it was about capitalism that created this ideological need, this need for what amounts to a theory of natural, not just conventional, slavery. And at least part of the answer must lie in a paradox. While colonial oppression and slavery were growing in the outposts of capitalism, the workforce at home was increasingly proletarianized; and the expansion of wage labor, the contractual relation between formally free and equal individuals, carried with it an ideology of formal equality and freedom. In fact, this ideology, which on the juridical and political planes denies the fundamental inequality and unfreedom of the capitalist economic relation, has always been a vital element in the hegemony of capitalism.

In a sense, then, it was precisely the structural pressure *against* extra-economic difference which made it necessary to justify slavery by excluding slaves from the human race, making them non-persons standing outside the normal universe of freedom and equality. It is perhaps because capitalism recognizes no extra-economic differences among human beings that people had to be rendered less than human in order to accommodate the slavery and colonialism which were so useful to capital at that historical moment. In Greece and Rome, it was enough to identify people as outsiders on the grounds that they were not *citizens*, or that they were not Greeks (the Romans, as we have seen, had a rather less exclusive conception of citizenship). In capitalism, the criterion for excommunication seems to be exclusion from the main body of the human race.

Or consider the case of gender oppression. The contradictions here are not quite so glaring. If capitalism has been associated with a racism more virulent than ever before, I for one would find wholly unconvincing any claim that capitalism has produced more extreme forms of gender oppression than existed in precapitalist societies. But here too there is a paradoxical combination of structural indifference to, indeed pressure against, this extra-economic inequality, and a kind of systemic opportunism which allows capitalism to make use of it.

Typically, capitalism in advanced Western capitalist countries uses gender oppression in two kinds of ways: the first it shares with other extra-economic identities, like race or even age, and it is to some extent interchangeable with them as a means of constituting underclasses and providing ideological cover. The second use is specific to gender: it serves as a way of organizing social reproduction in what is thought (maybe incorrectly) to be the least expensive way.[4] With the existing organization of gender relations, the costs to capital of reproducing labor power can be kept down—or so it has generally been thought—by keeping the costs of childbearing and childrearing in the private sphere of the family. But we have to recognize that, from the point of view of capital, this particular social cost is no different from any other. From the point of view of capital, maternity leaves or daycare centers are not qualitatively different from, say, old-age pensions or unemployment insurance, in that they all involve an undesirable cost.[5] Capital is in general hostile to any such costs—though it has never been able to survive without at least some of them; but the point is that in this respect it is no more incapable of tolerating gender equality than of accepting the National Health Service or social security.

Although capitalism can and does make ideological and economic use of gender oppression, then, this oppression has no privileged status in the structure of capitalism. Capitalism could survive the eradication of all oppressions specific to women as women—while it would not, by definition, survive the eradication of class exploitation. This does not mean that capitalism has made the liberation of women necessary or inevitable. But it does mean that there is no specific structural necessity for, nor even a strong systemic disposition to, gender oppression in capitalism. I shall have some things to say later about how capitalism differs in this respect from precapitalist societies.

I have cited these examples to illustrate two major points: that capitalism does have a structural tendency away from extra-economic inequalities, but that this is a two-edged sword. The strategic implications are that struggles conceived in purely extra-economic terms—as purely against racism or gender oppression for example—are not in themselves fatally dangerous to capitalism, that they could succeed without dismantling the capitalist system but that, at the same time, they are probably unlikely to succeed if they remain detached from an anticapitalist struggle.

CAPITALISM AND THE DEVALUATION
OF POLITICAL GOODS

The ambiguities of capitalism are particularly evident, as we have seen, in its relationship with democratic citizenship. Here, I want to explore the ambiguities of capitalist democracy as they relate to the question of "extra-economic" goods in general and the position of women in particular.

It has always been a major question for socialism what strategic importance should be attached to the fact that capitalism has made possible an unprecedented extension of citizenship. Almost from the beginning there has existed a socialist tradition which assumes that the formal juridical and political equality of capitalism, in combination with its economic inequality and unfreedom, will set up a dynamic contradiction, a motivating force for a socialist transformation. A basic premiss of social democracy, for example, has been that the limited freedom and equality of capitalism will produce overpowering impulses toward complete emancipation. There now exists a strong new tendency to think of socialism as an extension of citizenship rights, or—and this is increasingly common—to think of "radical democracy" as a *substitute* for socialism. As *democracy* has become the catchword of various progressive struggles, the one unifying theme among the various emancipatory projects of the left, it has begun to stand for all extra-economic goods together.

The idea of regarding socialism as an expansion of democracy can be very fruitful, but I am not at all impressed by the new theoretical trappings of the very old socialist illusion that the ideological impulses of capitalist freedom and equality have created irresistible pressures to transform society at every level. The effects of capitalist democracy have been much more ambiguous than that, and this conception of social transformation is just a sleight of hand which invites us to imagine, if not a smooth transition from capitalist democracy to socialist (or "radical") democracy, then a substantial realization of democratic aspirations within the interstices of capitalism.

The first requirement here is to have no illusions about the meaning and effects of democracy in capitalism. This means understanding not only the limits of capitalist democracy, the fact that even a democratic capitalist state will be constrained by the demands of capital accumulation, and the fact that liberal democracy leaves capitalist exploitation essentially intact, but more particularly the *devaluation* of democracy discussed in our earlier comparisons between ancient and modern democracy.

The critical point is that the status of political goods is in large part determined by their particular location in the system of social property relations. Here again, the contrast with precapitalist societies of various kinds is instructive. I have suggested in previous chapters that in precapitalist societies, where peasants were the predominant exploited class and exploitation typically took the form of extra-economic, political, juridical, military domination, the prevailing property relations placed a special premium on juridical privilege and political rights. So just as medieval lordship inseparably united political and economic power, so too peasant resistance to economic exploitation could take the form of demanding a share in the privileged juridical and political status of their overlords—as for example, in the famous English peasant revolt in 1381 provoked by the attempt to impose a poll tax, in which the rebel leader Wat Tyler formulated peasant grievances as a demand for the equal distribution of lordship among all men. This, however, would have meant the end of feudalism. In contrast to capitalism, the salience of political rights imposed an absolute limit on their distribution.

For peasants economic power against exploitation depended to a great extent on the scope of jurisdiction permitted to their own political community, the village, as against the powers of landlord and state. By definition, any extension of the village community's jurisdiction encroached upon and circumscribed the landlord's powers of exploitation. Some powers, however, were more important than others. In contrast to capitalism, the precapitalist landlord or the surplus-extracting state did not depend on controlling the process of production as much as on coercive powers of surplus extraction. The precapitalist peasant, who retained possession of the means of production, generally remained in control of production both individually and collectively through his village community. It was a characteristic of feudalism, as of other precapitalist forms, that the act of appropriation was generally much more clearly separate from the process of production than it is in capitalism. The peasant produced, the landlord then extracted rent, or the state appropriated tax; or else the peasant produced one day on his own plot and for his own household needs, and on another day on the landlord's demesne, or in some kind of service for the state. So the appropriative powers of landlord or state could be preserved even with a considerable degree of independence for peasants in organizing production, so long as the jurisdiction of the peasant community did not cross the line to control of the juridical and political mechanisms of surplus extraction.

Peasant communities have from time to time pressed hard against those barriers, achieving a substantial degree of independence in their local political institutions, setting up their own local magistrates in place of landlord representatives, imposing their own local charters, and so on. And to the extent that they have achieved this degree of *political* independence, they have also limited their *economic* exploitation. But the barrier between village and state has generally defeated attempts to overcome the subjection of the peasant; and Athenian democracy may be the one case where that final barrier was breached and where the village community did not remain outside the state, and subject to it, as something alien.[6]

I have argued that by far the most revolutionary aspect of ancient Athenian democracy was the unique, and never equalled, position of the peasant as *citizen*, and with it the position of the village in its relation to the state.[7] In sharp contrast to other peasant societies, the village was the constituent unit of the Athenian state, through which the peasant became a citizen. This represented

not just a constitutional innovation but a radical transformation of the peasantry, unrivalled in the ancient world, or indeed anywhere else at any time. If the
peasant is, as Eric Wolf has said, a rural cultivator whose surpluses in the form
of rent and tax are transferred to someone who "exercises an effective superior
power, or domain, over him,"[8] then what characterized the Athenian smallholder was an unprecedented—and later unequalled—independence from this
kind of "domain" and hence an unusual degree of freedom from rent and tax.
The creation of the peasant citizen meant the liberation of peasants from all
forms of tributary relationship which had characterized the Greek peasantry
before, and continued to characterize peasantries elsewhere. Democratic citizenship here had political and economic implications at the same time.

The ancient democracy differed radically from other advanced civilizations
of the ancient world, in the Near East and Asia, as well as Bronze Age Greece,
in respect to the relation between rulers and producers; the democratic polis
diverged sharply from the widespread pattern of appropriating states and subject villages of peasant producers, and from the rule "universally recognized
everywhere under Heaven," that "those who work with their minds rule, while
those who work with their bodies are ruled." It was no accident that, when anti-
democratic Greek philosophers like Plato and Aristotle depicted their ideal states,
they very consciously and explicitly reinstated the principle of division between
rulers and producers, a principle whose violation they clearly regarded as essential to Athenian democracy.

In fact, the surplus-appropriating state acting in what Robert Brenner has
called "class-like" ways was probably more a rule than an exception in advanced
precapitalist societies.[9] We cannot understand, say, French absolutism without
recognizing the role of the state as a means of private appropriation, with its
vast apparatus of lucrative offices and its extraction of taxes from the peasantry,
a proprietary resource for those who possessed a piece of it. For that matter, we
cannot understand an upheaval like the French Revolution without recognizing
that a major issue in it was access to this lucrative resource.[10]

If these very diverse cases have in common a unity of political and economic power which gives political rights a special value, the devaluation of
political goods in capitalism rests on the separation of the economic and the
political. The status of political goods is bound to be diminished by the
autonomy of the economic sphere, the independence of capitalist exploitation
from direct coercive power, the separation of appropriation from the performance of public functions, the existence of a separate purely "political" sphere
distinct from the "economy," which makes possible for the first time a democracy" that is only "political," without the economic and social implications
attached to ancient Greek democracy.

To put the point differently, the separation of the political and the economic
in capitalism means the separation of communal life from the organization of
production. For instance, there is nothing comparable to the communal regulation of production exercised by the village community in many peasant

economies. And political life in capitalism is separated from the organization of exploitation. At the same time, capitalism also brings production and appropriation together in an inseparable unity. The act of appropriation in capitalism, the extraction of surplus value, is inseparable from the process of production; and both these processes have been detached from the political sphere and, so to speak, privatized.

All this has implications for the conditions of resistance. There is, for example, no parallel in capitalism to the function of the village commune as a form of peasant class organization in the struggle against lordly exploitation—that is, a form of class organization that is inseparably economic and political at once. In capitalism, a great deal can happen in politics and community organization at every level without fundamentally affecting the exploitative powers of capital or fundamentally changing the decisive balance of social power. Struggles in these arenas remain vitally important, but they have to be organized and conducted in the full recognition that capitalism has a remarkable capacity to distance democratic politics from the decisive centers of social power and to insulate the power of appropriation and exploitation from democratic accountability.

To sum up: in precapitalist societies, extra-economic powers had a special importance because the economic power of appropriation was inseparable from them. One might speak here of a scarcity of extra-economic goods because they were too valuable to be widely distributed. We might, then, characterize the situation of extra-economic goods in capitalism by saying that it has overcome that scarcity. It has made possible a far wider distribution of extra-economic goods, and specifically the goods associated with citizenship, than was ever possible before. But it has overcome scarcity by devaluing the currency.

THE POSITION OF WOMEN

What I have said about the devaluation of political rights applies, of course, to everyone, men and women alike; but it has some interesting consequences for women in particular, or rather for gender relations, which go well beyond purely political questions. First, there is the obvious fact that women under capitalism have achieved political rights undreamed of in earlier societies; and I think it is safe to say that the general tendency toward at least formal equality has created pressures in favour of women's emancipation with no historical precedent. This achievement was not, needless to say, won without a considerable struggle; but the very idea that political emancipation was something women could aspire to and struggle for was fairly late in its appearance on the historical agenda. In part, this development can be put down to the general devaluation of political goods which has made it possible for dominant groups to be less discriminating about their distribution. But in this case, there is much more at stake than formal rights of citizenship.

Let us return to our precapitalist examples. We have focused our attention on the typical combination of peasant production and extra-economic exploitation.

Now we can consider what this meant for the position of women. Here it is important to keep in mind that where peasants have been the primary producers and sources of surplus, as they typically have been in precapitalist societies, it is not just the peasant himself but the peasant *household* that has constituted the basic unit of production, as well as—and this point needs to be stressed—the basic unit of exploitation. The labor appropriated by landlords and states from the peasantry has been family labor, and it has taken the form not only of productive rent- or tax-producing services performed collectively by the peasant family, or other kinds of labor services both private and public, but also domestic labor in the master's household and, of course, the reproduction of the labor force itself, the bearing and rearing of children, the future laborers, servants and soldiers in the fields, households and armies of the dominant classes. The division of labor within the peasant family, then, has been deeply and inextricably linked to the demands placed upon the household unit by its role in the process of exploitation. Whatever may have been the historical reasons for particular sexual divisions of labor within the household, in class societies they have always been distorted by hierarchical, coercive, and antagonistic production relations between the household and forces outside it.

It is particularly important to remember that precapitalist peasants generally kept control of the production process, while landlords increased their surpluses not so much by directing production as by employing and enhancing their powers of surplus-*extraction*—that is to say, their jurisdictional, political, and military powers. Apart from the general implications of this fact for the distribution of political rights, it also had implications for gender relations within the peasant household. The critical point can be summed up by saying that wherever there is exploitation there has to be hierarchy and coercive discipline, and that in this case they are concentrated in the household and become inseparable from the day-to-day relations of the family. There can be no clear separation here between family relationships and the organization of the workplace of the kind that has developed under capitalism. It has been said that the peasant's "dilemma" is that he is both an economic agent and the head of a household, and the peasant household is "both an economic unit and a home." On the one hand, the household must meet its own demands as a unit of consumption and as a set of affective relationships, and also the demands of the peasant community of which it is a part; on the other hand, from the point of view of the exploiter, the peasant household is, as Eric Wolf has put it, "a source of labor and goods with which to increase his fund of power."[11] One consequence of this contradictory unity seems to be that the household reproduces the hierarchical and coercive relations between exploiter and exploited. As the organizer of production, the head of the household in a sense acts as the agent of his own exploiter.

It is possible, of course, to say that there is no absolute necessity for that hierarchical structure to take the form of male dominance, though it has generally, if not universally, done so. But apart from any other factors that may encourage this particular form of hierarchy—such as differences in physical strength, or the reproductive functions that occupy the woman's energies and time—there is a disposition to male dominance inherent in the relation between the precapitalist peasant household and the world of landlords and the state.

Again, that relation is inseparably economic and political at once. Since the exploitative powers confronting the peasant household are typically "extra-economic"—that is, juridical, political and military—they are inescapably linked to the one social function that has been most universally a male monopoly, armed violence. In other words, the organization of society in general, and specifically the nature of the ruling class, places a special premium on male dominance. The power and prestige attached to the male role in the society at large and in the dominant ideology of the ruling class have typically had the effect of reinforcing the authority of the male both in political and ceremonial functions within the peasant community and inside the household. If inside the household the head is the agent of landlord and state, outside it he is also the household's political representative, in the encounter with the male-dominated extra-economic powers of landlords and state. So the extra-economic, political coercive character of precapitalist exploitation tends to reinforce any other dispositions to male dominance within the peasant household.

Incidentally, one significant test of these propositions might be to imagine a dependent family of producers in which the male has no such political role outside the household, or where the surrounding social relations are not of this extra-economic kind. The closest approximation is perhaps the slave family of the American South, a group of people completely deracinated, cut off from their communal roots, without juridical and political standing, and inserted into a capitalist economy. And it turns out that one of the distinctive characteristics of the American slave family, even in the midst of a society where male dominance remained very tenacious, was the unusual authority of the woman.

At any rate, in capitalism the organization of production and exploitation is generally not so closely connected with the organization of the household, nor is the power of exploitation directly extra-economic, political, or military. Although capitalism has an unprecedented drive for accumulation, it fills this need mainly by increasing labor productivity rather than by means of directly coercive surplus extraction. Of course the compulsion to maximize productivity and profitability, and the resulting antagonism of interest between capital and labor, create a need for a hierarchical and highly disciplined organization of production; but capitalism does not concentrate these antagonisms, this hierarchical and coercive organization, in the household. They have a separate locale in the workplace. Even where the home is more closely tied to the workplace, as, say, in the small family farm, the capitalist market creates relations of its own with the outside world which differ from and supersede the old relations with the peasant community and the political, juridical, and military powers of precapitalist landlords and states. These new relations have typically had the effect of weakening patriarchal principles.

The major factors disposing feudalism to male domination are missing here—that is, the unity between the organization of production and exploitation and the organization of the family, the extra-economic relation between exploiters and exploited, and so on. Where feudalism operated through a relation between lord or state and the household, mediated through the male, capital strives for direct and unmediated relations with *individuals*, male or female, who from the point of view of capital take on the identity of abstract labor. Men who are interested in maintaining old patterns of male domination have been forced to defend them *against* the dissolving effects of capitalism—for instance, against the effects of growing numbers of women leaving the household to enter the wage-labor force.

CAPITALISM AND THE CONTRACTION OF THE EXTRA-ECONOMIC DOMAIN

These, then, are the various consequences of capitalism's separation of economic exploitation from extra-economic power and identities. There remains something more to be said about its ideological effects. It has become commonplace among "post-Marxist" theorists and their successors to say not only that capitalist democracy has produced powerful ideological impulses toward every kind of freedom and equality, but also that the "economy" has a limited importance in people's experience, that the autonomy of politics and the openness of social identities are the essence of our current situation in the capitalist West. Let us look at the features of capitalism to which these propositions apparently refer.

Paradoxically, yet again, the very features that have devalued extra-economic goods in capitalist societies have given the appearance of *enhancing* the extra-economic domain and widening its scope. This appearance has been taken for reality by capitalist ideologues who assure us that liberal capitalism is the last word in freedom and democracy (not to mention the end of History), and it now appears that people on the left are, for better or worse, accepting it too. On the face of it, capitalism seems to leave very large free spaces outside the economy. Production is enclosed in specialized institutions, factories, and offices. The working day is sharply marked off from non-working hours. Exploitation is not formally associated with juridical or political disabilities. There seems to be a wide range of social relations that lie outside the framework of production and exploitation and create a variety of social identities not immediately connected to the "economy." Social identities seem much more "open" in this sense. So the separateness of the economy may appear to give a wider scope, a freer hand, to the world outside it.

But, in fact, the economy of capitalism has encroached upon and narrowed the extra-economic domain. Capital has gained private control over matters that were once in the public domain, while giving up social and political responsibilities to a formally separate state. Even all those areas of social life that lie outside the immediate spheres of production and appropriation, and outside the direct control of the capitalist, are subjected to the imperatives of the market and the commodification of extra-economic goods. There is hardly an aspect of life in capitalist society that is not deeply determined by the logic of the market.

If politics in capitalism has a specific autonomy, there is an important sense in which that autonomy is weaker, not stronger, than the autonomy of pre-capitalist politics. Because the separation of the economic and the political has also meant the transfer of formerly political functions to the separated economic sphere, politics and the state are if anything more, rather than less, constrained by specifically economic imperatives and the demands of appropriating classes. Here we may recall our earlier examples of precapitalist states which were free from dominant classes to the extent that they were themselves "class-like," competing with other class appropriators for the same peasant-produced surpluses.

It used to be a truism for the left that social life in capitalism is uniquely subordinate to and shaped by the imperatives of the "economy," but the latest trends in social theory on the left seem to have abandoned this simple insight. In fact, it is not too much to say that they have been taken in by the mystifying appearances of capitalism, by the one-sided illusion that capitalism has uniquely liberated and enriched the extra-economic sphere. If the autonomy of politics, the openness of social identities, and the wide distribution of extra-economic goods are part of the truth, they are indeed only part of it, and a small and contradictory part at that.

It has to be said, nevertheless, that there is nothing surprising about the tendency to see only part of the picture. It is one of capitalism's most notable characteristics, this capacity to hide its face behind a mask of ideological mystifications. What is more surprising, when one comes to think of it, is that a convention has developed according to which capitalism is supposed to be unusually *transparent* in its relations of economic exploitation and domination. We are often told by social scientists that, unlike precapitalist modes of production, in capitalism relations of class are sharply delineated, no longer masked by non-economic categories like status-differences or other non-economic principles of stratification. Economic relations stand out in sharp relief, as the economy is no longer embedded in non-economic social relations. It is only now, if ever, they say, that it has become possible to speak of *class* consciousness.

Even those who deny the importance of class in capitalist society—as only one of many "identities"—may still subscribe to this view. They can agree about the distinctness of the economic sphere in capitalism and about the clarity of class as a distinctly economic category, and then they can go on to treat its separateness as an *isolation* and relegate it to an insular periphery, on the grounds that, while people may belong to classes, class identities are of limited or even marginal importance in the experience of human beings. People have other identities which have nothing to do with class and are equally or more determinative.

Again, there is a grain of truth in some of this, but again it is only part of a contradictory truth, so partial as to be a gross distortion. Of course people have social identities other than class, and of course these shape their experience in powerful ways. But this simple truism will not advance our understanding very far, and it certainly will not tell us much about how these identities should figure in the construction of a socialist politics—or indeed any emancipatory program—as long as we remain vague about what these identities mean, not only what they reveal about people's experience but also what they conceal.

Far too little attention has been given to capitalism's unprecedented capacity to mask exploitation and class—or rather, there is a growing failure to acknowledge that this mask is precisely a mask. Capitalist exploitation, far from being more transparent than other forms, is more opaque than any other, as Marx pointed out, masked by the obscurity of the relation between capital and labor in which the unpaid portion of labor is completely disguised in the exchange of labor power for a wage, where the capitalist pays the worker in contrast, for example, to the peasant who pays rent to a lord. This is the most elemental false appearance at the heart of capitalist relations, but it is only one of many. There is also the familiar "fetishism of commodities" which gives relations among people the appearance of relations among things, as the market mediates the most basic of human transactions; there is the political mystification that civic equality means that there is no dominant class in capitalism; and so on.

All this is familiar enough, but it needs to be emphasized that capitalist exploitation and unfreedom are in many ways less, not more, transparent than precapitalist domination. The exploitation of the medieval peasant, for example, was made more rather than less visible by feudalism's juridical acknowledgment of his dependence. In contrast, the juridical equality, contractual freedom, and citizenship of the worker in a capitalist democracy are likely to obscure the underlying relations of economic inequality, unfreedom, and exploitation. In other words, the very separation of the economic from the extra-economic which is supposed to unmask the realities of class in capitalism is, on the contrary, what mystifies capitalist class relations.

The effect of capitalism may be to deny the importance of class at the very moment, and by the same means, that it purifies class of extra-economic residues. If the effect of capitalism is to create a purely economic category of class, it also creates the appearance that class is only an economic category, and that there is a very large world beyond the "economy" where the writ of class no longer runs. To treat this appearance as if it were the unmasked and ultimate reality is certainly no advance in the analysis of capitalism. It mistakes a problem for a solution, and an obstacle for an opportunity. It is less illuminating than the most uncritical pre-Marxist political economy; and to build a political strategy on a retention of this mystification instead of an effort to overcome it must surely be self-defeating.

What, then, does all this mean for extra-economic goods in capitalist society and in the socialist project? Let me sum up: capitalism's structural indifference to the social identities of the people it exploits makes it uniquely capable of discarding extra-economic inequalities and oppressions. This means that while capitalism cannot guarantee emancipation from, say, gender or racial oppression, neither can the achievement of these emancipations guarantee the eradication of capitalism. At the same time, this same indifference to extra-economic identities makes capitalism particularly effective and flexible in using them as ideological cover. Where in precapitalist societies extra-economic identities were likely to highlight relations of exploitation, in capitalism they typically serve to obscure the principal mode of oppression specific to it. And while capitalism makes possible an unprecedented redistribution of extra-economic goods, it does so by devaluing them.

What about socialism then? Socialism may not by itself guarantee the full achievement of extra-economic goods. It may not by itself guarantee the destruction of historical and cultural patterns of women's oppression or racism. But it will do at least two important things in this regard, apart from abolishing those forms of oppression that men and women, black and white, share as members of an exploited class. First, it will eliminate the ideological and economic needs that under capitalism can still be served by gender and racial oppressions. Socialism will be the first social form since the advent of class society whose reproduction as a social system is endangered rather than enhanced by relations and ideologies of domination and oppression. And second, it will permit the revaluation of extra-economic goods whose value has been debased by the capitalist economy. The democracy that socialism offers is one that is based on a reintegration of the "economy" into the political life of the community, which begins with its subordination to the democratic self-determination of the producers themselves.

NOTES

1. Isaac Deutscher, "Marxism and the New Left," in *Marxism in Our Time* (London: Jonathan Cape, 1972), 74. This essay is based, with some modifications, on my Isaac Deutscher Memorial Lecture, delivered on 23 November 1987.
2. This observation may seem less plausible now than it did when I first made it, before American militarism had been overshadowed by the collapse of Communism, the apparent acceptance by U.S. governments that the Cold War is over, and dramatic outbreaks of so-called ethnic violence, notably in the former Yugoslavia. I contemplated taking out or somehow modifying this bald statement about the destabilizing effects of capitalism and American aggression, or saying something about the new forms of militarism associated with the role of the U.S. as the sole superpower and guardian of the "new world order". But nothing that has happened in the last few years changes the fact that there has hardly been a major regional conflict anywhere since the Second World War that has not been initiated, aggravated, or prolonged by U.S. intervention, open or clandestine; and it is far too soon to say that this pattern of adventurism has been finally repudiated—never mind new forms of military intervention such as Desert Storm.
3. For example, the Roman jurist Florentinus wrote that "Slavery is an institution of the

ius gentium whereby someone is subject to the *dominium* of another contrary to nature."
See M. I. Finley, "Was Greek Civilization Based on Slave Labour?" and "Between
Slavery and Freedom," in *Economy and Society in Ancient Greece* (London: Chatto &
Windus, 1981), 104, 113, 130. For an emphatic rejection of the view that Christianity
introduced "an entirely new and better attitude towards slavery," see G. E. M. de Ste
Croix, *The Class Struggle in the Ancient Greek World* (London: Duckworth, 1981), 419.

4. I have qualified this statement because I am told that there has been important work
   suggesting that state-funded childcare may be *less* expensive to capital.

5. There is evidence that a growing burden is being placed on age as distinct from sex
   or race, at least in the sense that structural youth unemployment combined with
   growing threats to social security and old-age pensions bear the brunt of capitalist
   decline. Which of these extra-economic identities will be made to carry the heaviest
   burden is largely a political question which has little to do with the structural disposition of capitalism to choose one rather than another form of extra-economic
   oppression.

6. On the village community as outside the state and subject to it as an alien power, see
   Teodor Shanin, "Peasantry as a Political Factor" and Eric Wolf, "On Peasant Rebellions," in T. Shanin, ed. *Peasants and Peasant Societies* (Harmondsworth: Penguin, 1971),
   especially 244 and 212.

7. This is a contentious point which is difficult to make clear in this limited space. The
   well-known evils of Athenian democracy, the institution of slavery and the position
   of women, cannot help but overshadow any other more attractive features; and it
   undoubtedly seems perverse to argue, as I do, that the essential characteristic of
   Athenian democracy, indeed perhaps its most distinctive one, is the extent to which
   it *excluded* dependence from the sphere of production—that is, the extent to which
   the material base of Athenian society was free and independent labor. There is a
   more detailed exposition in my book *Peasant Citizen and Slave: The Foundations of Athenian
   Democracy* (London: Verso, 1988), where I discuss slavery at length and also deal with
   the position of women in Athens. I am not asking people to discount or underesti-
   mate the importance of slavery or the status of women but simply to consider the
   unique position of the Athenian peasantry.

8. Eric Wolf, *Peasants* (Englewood Cliffs, NJ: Prentice-Hall, 1966), 9–10.

9. Robert Brenner, "Agrarian Class Structure and Economic development in Pre-
   Industrial Europe," in T. H. Aston and C. H. E. Philpin, eds., *The Brenner Debate:
   Agrarian Class Structure and Economic Development in Pre-Industrial Europe* (Cambridge:
   Cambridge University Press, 1985), 55–57.

10. On this point, see the ground-breaking study by George Comninel, *Rethinking the
    French Revolution: Marxism and the Revisionist Challenge* (London: Verso, 1987), especially
    196–203.

11. Wolf, *Peasants*, 12–17.

MILITARIZING WOMEN'S LIVES

CYNTHIA ENLOE

Over the past decades I have found that it is only by lots of us piecing together all sorts of information that we can get the full sense of how militaries rely both on women and on presumptions about femininity. And still I keep learning things that surprise me.

During the post-Vietnam War era in American popular culture, Sylvester Stallone wasn't the only one reconstructing war on the silver screen. Goldie Hawn was starring as Private Benjamin, a young widow making a new life for herself by joining the army. I can recall the skepticism with which European feminist friends greeted *Private Benjamin* when the film opened in Amsterdam. Were American women really this lacking in consciousness? Did they really imagine that the military offered just one more job opportunity, no different from the chance to work on a construction site or in a law firm? Yet it was a time, too, when American women peace activists were encircling the Pentagon with ribbon, while draftee-deprived officials on the inside were designing advertisements to enlist women volunteers to make up for their lost male conscripts.

Women *in* the military has never been an easy topic. It shouldn't be. Sexism, patriotism, violence, and the state—it is a heady brew. Women *in* the military provides the focus for only one chapter in the larger saga of women *and* the military. Furthermore, I now believe more firmly than ever that the military is only one part of the story of militarization.

One needs to take seriously the complicated militarized experiences of women as prostitutes, rape victims, mothers, wives, nurses, and feminist activists in order to make full sense of what happens when women are permitted in limited numbers to soldier in still-masculinized militaries. To invest one's curiosity solely in women as soldiers is to treat the militarization of so many other women as normal. If I slipped into that naive presumption, I probably would be allowing my own curiosity to become militarized.

I am even more convinced now than I was a decade ago that militaries need women to do a lot more than simply fill gaps in the ranks when their supply of "reliable" men runs short. Yet I also have been persuaded by the evidence that militaries and militarized civilian elites do not always get the results they so energetically pursue.

If we adopt the mainstream media's fascination with women-as-soldiers, and thus devote only meager attention and thought to all the other militarized women, we will, by our own very inattention, I think, perpetuate militarized officials' capacity to manipulate many women's hopes and fears and skills. Any militarized government's manipulative capacity has relied on most people not being interested in military wives; on most people labeling as "trivial" the mixed feelings of military girlfriends; on most people turning military mothers, wartime rape victims, and military prostitutes into either abstract nationalist icons or objects of shame and exclusion. *In*attention is a political act.

Militaries rely on women, but not all women experience militarization identically. Militaries have needed, and continue to need, some women to provide commercialized sexual services to male soldiers, other women to commit themselves to marital fidelity in military families; simultaneously, they need still other women to find economic security and maybe even pride in working for defense contractors. At times governments even need some civilian women to act as feminist lobbyists promoting women's right to serve in the state's military.

Women who serve militaries' needs differently usually do not see themselves as bound together by their shared womanhood or even by their shared militarization. In fact, some militarized women will see their own respectability, income, or career chances thrown into jeopardy by the actions of other militarized women. Mothers of soldier-sons, for instance, do not have any automatic political affinity with women soldiers. A woman who is a military wife may go to considerable lengths *not* to ask her soldier-husband about the women who work in the discos around his base. Feminists working to help women soldiers overcome the institutional barriers of sexual harassment and homophobia inside the military may not give much thought at all to women as militarized mothers, wives, and prostitutes. Women devoting their energies to peace activism may think that the only militarized women worthy of serious intellectual attention are those women who have been uprooted or raped in wartime. In the 1980s I almost took for granted this separateness among the varieties of militarized women and their advocates. Today I am more interested to discover just how those divisions between groups of militarized women are maintained and what happens if tentative efforts are made to dismantle those divisions. The very disparateness of women's experiences of militarization has posed acute problems for feminist theorizing and feminist strategizing.

Military officials and their civilian supporters go to great lengths in order to ensure that each of these groups of women feels special and separate. Militarized officials need women themselves to nurture the boundaries that separate them from one another. Militaries have counted on military officers' wives to look down on the wives of enlisted men, and on all military wives to look down on women working in the discos around a military base. Militarized civilian officials have needed women raped by other regimes' soldiers to remain suspicious of antiwar women and, instead, to be willing to serve as nationalist symbols. Militaries have depended on women soldiers who imagine their service to be superior to that of both wives and prostitutes, and even of military nurses. The more distanced each group of women has felt from the other, the less likely any of them would be to notice how the political manipulations of gender affected them all. Thus the less likely any of them are to think about militarism.

Government officials have been remarkably successful in these divisive efforts. There are very few instances in any country of military wives joining in an alliance with military prostitutes and together devising a joint action along with women soldiers, all for the sake of dismantling the usually elaborate ideology of femininity constructed by military authorities to serve their own institutional interests.

For militaries and their supporters in both government and the general public have needed not only women, flesh and blood creatures. They also have needed ideas, especially ideas about femininity. Just as important to the maintenance of military life as has been the ideology of manliness, just as important as parades, alliances, and weaponry, have been certain feminized ideas—"the fallen woman," "patriotic motherhood," "marital fidelity," "racial purity," "national sacrifice," and sexualized "respectability." Sometimes militaries even have needed a very particular version of the idea "liberated woman."

Paradoxically, these ideas turn out to be as potent as a B-52 bomber, while simultaneously they are as fragile as domestic harmony. The dynamics of this paradox create a peculiar narrative of our time: the military sex scandal. Military scandals occur—not just the globally headlined American military scandals, but those less internationally featured that have occurred recently in Canada, Italy, Chile, and Australia—when those delicate maneuvers that have been designed to make ideas about gender work for military ends become confused, and when that confusion becomes visible to the public. The whole story of the political efforts to get women to act and think in ways that sustain the military turns out to be riddled with this paradox: the gendering of any country's military involves some of society's most powerful actors, senior officials of the state; but they often act as though they were on the verge of losing control, losing control of women. Sometimes they are.

Feminists have devoted increasing intellectual energy and scarce organizational resources to making sense of the militarization of women's lives. Indian feminists have sought to explain why so many Indian Hindu women have supported their new regime's nationalist policy of nuclear weapons testing. Serbian feminists have courted the Milošević regime's repression when they have developed nonviolent forms of political protest. American feminists have struggled to craft strategies that support sexually harassed women soldiers without leaving deeper issues of American militarism unexamined. Okinawan feminists have tried to build alliances with male peace activists so as to challenge the U.S. bases on their island effectively without allowing those male peace activists to turn the rape of local women into merely a symbolic nationalist issue. Creating feminist theories and strategies to respond effectively to militarization's surprisingly multiple forms is not easy.

The American military has been so powerful in its Hollywood, CNN, and NATO versions that sometimes it seems as if it were the only military worth talking about. This dominance poses a risk. It tempts one (me) to think too simply. Treating the American military's attempts—often slick, occasionally bungling—to secure women's cooperation in its mission as *the* feature story once again places this institution at the center of the analytical universe, either as the archetypal villain or, more suspiciously, as the model of modernity and enlightenment. Such a centering of the American story is, I think, analytically dangerous.

At the start of this new century, the American military, admittedly, is preeminent in the creation of roles for, and ideas about, militarized women. On a recent transatlantic flight I was seated next to a pleasant man in his late thirties. We exchanged a few words before each of us became absorbed in the contents of our respective knapsacks. He seemed totally familiar with the rituals of a seven-hour flight. A regular. It was only later, as the captain announced our approach to Heathrow, that we struck up a conversation, now assured we wouldn't be intruding on the other's in-flight reverie. He was returning to his home in England, to one of the big American military bases that have survived the post-Cold War overseas base closures. An African American, he had made a career of soldiering, rising to the rank of senior sergeant. He thought it had been a good life for a family man. His wife liked it too. He confessed, though, that she didn't care for these frequent month-long trips he now had to make. He was a trainer. Ever since the collapse of the Soviet Union and the breakup of Yugoslavia, his skills had been in special demand. He already had helped train the new army of Lithuania. He was just completing a tour in Slovenia. The American military was offering itself up as a model to be emulated, and officials in charge of many new governments were accepting the offer.

Precisely because the U.S. military has become so physically and ideologically influential in today's post-Cold War world, we do need, I think, to pay special heed to American manipulations of ideas about women and to the appeal that those militarized ideas have for so many women. In the late 1990s the American armed forces provided not only traveling trainers, but their own formulas for AIDS prevention and peacekeeping. The U.S. also has become the world's leading exporter of weaponry. Each one of these international military programs is providing a site for the export of American ideas about what should be expected of a man, what should be expected of a woman—not just of a woman in uniform, but a woman in a soldier's home and a woman in a militarized off-base disco.

Yet, for all its influence, the American military is distinct, just as American feminisms are distinct. It is to underscore this distinctness that I compare American women's militarized experiences as wives, prostitutes, soldiers, nurses, mothers, and feminists with the experiences of women from Britain, Russia, Germany, the former Yugoslavia, Chile, Canada, the Philippines, Rwanda, Indonesia, South Africa, Israel, South Korea, Vietnam, and Japan. The American military's current pre-eminence has not made a comparative curiosity obsolete. In this new century, it has made non-parochial investigation an even more urgent enterprise. The processes of gendered militarization today operate internationally. We need, therefore, to develop our curiosities internationally.

There are routes toward a distinctly feminist form of action on militarization that can look quite unlike the much talked-about American liberal feminist route. For instance, British women's advocates have not spent much time and political energy trying to widen the roles of British women in the military. Among British women legislators—even after the celebrated 1997 influx of 160 women into the masculinized domain of the British House of Commons—there is no equivalent of recently retired Congresswoman Patricia Schroeder. No British woman parliamentarian, that is, has invested so much of her political currency in promoting women as equal members of her country's military: in the late 1990s House of Commons it just has not been a political priority. Likewise, it has been German, South Korean, and Okinawan women as well as British women, not their American counterparts, who have had to cope with the men from two militaries—their own and a foreign military—living in and around their hometowns. As a result, it has been feminists from these countries who have been tutoring their American counterparts about militarized gendered nationalism, about the pitfalls of organizing against foreign soldiers' abuses of local women in ways that rekindle a local brand of masculinized nationalist militarism. American women have a lot to learn.

Today American feminists are starting to absorb the hard lesson for women of any international superpower: they will be weaker analytically and strategically if they don't take seriously the gendered experiences and feminist theories developed by women in other countries. For example, America's well-developed anti-domestic violence movement only belatedly struggled to introduce the issue of violence onto its country's military bases. In Chile, the sequence was reversed: it was Chilean feminists' daring participation in their country's movement to oust an oppressive military regime in the 1980s that led them thereafter to raise the issue of domestic violence in civilian society. The result has been that American feminists have invested enormous energy in stopping domestic violence, yet many of them do not see their country's military policies as "their issue"; by contrast, Chilean feminists today constantly think analytically about militarism *because* they are concerned about misogynist violence against women. Questions are whetted, too, by a newly internationalized curiosity. For instance, why have no American mothers been documented doing what scores of Russian mothers did in 1995 and 1996—traveling to a war zone, Chechnya in this instance, to retrieve their soldier-sons from what they deemed to be an unjust military operation? The morning of a new century is no time for parochialism.

DEMOCRATIZATION: REFLECTIONS ON GENDERED DISLOCATIONS IN THE PUBLIC SPHERE

MARY E. HAWKESWORTH

Democratization has been celebrated by politicians, political scientists, and political theorists as one of the singular achievements of the late twentieth century. In its most rudimentary form, democratization is defined as a transition from various types of authoritarian regime and command economies to liberal democracy and capitalism. In Africa, Asia, Eastern Europe, Latin America, and Russia, democratization is characterized as a process of transition through which regimes that have been bureaucratic authoritarian, military dictatorships, and/or state socialist move toward an elective system of governance and a capitalist market (Saint Germain 1994).

To all who have been taught that democratic governance respects the dignity of human beings, affords rights and immunities to individuals, prevents abuse of power by government officials (or provides remedies for removal of abusive governments), fosters individual freedom, encourages collective action to achieve political benefits, provides opportunities for political innovation, and maintains mechanisms through which citizens can hold governments accountable, democratization does indeed seem an accomplishment worth celebrating. The establishment of fundamental freedoms for citizens through the constitutional protection of certain civil liberties (freedom of thought, speech, press, association; freedom from particular forms of governmental abuse; and freedom to participate in politics by voting and standing for election) and the provision of fundamental fairness through the rule of law and a range of entitlements to certain standards of living secured by the state certainly seem to be hallmarks of progress. When considered in the context of the claim advanced by some International Relations scholars that in the twentieth century democratic governments did not make war against one another, the growth of democracies across the globe seems to hold the promise of a new era of peace in international affairs.

Given such optimistic expectations for democratization, the recent findings of feminist scholars come as something of a shock. Evidence drawn from women's lives around the globe suggests that democratization produces gendered redistributions of resources and responsibilities that make women worse off. "In Central and Eastern Europe, the level of women's participation in national legislatures fell precipitously when democratic elections were held, ranging from 20–30 percent in 1987 ... to less than 10 percent in Poland, Czechoslovakia and Hungary in 1990" (Jaquette and Wolchik 1998: 10). In the 1995 elections, women constituted 10 percent of the legislators in the Czech Republic, 18 percent in Slovakia, 11 percent in Hungary, and 13 percent in Poland and Bulgaria (Jaquette and Wolchik 1998: 11). In Latin America, women are also markedly underrepresented in elective offices, holding only 5 percent of the seats in the legislative assembly in Brazil, 9 percent in Peru, and 14 percent in Argentina (Jaquette and Wolchik 1998: 11). Despite two hundred years of feminist political mobilization, women hold less than 12 percent of the formal political offices in nations across the globe. In more than one hundred countries women hold no elected offices in their national assemblies (Nelson and Chowdhury 1994).

The economic indicators of democratization are also troubling. The United Nations 1997 Human Development Report notes that the economies of more than one hundred nations were better off fifteen years ago than they are at present. In Central and Eastern Europe women's unemployment has skyrocketed[1] as access to childcare and reproductive freedom have been severely constricted (Bystydzienski 1992; Rai, Pilkington and Phizacklea 1992). Some Eastern European women have resorted to prostitution as a means of survival as the global "traffic in women" surges despite the rampant dangers of AIDS. In Africa, Asia, and Latin America structural adjustment policies since the 1970s have imposed drastic cuts in social spending, contributing to the growing impoverishment of women and children. According to UNIFEM women constitute nearly 70 percent of the world's 1.3 billion poor. The 564 million rural women living in poverty in 1990 represented a 47 percent increase above the number of poor women in 1970. Structural adjustment policies increase women's participation in waged labor at a time when global competition is driving wages down. Thus women find themselves working more hours in paid labor, playing crucial roles in the informal sector, and assuming increased responsibility for family subsistence. "These shifts in work patterns often have an impact on gender relations in the home not always to the benefit of women" (Craske 1998: 106).

In a period coincident with the increasing strength of feminism as a global movement, how can we make sense of democratization's gendered dislocations? If democracy is understood as a mode of governance that respects the dignity of human beings, affords rights and immunities to individuals, fosters individual freedom and development, and encourages collective action to achieve political benefits, then why are these gendered effects so palpable? And how can such blatant inequities continue to fall below the threshold of visibility and concern for mainstream social scientists, politicians, and the press?

The failure of social scientists to notice growing political and economic inequities may be related to an ideological immunity afforded by certain analytic

concepts accredited within the social science disciplines. A gulf separates popular understandings of key political concepts such as democracy from social
science definitions of these concepts. Since the eighteenth century, for example,
liberal political theorists have routinely argued that pragmatic considerations
such as population size, time constraints, limited citizen knowledge or interest,
and the need for stability, necessitate that democracy be understood as a system
of representative government. Within social science, the conception of democracy as "rule of the people, by the people and for the people" has been supplanted by a conception of democratic elitism, rule by an elite chosen through
popular participation in free and fair elections. Mainstream social scientists
confidently assert that prime ministerial/parliamentary systems and presiden-
tial/republican systems converge on this point: contemporary meaningful democracy is synonymous with rule by a popularly elected elite. Thus as operational
indicators of democratization, social scientists tend to focus upon the existence
of "free and fair elections." But in focusing on "popular participation in elections," mainstream social scientists have been remarkably gender-blind. Examining the political behavior of men but advancing claims about citizens, women's
participation as voters, candidates, or elected officials disappears. Assumptions
about the normalcy of hierarchy and research methods insensitive to gender
may explain why democratization's gendered dislocations fail to be noticed by
mainstream scholars, or by the press and politicians who ground their analyses
in scholarly accounts of political transformations. But how are we to make sense
of the gendered dislocations themselves? Why is democratization making women
worse off?

Feminist theory can help us understand some of the factors contributing to
democratization's gendered dislocations. Feminist scholarship has demonstrated
that claims concerning the "neutrality," "objectivity," and "inclusivity" of mainstream approaches in political theory and social science are deeply suspicious. A
hallmark of feminist critique within the humanities, social sciences, and natural
sciences has been the identification of androcentrism in theories, methodolo-
gies, and substantive research findings. The notion of androcentrism suggests
that assumptions, concepts, beliefs, arguments, theories, methods, laws, policies,
and institutions may all be "gendered." They may tacitly or explicitly privilege
one gender at the expense of the other.[2] Social practices may be gendered in
diverse ways. Exclusionary practices that bar women from participation lie at the
most overt end of a gendered spectrum. But practices that are officially "gender-
blind," "gender-neutral," or "equal opportunity" may also be gendered if they
are rooted in experiences typically associated with men but not with women or
if certain factors make it more difficult for women than for men to achieve the
same outcome by following the same procedures.

Many of the processes associated with democratization are gendered. The
model of liberal democracy that democratizing nations are urged to emulate is
drawn from Euro-American experiences. The most advanced of the Western
liberal democracies have very poor records in areas of gender equity. With the

exception of the Scandinavian nations, which are perhaps better categorized as social democracies, women are drastically underrepresented in positions of power in liberal democratic nations, holding only 12–21 percent of the positions in the legislative bodies. In the most advanced capitalist economies (e.g. the G7 nations), women are still confronting a glass ceiling that is remarkably low. Very few women are able to translate their education and professional experience into positions in the highest ranks of the corporate sector. Less than 5 percent of the senior management positions in the corporate sector are held by women. At the opposite end of the economic spectrum within advanced capitalist nations, women are overrepresented among the poor. In the United States, for example, women and their children constitute 80 percent of the poor, a higher percentage than exists globally.

If democratizing nations are seeking to replicate the Euro-American model of male-dominant democratic elitism within a capitalist economy, then perhaps it should not be such a surprise that women are faring less well than men. Many of the tools that democratizing nations are being offered to guide their transitions have been criticized by feminist scholars for perpetuating gender inequities.

Consultants currently offering advice on democratic consolidation are drawing heavily on "modernization theory," which assumes that capitalism will itself produce liberal democracy, which in turn will elevate women's status. On this view, integrating women into the modern labor force is deemed the basis for their liberation. This assumption is predicated upon a belief that modern methods of production will generate modernist belief systems, including commitments to representative government. Specifically, the adoption of modern machine technologies is expected to promote norms of rationality, universalism, and egalitarianism, which in turn engender mobility and achievement. In principle, these rules of "modern" society negate ascription standards—including gender—as determinants of the individual's socioeconomic and political status. Thus opportunities for women are expected to expand as technological advancement makes production less a function of physical strength. Greater employment opportunities supposedly contribute to higher aspirations and expectations as women begin to recognize their own economic power. On this view, inclusion of women in the modern industrial economy contributes to a greater open-mindedness, resulting in the destruction of the patriarchal ideology that has justified women's exclusion from the "socially valued" productive sphere and from participation in the institutions of state.

The assumptions that inform modernization theory (i.e. the process is linear, cumulative, expansive, diffuse, and fundamentally occupied with the modern/ traditional value dichotomy) inform democratization as well. According to this model, remedies for gender inequity in developing societies require only legal and institutional reforms. Observable differences between men and women in developing, or developed, societies is said to be merely a failure of the diffusive element of the model, not a problem in the process of democratization or the economic restructuring central to it.

Feminist scholars who have studied women in development have found that the assumptions of modernization theory have not been borne out in development projects in the global South (or for that matter in the industrialized nations). Inclusion of women in industrial production can coexist with traditional belief systems and traditional patterns of women's subordination. Indeed, inclusion of women in industrial production need not supplant women's performance of traditional roles. Feminist political economists are in the process of documenting the simultaneous growth of the formal, informal, and subsistence economies. Many women in the global South and in former Soviet-bloc states are simultaneously involved in light industry jobs, provision of a range of services within the informal sector, and subsistence agriculture to produce the food to keep their families alive. Such a "triple shift" need not challenge established patterns of women's subservience. Feminist scholars have also demonstrated that "development" is far from linear and cumulative. A modicum of progress in one aspect of social transition can be offset by setbacks in other areas of life. Consider, for example, the increase in domestic violence that can be coincident with a woman's increasing economic independence.[3] Or consider the astonishing transformation of some young male anti-apartheid activists in South Africa, who since 1995 have renamed themselves the South African Rapists Society and adopted sexual violence against women as the outlet for their "displaced political energy."[4] Contrary to the assumptions of modernization theory, the impressive political empowerment of South African women under the ANC government and the dramatic increase in the number of women in the South African parliament since the creation of the new constitution coexists with a huge increase in violence against women. Indeed South Africa now has the highest percentage of violence against women in the world: 60 percent of intimate relationships involve violence.

Modernization theory also fails to acknowledge the extent to which Westerners implementing development projects in the global South have replicated Western patterns of male dominance in their choice of trainees and employees in both industrial and agricultural development projects. Indeed, the assumptions of Western development "experts" that farming is men's work led to the displacement of women subsistence farmers and the spread of mass starvation and environmental crises as land farmed by women for subsistence crops was taken over for male-controlled production of export crops. In addition to structural adjustment policies developed in response to the international debt crisis that require countries to increase productivity and exports while decreasing government spending on social welfare, and colonial land policies that accorded men legal entitlement to land, misguided development policies have created food, fuel, and water crises in rural areas in the global South that have made women's lives vastly more difficult. However erroneous the assumptions underlying modernization theory, feminist scholars point out that Western "experts" continue to recommend adoption of key tenets of modernization theory as part of the process of democratization. As a result, democratization is producing gendered patterns of skilling and deskilling, gendered differences in political rights and economic opportunities, gender-specific political visibility and invisibility, while subtly and unsubtly regendering the identities of citizens (Alvarez 1990; Funk and Mueller 1993; Jaquette 1989; Miller 1991; Nelson and Chowdhury 1994; Radcliffe and Westwood 1993; Saint Germain 1994; Peterson and Runyon 1999).

In recent work, a number of scholars have emphasized the importance of the development of "civil society" to insure the success of democratization. Within the works of Western democratization experts, civil society is typically conceived in terms of a voluntary sector of organizations and interest groups that provide a means for organized citizen action. The cultivation of civil society is said to be beneficial because it encourages citizens to organize to promote their interests and fosters ties among like-minded people across divisions of race, class, ethnicity, and gender. Private interest organizations create alternative power centers outside the state, provide an opportunity for learning leadership and developing political skills, and can provide not only a means of political communication but a mechanism for tracking government performance and holding governments accountable. Like the popular construction of democratization, such an account of civil society sounds uniformly beneficial.

Discussions of civil society have been proliferating over the past decade. Some commentators use the term broadly to encompass all civic, economic, religious, and voluntary institutions that fall outside agencies of government. Such an encompassing definition makes sense in describing the emergence of a host of institutions in the aftermath of the fall of authoritarian regimes. But the conception of civil society that dominates the discussions of American democratization experts has a narrower and more pluralist cast. Incorporating assumptions from theorists such as Hobbes, Locke, Hume, Madison, Hegel, and Tocqueville, this narrower conception of civil society should give feminist scholars cause for concern. Feminist critiques of the conceptions of human nature informing classic liberal and republican conceptions of civil society suggest that some of the core concepts are gendered in subtle and not-so-subtle ways (Brown 1988; Di Stefano 1996; Hirschmann 1992; Scott 1996; Tronto 1993). The notion of the autonomous individual as a self-interested maximizer who forms bonds with others to advance private interests haunts these discourses. Construing the "self-made" individual as someone with no ties to family or community gives rise to a notion of association as purely instrumental. The individual joins only those groups that will advantage him/her and abandons any group that fails to accomplish that end. Positing the pursuit of private interest as the primary concern of the individual in civil society, politics itself is construed instrumentally as a limited public process of interest accommodation.

Feminist scholars have suggested that the radical individualism underlying the instrumental model of civil society and of politics is fundamentally at odds with women's experiences, the life cycle and needs of citizens, and the beliefs of women political activists about the appropriate reasons for participation in social groups (Hirschmann 1992; Flammang 1997; Jaquette and Wolchik 1998). The gendered dislocations associated with democratization provide good reason for interrogating the productive power and exclusionary effects of "scientific" discourses promoting radical individualism and instrumental politics. In an excellent study of women and democratization in Latin America, and Central and Eastern Europe, Jane Jaquette and Sharon Wolchik point out that women were actively involved in the initial and most dangerous stages of democratization, organizing against oppressive regimes, mobilizing as citizens demanding the transformation of the political system, and standing publicly against authoritarian rule. In this critical stage of democratization, women understood their political roles to be very different to those of autonomous individuals. Like the Mothers of the Plaza de Mayo in Argentina, women came to the political arena as members of families, carrying obligations and aspirations that could not be subsumed under the rubric of self-interest. They understood their political project to be very different from private interest group activity, seeking not personal advantage but a much broader social goal of changing both the substance and style of political activity (Jaquette and Wolchik 1998: 13).

Rather than rejecting the self-understandings of these courageous women activists and subsuming their political engagement under the rubric of some form of "enlightened self-interest" to fit democratization experts' model of civil society, it is useful to consider the implications of their self-understandings in relation to their glaring absence from later stages of democratization. Jaquette and Wolchik document the displacement of women in Latin America, Central and Eastern Europe from political activity after the downfall of the old regime and during the period of "democratic consolidation." In tracing this displacement of women, Jaquette and Wolchik note that women's growing absence can be tied to the resurrection of traditional party apparatus and politician–client relations, which supplant the large-scale, participatory, citizen coalitions crucial to the overthrow of the old regimes. While political parties come in many different varieties, the kinds "of parties being fostered by U.S. democratization experts are the "non-ideological," undisciplined, "pragmatic" interest-accommodating parties characteristic of American political life.[5] Women and politics scholars have amassed a great deal of evidence that such political parties are more hostile to women's political participation than are average citizens. Thus the resurgence of interest-accommodationist party activity, mandated by democratization experts as essential to competitive elections, may help explain some of democratization's gendered dislocations. For it signifies an extinction of hopes. Women's hopes for a different kind of politics—more participatory, more oriented toward social justice, and less dependent on self-interest and money—are eradicated with the institutionalization of an old (and traditionally hostile to women) political organization. As women's "interests" are aggregated by political parties, they are "tamed," stripped of any transformative content. Parties' efforts to aggregate interests, to devise platforms that can appeal to a wide range of voters, including conservative men and women, require the elimination of "nonconsensual issues," such as reproductive freedom and economic justice, from the partisan agenda (Valenzuela 1998). Indeed, the insistence of many autonomous women's movements that issues of justice must be addressed in politics has provided grounds for accommodationist political parties to resist the integration of women into politics, especially in key decision-making positions. Appealing to the need for "political realism" and the necessity of "compromise," male party elites can reject women candidates ostensibly for their lack of pragmatism. Praise for women's "superior ethical standards" can thus serve to marginalize women as traditional parties simultaneously insist that politics is not an arena for ethical purists. Under the banner of neoliberalism, seasoned party cadres can insist that the role of government is to foster "self-help strategies," not social justice (Craske 1998).

Democratic consolidation has also been characterized by a shift in the kinds of political engagements deemed to be effective, or even possible, for women. During the earliest stages of democratization, women mobilized across class and ethnic divisions in participatory movements that emphasized the importance of solidarity and skills-building for all participants. For participants in autonomous women's movements the creation of a "democratic space" in which women could learn and grow through participation in decision-making was crucial to the politicization of women. For it helped women cultivate the skills to transform their everyday lives and practices. Under democratic consolidation, non-governmental organizations (NGOs), staffed by well-educated professionals and funded by international agencies, become the primary vehicle for women's interaction with governmental institutions. NGOs have been extremely important in keeping women's issues on the political agenda and in providing essential services for women in democratizing nations. Yet, the efficiency and professionalism required for NGOs' success exists in uneasy tension with the inclusive solidarity of participatory women's movements.

Teresa Caldeira (1998) has pointed out that the emergence of NGOs as the premier women's organizations under democratic consolidation raises important concerns. Because NGOs are dependent upon external funding, granting agencies have the power to set priorities for NGO activity. No matter how beneficial these priorities may be for women, priorities set by international agencies disempower local women, who can no longer set their own agendas. Sabine Lang (1999) has noted that although feminist NGOs may have been created out of participatory social movements, several factors mitigate their ability to maintain social movements. At the most minimal level, because NGOs are dependent upon soft money, they must develop the fixed organizational structures, professional staff, and fiscal accountability necessary to be entrusted with major grants by funding agencies. They can not afford the fluidity of a mass-based voluntary movement. Their agendas must be narrowly focused and presented in terms of realizable goals and objectives in order to demonstrate their efficacy. The energy required for the grant-writing essential to organizational survival leaves little time for mass mobilization. In some circumstances, the competition among NGOs for funds could hinder strategic coalition-building, placing NGOs in the uncomfortable position of being financially dependent upon institutions and organizations that pure political principle would lead them to confront (e.g. tobacco money, Nestlé, Dalkon Shield). In addition, the professionalization of NGO staff necessary to attain the respectability required not only to receive funds from international agencies but also to establish a reputation as an authoritative voice on women's needs and interests replicates inequalities and privileges among women rather than eroding them.

Although cautioning against any "blanket assessments of feminist NGOs as handmaidens of neoliberal planetary patriarchy," Sonia Alvarez has noted several recent developments that threaten NGOs' ability to "advance a progressive policy agenda while simultaneously articulating vital linkages among larger women's movement and civil society constituencies" (1999: 181). Under democratic consolidation as the political rewards and material resources to support consciousness-raising and women's political empowerment dry up, feminist NGOs are increasingly pressed into the role of "gender experts." As global pressures are brought to bear upon governments to develop "gender sensitive policies," feminist NGOs who possess policy-specialized staff, previous experiences with UN programs, and a record of international funding are recruited by governments to provide technical-advisory services. In keeping with neoliberal privatization efforts, NGOs are hired as consultants for gender policy assessment, project execution, and social services delivery, especially in the area of poverty alleviation policies. But this changed relationship to the state also changes NGOs' relationship with autonomous women's organizations. "Consulted as experts who can evaluate gender policies and programs rather than as movement organizations that might facilitate citizen input and participation in the formation and design of such policies, feminist NGOs' technical involvement in policy assessment ... does not necessarily translate into effectual gender policy or women's rights advocacy" (Alvarez 1999: 192). Indeed, increasing dependence upon government grants for their very livelihood may undermine the ability of feminist NGOs to criticize government policy and "to pursue more process-oriented forms of feminist cultural-political intervention—such as consciousness-raising, popular education, or other strategies aimed at transforming those gender power relations manifest in the realms of public discourse, culture, and daily life—forms of gendered injustice that defy gender-planning quick fixes" (Alvarez 1999: 198).[6]

Reviewing twenty-five years of transnational women's activism, Amrita Basu has suggested that women's NGOs have been particularly effective when a national government's repression or indifference constrains local feminist activism and an international appeal involving civil and political rights can provide a remedy. Operating in the post-Cold War era, NGOs' likelihood of success increases when their goals can be formulated in the language of liberal human rights. Noting that the hegemonic rhetoric of human rights is fast becoming the discursive limit of permissible social change, Basu points out that women's

NGOs have been much less effective in addressing economic justice i issues of water, firewood, land, and employment that have been the f(of so much local feminist activism. To note that transnational feminis: however dedicated, have not succeeded in overthrowing global capitalism or the devastating structural adjustment policies imposed by the IMF and the World Bank hardly seems a scathing indictment. For what fair-minded person could expect feminist NGOs to accomplish in a decade what socialist revolutionaries have failed to do over the past 150 years.

But if our goal is to understand democratization's dislocation of women, then perhaps there is more to be said about the circumscribed sphere of feminist NGOs success. Again, the insights of Theresa Caldeira (1998) are particularly helpful. Caldeira has suggested that operating within the boundaries of "public/private" set by neoliberal conceptions of civil society, NGOs provide services that the state is unwilling or unable to provide. Once accepted within the purview of NGO activity, what might once have been considered a matter of public policy is subtly redefined as a project of a private organization. Thus the context of women's struggles subtly changes. What was once understood as a political struggle of citizens about the boundaries of justice can now be construed as a dispute over private resources. In changing the framing assumptions from a discourse of citizenship and justice to a discourse of competition for scarce resources or material provision to meet private need, women's goals are resignified as "private." In working with NGOs on projects vital to their physical safety and economic survival, women in democratizing nations are re/ privatized. Although hailed as the hallmark of women's incorporation into the new civil society, NGOs simultaneously manifest the tendencies toward privatization and growing inequalities characteristic of neoliberal political systems. NGOs must be understood, then, as both crucial vehicles for the advancement of certain women's interests under resurgent capitalism and as an effect of the dismantling of welfare state structures, and as such complicit in the delegitimation of social rights and the privatization of women. In their mode of operation and in the unintended consequences of their action, NGOs affirm entrepreneurial individualism as a privileged mode of political agency and displace participatory politics.

The institutionalization of a particular liberal conception of civil society, the incorporation of women into civil society through NGOs, and the promotion of accommodationist political parties as the central elements of democratization are routinely depicted as progressive developments, but this may be another instance where structures that count as progressive for men have markedly different consequences for women. Indeed, it might be helpful to understand the resurrection of civil society and the accreditation of accommodationist parties as active processes of gendering public space. By valorizing institutions at odds with women's hopes for participatory politics and long associated with the exclusion of women as the key components of democratization, public space is symbolically reclaimed as male space.

To illuminate the process of gendering public space, it might be useful to consider two contemporary examples at great remove from democratization, the Serbian incursion in Bosnia and the regime of the Taliban in Afghanistan. The genocidal war in Bosnia was gendered. As women's rights activists have documented, rape was used as a strategic weapon in that war. The Serbian army made a strategic decision to rape Muslim women as a means of demoralizing the Bosnian men. The citizenship of women (Serb or Bosnian) was not at issue; women were viewed as mere means to achieve psychological and military objectives. Such an intentional dehumanization constitutes political space as male space. Indeed the sphere of political contestation is actively created as a threat to women, as a space in which to dehumanize and violate women. In Afghanistan, on attaining power the Taliban issued edicts prohibiting women from showing themselves in public unless fully veiled and accompanied by a man. They also prohibited girls and women from attending schools and practicing professions. The forced enclosure of women was to be implemented by publicly administering heinous punishments, including death, to any who refused to comply. The Taliban invented a version of Islam at great remove from the foundational texts of their religion and the lived religious practices in their nation. On the basis of this invention, they attempted to forge gendered political identities by enacting them with brutal force. Through this process they produced political space as exclusively male.

A process so blatantly enacted by the Serbs and the Taliban can also have far more subtle manifestations. I would like to suggest that the incorporation of certain gendered concepts within the neoliberal definition of democratization and the entrenchment of gendered institutions as the defining characteristics of democratization contribute to a very subtle structuring of public space as male terrain. The construction of women committed to participatory politics and economic justice as too idealistic or too unrealistic for political life marginalizes women just as successfully as did the Victorian pedestal. Working in two directions at once, it supports men's claims that idealistic women are inappropriate political actors, while simultaneously convincing women that the tawdriness of interest group politics is not worth their time and effort. The perpetration of violence against women by some men provides justification for other men to assume the familiar mantle of women's protector, while leaving women wondering how politics can help them when violence ensnares them in their most intimate relationships.

The gendered dislocations accompanying democratization are indisputable. Does it make sense to interpret them in terms of a subtle restructuring of political space as male terrain? I believe that there are two compelling reasons to do so. The first reason draws upon recent work by feminist historians that suggests that this has happened before. In the eighteenth and nineteenth centuries, a universalist rhetoric of democracy afforded a mechanism for men to claim exclusive political rights and entrench those claims in a wave of constitution-making. In the case of the American Revolution, the French Revolution, and

again in the U.S. in the period of Reconstruction, some men accorded themselves exclusive constitutional privileges and immunities against the vocal opposition of women who had participated intensively in the overthrow of the old
regimes. In establishing male gender as a constitutional criterion for full citizenship, some women who had rights of participation, including voting privileges,
lost those rights (McDonagh 1999; Case 1999; Barkley Brown 1997). Such
powerful historical precedents caution against dismissing democratization's
displacement of women as inconsequential.

The second reason to take this interpretive frame seriously looks to the
future rather than the past. If those in the global community committed to the
full realization of women's citizenship understand democratization as a process
of reclaiming public space as male, then it might be possible to identify national
and international strategies more supportive of women's political inclusion.

Some of the tactics adopted by contemporary women's rights advocates can
be read as an effort to thwart the reconstitution of political space as male space.
Rather than relinquish political parties and elective offices to men, feminists in
a number of nations have pressed for the creation of policies to break male
control of party apparatus and elective offices. In response to this pressure,
some seventy-five political parties in more than thirty nations have established
quotas to insure that women are recruited as party candidates at least in proportion to their membership in the party (Leijenaar 1998). Some nations have
established constitutional provisions mandating equitable representation of
women. India, for example, requires that women hold one-third of local elective
offices. (Similar legislation at the federal level was defeated, in part, because
lower-caste parties feared that the legislation would privilege higher caste
women.) France has just passed a constitutional amendment guaranteeing women
equal access to governing offices and now moves into the enormously complex
stage of statutory implementation.

The Platform for Action based on the Fourth World Conference in Beijing
called upon governments "to commit themselves to establish the goal of gender
balance in governmental bodies and committees, as well as in public administrative entities, and in the judiciary, including inter alia setting specific targets
and implementing measures to substantially increase the number of women with
a view to achieving equal representation of women and men" (paragraph 190a).

Feminists in autonomous women's movements and in some NGOs have
attempted to contest prevailing assumptions concerning civil society. Rather
than accept norms of self-interested actors, they have struggled to reclaim civil
society as a space for women's empowerment and collective action. Feminist
activists have pressed governments and international agencies to complete "gender impact analysis" prior to the adoption and implementation of policies.
Monique Leijenaar (1998) has suggested that democratizating states and international consultants working with them should conduct gender impact analyses
of all aspects of democratization in order to identify "best practices" to foster
women's political participation. Feminist activists have also used litigation in

international tribunals in an effort to hold their governments accountable for violations of women's rights recognized in international treaties, such as the Universal Declaration of Human Rights, and the Convention on the Elimination of All Forms of Discrimination Against Women (CEDAW).

Widespread awareness that democratization currently institutionalizes practices that are hostile to women, hamper or preclude women's inclusion, and regulate women's access to decision-making could bring new life to these feminist efforts. Contesting the reconstitution of political space as male space can illuminate the gulf between democratization and democracy in ways that may help women in "mature" liberal democracies learn from the experiences of women in democratizing nations. Governments cannot continue to claim to be democratic if they allow half their populations to be grossly underrepresented. Emerging liberal democracies, like their mature counterparts, have embraced a rhetoric of equal opportunity only to mask systemic inequality. By construing women's absence as a deprivation of public roles, women's rights advocates have a powerful means to challenge the legitimacy of any democratic consolidation that privileges men. Contesting gender power in liberal democratic institutions may help feminists repoliticize their emancipatory struggles. Holding political parties and elected officials accountable to inclusive norms of democracy may be one way to reopen the very old question of whose lives are to count politically and whose interests are to be served through democratic decision-making. Perhaps it might also reopen the question of what kind of democracy is possible in the twenty-first century, thereby resurrecting the emancipatory impulse of feminist social movements.

NOTES

1. In certain parts of the former Soviet bloc, women's unemployment reached 80 percent in the aftermath of democratization. A decade later the majority of women remain out of paid work in Russia (see Jaquette and Wolchik 1998; Sperling 1998.)

2. In principle, a gendered practice could privilege men or women. But the history of male dominance has resulted in systematic male power advantages across diverse social domains. Feminist usage of the adjective "gendered" reflects this male power advantage. Hence a gendered practice is synonymous with androcentric practice in common feminist terminology. This equation also draws upon linguistic terms which characterize the male as unmarked/universal and the female as marked/other. Within this framework, the allegedly neutral and inclusive term "gender" reflects the universal/male norm.

3. A good deal more research is needed to make sense of such increasing violence against women. Since the issue of domestic violence was politicized only in the 1970s, it is difficult to know to what extent the rate of violence has increased and to what extent increased rates of reporting and changed police practices account for an apparent increase. In some nations undergoing democratization, local feminist activists have argued that increasing male frustration related to economic strains are producing an increase in domestic violence; others have linked the increase in domestic violence to a form of "backlash" against the increasing independence of women.

4. Sheila Meintjes, "Mobilizing Against Violence Against Women in South Africa," paper presented at the International Conference on Politics, Rights, and Representation, University of Chicago, 17 October 1999.
5. These stand in marked contrast to the programmatic and disciplined parties characteristic of many European social-democratic states.
6. Alvarez notes that depending on the size and mission of the institution, as well as its technical profile, state funds account for 10–25 percent of feminist NGOs' operating budgets in Chile and 40–50 percent of feminist NGOs' budgets in Colombia (Alvarez 1999: 196).

REFERENCES

Alvarez, Sonia. 1990. *Engendering Democracy in Brazil: Women's Movements in Transition Politics.* Princeton: Princeton University Press.

Alvarez, Sonia. 1999. "Advocating Feminism: The Latin American Feminist NGO 'Boom'," *International Feminist Journal of Politics* 1, no. 2: 181–209.

Barkley Brown, Elsa. 1997. "Negotiating and Transforming the Public Sphere: African American Political Life in the Transition from Slavery to Freedom," in Cathy Cohen, Kathleen Jones, and Joan Tronto, eds., *Women Transforming Politics*, 343–76. New York University Press.

Brown, Wendy. 1988. *Manhood and Politics.* Totowa, N.J.: Rowan & Littlefield.

Bystydzienski, Jill, ed. 1992. *Women Transforming Politics: Worldwide Strategies.* Bloomington: Indiana University Press.

Caldeira, Teresa. 1998. "Justice and Individual Rights: Challenges for Women's Movements and Democratization in Brazil," in Jane Jaquette and Sharon Wolchik, eds., *Women and Democracy: Latin America and Central and Eastern Europe.* Baltimore: Johns Hopkins University Press.

Case, Mary Anne. 1999. "Assessing the Categories: Should Political Representation Be Organized by Race, Gender, or Sexuality." Paper presented at International Conference on Politics, Rights, and Representation, University of Chicago, 14 October.

Craske, Nikki. 1998. "Remasculinisation and the Neoliberal State in Latin America," in Vicky Randall and Georgian Waylen, eds., *Gender, Politics, and the State.* London and New York: Routledge.

Di Stefano, Christine. 1996. "Autonomy in the Light of Difference," in Nancy Hirschmann and Christine Di Stefano, eds., *Revisioning the Political*, 95–116. Boulder, CO: Westview Press.

Flammang, Janet. 1997. *Women's Political Voice: How Women are Transforming the Practice and Study of Politics.* Philadelphia: Temple University Press.

Funk, Nanette and Magda Mueller. 1993. *Gender Politics and Post-Communism.* New York: Routledge.

Hirschmann, Nancy. 1992. *Rethinking Obligation.* Ithaca: Cornell University Press.

Jaquette, Jane, ed. 1989. *The Women's Movement in Latin America: Feminism and the Transition to Democracy.* Boston: Unwin Hyman.

Jaquette, Jane and Sharon Wolchik. 1998. *Women and Democracy: Latin America and Central and Eastern Europe.* Baltimore: Johns Hopkins University Press.

Lang, Sabine. 1999. "The NGOization of Social Movements." Paper presented at the International Conference on Politics, Rights and Representation, University of Chicago, 17 October.

Leijenaar, Monique. 1998. "Gender and Good Governance." Paper presented at the Annual Meeting of the American Political Science Association, Boston, 3–6 September.

McDonagh, Eileen. 1999. "Democratization and Gender in American Political Development: Woman Suffrage and the Contradiction Model." Paper presented at conference on Framing Equality: Inclusion, Exclusion and American Political Institutions," Eagleton Institute of Politics, Rutgers University, 25–26 March.

Miller, Francesca. 1991. *Latin American Women and the Search for Social Justice*. Hanover, NH: University Press of New England.

Nelson, Barbara and Najima Chowdhury, eds. 1994. *Women and Politics Worldwide*. New Haven: Yale University Press,

Peterson, V. Spike and Anne Sisson Runyon. 1999. *Global Gender Issues*, 2d ed. Boulder, CO: Westview Press.

Radcliffe, Sara and Sallie Westwood, eds. 1993. *Viva: Woman and Popular Protest in Latin America*. New York: Routledge.

Rai, Shirin, Hilary Pilkington, and Annie Phizacklea, eds. 1992. *Women in the Face of Change: The Soviet Union, Eastern Europe and China*. London: Routledge.

Saint Germain, Michelle. 1994. "Women, Democratization, and Public Policy," *Policy Sciences* 27: 269–76.

Scott, Joan. 1996. *Only Paradoxes to Offer: French Feminists and the Rights of Man*. Cambridge, MA: Harvard University Press.

Sperling, Valerie. 1998. "Gender Politics and the State during Russia's Transition Period," in Vicky Randall and Georgian Waylen, eds., *Gender, Politics, and the State*. London and New York: Routledge.

Tronto, Joan. 1993. *Moral Boundaries*. New York: Routledge.

Valenzuela, Maria Elena. 1998. "Women and the Democratization Process in Chile," in Jane Jaquette and Sharon Wolchik, eds., *Women and Democracy: Latin America and Central and Eastern Europe*. Baltimore: Johns Hopkins University Press, 1998.

MAPPING GENDER
IN AFRICAN-AMERICAN
POLITICAL STRATEGIES

LEITH MULLINGS

Issues of gender have always been intertwined with national and ethnic processes (West 1992; Walby 1992), as women are involved in struggles of nations, ethnic groups, or national minorities against oppression (Anthias and Yuval-Davis 1989; Jayawardena 1986). For women of African descent in the United States, like their sisters around the world, efforts to challenge gender subordination have been integrally linked to the larger struggle for equality.

This has meant that for African-American women efforts at empowerment have differed fundamentally from those of many Euro-Americans—particularly middle-stratum and elite women—in their groundedness in national liberation struggles. Because African-American women have been involved in the construction of an identity within a context of inequality defined by relations of race and class as well as gender, their efforts have been part of the larger struggle of African Americans to define their collective identity and to address the structure of hierarchy.

Given this distinct history, there is no doubt that common features of history and culture have produced an emerging identifiable African-American women's consciousness and construction of gender. One scholar who speaks to this, charting the manner in which African Americans have constructed race, class, and gender in opposition to the views of the dominant class and how this consciousness expresses itself in everyday life, is Patricia Hill Collins. But critics of her pioneering work *Black Feminist Thought* (1991) argue that her central paradigm is essentialist and even reductionist in its projection of an Afrocentric notion of gender (see White 1990; Thorne 1992).

There is some truth to this. As Collins herself admits, in emphasizing the commonalities she has muted variation, presenting a less nuanced account of the debate about roles of women. But even as we struggle together, we must consider the different ways in which African Americans have defined their collective identity and sought to empower themselves, and the implications of these differences for gender construction.

This essay will suggest that there are distinct but overlapping paradigms through which African Americans have thought about the liberation project. I will first briefly discuss these approaches, their alternative solutions to the problem of gender, and their implications for issues such as reproduction and family and the participation of women in the liberation project. I will analyze several recent events, including the 1995 Million Man March and the 1991 appointment of Clarence Thomas to the Supreme Court, suggesting that these occasions, however diverse, speak to the central themes of the role of women in struggle and how gender is constructed in African-American culture, society, and politics. Though conscious that I run the risk of overstating the differences in African Americans' constructions of race, class, and gender, as Collins may have overstated the commonalities, I would nevertheless argue that while gender has been constructed through common struggles for political empowerment in the African-American community, it manifests itself in strikingly different ways.

THE DEEP STRUCTURE OF AFRICAN-AMERICAN POLITICS

Most political theorists have described two perspectives through which African Americans have organized their struggle for equality: integrationist versus nationalist.[1] While the bipolar approach has the elegance of symmetry, it fails to grasp the underlying structure of political culture among African Americans. Though there often appear to be two conflicting political ideologies and cultures, an analysis of the deep structure of African-American politics suggests that there are three overlapping paradigms through which African Americans have understood the past and attempted to realize their future: inclusion, autonomy, and transformation. These three approaches, which are the subject of collaborative work I have done with Manning Marable, are discussed in more detail in earlier works (see Marable and Mullings 1994; Marable 1995). Before exploring constructions of gender, I will briefly summarize the contours of each tradition.

In posing this tripartite structure, I recognize that the use of models is inherently limited; that the process of struggle is not static but dynamic; and that these represent orientations within political culture and social development that are neither all-inclusive nor mutually exclusive. Nevertheless, these models reflect significant differences in underlying assumptions about identity—how African Americans define themselves, as well as strategies and goals of the liberation project.

INCLUSION

The inclusionist vision assumes that African Americans are Americans who happen to be black. Its historical roots are found in the aspirations of the free Negro communities of the North before the Civil War, in the politics of the younger Du Bois and the older A. Philip Randolph. It incorporates the traditional integrationist vision of sectors of the civil rights struggle as well as the neoliberal currents of the post-civil rights period.

The central strategic objective of the inclusionists is integration of African Americans into Euro-American civil society and the expansion of equal opportunities for minorities within the existing capitalist system. Equal opportunity or access is thereby generally sought through struggles within the confines of the social and legal system. The general order of the economic system is rarely questioned except as it relates to exclusion and the failure to live up to the "democratic principles" upon which the United States was allegedly founded.

But therein lie the seeds of a critique. Integrationists may be either conservative or militant; they may seek accommodation or change. Their attempts to change the system may lead to efforts to transform it; in the course of trying to reform the system, activists sometimes discover that hierarchical race relations are not an aberration but a fundamental aspect of the socioeconomic system; Martin Luther King, Jr., for example, became very critical of capitalism as an economic system.

AUTONOMY

The second perspective is perhaps the most difficult to characterize. Popular usage usually designates this current as "black nationalist,"[2] but "autonomist" may be a more accurate label for those movements and people that seek free social space: autonomous geographic, institutional, or cultural space that allows them to participate as equals, either within the parameters of the state or in an altered political relationship with Euro-American civil society. Elements of nationalism can be found in empowerment strategies having to do with group identity, no matter what model they are part of. The back-to-Africa strategies of Martin Delaney in the nineteenth century and Marcus Garvey's Universal Negro Improvement Association in the early twentieth century are well-known historical examples of the call for territorial autonomy.

Given the deeply felt pessimism about the ability or willingness of white civil society to transform itself in order to accept the demands of people of color, nationalist strategies seek empowerment through autonomously controlled institutions that address the needs of African Americans and buffer them from the racism of Euro-Americans. There is often an unwillingness to engage in measures that challenge the basic economic and political system of the state; rather, nationalists often choose to demand autonomous space—hence the demand for territorial integrity, as in the Nation of Islam or the Republic of New Afrika; for economic space, as in the black capitalism of the Congress of Racial Equality; or for the substitution of cultural space for geographic separation, as expressed in the cultural nationalism of Maulana Karenga or in the cultural theory of Afrocentrism.

Among nationalists there is a range of activities and philosophies. At one end of the spectrum one can find the black capitalism of the Congress of Racial

Equality, and at the other the League of Revolutionary Black Workers or the Black Panther Party in its early stages, both of which include some form of class analysis (see Marable 1995: 76). What unites these various movements and perspectives is their emphasis on race as the fundamental variable in the distribution of power and consequently as the primary basis for mobilizing people, capital, markets, or politics. Like the inclusionist paradigm, racial categories are assumed to be largely fixed—African Americans are Africans who happen to live in America. White racism is seen as a permanent reality of America's cultural and social landscape, one that will never change.

TRANSFORMATION

Though relations between nationalists and the left are frequently fractious, African Americans holding a transformationalist perspective share key elements with autonomists in their identification with people of African descent and their desire to build black institutions and to oppose Euro-American cultural hegemony. However, they differ from both nationalists and inclusionists in their commitment to challenge the fundamental institutions of power, privilege, and ownership on which the contemporary state is based. The historical roots of this tradition may be found in the militancy of Nat Turner and Harriet Tubman, who sought to destroy slavery, as well as the radicalism of the older W. E. B. DuBois and the younger A. Philip Randolph. Other arenas for the enactment of this vision have been manifested, to varying extents, in African-American participation in the radical elements of the labor movement, the Southern Youth Congress, the Communist Party, the Black Workers Congress, and recent political movements such as Harold Washington's mayoral campaigns in Chicago in 1983 and 1987, the radical tendency of the anti-apartheid movement in the 1980s, and the left wing of Jesse Jackson's Rainbow Coalition.

The objective of this strategy is to dismantle all forms of inequality. Hence race is perceived not in biological or genetic terms but as an unequal relationship between collectivities, held in place by violence and power. African-American liberation is simultaneously central to the larger struggle to reorganize power and resources on a global basis and dependent on changing the larger power relationships. Consequently, commitment to African-American liberation is expressed not only through attempts to reorganize larger structures of power but also through transformative strategies directed toward specific class relationships that directly affect African Americans.

INTERRELATIONSHIPS

It is extremely important not to oversimplify or reify what are in fact broad, overlapping traditions. First and foremost, each perspective is an attempt to address the problem of racism in American society, and each grapples with the question of empowerment of African Americans. All three traditions include both accommodationist and radical possibilities. Within each current we find individuals dedicated to the liberation of African Americans and who have been willing to die for this commitment.

Hence there have always been, and will always be, grounds for unity among those approaching the empowerment of African Americans from different perspectives. Indeed, political activists working within each of the three paradigms frequently utilize identical discourses, slogans, and forms of representation. For example, within each critical perspective, the empowerment of African Americans is phrased as the quest for "freedom." However, the meaning of freedom may differ significantly; those advocating inclusion into, autonomy from, and transformation of American society often work with very different strategic models about economics, politics, structure, culture, family life, and the role of women.

Real movements and real people frequently embody elements of various political directions, as was the case with the civil rights movement of the 1960s. Individuals may begin their activist careers with one set of perspectives and move to another. Today's inclusionist or nationalist may be tomorrow's transformationist. For example, Martin Luther King, Jr. began his career by attempting to achieve integration through civil disobedience. By the final two years of his life, his confrontation with the machinery of the state had led him to question the basic premises of capitalism. He took an active stand in opposition to the Vietnam War and was assassinated as he was in the process of organizing the 1968 Poor People's March on Washington. From another direction, Malcolm X, as a young minister of the Nation of Islam, called for strict racial separation, non-involvement in political affairs, and a solution to U.S. racial problems through creation of a black state. By the end of his life, he had acquired elements of a transformationist perspective. He was a staunch critic of capitalism, strongly opposed the war in Vietnam, and favored a strategy of African-American empowerment that would ultimately make national and international alliances with forces outside of the African-American community.

Furthermore, the majority of African Americans do not narrowly define themselves as belonging exclusively in one ideological camp or another, but may be influenced by the particular juncture of personal, political, historical, and economic forces in their lives at a given point in time. If we were to think of these currents as overlapping spheres, most African Americans, much of the time, might place themselves at the center—the nexus where all three ideologies overlap.

THE CRUCIBLE OF GENDER

Each paradigm has very different implications for the construction of gender. Gender is not just about women; it is about the social *relationship* between men and women and the dialectical, reciprocal, and cultural construction of femininity and masculinity.

Recognition of a unique historical experience concerning gender informs the perspectives of African Americans of various political persuasions. This history incorporates a land of origin with certain common principles about gender and family (Mullings 1997: chap. 4). It also encompasses the African-American experience in the United States where the denial of many "protections" offered by gender roles and indeed sometimes inversion of such roles was a means of maintaining control (Mullings 1997: chap. 6). Hence asserting the right to assume gender-based roles of husband, father, wife, and mother paradoxically was an act of resistance. The manner in which African-American people have envisioned relationships of gender in light of that history has expressed itself in markedly different forms.

"I AM A MAN"

For those who believe that African-American empowerment is best achieved through integration into U.S. society, the vision of ideal gender roles is generally developed against the backdrop of the dominant Euro-American model, and the struggle for inclusion in Euro-American civil society includes the "privileges" of gender. Freedom is frequently identified with masculinity. Consequently the right to be treated like a "man" was a recurrent theme in the civil rights movement. Slogans ("I am a man"[3]) and songs ("How many roads must a man walk down before you call him a man?") metaphorically equated manhood with equality. While these examples in part reflect the semantics of generic usage, the thrust of the inclusionist current has been to seek gender privileges within the dominant paradigm: to claim for African-American men the privileges of manhood and to seek for African-American women the protections of patriarchy denied to them by the dominant culture.

Historically, African-American women, like other working women (see Laslett and Brenner 1989), have used appeals to the traditional gender role model to demand family wages for men. During the period of sharecropping or debt peonage, working women used the language of traditional gender roles (Gutman 1976: 167) to exert some control over their labor, emphasizing their roles as homemakers rather than as workers. Similarly for middle-stratum African-American women, "gender-defined work and domestic responsibilities were symbolic of their new status" (Harley 1978: 170), and women in organizations such as the National Association of Colored Women strongly encouraged conformity to Euro-American models of womanhood (Higginbotham 1992: 271).

In the church, despite Brown's (1994) contention that Afro-Baptists, for example, perpetuate African cultural values of complementarity rather than the androcentric bias of the Pauline scriptures, Christianity has helped to shape the representation of women primarily as mothers and helpmeets to men. Reverend Martin Luther King, Jr. once wrote, "The primary obligation of the woman is motherhood" (quoted in Fairclough 1987: 50).

In keeping with the view that African Americans are Americans who happen to be black, the inclusionist strategy seeks for Americans of African descent the rights, obligations, and roles of Euro-American society as they are defined by gender. For many this is mediated by recognition of the special history of African-American women. Furthermore, as traditional Euro-American gender roles are themselves challenged by the civil rights and women's movements, there is often a tendency to favor the extension of democratic rights to women, but generally within the parameters of the economic, political, and legal system of capitalism. However, the implicit acceptance of the foundations of capitalism inevitably reproduces patriarchal relationships.

WOMEN, MEN, AND NATION

Patriarchal gender relationships are characteristic of many nationalist positions; the referent, however, is not Euro-American models of gender but "traditional" societies, religions, or philosophies. For those seeking territorial and/or cultural autonomy, the gender relations of a Eurocentric society are to be rejected as African Americans re-establish alternative gender relations that have their origins in a traditional "golden age" (Mullings 1997: chap. 6). In this view, gender relations become an aspect of the larger project of building autonomous black institutions, culture, and society. In this construction of the past, men and women have complementary, harmonious roles.

Nationalist gender relationships, though phrased in terms of complementarity, tend to be largely patriarchal even when the discourse is gender-neutral. Women are thought to have different, but complementary, spheres of work, intellects, abilities, and sensitivities. Among the more enlightened who have tried to come to terms with gender, the woman's sphere may be considered as important as the man's. Molefi Asante, for example, emphasizes complementarity. Men and women, who

> are equally the source of our strength and indeed our genius ... in a relationship must be attuned to the primary objective of all Afrocentric unions: the productive and creative maintenance of the collective cognitive imperative. (Asante 1981: 77–78)

While I have argued elsewhere that complementarity in and of itself need not result in inequality (Mullings 1976), assumptions about inferiority and superiority are usually implicit in frameworks of complementarity that operate within the context of a hierarchical society. This is more clearly expressed in a classic statement from *Mwanamke Mwananchi* (The Nationalist Woman), a pamphlet published in the early 1970s:

> We understand that it is and has been traditional that the man is the head of the house. He is the leader of the house/nation because his knowledge of the world is broader, his awareness is greater, his understanding is fuller and his application of this information

is wiser.... After all, it is only reasonable that the man be the head of the house because he is able to defend and protect the development of his home.... Women cannot do the same things as men—they are made by nature to function differently. Equality of men and women is something that cannot happen even in the abstract world. (Quoted in Combahee River Collective 1982: 19)

The perception of women as different and inferior is not merely a product of a prefeminist period. The diatribe by nationalist Shahrazad Ali in a widely publicized (though self-published) volume, *The Black Man's Guide to Understanding the Black Women*, holds women, whose "brain is smaller than the Black man's" (Ali 1989: 177), responsible for the problems of African-American men and advocates physical violence against them if they are not acquiescent.

Whether "complementarity" is phrased frankly as superiority and inferiority or in more gender-neutral language, women are associated primarily with the domestic sphere. Their reproductive capacity is essentialized and becomes the primary aspect of their identity. Hence Molefi Asante refers to "a woman's time to create and a man's time to produce" (Asante 1981: 78). Nationalist scholar Nathan Hare expresses these assumptions in policy recommendations: "The most basic solution to the black or oppressed female's condition ... will be unavoidably in the reproductive/sexual realm, while the solution to the male's condition will be notably in the sphere of productive/social instrumentality" (Hare 1989: 169).

Furthermore, the common denominator of most of these perspectives is an idealist approach to gender roles. The discourse about gender is generally not grounded in the material history of African-American women but rather in metaphysical constructions of a traditional golden-age society. Women are essential to the ultimate and overriding project of building autonomous spaces—institutions, culture, society. But for this reason there is also an implicit need to control women.

Consequently the nexus between motherhood, family, and nationhood means that women may be seen as guardians of the nation and national culture and are granted an honored place in the national project. The attractions of the sense of dignity and protection inherent in this representation should not be lightly dismissed. To women of African descent, who have historically borne the double burdens of work and home, a language of complementarity, protection, or even frank patriarchy may be very seductive.

However, the other side of the coin of protection may be control. Hence, in *Message to the Blackman*, Elijah Muhammad, longtime patriarch of the Nation of Islam, asserts that the first step in self-knowledge is "the *control*, and the protection of our own women" (Muhammad 1965: 59; stress added). While protection may be suffused with benevolence and control associated with coercion, the two are linked by notions of women as property; Elijah Muhammad writes, "The woman is the man's field to reproduce his nation" (Muhammad 1965: 58).

STANDARDS FOR A NEW WOMANHOOD

Activists who represent the transformationalist approach have generally advocated dismantling relations of patriarchy as well as other structures of inequality, which are seen as inextricably linked.[4] For those within this tradition, gender is constructed, in the first instance, from the materiality of the experiences of African-American women as workers and participants in the struggle as well as mothers.

For example, W. E. B. DuBois was, in his political and public life, if not in his intimate relationships, consistently committed to women's rights. He wrote several essays calling for "the emancipation of women" in *Crisis*, the journal he edited from 1910 to 1934. In 1912 he authored a pamphlet entitled *Disenfranchisement*, published by the National American Woman Suffrage Association, in which he asserted women's right to vote as a necessary precondition for the realization of democracy. He was an enthusiastic supporter of women workers, and he also urged African-American husbands to "share housework" (Marable 1983: 82–83). Reviewing DuBois's sizable body of work on African-American women, Morton (1991: 64) notes, "In his own era DuBois was a pioneer in the transformation of even the most dehumanizing images of black womanhood into empowering symbols of worth." Similarly, Angela Davis's work on women, race, and class attempts to examine the social construction of gender within the context of class and race relations. As a historical materialist analysis, it simultaneously addresses not only the reality of gender inequality and its meaning to African Americans but also issues of class and race. Exploring the material history of African-American women, "the accumulated experiences of all those women who toiled under the lash for their masters, worked for and protected their families, fought against slavery, and who were beaten and raped, but never subdued," she suggests that they have passed on "a legacy spelling out standards for a new womanhood" (Davis 1981: 29).

But it is also true that among those who call for dismantling all forms of inequality, there have been sharp differences about how gender subordination is linked to other forms of inequality. Conflicts may take the form of romanticizing sexism in the working class or relegating various aspects of the struggle for women's rights to "bourgeois feminism." Efforts to gain equality for women may be seen as a diversion from the struggle against race and class oppression.

Notions of gender are fluid, and people modify their views in light of their experiences. For example, though Malcolm X never became an active advocate for women's equality, he struggled against the misogyny and patriarchal notions of his earlier years. In the latter years of his life, he appears to have changed his ideas about women, as he did about other things. Following his second African trip, he said:

> So one of the things I became thoroughly convinced of in my recent travels is the importance of giving freedom to the woman, giving her education, and giving her the incentive to get out there and put that same spirit and understanding in her children.

And I frankly am proud of the contribution that our women have made in the struggle for freedom and I'm one person who's for giving them all the leeway possible because they've made a greater contribution than many of us men. (Malcolm X 1970: 179)

WOMEN'S PLACE

The different approaches to gender outlined above may manifest themselves in policy alternatives. This may be illustrated by examining two salient issues: reproductive rights and the participation of women in the liberation project. For each of these, after noting areas of unity, I will indicate some of the differences in public positions of individuals and organizations associated with inclusionist, autonomist, and transformationist traditions.

REPRODUCTION AND FAMILY

As people seek to reproduce themselves, they often do so within a context of "stratified reproduction," where some populations are empowered to reproduce and others are not (Ginsburg and Rapp 1995: 3). For African Americans, issues of reproduction have not been relegated to the private sphere, but have often been in the public arena.[5] Pressures to encourage or limit reproduction have varied with the historical moment: for example, during slavery African-American women were often forcibly encouraged to reproduce the labor force, but in the contemporary period of deindustrialization and rising unemployment their reproductive capacity has become a matter for national attention (Mullings 1997: chap. 5). For many African Americans, regardless of their political orientation, issues about continuity and genocide have been real concerns.

Reproduction takes place within a complex set of social arrangements, and African Americans of most political persuasions would probably agree that the family has been a buffer from slavery and racism and that the struggle for family is part and parcel of the liberation struggle. But as Rapp (1987) reminds us, people mean different things by "family."

It is not surprising that questions of reproductive choice are strongly debated. The disagreements we find in the general population are reflected in microcosm in those who favor the strategy of integration. For example, there is a national organization of African Americans opposed to abortion, and African-American clergymen have often been conservative on this issue. African-American politicians, however, have generally supported reproductive rights.

While many inclusionists favor reproductive rights, often attending to the theoretical and tactical relationship between civil rights and women's rights, this concession does not necessarily extend to rethinking the premises of the patriarchal family. Though recognizing the variety of family forms and the strains on such families, inclusionists have generally supported the patriarchal nuclear family as ideal. They are frequently uncritical of the right-wing call for "family values," implicit in which is the notion that the decline of the "traditional" nuclear family is at the heart of increasing poverty among African Americans.

Uncritical acceptance of the dominant society's model of gender and family roles is perhaps most clearly evident in the work of sociologist William Julius Wilson (1987). While Wilson's analysis of conditions that produce increasing rates of households headed by women is very useful, he does not problematize the normative gender roles underlying his analysis. Documenting the relationship between the rising numbers of households headed by women and skyrocketing male unemployment among African Americans, his policy proposals are directed toward increasing the number of marriageable black males by giving priority to employment and education opportunities for African-American men. While few would deny the importance of addressing male joblessness, Wilson's proposals accept and reinforce the traditional model of gender roles as an effective solution to the social problems facing African-American households (Mullings 1997: chap. 8).

Given the centrality of reproduction in the nationalist project, it is not surprising that their position on reproductive rights is often conservative. Historically, nationalists have not been supportive of a woman's right to choose. For example, in 1934 Marcus Garvey's Universal Negro Improvement Association issued a resolution condemning the use of birth control for African Americans (Marable 1983: 83). The pronouncement of Louis Farrakhan, national leader of the Nation of Islam, that "when the black woman kills her unborn child she is murdering the advancement of her nation" (quoted in Marable 1983: 84–85) is a logical consequence of Elijah Muhammad's view that "the woman is man's field to reproduce his nation" (Muhammad 1965: 58).

Reproductive functions are ideally organized in the context of the patriarchal, perhaps polygynous, family. For nationalist groups that practice polygyny, it may be seen as both a return to African traditions and a response to the scarcity of African-American men. Black poet and cultural critic Haki Madhubuti, for example, calls for "the quality of sharing" in the wake of the shortage of black men. His extension of this "choice" to women as well is perhaps somewhat disingenuous, given that the actual constraints of demography would insure that the "sharing" is done almost exclusively by women. Despite what appears to be balance in his discussion, women are nonetheless viewed as markers of ethnic boundaries and the property of the African-American community: black women forming families with white men (in the absence of available black men) results in "a very serious consequence in terms of Black genocide" (Madhubuti 1978: 144).

A woman's rights over her own body need not always be juxtaposed to racial genocide. At the same time that Marcus Garvey condemned African-American women's right to use birth control, DuBois strongly endorsed Planned Parenthood and invited Margaret Sanger to contribute articles on birth control to *Crisis*. Similarly, Manning Marable (1991) presents a very nuanced view of reproductive rights, noting that in light of African-American history, the fear of genocide is not unreasonable. Nonetheless, he insists on women's right to choose in the context of freedom and responsibility. Reverend Jesse Jackson has also supported reproductive rights, appearing at rallies and marches in support of choice in reproductive matters.

For those who seek to undermine patriarchal relations, the traditional family may be an arena in which these relationships are produced and reproduced. Contemporary family organization and function are seen not as "natural" or given but as historically determined. As Johnetta Cole suggests,

> The nature and state of "the American family" cannot be understood without a recognition of the diversity of the groupings which bear the label "family" and the varied, complex, and often contradictory place of women within them. (Cole 1986: 116)

In this view public policy need not be based on reproducing the "traditional" patriarchal family.

WOMEN'S ROLES IN THE LIBERATION PROJECT

African Americans across the political spectrum would agree that three themes have been characteristic of the liberation project historically. First, for most women as well as men, the struggle for African-American liberation took priority over struggles around gender. Furthermore, most recognize the unprecedented role played by women in the liberation project and simultaneously the denial of traditional Euro-American masculine roles to African-American men. Though African Americans have different takes on how this history should inform contemporary relationships, in most inclusionist and autonomist organizations this experience, as well as the dominant ideology, has become part of the rationale for limiting the participation of women.

In the African-American church, for example, though women often constitute the bulk of the congregations, the ministry is a vehicle of social mobility for men. In the mainstream denominations, biblical ideology promotes the subordination of women, who are not proportionally represented in leadership. A survey of the clergy of 2,150 African-American "mainline" congregations in 1990 revealed that only 66, or 3.7 percent, were women (Baer 1993: 67). Even among the Afro-Baptists, where women are most active, women pastors, preachers, or evangelists are rare. Indeed, Brown suggests, "With the active complicity of women, men monopolize corporate leadership in the home and church" (Brown 1994: 173).

Similarly, if we examine the involvement of women in inclusionist political organizations, women have played more significant roles than in comparable Euro-American organizations and have generally unhesitatingly supported men and the struggle for the greater good of African Americans (see, for example, Jones 1985). But though they often constituted the shock troops in voter registration, boycotts, and civil disobedience and played major roles in initiating the militant actions around the Montgomery bus boycott, women rarely hold leadership positions in traditional civil rights organizations such as the Southern Christian Leadership Conference (SCLC), the Congress of Racial Equality (CORE), and the Student Nonviolent Coordinating Committee (SNCC) (see Giddings 1984: 313–14; Jones 1985). For example, the two women who served on the executive staff of the SCLC both complained of the ways in which male chauvinism limited their leadership (Fairclough 1987: 49–50). Though women were represented in leadership and decision-making in SNCC, Stokely Carmichael's infamous (and, it is to be hoped, joking) 1964 rebuttal to a position paper criticizing SNCC's treatment of women—"The only position for women in SNCC is prone" (Giddings 1984: 302; Jones 1985: 283)—did little to advance the issue of gender equality.

The traditional civil rights organizations have not made much progress in this area. For example, in the National Association for the Advancement of Colored People (NAACP) in 1994, ten of the twelve top executive positions were held by men, despite the fact that approximately two-thirds of the membership are female. Similarly, in 1994 the SCLC and the Urban League were both led by men.

In many autonomist projects women's roles are circumscribed. In the 1970s Amiri Baraka, for example, insisted that women should not be involved in men's discussions. (He has since changed his position.) The Republic of New Afrika called for a return to a male patriarchal system where men made decisions (Giddings 1984). Angela Davis described her encounters with Karenga's organization US while organizing for a rally in San Diego in 1967:

> I was criticized very heavily, especially by male members of Karenga's organization, for doing a man's job. Women should not play a leadership role, they insisted. A woman was supposed to "inspire" her man and educate his children. The irony of their complaint was that much of what I was doing had fallen to me by default. (Davis 1974: 161)

Today, with some notable exceptions—such as Shahrazad Ali's suggestion that women who defy men's leadership should be offered "a sound open-handed slap in the mouth" (1989: 170)—the public representation of women's roles in the liberation struggle is usually phrased in terms of complementarity and protection, as participants seek to reclaim leadership roles for men that existed in an ancestral society.

One of the most significant expressions of public activism around representations of gender in contemporary African-American politics was the Million Man March. On October 16, 1995, perhaps as many as a million African Americans went to Washington, D.C. for a day of racial unity and "atonement."[6]

The process of organization leading up to the march embodied the twin themes of protection and control of women and demonstrated points of unity in the nationalist and inclusionist perspectives on gender. The overwhelmingly male march was called by Minister Louis Farrakhan, the national leader of the Nation of Islam, after holding mass meetings of African-American men in major cities across the United States at which women were often turned away at the door. Reverend Benjamin Chavis, after being stripped of his position as national secretary of the NAACP ostensibly for using organizational funds for the settlement of a sexual harassment lawsuit, became national director of the march.

The Nation of Islam requested that the march be confined to men only; women were to stay at home, watch the children and pray. According to Farrakhan,

> We are asking the Black woman, particularly our mothers, to be with our children, teaching them the value of home, self-esteem, family and unity; and to work with us to ensure the success of the March and our mission to improve the quality of life for our people. We take this historical moment to recognize the major contributions that the Black woman has made and continues to make, toward the advancement of our people.[7]

When asked about the participation of women in the African National Congress and Frelimo, Conrad Muhammad, leader of the Nation of Islam's Harlem temple, explained:

> The Honorable Minister Louis Farrakhan and the Nation of Islam genuinely believe it's a sad man that sends his women into battle before himself … we believe as men it is our duty to go out on the front line.[8]

While the public discourse of the march leaders emphasized the protection of women, others seemed more concerned with control. A. Asadullah Samad, in a column in the *Los Angeles Sentinel*, defended the male-only composition of the march:

> Sisters gotta stay home on this one. I know you ain't used to anybody telling you what you can do or where you can go. That might be part of the problem (more on this later).… Until the black man regains the respect (*and control*) of his women, he will never regain the respect of the larger society. (Samad 1995: A7; stress added)

The march was supported by a wide spectrum of the African-American community. Many African-American women, including elected officials, officials of civil rights organizations, and members of sororities, enthusiastically supported the male-only march. This is not surprising given the historical burden of work and family carried by African-American women throughout their history. To many women, the call for men to take responsibility was a welcome one.

Progressives argued that while there is no inherent contradiction in single-sex movements, the march perpetuated divisions based on gender. As criticism mounted, the march leaders modified their stand on gender, and the widows of Martin Luther King, Jr., Medgar Evers, and Malcolm X were asked to "represent" women in the march. Rosa Parks, the catalyst of the Montgomery bus boycott, poet Maya Angelou, and a few other women were added to the speakers' platform. Nevertheless, the underlying paradigm of the march, based on the patriarchal world-view of the Nation of Islam, was not significantly transformed.

In a national context of mounting racism, the call for a march struck a chord among the majority of African Americans. The march was a massive demonstration against the demonization of African-American men and was successful in promoting and renewing feelings of solidarity, unity, and purpose among those who participated. It is nevertheless true that the organizers conceived of the Million Man March in terms of a patriarchal vision—a collective statement of manhood and self-assertion on the part of African-American men, with women deliberately relegated to arenas outside political and social confrontation. This framework is compatible with the patriarchy of both the inclusionist and the autonomist perspectives. Hugh Price, the president of the National Urban League, referred to the Million Man March as "the largest family-values rally in the history of the United States" (Gates 1996: 128).

Those organizations seeking radically to alter the structure of hierarchical relationships have not been immune from the influence of the "Moynihan thesis"—that the activist roles played by African-American women have emasculated African-American men. The Black Panther Party, for example, presents a complex case. Though the party was certainly characterized by serious problems of misogyny and sexism, women were integrated into the party leadership, and party members were influenced by leftist liberation movements that projected progressive views about the participation of women. For example, a Black Panther woman leader stated: "We feel that the example given us by the Vietnamese women is a prime example of the role women can play in the revolution" (Black Panther Party 1969: 22). At the founding of the party, one of the "Eight Points of Attention" was "Do not take liberties with women."

In the more traditional leftist movements, certainly ideology (if not always practice) supported the participation of women in political projects. Though practice was often inconsistent, leftist organizations with significant African-American membership, such as the Communist Party, could boast of an array of African-American women leaders, including Claudia Jones, Charlene Mitchell, and Angela Davis. Though the Marxist paradigm presented some limitations for the analysis of gender and gender oppression, these organizations differ significantly from the others discussed here in placing women in leadership positions as well as in giving ideological support to the deconstruction of patriarchy.

What preliminary conclusions can we draw from this? One aspect of inequality has been the dominant class's attempt to deny the humanity of Africans and African Americans by refusing them the attributes of gender. Within each political tradition, African Americans have challenged this by imagining and constructing gender relationships in distinct ways.

Literally coming from different places, those seeking inclusion and autonomy appear to construct very different models of gender relationships. Inclusionists seek equal opportunity and access to the gender privileges of the dominant Euro-American society, and many would support an expansion of women's rights within the confines of the existing legal system. Autonomists, on the other hand, reject the Eurocentric framework and seek to establish or re-establish gender relationships based on an ancestral tradition. Phrased in the language of complementarity (which easily shades into inequality), the division of labor, in which women's primary sphere is the domestic arena, is not a result of mutual agreement but rather is assumed to be a natural consequence of women's reproductive capacities. By reifying the cultural alternative, the material conditions of African-American women's experiences and struggles as workers are often obscured.

Dissimilar as they seem, there are underlying continuities between the inclusionist and autonomist perspectives. The final product of both strategic visions is a patriarchal model of gender roles in which masculinity is defined by the dependence of women. Within both currents, gender, like race, appears to be essentialized and fixed rather than historically and socially constructed. Though each attempts to grant women the protection and respect that was not forthcoming in the dominant society, this form of resistance accommodates and reproduces gender inequality. Thus the patriarchal theme put forward by the organizers of the Million Man March, for example, contradicted neither the Eurocentric patriarchy of the inclusionists nor the traditional model of patriarchy subscribed to by many nationalists, including the Nation of Islam.

While the nationalists pose an alternative model of gender roles, those within the transformationist perspective pose an oppositional model. However unsuccessful they may be in implementing it, they seek to deconstruct a definition of masculinity defined by the dependence of women. In this sense gender, like race, is seen as a social construction, based on historically unequal social relationships.

THE NOMINATION OF CLARENCE THOMAS:
RACE AND GENDER

In addition to the Million Man March, several public controversies have clearly demonstrated both the tensions around race and gender for African-American women and the varied approaches to configuring these relationships. One of the most momentous events—one with profound implications for the future—was the national debate concerning the nomination of Clarence Thomas to the U.S. Supreme Court. Though this topic has been analyzed in tedious detail (see, for example, Morrison 1992; Hill and Jordan 1995), it is a good example of how the different constructions of gender can play themselves out in a situation that has repercussions for millions of people.

On July 1, 1991, Clarence Thomas, a black conservative Republican, was nominated by then-President Bush to replace Thurgood Marshall on the Supreme Court. After being contacted by staff members of the congressional judiciary Committee, Anita Hill, an African-American attorney who had worked with Thomas, confirmed that Clarence Thomas had sexually harassed her. Congressional hearings on the nomination were carried live on several television networks. Thomas denied any sexual misconduct, labeling the hearings a "high-tech lynching for uppity blacks." Despite several corroborating witnesses and a lie detector test passed by Hill, the Senate voted 52–48 to confirm Clarence Thomas as an associate justice of the Supreme Court on October 16, 1991.

The nomination of Clarence Thomas to the Supreme Court highlighted tensions around race and gender. Most African Americans of various political stripes—with the exception of the sociologist Orlando Patterson, who suggested that the televised hearings "reconfirmed" the democratic process and won African Americans "unambiguous inclusion; unquestioned belonging" in American society (Patterson 1991: 79)—were concerned about the manner in which the televised spectacle could be used against African Americans. An unwillingness to demonstrate disunity publicly was one of the central factors responsible for the majority support Thomas received in the African-American community.

Though divided, a wide spectrum from inclusionists to nationalists embraced the notion that Clarence Thomas's elevation to the Supreme Court was a necessary evil. This included scholars such as Jacquelyne Johnson Jackson, who stated, "I supported Thomas' confirmation … because he was George Bush's only black star" (Jackson 1991–92: 49).

The inclusionist organizations, particularly the traditional civil rights organizations, either voted to confirm or did not effectively oppose the nomination. Though the Congressional Black Caucus Foundation eventually voted to oppose the nomination, the NAACP, while finally coming out against Thomas, issued an equivocal statement and did not take the lead in mobilizing opposition.

Inclusionist organizations supported Thomas on the basis of what Marable (1995) has termed "symbolic representation," the underlying assumption that the appointment of one of their own would inevitably work for the benefit of all African Americans. Hence the Southern Christian Leadership Conference voted to confirm the nomination, claiming that Thomas's experience as a black man "has subjected him to the 'Black Experience' that will help him to continue to grow more and more sensitive to the responsibility of the Supreme Court to insure justice for all" (Lowery 1991–92: 152). The Urban League voted neither to support nor to oppose him, expressing the hope that Thomas's "life experiences will lead him to closer identification with those in America who are victimized by poverty and discrimination" (Jacobs 1991–92: 153).

Nationalists supported Thomas on the basis of racial solidarity. Niara Sudarkasa, the president of Lincoln University, testified before the Senate Judiciary Committee on Thomas's behalf, closing with the plea that "we must not rest until Dr. King's dream becomes a reality" (Sudarkasa 1991–92: 102). For both inclusionists and autonomists, race outweighed other considerations, and the acceptance of a patriarchal model rationalized the disregard for issues of gender discrimination. Karenga, for example, neither strongly indicted Thomas's politics nor gave sufficient attention to gender, painting Clarence Thomas and Anita Hill as "a pathetic pair of seduced, opposing surrogates" of white conservatives and feminists (Karenga 1991–92: 68). Counterposing race and gender, he asked whether women should make a claim that will result in "collateral and devastating damage to African people" (60), calling for unity, "for a house divided among itself is a gift to the enemy" (62) and asserting that the African-American movement must continue to give weight to gender issues, but not at the expense of the African-American struggle (64).

In general, those holding a transformationist perspective challenged the nomination of Clarence Thomas. Reverend Jesse Jackson opposed it. Scholars such as Gerald Horne (1991–92) and Barbara Ransby urged consideration of class and gender as well as race. For Ransby the "hearings highlighted … the increasing hostility toward and scapegoating of black women … [and] the rise … of black neo-conservatives" (Ransby 1991–92: 82). Ransby and others organized a statement, signed by 1,603 women of African descent, entitled "African American Women in Defense of Ourselves," which appeared in the *New York Times* on November 17, 1991. The text indicted the Bush administration for the nomination and addressed the interrelationship of class, race, and gender issues, noting:

> The consolidation of a conservative majority on the Supreme Court seriously endangers the rights of all women, poor and working class people and the elderly. The seating of Clarence Thomas is an affront not only to African American women and men, but to all people concerned with social justice.[9]

Clarence Thomas was confirmed by the Senate committee on October 16, nearly a month before this statement appeared. I suggest that what Karenga described as "devastating damage" to African Americans lay not in Anita Hill's accusations but rather in the uncritical view of racial unity adopted by many inclusionists and nationalists and their failure to address gender issues (or, frankly, sexism), which has helped to produce a disaster of unmitigated proportions. In less than four years on the court, Thomas had supported—indeed, sometimes as the swing vote—measures that undercut democratic rights and opportunities for African Americans, women, poor and working people, and all Americans.

Thomas has voted with the majority to refuse to stay the deportation of Haitian refugees; to limit the scope of the Voting Rights Act in an Alabama case in which newly elected black representatives were stripped of power by white commissioners before they could take their seats; and to weaken the National Labor Relations Board act that allowed union organizers to leaflet in parking lots adjacent to stores they are trying to organize.

When this conservative court has been too liberal for his tastes, he has issued dissenting opinions. He signed onto the dissenting opinion in *Planned Parenthood* v. *Casey*, asserting that the *Roe* v. *Wade* decision should be overruled and that states should be free to permit or ban abortion. At a point in history when one in three African-American men between the ages of twenty and twenty-nine are involved in the criminal justice system[10] and prisons serve as warehouses for unemployed African-American and Latino youth, Thomas was one of two Supreme Court justices to dissent when the court held that the use of excessive physical force against a prisoner can violate the Eighth Amendment ban on cruel and unusual punishment. His dissent on this issue prompted a *New York Times* editorial entitled "The Youngest, Cruelest Justice" (Rosenthal 1992) and Justice Sandra O'Connor to write in her majority opinion that Thomas's dissent ignored "concepts of dignity, civilized standards, humanity and decency that animate the Eighth Amendment" (quoted in Coyle 1992: 40).

Most significant in retarding the gains of the civil rights movement, Thomas was the swing vote in 5–4 decisions that curbed affirmative action programs allowing federal benefits to members of minority groups and invalidated Georgia's 11th Congressional District, a majority black voting district, laying the groundwork for eliminating several majority black districts and decreasing the number of African Americans in Congress. Thomas was the swing vote in the decision holding that lower federal courts acted improperly in ordering the state to pay for a school desegregation plan in Kansas City, which is expected to open the door for decreasing federal involvement in school desegregation and even the rethinking of *Brown* v. *Board of Education.* According to the *National Law Journal,* Thomas has proven "more than willing to join those justices pushing hardest to the right" (Coyle 1992: 40).

The Thomas fiasco illustrates the theoretical and practical limitations inherent in some autonomist and inclusionist perspectives as they relate to gender. In both instances, those adopting these positions failed to understand how Thomas's elevation to the Supreme Court directly contradicted efforts to improve the status of African-American women and by extension undermined the entire struggle for freedom for all African Americans. Inherent in an essentialist view of race and an uncritical vision of racial solidarity is the necessity to exercise power over women. However, by failing to give attention to issues of gender and class, the larger project of African-American liberation is endangered.

WHERE ARE WE GOING? A PERSONAL POSTSCRIPT

What are the implications of this exploration, and where do we go from here? Historically African Americans, as individuals and as a people, have moved between various political visions and strategies. What are the conditions that produce the dominance of one or the other strategy, and what are the consequences for gender?

The 1960s and 1970s saw the rise of the civil rights movement, which employed various forms of civil disobedience to force changes in the state structure. This was a heroic—indeed in some instances revolutionary—movement, including streams of transformationist, inclusionist, and nationalist strategies. Its successes in democratizing access to and opportunity in housing, education, healthcare, immigration, and employment redounded to the benefit of all Americans. African-American women were major participants in the struggle, if not in the leadership, and heroines such as Fannie Lou Hamer and Rosa Parks were pivotal to the movement.

With the Civil Rights Act of 1964 and the Voting Rights Act of 1965, the struggle took an inclusionist direction, emphasizing change through legal channels and electoral strategies. In many of the civil rights and black power organizations, capitulation to the representation of "emasculating" African-American women led to increased identification of the struggle for equality with masculine privilege.

The 1970s brought with a vengeance the consequences of growing inequality, deindustrialization, and cutbacks in government services. As income inequality has increased, the middle class has expanded, but so has the number of those living below poverty, particularly poor women heading households. In addition, these conditions have given birth to a population of urban youth who have never seen successful struggle for change and have few job prospects in an economy where black youth unemployment is as high as 50 percent in some cities. The growth of a "ghettocentric" culture, including the musical form of hip-hop, in part reflects and expresses this experience. Initially embodying a serious critique of contemporary society, rap music quickly developed various currents that differ in their representation of politics and gender. But there is a major trend that is clearly politically conservative and misogynist. In gangsta rap, for example, women are frequently referred to as "bitches" and "hos."

In light of contemporary conditions, the inclusionist vision has proven unrealizable. An inherently unequal system cannot be expanded to produce opportunities for everyone, including African Americans. In an international context characterized by serious (if temporary) reversals for the left, the return of ethnic fundamentalism and racial essentialist explanations of social reality, and the consolidation of international capitalism, those individuals and organizations calling for transformationist strategies have been for the moment weakened.

In this void, there is a rising popularity of nationalist approaches, with the call for turning inward. Tempting as it may seem to shake the sand off our feet and turn our backs on Sodom and Gomorrah, this strategy is unlikely to succeed. The problems of the "skin strategy" are evident on the local level in the rise of a small but actively promoted group of conservative African Americans such as economist Thomas Sowell, Clarence Thomas, and Republican politician Alan Keyes, who cannot be trusted to promote the interests of African-American liberation. On the international level, the consolidation of globalized capitalism, with new forces of technology, renders narrow national struggles obsolete.

Furthermore, inherent in the nationalist project, in its essentialization of race and its prioritization of the black social order, is the necessity to "control" women, who reproduce the social order and mark its boundaries. Our historical struggle has clearly demonstrated that the pursuit of African-American libera-tion is inextricably connected to realizing the full potential of African-American women. The struggle against class exploitation, racial discrimination, and gender subordination must be integrated in theory and practice in order for any one element to be realized. As a people, we cannot afford to exclude women from full and equal participation in our struggle. Or, as an African brother said to me, paraphrasing a Ghanaian proverb: "We need all hands on deck."

NOTES

1. Scholars and commentators usually employ some variant of this dichotomous model. Krauthammer, for example, in an op-ed piece in *Time* magazine, categorized African-American political responses as "mainstream" versus "rejectionist" (1990: 80).
2. While many in this current refer to themselves as nationalists, "nationalism" is a contested term. Social theorists have distinguished between bourgeois nationalism, progressive nationalism, and revolutionary nationalism; or between cultural nationalism and political nationalism (Hutchison 1992). West (1992: 256), for example, defining nationalism as based on the development of group solidarity and the assertion of identity rights, suggests that nationalist movements may include political movements seeking to exercise state power; social movements that develop in response to colonialism; affirmations of cultural identity not necessarily linked to territorial sovereignty; and minority movements for identity rights and political inclusion.
3. This caption of a poster publicizing the struggle of Memphis sanitation workers became a rallying cry for the civil rights movement.
4. The different streams from which this critique emerges, including some feminist scholarship and lesbian writing as well as the action-oriented Marxist movements, often differ on the weight and position they give to various relationships of oppression.
5. This has also been true for poor and working-class Euro-American women. For example, the Eugenics movement at the turn of the century was concerned with limiting reproduction among immigrant women, particularly those from southern and eastern Europe.
6. The Parks Department estimated 400,000; the march organizers claimed at least 1,000,000. Boston University's Center for Remote Sensing estimated the crowd to be 837,214 with a 20 percent margin of error.
7. *Final Call* 14, no. 22 (1995): 19.
8. Forum on the Million Man March, held at Columbia University Institute for Research in African American Studios, 31 October 1995.
9. *New York Times*, 17 November 1991: A53.
10. *USA Today*, 5 October 1995: 1.

REFERENCES

Ali, Shahrazad. 1989. *The Black Man's Guide to Understanding the Black Woman*. Philadelphia: Civilized Publications.

Anthias, Floya, and Niral Yuval-Davis. 1989. "Introduction," in Floya Anthias and Niral Yuval-Davis, eds., *Woman—Nation—State*. London: Macmillan.

Asante, Molefi K. 1981. "The Black Male and Female Relationships: An Afrocentric Context," in Lawrence E. Gary, ed., *Black Men*. Beverly Hills: Sage Publications.

Baer, Hans A. 1993. "The Limited Empowerment of Women in Black Spiritual Churches: An Alternative Vehicle to Religious Leadership," *Sociology of Religion* 54, no. 1: 65–82.

Black Panther Party. 1969. *Black Panther Sisters on Women's Liberation*. N.p.: Black Panther Party.

Bookman, Ann, and Sandra Morgen, eds. 1988. *Women and the Politics of Empowerment*. Philadelphia: Temple University Press.

Brown, Audrey Lawson. 1994. "Afro-Baptist Women's Church and Family Roles: Transmitting Afrocentric Cultural Values," *Anthropological Quarterly* 67, no. 4: 173–86.

Busby, Margaret. 1992. *Daughters of Africa: An International Anthology of Words and Writings by Women of African Descent from Ancient Egypt to the Present*. New York: Pantheon Books.

Cole, Johnetta, ed. 1986. *All American Women: Lines That Divide, Ties That Bind.* New York: Free Press.

Collins, Patricia Hill. 1991. *Black Feminist Thought: Knowledge, Consciousness, and the Politics of Empowerment.* New York: Routledge.

Combahee River Collective. [1977] 1982. "A Black Feminist Statement," in Gloria Hull, Patricia Bell Scott, and Barbara Smith, eds., *All the Women Are White, All the Blacks Are Men, But Some of Us Are Brave.* Old Westbury, NY: Feminist Press.

Coyle, Marcia. 1992. "The Court Confounds Observers." *National Law Journal* 13, no. 1.

Davis, Angela. 1974. *An Autobiography.* New York: Random House.

Davis, Angela. 1981. *Women, Race, and Class.* New York: Random House.

Fairclough, Adam. 1987. *To Redeem the Soul of America: The Southern Christian Leadership Conference and Martin Luther King, Jr.* Athens: University of Georgia Press.

Gates, Henry Lewis. 1996. "A Reporter At Large: The Charmer." *New Yorker*, 29 April–6 May: 116–26.

Giddings, Paula. 1984. *When and Where I Enter: The Impact of Black Women on Race and Sex in America.* Toronto: Bantam.

Ginsburg, Faye, and Rayna Rapp. 1995. "Introduction: Conceiving the New World Order," in Faye Ginsburg and Rayna Rapp, eds., *Conceiving the New World Order: The Global Politics of Reproduction.* Los Angeles: University of California Press.

Gutman, Herbert G. 1976. *The Black Family in Slavery and Freedom, 1750–1925.* New York: Pantheon.

Hare, Nathan. 1989. "Solutions: A Complete Theory of the Black Family," in Nathan Hare and Julia Hare, eds., *Crisis in Black Sexual Politics.* San Francisco: Black Think Tank.

Harley, Sharon. 1978. "Northern Black Female Workers: 'Jacksonian Era'," in Sharon Harley and Rosalyn Terborg-Penn, eds., *The Afro-American Woman: Struggles and Images.* Port Washington, NY: National Universities Publications.

Higginbotham, Evelyn. 1992. "African American Women's History and the Metalanguage of Race," *Signs: Journal of Women in Society and Culture* 17, no. 2: 251–74.

Hill, Anita Faye, and Emma Coleman Jordan, eds. 1995. *Race, Gender, and Power in America: The Legacy of the Hill–Thomas Hearings.* New York: Oxford University Press.

Horne, Gerald. 1991–92. "The Thomas Hearings and the Nexus of Race, Gender and Nationalism," *The Black Scholar* 22, no. 1–2: 45–47.

Hutchison, John. 1992. "Moral Innovators and the Politics of Regeneration: The Distinctive Role of Cultural Nationalists in Nation-Building," *International Journal of Comparative Sociology* 33, no. 1–2: 101–17.

Jackson, Jacquelyne Johnson. 1991–92. "'Them Against Us': Anita Hill v. Clarence Thomas," *The Black Scholar* 22, no. 1–2: 49–52.

Jacobs, John E. 1991–92. "Clarence Thomas: Affirmative Action and Merit," *The Black Scholar* 22, no. 1–2: 153–54.

Jayawardena, Kumari. 1986. *Feminism and Nationalism in the Third World.* London: Zed Books.

Jones, Jacqueline. 1985. *Labor of Love, Labor of Sorrow: Black Women, Work, and the Family from Slavery to the Present.* New York: Basic Books.

Karenga, M. Ron. 1978. *Essays on Struggle: Position and Analysis.* San Diego, CA: Kawaida Publications.

Karenga, M. Ron. 1991–92. "Under the Camouflage of Color and Gender: The Dread and Drama of Thomas–Hill," *The Black Scholar* 22, no. 1–2: 59–65.

Krauthammer, Charles. 1993. "The Black Rejectionists." *Time*, 23 July: 80.

Laslett, Barbara, and Johanna Brenner. 1989. "Gender and Social Reproduction: Historical Perspectives," *Annual Reviews of Sociology* 15: 381–404.

Lowery, Joseph E. 1991–92. "The SCLC Position: Affirmative Action and Merit," *The Black Scholar* 22, no. 1–2: 151–52.

Madhubuti, Haki R. 1978. *Enemies: The Clash of Races.* Chicago: Third World Press.

Malcolm X. 1970. *By Any Means Necessary,* ed. George Breitman. New York: Pathfinder Press.

Marable, Manning. 1983. *How Capitalism Underdeveloped Black America: Problems in Race, Political Economy and Society.* Boston: South End Press.

Marable, Manning. 1997. "The Abortion Debate," in *Black Liberation in Conservative America.* Boston: South End Press.

Marable, Manning. 1995. *Beyond Black and White: Transforming African American Politics.* London and New York: Verso.

Marable, Manning, and Leith Mullings. 1994. "The Divided Mind of Black America: Race, Ideology and Politics in the Post Civil Rights Era," *Race and Class* 36, no. 1: 61–72.

Morrison, Toni, ed. 1992. *Race-ing Justice, En-gendering Power: Essays on Anita Hill, Clarence Thomas, and the Construction of Social Reality.* New York: Pantheon.

Morton, Patricia. 1991. *Disfigured Images: The Historical Assault on Afro-American Women.* New York: Greenwood Press.

Muhammad, Elijah. 1965. *Message to the Blackman in America.* Philadelphia: Hakim's Publications.

Mullings, Leith. 1976. "Women and Economic Change in Africa," in Nancy Hafkin and Edna Bay, eds., *Women in Africa.* Stanford: Stanford University Press.

Mullings, Leith. 1997. *On Our Own Terms: Race, Class & Gender in the Lives of African American Women.* New York: Routledge.

Patterson, Orlando. 1991–92. "Race, Gender and Liberal Fallacies," *The Black Scholar* 22, no. 1–2: 77–80.

Ransby, Barbara. 1991–92. "The Gang Rape of Anita Hill and the Assault Upon All Women of African Descent," *The Black Scholar* 22, no. 1–2: 82–85.

Rapp, Rayna. 1987. "Urban Kinship in Contemporary America: Families, Classes, and Ideology," in Leith Mullings, ed., *Cities of the United States: Studies in Urban Anthropology.* New York: Columbia University Press.

Rosenthal, Jack. 1992. "The Youngest, Cruelest Justice," *New York Times,* 27 February: A24.

Samad, A. Asadullah. 1995. "One Million Reasons for Black Men to March (Without Our Women)," *Los Angeles Sentinel,* 31 August: A7.

Sudarkasa, Niara. 1991–92. "Don't Write Off Thomas," *The Black Scholar* 22, no. 1–2: 99–102.

Thorne, Barrie. 1992. "Review of *Black Feminist Thought: Knowledge, Conciousness, and the Politics of Empowerment* by Patricia Hill Collins," *Gender and Society* 6, no. 3: 515–17.

Walby, Sylvia. 1992. "Women and Nation," *International Journal of Comparative Sociology* 33, no. 1–2: 80–99.

West, Lois A. 1992. "Feminist Nationalist Social Movements: Beyond Universalism and Towards a Gendered Cultural Relativism," *Women's Studies International Forum* 15, no. 5–6: 563–79.

White, E. Frances. 1990. "Africa on My Mind: Gender, Counter Discourse and African-American Nationalism," *Journal of Women's History* 2, no. 1: 73–97.

Wilson, William Julius. 1987. *The Truly Disadvantaged: The Inner City, the Underclass, and Public Policy.* Chicago: University of Chicago Press.

INTERSECTIONS, LOCATIONS, AND CAPITALIST CLASS RELATIONS: INTERSECTIONALITY FROM A MARXIST PERSPECTIVE

JOHANNA BRENNER

In feminist theory "intersectionality" has emerged as an analytic strategy to address the interrelation of multiple, crosscutting institutionalized power relations defined by race, class, gender, and sexuality (and other axes of domination). Most intersectional analysis focuses at the level of social location, a "place" defined by these intersecting axes of domination, and asks how a social location shapes experience and identity. If feminism is to become a powerful movement again, working-class women will have to organize across the divides of race/ethnicity and sexuality. It is therefore of political importance to understand how class locations, in intersection with race/ethnicity and sexuality, shape women's survival projects, their strategies for claiming self-worth and exercising public authority, their uses of motherhood as an identity, and their responses to cultural constructions of their sexuality. Due account must be taken of class differences within racial/ethnic groups as well as class similarities across racial/ethnic divides as a route toward delineating the potential common ground for a working-class women's politics and for a feminist politics of class.[*]

The following analysis shifts the focus to consider class as social relations of production. It shows how the possibilities for resistance in different class locations develop within a political context which is in turn shaped by capitalist relations of production, by the dynamics of the capitalist economy and the powers of the capitalist class. I argue that global capitalist restructuring has reconfigured the political terrain in the U.S., with profound strategic implications for feminism and other movements of liberation.

CAPITALIST CLASS POWER AND
THE POLITICS OF RESISTANCE

The civil rights and feminist movements combined revolutionary and reformist aims, their radical wings seeking to redistribute economic and political power. Though falling far short of this goal, the movements did dismantle the old gender and racial orders and opened the field for other movements against oppression (for example, gay/lesbian rights, disability rights). They have made it possible for a new left challenge, when it develops, to be far more self-consciously and powerfully anti-racist, anti-sexist, and anti-heterosexist than any that has gone before.[1] On the other hand, by almost any measure, neither racial oppression nor male domination have disappeared from the scene. They have, however, been fundamentally reorganized. Both operate, now, not through an explicit, legally and culturally authorized system of exclusion, but through a process of incorporation that systemically reproduces disadvantage. Elsewhere I have made the argument for this claim in the case of male dominance.[2] Here, I briefly recapitulate it, and then lay out the parallel for the reorganization of institutionalized racism.

The exclusion of women from higher-paid occupations and the male-bread-winner/female-housewife family, which underwrote patriarchal power, have been overturned. Yet male dominance continues, because feminism has been signally unable to win significant changes in the organization of social reproduction. Caregiving remains the privatized responsibility of family/households. No matter how women restrict their childbearing, the needs of adults and children continue to weigh heavily on their shoulders. Women in the upper reaches of the class structure—women in the higher professions and management positions—can buy their way out of responsibilities, but most women cannot. Men and women are negotiating different kinds of bargains about how to share caregiving responsibilities.[3] But so long as these responsibilities remain individual rather than social, households will be forced to organize a division of labor around them and women will continue to be disadvantaged relative to men in the labor market. Further, so long as solo motherhood remains so very difficult, while women will choose it when they need to, the double burden of being a bread-winner and caregiver will continue to underwrite not only a backward-looking political and cultural nostalgia about the nuclear family but also women's investments in and tolerance for reformed, but still "patriarchal," bargains in family households.[4]

The forces arrayed against changing this underpinning of male dominance are formidable. To make social reproduction a more collective responsibility would require a serious redistribution of wealth. Thus feminism's next wave will have to make common cause with and be part of a broad, anticapitalist, rainbow movement, including trade unions that are truly social-movement organizations.

In her analysis of the impasse facing black feminism, Patricia Hill Collins argues similarly that the gains of the civil rights and feminist movements have contributed to a reorganization of the racial order rather than the demise of institutionalized racism and racialized politics. Although successful in breaking down the explicit, legalized, and culturally sanctioned segregation that defined the horizons of black life for over a century, the civil rights movement, like the feminist movement, has not been able to improve significantly the lives of the majority of black people, while opening up previously unthinkable opportunities for a relatively small group. Class divisions among black women have grown wider. The upward mobility of the black middle class has weakened the community base of the civil rights movement, and the visible success of some black women obscures and mystifies the continuing systemic and institutionalized racism that disadvantages the majority. Increased access to political, residential, and employment spaces for some black women, she argues, is paired with the intractable impoverishment of the majority. Further, the breakup of black civil society—the loss of institutions that developed in the segregated communities which defined black life up through the civil rights era—have undermined the practices, such as community work, that fostered a black women's tradition of resistance. To address this new impasse, Collins says, black feminists have to recommit themselves to supporting, organizing for, and representing the needs of working-class and poor black women. She argues secondly for a break from the sexism and homophobia that have infused Afrocentrism, calling for a racial solidarity that is sensitive to black heterogeneity and difference and prepared to engage in principled coalitions.[5]

Thus, the problems facing the feminist and civil rights movements are parallel. In both instances, tremendous gains for the middle class are matched by continuing difficulties for an increasingly impoverished working class.[6] My point is not at all to refocus our attention on class to the exclusion of race or gender. The persistence of race and gender discrimination is well documented, even for the middle class.[7] Many African Americans' foothold in the middle class is certainly more tenuous than that of white men. While having moved out of the urban ghettos, black people live in segregated suburbs that are less affluent than white suburbs.[8] Still, the rise of a black intelligentsia, of black professionals, political office holders, corporate managers, and high-level state administrators is a historic change. The question remains, though, why hasn't it been possible for the black working class to take advantage of the same openings? For the African-American working class to reach even the distressed levels of the white working class would require a serious redistribution of income and wealth, through expansion of public investment in communities and housing, in schooling and access to higher education, and by the creation of living-wage jobs. If the potential for state intervention to end black poverty was undermined by racism during the 1960s,[9] it surely will not be fulfilled until the political balance of forces is shifted decisively leftward and with a much more heightened awareness of how institutionalized racism has scuttled previous efforts. The way out of the impasse facing the black working class cannot be found in reinvigorating the political thrust of the single-issue politics of the 1960s. At least in its assimilationist goals, that strategy has come up against structural and political limits. The successful political campaigns against affirmative action; the reinvigorated racist political discourses around crime, welfare, and immigration; the cutbacks in spending for social services and housing—these are not a simple "political backlash," a pendulum-swing to the right which is bound to move back. They are the political effects of profound changes in the economy. The drift of politics in the U.S. steadily to the right over the past twenty years will only be halted by a broad-based, multi-issue movement that combines the forces of many different groups in order to confront capital's formidable political and economic power.

The civil rights revolution failed to carry the majority of black people into the mainstream of the U.S. economy because, to put it simply, by the time the black working class finally got a ticket to ride the train that had carried other excluded groups into the mainstream, the train was no longer running. As Karen Brodkin so persuasively shows, in the post-Second World War era the combination of government intervention (especially the GI bill and housing programs) and unprecedented economic growth and prosperity laid the basis for the men of previously denigrated and excluded ethnic groups, and particularly Jews, to "become white."[10] The war against fascism had perhaps helped to undermine popular anti-Semitism, but we should not put too much weight on this factor. In many communities prejudice toward Jews remained quite strong, even after the war. Yet although the anti-communist right fulminated against Jews, by the early 1950s, in the context of a booming economy and what amounted to an affirmative action program which addressed broad segments of the working class, their anti-Semitism had little political purchase. However, blacks were systematically denied access to the government programs that provided suburban home-ownership, college education, and thus occupational upward mobility for many working-class ethnic males.[11] The gains made by ethnic groups of European origin, accrued in the 1950s, were passed down to the next generations and then used to sustain racist myths about the inferiority of black culture.

By the time the civil rights movement finally won for black people even a small part of the kind of consistent federal support that had propelled Jews and other "Euro-American" men into the middle class and across the color line, the economic conditions that had allowed for such upward mobility were about to disappear. Almost as the movements were coming into their own—from the mid-1960s through the early 1970s—the U.S. economy was entering into a sea change which culminated in the current reconfiguration and dominance of capitalist class power. As the postwar hegemony of U.S. corporate capital began to give way with the rise of new and quite powerful international competitors, profit margins began to narrow, and the corporations launched an offensive on wages and working conditions as a strategy to restore profits.[12] The bureaucratized labor unions were totally unprepared for this "new class war" and unwilling to take the risks involved in breaking away from the corporatist strategies that had allowed them to build their organizations in the period of prosperity.[13] The employers' offensive sparked defensive rank-and-file revolts and an upsurge in militancy in the early 1970s. But, with the exception of the black revolutionary union movements in Detroit, these revolts only rarely connected with the student, civil rights, feminist, and antiwar movements of their time. And they failed to shift fundamentally the "business union" strategies of their ossified union leaderships. By the 1980s, many corporations had turned away from squeezing manufacturing workers to simply dumping them altogether. Deindustrialization in the old centers of production, movement of manufacturing to the south and overseas, then the emergence of more flexible production processes and outsourcing—all pushed organized workers further onto the defensive.[14] There were many inspiring struggles by working-class communities in these years. And some activists, as they reached out across the country for support, found new allies among the other movements, in the course of their struggle expanding and even radicalizing their own political world-views.[15] But these battles were almost all lost. Plants just shut down. And if they didn't, the employers were able to force workers into harsh bargains that included wage cuts, changes in work rules, loss of control over schedules, speed-ups, and so on. Between 1980 and 1984, union membership in the private sector declined from 20.1 percent to 15.6 percent of the workforce. By 1996 only 10.2 percent of workers in private industry were unionized.[16]

As the old industrial centers died, so did the communities dependent on them. This was, of course, especially fateful for black urban communities dependent on stable, unionized working-class jobs.[17] During the 1970s, while affirmative-action policy and anti-discrimination legislation was opening up opportunities for higher education and professional/managerial employment to middle-class white women and people of color, good blue-collar jobs were disappearing. Urban renewal and deindustrialization, along with expanding opportunities for residential mobility for blacks who had the means to move out further, undermined the economic base of inner-city neighborhoods. White flight and suburbanization did the rest of the job, so by the time black urban residents were able to use the political muscle won through their civil rights struggle, they found themselves holding power in cities with a shrinking economic base in states where legislatures were increasingly hostile.

The political hostility, the intensified and racialized conflict between suburb and city, and the movement of white working-class communities away from the Democratic Party also had their roots in the employers' offensive.[18] The civil rights and women's movements really did threaten white male monopolies. Although this challenge would have always produced resistance, economic expansion, such as in the post-Second World War years, which saw real improvements in the standards of living of almost all working-class people, would also have softened the blow and helped to undercut the racist appeals of the right. Instead, working-class communities faced declining wages, job loss, shrinking opportunities, and increasing economic insecurity. Increasing economic competition intensifies reliance on existing group solidarities, solidarities that arise out of the ways that people come together to organize their everyday survival. These survival projects, organized through kin and other social networks as well as in the workplace, will in the ordinary course of events reproduce rather than disrupt the occupational and residential racial/ethnic segregation which is the basis for racial/ethnic conflict. To be clear: this is not an argument against anti-racism political strategies or for supposedly "universal" as opposed to "targeted" government programs. It is rather to say that economic and political conditions are related, that the past gains were made under conditions which will not return, and that a new antiracism offensive will only be possible if it is tied to an anticapitalist politics—allied to a broad coalition for economic and social justice.

Without the capacity to organize a collective response to the employers' offensive, white working-class people inevitably were mobilized to hold onto whatever advantages they could command, displacing their anger and fear onto the most vulnerable and powerless segments of society. Obviously, this is not the first time racist appeals and scapegoating have successfully divided U.S. working people.

In the absence of a more collective and inclusive response to economic instability, group resentment and political mobilization on the basis of narrow group interests are the order of the day. Omi and Winant make the point that even if white racism is deeply rooted, nonetheless a white backlash was not inevitable. "A more comprehensive series of reforms, for example, might have extended to redistribution initiatives and full-employment commitments, which could have cushioned the blow that whites located in marginal neighborhoods, school districts, jobs, etc. received when affirmative action and similar programs increased competition for semiskilled work, public education, and affordable housing."[19] Of course, the major cause of white workers' deteriorating living standards was the employers' offensive against workers' wages, jobs, and working conditions, an assault which weighed even more heavily on the black working class. However, the policies and programs that would have helped protect workers from the consequences of this assault were certainly not in the cards. As the economic room for contesting corporate power shrank, so did the political space for countering corporate interests. A full-employment policy, proposed during the 1970s and 1980s by the trade unions to soften the blows of dislocation and to strengthen the bargaining position of workers, never got off the ground. Instead, federally enforced legal protections for organizing were gutted.[20]

The right's mobilization of racist feelings and ideologies took form not only in an attack on aggressive state intervention to redress racial discrimination (especially campaigns against affirmative action, bilingual education, etc.) but also in an attack on the public sector more generally—both public-sector workers and users of social-welfare programs (especially clear in welfare reform and anti-immigration legislation). The mobilization of anti-immigrant sentiment has not been limited to the white working class; increasing competition between nonwhite racial/ethnic groups and increasing class division within them has also been the basis for attacks on immigrants as part of a broader assault on the "undeserving" poor.[21]

As the drift to the right has gained momentum, conservative interest groups have been able to capture increasing shares of the state budget. Thus, not only was funding for public services—especially those directed to the poor (in the hegemonic figuration of the class system, an "underclass" made up predominantly of people of color)—generally under attack. The 1980s and 1990s also saw increasing shifts away from social spending and toward spending on the coercive arm of the state—a rise in military spending as a portion of the federal budget and the rapid growth of prisons to the point that it makes sense to speak of a prison-industrial complex.[22]

This rise of the right through a politics of opposition to the "liberal" welfare state also has its origins in the employers' offensive. The expansion of the welfare state began in the 1950s but accelerated in the 1960s as a response to the urban rebellions and the increasingly well-organized groups making claims for state services.[23] Increased government spending, whether at the federal, state, or local level, was never financed by serious transfers of wealth. After averaging 45 percent in the 1950s, corporate tax rates began a sharp decline in the 1960s, reaching 24 percent in 1994.[24] Effective tax rates on the incomes of the wealthy were only very mildly redistributive and since the mid-1970s have become much less so.[25] The burden of funding for the U.S. welfare state falls on wage and salary incomes—a system of financing which emerged from the defeat of more interventionist strategies. Although during the 1930s there was real debate in policy circles over strategies to manage the economy, by the end of the Second World War an interventionist model of the state had been decisively marginalized in favor of what has been called "growth liberalism."[26] In this approach, government's role is confined to using fiscal power—its capacity to tax and spend—to maintain purchasing power and to fuel economic expansion. Management of the economy through wage-setting, powerful regulatory institutions, or publicly owned production was rejected in favor of demand stimulation and restrained social welfare spending. In comparison to the social-democratic regimes that emerged in many other capitalist economies, the postwar accord between labor and capital created a segmented system of income security, pensions, and health benefits. Unionized workers earned pension and health benefits through their contracts, leaving those in the lower tiers of the working class dependent on the public sector.[27]

This system worked relatively well during the prosperous postwar boom years. A rising tide did lift all boats, although not equally, and it was possible to build a "guns and butter" state through taxing the working class and middle class. With real income rising, taxation did not loom large as a political issue. The employers' offensive, however, quickly exposed the fundamental weaknesses of this foundation for welfare-state liberalism. During the 1970s, while median real family income declined by 16 percent, taxes increased as a proportion of workers' income. The revolts against property taxes in the late 1970s were simply the beginning of a successful conservative mobilization around the issue of taxation and spending.[28]

The conservative movement that emerged in the 1970s but took over U.S. politics in the 1980s was an alliance of two overlapping but distinct political movements. The religious right created its strength out of the Christian churches and on the basis of a backlash against feminism and gay/lesbian rights movements. The modernizing right has staked its claim much more firmly in a classic liberal political world-view. Thus, their neoliberalism has incorporated the individual-rights discourses of the civil rights movements rearticulated as the right to fair competition on the market. Although the religious right has caused feminism and the gay/lesbian movement a lot of pain, the real conservative success story lies in the dominance of the modernizing right's world-view. Clinton's rhetoric on welfare in the 1992 campaign captured this shift very well, particularly the celebration of work as a moral issue (working mothers are good role models who break the "cycle of dependence"), which reproduced rather than challenged the now standard and pervasive representation of black poor single mothers as undeserving welfare queens. The modernizing right's discourse depends on the contrast between the deserving—those who wish to make it through their own efforts (a hand up)—and the undeserving—namely, those who argue for group support (a hand out). Efforts by the government to improve the lives of people collectively are delegitimized by this framing. Instead, the role of the state is to "help" those who need it to enter into the market and to enjoy the supposedly equal opportunities for upward mobility awaiting those willing to make the effort. While New Democrats put a slightly more populist spin on this basic conservative message, they have essentially adopted it. As civil rights and women's organizations are forced to struggle on this terrain, they have pragmatically adapted to the limits of available discourses, reproducing rather than challenging the conservative terms of the debate.

As I argued in my analysis of the political consensus on welfare reform, the "middle-class" representatives advocating for communities of color—directors of nonprofit organizations, social-service providers, public health workers, and so on—shifted their political strategies in response to the rapid decline of support for government investments in their communities. Navigating within increasingly conservative political waters and without a politically mobilized social base, they adapted their political rhetoric and demands to suit the times. Mainstream civil rights organizations have joined with black conservatives and black nationalists to justify social-service programs in terms of their value for morally uplifting the black working class, now redefined as an underclass. This shift has also been fueled by a masculinist political current that has been historically dominant in communities of color.[29] The crisis of the black male, like the panic about (black) teen pregnancy, comes to justify state funding for services that target behavioral reform.[30] Whatever successes advocates may have in grasping some of the shrinking state funds for their own programs, they pay for these gains in reinforcing the very ideologies which have justified funding cutbacks in the first place. That is, the focus on the "bad character" of the "underclass" supports eliminating hard-won public programs, now disparaged as entitlements that breed "dependence" in favor of the bracing independence and self-help of the market economy. At the same time, as Barbara Omolade argues, political statements, such as the Million Man March, which mobilize around themes of black male responsibility, strike a responsive emotional chord among women who struggle with single parenthood and extremely conflictual gender relations.[31] Here, too, we see the political consequences of our movements' failure to wrest concessions from the state that would lighten women's burdens of caregiving.

Advocates' failure to move resources into their communities leaves their working-class base stranded.[32] The pattern of dramatic class cleavage within the black community has been repeated in many others as a consequence of global capitalist restructuring, and the recent wave of immigration to the U.S., particularly into "Asian" and "Latino" communities. Bringing very different cultural capitals and economic resources with them, and in certain instances benefiting from large federal subsidies, some new immigrants have done quite well, while many others have filled the ranks of the expanding working class.[33] At the same time, political openings in the state apparatus and elective offices increase opportunities for individuals to play a brokering role as representatives of their respective racial/ethnic groups. New relationships between the local state and urban racial/ethnic enclaves have created more complex power structures internally, while at the same time increasing competition among racial/ethnic groups jockeying for position with regard to public spending and investments.[34]

The working classes in these communities have spoken politically and sporadically through riots/rebellions, mobilizations for immigrant rights, community–labor coalitions around union organizing drives, and other grassroots struggles.[35] But their voices are muted compared to those of their middle-class spokespeople.[36]

To understand, then, both the gains and impasses of the civil rights and women's movements, their ability to challenge so thoroughly and to change ways of thinking about race and gender and their inability to sustain this challenge, it is helpful to put them in the context of the periods of capitalist economic transformation. The economic changes that were already reshaping the political landscape in the 1970s and 1980s accelerated in the 1990s: the expansion of markets and production, the increase in labor migration both within and across national borders, the flexibility and mobility of investment/production, the penetration of global firms into the U.S. economy not only in goods but in services, the increasing freeing of global firms from control and regulation by national states. The capitalist restructuring that first undermined the conditions of blue-collar workers in core manufacturing industries now threatens security and stability of jobs in many sectors—from middle-managers and supervisors to production workers.

At the core of these changes are not simply globalization but capital's increasing flexibility, mobility, and concentrated power, as well as the intensity of capitalist competition and the employers' drive to squeeze ever more out of the workforce. A highly competitive and turbulent economy now dominates life in the U.S. As in the significant periods of capitalist restructuring that preceded this one, the institutions of working-class political and economic defense that had been built up under the old paradigm and that might have worked (although not all that well) previously are now utterly unable to respond to new conditions. Until some alternatives develop, the political hegemony of the modernizing right can be expected to remain in place.

Even if no quick or easy solution seems to be on the horizon, the situation is not without realistic hopes and expectations for renewed contestation and political organization. The U.S. working class has become more immigrant, more racially/ethnically diverse, more low-waged, and more female. And the trade unions, although weak in terms of the percentage of the labor force who are members of unions, are groping toward new, more militant, more democratic, more political, and more community-based modes of struggle. In response to global capital's vicious exploitation of the environment as well as the workforce, coalitions of environmental groups and trade unions have been formed.[37] Labor is changing partly because it has no choice, partly because new groups of workers have organized within the trade unions to make new demands: gay/lesbian workers have organized for their unions to take a stand on and contribute to campaigns for lesbian/gay rights; feminist union members have forced their unions to "come out" for abortion rights, to see support for these rights as a union issue; immigrants are organizing. Grassroots worker solidarity organizations, like Jobs With Justice, have built international labor solidarity and raised the consciousness of U.S. workers through cross-border organizing campaigns.[38] New community-based organizations which bridge trade-union organizing with struggles for racial justice have emerged.[39] For the first time there is a real possibility for a coalitional politics, for a rainbow movement organized around a broad agenda of social and economic justice.[40] Of course, there are currents running in a very different direction, and they are, right now, the stronger. Still, we, all of us who won't settle for what the powerful intend, have no choice but to stake our future on this possibility, engaging in the "visionary pragmatism"[41] that has animated resistance to oppression and the struggle for justice in every generation.

NOTES

* This study originally comprised two parts: the first follows the usual approach of intersectional analysis by concentrating on social location; the second shifts the terrain to focus on class as social relations of production. The present text reproduces the latter part. The full essay is published in Johanna Brenner, *Women and the Politics of Class* (New York: Monthly Review Press, 2001).

1. On anti-sexist consciousness in new Latino/a student movements, see Elizabeth Martinez, *De Colores Means All of Us* (Cambridge, MA: South End Press, 1998), 216–17, 165–69.
2. In Brenner, *Women and the Politics of Class.*
3. Stephanie Coontz, *The Way We Really Are* (New York: Basic Books, 1997), chap. 3; Louise Lamphere, Patricia Zavella, and Felipe Gonzales, with Peter B. Evans, *Sunbelt Working Mothers: Reconciling Family and Factory* (Ithaca: Cornell University Press, 1993).
4. Judith Stacey, "What Comes After Patriarchy? Comparative Reflections on Gender and Power in a 'Post-Patriarchal' Age," and Linda Gordon and Alan Hunter, "Not All Male Dominance is Patriarchal," both in *Radical History Review* 71 (1998): 63–83.
5. Patricia Hill Collins, *Fighting Words: Black Women and the Search for Justice* (Minneapolis: University of Minnesota Press, 1998), 30–32, 182–83.
6. White women's gains have been greater proportionally, because they are more evenly distributed within the class structure.
7. Sharlene Hesse-Biber and Gregg Lee Carter, *Working Women in America: Split Dreams* (New York: Oxford University Press, 2000), 40–52.
8. Dennis R. Judd, "Symbolic Politics and Urban Policies: Why African Americans Got So Little from the Democrats," in Adolph Reed, Jr., ed., *Without Justice for All: The New Liberalism and Our Retreat from Racial Equality* (Boulder, CO: Westview Press, 1999), 144–47.
9. Jill Quadagno, *The Color of Welfare: How Racism Undermined the War on Poverty* (New York: Oxford, 1994).
10. Karen Brodkin, *How Jews Became White Folks and What That Says About Race in America* (New Brunswick, NJ: Rutgers University Press, 1998), chap. 1.
11. Ibid.; see also Judd, "Symbolic Politics and Urban Policies," 126–31.
12. Aaron Brenner, "Rank and File Rebellion, 1966–1975" (Ph.D. dissertation, Columbia University, 1996), 30–49.
13. Ibid., 56–62.
14. Kim Moody, *Workers in a Lean World* (London: Verso, 1997), 51–113.
15. Ibid., 23–31; Neala J. Schleuning, *Women, Community, and the Hormel Strike of 1985–86* (Westport, CT: Greenwood Press, 1994).
16. Moody, *Workers in a Lean World*, 183; Mike Davis, *Prisoners of the American Dream* (London: Verso, 1986), 147.
17. On the impact of deindustrialization on the Black community in Los Angeles, Detroit, and Birmingham, see Mike Davis, "Los Angeles: Civil Liberties between the Hammer and the Rock," *New Left Review* 170 (July–August 1988): 37–60, esp. 47–52; Tomas J. Sugrue, *The Origins of the Urban Crisis: Race and Inequality in Postwar Detroit* (Princeton: Princeton University Press, 1996); Robin D. G. Kelly, *Race Rebels: Culture, Politics, and the Black Working Class* (New York: The Free Press, 1994), chap. 4, esp. 93–100.
18. I am interested here particularly in the inroads of the right in the working-class base, the ways in which race divided working-class people. This is not intended as an overall analysis of the rise of the right in U.S. politics.
19. Michael Omi and Howard Winant, *Racial Formation in the United States: From the 1960s to the 1990s*, 2d ed. (New York: Routledge, 1994), 208 n.63.
20. Davis, *Prisoners of the American Dream*, 131–35, 138–40.
21. Martinez, *De Colores Means All of Us*, 200–01, 243–44.
22. Angela Y. Davis, "Race and Criminalization: Black Americans and the Punishment Industry," in Wahneema Lubiano, ed., *The House that Race Built* (New York: Vintage, 1998), 264–79.

23. Francis Fox Piven, "The Welfare State as Work Enforcer," *Dollars and Sense*, September–October 1999: 32–34.

24. Nancy Folbre and the Center for Popular Economics, *The New Field Guide to the U.S. Economy* (New York: The New Press, 1995), 5.12.

25. Lawrence Mishel, Jared Bernstein, and John Schmitt, *The State of Working America, 1998–99* (Ithaca: Cornell University Press, 1999), 99–118; Joseph Pechman, *The Rich, the Poor, and the Taxes They Pay* (Boulder, CO: Westview Press, 1986), 31–39.

26. Alan Brinkley, "The New Deal and the Idea of the State," in Steve Fraser and Gary Gerstle, eds., *The Rise and Fall of the New Deal Order: 1930–1980* (Princeton: Princeton University Press, 1989), 85–121.

27. For an analysis of labor's defeat and the emergence of this accord, see Nelson Lichtenstein, "From Corporatism to Collective Bargaining: Organized Labor and the Eclipse of Social Democracy in the Postwar Era," in Fraser and Gerstle, eds., *The Rise and Fall of the New Deal Order*, 122–52.

28. Michael K. Brown, "The Segmented Welfare System: Distributive Conflict and Retrenchment in the United States, 1968–1984," in Michael K. Brown, ed., *Remaking the Welfare State: Retrenchment and Social Policy in America and Europe* (Philadelphia: Temple University Press, 1988), 182–210.

29. Leith Mullings, *On Our Own Terms: Race, Class, and Gender in the Lives of African American Women* (New York: Routledge, 1997), 135–46; see also Martinez, *De Colores Means All of Us*, 172–81.

30. Willie M. Legett, "The Crisis of the Black Male: A New Ideology in Black Politics," and Preston H. Smith, "'Self-Help,' Black Conservatives, and the Reemergence of Black Privatism," both in Reed, ed., *Without Justice for All*.

31. Barbara Omolade, *The Rising Song of African American Women* (New York: Routledge, 1994), chap. 5; see also Mullings, *On Our Own Terms*, 146–48.

32. The politics of urban regimes and the failure of even those controlled by black mayors to shift substantial resources to the urban working class and poor is a complex issue. For a subtle and perceptive analysis of the politics and policies of black office holders and public managers, see Adolph Reed, Jr., *Stirrings in the Jug: Black Politics in the Post-Segregation Era* (Minneapolis: University of Minnesota Press, 1999); on their adaptation to the political climate, see 204–05.

33. On the impact of "massive state assistance" for middle-class Cuban immigrants, as well as the class relations internal to the Miami Cuban community, see Alex Stepick III and Guillermo Grenier, "Cubans in Miami," in Joan Moore and Raquel Pinderhughes, eds., *In the Barrios: Latinos and the Underclass Debate* (New York: Russell Sage Foundation, 1993), 79–100. On differential fates of Asian immigrants, see Paul Ong, Edna Bonacich, and Lucie Cheng, eds., *The New Asian Immigration in Los Angeles and Global Restructuring* (Philadelphia: Temple University Press, 1994). On class differences and the new immigration, see Jan Lin, *Reconstructing Chinatown: Ethnic Enclave, Global Change* (Minneapolis: University of Minnesota Press, 1998).

34. On divisions among communities of color, see, for example, "Melvin L. Oliver, James H. Johnson, Jr., and Walter Farrell, Jr., "Anatomy of a Rebellion: A Political-Economic Analysis," in Robert Gooding-Williams, ed., *Reading Rodney King, Reading Urban Uprising* (New York: Routledge, 1993); Alejandro Portes and Alex Stepick, "A Repeat Performance? The Nicaraguan Exodus," in Mary Romero, Pierrette Hondagneu-Sotelo, and Vilma Ortiz, eds., *Challenging Fronteras: Structuring Latina and Latino Lives in the U.S.* (New York: Routledge, 1997); Martinez, *De Colores Means All of Us*, 75–80. On the brokering role of the middle class, see Reed, *Stirrings*; Yen Espiritu and Paul Ong, "Class Constraints on Racial Solidarity among Asian Americans," in Ong et al., *The*

New Asian Immigration, 295–321.

35. Eric Mann, "Class, Community and Empire: Toward an Anti-Imperialist Strategy for Labor," in Ellen Meiksins Wood, Peter Meiksins, and Michael Yates, eds., *Rising From the Ashes? Labor in the Age of "Global" Capitalism* (New York: Monthly Review Press, 1998), 100–09; Moody, *Workers in a Lean World*, 170–78.

36. On middle-class bias in Asian-American organizations, see Espiritu and Ong, "Class Constraints."

37. Martinez, *De Colores Means All of Us*, 108–16. For those of us participating in the truly massive demonstrations that disrupted the meetings of the World Trade Organization in Seattle, November 29–30, 1999, this potential for a broad coalition of labor, environment, and social justice groups seemed to be closer to reality than ever.

38. These grassroots organizations as well as the reform movements within the official trade unions, such as Teamsters for a Democratic Union, represent a force for challenging the economic nationalism of the trade-union officialdom (and for winning rank-and-file workers to more internationalist perspectives). For an analysis of these political prospects, see Kim Moody, "Global Capital and Economic Nationalism: Protectionism or Solidarity?" *Against the Current* 14, no. 3 (July–August 2000): 34–38, and "Global Capital and Economic Nationalism: Finding Protection in the Crowd," *Against the Current* 14, no. 4 (September–October 2000): 25–29.

39. For example, the Workers Organizing Committee in Portland, Oregon; the Chinese Staff and Worker Association in New York City; the Bus Riders Union in Los Angeles; Black Workers for Justice in Rocky Mountain, North Carolina. Lin, *Reconstructing Chinatown*, 192–93; Mann, "Class, Community and Empire," 103–06.

40. For explorations of such a coalitional politics, see Iris Young, "Polity and Group Difference: A Critique of the Ideal of Universal Citizenship," and Bernice Johnson Reagon, "Coalition Politics: Turning the Century," both in Anne Phillips, ed., *Feminism and Politics* (New York: Oxford University Press, 1998); Chela Sandoval, "Mestizaje as Method: Feminists-of-Color Challenge the Canon," in Carola Trujillo, ed., *Living Chicana Theory* (Berkeley: Third Woman Press, 1998), 352–70.

41. I borrow this phrase from Stanlie M. James and Abena P. A. Busia, eds., *Theorizing Black Feminisms: The Visionary Pragmatism of Black Women* (London and New York: Routledge, 1993).

PART VI

NATURE, SOCIETY, AND KNOWLEDGE

THE FEMINIST STANDPOINT REVISITED

NANCY HARTSOCK

I first wrote a draft of my essay "The Feminist Standpoint", then subtitled "Developing the Ground for a Specifically Feminist Historical Materialism," in December 1978 as a commentary on a paper Sandra Harding presented at the American Philosophy Association annual meeting. I continued to rewrite it until the summer of 1981, when it assumed a form close to its published version. In the years since I wrote the essay, the many arguments in feminist theory have included those centered on standpoint theory, as opposed to postmodernism and critiques of standpoint theory on postmodernist grounds. I am not, of course, the only person to have made standpoint-type arguments; a number of people who have commented on my essay have characterized others as standpoint theorists as well.[1] As the debate has widened, it has become possible to find discussions of standpoint theory as a general category of feminist analysis with no names attached.[2] And in these cases, the account of standpoint theory is sometimes fanciful. On more than one occasion I found myself wondering what possible sources the author could be referring to.

MY PROJECT

Here, then, I want to clarify the points I was trying to make, and rewrite and update the argument to correct some of what I see as its important flaws. Many of the published critiques of my work seem to represent significant misreadings of the project. I was attempting to follow the lead of Marx and Lukács. I wanted to translate the concept of the standpoint of the proletariat, by analogy, into feminist terms. Marx, in *Capital*, adopted a simple two-class model, in which everything exchanged at its value. And only a few pages before the end of Volume 3, he stated, "At last we come to the problem of class," which he would show to be more complicated and demanding of subtle treatment. The manuscript, however, breaks off without presenting such an analysis. But given the fruitfulness of Marx's strategy, I adopted by analogy a simple two-party opposition between feminists and masculinist representatives of patriarchy. Following Lukács's essay, "Reification and the Standpoint of the Proletariat,"[3] I wanted to translate the notion of the standpoint of the proletariat (including its historic mission) into feminist terms. I wanted to reformulate his arguments in my essay, in the light of his corrective 1967 introduction to *History and Class Consciousness*, which makes some important self-critical points. In particular there Lukács noted the importance of his failure to begin his analysis with labor rather than with the reified forms of commodities in capitalism—that is, to begin his analysis with human activity itself.

I was arguing that, like the lives of proletarians in Marxist theory, women's lives also contain possibilities for developing critiques of domination and visions of alternative social arrangements. By examining the institutionalized sexual division of labor, I argued that a feminist standpoint could be developed that would deepen the critique available from the standpoint of the proletariat and allow for a critique of patriarchal ideology and social relations that would provide a more complete account of the domination of women than Marx's critique of capitalism.

There were several contentions involved in my formulation of the idea of a feminist standpoint. Most important, I posited a series of levels of reality in which the deeper level both includes and explains the surface or appearance. I have come to understand that the notion of levels of reality is very unpopular and that surfaces are all that is credible now. But the surface and depth metaphor is not necessary to feminist standpoint projects; nor are the psychoanalytically based theories of Nancy Chodorow. Still, I think that standpoint projects are important and useful for most oppressed groups.

The most important aspects of standpoint theory bear repeating here.

1. Material life (class position in Marxist theory) not only structures but also sets limits on understandings of social relations.

2. If material life is structured in fundamentally opposing ways for two different groups, one can expect that the understanding of each will represent an inversion of the other, and in systems of domination the understanding available to the ruling group will be both partial and perverse (by which I mean to suggest both strange and harmful).[4] I would add as a reformulation that there are a variety of inversions that "match" the variety of dominant and subordinate groups.

3. The vision of the ruling group can be expected to structure the material relations in which all people are forced to participate and therefore cannot be dismissed as simply false consciousness. Not only do we all have no choice but to participate in the market, but today we also hear and read incessantly about the virtues of the market in solving all problems and promoting democracy.

4. In consequence, the vision available to an oppressed group must be struggled for and represents an achievement that requires both systematic analysis and

the education that can only grow from political struggle to change those relations.

5. As an engaged vision, the potential understanding of the oppressed, the adoption of a standpoint, makes visible the inhumanity of relations among human beings and carries a historically liberatory role.[5] For Marx, the liberatory role of the proletariat was in part a function of its historical mission. I would like to substitute for that understanding bell hooks's phrase of yearning for a better and more just world.[6]

As I have thought through the criticisms and reassessed my own argument, I have been struck by a paradox. First, the critiques are enabled and supported by a failure to recognize the Marxist dimension of my work, with its emphasis on historically specific social relations among groups rather than individuals. Thus, a number of the critiques read my essay in ways that locate it within a liberal humanist tradition. At the same time, I believe that the flaws in my argument are directly attributable to my efforts to locate the argument within the Marxist tradition, efforts that took the specific form of an attempt to theorize women's position by analogy to that of the proletariat and that depended on a too-literal reading of Marx's own too-schematic two-class model of society. The debates around my essay, then, and debates about standpoint epistemologies more generally have suffered from, on the one hand, a reading of the argument uninformed by familiarity with Marxist traditions and, on the other, my too-rigid insistence on the applicability of the two-class model of society to the situation of women in advanced capitalism.

As I have reflected on both these and other discussions of standpoint theories over the years, I have come to believe that it is this intertwining of issues of politics with more traditional philosophical questions concerning truth and knowledge, along with their conflicting criteria for claims of epistemological validity, that has been responsible for much of the controversy. That is, standpoint theories must be recognized as essentially contested in much the same way that I have argued the concept of power is essentially contested: arguments about how to understand power rest on differing epistemologies. These same issues being in play may account for the existence of so many (conflicting) interpretations of the meaning of feminist standpoint theories. Still, I prefer now to see this proliferation of interpretations as an indication that standpoint theories provide a fertile terrain for feminist debates about power, politics, and epistemology.

REFORMULATIONS

But there are problems with my argument; in particular, it worked to subsume the "marked" categories of feminists (feminists of color) under the unmarked and therefore white feminist, and lesbian under the category of straight, just as women have been subsumed under the category "man." That is, in following

Marx's procedure of reducing the world to a two-class, two-man model, I ended up with a problem similar to his own—that is, unable to see important axes of domination, even while recognizing their operation. Thus, Marx was clear that widows were part of the lower layer of the reserve army of the unemployed. At the same time, he lost track of women's labor in reproducing the working class. So whereas I too took note of some race and class differences in terms of the sexual division of labor, I made no theoretical space that would have accorded them proper significance.

In revisiting the argument I made for a feminist standpoint, I want both to pluralize the idea and to preserve its utility as an instrument of struggle against dominant groups. I believe that the task facing all theorists committed to social change is that of working to construct some theoretical bases for political solidarity. Such theoretical bases are no substitute for collective action and coalition building but are a necessary adjunct to them. In revising the notion of feminist standpoint theory, I gain encouragement from a number of similar efforts by others who argue for a specific view from below.[7]

The work of Fredric Jameson has been particularly useful in my rethinking of the nature of a standpoint. He states that "the presupposition is that, owing to its structural situation in the social order and to the specific forms of oppression and exploitation unique to that situation, each group lives the world in a phenomenologically specific way that allows it to see, or, better still, that makes it unavoidable for that group to see and to know, features of the world that remain obscure, invisible, or merely occasional and secondary for other groups."[8] Jameson is clear that in each case the issue is the condition of possibility of new thinking inherent in each social location. It is not a matter of the aptitude of individual workers and still less "the mystical properties of some collective proletarian 'world view'."[9] Jameson stresses the prerequisites of Marxist analysis: the diagnoses of blocks and limits to knowledge as well as positive features such as the capacity to think in terms of process.

Jameson also takes up feminist standpoint theories to argue that the experience of women generates new and positive epistemological possibilities. (Stress should be placed on the idea of possibilities and potentials.) Standpoint theory, he argues, demands a "differentiation between the various negative experiences of constraint, between the *exploitation* suffered by workers and the *oppressions* suffered by women."[10] If one begins from a feminist project, one can argue that it is important to differentiate situations that can be characterized as those of constraint. Jameson takes particular note of the Central European Jewish experience, which he characterizes as one of fear that crosses class and gender lines. Other groups, he suggests, experience fear, but for this group it is constitutive.[11] Thus, he indicates that it is important to dissolve the concept of oppression into the "concrete situations from which it emerged" and to examine the various structured constraints lived by dominated groups. But in the process, each form of domination must be understood to produce its own specific epistemology, or view from below.[12]

We need a revised and reconstructed theory, indebted to Marx, among others, and containing several important features of standpoint theories, as opposed to postmodernism theories. First, rather than getting rid of subjectivity, oppressed groups need to engage in the historical, political, and theoretical process of constituting ourselves as subjects as well as objects of history. We need to sort out who we really are and in the process dissolve this false "we" into its real multiplicity and variety. Out of this concrete multiplicity, it should be possible to build an account of the social relations as seen from below. I am not suggesting that oppression creates "better" people; on the contrary, the experience of domination and marginalization leaves many scars. Rather, it is to note that marginalized groups are less likely to mistake themselves for the universal "man"; and to suggest that the experience of domination may provide the possibility of important new understandings of social life.

Second, it is important to do our thinking on an epistemological base that indicates that knowledge is possible—not just conversation or a discourse on how it is that power relations work to subject us. We will not have the confidence to act if we believe that we cannot know the world. This does not mean that we need to believe that we have absolute knowledge, but rather that we need to have "good enough" certitude.[13]

Third, we need an epistemology that recognizes that our practical daily activity contains an understanding of the world—subjugated perhaps, but present. Here I refer to Gramsci's argument that all men are intellectuals and that everyone has a working epistemology. The point, then, is to read out the epistemologies contained in our various practices. In addition, we must not give up the claim that material life not only structures but also sets limits on understandings of social relations, and that in systems of domination the vision available to the ruling groups will be partial and will reverse the real order of things.

Fourth, our epistemology needs to recognize the difficulty of creating alternatives. The ruling class, race, and gender actively structure the world in a way that forms the material-social relations in which all parties are forced to participate; their vision cannot be dismissed as simply false or misguided. Oppressed groups must struggle to attain their own, centered, understanding, recognizing that this will require both theorizing and the education that can come only from political struggle.

Fifth, the understanding of the oppressed exposes the real relations among people as inhumane. Thus there is a call to political action.

In light of these needs, following Jameson's extension of standpoint arguments, and in the spirit of attempting to develop theoretical bases for coalitions, I propose to read a number of statements of the view from below, or the perspectives of subaltern groups. I believe that although the phenomenological specifics differ, there are a number of connections to be made and similarities to be seen in the epistemologies contained as possibilities in the experience of dominated groups. In particular, I want to suggest that white feminists should learn the possibilities of solidarity from U.S. feminists of color and postcolonial subjects.

There are several important issues on which a great deal more work needs to be done. First, there is the question of the status of "experience" and its interpretation, and, most important, the political consequences of treating experience in different ways. Second, in the particularly American (or perhaps Anglophone) context, much more needs to be learned about the construction of groups, which must be thought of not as aggregations of individuals but as groups formed by their oppression and marginalization, groups whose members share enough experience to have the possibility of coming to understand their situations in ways that can empower their oppositional movements. Third, I believe there is a great deal of work to be done to elaborate the connections between politics, epistemology, and claims of epistemic privilege and to develop new understandings of engaged and accountable knowledge.

To understand these perspectives and the knowledges they support, generate, and express, we must understand at least the outlines of the situations of oppression from which they emerge, or, put more clearly, the existential problems to which the world-views of the oppressed must respond. Most fundamentally, the dominated live in a world structured by others for their purposes—purposes that at the very least are not our own and that are in various degrees inimical to our development and even existence. This takes a variety of forms, both globally and locally. There is an implicit "assumption of 'the West' as the primary referent in theory and practice." At the very least, as Carlos Fuentes put it from the perspective of Mexico, "The North American world blinds us with its energy; we cannot see ourselves [because] we must see YOU."[14]

As a result of this definition, dominated groups experience a series of inversions, distortions, and erasures that can become epistemologically constitutive. "The presupposition is that, owing to its structural situation in the social order and to the specific forms of oppression" inherent in that situation, each group lives the world in a way that allows it to see, or rather "makes it unavoidable to see and to know, features of the world that remain obscure, invisible, or merely occasional and secondary for other groups."[15]

Let us look more specifically at a very powerful experience of inversion. One of the most frequently mentioned features of the consciousness of the dominated as they become conscious of both relations of domination and possibilities for change is a recognition of the "insanity" or "unreality" of the "normal." Thus, Michelle Cliff writes of light-skinned, middle-class Jamaicans: "We were colorists and we aspired to oppressor status. ... We were convinced of white supremacy. If we failed, ... our dark part had taken over: an inherited imbalance in which the doom of the Creole was sealed." She steps back to look at what she has written and states that this "may sound fabulous, or even mythic. It is. It is insane."[16] Or consider a U.S. black woman who told her interviewer, "I have grown to womanhood in a world where the saner you are, the madder you are made to appear."[17]

Eduardo Galeano, writing of the situation in Latin America, noted, "'Freedom' in my country is the name of a jail for political prisoners and 'democracy' forms part of the title of various regimes of terror; the word 'love' defines the relationship of a man with his automobile, and 'revolution' is understood to describe what a new detergent can do in your kitchen."[18] He added: "Why not recognize a certain creativity in the development of a technology of terror? Latin America is making inspired universal contributions to the development of methods of torture ... and the sowing of fear."[19]

This sort of understanding of the inversions created for the oppressed leads to a renewed understanding of the dominant group. As this understanding changes, it is striking how similar the descriptions are. Thus, one can begin to ask questions and formulate descriptions that are vastly different. Thus, we find questions raised among feminist, Third World, and postcolonial writers. "Besides possessing more money and arms is it that the 'First World' is qualitatively better in any way than our 'underdeveloped' countries? That the Anglos themselves aren't also an 'ethnic group,' one of the most violent and anti-social tribes on this planet?"[20] And there is also the observation by a student of black radicalism that "there was the sense that something of a more profound obsession with property was askew in a civilization which could organize and celebrate—on a scale beyond previous human experience—the brutal degradations of life and the most acute violations of human destiny." He added that the suspicion was mounting that "a civilization maddened by its own perverse assumptions and contradictions is loose in the world."[21]

The result of this kind of experience for knowledge and epistemology is expressed in Gabriel García Márquez's Nobel Prize address. He presented a rich statement that "our crucial problem has been a lack of conventional means to render our lives believable. This, my friends, is the crux of our solitude. ... The interpretation of our reality through patterns not our own serves only to make us ever more unknown, ever less free, ever more solitary."[22] The result is that the dominated and marginalized are forced to recognize (unlike whites, males, and Europeans) that they inhabit multiple worlds. W. E. B. DuBois described this situation from an African-American perspective: "It is a peculiar sensation, this double consciousness, this sense of always looking at one's self through the eyes of others, of measuring one's soul by the tape of a world that looks on in amused contempt and pity."[23]

The significance of this experience for developing knowledge and experience has been described in a number of ways. I argued in my feminist standpoint essay that for (white) women in Western industrial society, the experience of life under patriarchy allows for the possibility of developing both an understanding of the falseness and partiality of the dominant view and a vision of reality that is deeper and more complex than that view. Others have made similar arguments about the nature of the knowledge available to the subjugated. Thus, Sangari writes that for "Third World" people, the difficulty of arriving at fact through the "historical and political distortions that so powerfully shape and mediate it" leads them to assert a different level of factuality, "a plane on which the notion of knowledge as provisional and of truth as historically circumscribed is not only necessary for understanding but can in turn be made to work from positions of engagement within the local and contemporary." She argues that marvelous realism operates because "if the real is historically structured to make invisible the foreign locus of power, if the real may thus be other than what is generally visible, ... then marvelous realism tackles the problem of truth at a level that reinvents a more comprehensive mode of referentiality."[24]

Gloria Anzaldua, writing out of the experience of a Chicana living on the Mexico–Texas border, describes a similar phenomenon in terms reminiscent of Sangari's discussion. She points not only to the experience of living in two realities and thus being forced to exist in the interface but also to "la facultad," the capacity to see in surface phenomena the meanings of deeper realities, to see the "deep structure below the surface." And she argues that "those who are pounced on the most have it the strongest—the females, the homosexuals of all races, the dark skinned, the outcast, the persecuted, the marginalized, the foreign." It is a survival tactic unknowingly cultivated by those caught between the worlds, but, she adds, "it is latent in all of us."[25]

The knowledges available to these multiple subjectivities have different qualities from that of the disembodied and singular subject of the Enlightenment. Moreover, despite the specificity of each view from below, several fundamental aspects are shared. Among these are the qualities of multiplicity, of being locatable in time and space and particular cultures, of being embodied in specific ways, and, finally, of operating as social and collective points of view—indeed, operating as standpoints. Although I cannot discuss these qualities in detail, I can lay out a few of their general outlines.

These are knowledges located in a particular time and space—situated knowledges.[26] They are therefore partial, the knowledges of specific cultures and peoples. As an aspect of being situated, these knowledges represent a response to an expression of specific embodiment. The bodies of the dominated have been made to function as the marks of our oppression.

One can describe the shape of these knowledges by attending to the features of the social location occupied by dominated groups. Because of these features, these knowledges express a multiple and contradictory reality; they are not fixed but change, and they recognize that they change with the changing shape of the historical conjuncture and the balance of forces. They are both critical of and vulnerable to the dominant culture, both separated from and opposed to it and yet contained within it. Gloria Anzaldua's poem expresses these characteristics:

> To live in the Borderlands means
> you are at home, a stranger wherever you are
> the border disputes have been settled
> the volley of shots have shattered the truce
> you are wounded, lost in action
> fighting back, a survivor[27]

All these mark achievement through struggle, a series of ongoing attempts to keep from being made invisible, to keep from being destroyed by the dominant culture.

Even more than this, however, the development of situated knowledges can constitute alternatives: They open possibilities that may or may not be realized. To the extent that these knowledges become self-conscious about their assumptions, they make available new epistemological options. The struggles they represent and express, if made self-conscious, can go beyond efforts at survival in order to recognize the centrality of systematic power relations. They can become knowledges that are both accountable and engaged. As the knowledges of the dominated, they are "savvy to modes of denial," which include repression, forgetting, and disappearing.[28] Thus, while recognizing themselves as never fixed or fully achieved, they can claim to present a truer, or more adequate, account of reality. They can form what Jameson has termed a "principled relativism." As the knowledges that recognize themselves as the knowledges of the dominated and marginalized, these self-consciously situated knowledges must focus on changing contemporary power relationships and thus point beyond the present.

NOTES

1. The list usually includes Dorothy Smith, Mary O'Brien, Hilary Rose (and formerly also Elizabeth Fee and Jane Flax), and more recently theorists such as Alison Jaggar, Sandra Harding, and Patricia Hill Collins, who have more complicated relationships to standpoint theory. Missing are writers such as Donna Haraway, Chela Sandoval, bell hooks, and Paula M. L. Moya, who I see as involved in versions of standpoint projects. There are also issues to be taken up about "feminist" as opposed to "women's" standpoints. On this point, see N. Hartsock, "Standpoint Theories for the Next Century," *Women and Politics* 18, no. 3 (Fall 1997).

2. For example, Norma Alarcon, "The Theoretical Subject(s) of *This Bridge Called My Back*," in Gloria Anzaldua, ed., *Making Face/Making Soul* (San Francisco: Aunt Lute Foundation, 1990), discusses an unnamed group of "standpoint epistemologists." Later in the essay she cites Harding and Jaggar as standpoint theorists.

3. Georg Lukács, *History and Class Consciousness* (Boston: Beacon Press, 1971).

4. I did intend to privilege the perspective available as a possibility within women's lives, though not to argue for a ranking of oppressions such that the vision available to the most oppressed group provided the best account. Katie King seems to read inversion in this way. See *Theory in Its Feminist Travels* (Bloomington: Indiana University Press, 1994), 62.

5. These five points are my restatement with only a few changes of the formulation that appeared in *Money, Sex, and Power: Toward A Feminist Historical Materialism* (New York: Longman, 1983; Boston, Northeastern University Press, 1984), 232.

6. bell hooks, *Yearning* (Boston: South End Press, 1994). See also Donna Haraway, *Modes_Witness@Second_Millennium.FemaleMan©Meets_OncoMouse*™ (New York: Routledge, 1997), 127–29, which reminds me very much of this work.

7. See, for example, work by Patricia Hill Collins on a Black feminist standpoint, Marilyn Frye, Teresa De Lauretis, Molefi Asante, Sandra Harding, Chela Sandoval, and Donna Haraway.

8. Fredric Jameson, "History and Class Consciousness," *Rethinking Marxism* 1, no. 1 (1988): 65.

9. Ibid., 66.

10. Ibid., 70.

11. Ibid.

12. Ibid. He went on to state that it was a project that would sound like relativism, but termed it a principled relativism.

13. See, for example, Ludwig Wittgenstein, *On Certainty* (New York: Harper & Row, 1969), and *Remarks on the Foundations of Mathematics* (Cambridge: MIT Press). See also Ilya Prigogine, *The End of Certainty* (New York: The Free Press, 1996).

14. Carlos Fuentes, "How I Started to Write," in Rick Simonson and Scott Walker, eds., *Graywolf Annual Five: Multicultural Literacy* (St. Paul, MN: Graywolf Press, 1988), 85.

15. Jameson, "History and Class Consciousness," 65.

16. Michelle Cliff, "A Journey into Speech," in *Graywolf Annual Five*, 78.

17. From Edward Gwaltney, *Dryongso,* cited in Patricia Hill Collins, "The Social Construction of Black Feminist Thought," *Signs: Journal of Women in Culture and Society* 14, no. 4 (1989): 748.

18. "In Defense of the Word: Leaving Buenos Aires," *Graywolf Annual* (June 1976), 124–25.

19. Ibid., 114–15. See also his remarks about the importance of the consumption of fantasy rather than commodities (117).

20. Guillermo Gómez-Peña, "Documented /Undocumented," in *Graywolf Annual Five*, 132.

21. Cedric Robinson, *Black Marxism* (London: Zed Books, 1984), 442 and 452 respectively.

22. Quoted in Eduardo Galeano, *Century of the Wind* (New York: Pantheon, 1988), 262. Marquez's work makes important points about incommensurable realities. He argued that ordinary people who have read *One Hundred Years of Solitude* have found no surprise, because "I'm telling them nothing that hasn't happened in their own lives." *The Fragrance of Guava*, 36, cited in Kumkum Sangari, "The Politics of the Possible," *Cultural Critique* 7 (Fall 1987): 164.

23. W. E. B. DuBois, *The Souls of Black Folk,* 2d ed. (New York: Fawcett World Library, n.d.), 16, cited in Joyce Ladner, *Tomorrow's Tomorrow* (New York: Anchor Books, 1971), 273–74.

24. Sangari, "The Politics of the Possible," 161 and 163 respectively.

25. Gloria Anzaldua, *Borderlands* (San Francisco: Spinsters, Aunt Lute, 1987), 37–39.

26. I have been very much influenced by Haraway's essay "Situated Knowledges," in *Simians, Cyborgs, and Women* (New York: Routledge, 1991).

27. Anzaldua, *Borderlands*, 14.

28. These are Donna Haraway's terms (in *Simians, Cyborgs, and Women*).

A MARXIST THEORY OF WOMEN'S NATURE

NANCY HOLMSTROM

Debates about women's nature are very old but far from over. In fact they have acquired a new urgency with the rise of the women's movement and with the dramatic increase in the number of women in the workforce. Conservatives claim that there is a distinct women's nature that puts limits on the extent to which the traditional sexual/social roles can and should be altered. Feminists usually reject the idea, correctly pointing out that it has been used to justify women's oppression for thousands of years.

Here I attempt to develop a Marxist approach to the question. Marx held human nature to be determined by the social forms of human labor. I will bring out his general realist methodology and his perspective on the relation between the biological and the social. Given my interpretation of the facts about psychological differences between the sexes and the probable dependence of these differences on the sexual division of labor, this approach entails that women probably do have distinct natures. (It similarly entails that men probably have distinct natures since there is no reason to take men as the norm.) However, contrary to the usual assumption, it does not follow that sexual/social roles cannot or should not be radically altered, for men's and women's natures are socially constituted and historically evolving. Marx's approach, though novel in certain respects, accords with the methodology employed in biological classifications.

I

Just as the nonhuman natural world consists of biological, chemical, and physical structures for which different sorts of explanations are appropriate, so there are many levels of explanation appropriate to human beings. The nature of a human being as a biological being would be the genotype. The philosophical question of human nature is of the nature of human beings qua social beings. According to Marx's theory, human beings have certain basic needs and capacities which are biological in origin but to some extent socially constituted:[1] "Hunger is hunger but the hunger gratified by cooked meat eaten with a knife and fork is a different hunger from that which bolts down raw meat with the aid of hand, nail and tooth."[2] Some human needs and capacities are unique to human beings, but even those that are not take uniquely human forms. As new needs and capacities are continually being created, biology remains an important determining factor, but human life progressively becomes less directly tied to its biological base.

Since human needs and capacities are expressed, shaped, and even created through the activity of satisfying needs (i.e. through labor), Marx concentrated on the form of labor characteristic of the human species. Though this species can be distinguished from others on a number of criteria, Marx says that human beings in fact begin to distinguish themselves from other species when they begin to produce their means of subsistence. Because the labor of society is institutionalized into sets of social practices and social relations, by their labor people are thereby producing their whole life. The general capacity of human beings to labor in a social and purposive way takes a variety of specific forms throughout history, which in turn affect and even create other human needs and capacities.

Now obviously there are biological structures that make possible the kinds of labor that human beings do. However, the relation between biology and activity in human beings differs from that in other species in two ways: first, human biology makes possible more than just a narrow range of behavior, even within a particular historical period; and second, rather than determining the forms of human labor, human biology does no more than make possible its forms. Our large brain size, the basis of the flexibility and plasticity of human behavior and consciousness, resulted from evolution, a major determinant of which was labor. This is the basis of Engels's remark that "labor created man himself." On Marx's theory, labor is the key to an explanation of social life and social change. Since this was his concern, he emphasized the labor and not the biology.

Compare the methodology employed in biological classifications: animals are classified into the same or different species not simply on the basis of their similarities and differences but also according to the importance of these features within biological theory. For this reason, Chihuahuas and St. Bernards are classified as belonging to the same species, although there are greater differences between them than there are between many dogs and wolves. In analogous fashion, the differentiating characteristic of social beings should be determined by its importance in social theory. As the forms of human labor (and the resultant social practices and institutions) change, new mental and physical capacities are developed, some remain undeveloped, and others are destroyed. Hence different behavioral and psychological generalizations will be true of people who do different sorts of labor in different modes of production.

A nominalistic–empiricist approach would leave the discussion of human nature at that. However, I take Marx to have a realist approach to the philosophy of the natural and social sciences. Realists maintain that the concept of a nature—stripped of outmoded metaphysical assumptions—often plays an important explanatory role in answer to such questions as, Why do the generalizations hold? and What is the basis of the observed similarities? Biological theories, which back up some generalizations and not others, should provide some account of the mechanisms that generate the regularities. For example, realists argue that it is necessary to posit some underlying structure, common to the things defined as one species, that generates the disjunctive set of properties defining a species and causes variations in different individuals within that species.[3] (This demand is satisfied by the concept of the gene pool.) In traditional terminology, the set of properties which justify the use of the common term is called the nominal essence; the internal constitution which generates these manifest properties in accordance with laws is called the real essence.

Marx assumed the same perspective on the social world. He believed that the distinction between accidental and lawful generalizations applied to social phenomena and that certain social entities had natures, saying repeatedly that science was necessary to uncover the hidden laws of motion of capitalist society. Socioeconomic classes are not mere collections of individuals with some common economic feature—not classes simply in the logical sense. The realist methodology implies that there must be certain characteristic differences in the psychophysical structures of people who do very different sorts of labor in different modes of production to account for the observed personality and behavioral differences between them.[4] These psychophysical structures would generate and explain a wide range of human behavior within that mode of production, which the transhistorical features of human beings would not be able to do. To say in detail what these historically specific structures are and how they work would require a more adequate psychological theory than presently exists, one that integrates social and historical factors. However, an explanation of the varieties of human personality and behavior requires some such hypothesis of historically specific structures. This indicates a line of future research.[5]

Talk of "determining structures" is not inconsistent with Marx's conception of human beings as historical agents. Individually and collectively, human beings often do what they do because of their beliefs, desires, and purposes. Human beings are free in this sense. But Marx stresses that human freedom is exercised only within certain constraints—set by social, historical, and economic conditions as well as biological facts. Talk of social groups with natures is a way of bringing out those constraints. For example, we can better predict John Smith's economic behavior by knowing that he is a capitalist than by knowing his personality and character traits.

The psychophysical structures produced by the sorts of labor that people do and the resultant social relations would constitute the nature of human beings qua social beings. Although there are certain features common to these structures, they vary as a whole from one mode of production to another. Marx is denying that there is a human nature in the traditional, transhistorical sense. On his view, however, there are historically specific forms of human nature—that is, human nature specific to feudalism, to capitalism, to socialism, and so on. In traditional terminology, the (variable) psychophysical structures would be the (variable) real essence of human beings qua social beings, and the forms of personality and behavior to which they give rise would be the nominal essence.

This acceptance of natures in the social world implies that, contrary to traditional assumptions, natures can change. Even for biological natures, however, the assumption that natures must be unchanging became less plausible after the discovery of evolution. If species can be understood as evolving sorts of things, why must natures be understood as unchanging? In Marx's view, the contrast of the social with the natural and unchanging is particularly inappropriate to human beings since they are by nature social beings with a history.

II

Let us try to apply this approach to the question of whether women (and men) can be said to have distinct natures. Distinct sex-linked natures are supposed to account for (and to justify) the distinct social roles of women and men. It is important to see first of all that the defining biological differences between men and women cannot by themselves play this explanatory role, much less the justificatory one. A woman is defined as a typical member of the female sex, which is distinguished from the male sex by its ability to conceive and bear children. Whether these biological differences cause the social differences is an empirical question that we shall discuss shortly. However, to say that men and women have distinct natures so defined would be to utter a tautology. We are looking for the nature of women and men as social groups, not as biological groups.

Do, then, men and women as social beings have distinct natures? If there are generalizations subsumable under a theory, explanatory of behavior distinctive of a given social group, this suggests that the group has a distinct nature. Indeed there are many generalizations we can make about women's behavior and roles within given cultures and many that are true cross-culturally as well. Compared to men, women spend more time taking care of children and doing other household tasks; they have less social, economic, and political power in society at large and in almost every subgroup in society; their work outside the home, if any, is usually related to the work they do inside the home; they tend to cry more easily, dress and adorn themselves distinctively, to have distinct recreations and pleasures, and so on.

What is the explanation? Discrimination and direct social pressure are undoubtedly part of it. But are there differences between men and women themselves that underlie the behavioral differences? Many claim that biological differences between the sexes are the most important part of the explanation.[6] However, it is highly implausible that biological differences could directly determine the social differences. If biological facts are critical determinants of sexual/social roles, the connection is most likely to run through psychology; that is, biological differences cause or predispose psychological differences, which in turn cause differences in social roles. The first question, then, is whether there are psychological differences between the sexes that are relevant to their respective social roles: for example, that women are more nurturant than men and hence are more appropriate caretakers of children. If there are such differences, the next question will be about their source.

Both these questions are controversial, even among the experts. Despite this and my own serious reservations about much of the research,[7] I believe that research to show that there exist statistically significant psychological sex differences of a sort that are relevant to the different social roles men and women play.[8]

Any position regarding the source of these differences is necessarily somewhat speculative since, by and large, the researchers look only for statistically significant relationships and do not try to establish cause and effect. The prevailing hostility among academic research psychologists to any theoretical framework makes it difficult to assess the data, since the significance of the data and even what needs to be explained are to some extent dependent on a theory. But the following findings strongly support the view that social factors are the primary determinants:[9] (1) Black males and white females, different biologically but with similar social handicaps, are similar in patterns of achievement scores and fear of success.[10] (2) The same physiological state can yield very different emotional states and behavior, depending on the social situation. Adrenalin produces a physiological state very much like that present in extreme fear, yet subjects injected with it became euphoric when around another person who acted euphorically and very angry when around another person who acted very angrily.[11] Thus even if sex hormonal differences between men and women affect brain functioning, as some psychologists contend, it does not follow that there necessarily will be consistent emotional and behavioral differences between men and women. (3) Different behavioral propensities, thought by many to be biologically based, disappear given certain social conditions. In one study, when both sexes were rewarded for aggressive behavior, the sex difference disappeared.[12] (4) Psychological sex differences are least pronounced in early childhood and old age, when sex-role stereotypes are least powerful.[13] Furthermore, the principle of methodological simplicity supports taking environmental factors as decisive. We have at present ample evidence of environmental shaping of sex-differentiated behavior, so ample in fact that it is sufficient to account for the cognitive and personality differences we observe in children and adults. Although it is possible that future research will discover biological factors as well, there is no reason to expect this will happen.

The social roles of men and women that are related to psychological sex differences are not universal cross-culturally, but they are very prevalent. Sex-differentiated socialization patterns also show little cross-cultural variation, with girls being trained for nurturance and responsibility and boys for achievement and self-reliance in both developed and underdeveloped societies.[14] This strongly suggests that many, though not all, of the psychological differences between men and women are very prevalent, though not universal, cross-culturally. They are not universal to all women even within this culture. Something like the following is probably true: there is a common core of psychological traits found more among women than among men throughout the world, but women belonging to different cultures or subcultures have different subsets of this common core of traits. Though there is not enough rigorous cross-cultural psychological research to say for sure, this opinion accords with the anthropological data we do have.[15]

There seem, then, to be several levels of generalizations (sociological, psychological, etc.) that are distinctive of women. By itself, however, this by no means implies that there is a distinct women's nature. As we saw in our discussion of taxonomy, the differences must be of a kind that is theoretically important. Following Marx's approach, we should expect psychological differences to be connected to differences in the sorts of labor that women do in society and to the resulting differences in social relations. Universally there is and has always been a sexual division of labor. Although there are some variations as to what labor each sex does, men generally have primary responsibility for subsistence activities; women's contribution to this varies. What does not vary is that, whatever else they do, women have primary responsibility for childcare and most of the everyday household work. Their contribution to subsistence depends on its compatibility with childcare.[16]

Several cross-cultural studies support the Marxist assumption that it is women's distinctive labor and the different social relations resulting from it that are critical in determining these personality differences.[17] Striking parallels exist between cultural and sexual differences; that is, cultures differ along the same lines as those along which men and women differ in most societies. Some cultures exhibit the sort of behavior and personality usually considered masculine: everyone tends to be independent, achievement oriented, and assertive (although women still are less so than men are in the culture). In other cultures everyone tends to be compliant, obedient, and responsible—the sort of personality associated with women. Critical for us is that the differences in the "personalities" of cultures are correlated with different economies. Where animal husbandry and agriculture are the primary sources of subsistence, obedience and responsibility are essential whereas experimentation and individual initiative would be dangerous. But societies which depend largely on hunting and fishing benefit from experimentation and individual initiative and are less threatened by disobedience and irresponsibility. Women in the latter societies tend both to fish and to have their more traditional responsibilities. Though more "masculine" than men and women in other cultures, they are less "masculine" than men in their own cultures. It seems plausible to say therefore that the differences between men and women can be explained by the different sorts of labor that they do.

Within our own society, certain psychological differences between young black and young white women lend support to the hypothesis. While wealthy black adolescent girls share the traditional (white) version of femininity,[18] black adolescent girls from poor and working-class families (i.e. the majority) accept the very different values for women of strength and independence.[19] It is difficult to avoid the conclusion that the psychological differences between young black and young white women reflect the fact that black women have historically almost always been employed outside the home.

Now the Marxist view is not that there is a direct causal connection between the type of labor people do and their personality structure. Rather, the type of labor people do puts them into certain social relations, and these relations are institutionalized into sets of practices, institutions, cultural agencies, and so on. In the case of the sexual division of labor, the most important of these institutions is the family. Women are first of all raised primarily by a woman in a family. They then usually have a family of their own. Although fewer women today are full-time domestic workers than in the past, they still tend to think of their primary work and role as those of wife and mother. Their role in the family helps keep them in an inferior economic and social position. Their work outside the family, if any, is most often related to their role inside the family. Even the rare woman who both has an untraditional job and does not have a family is still shaped by the social and cultural institutions from which she is deviating. Men who for a long time do unskilled work and are treated in a paternalistic manner at work are also psychologically affected by it, but the effect is counteracted by their dominant role in the family and by the ideology of male supremacy.

The Marxist view, then, is that the different generalizations true of men and women can be explained by the sexual division of labor institutionalized into sets of practices and social and cultural institutions, and that this in turn can be subsumed under a theory explaining the sexual/social division of labor. The two explanations are provided by different aspects of historical materialism. In a society where there was a significantly different sexual division of labor, different generalizations would be true of men and women. In a society where there was no sexual division of labor, there would probably be few if any generalizations that were true of men but not women, except biological ones, and there would be fewer even of these.

The generalizations true of women and not men describe emotions and behavior that reflect specific cognitive/affective structures more often found among women. My contention is that there is probably a common core of psychological traits found more often among women than among men throughout the world, of which women of different (sub)cultures have different subsets. The cognitive/affective structures generate the different sets of traits under different conditions. Although our knowledge at this point is too meager to say much about these structures, an adequate explanation of the differences requires that we posit such structures. What we need is a psychological theory supplemented by social and historical considerations of the kind discussed here.[20] In the traditional terminology the cognitive/affective structures would be the real essence; the disjunctive set of traits would be the nominal essence. Although the underlying structures which give rise to the different traits would more properly be called the distinct nature of women, for ordinary purposes the nature of women could be taken to be the systematically related sets of properties to which these structures give rise.

That these properties are not universal is not a reason to reject the claim that they constitute a nature. This might seem surprising, but actually it accords with the approach used in taxonomy. Contrary to Aristotelian essentialism, classifications made in biology do not require that the defining characteristics be individually necessary and jointly sufficient. The actual distribution of properties among organisms is such that most taxa names can be defined only disjunctively. Any of the disjuncts is sufficient, and the few necessary properties are far from sufficient. This makes most concepts of so-called natural kinds what are called "cluster concepts." There seems no reason to apply stricter criteria in the social sphere. The account given here of women's nature makes it just such a cluster concept.

There is, then, what Marxists would call a dialectical interaction between women's labor and their nature. The sexual/social division of labor is the cause of the distinctive cognitive/affective structures that constitute women's nature, and these structures are at least a partial cause of a variety of personality traits and behavior distinctive of women, including the sorts of labor they do.

III

Now some might try to extend my argument and claim not only that the differences in natures between men and women are social and historical in origin but also that the very division into men and women is social and historical in origin. After all, there is an enormous physical variety among infants and among adults. And physical similarities and differences do not by themselves determine any particular division into groups. Rather, it is the significance that society gives to the physical characteristics that does this. Similar arguments regarding the classification of humanity into races are generally accepted today by informed people.

Though interesting, this argument goes wrong in its assumption as to what constitutes a biological or "natural" distinction as opposed to one that is social or historical in origin. Nothing is a "given fact of nature" in the sense presupposed in the argument. It is true that it is the significance of physical similarities and differences, rather than the physical similarities themselves, that determines a classification. Nevertheless, given that the sex difference is what allows for physical reproduction of most kinds of things, and that the distinction between things that reproduce sexually and those that reproduce by some other means is a very important one in biology, the division into two sexes has great importance for biological theory. The basis of the division into two sexes, then, is much the same as the division into species. Why should the sexual division not be called a natural distinction as well?

IV

It must not be forgotten that the similarities between men and women are greater than their differences. These similarities constitute their common human nature, as both biological and social beings. But within the sociohistorical category of human beings, I have argued that there are sex-differentiated natures. An individual woman will have this women's nature as a part of her human nature. She is, of course, a particular woman and more than just a woman. Aside from being human, she is, among other things, of a particular social class, race, and culture. These are categories that cut across sex lines, and some will be as important as her sex or more important. Given the methodology I am using, this means that every individual has or is constituted by several natures. There is no contradiction in this. It simply shows that there are several different sorts of facts about people and that these require different sorts of explanations, however these facts and explanations are ultimately related. There need be no conflict between the different sorts of explanations; different areas of a woman's behavior can be explained by different aspects of her total nature. In certain conditions, however, there might be a conflict. A woman who is a wife and mother and also a wage worker will have needs and propensities based on these social relations. These will sometimes conflict, such as when she has a union meeting and responsibilities at home at the same time. Particular conditions will also make a difference: if there is a strike going on she will be more likely to go to the union meeting than at other times. We should look for theories to explain under what conditions each factor will be most important, how factors interact, and how these correlations could change given other conditions. Our theories should also explain why all this is so. Different individuals may respond somewhat differently to the same factors because of the particular conditions of their lives and their particular socialization experiences. The theories are about groups, not individuals. This is why many of the generalizations about the different social groups of which a person is a member are statistical and not universal.

It is important to make clear that the sense in which women have a distinct nature does not carry many of the usual implications of such a statement and has no implications to which feminists should object. This nature is not fixed and inevitable; natures in this sense can change. Although there is a biological element as part of its basis, the crucial determinants are not biological but social. (As we saw, even if it were entirely biological this would not make it inevitable. Not only can the biological facts be changed but also, much more important in the short run, their effects can be altered by human intervention.) That there is a distinct women's nature in my sense does not mean that every woman has this nature. The cluster of psychological traits that constitutes the nature of women as social beings need not belong to all biological females, though it would be an unusual woman to have none of the traits. Though a woman's nature would explain some of women's behavior (indeed this is required for use of the concept of nature), it would not necessarily be more determinant than other aspects of her nature. Thus a woman could, over all, have more in common with a man who shared other aspects of her nature than with another woman with whom she shared this women's nature. Most importantly, a women's nature in this sense carries no moral implications about how women ought or ought not to live. Whether a type of behavior characteristic of women is morally or socially desirable is a normative issue. A further normative question is whether desirable traits should be divided up along sexual lines. Personally, I see no justification for this. In my opinion some traits more characteristic of women, such as nurturance, are desirable for everyone, while others, like passivity, are undesirable for everyone. But any opinion on this would need argumentation independent of the facts about how men and women tend to behave. The existence of socially constituted sex-differentiated natures might be relevant to the normative questions but hardly decisive.

Though talk of women's nature does not, on my account, imply that it is immutable, it does imply that it is not easily changed. The Marxist conception of a thing's nature is of something underlying and explanatory of its observable behavior. But being explanatory is not sufficient to be part of a thing's nature. Only those traits belong to a thing's nature that are systematically related, explain a variety of systematically related behavior, and are subsumable in a theoretical framework. Such features do not easily and suddenly change. A sexual division of labor with resultant psychological sex differences has been near to universal, despite variations. Today, however, things may be changing. Only a small minority of Americans (11 percent) live in the traditional nuclear family of breadwinning father, homemaker mother, and two or more children. Women comprise 45 percent of the workforce. On the other hand, the jobs that women do for wages tend to be related to their traditional and subordinate social role: they assist, nurse, teach, serve, and clean up after others in their wage work as well as in the home. Moreover, women still do most of the parenting and housework whether or not they do wage work.[21] How much this can change within capitalism is a complicated and controversial question. And how quickly the psychological differences between the sexes would disappear if the social differences were removed remains to be seen.

In neither capitalist nor noncapitalist societies has the entry of women into paid labor been sufficient to change traditional sex roles.[22] Although one part of the traditional sexual division of labor has changed, the most important part has not. Women are oppressed by their "double duty" in both forms of society. That women working outside the home still do most of the childcare and housework has to be attributed in part to psychological differences between the sexes. Even women leading fairly untraditional lives still tend to hold many of the traditional assumptions, values, expectations, and self-conceptions on a deep level. So I do not think the psychological changes will be so rapid as to refute my talk of them as "natures." On the other hand, these psychological attributes seem to be very much dependent on the objective economic power relations between men and women. Thus, in the working class, where women's wages are a higher proportion of family income than they are in the middle class, studies show that women gain more power from employment.[23] And even women working in low-level traditional women's jobs have more feminist consciousness than do full-time housewives.[24] Thus there is a basis for believing that, to the extent that the sexual division of labor in society was reduced or eliminated, psychological sex differences would follow suit. As these social changes occur we are likely to see contradictions develop in the psychic structures of men and women. Using "contradiction" in the Marxist sense of structures with incompatible tendencies, the presence of contradictions in periods of change is perfectly consistent with the idea that these structures constitute natures. The difficulty of changing male and female natures does not imply that we should not try to change them. On the contrary, if they are judged to be undesirable, as I believe they are, the difficulty of change would entail that extra efforts ought to be made.

V

In the concluding section of this essay I should like to explore a contrast between Marx's approach to human nature and my approach to women's nature. Although my perspective has been based on Marx's theory of human nature, there is an interesting difference on one point. The fact that human beings cannot, under capitalism, fulfill certain capacities unique to human beings is taken by many Marxists (and Marx) to be a criticism of capitalism. The fact that these aspects of their nature will be fully realized only in socialism and communism is taken to be a key reason why socialist and communist societies are in some sense better than all previous ones. Yet I have rejected any normative implications of my account of women's nature. Why is it good that human beings should fulfill their nature or aspects of their nature? And if it is good, why doesn't it follow that women should fulfill their natures too? Or is this Marxist-feminist position I have developed lacking in any consistent theoretical basis? It says that natures should be developed when I like what is part of the natures and rejects the idea when I don't like the natures.

I think there is a consistent theoretical reason for the difference on this point. It is true that of the different historical forms of human nature, such as those of feudalism, capitalism, and socialism/communism, Marx evinces a preference for the last. He often talks as if it is better that this nature should be realized and even, at times, that it is in some sense more truly human nature. What underlies this preference is not that this human nature is unique to human beings or that it differs most from the nature of other species. There is no particular reason why a group or a person should develop what is unique or special to it. Rather, Marx's preference has to do with freedom conceived as the power to act on one's own beliefs and desires. In Marx's theory, consciousness and much of what is taken to be human nature are formed by the social system in which people live. This is not to say that they are formed in every detail or that human beings are mere passive products of their society. It is to say that the broad outlines, the limits, are set by the mode of production and one's place in it. Until the institution of socialism/communism, the mode of production is not under the control of the people who live under it; social relations are exploitative and oppressive. Under socialism/communism, social relations are not exploitative because the mode of production is under conscious collective control. This means that the social determinants of human nature are under human control. Consequently there is a basis for saying that the needs, wants, and capacities that constitute the human nature of socialism and communism are acquired more freely than are those that constitute the human nature of other epochs.

There is another reason—also having to do with freedom—why Marx had a preference for the human nature of socialism and communism. As we have seen, of all the different features of a species, Marx emphasized the characteristic form of life activity as key to the nature of that species. Free, conscious activity is a transhistorical capacity of human beings that is unique to them, but it is only fully developed and realized in socialism and communism. Only when social need is the basis of production, and production is under conscious collective control, will there be a significant reduction of necessary labor time, beyond which, Marx says, "begins that development of human energy which is a need in itself, the true realm of freedom." He refers to this sort of labor which is only possible for most people under socialism and communism as "self-realization, objectification of the subject, hence real freedom."[25]

Thus the human nature of socialism and communism can be said to be more free than that of previous societies in two senses: first, a key aspect of this human nature is the expression of freedom, and second, the determinants of many other aspects of human nature are under people's conscious, collective control for the first time. For this reason and because it is the most developed form of what is peculiar to human beings, Marx sometimes referred to it as the most truly human nature.[26] A higher value is put on a society in which human nature takes this form because freedom is a basic value.

The women's nature discussed in this paper is disanalogous to human nature in many respects. Most important is the fact that, while there will always be a distinctive human nature, even in socialism/communism, it seems unlikely that there will always be a distinctive women's nature. Except as a remnant of the past, there seems little reason to think that there would still be a women's nature in socialism/communism, either the present one or one specific to that society. The biological differences between men and women would remain, but this does not constitute a difference in nature for reasons discussed earlier. Moreover, the biological differences do not by themselves determine the present psychological differences between men and women. Rather, it is the sexual/social division of labor and the resulting sexually differentiated social relations and socialization that explain the differences. In Marx's theory this is determined not by biology but primarily by oppressive social, economic, and historical conditions which are not present in socialism/communism. Socialism/communism for Marx is a society of self-governing producers, the self-emancipation of the working class. Since this can come into being and survive only with the full participation of both sexes, a struggle for women's liberation is integral to the struggle for socialism. Furthermore, in a socialist society in Marx's sense there is no economic basis for women's oppression as there is in capitalism. While there might be some lingering material and psychological basis in the advantages to men, the nature both of a successful struggle for socialism and of a genuinely socialist society would substantially reduce the strength, efficacy, and longevity of such tendencies.

Now it is not impossible that the biological differences between men and women would still produce psychological differences under socialism/communism. Free, conscious activity will not take the same concrete form for everyone, and it is possible that these forms will differ along sexual lines. However, since there does not appear to be a direct biological-psychological link now, why should there be then? One could say that there would always have to be some differences in men's and women's experience of themselves as physical beings, but exactly what this means or how one would determine it is somewhat obscure. In any case, unless they were expressed in social practices and institutions, such differences, if they existed, would not have the kind of importance that would warrant speaking of them as distinct men's and women's natures. The sexual and reproductive choices women make would not have the kind of profound social consequences for women as opposed to men that they do now. So women's needs and interests, in this central and currently sex-differentiated realm, would differ very little from men's.

As we saw, the reason Marx gave a preference to the human nature of socialism and communism is that it is more freely acquired than previous forms of human nature, and freedom is a key constituent of human nature. Neither of these considerations applies to the present (and past) sex-related natures. Freedom is not constituent of (present and past) sex-related natures, and there is no basis for saying that they were freely acquired. There is little reason to think that what is truly unique to women, bearing children, is what they would freely choose to do more than anything else. The biological differences are the basis, along with economic, social, and historical conditions, for the sexual/social division of labor and the resulting social relations—none of which is under their control. Thus the psychological sex differences that result and that constitute sex-differentiated natures are not under their control. Furthermore, ignoring the legal restrictions that exist or that have been lifted only recently, women's traditional social role and the nature associated with it involves less freedom than men's. Being a wife and mother is supposed to be women's primary aim and self-definition, and the traits desirable for women are those that make them better able to fulfill this role—being attractive to men and able to satisfy a family's needs. Leaving aside for the moment the question of whether this life is inherently less challenging and empowering than most men's lives (hence less free in Marx's sense), the point is that this is only one choice. In developed countries, at least, men have many more choices. And though, obviously, as many men are fathers as women are mothers, men are first and foremost doctors, lawyers, tailors, and sailors. Unless this is what women would be inclined to do anyway, this implies that there are greater social pressures on women than on men. When women do take on other jobs, they are still constrained by the traditional values and expectations. Standing in the way of women's whole-hearted pursuit of other options are not only the objective constraints of sex discrimination and family responsibilities but, in addition, their own conflicting feelings of obligation, conflicting desires, and even habits (for example, spending a lot of time on their personal appearance). Women's lives are less free than men's are both because they are dependent on men and because they have children dependent on them. Traditional sexual values constrain women more than they do men. And women, being as a rule more passive and oriented to other people's wishes than men, are less able to act to realize their own desires. In all these ways the present women's nature lacks the freedom involved in the human nature of socialism/communism as envisioned by Marx.

But any women's nature or indeed any sex-differentiated nature would lack this freedom. Indeed there is a contradiction in the very idea of a society in which the human nature distinctive of socialism/communism and this distinctive women's nature are both fully realized. Women (and men) are human beings. They could not simultaneously realize a limited nature determined by limiting social conditions and a nature whose essence is freedom. By definition, any sex-differentiated nature would be more limited than one not so differentiated. And while there is nothing that absolutely precludes sex-differentiated natures from being freely acquired, there seem very good empirical grounds for rejecting the idea that they could be.

NOTES

My thanks to Milton Fisk and Karsten Struhl for their helpful comments. This essay originally appeared in *Ethics* 94 (April 1984).

1. As is well known, one of the most controversial areas of Marxist scholarship is whether Marx had a theory of human nature in his later work and, if so, whether it is significantly different from his earlier one. The interpretation I give below is consistent with both his early and his later work (as indicated by references). So there is some common theory of human nature, although there are also differences between his early and late ideas which are not relevant to my concerns in this essay.
2. Karl Marx, *Grundrisse* (Harmondsworth: Penguin, 1973), 92.
3. D. L. Hull, "Contemporary Systematic Philosophies," in *Annual Review of Ecology and Systematics*, ed. Richard Johnson (Palo Alto, CA: Annual Reviews, 1970), 19–54; "The

Metaphysics of Evolution," *British Journal of the History of Science* 3 (1966–67): 309–37; and "The Effect of Essentialism on Taxonomy: 2000 Years of Stasis, Parts 1, 2," *British Journal of the Philosophy of Science* 15 (1965): 314–26; 16 (1966): 1–18.

4. By "psychophysical" I mean to include phenomena to be explained in physical terms, psychological terms, or any mixture thereof, whatever the ultimate relation between the physical and the psychological.

5. Some fascinating work along these lines was done by the early Soviet psychologists, Lev Vygotsky and A. R. Luria, who defined psychology to mean "the science of the socio-historical shaping of mental activity and of the structures of mental processes which depend utterly on the basic forms of social practice and the major stages in the historical development of society." *Cognitive Development: Its Cultural and Social Foundations* (Cambridge, MA: Harvard University Press, 1976), 164. In a study of Central Asian peasants in the early 1930s, they discovered significant differences in the mode as well as the content of cognition between those living on a collective farm for two years and those engaged in traditional peasant agriculture. Specifically, the latter had difficulty with simple syllogisms while the former did not; and the latter classified objects according to what Luria called a "graphic-functional" mode as opposed to the "abstract-theoretical" mode used by the former. In attempting to give a material basis for his approach, Luria made innovative contributions to neuropsychology. Unfortunately, they did not explore the connections between social structure and noncognitive aspects of mental life. These seminal ideas have never really been developed. They were suppressed in the Soviet Union until recently and remained unknown in the West until many years later. See also A. R. Luria, *The Working Brain: An Introduction to Neuropsychology* (New York: Basic Books, 1973), and *Higher Cortical Functions in Man* (New York: Basic Books, 1966); Lev Vygotsky, *Thought and Language* (Cambridge, MA: MIT Press, 1982).

6. An academic example of this point of view is Judith Bardwick, *Psychology of Women* (New York: Harper & Row, 1971); a more popular example is Steven Goldberg, "The Inevitability of Patriarchy," in Jane English, ed., *Sex Equality* (Englewood Cliffs, NJ: Prentice-Hall, 1977).

7. These reservations are based on the following objections: First, the research is confined to artificial situations and narrow cultural contexts. Second, it concentrates on statistically significant differences and ignores the magnitude, overlap, and importance of the features. And third, it lacks a theoretical framework with which to evaluate the findings.

8. For example, women tend to have greater needs to be close to people (L. E. Tyler, *The Psychology of Human Differences* [New York: Appleton-Century-Crofts, 1965]; E. Maccoby, "Sex Differences in Intellectual Functioning," in E. Maccoby, ed., *The Development of Sex Differences* [Stanford, CA: Stanford University Press, 1966], 25–55); to be less aggressive (E. Maccoby and L. Jacklin, *The Psychology of Sex Differences* [Stanford, CA: Stanford University Press, 1974]); more suggestible (Tyler, *The Psychology of Human Differences*; Maccoby, "Sex Differences"); to be motivated more by a desire for love than by a desire for power (L. Hoffman, "Early Childhood Experiences and Women's Achievement Motives," *Journal of Social Issues* 28 [1972]: 129–55); to have greater verbal and less visual/spatial ability (Tyler, *The Psychology of Human Differences*; Maccoby, "Sex Differences"; Maccoby and Jacklin, *The Psychology of Sex Differences*). These differences are clearer and more significant among adolescents and adults than among young children (J. Block, "Issues, Problems and Pitfalls in Assessing Sex Differences: A Critical Review of *The Psychology of Sex Differences*," *Merrill-Palmer Quarterly* 22 [1976]: 283–308), with newborn boys and girls showing no clear

psychological differences (N. Romer, *The Sex-Role Cycle* [New York: Feminist Press/ McGraw-Hill, 1981], 7). These findings of statistically significant differences simply show that women have a trait to a higher degree than men. This is consistent with some men having it more than most women and even with a majority of women lacking it.

9. Critics of sociobiology have raised serious doubts that any specific and variable human behavioral traits are under genetic control. See in particular Stephen Jay Gould, "The Non-Science of Human Nature" and "Biological Potentiality vs. Biological Determinism," in *Ever Since Darwin* (New York: W. W. Norton, 1977), 237–42, 251–59; Arthur Caplan, ed., *The Sociobiology Debate* (New York: Harper & Row, 1978).

10. Regarding achievement scores, see S. R. Tulkin, "Race, Class, Family and School Achievement," *Journal of Personality and Social Psychology* 9 (1968): 31–37; A. R. Jensen, "The Race × Class × Ability Interaction" (Ph.D. diss., University of California, Berkeley, 1970). Regarding fear of success, see P. Weston and M. Mednick, "Race, Social Class and the Motive to Avoid Success in Women," *Journal of Cross-cultural Psychology* 1 (1970): 284–91.

11. S. Schachter and J. E. Singer, "Cognitive, Social and Physiological Determinants of Emotional State," *Psychological Review* 69 (1962): 379–99. A philosopher might argue that a finer analysis would show that it was not the *same* physiological state which yielded the different results but two different states. Regardless, the study shows that the social situation is more important than the physiological factor.

12. W. Mischel, "A Social-Learning View of Sex Differences in Behavior," in Maccoby, ed., *The Development of Sex Differences*, 56–81.

13. Romer, *The Sex-Role Cycle*, 7, 124. Studies show that parents (as well as society) project fewer clear sex-role expectations on babies than on young children and adolescents. However, such stereotypes are projected throughout the human life: there is no time that can safely be said to be prior to socialization. Studies show that parents describe newborns in sex-stereotypic ways, even though hospital records show no objective differences, and that parents behave differently toward boy and girl babies even though they are unaware of it. Cited in ibid., 139–40, nn. 3, 4, 5, 6.

14. H. Barry III, M. K. Bacon, and I. I. Child, "A Cross Cultural Survey of Some Sex Differences in Socialization," *Journal of Abnormal and Social Psychology* 55 (1957): 327–32.

15. Margaret Mead's ground-breaking research provides dramatic examples of societies where sex roles are very different from those familiar to us: *Sex and Temperament in Three Primitive Societies* (New York: William Morrow, 1935).

16. See Judith K. Brown, "An Anthropological Perspective on Sex Roles and Subsistence," in Michael S. Teitelbaum, ed., *Sex Differences* (Garden City, NY: Doubleday, 1976), 122–38, for a survey of the research on sex roles and subsistence activities. "Though men typically make a predominant contribution ... there are numerous societies in which women make a predominant contribution" (125). This variation is not random but seems to depend on two other activities which are universally sex-linked. Warfare is everywhere a predominantly male activity, and childcare is everywhere a predominantly female activity. Women do more subsistence work when men are occupied by warfare and when it is compatible with childcare responsibilities. Thus societies in which women predominate in subsistence activities are those which depend almost entirely on gathering or hoe cultivation.

17. See Nancy Chodorow, "Being and Doing: A Cross Cultural Guide to the Socialization of Males and Females," in V. Gornick and B. Moran, eds., *Woman in Sexist Society* (New York: Basic Books, 1971), 173–97.

18. C. B. Thoy, "Status, Race and Aspirations: A Study of the Desire of High School Students to Enter a Profession or a Technical Occupation," *Dissertation Abstracts International* 2 (1969): 10-A, abstract 3672.

19. Joyce Ladner, *Tomorrow's Tomorrow* (Garden City, NY: Doubleday, 1972).

20. Dorothy Dinnerstein's *The Mermaid and the Minotaur* (New York: Harper & Row, 1977) and Nancy Chodorow's *The Reproduction of Mothering* (Berkeley: University of California Press, 1978) fit this approach in that they argue that the near universal fact that women "mother" (in a psychological sense as well as the many physical ways) is the key to adult male and female personality structures. I disagree, however, with many of the specifics of the theories—in particular, the primary emphasis put on early childhood and the psychological aspects of the division of labor.

21. One showed that women wage workers work an average of 69 hours per week (40 paid, 29 unpaid), while male wage workers work an avenge of 53 hours per week (44 paid, 9 unpaid). Cited in E. Currie, R. Dunn, and D. Fogarty, "The New Immiseration: Stagflation, Inequality and the Working Class," *Socialist Review* 10 (1980): 7–32.

22. See Hilda Scott, *Does Socialism Liberate Women?* (Boston: Beacon Press, 1974); Maxine Molyneux, "Socialist Societies: Progress towards Women's Emancipation?" *Monthly Review* 34 (1982): 56–100.

23. See S. J. Bahr, "Effects on Family Power and Division of Labor in the Family," in L. Hoffman and F. I. Nye, eds., *Working Mothers* (San Francisco: Jossey-Bass, 1974).

24. Myra Marx Ferree, "Working Class Jobs: Housework and Paid Work as Sources of Satisfaction," *Social Problems* 23 (1976): 431–41.

25. Karl Marx, *Capital*, vol. 3 (Moscow: Progress Publishers, 1974), 820; and Marx, *Grundrisse*, 611.

26. Although this way of thinking about it is quite understandable, it should not be taken as negating the more relativistic analysis given earlier in the essay. See my "Free Will and the Marxist Concept of Natural Wants," *Philosophical Forum* 6 (1975): 423–45, for a fuller discussion of some of these issues, though with a more universalistic interpretation of Marx's theory of human nature.

THE ECOPOLITICS DEBATE
AND THE POLITICS OF NATURE

VAL PLUMWOOD

What might loosely be called "green theory" includes several subcritiques and positions whose relationship has recently been the subject of vigorous and often bitter debate, and which have some common ground but apparently a number of major divergences. The ecopolitics debate seems to have revealed that the green movement still lacks a coherent liberatory theory which enables opposition to both the domination of humans and the domination of nonhuman nature. Yet such a perspective connecting human and nonhuman forms of domination seems both possible and essential to do justice to the concerns the movement has articulated in the last two decades. Many environmental critiques have shown how control over and exploitation of nature is linked to control over and exploitation of human beings (Plumwood and Routley 1982; Hecht and Cockburn 1990; Shiva 1989, 1992). High-technology agriculture and forestry in the Third World which is ecologically destructive also strengthens the control of elites and social inequality, increasing for example men's control over the economy at the expense of women, and it does these things in a way which reflects structure, not coincidence. As the free water we drink from common streams, the free air we breathe in common become increasingly unfit to sustain life, the biospheric means for a healthy life are increasingly privatized and become the privilege of those who can afford to pay for them. The losers will be (and in many places already are) those, human and nonhuman, without market power, and issues of human justice and issues of the destruction of nature must increasingly converge.

Unless we are to treat human and nonhuman forms of domination as in only temporary and accidental alliance, an adequate green philosophy must cater for both human and nonhuman concerns, and give an important place to understanding their mutual determination and mutual development. Behind the failure of the green movement to articulate such a theory stands the broader failure of radical social change movements to build a coherent theoretical basis for political alliances. For the three main ecopolitical positions that have been involved in this dialogue—social ecology, deep ecology, and ecological feminism—each has links to critiques of capitalism, to environmentalism, and to the women's movement respectively. Thus deep ecology is perhaps the best known branch of what has been called "deep green theory,"[1] a set of positions or critiques treating anthropocentrism or human centeredness as one of the major roots of environmental problems (Naess 1973, 1987): Social ecology, whose best-known exponent is Murray Bookchin, draws on Western radical traditions, especially anarchist tradition, and focuses on an analysis of ecological problems in terms of human social hierarchy. Many ecological feminists have seen the domination of nature and the domination of women as arising from the same problematic and as sharing a common ideological foundation (Ruether 1975; Plumwood 1986, 1992; Warren 1987, 1990). Thus what is at stake in the internal green debate on this issue of political ecology is also the larger question of liberatory coherence and of cooperative relationship between the radical movements and critiques of oppression each of these internal green positions is aligned with. The quest for coherence is not the demand that each form of oppression submerge its hard-won identity in a single, amorphous, oceanic movement or party.[2] Rather it asks that each form of opposition develop sensitivity to other forms of oppression, both at the level of practice and that of theory, and develop a basis for understanding connections.

The ecopolitics debate has involved issues of great importance, but there are a number of reasons why it has been problematic and unnecessarily polarized. The prominent male theorists aligned with social ecology and deep ecology have persistently conducted the debate as a dialogue for two (Zimmerman 1993), as if their two positions were the only starters in the green theory stakes, and have neglected the important contribution feminist and ecological feminist theory has made and continues to make to the construction of a coherent liberatory perspective which includes the green movement (Bookchin 1988, 1989, 1990, 1992; Chase 1991; Bradford 1993; Clark 1993; Kovel 1993; Sessions 1993). The resulting focus, as I argue below, has distorted their analysis in a number of ways, especially by suppressing the potential for a fully political understanding of the human domination of nature, an understanding of the sort an ecological feminist position can provide. The debate has also been largely conducted in a spirit of competitive reductionism and has often had an unnecessarily dismissive character. This style of debate has helped to generate a general climate of competition and false choice between approaches which critique anthropocentrism, on the one hand, and approaches which focus primarily on forms of human domination, on the other. It has helped to obscure the fact that there are ways of developing the critique of human domination of nature which are in no way incompatible with older critiques which reject human hierarchy, and which complement and make more complete our understanding of this hierarchy. I illustrate this further below.

An example will illustrate what I mean by "reductionism" here. Back in the days when Marxism was king of radical discourses, other discourses and critiques, such as those of the women's movement and the environment movement, were reduced to subject status, to be subsumed, incorporated into the kingdom of the sovereign. Their insights and problems were recognized and accorded legitimacy and attention just to the extent that they could be so absorbed (e.g. those aspects of the feminist critique which could plausibly be reduced to questions of "class" or of capitalism). Such an approach is a form of colonization, creating a hierarchy of oppressions (Haraway 1991a). It is incapable of providing a framework which can adequately recognize the multiplicity and interrelationship of forms of oppression.

THE INADEQUACY OF EXISTING ACCOUNTS: SOCIAL ECOLOGY

Social ecology, which draws on the radical tradition for an analysis of ecological problems in terms of human social hierarchy and market society, seems initially to be a promising place to look for a coherent liberatory perspective. But social ecology, as articulated in the recent work of Murray Bookchin, tries to resolve the problem of the relationship between these forms of exploitation in the familiar but deeply problematic move of creating a hierarchy of oppressions. Bookchin's work has developed, often in a powerful way, a critique of the role of intrahuman hierarchy and centralization in ecological destruction, and of the need to maintain a critique of fundamental social structures. But his recent work has been unable to accommodate a thoroughgoing critique of human domination of nature or to acknowledge a notion of human difference not linked to hierarchy. Recent attempts at public reconciliation (Chase 1991) have not convincingly bridged the theoretical chasm between critiques of human and of nonhuman domination. Bookchin's recent work leaves little room for doubt that his theory is for the most part hostile to the new rival critique of anthropocentrism, and eager to subsume it under some form of human domination. The domination of nature, he assures us, came after the domination of human by human and is entirely secondary to it (Bookchin 1993: 365). Thus he asserts a historical reduction thesis:

> All our notions of dominating nature stem from the very real domination of human by human.... As a historical statement [this] declares in no uncertain terms that the domination of human by human preceded the notion of dominating nature. (Bookchin 1989: 44)

It is prior in other senses too, according to Bookchin. Although his account stresses human liberation, he claims that it is strategically prior to (1989: 601), and must come before, the liberation of nature, which is demoted to the status of a "social symptom rather than a social cause" (1989: 25). Bookchin can be read as suggesting that we must first create a society in which all forms of human hierarchy are eliminated before we can hope to achieve a truly rational, ecological society (1989: 44). Although social ecology stresses its radical political orientation, Bookchin's version of it seems to see politics as confined to intrahuman relationships, and his textual practice appears insensitive to the colonizing politics of Western accounts of the human–nature relation. Thus in *Remaking Society* (1989) Bookchin rarely mentions nonhuman nature without attaching the word "mere" to it. (Thus deep ecologists want to "equate the human with mere animality," to "dissolve humanity into a mere species within a biospheric democracy," and to reduce humanity "to merely one life form among many" [1989: 42].) A more egalitarian approach is roundly condemned as debasing to humans and involving a denial of their special value-making quality of rationality.

For Bookchin, the ecological crisis demands the defense of the Western tradition and of the supremacy of reason against its critics, including its recent philosophical, feminist, and postmodernist critics who have argued that Western cultural ideals of reason have defined themselves in opposition to the feminine and to the sphere of nature and subsistence (Midgley 1980; Harding and Hintikka 1983; Harding 1984, 1986; Lloyd 1984; Fox Keller 1985). These critics of oppositional and colonizing forms of reason have not sought to reject reason as such, but rather to reject its traditional Western "rationalist" construction as inferiorizing, opposing, and controlling other areas of human and nonhuman life (usually those counted as "nature"). Bookchin's recent work can be described as an ecological rationalism in that it retains much of the traditional role of reason as the supreme source of value, the basis of human difference and identity, and the chief justification of superiority over those others cast as nature. Many ecological critics of anthropocentrism (e.g. Dodson Gray 1979: 19) have argued that the dominant tendency in Western culture has been to construe difference in terms of hierarchy, and that a less colonizing approach to nature does not involve denying human reason or human difference but rather ceasing to treat reason as the basis of superiority and domination. Bookchin, however, presents the denial of human superiority as the denial of human difference, just as he presents the critique of colonizing forms of reason as the rejection of all rationality.

Social ecologists, including Bookchin, may not be wrong in their conviction that Western radical traditions can offer valuable insights into our ecological plight. But the best radical traditions of the West, at least in their more self-critical phases, must surely be uneasy with the politics of a rationalist philosophy which places an implicitly Western, "rational" culture at the apex of evolution. Ecological rationalism merely puts a new, "radical" spin on the old reason supremacy of the Western tradition which has underlain so much of its history of colonization and inferiorization of those "others" cast as outside reason. Reason supremacy, a rational hierarchy with the most rationalized and intellectualized human individuals and cultures at the top, is the logical outcome of a world-view which understands the significance of the world in terms of "the vast evolution of life toward greater subjectivity and ultimately human intellectuality" (Bookchin 1992: 26). Many recent thinkers have critiqued the escalator account of evolution (Midgley 1983), an arrogant and unidimensional world-view which judges the whole great diversity of earth life as a mere "stage" along the way to human intellect, as merely falling short of the human ideal. Bookchin's neo-Hegelian ecological rationalism turns its back on this important critique, and fails to come to terms with the re-evaluation of the complex of Western-centered rationalist concepts which inferiorize the sphere of nature and non-Western culture—rationality, progress, "primitivism," development, and civilization. It fails to confront the chief myth of progress and the other ideologies which surround colonialism, namely the confrontation with an inferior past, an inferior non-Western other, and the associated notion of indigenous cultures as "backward," earlier stages of our own exemplary civilization. The retention of an oppositional concept of reason and the continued fear and denial of its exclusions are represented in the constant dark references his work makes to "atavism" and "primitivism."

Although social ecology prides itself on the thoroughness of its political critique, its political sensitivity is not extended to the nonhuman sphere. Indeed social ecologists (Bradford 1993: 431) join environmental ethicists (Rolston 1987: 264) and deep ecologists (Fox 1990) in denying that our relations to nature can be understood in political terms which approximate those of other forms of oppression. Bookchin seeks a resolution of the ecological crisis through an ecological society where humans, representing "second nature"—defined as "first nature rendered self-reflexive, a thinking nature that knows itself and can guide its own evolution" (1990: 182)—can realize their potential as the "rational voice of nature" (1992: 23), rational "stewards" managing nature for its own best interests. Although human difference (as rational) from nature is stressed in order to establish the human right to control, the difference of nature is subtly erased when it comes to establishing that it has no independence of being or interest which could properly impose constraints on human interference. Thus we do not need to leave space for this other on the earth, since it is never "natural" to exclude the human species, even from pristine wilderness (Bookchin 1992: 27). The incorporation of nature into the human sphere by defining humanity as "nature rendered self-conscious" makes a political conception of human–nature relations impossible, because it leaves no space for independence, difference, and self-directedness on the part of first nature, defining out of existence conflicts of interest between rational "second nature" and "first" nature. Any attempt to conceive the human domination of nature as comparable to other forms of oppression will have to resist such an incorporation, and recognize beings in nature as others deserving (both as individuals and as nations) respect in their own right.

Bookchin's version of social ecology, then, focuses on some of the forms of hierarchy within human society, but inherits many problematic aspects of the rationalist, Enlightenment, and Marxist traditions (Plumwood 1981; Clark 1984, 1993; Benton 1990). It defends assumptions associated with the human colonization of nature and retains forms of intrahuman hierarchy which draw on this. Although social ecology presents itself as offering a way of reconciling the various critiques of domination, Bookchin's version at least falls well short of that objective.

DEEP ECOLOGY AND LIBERATION

The critique of anthropocentrism or human domination of nature is a new and, in my view, inestimably important contribution to our understanding of Western society, its history, its current problems, and its structures of domination. However, as it is currently represented by its leading exponents in deep ecology, it fails to present a coherent liberatory perspective and is equally intent on a strategy of subsuming or dismissing other green perspectives. Thus leading deep ecologist Warwick Fox makes repeated counterclaims to "most fundamental" status for his own critique of the domination of nature, arguing that oppression as "nature" accounts for forms of human domination also. (There is an important point here, though in fact it is not deep ecology but ecological feminism which has provided the account of how the construction of certain categories of humans as "nature" has naturalized their domination (Ruether 1975; Mies 1986; Plumwood 1986, 1991, 1993; Shiva 1990, 1992.) At the same time (and inconsistently) Fox treats critiques of other forms of domination as irrelevant to environmental concern, on the grounds that overcoming them is not sufficient for overcoming anthropocentrism. Feminism, for example, is said to have nothing to add to the conception of environmental ethics (Fox 1989: 14). Hierarchy within human society is declared to be irrelevant to explanations of the destruction of nature.

If social ecology fails to reconcile the critiques because it fails to understand that human relations to nonhumans are as political as human relations to other humans, deep ecology as articulated here also suppresses the potential for an adequate political understanding of its theme of human–nature domination, although it achieves this suppression of the political by a route which is partly different. Like social ecology, deep ecology suppresses the difference of nature by incorporation into the self (or Self), as I have argued elsewhere (Plumwood 1991, 1993). But it also suppresses the political dimension by providing a politically insensitive account of the core relationship to nature which provides the basis for its account. Thus dominant forms of deep ecology choose for their core concept of analysis the notion of identification, understood as an individual psychic act rather than a political practice, yielding a theory which emphasizes personal transformation and ignores social structure. The account is both individualist (failing to provide a framework for change which can look beyond the individual) and psychologistic (neglecting factors beyond psychology).

A similarly apolitical understanding is given to its core concept of ecological selfhood; here the account, while drawing extensive connections with various eastern religious positions, seems to go out of its way to ignore the substantial links which could fruitfully be made with feminist accounts of the self and with feminist theory (Cheney 1987, 1989; Warren 1990). The result is a psychology of incorporation, not a psychology of mutuality. Fox suggests that selfishness in the form of excessive personal attachment, which he conflates with psychological egoism, is the fundamental cause of "possessiveness, greed, exploitation, war and ecological destruction" (Fox 1990: 262). An analysis that exhorts us to consider nature by transcending the egoism of personal attachment matches in its depth of political insight the sort of social analysis that exhorts us to resolve problems of social inequality through acts of individual unselfishness. Such an analysis also uncritically assumes an account of personal attachment as antithetical to moral life, which has increasingly and deservingly come under attack recently, especially from feminists (Plumwood 1992). Deep ecology in this standard form makes a good religious or spiritual garnish for an eclectic green stew of liberal political theory (Elkins 1989; Bradford 1993).[3]

The strategies followed by both social and deep ecology critiques for excluding common ground and maintaining territories are both bad methodology and bad politics. They are bad methodology because they involve a false choice between human and nonhuman domination, and bad politics because they pass up important opportunities for connection and strengthening. They are bad politics also because it is essential for critiques which purport to treat hierarchy to be prepared to meet others on a basis of equality, not with an agenda of inferiorizing or absorbing them. Maximizing chances for change must involve broadening the base of those who desire change, who can see how change is relevant to their lives, and this involves maximizing connection with a wide variety of issues and social change movements.

At first glance, each of the three positions in the ecopolitics debate appears to share an approach employing the concept of domination, which thus provides the potential for a new synthesis and a common political understanding. But the two positions that have occupied most of the space in the debate have squandered this potential. From a third perspective which sees human and nonhuman domination as cut from the same cloth, many of the criticisms deep ecology and social ecology have made of each other seem valid, but can be avoided by such a third position. Thus deep ecology has, on this view, been right in criticizing social ecology's human chauvinism and continued subscription to traditional doctrines of human supremacy. But social ecology is similarly correct in its criticism of the insensitivity of deep ecology to intrahuman politics and of its failure to understand the role of human hierarchy in creating environmental problems.

FEMINIST FRAMEWORKS FOR GREEN THEORY

Despite its neglect and even depreciation (Fox 1990; Sessions 1993)[4] by prominent green theorists, feminist theory provides a very promising foundation for a green theory which can resolve these problems of coherence and which can provide a recognition of multiplicity without setting up a hierarchy of oppressions. The formulation of a theoretical framework that takes account of the oppression of women in the context of a multiplicity of oppressions has been a major concern of many feminist theorists in the last decade.[5] This framework includes sophisticated developments of liberation theory which address the interconnection of all forms of domination, focusing especially on race, class, and gender issues, and including also nature (hooks 1981, 1984, 1989). Thus bell hooks writes:

> Feminism, as liberation struggle, must exist apart from and as a part of the larger struggle to eradicate domination in all its forms. We must understand that patriarchal domination shares an ideological foundation with racism and other forms of group oppression, that there is no hope that it can be eradicated while these systems remain intact. (hooks 1989: 22)

Ecological feminists have been addressing the domination of nature in a context of recognizing the multiplicity of oppressions for nearly two decades. They have mainly been concerned, like socialist and black feminists, with cooperative rather than competitive movement strategies.[6] The domination of women is of course central to any feminist understanding of domination, but is also an illuminating and well-theorized model for many other kinds of domination, since the oppressed are often both feminized and naturalized. The ecologically oriented feminism of writers such as Rosemary Ruether has always stressed the links between the domination of women, of human groups such as blacks, and of nature. "An ecological ethic," Ruether writes, "must always be an ethic of ecojustice that recognizes the interconnection of social domination and the domination of nature" (Ruether 1989). Karen J. Warren writes that a more complete feminism "would expand upon the traditional conception of feminism as a movement to end women's oppression by recognizing and making explicit the interconnections between all systems of oppression" (1987: 18). Thus the work of many feminists and ecological feminists has foreshadowed the development of a form of liberation theory which provides a coherent theory of oppression.

LIBERATION THEORY AND THE NETWORK OF OPPRESSION

As feminist theorists working on the connections between race, class, and gender oppressions have shown, there is a certain construction of "colonized" identity which is common to these oppressed groups and which arises from the perspective of a dominant master elite, from their ability to control culturally mediated perception and construct identities (Hartsock 1990). This reflects oppression in the cultural structures of dualism, which casts oppressed groups as part of a separate lower order whose domination is natural, part of the order of nature. The interwoven dualisms of Western culture, mind/body, male/female, reason/emotion, and subject/object, have been involved here to create a logic of interwoven oppression consisting of many strands coming together. This common framework of dualism that structures human oppressions also extends to include human/nature and reason (civilization)/nature dualism, which construct human identity as sharply separate from the inferiorized, backgrounded, instrumentalized, and homogenized sphere of nature. This common structure is one reason for seeing the domination of nature as of the same general kind as intrahuman forms of domination, although the latter have, of course, specific features of their own.

As bell hooks notes, these areas of oppression are linked by a common ideology which is associated with this structure. The core of this common ideology, I have argued (Plumwood 1991, 1993), is the ideology of the control of reason over nature, for what these oppressed groups particularly have in common is that each has been counted as part of the sphere of nature. As "nature," oppressed groups have been located outside the sphere of reason the sphere Western elites have particularly seen themselves as representing. The story of the control of the chaotic and deficient realm of "nature" by mastering and ordering "reason" has been the master story of Western culture. An examination of this story reveals that this ideology of the domination of nature plays a key role in structuring all the major forms of oppression in the West, which are thus linked through the politics of nature. It has supported pervasive human relations of domination within Western society and of colonization between Western society and other societies, as well as supporting a colonizing approach toward nonhuman nature itself. Those of us who have been desensitized in the nonhuman case to the colonizing politics built into the ideology of reason and nature can perhaps best be brought to feel it by considering examples of the application of this ideology to the human case.

THE POLITICS OF THE "PRIMITIVE"

Ecological feminism has particularly stressed that the treatment of nature and of women as inferior has supported and "naturalized" not only the hierarchy of male to female but the inferiorization of many other groups of humans seen as more closely identified with nature. As "nature," women have been distanced from reason and counted as disorderly, emotional, and subject to a physicality conceived as chaotic and animal. The same ideology has been used to justify the supposed inferiority of black races (conceived as more animal), the supposed inferiority of uncivilized" or "primitive"' cultures, and the supposed superiority of master to slave, boss to employee, mental to manual worker. Western colonizers have seen themselves as carrying the torch of reason and civilization (in its more modern form "development") to alien lands. In their ideology, the indigenous peoples they encountered were outside reason in the form of Christian civilization, and were seen as "primitive," childlike, and closer to the animal, an earlier form of the exemplary civilization of the West which represented the pinnacle of human development. From the time of Columbus, the conception of indigenous peoples as "nature" has justified invasion, enslavement, and slaughter. The Spanish priest Las Casas, historian of Columbus's conquests, noted that the Christians despised the natives and held them as fit objects for enslavement "because they are in doubt as to whether they are animals or beings with souls" (Turner 1986: 142). To deal with these examples as merely errors of classification is to miss the way in which this politics has constructed reason, mind, and spirit as the domain of the colonizer, and builds domination into the basic concepts of reason and nature, in terms of which Western culture has framed the world.

TASMANIA AND THE NETWORK OF OPPRESSION

The example of the sealing industry in Tasmania, the first form of accumulation witnessed on the Australian continent, will serve to illustrate both this ideology and its practical correlate of linked oppressions. The history of the convicts, of the Aborigines who suffered invasion, and of the seals and whales whose deaths fueled these processes of human oppression is interwoven at both ideological and material levels. The convict system helped maintain the savagely repressive internal order of the class and property structure of Britain, the product of a long-term previous accumulation process. The slaughter of seals and whales provided fuel, oil, and a commercial basis for the convict transportation industry.

The population of seals on the islands of Bass Strait and Tasmania in the 1700s was in the hundreds of thousands. It took Australia's first export industry a mere eight years from the first sealing expedition in 1798 to reduce their numbers there below the levels capable of commercial exploitation. After each depletion, the sealers moved on, to other states and to New Zealand. Sealers typically killed all sizes and ages, clubbing or stabbing seals as they came ashore and not hesitating to destroy breeding colonies. Some species, such as the elephant seal, were locally wiped out and are only just returning to Australian coasts. From 1806, when William Collins set up a bay whaling station in the Derwent (where whales were reported to be so thick in season that collisions with boats were a problem), the seal story was immediately repeated with whales. Female southern right whales (or bay whales)—now some of the world's rarest whales—were killed along with their young when they entered the bays to give birth. Within a few decades the industry could boast the virtual local extinction of bay whales. Again the industry moved on to repeat the same story in New Zealand.

The ships which had delivered their human cargoes of convicts went sealing or whaling and returned profitably to the "civilized" world with holds filled with oil or skins. In turn, the runaway convicts and soldiers provided suitably hardened and desperate workers for these industries and helped clear the country of the despised natives, described by the *Hobart Town Gazette* of 1824 as "the most peaceful creatures in the world." The industry involved the abduction and enslavement of large numbers of Aboriginal women, who were subjected to cruelty and to rape, and the killing of Aboriginal men and children during their capture. Settlement along these lines led to the near annihilation of Aboriginal Tasmanians, who survive today as a distinct grouping with mixed ancestry, claiming Aboriginal identity but almost entirely dispossessed of their culture and lands.

The ideology that linked these common practices of oppression stressed the inferiority of the order of "nature," which was construed as barbaric, alien, and animal, and also as passive and female. It was contrasted with the truly human realm, marked by patriarchal, Eurocentric, and body-hating concepts of reason and "civilization," maximally distanced from "nature." Aborigines were seen as part of this inferior order, supposedly being "in a state of nature," and without culture. Aborigines "lived like the beasts of the forest," writes Cook at Adventure Bay in 1770; they were "strangers to every principle of social order" (Bonwick 1870). Early journal reports consistently stressed Aboriginal nudity and propensity to leave open to public view "those parts which modesty directs us to conceal." Where clothes are construed as the mark of civilization and culture, nudity confirms an animal and cultureless state, a reduction to body. The ideology of nature, reason, and civilization made it possible to deny kinship and see those classed as part of the inferior realm of nature as open to merciless exploitation. The unclothed bodies of Aborigines and the technological economy of Aboriginal life meant that they could be seen in terms of such an ideology as not fully human, but as part of the realm of nature, to be treated in much the same way as the seals.

NATURE AND TERRA NULLIUS

Such was the philosophical basis not only for the destruction of Tasmanian Aborigines but for the annexation of Australia under the rubric of terra nullius, a land without occupiers, under which Australians lived until very recently.[7] The doctrine of terra nullius provided a basis for annexing without a treaty land classed as uninhabited. It was used in parts of Africa as well as in Australia, classing the occupants of these lands as less than human and erasing from the European record their history of resistance and struggle. The category of "nature" has been above all a political category, one which has allowed its occupants to be erased from consideration as others to be acknowledged and respected, constituted as objects whose rights are not recognized and which are allowed to place no limits on those of the colonizer. In this capacity it continues to function to justify oppression in both the human and nonhuman spheres.

These connections are not just historical curiosities. Aboriginal people in many parts of the world (including Australia) are still inferiorized, killed, or deprived of access to the means of life, under the influence of the same ideology.[8] In Tasmania seals too are now legally "protected," but the slaughter of seals in large numbers continues into the present.[9] The denial of dependence on and contempt for the processes of life and reproduction involved in the systematic wiping out of mammal breeding colonies and the killing of whales and seals in the very act of giving birth continues to underlie our treatment of humans as outside of nature and our treatment of nature as limitless provider. The heart of the problem of sustainability lies in this Western master consciousness deny-ing dependence on the sphere of nonhuman life, the body, women's labour, and reproduction. The opportunistic ideology proclaiming the supremacy of reason over nature changes its sites but not its political colors. Now it naturalizes the fate of the poor, distanced from reason (increasingly defined in the market) as childishly improvident, animal-like in their incapacity for deferred gratification, and insufficiently qualified or rationally self-developed (Ehrenreich 1989). The network of oppression stretches from the past into the present.

A COOPERATIVE MOVEMENT STRATEGY: METHODOLOGY AND POLITICS

The conception of oppression as a network of multiple, interlocking forms of domination linked by a flexible, common ideology and structure of identity raises a number of new methodological dilemmas and requires a number of adjustments for liberation movements. The associated critiques cannot simply be added together, for there are too many discrepancies between them. Should we say for example that opposition struggle involves one movement or many? Each answer to the one/many dilemma has its problems.

One way to deal with the multiplicity of oppressions is to say that each involves all—for example, that feminism should be thought of as a movement to end all forms of oppression (Warren 1987: 133). But we should not under-stand by this an oceanic view of the movements as submerged and indistin-guishable in a single great movement—for example, that there should not and cannot be an autonomous women's movement concerned primarily with women's oppression (or indeed any other autonomous movement). This would be prob-lematic if it denied the specificity of women's oppression, for example, and the need for accounts to relate to lived experience, as well as the possibility of difference of direction and conflicts of interest between movements (e.g. ethnic, race, and sexual oppression). And even if struggles have a common origin point, a common enemy or conceptual structure, it does not follow that they then become the same struggle. The women's movement especially has had good historical reason to distrust the submergence of women's struggle in the strug-gles of other movements, and has wanted to insist on the importance of move-ment autonomy and separate identity. And if a struggle which is too narrow and aimed at only a small part of an interlocking system will fail, so too will one which is too broad and lacking in a clear focus and a basis in personal experi-ence. On the other hand, treating the women's movement as isolated from other struggles is equally problematic, because there is no neutral, apolitical concept of the human or of society in which women can struggle for equality, and no pure, unqualified form of domination that is simply male and nothing else, which oppresses them. And since women are oppressed in multiple ways, as particular kinds of women (Spelman 1988), the struggle for most women is inevitably interlinked with other struggles.

The dilemma is created by setting up a choice between viewing liberation struggles as a shifting multiplicity only fortuitously or fleetingly connected (as in poststructuralism) versus viewing them as a monolithic, undifferentiated, and unified system. But if there are reasons for seeing the structure both as multiple and as unified, any model which does not recognize both these aspects is distorting. It is possible to bypass this one/many dilemma if these forms of oppression are seen as very closely, perhaps essentially, related, and working together to form a single system without losing a degree of distinctness and differentiation. One working model which enables such an escape from the one/many dilemma pictures oppressions as forming a network or web. In a web there are both one and many, both distinct foci and strands with room for some independent movement of the parts, but a unified overall mode of operation, forming a single system.[10]

The objections that some feminists have raised to what has been called "dual systems theory" in the case of capitalism and patriarchy (Young 1980; Mies 1986: 38) focus on the links and unified operation of the web rather than on the differentiated aspects of the structure. The interconnectedness of forms of oppression provides another reason for viewing these oppressions as forming a single mutually supporting system. The sorts of considerations that tell against the oceanic view provide a reason for viewing them as forming a differentiated system, with distinct parts that can and must be focused upon separately as well as together, as in a web. bell hooks's conception of feminism as retaining a separate identity but as necessarily overlapping with and participating in a wider struggle (hooks 1989: 22) captures the politics implied by the weblike nature of oppression and enables a balance between the requirements of identity politics and the requirements of connected opposition which arises from the connected nature of oppressions.

LIBERATION AND THE WEB

If oppressions form a web, it is a web which now encircles the whole globe and begins to stretch out to the stars, and whose strands grow ever tighter and more inimical to life as more and more of the world becomes integrated into the system of the global market and subject to the influence of its global culture. In the methodology and strategy for dealing with such a web it is essential to take account of both its connectedness and the capacity for independent movement among the parts. Rarely if ever can it be said, "Once we have cut this section, solved this problem, all the rest will follow, other forms of oppression will wither away." A web can continue to function and repair itself despite damage to localized parts of its structure. The parts can even be in conflict and perhaps move for a limited time in opposite directions.

The strategies for dealing with such a web require cooperation, the creation of political alliances. A cooperative movement strategy suggests a methodological principle for both theory and action, that where there is a choice of strategies or of possibilities for theoretical development, then, other things being equal, those strategies and theoretical developments which take account of or' promote this wider, connected set of objectives are to be preferred to ones which do not. This could be regarded as a minimum principle of cooperative strategy. But even as a minimum principle it is one which the major green positions of social and deep ecology currently fail.

Thus deep ecology has chosen the company of American nature mysticism and of religious eastern traditions such as Buddhism over that of various radical movements, including feminism, that it might have kept better company with. Elsewhere I have argued (Plumwood 1991) that deep ecology gives various accounts of the ecological self, as indistinguishable (holistic), as expanded, and as transpersonal, and that all of these are problematic both from the perspective of ecological philosophy and from that of other movements. Deep ecology could have provided an account of the ecological self in terms of a different account of the self as relational which does form a relevant connecting base for other movements. Social ecologists have rightly pointed to some of the political implications of its choice, which lead away from connections with the radical movements and traditions, and lead toward those being seen as only accidentally connected to environmental concerns.

If there is some reason for hope in our current situation, I believe it mainly lies in this: that we now have the possibility of obtaining a much more complete and connected understanding of the web of domination than we have ever had before, and hence a much more comprehensive and connected oppositional practice. What may be especially significant about this point in history is not only that the now global power of the web places both human and biological survival itself for the first time in the balance, but that several critically important parts of its fabric have recently become for the first time the subject of widespread conscious, self-reflective opposition. An understanding of its common structure and ideology of reason and nature can help provide a broader, deeper, and more complete basis of oppositional theory and practice, and fill out some crucial connections.

We who hope to break the power of the web must pursue with vigor the critique of older oppositional theories, such as Marxism, which had such an incomplete, reductionistic, and fragmentary understanding of it. We can trace much of their failure, in practice as well as in theory, to that very incompleteness, the blindspots which left domination ever ready to renew and consolidate itself in a different but related form, as state and bureaucratic tyranny, as sexism, as militarism, as power over nature. So much radical theory, especially Marxist theory, remained still caught within the ideology of reason and nature, an ideology we can still trace in existing green alternatives such as ecological rationalism. This does not mean that we should abandon the entire set of radical traditions, and turn to apolitical or mystical ones, but rather that we must come to an understanding of them as limited and partial. The problems of human inequality and hierarchy that the radical traditions addressed over the centuries have not gone away and are taking new and ever more sinister "environmental" forms. Their visions of human equality and the immense creative and intellectual energies they harnessed over long periods of history have helped to form the vision of a world where all the nations (including those of roots and wings and fur) live in freedom. We must somehow balance recognition of the power and strength of past radical traditions with recognition of the need for major revision and reworking, and so come to build better.

NOTES

1. The terminology "light" to "dark" or "deep" green theory is widely used in this context, but there has been contention over the issue of whether the difference can be represented as a spectrum or not. I use it here not to reinforce the idea of a spectrum, but mainly to allow terminologically for the idea that the critique of anthropocentrism or "deep green theory" is much wider and more diverse than the particular development given it by Naess, Sessions, Devall, Fox and others, who call themselves "Deep Ecologists," and includes such deep ecology as a proper subset. This issue has been a potent source of confusion and conservativism. Another way to make this point, which I shall not adopt here, is to capitalize the particular development of the position as "Deep Ecology," and refer to the generic position challenging anthropocentrism as "deep ecology" (see Chase 1991). For the term "Deep Ecology," see Naess 1973, 1987; Devall and Sessions 1985; Fox 1990. For development of deep green theory which is not deep ecology, see Plumwood 1975, 1980; Plumwood and Routley 1979.

2. Many postmodernist writers on the topic of movement connection object strenuously to absorption or "totalization," but are unable to envisage interaction in any more positive terms than "mutual disruption," "disintegration," or "destabilization" (Quinby 1990). This is indeed "a philosophical insurance policy" (Brennan 1991) against effective opposition to the master subject.

3. Biehl (1988a), another social ecologist, retains Bookchin's heavy emphasis on the defense of an oppositional conception of rationality and on Enlightenment humanism. Biehl endorses Bookchin's thesis of the secondary character of the domination of nature and is dismissive of its critique (Biehl 1988b). Some other social ecologists adopt less extreme positions. Thus both Tokar and Bradford, although heavily critical of present forms of deep ecology and its political orientation, go some way toward endorsing the generic critique of human domination of nature (Tokar 1989; Bradford 1989). On the ecopolitics debate between social ecology, ecofeminism, and deep ecology, see especially Biehl 1987, 1988a, 1988b, 1991; Bookchin 1988, 1989, 1991; Bradford 1989; Cheney 1987; Eckersley 1989; Fox 1989, and Plumwood 1991. A useful contribution is Tokar 1989.

4. Fox 1989: 525; on the irrelevance of feminism see 14, n. 22. See also Eckersley 1989: 101. For a discussion of this point, see Warren 1990 (144–45); and Plumwood 1991.

5. Social ecological feminists join black feminists in seeing women's oppression as one among a number of forms of oppression (hooks 1981, 1984, 1989; Eisenstein 1978). Social ecological feminism draws especially on black and anticolonial feminism and socialist feminism (Ruether 1975; Hartsock 1983; Mies 1986; Warren 1987, 1990; Spelman 1988; Haraway 1989, 1991b; King 1989, 1990; Shiva 1989, 1992). But unlike those forms which are concerned exclusively with race, class, and gender (Wajcman 1991; Walby 1992), they integrate a concern with nature into their investigation of

multiple grounds of exploitation and show how all these types of exploitation mutually determine and support one another. This form of ecological feminism is not committed to the thesis that women's struggle is identical with the struggle for nature, or that fixing one problem would automatically fix the other, which is a causal fallacy for most linked phenomena (see Plumwood 1991).

6. See the work of ecofeminists such as Ruether (1975), Warren (1987, 1990), and King (1989, 1990). Ecological feminism is a very diverse position: there are ecofeminists who are closely associated with deep ecology and others who are close to social ecology, as well as some close to radical feminism. Some forms of feminism and ecological feminism, principally those emerging from radical feminism, have had a reductionist slant of their own, taking patriarchy to be the basis of all hierarchy, the basic form of domination to which other forms (including not only the domination of nature but capitalism and other forms of human social hierarchy) can be reduced. However, to consider ecological feminism as if it were all of this reductionist bent (Fox 1990; Sessions 1993) certainly involves major representation. Unlike the other two positions, ecofeminism as a general position is not committed to reducing or dismissing either the critique of anthropocentrism and the domination of nature with which deep ecology is concerned or that of the human hierarchy with which social ecology is concerned.

7. The judgment of the High Court of Australia in the Mabo Case (3/6/92) has been welcomed by white political leaders as bringing to an end the colonial dispossession of Aboriginal people in Australia, but there are many reasons to treat this claim with caution; see Pitty 1992; Reynolds 1992.

8. Despite numerous reports and inquiries, deaths of Australian Aboriginal people in police custody remain at very high levels and in some states continue to increase. For an account, see Langford 1988: 256–58.

9. See Darby 1991. As many as 3,000 fur seals are killed by the Tasmanian fishing industry each year, many in macho shootouts which wipe out whole colonies. Others are killed even more cruelly, as their playfulness leads them to become entangled in the plastic fish bait packaging and discarded nets tossed overboard from boats. The industry dumps plastic garbage of all kinds, which is a killer of marine life and is found on the most remote beaches.

10. The net or web analogy is an alternative to the pillar analogy of some ecofeminists, as in "Racism, sexism, class exploitation and ecological destruction form interlocking pillars upon which the structure of patriarchy rests" (Sheila Collins, quoted in Warren 1987: 7). Another analogy is that of a body, as in Perlman 1983. For further models, see Albert et al. 1986. The web model was of course suggested by Foucault (1980: 234); his version has recently been criticized by Hartsock (1990).

REFERENCES

Albert, M. et al. 1986. *Liberating Theory*. Boston, MA: South End Press.

Benton, T. 1990. "Humanism = Speciesism? Marx on Humans and Animals," in S. Sayers and P. Osborne, eds., *Socialism, Feminism and Philosophy: A Radical Philosophy Reader*. London: Routledge.

Biehl, J. 1987. "It's Deep, but is it Broad? An Ecofeminist Looks at Deep Ecology," *Kick It Over*, Special Supplement, Winter.

Biehl, J. 1988a. "What is Social Ecofeminism?," *Green Perspectives* 11 (October): 57.

Biehl, J. 1988b. "Ecofeminism and Deep Ecology: Unresolvable Conflict?" *Our Generation* 19: 19–31.

Biehl, J. 1991. *Rethinking Ecofeminist Politics.* Boston, MA: South End Press.

Bonwick, J. 1870. *The Last of the Tasmanians.* London.

Bookchin, M. 1982. *The Ecology of Freedom.* Palo Alto, CA: Cheshire Books.

Bookchin, M. 1988. "Social Ecology versus Deep Ecology," *Kick It Over,* Special Supplement, Winter.

Bookchin, M. 1989. *Remaking Society.* Montreal: Black Rose Books.

Bookchin, M. 1990. *The Philosophy of Social Ecology.* Montreal: Black Rose Books.

Bookchin, M. 1991. *Defending the Earth: A Dialogue Between Murray Bookchin and Dave Foreman,* ed. S. Chase. Boston: South End Press.

Bookchin, M. 1992. "The Population Myth," *Kick It Over* 29 (Summer): 20–27.

Bookchin, M. 1993. "What is Social Ecology?," in M. Zimmerman, ed., *Environmental Philosophy: From Animal Rights to Radical Ecology.* Englewood Cliffs, NJ: Prentice-Hall.

Bradford, G. 1989. *How Deep is Deep Ecology?* Ojai, CA: Times Change Press.

Bradford, G. 1993. "Towards a Deep Social Ecology," in M. Zimmerman, ed., *Environmental Philosophy: From Animal Rights to Radical Ecology.* Englewood Cliffs, NJ: Prentice Hall.

Brennan, T. 1991. "Introduction," in J. F. McCannell, ed., *The Regime of the Brother.* London: Routledge.

Chase, S., ed. 1991. *Defending the Earth: A Dialogue Between Murray Bookchin and Dave Foreman.* Boston, MA: South End Press.

Cheney, J. 1987. "Ecofeminism and Deep Ecology," *Environmental Ethics* 9, no. 2: 115–45.

Cheney, J. 1989. "The neo-Stoicism of Radical Environmentalism," *Environmental Ethics* 11, no. 4: 293–325.

Clark, J. 1984. *The Anarchist Moment.* Montreal: Black Rose Books.

Clark, J. 1989. "Marx's Inorganic Body," *Environmental Ethics* 11, no. 3: 243–58.

Clark, J. 1993. "Social Ecology: Introduction," in M. Zimmerman, ed., *Environmental Philosophy: From Animal Rights to Radical Ecology.* Englewood Cliffs, NJ: Prentice-Hall.

Darby, A. 1991. "Seal Kill: The Slaughter in our Southern Seas," *The Good Weekend,* 5 January.

Devall, B. and G. Sessions. 1985. *Deep Ecology: Living As If Nature Mattered.* Salt Lake City, UT: Gibbs M. Smith.

Dodson Gray, E. 1979. *Green Paradise Lost: Remything Genesis.* Wellesley, MA: Roundtable Press.

Eckersley, R. 1989. "Divining Evolution: The Ecological Ethics of Murray Bookchin," *Environmental Ethics* 11, no. 2: 99–116.

Ehrenreich, B. 1989. *Fear of Falling: The Inner Life of the Middle Class.* New York: HarperCollins.

Eisenstein, Z. R. 1978. "Combahee River Collective," in *Capitalist Patriarchy and the Case for Socialist Feminism.* Boston, MA: South End Press.

Elkins, S. 1989. "The Politics of Mystical Ecology," *Telos* 82, no. 22, 4: 52–70.

Foucault, M. 1980. "Disciplinary Power and Subjection," in C. Gordon, ed., *Power/Knowledge: Selected Interviews and Other Writings of Michel Foucault, 1972–1977.* Brighton: Harvester.

Fox, W. 1989. "The Deep Ecology—Ecofeminism Debate and its Parallels," *Environmental Ethics* 11, no. 1: 5–25.

Fox, W. 1990. *Towards a Transpersonal Ecology: Developing New Foundations for Environmentalism.* Boston. MA: Shambala.

Fox Keller, E. 1985. *Reflections on Gender and Science.* New Haven, CT: Yale University Press.

Griscom, J. L. 1981. "On Healing the Nature/History Split in Feminist Thought," *Heresies* 13, no. 4: 4–9.

Haraway, D. 1989. *Primate Visions: Gender, Race, and Nature in the World of Modern Science.* New York: Routledge.

Haraway, D. 1991a. "A Manifesto for Cyborgs," in L. J. Nicholson, ed., *Feminism/Post-modernism*. New York: Routledge.

Haraway, D. 1991b. *Simians, Cyborgs and Women*. London: Free Associations Books.

Harding, S. 1981. "What is the Real Material Base of Patriarchy and Capital," in L. Sargent, ed., *Women and Revolution*. Boston, MA: South End Press.

Harding, S. 1984. "Is Gender a Variable in Conceptions of Rationality?" in C. Gould, ed., *Beyond Domination*. Totowa, NJ: Rowan & Allanfeld.

Harding, S. 1986. *The Science Question in Feminism*. Ithaca, NY: Cornell University Press.

Harding, S. and M. B. Hintikka, eds. 1983. *Discovering Reality*. Dordrecht: Reidel.

Hartsock, N. C. M. 1983. *Money, Sex, and Power: Toward a Feminist Historical Materialism*. New York: Longman.

Hartsock, N. C. M. 1990. "Foucault on Power: A Theory for Women?" in L. J. Nicholson, ed., *Feminism/Postmodernism*. New York: Routledge.

Hecht, S. and A. Cockburn. 1990. *The Fate of the Forest*. London: Penguin.

hooks, b. 1981. *Ain't I a Woman*. Boston, MA: South End Press.

hooks, b. 1984. *Feminist Theory: From Margin to Center*. Boston, MA: South End Press.

hooks, b. 1989. *Talking Back*. Boston, MA: South End Press.

King, Y. 1989. "The Ecology of Feminism and the Feminism of Ecology," in J. Plant, ed., *Healing the Wounds: The Promise of Ecofeminism*. Philadelphia: New Society Publishers.

King, Y. 1990. "Healing the Wounds: Feminism, Ecology, and the Nature/Culture Dualism," in I. Diamond and G. F. Orenstein, eds., *Reweaving the World: The Emergence of Ecofeminism*. San Francisco: Sierra Club Books.

Kovel, J. 1993. "The Marriage of Radical Ecologies," in M. E. Zimmerman, ed., *Environmental Philosophy: From Animal Rights to Radical Ecology*. Englewood Cliffs, NJ: Prentice-Hall.

Langford, R. 1988. *Don't Take Your Love to Town*. Sydney: Penguin.

Lloyd, G. 1983. "Reason, Gender and Morality in the History of Philosophy," *Social Research* 50, no. 3.

Lloyd, G. 1984. *The Man of Reason*. London: Methuen.

Midgley, M. 1980. *Beast and Man: The Roots of Human Nature*. London: Methuen.

Midgley, M. 1981. *Heart and Mind*. London: Methuen.

Midgley, M. 1983. *Animals and Why They Matter*. Harmondsworth: Penguin.

Mies, M. 1986. *Patriarchy and Accumulation on a World Scale*. London: Zed Books.

Naess, A. 1973. "The Shallow and the Deep, Long-range Ecology Movement: A Summary," *Inquiry* 16, no. 1: 95–100.

Naess, A. 1987. "The Deep Ecological Movement: Some Philosophical Aspects," *Philosophical Inquiry*; reprinted in M. E. Zimmerman, ed., *Environmental Philosophy: From Animal Rights to Radical Ecology*. Englewood Cliffs, NJ: Prentice-Hall, 1993.

Perlman, F. 1983. *Against His-story, Against Leviathan*. Detroit, MI: Black & Red.

Pitty, R. 1992. "Terra Nullius: The Skeleton in Our Courts," unpublished.

Plumwood, V. 1975. "Critical Notice of Passmore's *Man's Responsibility for Nature*," *Australasian Journal of Philosophy* 53, no. 2: 171–85.

Plumwood, V. 1980. "Social Theories, Self-management and Environmental Problems," in D. S. Mannison, M. A. McRobbie, and R. Routley, eds., *Environmental Philosophy*. Canberra: Department of Philosophy, Research School of Social Sciences, Australian National University.

Plumwood, V. 1981. "On Karl Marx as an Environmental Hero," *Environmental Ethics* 3: 237–44.

Plumwood, V. 1986. "Ecofeminism: An Overview and Discussion of Positions and Arguments," *Australasian Journal of Philosophy* 64 (Supplement, "Women and Philosophy"): 120–38.

Plumwood, V. 1991. "Nature, Self and Gender: Feminism, Environmental Philosophy and the Critique of Rationalism," *Hypatia* 6, no. 1: 3–27.

Plumwood, V. 1992. "SealsKin," *Meanjin* 51 (Spring): 45–57.

Plumwood, V. 1993. *Feminism and the Mastery of Nature.* London: Routledge.

Plumwood, V. and R. Routley. 1979. "Against the Inevitability of Human Chauvinism," in K. E. Goodpaster and K. M. Sayre, eds., *Ethics and Problems of the 21st Century.* Notre Dame, IN: University of Notre Dame Press.

Plumwood, V. and R. Routley. 1982. "World Rainforest Destruction—The Social Factors," *The Ecologist* 12, no. 1: 4–22.

Quinby, L. 1990. "Ecofeminism and the Politics of Resistance," in I. Diamond and G. F. Orenstein, eds., *Reweaving the World: The Emergence of Ecofeminism.* San Francisco: Sierra Club Books.

Reynolds, H. 1992. "Implications of Mabo," *Aboriginal Law Bulletin* 2 (December): 39.

Rolston, III, H. 1987. "Duties to Ecosystems," in J. B. Callicott, ed., *Companion to a Sand County Almanac.* Madison: University of Wisconsin Press.

Ruether, R. R. 1975. *New Woman, New Earth.* Minneapolis, MN: Seabury Press.

Ruether, R. R. 1989. "Toward an Ecological-Feminist Theology of Nature," in J. Plant, ed., *Healing the Wounds: The Promise of Ecofeminism.* Philadelphia: New Society Publishers.

Sessions, G. 1993. Introduction," in M. E. Zimmerman, ed., *Environmental Philosophy: From Animal Rights to Radical Ecology.* Englewood Cliffs, NJ: Prentice-Hall.

Shiva, V. 1989. *Staying Alive: Women, Ecology and Development.* London: Zed Books.

Shiva, V. 1990. "Development as a New Project of Western Patriarchy," in I. Diamond and G. F. Orenstein, eds., *Reweaving the World: The Emergence of Ecofeminism.* San Francisco: Sierra Club Books.

Shiva, V. 1992. "The Seed and the Earth: Women, Ecology and Biotechnology," *The Ecologist* 22, no. 1: 4–7.

Spelman, E. 1988. *Inessential Woman: Problems of Exclusion in Feminist Thought.* Boston, MA: Beacon Press.

Tokar, B. 1989. "Exploring the New Ecologies: Social Ecology, Deep Ecology and the Future of Green Political Thought," *Fifth Estate* 24, no. 1: 5–21.

Turner, F. 1986. *Beyond Geography: The Western Spirit Against the Wilderness.* New Brunswick, NJ: Rutgers University Press.

Wajcman, J. 1991. *Feminism Confronts Technology.* Cambridge: Polity Press.

Walby, S. 1992. "Post-Post-Modernism? Theorising Social Complexity," in M. Barrett and A. Phillips, eds., *Destabilising Theory.* Cambridge: Polity Press.

Warren, K. J. 1987. "Feminism and Ecology: Making Connections," *Environmental Ethics* 9, no. 1: 3–20.

Warren, K. J. 1990. "The Power and the Promise of Ecological Feminism," *Environmental Ethics* 12, no. 2: 121–46.

Warren, K. J. and J. Cheney. 1991. "Ecological Feminism as Ecosystem Ecology," *Hypatia* 6, no. 1: 179–97.

Young, I. 1980. "Beyond the Unhappy Marriage: A Critique of Dual Systems Theory," in L. Sargent, ed., *Women and Revolution.* Boston, MA: South End Press.

Zimmerman, M .E. 1987. "Feminism, Deep Ecology, and Environmental Ethics," *Environmental Ethics* 9, no. 1: 22–44.

Zimmerman, M. E., ed. 1993. *Environmental Philosophy: From Animal Rights to Radical Ecology.* Englewood Cliffs, NJ: Prentice-Hall.

WOMEN AND THE THIRD WORLD: EXPLORING THE DANGERS OF DIFFERENCE

MEERA NANDA

I will begin with a real-life story from Shashi Tharoor's 1998 book, *India: From Midnight to the Millennium*. In this passage, Shashi, an upper-caste, very liberal-left urbanite from Bombay is talking to Charlis, a dalit from a small village in Kerala. The two men have known each other since they met as boys in Shashi's ancestral village. Shashi had befriended the untouchable boy out of a sense of outrage against his more traditional, caste-bound cousins who would not allow Charlis to play with them. At the time of this conversation, Shashi is attending an elite English-language college in Delhi, which will then take him to the U.S. and to the UN (where he works as a senior officer in the office of Kofi Annan). Charlis is pulling himself up by his bootstraps: determined to get an education, he has made it to a provincial college near his village—the first in his community to come this far. Their conversation touches on Rudyard Kipling and two of his fictional characters:

> "For the Colonel's lady and Judy O'Grady," he [Charlis] declaimed at one point, "are sisters under their skins!—Rudyard Kipling," he added. "Is that how you are pronouncing it?"
>
> "Rudyard, Roodyard, I haven't a clue," I confessed. "But who cares Charlis? He is just an old imperialist fart. What does anything he wrote have anything to do with any of us today, in independent India?
>
> Charlis looked surprised then slightly averted his eyes. "But are we not," he asked softly, "are we not brothers under our skins?"
>
> "Of course," I replied, too quickly. And it was I who could not meet his gaze.

Dead white men's poems: words of "imperialist farts" for the upper-caste Shashi; an affirmation of egalitarianism for the untouchable, Charlis. This conversation highlights the disjuncture between the postcolonial critics of modernity and development, and the women on whose behalf they claim to speak.

I will treat Shashi Tharoor as a stand-in for the broad class of intellectuals in and from the postcolonial world who are intimately familiar with the West, but who feel compelled to say "No" to it, or who, at the very least, feel compelled to approach the West with a presumption of radical difference. Given the limited and uneven reach of development, these intellectuals have come to see their own access to modern scientific learning and modern institutions as a source of their alienation from the lifeworld of the non-modern masses. Not only do these angst-ridden intellectuals desperately wish to speak in a popular idiom derived from shared symbols and myths of the masses; they believe that this idiom can provide templates for different sciences, different institutions and, indeed, different ways of being altogether. These differences are valued as seedbeds of alternatives to both capitalism and socialism.

But what of Charlis? Going by his passionate engagement with the words of dead white males, it is clear that he does not approach them with a presumption of radical difference. Far from it: he finds in them intellectual resources to combat the difference he has suffered all his life at the hands of upper castes. Contrary to the postcolonial intellectuals who look to "Third World difference" as a source of salvation, Charlis-the-subaltern is not interested in affirming any difference: *he wants to put difference out of business altogether.* After all, it is not the Kipling who declared the impossibility of the East meeting the West but the Kipling who declares "sisterhood under the skin" who has captured Charlis' imagination.

I want to explore a most peculiar twist in this encounter: the postcolonial intellectual justifies her presumption of radical difference toward the West in the name of the subaltern who, if Charlis is our guide, seems to be making a presumption of universalism toward the West. So the question to ask is simple: how do discourses of difference actually play out in Third World societies? Can we simply assume the consent of the subalterns for embracing "their own" local knowledge? Can we, to borrow Nancy Fraser's question, assume that a struggle for recognition of non-Western, non-modern difference will help bring about a *redistribution of* economic and cultural power within these societies?

Limiting myself to my native India, I will examine three case studies. First, that of Viramma, a remarkable dalit woman whose first-person narrative of her life has recently appeared as a book. Here we ask how deep is the difference between Viramma and Western or Westernized Indian women? Is Viramma "like us, only more so," as Susan Moller Okin has affirmed? Or does any presumption of shared knowledges and needs between Viramma and the Western women amount to "discursive colonization" or "feminist Orientalism" as Chandra Talpade Mohanty and Frederique Marglin, respectively, have charged? For our next two cases, we move from the subaltern to the intellectuals and their acts of commission and omission. The acts of commission take us to the arguments for Third World ecofeminism made most prominently by Vandana Shiva. I ask who exactly is pushing for Shiva's neo-Hindu notions of *prakriti* and *Shakti*—the subaltern women like Viramma or the landed, upper-caste exploiters of these women? I will argue that far from empowering women like Viramma, ecofeminism has come to serve as a mobilizing ideology of surplus-producing, landowning farmers. Finally, for the acts of omission of difference-oriented theorists, we go to Prem Chowdhry's study titled *The Veiled Women*, which offers a cautionary tale for all those who denounce modern technology *itself* as fundamentally patriarchal. Chowdhry shows how the pre-existing, religion- and culture-sanctified patriarchal bargains are literally soaking up the liberatory aspects of the shift from private to public patriarchy made possible by the Green Revolution.

But before proceeding with my case studies, I need to define more precisely who my interlocutors are and what exactly concerns me about their critiques of development. Defining postcolonial intellectuals as those who say "no" to the West is to cast too wide a net. There are those who may say "no" to particular economic and political policies of the West, and many others who may be troubled by the uneven and exploitative mode of development under capitalism. I have nothing to say about these critics, except that I count myself as one of them. My concern is limited only to those critics who are postcolonial or post-developmentalist in a strong sense of the word; that is, who bring a post-Enlightenment world-view to bear on the problems of development. I include here critics with very different theoretical orientations, including Gandhian communitarians like Ashis Nandy, Vandana Shiva, and Claude Alvares; Foucauldians like Arturo Escobar; ethno-sociologists like the Marglins; and feminist critics like Jane Parpart, Mariaane Marchand, Mitu Hirschman, and Geeta Chowdhry, who seem to be deeply influenced by feminist theories of difference. These critics see development as a source of violence, both real and symbolic, on non-Western people. The violence comes from subjecting non-Western people to a culturally alien, ethnocentric, and colonial imaginary of what it means to be developed; forcing them to measure the worth of their lives and their communities by Western norms; and, in the process, silencing their own norms of a good society.

The source of this symbolic violence, or "the motor of the crisis," as Rosi Braidotti and her colleagues put it, is modern science itself. Scientific rationality, the critics claim, has hidden its Eurocentric and patriarchal interests behind its claims of objective and universally valid knowledge. Riding on false claims of objectivity and propelled by imperialist interests, modern science has established itself as the norm of what it means to be rational and objective. All other ways of comprehending the world have been delegitimized. Post-developmentalist critics ask not for better implementation of this or that development policy, but for pluralizing the norms of development themselves, for allowing non-Western people to define development in their own culturally grounded conceptual categories and meeting these needs through their own local sciences and technologies.

I fully welcome the idea of using local cultural discourses to enable and encourage a more participatory and egalitarian modernization. But the kind of emphasis one finds in post-developmentalist discourse goes far beyond such a strategic use of culture and verges on culturalism which regards the conceptual and imaginary representations of existing cultures in modernizing societies to be the ultimate and irreducible force in development. Protestations to the contrary, I believe that the kind of culturalism one finds in post-developmentalist discourse reifies non-Western cultures by setting them as the "other" of the West and not examining the content and actual practices that give substance—often a highly oppressive and illiberal substance—to the traditions of these cultures. The post-developmentalist notion of the non-Western cultures, I contend, is shaped by the ideological needs of *Western* intellectuals (and their "anti-imperialist" cultural nationalistic allies in the Third World) to invest other cultures with critical force against their own supposedly hyper-rational, one-dimensional scientistic culture. This radical xenophilia of Western intellectuals has scarified, or at least minimized, the theoretical space for a critical assessment of non-Western cultures.

Let us return, for the moment, to where we started from in our Shashi–Charlis dialogue. Post-development critics make a presumption of radical difference toward rationality itself. Norms of what is rational, warranted, and truthful are "completely constituted by the distinctive cultural inheritance of different cultures," as Sandra Harding has declared in her recent book, *Is Science Multicultural?*, or as Marshall Sahlins concluded in his *How Natives Think?*, or as Ashis Nandy put it much before them in his *Intimate Enemy*. The question before us is, what would Charlis say? Would *he* feel content to rediscover his own definition of what is rational? More importantly, will his own culturally constructed rationality be so different from modern scientific rationality that will feel violated and silenced by it? Does Charlis see modern scientific rationality and world-view as an enemy or an ally in his fight against his local oppressors?

It will be useful to dwell upon the larger debate on scientific rationality because the culturalism of post-development discourse uses the idea of "different cultures, different rationalities, different sciences" to legitimate itself. The argument that all of us—and not just Charlis—should prefer Charlis' own standards of rationality in order to get a "strong objectivity" against the supposedly phony objectivity of science has been made most forcefully by Sandra Harding, most recently in her *Is Science Multicultural?*, where she extends standpoint epistemology into postcolonial concerns. Harding is emphatic that "modern science is at an epistemological par with other cultures' traditions of systematic knowledge: they are all equally local knowledge systems, for they are all completely constituted by their respective local cultures. Thus there could be many universally valid but culturally distinct sciences." What is more, Harding insists that the distinct sciences of different cultures are not parts of a puzzle that will all eventually fit together, but are, as she puts it, "fundamentally incompatible knowledge claims, encoding different norms shaped by each culture's distinctive discursive inheritance." Harding is hardly alone: similar claims are the staple of contemporary cultural and social constructivist studies of science.

Since this essay is not about the philosophy of science, I will not go on to refute Harding's claim here. I will only point out what troubles me about this thesis of cultural construction of the very norms of rationality: *treating rationality and knowledge as completely constructed by culture puts culture beyond a reasoned critique.* If at no point in our inquiry can we go beyond, or refute, the cultural categories that we inherit, how can we obtain any critical distance from these categories? Of course, Harding, Donna Haraway and their sympathizers would say that we *can* go beyond inherited cultural assumptions through purposefully adopting the standpoint of the underdog. Underdogs don't need value-neutrality, or objectivity, which are Western cultural values anyway. They can legitimately claim the status of science for inquiry based upon their own culturally embedded assumptions—say, of treating nature as sacred, as Shiva argues, or treating the natural and the supernatural as one and the same, as Frederique Marglin argues. Once these local ways of knowing are positively evaluated as sciences and not just folk beliefs, the subaltern and their sympathizers can use them as legitimate norms of rationality against which they measure modern science's assumptions, methods, and claims. Well, seeing modern science from the underdog's standpoint will reveal differences. But why should it follow that the underdog will reject the difference as alien and undesirable? Moreover, even if adopting a local standpoint can help the underdog to see through "western science," it still evades the issue of how it can help them see through their own religion- and tradition-sanctified dominant ideologies.

The insistence on local rationalities as progressive standpoints of the oppressed flies in the face of *real* movements of the oppressed, the most radical of which have all been firmly in the Enlightenment mode. Take the anti-caste movement of B. R. Ambedkar, which, in sharp contrast to Gandhi's reformist overtures to the untouchables, was a radical attack on the ideology of caste itself. Ambedkar and his dalit followers challenged the Brahmanical knowledge about the natural world not in the name of their own dalit caste-myths and origin stories but in the name of scientifically obtained objective truth. Unlike their academic sympathizers, the organic intellectuals of dalits and women—say an Ambedkar, or a Pandita Rama Bai, people who personally suffered the worst insults and degradations of the traditional Hindu order—were never content to build a counter-hegemony around the standpoint of the dalits or women. As Ambedkar repeatedly emphasized, annihilation of caste would require a challenge to the entire Hindu cosmology, which assumes the sacredness of nature and the continuity of the natural and the supernatural—precisely because this kind of "local knowledge" was used to justify the rationality of Karma and caste. Ambedkar, in other words, linked the liberation of dalits to *overturning* the kind of cultural assumptions about sacredness and holism that people like Harding, Marglin, and Shiva see as the standpoint of the oppressed. Ambedkar was convinced that only a *secularization of consciousness* through a rigorous application of reason and scientific temper could bring about a *transformative* change. If Charlis has been influenced in any way by Ambedkar, as most progressive dalits are, I am ready to bet that he would any day opt for modern science over Hindu cosmology as his own standpoint.

But let us get down to the specifics. Viramma is a Tamil-speaking dalit woman in her sixties who narrated the story of her life and the life of her community to two ethnographers, who published the entire narrative in her own voice. From the opening sentence, "My paternal grandfather was a serf of the Reddi," we meet this energetic, life-loving, sharp-witted, and sharp-tongued woman, who is simultaneously a mother, a wife, a farm worker, a midwife, a devout believer in a whole pantheon of goddesses, a singer of songs, a lead organizer of religious festivals—all in all, a pillar of her community. Viramma's ability to create a life of love, laughter, and meaning is all the more remarkable in that she has had more than her share of avoidable misery, losing nine of her twelve children to perfectly curable, ordinary infectious diseases. And she has had more than anyone's share of humiliations at the hands of the upper-caste landlords. No one's fool, Viramma understands perfectly well that the upper castes exploit her labor, and feels perfectly justified in stealing from them. But her everyday resistance is bounded by her internalization of the idea of purity and pollution. She sees caste humiliations as deserved because of the sins in past lives of her entire community.

I want to bring the concerns of the critics of modernity and modern science to bear upon Viramma's life. Is it the case that Viramma experiences modern institutions and knowledge as alien impositions contrary to her own practical and strategic interests? Is it the case that Viramma's local knowledge as a mid-wife is embedded in a wholly different and more enabling rationality?

Viramma's relationship with modern institutions and ideas is too complex to allow a neat for-or-against classification. She has lived through truly epochal changes, including India's independence, Indira Gandhi, the slow-but-sure loosening of caste hierarchy, the spread of wage labor over caste "duties," the rising aspirations of her son, the coming of the television and so on. While she loves the idea of a woman as a prime minister, and values the opportunity to send her son (not her daughters) to school, she finds the new militancy among the younger generation unnerving, and she abhors the television.

Being a midwife and a healer, Viramma's main contact with modern institutions is through public health workers who visit the village for vaccinations, family planning, and childbirth. Again, Viramma simultaneously reaches out and evades: she seems to appreciate the value of timely medical intervention, cooperates with the nurses, and seeks modern alternatives for all complicated pregnancies she attends (she herself opted for the modern method of abortion over her own traditional knowledge). But she hates the way the nurses and doctors treat the women: she finds them arrogant and full of caste prejudice. This love–hate relationship holds even with traditional healing practices that are deeply intertwined with religion. Viramma believes that diseases like smallpox, cholera, and hepatitis are caused by the presence of angry goddesses who must be appeased with worship and gifts. She is slow in accepting smallpox vaccination and continues to combine modern treatments with traditional worship.

Modern medicine is experienced as different, in part threatening and in part life-saving. The question is at what level does the difference operate: at the level of the rationality of modern medicine itself or at the level of institutions? Of course, even an analytical separation between rationality and institutions is unacceptable to critics like Marglin, Nandy, and their Foucauldian colleagues, who see knowledge and institutional power as co-constructing each other. They explain Viramma's discomfort with modern medicine as a reflection of her non-logocentric world-view in which the natural and the supernatural, health and disease are not separated from each other as polar opposites, but each contains elements of the other: nature is enchanted, and health includes disease and death. What is more, they have claimed that modern hospitals cannot, even in principle, meet Viramma's needs, for they incorporate a bipolar, logocentric reasoning.

But there is very little sign of non-logocentricity in Viramma's local knowledge. She invokes gods and goddesses in order to explain, predict, and control disease, just as we moderns invoke the germ theory of disease. There is no sign whatsoever that she offers prayers to the person afflicted with smallpox because she is simultaneously celebrating health, as Marglin has claimed. Whatever the outsiders may read into it, Viramma herself is very clear that her prayers are meant only to cajole the goddess to leave them alone. Absence of goddess is welcomed as absence of disease. If we take Viramma at her word, we will find that gods and goddesses serve fairly down-to-earth instrumental rationality that seeks freedom from suffering. There is no reason to insist that incommensurability of rationalities will forever make modern medicine alien and oppressive to Viramma. Pitching difference at the level of rationality ignores the possibility of institutional reform, and turns a blind eye to the fact that, after all, Viramma with all her expert local knowledge, and all her mother's love, could not prevent nine of her twelve babies from dying. To conclude, yes, Viramma resists modernization but not because of her standpoint epistemology, which actually contains elements of instrumental rationality expressed in a religious idiom.

Let us move to the best known case feminists have made for local knowledges: namely, Vandana Shiva's arguments for Third World ecofeminism. Elsewhere I have examined Shiva's essentialism and standpoint epistemology, and need not repeat these arguments. Here, I want only to deal with Shiva's much admired "politicization" of "Third World difference": even those who find Shiva's essentialism and romanticism troubling praise her for politicizing the issue of Third World women's subsistence needs and their culturally distinctive uses of nature. But this begs the question: must feminists welcome *all* politicization as progressive? Should we not ask *what kind of politicization of difference* has Shiva's ideas brought about in India? So I ask a simple question: what has happened to Shiva's idea of feminine principle in the decade since her book *Staying Alive* put it on the agenda of new social movements around the world? Which political constituencies have used it and to what end? I want to be clear that the remarks that follow are meant solely to assess the influence of the idea of ecofeminism and not the personal political beliefs of anyone involved.

Gail Omvedt, a sympathetic critic of ecofeminism, provides a fair summary of Shiva's influence in her recent book, *Reinventing Revolution*: "Shiva's articulation of the feminine principle that sees united action by women and men to transform society in a feminist, ecological and participatory direction finds its echoes in the themes of *stri shakti* [women's power] within the women's movement connected with the Shetkari Sanghathan and other rural organizations." Shetkari Sanghathan and other rural organizations that Omvedt mentions are powerful farmers' movements of landowning, surplus-producing commercial farmers who are simultaneously aligned against the state, from whom they demand higher subsidies for modern inputs and higher prices for their crops, and against the mostly dalit landless and migrant workers, who they don't pay even the barest minimum wages.

These farmers' movements differ in their caste, class, and ideological orientations. Media reports from India indicate that Shiva is personally involved as an advisor and supporter of the Gandhian, "anti-imperialist" movement KRRS in Karanatka, and has also lent at least her tactical support to the populist, upper-caste and severely patriarchal Bharatiya Kisan Union (BKU) in Uttar Pradesh, an organization that actively campaigned for Hindu fundamentalists in 1991 elections. Shiva's idea of *prakriti* and feminine principle has found a wider women's constituency in the more free-market oriented, neoliberal Shetkari Sanghathan in Maharashtra. The Sanghathan's "Laxmi Mukti" (Laxmithe-goddess liberation) is based upon ecofeminist principles and has won the support of well-known Indian feminists, including Gail Omvedt and Madhu Kishwar. Even Bina Agarwal offers words of praise for the ecofeminist elements of the Shetkari Sanghathan program in her otherwise remarkable book *A Field of Her Own.*

But if you place these movements in the larger class structure that prevails in the rural economy, it becomes clear that ecofeminism is serving the tactical and ideological interests of landed farmers rather than the strategic interests of either women or nature: Karnatka Rajya Raitha Sangh (KRRS), for instance, has used Gandhian and ecofeminist anti-modernism to cover up class and caste differences among the landowners and landless workers in order to demand concessions and subsidies from the state: the entire modern, urban industrial sector, inside India or outside, is declared to be the enemy of the entire traditional, rural, and agricultural "real India." While the Gandhian leadership of KRRS mobilizes large numbers of peasants to ransack offices of multinational corporations, it turns a blind eye to the atrocities against dalit farm workers that members of KRRS have continued to commit.

Movements like KRRS, BKU, allied new social movements, and their anti-modernist intellectual sympathizers end up conferring a seemingly secular, populist, and even progressive "anti-imperialist" gloss on a kind of reactionary nationalism that is no different in substance from the *swadeshi* (self-reliance) platform of the Hindu right. The movements (notably KRRS and BKU) have claimed, following the rhetoric made popular by Shiva and other anti-modernist intellectuals, that Western economic interests represented by multinational corporations and Western culture in general are the major contradiction in Indian society today and that a fight against the West is in the interests of the ordinary people in India. Western feminists and progressives more or less accept this underlying assumption as well. But such "anti-imperialism" is hardly warranted by actual economic facts. For much of its postcolonial history, India has been one of the most protected economies in South Asia. The Indian state and businesses have actually invested more abroad than any foreign corporation is allowed to invest in India. Even after the economic liberalization that started in the early 1990s, the total direct foreign investment in the whole of South Asia amounted to a mere 0.5 percent of GNP in 1996, a figure which compares poorly with 4.2 percent in East Asia and 1.9 percent in all other developing countries. Clearly, the overheated anti-Western, "anti-imperialist" rhetoric is serving the ideological need of rural and Hindu nationalistic elites to rally the masses across class and caste divides for their own, often shared, agendas.

Let us look at the much praised "Laxmi Mukti" program of Shetkari Sanghathan. Started in 1990 in response to women activists and feminist intellectuals, this program urges farmers to make a voluntary gift of a portion of their land to their wives on the condition that the wives can only use traditional organic farming techniques. The limited usefulness of such a gift can be readily granted: independent ownership does strengthen women's position in the family, although it is not clear if wives can actually sell or mortgage the gifted land if they want to. But I contend that such a program performs an ideological function by confining women's rights within the traditional framework of family and goddesses. What is worse, it makes the intra-family gift serve as a substitute for land redistribution to those without any assets at all. There are reports that many relatively large farmers are using it as a means to evade a legal land ceiling, which explains their enthusiasm for this program. Moreover, the restriction of women to organic and subsistence farming is a continuation of the sexual division of labor. Laxmi Mukti is clearly a middle peasant program that serves to absorb women's growing assertion of the right to land within the traditional patriarchal family, and prevents them from making common cause with landless women.

The partly willing and partly inadvertent co-option of ecofeminism by farmers' movements is a good example of the problems of valorizing symbolic differences over class differences. While it is true that the symbolic and the material can not be separated, it is not true that struggles over the terrain of symbols neatly translate into a more equitable redistribution in the terrain of the material. I am not suggesting that *all* struggles over recognition of difference are *necessarily* right wing or left wing. All I am saying is that, given India's balance of caste and class power, glued together by deeply inegalitarian Hindu norms, critiques pitched at the level of irreducible cultural differences with the West are strengthening the already formidable power of upper-caste, rich rural males, who are the most dubious "allies" that feminists and other secular democrats could ever want.

Finally, there are the acts of omission of Third Worldist intellectuals. Here we turn to Prem Chowdhry's *Veiled Women*. The women in the veil are farm laborers in Haryana who seem to be getting the worst of both worlds: they enjoy neither the freedom from hard labor on the farm that comes with the veil, nor the relative autonomy that comes with working for wages. Defying all generalizations by South Asian anthropologists and economists, women in Haryana have not experienced any improvement in their social worth, despite very high levels of wage labor participation encouraged by the Green Revolution. Indeed, the situation seems to be getting worse, with female feticide on the rise, leading to a high male ratio.

This dismal situation has been cited repeatedly by prominent feminist critics of development as an example of the "violence of science," or as evidence of the *fundamentally* patriarchal nature of modern technology, which supposedly imposes a wholly different, Western capitalist logic on the ecological and moral economy of the peasant. Prem Chowdhry's sensitive field studies show what this meta-level epistemological critique of technology leaves out. The great value of Prem Chowdhry's work is that she never lets you lose track of the ways in which supposedly Western technology is mediated through traditional, "Eastern" institutions. A few words of explanation are in order here.

Introduction of the Green Revolution has indeed set in motion social forces that are causally associated with, using Sylvia Walby's terminology, the transformation of the private patriarchy of peasant economy into the public patriarchy of market economy. Because of the adoption of new technology by small and marginal farmers, who now need to earn more cash to modernize, Haryana has seen a change of cultural norms. Before the Green Revolution, women of dominant-caste landowners were permitted to work only on family farms, while only lower-caste landless women worked for wages. In the late 1980s, 44 percent of upper-caste, small and marginal farmers allowed their women to work on other people's farms for hard cash. Important studies of women and work by scholars like Bina Agarwal, Kalpana Bardhan, and Barbara Miller in the agricultural sector, Karin Kapadia in the informal sector, Naila Kabeer and Swasti Mitter in the garment industry have clearly shown that independent income through wage work leads to a slow but steady enlargement of women's freedoms in South Asia. The reason it is not happening in Haryana has everything to do with the culture of female subordination, which has deep historical roots in the harsh desert-like ecology of part of the region, combined with hypergamy, imitation of upper caste practices, and the concept of male *izzat* (honor), which depends upon female propriety. Whatever other virtues this peasant culture may have in terms of ecological living, they were obtained not because of, but at the cost of, equality and autonomy of women. It is these deeply misogynist and illiberal cultural norms that are now acting as shock absorbers to maintain men's *izzat* at a time of rapid changes introduced by the Green Revolution.

An *enabling* critique of development must engage in a cultural challenge to this inherited discourse of patriarchy, caste, and other inequities justified by traditional cosmologies. And that challenge cannot proceed within the confines of local knowledges alone, for these knowledges simultaneously allow everyday resistance while conditioning the subalterns to accept their subordination. It is important to acknowledge that, like all cultures, non-Western cultures and traditions have progressive impulses toward autonomy and justice. But if we let traditions define what autonomy and justice are—that is, if we accept as justifiable that different cultures have different norms of what is true, just and good—we run the risk of easy appropriation by traditional patriarchs who are taking the lead in the rising tide of religious revivalism in many parts of the world. The task of feminism and other progressive social movements ought to be to challenge the terms of the debate. Modern science can assist in this challenge by enabling the subalterns to see through the mystification of their own inherited ideologies. To reduce science to a Western local story is not in the interests of the Virammas and the Charlises of this world, who have everything to gain from it.

NOTES

1. Dalit is the chosen self-description of the "untouchable" castes in India. The word *dalit* literally means "crushed," or "the oppressed."

2. Nancy Fraser, "From Redistribution to Recognition? Dilemmas of Justice in a 'Post-Socialist' Age," *New Left Review* 212 (July/August 1995).

3. Viramma, Josiane Racine, and Jean-Luc Racine, *Viramma: Life of an Untouchable* (London: Verso, 1997).

4. Susan Moller Okin. "Gender Inequality and Cultural Differences," *Political Theory* 22, no. 1 (1994): 5–24.

5. Chandra Mohanty, "Under Western Eyes: Feminist Scholarship and Colonial Discourses," *Feminist Review* 30 (1988), 61–88; and Frederique Marglin and Suzanne Simon, "Feminist Orientalism and Development," in Wendy Harcourt, ed., *Feminist Perspectives on Sustainable Development* (London: Zed Books, 1994): 26–45.

6. Prem Chowdhry, *The Veiled Women: Shifting Gender Equations in Rural Haryana, 1880–1990* (New Delhi: Oxford University Press. 1994).

7. For representative writings of this genre, see the entries in Wolfgang Sachs, *The Development Dictionary: A Guide to Knowledge and Power* (London: Zed Books, 1996).

8. Arturo Escobar, "Imagining a Post-Development Era? Critical Thought, Development and Social Movements." *Social Text* 31–32 (1992): 20–36.

9. Frederique A. Marglin and Stephen A. Marglin, eds., *Dominating Knowledge: Development, Culture and Resistance* (Oxford: Clarendon Press, 1990).

10. See the recent anthology edited by Marianna Marchand and Jane L. Parpart, *Feminism/Postmodernism/Development* (New York: Routledge, 1995).

11. Rosi Braidotti et al., eds., *Women, Environment and Sustainable Development: Towards a Theoretical Synthesis* (London: Zed Books, 1994).

12. For a trenchant critique of culturalism, see Aziz Al-Azmeh, *Islam and Modernities*

(London: Verso, 1993).

13. Sandra Harding, *Is Science Multicultural? Postcolonialisms, Feminisms and Epistemologies* (Bloomington: Indiana University Press, 1998), 44.

14. For recent works, see David Hess, *Science and Technology in a Multicultural World: The Cultural Politics of Facts and Artifacts* (New York: Columbia University Press, 1995); Sarah Franklin, "Science as Culture, Cultures of Science," *Annual Review of Anthropology*, 1995. Works by Frederique and Stephen Marglin, Ashis Nandy, and Ziauddin Sardar are well known.

15. See my "A Postcolonial Manifesto for the Brahmans? Sandra Harding's Epistemology for Ethnosciences," forthcoming in *Feminist Theory*.

16. See Frederique Marglin, "Smallpox in Two Systems of Knowledge," in Marglin and Marglin, eds., *Dominating Knowledge*.

17. See my "History is What Hurts: A Materialist Feminist Perspective on the Green Revolution and its Ecofeminist Critics," in Rosemary Hennessy and Chrys Ingraham, eds., *Materialist Feminism: A Reader in Class, Difference and Women's Lives* (New York: Routledge, 1997). Also "Is Modern Science a Western, Patriarchal Myth? A Critique of the Neo-populist Orthodoxy," *South Asia Bulletin* 9 (1991).

18. Gail Omvedt, *Reinventing Revolution: New Social Movements and the Socialist Tradition in India* (New York: M. E. Sharpe, 1993), 316.

19. For a complete analysis, see my "Who Needs Post-development? Discourses of Diference, the Green Revolution and Agrarian Populism in India," *Journal of Developing Societies*, June 1999.

20. See Achin Vanaik, *The Painful Transition: Bourgeois Democracy in India* (London: Verso, 1990), 12–13.

21. M. Pigato et al., eds., *South Asia's Integration into the World Economy* (Washington D.C.: World Bank, 1997).

22. Sylvia Walby, *Theorizing Patriarchy* (Oxford: Blackwell, 1989).

EXPANDING ENVIRONMENTAL JUSTICE: ASIAN-AMERICAN FEMINISTS' CONTRIBUTION

JULIE SZE

An Asian-American feminist movement for environmental justice is critical both for expanding the scope of environmental justice and for realizing a radical Asian women's politics and vision.[1] Among the social injustices that affect large numbers of Asian women in the United States and around the world are occupational health hazards, labor exploitation due to economic globalization, and anti-immigrant policies. Each of these poses an obstacle to the creation and protection of a healthy environment for Asian women.

A diversity of Asian-American communities face environmental risks such as high rates of lead poisoning on the job, lack of open space, elevated exposure to military toxics, and health hazards from fish consumption.[2] There is within the Environmental Protection Agency (EPA) a growing recognition of Asian environmental justice issues in the United States, according to Angela Chung, an environmental protection specialist from the EPA's Office of Environmental Justice.[3]

Asian women's organizing shares a number of similarities with environmental justice organizing. These similarities need to be recognized and built on to further the common goals of both movements.

THE ENVIRONMENTAL JUSTICE MOVEMENT

Environmental justice is a social movement led by and for people of color that views environmental issues as having social, public health, economic, political, and ideological components. It thus seeks not only environmental justice but also economic, political, and cultural justice, both in the United States[4] and abroad.[5]

Early catalyzing events for environmental justice include nonviolent direct action in 1982 against the proposed siting of a hazardous waste landfill in the predominantly African-American community of Warren County, North Carolina, and the 1987 publication of *Toxic Wastes and Race* by the United Church of

Christ Commission for Racial Justice, which documented the disproportionate location of toxic waste sites in communities of color. Environmental justice first came to prominence when advocates documented that people of color suffer from disproportionately high effects of environmental pollution, as well as unequal protection from the state. According to the Commission on Racial Justice, three-fifths of African and Hispanic Americans live in communities with uncontrolled toxic waste sites, and approximately half of all Asian/Pacific Islanders and Native Americans live in communities with uncontrolled toxic waste sites.[6] In one study, the EPA took 20 percent longer to identify Superfund sites in minority communities, and pollution in those neighborhoods resulted in fines only half as high as those in white neighborhoods.[7] Environmental justice activists attempt to remedy environmental damage and at the same time educate people of color about how power, knowledge, science, and authority are constructed.

Environmental justice repudiates elitist, racist, and classist wilderness/preservationist conceptions of the environment as being equal to "nature"—typically characterized as pristine, green space devoid of people.[8] Such conceptions often regard nature as being threatened by the sustaining activities of people in "underdeveloped" countries. Environmental justice foregrounds social categories and shifts the concept of the environment to include not just natural resources such as air, water, and land, but also public and human health concerns.

In a span of roughly fifteen years, the environmental justice movement has succeeded in changing what environmentalism means. In February 1994, President Clinton signed the Executive Order on Environmental Justice, provoked by the organizing of people of color, most notably at the historic 1991 People of Color Environmental Leadership Summit, at which the Principles of Environmental Justice[9] were introduced and adopted.

One of the key contributions of the environmental justice movement has been to challenge long-held assumptions about risks and hazards. Rather than considering risks and hazards to human health and the environment in isolation, environmental justice advocates consider cumulative risks—the combination and accumulation of hazards. While individual polluting sources may not pose fatal health hazards, their cumulative effect might. Consideration of cumulative risk is particularly important in urban settings: in rural areas, toxic sites are often the result of single, egregious polluters, whereas in an urban environment, toxic pollution is more often a problem of cumulative hazards.

ENVIRONMENTAL JUSTICE AND
ASIAN-AMERICAN WOMEN

I live in San Jose [California]. I assemble electronics parts and boards at my company. I've been there for ten years. I was a housewife in Korea.... We got very little training about health and safety. I have headaches, nausea, dizziness, shoulder aches, backaches.... I see everyone with the same problems in my department. Some women have Carpal

Tunnel Syndrome, high blood pressure, and kidney problems. It's difficult to learn about safety at work.... we lose our health.[10]

Korean electronics worker

A number of initiatives by Asian-American women have connected workers' rights and occupational health with environmental justice concerns. According to Pam Tau Lee of the University of California at Berkeley Labor Occupational Health Program, immigrant Asian women are disproportionately employed in hazardous industries such as the garment and the electronics/semiconductor industries. The hazards they face include exposure to toxic materials, low wages, and institutional neglect by the government, unions, employers, and consumers.[11]

Fifty-three percent of all textile workers and apparel workers in the United States are Asian women.[12] Garment workers face increased exposure to fiber particles, dyes, formaldehydes, and arsenic, leading to high rates of byssinosis and respiratory illness. Asian Americans—primarily women—comprise 43 percent of electronics workers in assembly line and operative jobs in Silicon Valley.[13] Asian and Latina immigrant women in the electronics/semiconductor industry suffer from "damage to the central nervous system, and possibly the reproductive system, as a result of using dangerous solvents to clean electronic components, as well as exposure to other chemicals," according to Lee. They suffer occupational illness at triple the rate of workers in general manufacturing.

The Asian Pacific Environmental Network (APEN) is the most prominent Asian environmental justice organization in the United States. Other organizations that work on Asian environmental justice issues include Asian Immigrant Women Advocates (AIWA), which organizes and empowers immigrant Asian garment and electronic workers, "so they can improve their living and working conditions," according to Helen Kim, an organizer from AIWA.[14]

Young Hi Shin, AIWA'S executive director, gave one of two major papers presented by an Asian woman at the first People of Color Environmental Leadership Summit (the other was given by Pam Tau Lee). It is no accident that its focus was also occupational health issues—many activists argue that occupational health is the number one environmental justice concern for Asian Americans.

Both Lee and Shin helped create innovative models to educate immigrant Asian women about occupational and environmental hazards—for example, by including political education in English classes. In these classes, immigrant women practice their English by translating warning information about chemicals they are routinely exposed to at work.[15] Lee explains how trainers in the Labor Occupational Health Program use graphics and risk-mapping—which enable workers to identify health hazards through visual means—to reach diverse linguistic communities.[16]

ENVIRONMENTAL JUSTICE ABROAD

Internationally, economic globalization necessitates further strategic alliances between radical Asian feminist, labor, and environmental justice movements. According to Lee,

> You will find women in the Philippines, Malaysia, and Japan and other parts of Asia working very hard to stop deforestation, organizing around military toxics, organizing around issues of health and safety.... Environmental justice efforts do not confine themselves to local efforts or national ones. Environmental justice activists also work in solidarity with those in Asia, Africa, Mexico, Central and Latin America against corporate greed and profits.[17]

Poor people and people of color both here and abroad have suffered from economic globalization orchestrated by governments and corporations and supported by mainstream environmental organizations in the United States. The World Wildlife Fund, Natural Resources Defense Council, National Audubon Society, and Environmental Defense Fund all supported the North American Free Trade Agreement (NAFTA), to the outrage of labor and social justice organizations.[18] While NAFTA claims to emphasize protection of natural resources, it encourages the degradation of human life by driving down wages and work standards to maximize corporate profit.

The links between occupational health and environmental justice will become increasingly relevant as more multinational corporations move their factories to countries with little or no worker or environmental protections. Asian countries such as Indonesia, Singapore, Vietnam, South Korea, Taiwan, Thailand, and China are low-wage countries where legions of workers—mostly women—face slave-like working conditions. One of the more egregious work situations led to the deaths in 1993 of 188 workers who were trapped in a fire at the Kader toy factory in Thailand.[19]

One of the leading theorists of the links between the exploitation of women, labor, and natural resources in an international development matrix is the Indian environmentalist Vandana Shiva, a leading spokesperson for radical Asian politics and environmental justice. Shiva, a physicist, philosopher, Science and Environment Advisor with the Third World Network, and Director of the Research Foundation for Science, Technology and Natural Resource Policy in Dehra Dun, India, has researched, written, and spoken extensively about how Third World women are particularly targeted in the logic of "maldevelopment" that exploits both women and nature as commodities.[20] According to Shiva,

> You really can't separate issues of ecology from feminism or from human rights or from development or from issues of ethnic and cultural diversity.... to me, the choice.... is between environmental justice and green imperialism, between a common future for all or continued economic and environmental apartheid.[21]

Shiva is also an activist with the International Forum on Globalization and with the Chipko movement, a women's movement in the Himalayas that successfully resisted World Bank deforestation projects. The "Chipko andolan" translates literally into "hugging movement."[22] In the United States, "tree hugger" is generally a pejorative term (used by people from across the political spectrum) to describe environmentalists who care more about trees than about people. People of color often level this charge of elitism against mainstream environmental organizers. Their critique is entirely valid and necessary, but the fact that many environmental justice advocates in the United States do not know the history of this term, which emerged from an integrated struggle for both human dignity and preservation of natural resources, suggests that the links and histories of environmental justice struggles in other countries need to be highlighted.

THE ANTI-IMMIGRATION ASSAULT ON ASIAN WOMEN

Shiva's critique of macro-level economic policies and their impact on individuals is reinforced by Cathi Tactaquin, Executive Director of the National Network for Immigrant and Refugee Rights. According to Tactaquin, in the United States immigrants and refugees are scapegoated for various social ills, such as "stealing" jobs or "ruining" the environment. Tactaquin points out that the real global threat is from "neo-liberalism—the globalization of poverty imposed by United States policies and by international financial institutions."[23]

Environmentally based anti-immigration and zero-population movements pose a serious threat to Asian and Asian-American women. A growing number of anti-immigrant and zero-population advocates argue that immigration should be limited because of environmental degradation. This argument—most developed in California—is another version of the "limited resource" argument that convinced voters in California to pass Proposition 187, an anti-immigration bill, in the fall of 1994. The "limited resource" perspective argues that finite resources—whether financial or environmental—are wasted on immigrants generally, and illegal immigrants specifically, who are purely a resource drain and make no contribution to their adopted society (regardless of the fact that they provide low-wage labor that is much used—and abused). Therefore, proponents conclude, the answer to a multitude of social and environmental problems is to reduce immigration.

For these activists, "environmentalism" is used to justify severe, punitive, and regressive calls for immigration moratoriums and changes in national immigration legislation. In 1995, Population Environment Balance, Californians for Population Stabilization, and Carrying Capacity Network called for a five-year immigration moratorium with a ceiling for all countries of 100,000 immigrants. Negative Population Growth placed advertisements in environmental magazines such as *E* and *Natural History* calling for an immigration moratorium.[24]

Anti-immigrant and zero-population advocates fuel a political and social atmosphere of hate and misinformation by pandering to the white electorate's fears of "Third Worldification" by Latinos and Asians. The fundamental assumptions that ground this argument are:

- More immigrants mean more environmental degradation and a lower quality of life.
- Population growth is the primary cause of environmental degradation, and high population density leads to ecological devastation.
- A rising population, fueled by immigration, is the cause of water quality and scarcity problems.
- Immigrants not only have higher rates of population growth, but quickly adopt resource-intensive lifestyles.
- The world's people of color cause overpopulation—birth rates for people of European descent are under control.[25]

On the contrary, the nation's single largest environmental polluter is the U.S. military. Rich people consume more resources than poor people. The United States has 5 percent of the world's population and uses 36 percent of the world's resources. The average American uses energy at the rate of 3 Japanese, or 6 Mexicans, or 12 Chinese, or 33 Indians, or 147 Bangladeshis, or 422 Ethiopians.[26] Rather than reducing wasteful consumption of natural resources by rich people generally, and of Americans specifically, these xenophobic "environmentalists" want to reduce human populations—specifically immigrants of color, even though immigrants are not the primary (nor for that matter, a significant) cause of environmental degradation.

Anti-immigration environmentalists' dangerous arguments have been absorbed by mainstream politicians. For example, Senator Reid from Nevada described the Immigration Stabilization Act of 1994—which called for more limits on and fewer benefits for illegal immigration and refugees—as "one of the most important bills for protecting the environment." According to Reid,

> Our environment is beset from all sides by the problems of the gravest and most intractable kind: vanishing ecosystems, acid rain, global warming, groundwater pollution, air pollution, and dwindling wetlands and farmlands. All of these problems have one root cause—too many people. If we have any hope of slowing our country's population growth, immigration must be reduced.[27]

The Political Ecology Group is a multiracial social justice organization based in San Francisco that fights anti-immigration and zero-population policies. It creates and disseminates fact-sheets that outline the myths and facts on immigration, population, and the environment.[28] The Political Ecology Group researches anti-immigration groups and other allied groups, such as the Federation for American Immigration Reform, to publicize their scapegoating statements and funding links to right-wing eugenicist foundations.

We need to expand our efforts to educate and mobilize Asian women to assert our right to live and work safely and productively wherever we choose.

CONCLUSION

Since Asian women are disproportionately affected by environmental and social injustice, we are also uniquely positioned to lead insurgent movements for justice. Our efforts pave the road for stronger domestic and international resistance against corporate and political agendas that exploit Asian women, our labor, and the natural environment.

Radical Asian women must continue to theorize about and organize around a wide range of issues, including: labor exploitation, healthcare, institutional violence, domestic violence, and cultural discrimination. Radical Asian women's movements, like environmental justice, envision multiracial, multi-ethnic, international/national movements for progressive social change.

International workers' rights and environmental justice movements need to share information, make organizational links, and coordinate campaigns against wage and environmental exploitation. Radical Asian women as labor organizers and environmental justice advocates need to organize across borders and recognize our common visions for justice, community-based self-determination, and a safe and healthy environment.

NOTES

1. Though I reject the notion that any static or essential Asian feminist perspective exists, I believe that race- and gender-specific analysis is critical. See, for example, Carl Anthony, "Why Blacks Should Be Environmentalists," in Brad Erickson, ed., *Call to Action* (San Francisco: Sierra Club Books, 1990).
2. Gwen Schaffer, "Asian Americans Organize for Justice," *Environmental Action*, Winter 1994.
3. Telephone interview with Angela Chung.
4. Robert Bullard, *Dumping in Dixie* (Boulder, CO: Westview Press, 1994); Robert Bullard, ed., *Confronting Environmental Racism* (Boston, MA: South End Press, 1993), and *Environmental Justice and Communities of Color* (San Francisco: Sierra Club Books, 1994); Richard Hofrichter, ed., *Toxic Struggles: The Theory and Practice of Environmental Justice* (Philadelphia: New Society Publishers, 1993); Marianne Lavelle and Marcia Coyle, "Unequal Protection: The Racial Divide in Environmental Law," in Hofrichter, ed., *Toxic Struggles*.
5. "The Global Connection: Exploitation of Developing Countries," in Hofrichter, ed., *Toxic Struggles*.
6. United Church of Christ Commission for Racial Justice, *Toxic Wastes and Race in the United States: A National Report on the Racial and Socio-Economic Characteristics of Communities with Hazardous Waste Sites* (New York: United Church of Christ, 1987).
7. Lavelle and Coyle, "Unequal Protection."
8. Marcy Darnovsky, "Stories Less Told: Histories of U.S. Environmentalism," *Socialist Review* 22, no. 4 (October–December 1992): 11–53.
9. "Principles of Environmental Justice," Proceedings from the First National People

of Color Environmental Leadership Summit (United Church of Christ, Commission for Racial Justice, 1992).

10. *Working Healthy*, Asian Immigrant Women Advocates brochure (Oakland, CA), 7.

11. "Principles of Environmental Justice." Lee is a former labor organizer and a board member of the Washington Office on Environmental Justice, the National Environmental Justice Advisory Council, and Asian Pacific Environmental Network.

12. Peggy Saika, "APEN Brings Asian Pacific Perspective to Environmental Justice," Washington Office on Environmental Justice Newsletter, Summer 1995.

13. Schaffer, "Asian Americans Organize for Justice."

14. Telephone interview with Helen Kim, 13 September 1996.

15. Schaffer, "Asian Americans Organize for Justice."

16. Sandra Swanson, "Can We Balance the Scales of Environmental Justice?" *Safety & Health*, October 1995.

17. Interview with Pam Tau Lee, 21 August 1996.

18. Tom Athanasiou, *The Divided Planet* (Boston: Little, Brown, 1996), 191.

19. Mitchell Zuckoff, "Trapped by Poverty, Killed by Neglect," *Boston Globe,* 10 July 1994.

20. Vandana Shiva, "Women and Nature," in Susan J. Armstrong and Richard G. Botzler, eds., *Environmental Ethics: Divergence and Convergence* (New York: McGraw Hill, 1993), and "Development, Ecology and Women," in Judith Plant, ed., *Healing the Wounds: The Promise of Ecofeminism* (Philadelphia: New Society Publishers, 1989).

21. Ethnic News Watch, *India Currents* 6, no. 4 (31 July 1992): MI5.

22. Vandana Shiva, *Staying Alive: Women, Ecology, and Development* (London: Zed Books, 1989), 67–77.

23. National Network For Immigrant and Refugee Rights, *Network News,* Summer 1996.

24. Penn Loh, "Creating an Environment of Blame: Anti-Immigration Forces Seek to Woo Environmentalists," *RESIST* newsletter, December 1995: 4.

25. Political Ecology Group Immigration and Environment Campaign Organizer's Kit.

26. *Environmental Action*, Summer 1994: 15.

27. Ibid., 23.

28. Political Ecology Group Immigration and Environment Campaign Organizer's Kit.

ACKNOWLEDGMENTS

Though it is a cliché to say that books, especially feminist books, are collective efforts, it is nonetheless true. I wish to thank the following people for their encouragement or their suggestions, whether or not I was able to follow them: Louise Antony, Jean Anyon, Mary Boger, Christine DiStefano, Tracy Edwards, Ann Ferguson, Sue Ferguson, Nanette Funk, Evelyn Nakano Glenn, Linda Gordon, Heidi Hartmann, Alison Jaggar, Kathy Johnson, Mecke Nagel, Ros Petchesky, Elayne Rapping, Nancy Romer, Gary Roth, Karen Brodkin Sacks, Eleni Varikas, Lise Vogel, Barbara Winslow, Iris Young and all the authors who were so generous with their work, although I was not able in the end to include them all. Most especially I want to thank my dear friend and comrade Johanna Brenner without whose generosity this book would probably not have come to be, or at least would certainly have been less good. Her knowledge of the field, her political insights, and her personal support were invaluable.

At Monthly Review Press I want especially to thank Christopher Phelps, who first approached me about doing the book when he was the editor at MR, and Danielle McClellan, who was so productive and congenial an editor. I enjoyed working with Martin Paddio and I appreciate the contributions of Andrew Nash, Lucy Morton and Robin Gable.

My politics have not developed in isolation or in academia, but through active involvement with various socialist and feminist groups and struggles that, at their best, represent the ideal of self-emancipation, the deepest and broadest liberatory vision and practice. I thank them for keeping the ideal alive. Finally I wish to express how deeply gratified I am by the new generation of activists, especially my daughter Alexandra, who start at a higher level and inspire me with hope.

The editor and publishers gratefully acknowledge the following sources:

"A Question of Class," by Dorothy Allison, © 1994, from Dorothy Allison, *Skin*, Firebrand Books, reprinted by permission of the author.

"Gender, Sexuality, Political Economy," by Micaela di Leonardo and Roger Lancaster, from *New Politics* 6, no. 1, New Series (Summer 1996), reprinted by permission.

"Premenstrual Syndrome, Work Discipline, and Anger," by Emily Martin, © 1987, 1992, extracted, from Emily Martin, *The Woman in the Body*, reprinted by permission of Beacon Press.

"Human Rights, Reproductive Health and Economic Justice: Why They Are Indivisible," by Rosalind P. Petchesky, from *Reproductive Health Matters* 8, no. 15 (May 2000), reprinted by permission.

"The Family is Dead, Long Live Our Families," by Judith Stacey, © 1994, from Craig Calhoun and George Ritzer, eds., *Sociology Database*, reprinted by permission of The McGraw-Hill Companies, Inc.

"Redefining the Home," by Purvi Shah, © 1997, extracted, from Sonia Shah, *Dragon Ladies: Asian American Feminists Breathe Fire*, reprinted by permission of South End Press.

"My Brother's Sex Was White, Mine Brown," by Cherríe Moraga, © 1983, extracted, from Cherríe Moraga, *Loving in the War Years*, reprinted by permission of South End Press.

"Revisiting Marx and Engels on the Family," by Stephanie Coontz, from *Against the Current*, January/February 1998, reprinted by permission.

"On Conceiving Motherhood and Sexuality: A Feminist-Materialist Approach," by Ann Ferguson, © 1991, extracted, from Ann Ferguson, *Sexual Democracy: Women, Oppression and Revolution*, reprinted by permission of Westview Press, a member of the Perseus Books Group.

"Bargaining with Patriarchy," by Deniz Kandiyoti, from *Gender & Society* 2, no. 3 (1998), reprinted by permission of Sage Publications, Inc.

"The Disappearing Fathers Under Global Capitalism," by Temma Kaplan, from *Radical History Review* 71 (Spring 1998), reprinted by permission.

"Women Workers and Capitalist Scripts: Ideologies of Domination, Common Interests, and the Politics of Solidarity," by Chandra Talpade Mohanty, © 1997, extracted, from Jacqui Alexander and Chandra Mohanty, *Feminist Geneologies, Colonial Legacies, Democratic Futures*, reprinted by permission of Routledge, Inc., part of The Taylor & Francis Group.

"The Hidden History of Affirmative Action: Working Women's Struggles in the 1970s and the Gender of Class," by Nancy MacLean, from *Feminist Studies* 25 (Spring 1999), reprinted by permission.

"Making Fantasies Real: Producing Women and Men on the Maquila Shop Floor," by Leslie Salzinger, from *NACLA Report on the Americas* 34, no. 5 (March/April 2001), reprinted by permission.

"Machos and Machetes in Guatemala's Cane Fields," by Elizabeth Oglesby, from *NACLA Report on the Americas* 34, no. 5 (March/April 2001), reprinted by permission.

"An International Perspective on Slavery in the Sex Industry," by Jo Bindman, © 1998 from Kamala Kempadoo and Jo Doezema, eds., *Global Sex Workers: Rights, Resistance and Redefinition*, reprinted by permission of Taylor & Francis, Inc./Routledge, Inc.

"Globalizing Sex Workers' Rights," by Kamala Kempadoo, © 1998, extracted, from Kamala Kempadoo and Jo Doezema, eds., *Global Sex Workers: Rights, Resistance and Redefinition*, reprinted by permission of Taylor & Francis, Inc./Routledge, Inc.

"Still Under Attack: Women and Welfare Reform," by Mimi Abramovitz, ©

1996, extracted, from Mimi Abramovitz, *Under Attack, Fighting Back: Women and Welfare in the United States*, Monthly Review Press.

"Toward a Strategy for Women's Economic Equality," by Chris Tilly and Randy Albelda, from *New Politics* 7, no. 3, New Series (Summer 1999), reprinted by permission.

"Public Imprisonment and Private Violence: Reflections on the Hidden Punishment of Women," by Angela Y. Davis, from *New England Journal of Criminal and Civil Confinement* 24, no. 2 (Summer 1998), reprinted by permission.

"Conceptualizing Women's Interests," by Maxine Molyneux, © 1986, extracted, from Richard R. Fagen, Carmen Diana Deere, and Jose Luis Coraggio, *Transition and Development: Problems of Their World Socialism*, Monthly Review Press.

"Appreciating Our Beginnings," by Sheila Rowbotham, © 1999, from Sheila Rowbotham, *Threads Through Time*, reprinted by permission of Verso.

"Listen Up, Anglo Sisters," by Elizabeth Martínez, © 1998, from Elizabeth Martínez, *De Colores Means All of Us*, reprinted by permission of South End Press.

"Capitalism and Human Emancipation: Race, Gender, and Democracy," by Ellen Meiksins Wood, © 1995, from Ellen Meiskins Wood, *Democracy against Capitalism: Renewing Historical Materialism*, reprinted by permission of Cambridge University Press.

"Militarizing Women's Lives," by Cynthia Enloe, © 1999, from Cynthia Enloe, *Maneuvers: The International Politics of Militarizing Women's Lives*, reprinted by permission of the Regents of the University of California.

"Democratization: Reflections on Gendered Dislocations in the Public Sphere," by Mary E. Hawkesworth, © 2001, from Rita Kelly, Jane Bayes, Brigitte Young, and Mary Hawkesworth, *Gender, Globalization, and Democratization*, reprinted by permission of Rowman & Littlefield Publishers.

"Mapping Gender in African-American Political Strategies," by Leith Mullings, © 1997, extracted, from Leith Mullings, *On Our Own Terms*, reprinted by permission of Taylor & Francis, Inc./Routledge, Inc.

"Intersections, Locations, and Capitalist Class Relations: Intersectionality from a Marxist Perspective," by Johanna Brenner, © 200o, extracted, from Johanna Brenner, *Women and the Politics of Class*, Monthly Review Press.

"The Feminist Standpoint Revisited," by Nancy Hartsock, © 1998, extracted, from Nancy Hartsock, *The Feminist Standpoint Revisited and Other Essays*, reprinted by permission of Westview Press, a member of the Perseus Books Group.

"A Marxist Theory of Women's Nature," by Nancy Holmstrom, extracted, from *Ethics* 94 (April 1984), reprinted by permission.

"The Ecopolitics Debate and the Politics of Nature," by Val Plumwood, © 1994, from Karen Warren, with the assistance of Barbara Wells-Howe, *Ecological Feminism*, reprinted by permission of Routledge, Inc., part of The Taylor & Francis Group.

"Women and the Third World: Exploring the Dangers of Difference," by Meera Nanda, from *New Politics* 7, no. 2, New Series (Winter 1999), reprinted by permission.

"Expanding Environmental Justice: Asian-American Feminists' Contribution," by Julie Sze, © 1997, from Sonia Shah, *Dragon Ladies: Asian American Feminists Breathe Fire*, reprinted by permission of South End Press.

INDEX